PUBLIC LAW AT THE McLACHLIN COURT

PUBLIC LAW AT THE McLACHLIN COURT

The First Decade

DAVID A. WRIGHT AND ADAM M. DODEK,
EDITORS

IRWIN LAW

Public Law at the McLachlin Court: The First Decade

Published in 2011 by

Irwin Law Inc.
14 Duncan Street
Suite 206
Toronto, ON
M5H 3G8

www.irwinlaw.com

ISBN 978-1-55221-214-1
e-book ISBN 978-1-55221-217-2

Cover photograph: © Ken Yuel Photography/Getty Images
Cover and interior design: Heather Raven

Cataloguing in Publication available from Library and Archives Canada

The publisher acknowledges the financial support of the Government of Canada through the Canada Book Fund for its publishing activities.

We acknowledge the assistance of the OMDC Book Fund, an initiative of Ontario Media Development Corporation.

Printed and bound in Canada.

1 2 3 4 5 15 14 13 12 11

Table of Contents

FOREWORD

The First Decade of the 21st Century: The Supreme Court of Canada in Context

THE RIGHT HONOURABLE CHIEF JUSTICE OF CANADA BEVERLEY McLACHLIN, P.C.

It is a daunting task, I must admit at the outset, for me to speak about the topic that this conference refers to as "The McLachlin Court's First Decade." I feel a little like a student being asked to evaluate her own performance on an exam. I strongly feel I should get an A-plus. But I know beyond a shadow of a doubt that there are likely to be other views on the subject. In such circumstances, a wise person might politely have refused this invitation. But—and you may draw your own conclusions about my wisdom—I did not, and the moment of self-evaluation is upon me.

Let me try to deflect the task by shifting the focus from me to the institution, from "McLachlin" to the Court. To label a court by one of its nine members serves as, no doubt, a convenient shorthand. I, myself, am guilty of referring to past eras of the Court as "the Laskin Court" or "the Dickson Court." But it is only a shorthand. The fact is that the work of the Supreme Court of Canada is the collective product of all nine of its members. Each brings his or her own work, experience, and knowledge of the law to every case. The Court's strength lies in how the nine members share their views with one another. We all contribute to the work of the Court and its jurisprudence.

I quickly discovered, upon being named Chief Justice Designate, that the phrase "the authority of the chief justice" is a perfect oxymoron. I learned that there is a literary sub-genre known as "chief justice" jokes. I cannot accurately estimate the size of this sub-genre, since I am certain that there

Address delivered at the CBA Conference, "The McLachlin Court's First Decade," 19 June 2009.

are many chief justice jokes that are never shared with the chief justice in question. But those I learned about all had the same theme—the ultimate powerlessness that the trappings of chief justice conceal. As an ex-chief from California put it, "They gave me the reins of power and then I discovered they weren't connected to anything."

But let's get to the question of the day—how has it been, this first decade? Here, as a Canadian, I find myself on more comfortable terrain. Have you noticed that Canadians seem to have a stock answer to the question "How was it?"—the same answer no matter what the circumstances?

"How's the weather?"

"Not bad."

"How's work?"

"Not bad."

"How was it for you?"

"Not bad."

It's our stock answer for everything, "Not bad."

So how was it for me—the first nine years and five months, that is?

Let me sum it up in two words: "Not bad."

One of the most gratifying aspects of my tenure as chief justice has been the honour and privilege to work with fourteen extraordinary Canadian jurists—each amazingly talented and gifted in his or her own way: Claire L'Heureux-Dubé, Charles Gonthier, Frank Iacobucci, Jack Major, Louise Arbour, Ian Binnie, Michel Bastarache, Louis LeBel, Marie Deschamps, Morris Fish, Rosie Abella, Louise Charron, Marshall Rothstein, and Tom Cromwell. Each of them has given me that great gift without which a chief justice can be neither happy nor successful—their unqualified friendship and support. To my wonderful colleagues, thank you.

Another gratifying aspect has been the privilege of working with chief justices from all across Canada on the Canadian Judicial Council. As a group, chief justices are a sadly misunderstood lot. To evoke the image of thirty-nine chief justices, associate chief justices, and senior judges meeting to discuss matters of mutual concern is to provoke at best a big yawn, at worst an immediate flight response. In fact, chief justices in Canada, much to my surprise, turned out to be neither boring nor intimidating. True, they can hardly be described as a docile lot. But they are smart, incisive, witty, and passionately dedicated to improving the justice system. And on rare judicial "let-your-hair-down" sessions—if that metaphor is not misplaced in describing a covey of senior judges of a certain age—they can be downright fun. The last ten years have seen a fundamental reorientation of the

Judicial Council, as it streamlined its complaints process and developed new policies with respect to legal education, the press, and access to justice. It has been an exciting and stimulating ride, with exciting and stimulating colleagues. To my friends on the Judicial Council and all who so ably support them, thank you. The same goes for Brian Lennox and everyone at the National Judicial Institute, which has emerged as a world leader in judicial education in the last ten years.

But I must return to the Court, which is the focus of this conference. What of the work of the Court? Again, let me say, "Not bad."

First—and not unimportant—we still have work. In 2007, a statistical blip led to jeremiads that the Court would soon be out of cases. Not so. Things picked up. In fact, we find ourselves quite occupied. The cases keep coming.

Second, we still have work of high quality and interest. The criminal law was sorted out, the big *Charter* questions had been decided, the doomsayers claimed. Indeed, for a while I must confess I worried that we would be left with nothing but judicial review, nine brilliant minds spinning out endless iterations of *Dunsmuir.*[1] But my fears proved groundless. *Singh,*[2] *Grant,*[3] and *Suberu*[4] came along, not to mention *Turcotte,*[5] *Clayton,*[6] and *Harrison.*[7] And on the constitutional scene, sections 91 and 92 of the *Constitution Act, 1867* emerged from long hibernation with signs of awakening. The old saws of "pith and substance" and "double aspect" bestirred themselves and revived to new life, in the face of the threat of "interjurisdictional immunity." And if that's not enough to excite you, I could go on and on.

Third, the Court's work in the last ten years has been marked by a high degree of consensus, judged by the standards of final courts of appeal. In the first year I was chief justice, consensus peaked at 82 percent—that is, in 82 percent of the cases we were unanimous in the result. Unfortunately, the stats have been somewhat downhill from then on. The honeymoon high was never again equaled. Still, our consensus rates remain high, varying from year to year but generally in the mid-70 percent range, as the Court calculates these matters. This compares favourably, for example, with

---

1 *Dunsmuir v. New Brunswick*, 2008 SCC 9, [2008] 1 S.C.R. 190.

2 *R. v. Singh*, 2007 SCC 48, [2007] 3 S.C.R. 405.

3 *R. v. Grant*, 2009 SCC 32, [2009] 2 S.C.R. 353.

4 *R. v. Suberu*, 2009 SCC 33, [2009] 2 S.C.R. 460.

5 *R. v. Turcotte*, 2005 SCC 50, [2005] 2 S.C.R. 519.

6 *R. v. Clayton*, 2007 SCC 32, [2007] 2 S.C.R. 725.

7 *R. v. Harrison*, 2009 SCC 34, [2009] 2 S.C.R. 494.

approximately 30 percent in the same period for the Supreme Court of the United States. The members of this Court, first and foremost its chief justice, believe strongly in the right of dissent and its significance in shaping the law. But we also believe in ironing out differences insofar as this can be done, to better fulfill our primary function—settling the legal questions of public importance that Canadian society brings up.

Fourth, the Court is working efficiently. This is nothing new. My predecessor Antonio Lamer prided himself on the efficiency of court operations, and justly so. Under Brian Dickson, he and his colleagues on the Court fashioned new rules to deal with the *Charter* era—time limits on hearings, an intervener process, and a paper-based leave to appeal process. Without these reforms, the Court would never have coped with the huge burden of *Charter* litigation that marked the last decade-and-a-half of the twentieth century.

In the last ten years, the Court has built on this legacy, meeting the new challenges to efficiency imposed by our own age. We have continued the drive for technological modernization. Over the past few years, the Court completed a renovation and modernization of the courtroom. All of the audio-visual equipment was replaced, improving sound quality in the courtroom, and improving broadcast quality of recordings of hearings. Computers have been installed on the bench, at the counsel tables, and at the media table, allowing lawyers, judges, and the press to call up electronic copies of the documents filed in an appeal during the course of argument. The lectern was replaced with one where the height can be adjusted to accommodate counsel in a wheelchair, or moved to fit counsel's height.

By and large, these changes have been smoothly implemented. It's true that we have moved monitor equipment into the courtroom to deal with the occasional heart attack of counsel caused by the new lectern being precipitously elevated or lowered when the wrong button is pushed. It's also true that we still haven't found a way to let counsel know precisely which judge is bearing down on them with a question. And it's true, I must admit, that even nine years after our invitation to address us simply as "Justice," confusion occasionally arises over whether we are lords, ladies, or some other species of judicial esoterica.

Not the least of the administrative accomplishments of the past ten years has been improving the quality of the coffee in the Supreme Court of Canada. The first promise I made to my colleagues upon becoming chief justice was to improve the quality of the courthouse coffee. Having made this announcement, I immediately delegated the task of accomplishing it to

Jack Major. Within a few weeks, we were all enjoying high-quality cappuccino. Whatever else they may say about my time as chief justice, I comfort myself with the knowledge that no one can dispute that the quality of the coffee has improved.

Fifth, I believe that the Court is increasingly accessible, understood, and accepted as an institution fundamental to Canadian democracy. I have already mentioned improved access through technological innovations like e-filing. But being accessible, understood, and accepted is more than a matter of technology. In 2004, the Court's media program was expanded to provide for media lock-ups in particularly complex cases of public interest.[8] This year, the Court began webcasting appeal hearings and posting factums in appeals online. Canadians, from law students to members of the public, are tuning into our hearings in real time. We are not yet giving Oprah a run in the afternoon ratings, it is true. But we are helping Canadians better understand the vital work of the Court and how we go about accomplishing it.

This brings me to public understanding and acceptance of the Court as a fundamental institution of Canadian democracy. The two decades following the adoption of the *Charter* saw a lively dialogue on the role of courts in Canadian democracy. One side of the debate focused on judicial activism—the fear that courts would overstep appropriate constitutional bounds and impinge on the proper functions of Parliament and the legislatures. Some went so far as to argue that unelected courts were imposing their own policy views on Canadian society. The other side of the debate took the position that in a constitutional democracy built on rights, courts must play a strong and independent role in upholding those rights, even if the result is the invalidation of laws passed by Parliament or the legislatures.

The last ten years have seen a shift in the debate. The stark either-or alternatives of absolute legislative power and court supremacy have increasingly given way to the recognition that in a mature democracy of rights, both institutions are vital. Parliament and the legislatures, as the elected representatives of the people, bear the major responsibility of legislating for the good of Canada.

It is inevitable that particular decisions of the Court will be criticized. My hope is not that everyone agrees with the Court's decisions—that can never be. My hope is more modest—that whether people agree with a particular decision or not, they accept that it is the role of the Court charged

8 Florian Sauvageau, David Schneiderman, & David Taras, *The Last Word: Media Coverage of the Supreme Court of Canada* (Vancouver: UBC Press, 2006) at 203.

with upholding the rule of law and the constitutional order to make the decision, and understand that the members of the Court have honestly wrestled with the difficult and complex issues at stake.

So for all these reasons, I respond to the question of how the last ten years have been with the quintessentially Canadian answer: "Not bad." Let me close with a historical perspective on where the Court stands, a decade after I became chief justice.

The Supreme Court of Canada is now 134 years old. In Canadian terms, that is a long and venerable time. Over that time, the Court has evolved in response to changes in the Canadian constitution and Canadian society. Roughly speaking, and acknowledging room for debate over where precise boundaries lie, the history of the Court can be divided into three periods—the initial colonial period from 1875 to 1949; the emerging independence period from 1950 to 1982; and the post-*Charter* period from 1982 to the present.

The Court did not get off to a scintillating start. Five of its six judges duly met in the Railway Committee room in the Parliament Building at the start of its first session on 17 January 1876. We are not sure what they did. All we know is what the record says: "There being no business to dispose of the Court rose."[9] Things got so bad that a couple of years later a private member brought a bill to have the Court abolished. To judge by the debates, it was a hotly contested issue, but in the end the prime minister, John A. Macdonald, successfully postponed a final judgment on the bill until the desire for abolition dissipated.[10]

Yet until 1949, when appeals to the Judicial Committee of the Privy Council were abolished, the so-called Supreme Court of Canada was not supreme. It was a colonial court. It was bound by precedent to do what the law lords in England ruled. This reflected Canada's status as a "dominion," a term that effectively avoided the obvious question—dominion of whom? Of Great Britain? Or of its own peoples?

The statistics available for the tail end of this period, 1944–54, under the leadership of Chief Justice Rinfret, show that nearly 60 percent of the precedents cited in Supreme Court of Canada decisions were British cases.[11]

9 Bora Laskin, "The Supreme Court of Canada, the First One Hundred Years: A Capsule Institutional History" (1975) 53 Can. Bar Rev. 459 at 462–63.

10 See James G. Snell & Frederick Vaughan, *The Supreme Court of Canada: History of the Institution* (Toronto: The Osgoode Society, 1985) at 28–34.

11 Peter McCormick, *Supreme at Last: The Evolution of the Supreme Court of Canada* (Toronto: James Lorimer & Company Ltd., 2000) at 24.

Nearly half of the constitutional cases decided by the Privy Council were appeals directly from the provincial courts of appeal.[12] For half the cases, the Supreme Court of Canada was not even a step on the way.

Yet a few people saw a more important future for the Court. In what can only be termed a brave act of faith in the future, Prime Minister McKenzie King approved plans to build the magnificent and enduring building on Wellington Street that still houses the Court. The Queen Mother laid the cornerstone in 1939, noting, in what is the only feminist speech by British Royals I know of, that it is only through the law that the true advancement of women can be secured.

In 1949, appeals to the Judicial Committee of the Privy Council were finally abolished and the Court entered its second period—the period of emerging independence. Like a young matron gathering up her new-found powers, the Court slowly took on an air of quiet confidence. To be sure, British law and British precedents still bulked large.[13] But new, uniquely Canadian law began to emerge. Building on the *Alberta Reference*'s affirmation of the implied constitutional right of free political speech,[14] the Court expanded the doctrine in *Saumur v. Quebec*[15] and *Switzman v. Elbling*.[16] It broke new ground on aspects of Canadian federalism, breathing new life into the Peace, Order and Good Government Power;[17] the federal trade and commerce power; and interjurisdictional power-sharing under the rubric of double aspect.[18] A distinctly Canadian jurisprudence was born.

The Court continued to gather strength under Chief Justices Bora Laskin and Brian Dickson. In 1975, the old monetary limits were replaced by a requirement of leave for all appeals except for criminal appeals as of right and references. This recognized a shift from an error-correcting role to a new role of establishing legal norms on issues of public importance,[19] and

---

12 Peter Hogg, *Constitutional Law of Canada*, looseleaf, 5th ed. (Toronto: ThomsonCarswell, 2007) at 8-3.

13 Under Kerwin C.J., 1954–63, 47 percent of precedents cited were British. Under Taschereau, Cartwright, and Fauteux C.JJ., 1963–73, 33 percent of precedents cited were British: McCormick, above note 11 at 47 and 71.

14 *Reference Re Alberta Statutes*, [1938] S.C.R. 100.

15 *Saumur v. Quebec*, [1953] 2 S.C.R. 299.

16 *Switzman v. Elbling*, [1957] S.C.R. 285.

17 *Johannesson v. Municipality of West St. Paul*, [1952] 1 S.C.R. 198.

18 *Re The Farm Products Marketing Act*, [1957] S.C.R. 198; *Murphy v. C.P.R.*, [1958] S.C.R. 626.

19 Hogg, above note 12 at 8-13; Laskin, above note 9 at 463–64; Diane Teeple, "The History and Role of the Supreme Court of Canada" (2002) 10 *Australian Law Librarian* 216 at 221–22.

for the first time gave the Supreme Court of Canada control over its docket. Bold new decisions reflected the new role. In the trilogy of *Thorson*, *McNeil*, and *Borowski*, the Court established a broader test for public-interest standing to challenge government action in cases where there was no other reasonable or effective means to bring an issue before the courts.[20] In the *Anti-Inflation Reference*, the Court considered extrinsic evidence of social and economic context in a division of powers case, paving the way for the contextual approach which the Court later followed in *Charter* cases.[21] In *City of Sault Ste. Marie*,[22] the Court synthesized the approach to *mens rea* in criminal law, outlining a spectrum of levels of *mens rea* from full *mens rea* offences, to strict liability, and then absolute liability. The Dickson and Lamer Courts would later expand on this approach in the constitutional analysis of *mens rea*. And who can forget the *Patriation Reference*,[23] which paved the way for repatriation of the Canadian Constitution and adoption of the *Charter of Rights and Freedoms*.

Even in dissent, the Court was breaking new ground. In the infamous case of *Murdoch v. Murdoch*,[24] the majority of the Court held that Mrs. Murdoch's contributions to running the family ranching business over many years were not sufficient to give her a property interest in the ranching business. Chief Justice Laskin's dissent held that Mrs. Murdoch's contributions through her labour over the years should give her an interest, and to deny her this would be inequitable. Although *Murdoch* was not a constitutional case, Laskin C.J.'s dissent foreshadows the development of our notions of gender equality the following decade under section 15 of the *Charter*.

In 1982, the Constitution was repatriated and the *Charter* adopted. The Court entered a third era, defined by a critical new responsibility. To the Court's constitutional roles of division of powers and administrative review was added the task of reviewing challenged government action or legislation for compliance with the fundamental rights and freedoms protected by the *Charter*.

In those early years of the *Charter*, the members of the Court charted the path for the interpretation of the rights and freedoms contained in it. The pundits who predicted that the Court would follow the conservative path it

---

20 *Thorson v. Attorney General for Canada*, [1975] 1 S.C.R. 138; *Nova Scotia Board of Censors v. McNeil*, [1976] 2 S.C.R. 265; *Minister of Justice v. Borowski*, [1981] 2 S.C.R. 575.

21 *Re Anti-Inflation Act*, [1976] 2 S.C.R. 373.

22 *R. v. City of Sault Ste. Marie*, [1978] 2 S.C.R. 1299.

23 *Reference re a Resolution to amend the Constitution*, [1981] 1 S.C.R. 753.

24 *Murdoch v. Murdoch*, [1975] 1 S.C.R. 423.

had trod with the Diefenbaker Bill of Rights were proved wrong. With vision and tenacity, the Court proclaimed that the *Charter* rights should be interpreted purposively and generously. We all know the cases that followed and set the framework within which we still work—*Oakes* and the doctrine of justification under section 1 of the *Charter*;[25] *Big M.* and the scope of freedom of religion;[26] *Ford* and *Irwin Toy* and their rich understanding of the right to freedom of expression rooted in democratic values;[27] the *Motor Vehicle Reference* and substantive due process under section 7 of the *Charter*;[28] and *Hunter v. Southam* and the right to be free from unreasonable searches and seizures.[29] All this was made possible by the procedural changes I mentioned earlier.

Some see the 1990s that followed as a decade of consolidation. And so it was in many ways. Still, as someone who joined the Court in 1989 on the eve of Lamer C.J.'s term, I can attest to the fact that these were heady times. *Hébert*,[30] *Brydges*,[31] *Bartle*,[32] and *Stinchcombe*[33] all broke new and important ground. Among the most significant developments of this era was the affirmation of Aboriginal rights and entitlements.[34] In a series of seminal cases, the Court articulated a vision of reconciliation, in which all Canadians, Aboriginal and non-Aboriginal, would move forward in respectful dignity. Chief Justice Lamer spoke for the country when he said, in *Delgamuukw*, "Let us face it, we are all here to stay."[35]

And so we arrive at the year 2000, and the decade that is the subject of this conference. How will history colour this decade, when it looks back? I leave that question for you to discuss. I must confess, however, to one hope: that when people look back, they see a Court of integrity, independence, and some modicum of common sense. When I became chief justice, I made a wish. It was a simple wish—that I leave the Court as strong as I found

---

25 *R. v. Oakes*, [1986] 1 S.C.R. 103; *Canadian Charter of Rights and Freedoms*, s. 1, Part I of the *Constitution Act, 1982*, being Schedule B to the *Canada Act 1982* (U.K.), 1982, c.11.

26 *R. v. Big M. Drug Mart*, [1985] 1 S.C.R. 295.

27 *Ford v. Quebec*, [1988] 2 S.C.R. 712; *Irwin Toy v. Quebec*, [1989] 1 S.C.R. 927.

28 *Re B.C. Motor Vehicle Act*, [1985] 2 S.C.R. 486.

29 *Hunter v. Southam*, [1984] 2 S.C.R. 145.

30 *R. v. Hébert*, [1990] 2 S.C.R. 151; *R. v. S. (R.J.)*, [1995] 1 S.C.R. 451; *British Columbia Securities Commissioner v. Branch*, [1995] 2 S.C.R. 3.

31 *R. v. Brydges*, [1990] 1 S.C.R. 190.

32 *R. v. Bartle*, [1994] 3 S.C.R. 173.

33 *R. v. Stinchcombe*, [1991] 3 S.C.R. 326.

34 *Delgamuukw v. British Columbia*, [1997] 3 S.C.R. 1010; *R. v. Van der Peet*, [1996] 2 S.C.R. 507.

35 *Delgamuukw, ibid.* at para. 186.

it. The support I feel from Canadians and indeed others around the world, leads me, modestly, to dare hope that thus far, my wish has been fulfilled.

This has been the most challenging and rewarding decade of my life. I have loved every minute of it. As a true Canadian might say, "Not bad."

Introduction: The McLachlin Court's First Decade—A Dynamic Time for Public Law

ADAM M. DODEK AND DAVID A. WRIGHT

When Beverley McLachlin was sworn in as the seventeenth chief justice of Canada on 7 January 2000, the Supreme Court was at somewhat of a crossroads. For several years, the Court had been accused of judicial activism, of being too eager to intervene in policy decisions that some felt were better left to governments than to courts. There were numerous blockbuster cases in the 1990s that garnered headlines, often negative, including *Askov*,[1] *Eldridge*,[2] and *M. v. H.*[3] The Lamer Court was frequently divided, often producing fractured opinions rather than coherent statements of the law. Near the end of the decade, the Supreme Court came together to produce what many believed to be a Solomonic judgment in the *Quebec Secession Reference*.[4]

Under such circumstances, it would have been easy for the members of the McLachlin Court to adopt a cautious or tentative approach. One commentator predicted that the principle of *stare decisis* would prevent the new chief justice from revisiting earlier court decisions.[5] This has not been the case. In fact, as evident from many of the contributions in this volume, the McLachlin Court has shown a remarkable willingness to revisit earlier decisions across the spectrum of public law. In its first decade, the McLachlin Court was a Court on the move.

---

1 *R. v. Askov*, [1990] 2 S.C.R. 1199.

2 *Eldridge v. British Columbia (Attorney General)*, [1997] 3 S.C.R. 624.

3 *M. v. H.*, [1999] 2 S.C.R. 3.

4 *Reference re Secession of Quebec*, [1998] 2 S.C.R. 217.

5 See Peter McCormick, *Supreme at Last: The Evolution of the Supreme Court of Canada* (Toronto: James Lorimer, 2000) at 158.

The McLachlin Court's public law jurisprudence leads us to characterize the Court as "a dynamic court." It was a court that was characterized by continuous change and activity. It has been a court that has reshaped existing doctrines and crafted new ones, such as the creation of the duty to consult in Aboriginal law. Elsewhere, the McLachlin Court has put the brakes on developments in other areas such as the unwritten constitutional principles, which, after the *Secession Reference,* held out the possibility of significantly refashioning constitutional law in Canada by adding a powerful weapon to the arsenal of constitutional litigators against government. However, with the McLachlin Court's decision in *Imperial Tobacco*[6] mid-way through its first decade, the Court poured cold water on the extent to which the unwritten constitutional principles could be used as an independent source of substantive rights.

La jurisprudence de la Cour McLachlin a attiré moins de publicité et moins de controverse dans les médias et auprès du grand public que celle de la Cour Lamer. Les jugements sont plus courts, et souvent contiennent moins d'élaboration de « grands principes » que certains jugements rendus par des Cours suprêmes précédentes. Les articles dans ce livre confirment que ce n'est pas à cause d'une réticence à prendre des décisions de grande portée ou à cause d'une absence de jurisprudence importante. Vingt-cinq ans après l'entrée en vigueur de la *Charte* et des arrêts qui ont révolutionné le droit public, tels que *Nicholson,*[7] *CUPE,*[8] *Oakes,*[9] *Sparrow,*[10] et *Sault Ste. Marie,*[11] le rôle de la Cour est différent, mais encore significatif.

Many of the contributions to this volume, both about general developments and particular areas of law, take up the theme of the Court's willingness to reconsider previous jurisprudence. This book had its origins in a CBA Conference on the McLachlin Court held in Ottawa in June 2009. We also issued a national call for papers and we were fortunate in the quality and the scope of the papers that we received. Each paper was subjected to a peer-review process and we thank the anonymous reviewers who were kind enough to contribute to this book through their work.

We each consider ourselves public law lawyers and scholars and we acknowledge the breadth of the field of public law. This book focuses on con-

---

6 *British Columbia v. Imperial Tobacco Canada Ltd.*, 2005 SCC 49, [2005] 2 S.C.R. 473.

7 *Nicholson v. Haldimand-Norfolk Regional Police Commission*, [1979] 1 S.C.R. 311.

8 *C.U.P.E. v. N.B. Liquor Corporation*, [1979] 2 S.C.R. 227.

9 *R. v. Oakes*, [1986] 1 S.C.R. 103.

10 *R. v. Sparrow*, [1990] 1 S.C.R. 1075.

11 *R. v. Sault Ste. Marie*, [1978] 2 S.C.R. 1299.

stitutional and administrative law decisions of the McLachlin Court. Thus, it does not include contributions on many important areas of public law: environmental law, immigration law, child protection, municipal law, tax, copyright, and similar areas. Sanda Rogers and Sheila McIntyre have recently published a book focusing on social justice issues at the McLachlin Court, *The Supreme Court of Canada and Social Justice: Commitment, Retrenchment or Retreat*.[12] For us to cover the span of public law would have filled several volumes and that project likely would not have been completed until the end of the McLachlin Court's second decade. Instead, our goal was to focus on familiar and often debated areas of constitutional law and administrative law in which the Court was particularly active and provide a basis for continued discourse in these areas. We leave discussion of other important areas of public law to future conferences and future books.

We are fortunate that the chief justice permitted us to publish her keynote address that was delivered at the CBA Conference on her first decade as chief justice. Entitled "The First Decade of the 21st Century: The Supreme Court of Canada in Context," the chief justice's comments and insight provide the perfect framework for the consideration of her Court's public law jurisprudence over that time.

The first section of the book addresses broader themes in the McLachlin Court's public law jurisprudence that are then later taken up in relation to specific areas of law. Thomson Irvine examines ten key decisions where the McLachlin Court reconsidered earlier doctrine, asking whether the Court was changing course or simply "trimming its sails." Marie-Claire Belleau, Anik Lamontagne, and Rebecca Johnson provide a statistical analysis of the McLachlin Court's decisions. In "The McLachlin Court and the Promise of Procedural Justice," Lorne Sossin demonstrates the Supreme Court's propensity under McLachlin C.J. to focus on procedural frameworks when complex substantive issues are brought before it.

Our next section focuses squarely on administrative law. David Mullan analyzes the continually changing standard of review of administrative decisions, asking whether the McLachlin Court has soothed this major irritant or whether it persists as an ongoing problem. Freya Kristjanson addresses an issue that she argues, in contrast, has not received sufficient attention from the Court: procedural fairness. Susan Gratton and Lorne Sossin examine the intersection between the *Charter* and administrative law, searching

12 Sanda Rogers & Sheila McIntyre, *The Supreme Court of Canada and Social Justice: Commitment, Retrenchment or Retreat* (Toronto: LexisNexis, 2010).

for coherence in the analytical approach to the intersection of these overlapping areas of public law.

The next section focuses on issues that could be described as "non-*Charter* constitutional law." In his article on federalism, Peter Oliver argues that the McLachlin Court has continued the trend of its predecessors in encouraging flexible, co-operative federalism whereby legislation is generally upheld and disputes allocated to the intergovernmental process. It is another area in which the Court has been willing to reconsider previous jurisprudence, significantly narrowing the doctrine of interjurisdictional immunity in *Canadian Western Bank*[13] and *Lafarge*.[14] Our next two chapters address the most important developments in Aboriginal law at the McLachlin Court. Constance MacIntosh analyzes the transformation of the doctrine of reconciliation from a limit on Aboriginal rights in the jurisprudence of Lamer C.J., to an obligation for the Crown to consult and work with Aboriginal peoples in the jurisprudence of the present Court. Lori Sterling and Peter Landmann examine the practical implications of the development of the duty to consult, specifically from the perspective of government.

Turning to the *Charter* outside of the criminal context, Nathalie Des Rosiers examines the McLachlin Court's freedom of religion jurisprudence. On equality, Daniel Proulx examines the landmark decision of *R. v. Kapp*[15] and how it recentred the section 15 inquiry on non-discrimination. Moving to another landmark decision, Thomas Kuttner reflects on the *B.C. Health Services*[16] decision and the right to freedom of association under the *Charter*.

In the last section of this volume, our contributors address the old and the new at the Supreme Court. Criminal law has always been a public law mainstay of the Supreme Court of Canada. It has remained a priority for the McLachlin Court and in Don Stuart's comprehensive assessment of the McLachlin Court's criminal justice jurisprudence, there are many more positive developments than negative ones. Over the past several decades, international law has played an increasingly important role at the Supreme Court of Canada. John Currie analyzes the use of international law in the jurisprudence of the McLachlin Court and its relationship with Canadian law. Currie concludes that the McLachlin Court has clarified certain issues

---

13 *Canadian Western Bank v. Alberta*, 2007 SCC 22, [2007] 2 S.C.R. 3.

14 *British Columbia (Attorney General) v. Lafarge Canada Inc.*, 2007 SCC 23, [2007] 2 S.C.R. 86.

15 *R. v. Kapp*, 2008 SCC 41, [2008] 2 S.C.R. 483.

16 *Health Services and Support—Facilities Subsector Bargaining Association v. British Columbia*, 2007 SCC 27, [2007] 2 S.C.R. 391.

but there are others that remain open, it is hoped, to be addressed by the McLachlin Court in its second decade.

Les trois articles introductifs proposent des thèmes principaux qui reviennent au cours du volume. Comme l'indique Irvine, la Cour a changé de façon significative certains principes importants du droit administratif, du fédéralisme, du droit autochtone, de l'égalité, et de la liberté d'association. La plupart des auteurs sont d'avis que les modifications apportées à la jurisprudence dans ces domaines sont positives. L'étude de données statistiques par Belleau, Lamontagne et Johnson met lumière sur l'influence de la juge en chef elle-même; comme le souligne certains autres articles, l'importance évidente des jugements qu'elle a écrit elle-même confirme son rôle important dans le développement du droit public canadien. Sossin met l'emphase sur la tendance de la Cour à ordonner des procédures de discussion et négociation au lieu d'imposer des correctifs substantifs spécifiques. D'autres articles, surtout ceux qui concernent le droit administratif, le droit autochtone et la liberté d'association font une évaluation préliminaire de l'efficacité de cette approche dans des domaines de droit particulières.

We are grateful for the work of our contributors, both for meeting tight deadlines and for their patience in dealing with a collective endeavour such as this one. We also thank Jeff Miller, president of Irwin Law, for his interest and support for this project. Irwin Law continues to expand and strengthen the field of legal scholarship in Canada. We had the assistance of a fabulous University of Ottawa law student, Samantha Newton, in the editing of this manuscript and our colleague and friend Michelle Flaherty assisted us with the editing of the French portions of the manuscripts with her usual combination of expertise, diligence, and good humour. Thank you so much, Michelle. Both of our families were patient with us as we poured over manuscripts, held conference calls, and coordinated emails. We appreciate their support in everything we do. Lastly, we are united by a strong public law force who brought us together and continues to inspire us. We each clerked for Claire L'Heureux-Dubé J. and her passion for public law and for justice was infectious. Madame, from each of us, thank you for everything. You often instructed us on the need to "*frapper quand le fer est chaud*" ("to strike while the iron is hot"). In compiling this collection, we have tried to do just that.

This volume attempts to capture the dynamism of the McLachlin Court. In many ways, this endeavour is like trying to describe the route travelled and the location of a vehicle that is still in motion. We leave it to the reader to judge the success of our endeavours. In any event, whether the second decade of the McLachlin Court will prove to be as dynamic as the first or whether it will be a time of consolidation remains to be seen. Those judgments and that book remain to be written.

PART ONE

Broad Perspectives

Changing Course or Trimming Sails? The Supreme Court Reconsiders

THOMSON IRVINE*

A. INTRODUCTION

When should a court of last resort reconsider its own decisions? In the past few years, the Supreme Court of Canada has demonstrated a remarkable willingness to review its own decisions and to reach new results. This tendency raises questions about the stability and predictability of the law set out by the Court, in a wide range of areas. On the other hand, it means that counsel advancing new issues and new approaches may find a receptive audience with the Court, particularly if they combine arguments based on principle with a pragmatic critique of the actual operation of the law. This is a time for creative arguments by counsel.

For example, in one recent case, the *Health Services* decision, the Court completely changed course and overruled four of its own cases decided under the *Canadian Charter of Rights and Freedoms*, relating to freedom of association and the right to collective bargaining. This decision is the clearest example of the Court's willingness to reconsider its own precedents. In other cases, the Court has re-examined some of its earlier decisions and changed its approach without overruling the earlier case—a trimming of

* The views expressed in this paper are my own, and do not necessarily represent the views of the Ministry. I would like to thank my colleague, Graeme Mitchell, Q.C., for his suggestions and also acknowledge the assistance provided by his article, "'Cleaning House' or *Stare Decisis* in the Supreme Court of Canada" (2007) 16 Policy Dialogue 18 (Saskatchewan Institute of Public Policy). I also wish to thank my wife, Sharon Pratchler, Q.C., for her professional comments and support, and also for her solo supervision of our very active son, Graeme Glen, at various times during the preparation of this article.

the sails. Recent cases dealing with tobacco advertising, judicial compensation commissions, judicial review of administrative action, and equality claims have all resulted in significant departures from the approaches that the Court had used in some of its earlier cases, without formally overruling those cases.

In reviewing the Court's decisions during the period of Chief Justice McLachlin's tenure, I have selected ten cases illustrating this tendency, all from 2005 and onwards. This is not intended as an exhaustive review of all cases where the Court has reconsidered its own decisions, but is aimed at those with a substantial public law impact. As well, since my focus is on the Court's willingness to reconsider its own decisions, this article is not intended to be a detailed review of the numerous legal and constitutional issues that arose in all of these cases.

B. THE TEN CASES

My list of ten cases, in (almost) chronological order, is as follows:

1. *Canada (Attorney General) v. JTI-Macdonald Corp.* (2007).[1]
2. *Provincial Court Judges' Association of New Brunswick v. New Brunswick (Minister of Justice)* (2005).[2]
3. *British Columbia v. Imperial Tobacco Canada Ltd.* (2005).[3]
4. *British Columbia (Attorney General) v. Christie* (2007).[4]
5. *Canadian Western Bank v. Alberta* (2007).[5]
6. *R. v. Hape* (2007).[6]
7. *Health Services and Support—Facilities Subsector Bargaining Association v. British Columbia* (2007).[7]
8. *Dunsmuir v. New Brunswick* (2008).[8]

---

1 *Canada (Attorney General) v. JTI-Macdonald Corp.*, [2007] 2 S.C.R. 610, 2007 SCC 30 [*JTI-Macdonald*].

2 *Provincial Court Judges' Association of New Brunswick v. New Brunswick (Minister of Justice)*, [2005] 2 S.C.R. 286, 2005 SCC 44 [*Provincial Court Judges' Association*].

3 *British Columbia v. Imperial Tobacco Canada Ltd.*, [2005] 2 S.C.R. 473, 2005 SCC 49 [*Imperial Tobacco*].

4 *British Columbia (Attorney General) v. Christie*, [2007] 1 S.C.R. 873, 2007 SCC 21 [*Christie*].

5 *Canadian Western Bank v. Alberta*, [2007] 2 S.C.R. 3, 2007 SCC 22 [*Canadian Western Bank*].

6 *R. v. Hape*, [2007] 2 S.C.R. 292, 2007 SCC 26 [*Hape*].

7 *Health Services and Support—Facilities Subsector Bargaining Association v. British Columbia*, [2007] 2 S.C.R. 391, 2007 SCC 27 [*Health Services*].

8 *Dunsmuir v. New Brunswick*, [2008] 1 S.C.R. 190, 2008 SCC 9 [*Dunsmuir*].

RÉSUMÉ

Depuis quelques années, la Cour suprême du Canada manifeste une volonté remarquable de réexaminer ses propres décisions. Le présent article passe en revue dix causes instruites entre 2005 et 2008, pour lesquelles la Cour suprême a réexaminé un certain nombre de ses causes précédentes. Dans toutes ces décisions, la Cour a modifié son approche analytique. Dans une affaire, la Cour a même infirmé quatre de ses premières décisions en vertu de la *Charte canadienne des droits et libertés.* L'article fait état des raisons avancées par le tribunal dans ces affaires en vue d'expliquer le réexamen de ses décisions antérieures. L'auteur conclut que la Cour suprême est actuellement très pragmatique en ce qui a trait à la révision de ses décisions et à sa volonté de réexaminer des approches qui ne semblent pas bien fonctionner en pratique. La Cour suprême est aussi ouverte aux arguments imaginatifs fondés sur les principes réclamant des changements à sa propre jurisprudence.

9. *Société des Acadiens et Acadiennes du Nouveau-Brunswick Inc. v. Canada* (2008).[9]
10. *R. v. Kapp* (2008).[10]

There are at least five points of interest about this list of cases. The first is that the topics are diverse: several different *Charter* issues are included, as well as a division of powers case and a non-constitutional case dealing with the judicial review of administrative tribunals and the employment rights of public employees. Given this diversity, I do not think that this trend can be explained solely as the Court re-examining its early *Charter* cases.

A second point is that in the first case on the list, *JTI-Macdonald Corp.* (a case which dealt with freedom of expression and tobacco advertising), McLachlin C.J. reached a decision diametrically opposed to one of her own earlier decisions. That decision is a clear indication that the chief justice is willing to reconsider her own decisions.

A third point of interest is that three cases on the list all relate to one of the landmark decisions of the Lamer Court, namely, the *Reference re Re-*

9 *Société des Acadiens et Acadiennes du Nouveau-Brunswick Inc. v. Canada*, [2008] 1 S.C.R. 383, 2008 SCC 15.

10 *R. v. Kapp*, [2008] 2 S.C.R. 483, 2008 SCC 41 [*Kapp*].

muneration of Judges of the Provincial Court of Prince Edward Island.[11] The Court under McLachlin C.J. appears to have pulled back considerably from the *Judges' Compensation Reference*, both in the application of that case to the issue of judicial compensation, and in the consideration of the underlying theory of unwritten constitutional principles espoused by Chief Justice Lamer in the Reference.

The fourth point is that it is not possible to characterize these cases easily as showing a "conservative/liberal" dichotomy nor an "activist/deferential" approach. Some of the decisions, such as the new judicial compensation case, pay considerable deference to government action. Others, notably the *Health Services* decision, markedly restrict government action in an area of sensitive social policy—health care reform. Still others show the Court struggling with difficult jurisprudential issues that do not fit into such dichotomies, such as the cases dealing with equality under section 15 or judicial review of administrative action.

The fifth and final point is that there is a strong streak of pragmatism running through these cases. The Court appears to be very willing to take the actual operation of its previous decisions into account. Analytical approaches that have proven difficult to apply in practice may be ripe for review and rejection by the Court. The Court wants to makes its decisions work.

C. ANALYSIS

1) *Canada (Attorney General) v. JTI-Macdonald Corp.*: The Court Upholds Federal Restrictions on Tobacco Advertising

I begin with this case, out of its chronological order, because in it, McLachlin C.J. reached a completely different decision than McLachlin J. had made twelve years earlier. It is one of the most interesting examples of the McLachlin Court re-examining an earlier decision of the Court. It also illustrates the chief justice's own willingness to reconsider her prior decisions.

The 1995 case was *RJR-MacDonald Inc. v. Canada (Attorney General)*.[12] At issue were the extensive restrictions on tobacco advertising which Parliament had enacted in the *Tobacco Products Control Act*.[13] The Court, in a 5:4

11 *Reference re Remuneration of Judges of the Provincial Court of Prince Edward Island*, [1997] 3 S.C.R. 3 [*Judges' Compensation Reference*].

12 *RJR-MacDonald Inc. v. Canada (Attorney General)*, [1995] 3 S.C.R. 199 [*RJR-MacDonald*].

13 *Tobacco Products Control Act*, S.C. 1988, c. 20.

decision, struck down the federal statute. Although several members of the Court wrote opinions, McLachlin J.'s opinion attracted majority support. There was little doubt that the restrictions infringed freedom of expression, guaranteed by section 2(b) of the *Charter*. The main issue was whether the federal government had justified the restrictions under section 1 of the *Charter*. Justice McLachlin held that the federal government had not satisfied its onus under section 1 and struck down the legislation.

Parliament responded by enacting new restrictions on tobacco advertising, set out in the *Tobacco Act* of 1997.[14] Although there were some differences in approach, the new legislation was generally similar to the former Act. The tobacco companies promptly challenged the new restrictions, relying on the Court's earlier decision. In 2007, in *Canada (Attorney General) v. JTI-Macdonald Corp.*, the Court ruled on the challenge. Speaking for the unanimous Court, McLachlin C.J. upheld the new federal advertising restrictions in their entirety.

In addition to the technical differences between the first and second federal tobacco acts, a key difference was the factual record before the Court in each case. In the 1995 case, the sufficiency of evidence to provide the justification under section 1 had been very much in issue.[15] In response, in the 2007 case the federal Attorney General had produced a voluminous evidential record aimed at proving the harm that tobacco causes, the fact that young people are particularly susceptible to picking up the tobacco habit, and that tobacco advertising induced young people and other vulnerable people to start smoking.[16]

In the 2007 case, McLachlin C.J. referred to this detailed body of evidence as a significant factor in reviewing the new law under section 1.[17] She held that the new evidence did not relieve the government of its obligation to justify the new measures under section 1, but she acknowledged that significant contextual changes could well lead to a different result under section 1.[18] In the result, McLachlin C.J. upheld the new law in its entirety, by a combination of statutory interpretation techniques and a justification of the law under section 1.

---

14 *Tobacco Act*, S.C. 1997, c. 13.

15 *RJR-MacDonald*, above note 12, paras. 83–108, La Forest J., dissenting; paras. 155–74, McLachlin J.

16 *JTI-Macdonald*, above note 1, paras. 12–17.

17 *Ibid.* at para. 9.

18 *Ibid.* at para. 11.

Given her decision striking down the earlier federal tobacco restrictions, the chief justice's decision in *JTI-Macdonald* in 2007 leads to interesting questions: was it simply the facts and the context which had changed? Or had the chief justice's own approach to *Charter* analysis developed over the intervening twelve years, as part of the Court's emphasis on contextual analysis and the concept of a *Charter* dialogue between the courts and Parliament? Was this decision simply an example of the McLachlin Court taking a more deferential approach to Parliament's decisions on matters of social policy? Or was it a relaxation of the standards for social sciences evidence needed for section 1 justification?

It is obviously difficult to attempt to answer these questions, since they delve into the motivations of the chief justice and the other judges of the Court. However, the chief justice's own reference to the detailed new evidence presented by the Attorney General of Canada is a clear indication of her thoughts on this point. Ever since the Court initially set out the framework for section 1 issues in *R. v. Oakes*,[19] section 1 analysis has been, and remains, a heavily fact-based inquiry.[20] There is certainly a sound basis to say that different facts can lead to a different result under section 1. As well, a perusal of the trial decision of the Quebec Superior Court reveals that the federal Attorney General's approach to the trial was heavily fact-based, as was the response of the tobacco companies.[21]

---

19 *R. v. Oakes*, [1986] 1 S.C.R. 103.

20 The Court emphasized this point in *MacKay v. Manitoba*, [1989] 2 S.C.R. 357 at 361–62:

> *Charter* decisions should not and must not be made in a factual vacuum. To attempt to do so would trivialize the *Charter* and inevitably result in ill-considered opinions. The presentation of facts is not, as stated by the respondent, a mere technicality; rather, it is essential to a proper consideration of *Charter* issues. A respondent cannot, by simply consenting to dispense with the factual background, require or expect a court to deal with an issue such as this in a factual void. *Charter* decisions cannot be based upon the unsupported hypotheses of enthusiastic counsel.

21 *J.T.I. MacDonald Corp. c. Canada (Procureure Générale)*, J.E. 2003-137, [2003] R.J.Q. 181, 102 C.R.R. (2d) 189 (Que. C.S.). As Denis J. noted:

> 100 Witnesses were heard from January to June 2002. Closing arguments were heard in September 2002, and the case was taken under advisement on September 19, 2002.
>
> 101 The hearing generated nearly 10,000 pages of stenographic notes, and 988 exhibits totalling hundreds of thousands of pages were entered into the record.
>
> 540 As already mentioned, this trial has been a most demanding one. No fewer than 22 lawyers from all parties took part in it.

See also the Appendices which Denis J. attached to his decision: Appendix 1 (Summary of Testimony); Appendix 3 (Interim Decision on the Use of Extrinsic Evidence); Appendix 4 (Health Canada Warnings); and Appendix 5 (Brazilian Warnings). I should mention that

At the same time, it is hard not to have the impression that the Court has moved towards a posture of greater deference to the policy decisions of the elected branch, at least in some matters of general social policy and in relation to social sciences evidence. The outcome of this case, where one federal law was upheld while a very similar had been struck down just twelve years earlier, points very strongly towards the adoption of a more deferential standard. This impression is strengthened by the Court's reconsideration of the issue of judicial salaries, the next case considered.

2) *Provincial Court Judges' Association of New Brunswick v. New Brunswick (Minister of Justice)*: Judicial Compensation Commissions—The Degree of Deference Revisited

The question of the authority of the judicial compensation commissions arose in *Provincial Court Judges' Association of New Brunswick v. New Brunswick (Minister of Justice)*.[22] Although this case built on the analytical framework that the Court had set out in the *Judges' Compensation Reference*, the result was to establish marked deference to the decisions of governments relating to judicial remuneration.

The *Judges' Compensation Reference* was one of the most significant cases decided by the Lamer Court. In a 6:1 decision, Lamer C.J. held that in order to protect judicial independence, the Constitution requires governments to set up commissions on a regular basis to hear submissions from the judiciary and the government on the appropriate level of salary for judges.[23] As well, the decisions of those commissions were to have "meaningful effect" on the determination of judicial salaries.[24] Governments would then be required to comply with those recommendations, unless there was a rational basis for departing from the recommendations.[25] If they did not follow the recommendations, governments would be required to justify their decision, "if necessary in a court of law."[26] Chief Justice Lamer believed that this commission process would depoliticize the issue of judicial compensation.[27]

I was counsel for the Attorney General for Saskatchewan in this case at the Supreme Court, and the breadth of evidence filed by the parties was striking.

22 *Provincial Court Judges' Association*, above note 2.

23 *Judges' Compensation Reference*, above note 11 at para. 147.

24 *Ibid.* at para. 175.

25 *Ibid.* at para. 183.

26 *Ibid.* at para. 180.

27 *Ibid.* at para. 147.

Eight years later, the issue of the authority of the judicial compensation commissions came before the Court again, in *Provincial Court Judges' Association of New Brunswick*. The unanimous decision by the Court began with the interesting comment that the commission process had not so far lived up to the hopes that it would end conflict over judicial compensation and depoliticize the process.[28] In several provinces, the process had actually exacerbated friction between judges and governments, resulting in litigation. The Court stated that the litigation was caused by the uncertainty about the scope of the powers of governments under the principles the Court itself had set out in the *Judges' Compensation Reference*.[29] This comment reflects a theme of pragmatic reappraisal which is echoed in several of the other cases examined in this paper.

The Court commented that the principles of the *Judges' Compensation Reference* remained valid.[30] However, the Court then noted that considerable disagreement had emerged about the statement in the Reference that the decisions of the commissions were to have a "meaningful effect" on the determination of judicial compensation. Some Provincial Court judges' associations had argued that "meaningful effect" meant that the commission decisions were generally binding on governments. Governments, on the other hand, had argued that "meaningful effect" meant an open process, but that they were not bound by the commissions' recommendations.[31]

It was also unclear what factors, if any, would justify a government's refusal to implement the recommendations of a commission. Chief Justice Lamer's strong wording in the Reference, including a comparison to *Reference re Anti-inflation Act* dealing with emergency situations,[32] suggested that only very exceptional circumstances could justify a government in refusing to follow the recommendations of a judicial compensation commission. It appeared that the commissions might in practice amount to a form of binding arbitration.

In *Provincial Court Judges' Association*, the Court resolved these questions in favour of the governments. It held that the Reference required an open process, not a binding one.[33] The Court emphasized that the commission

---

28 *Provincial Court Judges' Association*, above note 2 at para. 12.

29 *Ibid.* at para. 22.

30 *Ibid.* at para. 13.

31 *Ibid.* at para. 19.

32 *Reference re Anti-Inflation Act*, [1976] 2 S.C.R. 373; cited by Lamer C.J. in *Judges' Compensation Reference*, above note 11 at para. 183.

33 *Provincial Court Judges' Association*, above note 2 at para. 20.

process was consultative in nature[34] and that governments had the power to reject or vary a commission's recommendations.[35] Judicial review of a government's decision should be rare,[36] and if sought, the reviewing court should approach the government's decision with considerable deference.[37] The Court also stated that a government did not need exceptional circumstances to depart from a commission's recommendations,[38] which some had inferred from Lamer C.J.'s mention of the *Reference re Anti-Inflation Act*.

Although the Court stated it was following the general principles established in the *Judges' Compensation Reference*, the net effect of the decision was to return considerable discretion to the elected branches of government in determining judicial compensation. The Court made it clear that the commission process is consultative in nature. Governments retain the ultimate authority to determine if they will accept the recommendations of a commission.

3) *British Columbia v. Imperial Tobacco Canada Ltd.*: The Court Declines to Expand on Unwritten Constitutional Principles

Shortly after the *Provincial Court Judges' Association* case, the Court dealt with a case which considered a different aspect of the *Judges' Compensation Reference*: the concept of unwritten constitutional principles. In the Reference, Lamer C.J. had grounded the concept of judicial independence in the Preamble to the *Constitution Act, 1867*, which he referred to as "the grand entrance hall to the castle of the Constitution."[39] He held that the written text of the Constitution was neither comprehensive nor definitive.[40] Rather, the written provisions of the Constitution simply elaborated upon the Preamble's recognition of unwritten constitutional principles. He also held that the Preamble's unwritten constitutional principles give the courts the power to fill perceived gaps in the written text of the Constitution.[41]

Chief Justice Lamer's elaboration of the concept of unwritten constitutional principles grounded in the Preamble was a significant development in constitutional theory, and was not without controversy. Did Lamer C.J.'s

---

34 *Ibid.* at para. 21.

35 *Ibid.* at para. 25.

36 *Ibid.* at para. 28.

37 *Ibid.* at paras. 30 and 40.

38 *Ibid.* at para. 34.

39 *Judges' Compensation Reference*, above note 11 at para. 109.

40 *Ibid.* at paras. 89 and 109.

41 *Ibid.* at para. 95.

reliance on unwritten constitutional principles mark a sea change in constitutional interpretation? Some would argue that the legitimacy of judicial review comes from the fact that the courts are interpreting and applying the written text of a carefully drafted Constitution. Did Lamer C.J.'s concept of justiciable unwritten constitutional principles undermine that legitimacy?

In *British Columbia v. Imperial Tobacco Canada Ltd.*,[42] the Court was asked to infer additional unwritten constitutional principles, this time based on the rule of law. At issue was British Columbia legislation that authorized tort actions by the province against the major tobacco companies to recover health care costs. The legislation created a new statutory tort allowing the government to sue the tobacco companies for health care costs, and made this liability retroactive. Normal limitation periods did not apply, enabling the government to sue for costs alleged to have occurred years, if not decades, previously. The law also made various procedural and evidentiary innovations to assist the government to make its case against the tobacco companies, such as allowing aggregate claims, with a reversal of the onus of proof on certain elements.

The tobacco companies challenged the legislation on a variety of grounds, including a challenge based on the theory of unwritten constitutional principles. They relied on the Preamble to the *Constitution Act, 1982*, which provides that Canada is founded on principles that recognize the rule of law. They argued that the British Columbia statute violated the rule of law by its marked departures from normal principles of civil liability and judicial process, particularly since the changes were all designed to benefit the same government which had passed the law.

The Court unanimously rejected this argument and declined the invitation to flesh out the unwritten principles of the Constitution. Speaking for the Court, Major J. held that the Preamble's reference to the rule of law did not prohibit the government of British Columbia from establishing a retroactive system of tort liability for tobacco manufacturers. He rejected the argument advanced by the tobacco companies, commenting that if accepted, their approach would seriously undermine the legitimacy of judicial review under the Constitution.[43] He added:

> Put differently, the appellants' arguments fail to recognize that in a constitutional democracy such as ours, protection from legislation that some

42 *Imperial Tobacco*, above note 3.

43 *Ibid.* at para. 64.

> might view as unjust or unfair properly lies not in the amorphous underlying principles of our Constitution, but in its text and the ballot box. See *Bacon v. Saskatchewan Crop Insurance Corp.* (1999), 180 Sask. R. 20 (C.A.), at para. 30.[44]

Justice Major's analysis of this issue affirmed that constitutional interpretation must be based on the written text of the Constitution. He stated that the rule of law "requires that courts give effect to the Constitution's text, and apply, by whatever its terms, legislation that conforms to that text."[45] This analysis differs considerably from Lamer C.J.'s reliance on the "the grand entrance hall to the castle of the Constitution" as the source for enforceable unwritten constitutional principles.

4) *British Columbia (Attorney General) v. Christie*: The Court Again Declines to Expand the Unwritten Constitutional Principles

In *British Columbia (Attorney General) v. Christie,*[46] the Court again declined an invitation to use the rule of law to strike down a provincial statute. At issue was a provincial tax which applied to legal services provided by lawyers to their clients. The challengers argued that by taxing legal services, the province was burdening access to the administration of justice, contrary to the rule of law. The Court unanimously dismissed the argument, holding that such a reading of the rule of law would render redundant the right to counsel set out in section 10(b) of the *Charter.*[47] Nor could the rule of law be read generally to require a right to counsel in all cases.[48] Absent such a right, there was no basis to challenge the tax on legal services.

Taken together, *Imperial Tobacco* and *Christie* mark a considerable retreat from the broad concept of unwritten constitutional principles espoused in the *Judges' Compensation Reference.* These two cases suggest that the Court will not easily be persuaded to use unwritten constitutional principles to create enforceable constitutional rights, in spite of the very expansive language used by Lamer C.J. in the *Judges' Compensation Reference.*

---

44 *Ibid.* at para. 66.

45 *Ibid.* at para. 67.

46 *Christie*, above note 4.

47 *Ibid.* at para. 25.

48 *Ibid.* at paras. 23 and 27.

5) *Canadian Western Bank v. Alberta*: The Court Freezes the Interjurisdictional Immunity Doctrine

The decision in *Canadian Western Bank v. Alberta*[49] is the only division of powers case on my list. It resulted in the Court freezing the interjurisdictional immunity doctrine to apply only to situations already covered by precedent. The Court held that the doctrine cannot be expanded to apply to other situations. This decision marked a pulling back from a developing trend in which the Court seemed to be willing to expand the application of the doctrine. The Court's decision cast a sharp restraint on a constitutional doctrine which had been expanding over the past century.

The question in *Canadian Western Bank* was whether provincial insurance laws apply to federally chartered banks selling insurance products as part of their business, such as mortgage insurance or credit card insurance. There was no doubt that the insurance laws were *intra vires* the province, as an exercise of provincial jurisdiction over property and civil rights. However, the banks argued that even though the laws were constitutionally valid, the interjurisdictional immunity doctrine meant that the insurance laws did not apply to the federally chartered banks.

The interjurisdictional immunity doctrine has its roots in a series of cases from the early twentieth century, in which the Privy Council held that provincial laws could not sterilize the vital aspects of federally incorporated companies.[50] The Supreme Court later expanded the doctrine in cases such as *Commission du salaire minimum v. Bell Telephone Co. of Canada*[51] and *Bell Canada v. Quebec (Commission de la santé et de la sécurité du travail).*[52] In these cases, the Court held that the doctrine of interjurisdictional immunity went beyond the concept of sterilization and concluded that the core operations of federally regulated undertakings were immune from provincial workplace laws, such as labour standards and occupational health laws. More recently, in *Ordon Estate v. Grail*,[53] the Court had applied the doctrine of interjurisdictional immunity in a division of powers case relating to maritime law that did not involve federally regulated undertakings. In another case, *Law Society of British Columbia v. Mangat*,[54] the Court had considered

---

49 *Canadian Western Bank*, above note 5.

50 *John Deere Plow Co. Ltd. v. Wharton*, [1915] A.C. 330 (P.C.); *Great West Saddlery v. The King*, [1921] 2 A.C. 91 (P.C.).

51 *Commission du salaire minimum v. Bell Telephone Co. of Canada*, [1966] S.C.R. 767.

52 *Bell Canada v. Quebec (Commission de la santé et de la sécurité du travail)*, [1988] 1 S.C.R. 749.

53 *Ordon Estate v. Grail*, [1998] 3 S.C.R. 437.

54 *Law Society of British Columbia v. Mangat*, [2001] 3 S.C.R. 113, 2001 SCC 67.

applying the doctrine to business agents appearing before federal administrative tribunals, but ultimately resolved the case under the paramountcy doctrine.

The banks now argued that the doctrine also applied to their business activities, such as selling insurance. Several provinces and insurance groups intervened to oppose the position of the banks and to argue that the interjurisdictional immunity doctrine did not prevent provincial insurance laws from applying to the banks. One intervener, the Attorney General for Saskatchewan, went further and argued that the interjurisdictional immunity doctrine should be abolished completely, on the basis that it runs counter to well-established constitutional doctrines such as the double aspect doctrine, and also that it had the effect of incrementally increasing the scope of federal jurisdiction.[55]

The Court ruled unanimously that the provincial insurance laws applied to the banks, splitting 6:1 on the reasons. Speaking for the majority, Binnie and Le Bel JJ. held that the interjurisdictional immunity doctrine did not sit well with the general principles of the division of powers, notably the double aspect doctrine.[56] They also agreed that the doctrine could have an unintended centralizing tendency, favouring the federal government asymmetrically over the provinces.[57] They did not go so far as to accept Saskatchewan's invitation to abolish the doctrine, but they held that the doctrine was of limited application and in the future should be applied only in situations already covered by the Court's precedents. The doctrine should not be expanded further.[58]

Justice Bastarache wrote a concurring decision. He agreed that the banks were subject to provincial insurance laws, but he would have gone entirely in the other direction with respect to interjurisdictional immunity. Justice Bastarache concluded that the interjurisdictional immunity doctrine should be considered in all division of powers cases, not just cases involving federally regulated undertakings.[59] This approach would mean that interjurisdictional immunity would no longer be confined to its roots in federal undertakings, but would become a potential limitation on the application of provincial laws in every division of powers case.

---

55 In the interests of openness, I mention that I was counsel for the Attorney General for Saskatchewan in this case.

56 *Canadian Western Bank*, above note 5 at para. 42.

57 *Ibid.* at para. 45.

58 *Ibid.* at paras. 77 & 78.

59 *Ibid.* at para. 112.

The case is unusual because of the willingness of both the majority and the minority to depart from the Court's previous approach to a well-established constitutional doctrine. The majority acknowledged that the Court's earlier cases had recognized that in theory, the doctrine of interjurisdictional immunity could be given broader application.[60] They instead chose to confine the doctrine to cases already covered by precedent. That decision to pre-empt any further expansion of a constitutional doctrine is also somewhat unusual. By contrast, Bastarache J. was equally willing to depart from the Court's cases, but he would have greatly expanded the doctrine, making it part of the analysis in every division of powers case. Either way, all of the judges of the Court were willing to reconsider their earlier decisions on this significant constitutional doctrine.

6) *R. v. Hape*: The Court Reduces the Extraterritorial Application of the *Charter*

In *R. v. Hape*,[61] the Court decided an issue concerning the extraterritorial scope of the *Charter*, and in doing so, revisited a similar case decided in 1998, *R. v. Cook*.[62] Both cases concerned the application of the *Charter* to acts of Canadian police officers operating in a foreign country. Although the Court had previously held in *Cook* that the *Charter* could apply to extraterritorial actions by Canadian police officers, in *Hape* the Court by a 5:4 majority reversed course and held that the *Charter* did not apply extraterritorially, except in very limited circumstances.

In *Cook*, the issue was whether the accused had the right to be warned of the right to counsel under section 10(b) of the *Charter* before being interrogated by Canadian police officers operating in the United States. The Court had held that the *Charter* could apply to the actions of Canadian officials abroad, depending on two factors: whether the impugned act fell within the scope of section 32 of the *Charter*, and whether the application of *Charter* standards in the particular case would conflict with the concurrent territorial jurisdiction of the foreign state. The Court held in *Cook* that under that two-pronged test, the *Charter*'s counsel guarantee did apply. Since the Canadian officers had not advised the accused of his right to counsel before interrogating him, his statement was excluded.

60 *Ibid.* at para. 67.

61 *Hape*, above note 6.

62 *R. v. Cook*, [1998] 2 S.C.R. 597.

In *Hape*, the issue was whether evidence obtained in a warrantless search in the Turks and Caicos Islands had been obtained contrary to section 8 of the *Charter* and therefore should be excluded under section 24(2). Under Turks and Caicos law, a warrant was apparently not necessary for the search in question, and the search was therefore lawful there. However, a warrant would have been required for a similar search in Canada.

In a lengthy decision, LeBel J. for the majority reviewed the issue of extraterritorial application of laws and the treatment of that issue at international law. He criticized the majority in *Cook* for failing to take these principles into account, particularly the international law concept that one country's laws cannot apply in another country without the consent of that country.[63] He also emphasized the practical difficulties that arose from a case such as that before the Court, where the Canadian officers had been acting under the authority of the police in the foreign country and had complied with the legal requirements for a search in that country.[64] He concluded that the *Charter* would apply only if the actor in question were a Canadian state actor, and if there were an exception to the principle of sovereignty which would justify the extraterritorial application of the *Charter*.[65] Applying that test, he held that although the Royal Canadian Mounted Police (RCMP) officers were officers of the Canadian state, the searches took place in the Turks and Caicos Islands, outside the authority of the Parliament of Canada, and therefore the *Charter* did not apply.[66]

Justice Bastarache spoke for three of the minority justices. He agreed that there were difficulties with the reasons of the majority in *Cook*,[67] but he accepted *Cook*'s general principle that the *Charter* could have extraterritorial application.[68] He held that the *Charter* did apply to the actions of the RCMP officers in the Turks and Caicos Islands, but the accused had not established a breach of section 8 of the *Charter* because the RCMP officers had complied with the Turks and Caicos law authorizing searches.[69]

The fourth justice in the minority, Binnie J., wrote to similar effect, but strongly criticized the approach taken by LeBel J. He stated that in his opin-

63 *Hape*, above note 6 at para. 84.
64 *Ibid.* at paras. 86–90.
65 *Ibid.* at para. 113.
66 *Ibid.* at para. 118.
67 *Ibid.* at para. 158.
68 *Ibid.* at para. 178.
69 *Ibid.* at para. 179.

ion, the majority was effectively overruling *Cook*.[70] He also pointed out that none of the parties had challenged the analysis in *Cook* and that the Court was deciding an issue without the benefit of any reasons from the lower courts on the issue.[71] He concluded that the case could be decided under the principles set out in *Cook*, and that the accused had not brought himself within those requirements.[72]

Why did the Court feel a need to revisit this issue, even though it had not been raised by the parties or by the lower courts? It is hard not to conclude that the timing had something to do with this issue. *Cook* was decided in 1998, three years before 9/11. *Hape* was decided in 2007, six years after 9/11 and Canada's entry into the war in Afghanistan. While both cases involved Canadian police officers, it is not a stretch to see that the question of the extraterritorial application of the *Charter* may have implications for Canadian military and police operating abroad under national security mandates. Both LeBel J. and Binnie J. referred to this issue in their reasons.[73] The majority's reasons suggest that the *Charter* would not have extraterritorial effect in these situations.

7) *Health Services and Support—Facilities Subsector Bargaining Association v. British Columbia*: The Court Overrules Four of Its Own Decisions

In all of the cases discussed so far, the Court did not actually overrule any of its previous decisions, but instead either changed the scope or restricted the application of a prior decision. However, in one 2007 case—*Health Services*[74]—the Court formally overruled four of its own *Charter* decisions: the 1987 *Labour Trilogy*[75] as well as *Professional Institute of the Public Service of Canada v. Northwest Territories (Commissioner)*,[76] which had elaborated upon the principles set out in the *Labour Trilogy*. Those four cases had found that

70 *Ibid.* at para. 182.

71 *Ibid.* at paras. 187 and 189.

72 *Ibid.* at para. 181.

73 *Ibid.* at para. 95, LeBel J. and paras. 183–84, Binnie J.

74 *Health Services*, above note 7.

75 *Reference re Public Service Employee Relations Act (Alta.)*, [1987] 1 S.C.R. 313; *PSAC v. Canada*, [1987] 1 S.C.R. 424; and *RWDSU v. Saskatchewan*, [1987] 1 S.C.R. 460.

76 *Professional Institute of the Public Service of Canada v. Northwest Territories (Commissioner)*, [1990] 2 S.C.R. 367.

the *Charter*'s guarantee of freedom of association did not include a constitutional right to collective bargaining.

In the *Health Services* case, the Court unanimously reversed this conclusion and held that freedom of association included a constitutional right to collective bargaining. Chief Justice McLachlin and LeBel J. wrote the main set of reasons. They held that the four earlier decisions of the Court did not "withstand principled scrutiny and should be rejected."[77] Justice Deschamps agreed with this conclusion,[78] but dissented in part on the exact interpretation of freedom of association[79] and justification under section 1.[80]

Chief Justice McLachlin and LeBel J. found that the earlier decisions failed to recognize the history of collective bargaining in Canada;[81] that it was inappropriate for the Court to declare that an entire area of the law was outside the scope of the *Charter*;[82] that the earlier cases erred by focusing narrowly on individuals instead of recognizing that freedom of association protects inherently collective activities;[83] and that the earlier cases improperly linked the process of collective bargaining with the outcome of collective bargaining as a basis for excluding both aspects from the ambit of freedom of association.[84] They also noted that in a later case, *Dunmore v. Ontario (Attorney General)*, the Court had reconsidered the meaning of freedom of association and upheld a right to collective bargaining in a particular case.[85] In light of the Court's decision in *Dunmore* and the difficulties with the earlier cases, McLachlin C.J. and LeBel J. concluded that the earlier decisions could no longer stand.[86] They went on to hold that the *Charter* guarantee of freedom of association protected the process of collective bargaining generally.

Of all the cases considered in this paper, the *Health Services* case can best be explained as an example of the Court reconsidering a *Charter* issue in the light of twenty-five years of experience with the *Charter* and developments in *Charter* jurisprudence. Since the early years of the *Charter*, the

---

77 *Health Services*, above note 7 at para. 22.

78 *Ibid.* at para. 174.

79 *Ibid.* at para. 175.

80 *Ibid.* at para. 196.

81 *Ibid.* at para. 25.

82 *Ibid.* at para. 26.

83 *Ibid.* at para. 27.

84 *Ibid.* at para. 29.

85 *Dunmore v. Ontario (Attorney General)*, [2001] 3 S.C.R. 1016, 2001 SCC 94; *Health Services*, above note 7 at paras. 31–34.

86 *Health Services*, *ibid.* at para. 36.

Court has developed a rich, contextual-based approach to *Charter* issues. Looking back, the current members of the Court apparently felt that the early approach to freedom of association was too rigid and categorical. They evidently did not agree that an entire area of the law should be a *Charter*-free zone. Even so, the fact that the Court would unanimously state that four of its own relatively recent decisions did not "withstand principled scrutiny" is a remarkable statement. It indicates the current justices' willingness to re-examine their own decisions, but it is also a remarkably open criticism of the reasoning of some of their predecessors on the Court.[87]

To what extent does *Health Services* represent other factors, such as a nuanced understanding of the role of collective bargaining? This is a more difficult question to assess. One point that stands out is that the majority made a clear distinction between the process of collective bargaining, which is protected by freedom of association, and the goals and outcomes, which are not. The Court's view of freedom of association was process based, not substantive. As well, in *Health Services* the Court did not reconsider whether the right to strike is constitutionally guaranteed, which was the key issue in the *Labour Trilogy*. It may be that it was easier to view freedom of association as protecting procedure, while separating it from outcomes or remedies such as the right to strike.

8) *Dunsmuir v. New Brunswick*: Two Reconsiderations in One Case

a) The Two Issues

In *Dunsmuir v. New Brunswick*[88] the Court reconsidered not one, but two of its own prior decisions, in different areas of law: judicial review of administrative agencies, and the law governing dismissal of non-unionized public employees. On the first issue, all members of the Court agreed that the system of three standards of judicial review, which the Court had unanimously reaffirmed just five years before, was not working and needed reappraisal. However, the members of the Court could not agree on a new analytical framework to replace them. On the second issue, relating to the merits of the dismissal of Mr. Dunsmuir, the majority held that the arbitrator had erred by

---

87 The majority decisions for the six-judge panel in the *Labour Trilogy* were written by Le Dain J. (Beetz and La Forest JJ. concurring), with McIntyre J. writing separate concurring reasons. The majority in *Professional Institute* was written by Sopinka J., with additional concurring reasons written by Dickson C.J., and L'Heureux-Dubé and La Forest JJ.

88 *Dunsmuir*, above note 8.

following one of the Court's earlier decisions, *Knight v. Indian Head School Division No. 19.*[89] They held that *Knight* should not be followed in the future.

b) The Court Reviews Judicial Review of Administrative Tribunals

In recent years, judicial review of administrative tribunals has been one of the recurring themes of the Supreme Court's workload. In several cases, the Court has struggled to explain when reviewing courts should show deference to administrative tribunals, and when it is appropriate for the courts to intervene. In *Dunsmuir*, the Court returned to the issue and made a significant change relating to the standards of review, disavowing its own approach from only five years previously set out in *Law Society of New Brunswick v. Ryan.*[90]

In *Ryan*, the Court had responded to a suggestion from the lower court that there was a spectrum of standards that could be used in judicial review. Speaking for a unanimous Court, Iacobucci J. held that there were only three standards of review: correctness, reasonableness *simpliciter*, and patent unreasonableness.[91] The choice of the standard to apply in a particular case would depend on the pragmatic and functional approach the Court had set out in *U.E.S., Local 298 v. Bibeault.*[92]

In 2008, only five years later, the Court in *Dunsmuir* rejected the system of three standards of review it had reaffirmed in *Ryan*. Speaking for the majority, Bastarache and LeBel JJ. began their reasons with the frank statement that the Court's own decisions on the issue were complex, yet gave "no solutions that provide real guidance for litigants, counsel, administrative decision makers or judicial review judges."[93] Later on, they commented that even the Supreme Court judges themselves had found it difficult to apply their own distinction between reasonableness *simpliciter* and patent unreasonableness, "although this should have been self-evident under the existing test."[94] In an earlier decision, *Toronto (City) v. C.U.P.E., Local 79*, LeBel J. had commented at length on the difficulty of distinguishing between the two reasonableness standards and had raised the possibility of moving to a system of two standards of review.[95] Now, in *Dunsmuir*, the five

---

89 *Knight v. Indian Head School Division No. 19*, [1990] 1 S.C.R. 652.

90 *Law Society of New Brunswick v. Ryan*, [2003] 1 S.C.R. 247, 2003 SCC 20.

91 *Ibid.* at paras. 24–26.

92 *U.E.S., Local 298 v. Bibeault*, [1988] 2 S.C.R. 1048.

93 *Dunsmuir*, above note 8 at para. 1.

94 *Ibid.* at para. 41.

95 *Toronto (City) v. C.U.P.E., Local 79*, [2003] 3 S.C.R. 77, 2003 SCC 63 at paras. 63–134.

judges in the majority held that there would be only two standards of review: correctness and reasonableness (albeit with a great deal of nuance left in the issue of reasonableness).[96]

In addition to the majority decision, there were two other sets of reasons in *Dunsmuir*. Justices Binnie and Deschamps concurred in the result and agreed that the law governing judicial review needed reform, but they set out their own approaches to the issue.[97] Like the majority, Binnie J. highlighted the practical difficulties with the three standards of review previously established by the Court. He commented on the degree of analysis needed by counsel simply to establish the correct standard of review:

> The present incarnation of the "standard of review" analysis requires a threshold debate about the four factors (non-exhaustive) which critics say too often leads to unnecessary delay, uncertainty and costs as arguments rage before the court about balancing expertise against the "real" nature of the question before the administrator, or whether the existence of a privative clause trumps the larger statutory purpose, and so on. And this is all mere *preparation* for the argument about the actual substance of the case.[98]

However, Binnie J. was sceptical that the approach suggested by the majority would actually solve the problem, and suggested that it would simply be equivalent to shuffling traffic routes during rush hour.[99] While he agreed with the majority's adoption of only two standards of review, he argued that what was needed was "a more easily applied framework" of judicial review, for the benefit of both courts and litigants.[100] Justice Binnie suggested a two-fold approach: an increased focus on the context of the particular decision maker, with its implications for the scope of the "reasonableness" standard[101] and an initial presumption that the reasonableness standard would apply. The onus would always be on a litigant to demonstrate why this presumption should be displaced in favour of a correctness standard.[102]

---

96 *Dunsmuir*, above note 8 at paras. 43–50.

97 Justice Binnie wrote only for himself. Justice Deschamps attracted the support of Charron and Rothstein JJ.

98 *Ibid.* at para. 145 [emphasis in original].

99 *Ibid.* at para. 139.

100 *Ibid.* at para. 151.

101 *Ibid.* at paras. 150–55.

102 *Ibid.* at paras. 146–47.

Justice Deschamps took an entirely different approach. Like her colleagues, she emphasized the need to simplify the law of judicial review, which she stated not only needed repairs, but clearing of "superfluous discussions and processes."[103] Her approach was to focus on the nature of the question in issue. Drawing on the Court's recent analysis of appellate deference to fact-finding by trial courts,[104] Deschamps J. advocated different levels of deference for the decisions of administrative agencies, depending on whether the administrative decisions involved a question of fact, a question of law, or a question of mixed fact and law. For factual issues decided by an administrative agency, courts should automatically accord deference, just as with the fact-finding by trial courts.[105] By contrast, on questions of law, courts should have a greater freedom to intervene, since the interpretation of the law is a core function of the courts. Questions of law could nonetheless attract some degree of deference, due to the specialized expertise of the tribunal or the existence of a privative clause, evincing the legislature's clear intention to limit judicial review.[106] For questions of mixed fact and law, Deschamps J. concluded that the reviewing court should treat them in the same way as an appellate court would treat similar issues on appeal from a lower court.[107]

Of all the cases discussed in this paper, *Dunsmuir* is probably the least surprising. The Court had obviously been struggling with the issue of standards of review for many years, searching for a legal framework that could be applied to the multiplicity of administrative tribunals. The possibility of a change was foreshadowed in cases since *Ryan*, and particularly in LeBel J.'s extensive comments in *Toronto (City) v. C.U.P.E.* As well, there is a very strong pragmatic aspect to all three sets of reasons. All of them openly acknowledged that litigants, the lower courts, and the Supreme Court itself, had found it difficult to apply the three standards. As in *Provincial Court Judges' Association*, the Court acknowledged that practical difficulties with its own earlier approach would be a factor in deciding whether it would review its earlier decision and strike out in a new direction.

Given the chequered history of judicial review over the past thirty years and the divergent views of the justices, it remains to be seen if *Dunsmuir* is the final word on judicial review of administrative decisions. Nonetheless,

---

103 *Ibid.* at para. 158.

104 *H.L. v. Canada (Attorney General)*, [2005] 1 S.C.R. 401, 2005 SCC 25.

105 *Dunsmuir*, above note 8 at para. 161.

106 *Ibid.* at paras. 162–63.

107 *Ibid.* at para. 164.

the case stands as a clear example of the Court's willingness to review its own recent decisions if they are not working.

c) Dismissal of Public Employees: No Longer a Duty of Fairness

The majority's willingness in *Dunsmuir* to re-examine its earlier decisions did not stop at the question of the standard of review. It went on to reconsider a long-standing case dealing with the dismissal of public employees: *Knight v. Indian Head School Division No. 19*.[108] The Court held that while *Knight* was still correct as a statement of general principles governing the duty of fairness, it should no longer be followed in cases dealing with dismissals of public employees.

Dunsmuir arose from an arbitrator's decision. Mr. Dunsmuir had held a position in the New Brunswick public service and had been dismissed with pay in lieu of notice. The arbitrator held that as an employee under a statutory employment regime, Mr. Dunsmuir was entitled both to contractual remedies and to administrative remedies, such as the duty of fairness. In reaching this conclusion, the arbitrator relied on the Supreme Court's decision in *Knight*, which had held that statutory public employers were bound both by the common law of employment and the administrative duty of fairness.[109] Applying this principle, the arbitrator ruled that the dismissal violated the duty of fairness and ordered that Mr. Dunsmuir be reinstated.

The majority in *Dunsmuir* rejected this analysis. Justices Bastarache and LeBel emphasized the importance of the contractual nature of a public office. In most cases, public offices will be considered primarily contractual, with the result that disputes relating to dismissal should be resolved by the principles of contract law. There is no additional duty of administrative fairness.[110] While Bastarache and LeBel JJ. commented that *Knight* continues to stand for the general duty of fairness owed by a public authority, they also stated that "to the extent that the majority decision in *Knight* ignored the important effect of a contract of employment, it should not be followed."[111]

108 *Knight v. Indian Head School Division No. 19*, above note 89.

109 *Ibid.* at 668–77.

110 *Dunsmuir*, above note 8 at para. 113.

111 *Ibid.* at para. 114. Neither Binnie J. nor Deschamps J. commented on the application of *Knight* in their reasons.

9) *Société des Acadiens et Acadiennes du Nouveau-Brunswick Inc. v. Canada*: The Court Finds That the RCMP Can Be Subject to Provincial Constitutional Obligations

The RCMP, like other federal institutions, is subject to the bilingualism requirements set out in section 20(1) of the *Charter*. In *Société des Acadiens et Acadiennes du Nouveau-Brunswick Inc. v. Canada*,[112] the Court held that when the RCMP acted as a provincial police force under the policing agreement between the federal government and New Brunswick, the RCMP was also required to comply with the more expansive New Brunswick bilingualism requirements set out in section 20(2) of the *Charter*. The case is interesting because it holds that a federal agency can inadvertently contract into constitutional obligations.

While the case does not expressly reconsider any of the Court's previous decisions, the reasoning in this case is difficult to reconcile with an earlier Supreme Court case from Saskatchewan, *Scowby v. Glendinning*.[113] In that case, the Court had held that the RCMP was not subject to *The Saskatchewan Human Rights Code* when carrying out ordinary policing duties in Saskatchewan.

The Court did not mention *Scowby* in *Société des Acadiens et Acadiennes du Nouveau-Brunswick Inc.*, but the two cases do not appear to be consistent. The Court has repeatedly held that human rights laws are of quasi-constitutional status. If the RCMP is subject to provincial constitutional obligations when acting as a provincial police force, there would then be scope to argue that the RCMP would also be subject to the quasi-constitutional human rights standards of each province in which it operates as a provincial police force. On the other hand, it may simply be that *Société des Acadiens et Acadiennes* was decided solely as a question of language rights, and is not a precedent with respect to human rights generally.

10) *R. v. Kapp*: The Court Reconsiders Equality (Again)

Ever since the equality guarantee in section 15 of the *Charter* came into force in 1985, the Court has struggled with its meaning. It was not a surprise that the Court reconsidered its approach to section 15 in 2008, in *R. v. Kapp*.[114] What was surprising was that the Court unanimously backed away

112 *Société des Acadiens et Acadiennes du Nouveau-Brunswick Inc. v. Canada*, above note 9.

113 *Scowby v. Glendinning*, [1986] 2 S.C.R. 226.

114 *Kapp*, above note 10.

from the extensive and detailed analysis of section 15 set out by an equally unanimous Court only nine years previously, in *Law v. Canada (Minister of Employment and Immigration)*.[115] Instead, the Court in *Kapp* returned to the approach originally set out by McIntyre J. in 1989, in *Andrews v. Law Society of British Columbia*.[116] Like the Canadian Broadcasting Corporation (CBC) in one of its advertising campaigns announcing that *The National* was returning to its familiar ten o'clock spot, the Court was "boldly going where it had been before."

Andrews was the first Supreme Court case dealing with section 15. The Court split on its analysis, with three sets of reasons being delivered on behalf of a panel of six judges. The Court continued to be split in the next three major cases dealing with equality under section 15, decided in 1995: *Miron v. Trudel*;[117] *Egan v. Canada*;[118] and *Thibaudeau v. Canada*.[119] In *Miron*, which dealt with a claim of marital status discrimination brought by a common-law couple, the justices delivered three sets of reasons. In *Egan*, which dealt with a claim of discrimination on the basis of sexual orientation, there were five sets of reasons, and in *Thibaudeau*, which dealt with a discrimination claim, there were again five sets of reasons, this time from a panel of seven judges. In none of these cases did the Court have a clear majority on the interpretation of section 15. The Court was obviously having difficulty finding a consensus on a key provision of the *Charter*.

The Court's 1999 decision in *Law* appears to have been a determined attempt to produce a unanimous view of section 15. Unfortunately, in driving for unanimity, the Court produced an extremely technical and multifaceted test, set out in ten categories, with numerous subheadings within those categories. It also introduced the new concept of "human dignity" as a factor in the analysis.[120] From a practitioner's perspective, it was a very unsatisfying case, being far too technical and detailed to provide much practical guidance. Unanimity, rather than clarity of analysis, seems to have been the driving force.

Seen against this history, the Court's decision to revisit the equality analysis in *Kapp* was not a complete surprise. The Court's decision in *Law* had received considerable academic criticism over the intervening nine years,

115 *Law v. Canada (Minister of Employment and Immigration)*, [1999] 1 S.C.R. 497 [*Law*].

116 *Andrews v. Law Society of British Columbia*, [1989] 1 S.C.R. 143 [*Andrews*].

117 *Miron v. Trudel*, [1995] 2 S.C.R. 418.

118 *Egan v. Canada*, [1995] 2 S.C.R. 513.

119 *Thibaudeau v. Canada*, [1995] 2 S.C.R. 627.

120 *Law*, above note 115 at paras. 47–55, 59–75, and 88.

both for its complexity and for the concern that the inclusion of "human dignity" as a factor in the equality analysis actually made it more difficult for equality claimants to prove their cases. Speaking for the majority, McLachlin C.J. and Abella J. met these criticisms head-on, with two footnotes citing the extensive scholarly criticisms of *Law*.[121]

The Court in *Kapp* nodded politely to the *Law* decision, commenting that *Law* had reiterated and confirmed that section 15 is a guarantee of "substantive, not just formal, equality." They also stated that *Law*'s analysis of human dignity was an important development in the understanding of section 15.[122] However, they accepted the academic criticism that the practical effect of the decision was to add an additional requirement to the equality analysis, that of proving a breach of human dignity, which had the unintended consequence of making it more difficult for litigants to prove an equality claim.[123] They also acknowledged the complexity of the *Law* framework.[124] As a result, they returned to the simpler, more general statements of *Andrews* as the framework for section 15 claims.[125]

The Court's decision in *Kapp* was similar to the pragmatic approach taken in *Dunsmuir* the year before. The problem was not so much the general principle in issue, as it was the analytical framework that should be used to apply that general principle. In both *Kapp* and *Dunsmuir*, the Court acknowledged that its previous efforts had been too complex and had not provided the necessary guidance for the bar and the lower courts. This pragmatism echoed the Court's approach in *Provincial Court Judges' Association*, where the Court had acknowledged that the *Judges' Compensation Reference* had not had the desired effect of depoliticizing the issue of judicial compensation, and therefore the Court was willing to re-examine the analytical framework it had set out.

Will the Court's return to the *Andrews* test make equality issues easier to analyze? As with *Dunsmuir*, it remains to be seen if the new approach will be successful. Part of the problem in both areas is that the issues of judicial review and equality are inherently difficult in nature, and do not usually

121 *Kapp*, above note 10 at paras. 21 & 22.

122 *Ibid.* at para. 20.

123 *Ibid.* at para. 22.

124 *Ibid.* at para. 21.

125 The decision on this point was unanimous. Chief Justice McLachlin and Abella J. wrote with the support of six of their colleagues. The ninth judge, Bastarache J., would have decided the case under s. 25 of the *Charter*, but he stated that he was nonetheless "in complete agreement with the restatement of the test for the application of s. 15 that is adopted by the Chief Justice and Abella J. in their reasons for judgment." *Ibid.* at para. 77.

have obviously correct responses. The adopted analytical framework can go only so far in assisting in the resolution of these issues.

From the practitioner's perspective, the decision in *Kapp* is a welcome one, even if it raises new difficulties. The Court's ten-step test in *Law* was extremely difficult to use in practice. Although the Court in *Kapp* did bow politely to the contribution made by the *Law* analysis, in reality it appears to have jettisoned *Law*. For example, in the recent case of *Ermineskin Indian Band and Nation v. Canada*, Rothstein J. refers only to *Andrews* and *Kapp* in his equality analysis. *Law* appears to have disappeared.[126]

D. IMPLICATIONS FOR COUNSEL

The Supreme Court is clearly willing to re-examine its own decisions. What are the implications of this trend for counsel appearing before the Supreme Court? In considering this point, I return to the question I posed in the opening of this paper: When should a court of last resort reconsider its own decisions? Based on the ten cases examined in this paper, the Court's answer to that question relies on several factors, which counsel appearing in the Court should bear in mind:

- when the factual context of the cases changes significantly (*JTI-MacDonald*; *Hape*; *Société des Acadiens et Acadiennes*);
- when earlier cases do not appear to be responding to the problem needing to be addressed, or are difficult to apply in practice (*Provincial Court Judges' Association*; *Dunsmuir*; *Kapp*);
- when the analytical approach taken in the earlier cases does not fit with principles set out in related areas of law, or in light of more recent developments in other cases (*Health Services*; *Canadian Western Bank*); and
- when, on reconsideration, the Court concludes that an earlier case was too broadly expressed, and may conflict with other important constitutional principles (*Imperial Tobacco Canada*; *Christie*).

Reviewing these factors, it appears that the Court is focused on the twin goals of principled analysis and pragmatism. Overall, when the Court reconsiders one of its earlier cases, it is analyzing the intersection between

126 *Ermineskin Indian Band and Nation v. Canada*, [2009] 1 S.C.R. 222, 2009 SCC 9 at paras. 185–202. I am indebted to my colleague, Colleen Matthews, for pointing out this aspect of the *Ermineskin Indian Band and Nation* decision to me.

practicality, social change, and legal principles. Are the cases consistent with the principled analysis of the legal issues? Do the cases work? Do they solve the problem? Can they be applied in a principled fashion by the courts? Have there been significant changes in the factual background?

Counsel appearing before the Court should keep these points in mind. The Court is clearly receptive to new arguments and to reconsideration of its own decisions, but will not do so helter-skelter. Counsel pressing for a change to the law will need to marshal facts for support, show the difficulties with the current state of the cases, and offer a pragmatic solution. Above all, counsel must base arguments on principle. A successful combination of these factors may persuade the Court to reconsider one of its earlier cases.

The Supreme Court's willingness to reconsider its own cases does, however, pose a downside for counsel: the justices have shown that they will reconsider a case without any prompting from counsel, and without giving counsel any opportunity to make submissions on the need to reconsider a case. Justice Binnie levelled this criticism at the majority in *Hape*, commenting, "Neither the parties nor the intervener asked that *Cook* be revisited, much less overruled."[127]

Similarly, the parties in *Dunsmuir* and *Kapp* did not argue for a substantial re-evaluation of the Court's earlier decisions. In *Dunsmuir*, some members of the Court in oral argument raised the issue of the complexity of the three standards of review and invited comments from counsel, but at that late stage, neither counsel felt they could contribute since the case had not been argued on that basis.[128] Nor in *Kapp* did the Court raise the possibility with counsel that it might reconsider the basic framework for equality analysis. All counsel argued the case on the basis of the *Law* analysis.[129]

---

127 *Hape*, above note 6 at para. 187.

128 In fact, counsel appearing for Mr. Dunsmuir, Mr. J. Borden Petrie, Q.C., expressly declined the Court's invitation, trenchantly commenting: "Oh No! You're not going to get me into that! You got yourselves into this mess, and you are going to have to get yourselves out!" (E-mail from C. Clyde Spinney, Q.C., counsel for the Attorney General of New Brunswick in *Dunsmuir*, to Mr. Petrie and myself, 5 October 2009.) Note, however, that Mr. Spinney, counsel for New Brunswick, did suggest in written argument that the dissenting opinion from *Knight* could be either re-examined, or the majority decision distinguished, in the context of the *Dunsmuir* case: Factum of the Attorney General of New Brunswick at paras. 88–94. I am indebted to Mr. Spinney and Mr. Petrie for their comments to me about the *Dunsmuir* case.

129 Personal conversation with my colleague, Richard James Fyfe, counsel for the Attorney General for Saskatchewan in *Kapp*.

The Court's willingness to reconsider may thus catch counsel unaware. The fact that the Court may be willing to reconsider its own cases increases the onus on counsel to be sensitive to trends in the caselaw, and alert to the possibility that the Court may view a case as ripe for reconsideration.

E. CONCLUSIONS

Courts are normally conservative in their approach to precedent. While *stare decisis* is not as rigidly applied nowadays as it was in the nineteenth century, the need for stability and predictability in the law counts strongly in favour of a cautious approach to reconsideration of previous decisions. For that reason, the Supreme Court's willingness to reconsider its decisions in recent years is a significant development.

As noted at the beginning of this paper, the Court's approach cannot be easily categorized as liberal/conservative, or active/deferential. The Court in *Provincial Court Judges' Association* was extremely deferential to the financial and policy choices made by governments. By contrast, the Court's decision in *Health Services* had a major impact on the British Columbia government's attempt to reorganize the health care administration in that province. However, based on the retreat from the *Judges' Compensation Reference* in *Provincial Court Judges' Association, Imperial Tobacco,* and *Christie,* it is fair to say that in some areas the McLachlin Court appears to take a more cautious view of its own authority than the Court did under Lamer C.J.

Nor does it appear that the cases are simply a result of re-examining the *Charter* jurisprudence after twenty-five years of experience. That is an element in some of the cases, such as *Health Services,* but other cases involved a review of much more recent *Charter* cases. As well, some of the cases were not really surprising. The Court's struggles with the definition of equality and the appropriate standards of judicial review have been an ongoing theme of its cases in those areas.

The most satisfying explanation for these decisions is that the Supreme Court is open to principled criticism of its own decisions, from both academics and counsel. The justices also take into account the practical implications of their decisions and are willing to reconsider a decision that does not appear to be working well. This theme is most apparent in *Provincial Court Judges' Association, Kapp,* and *Dunsmuir,* but it also comes through in several of the other cases. In his comments at the closing plenary of the Canadian Bar Association Constitutional Law and Human Rights Conference, Binnie J. also highlighted the need for pragmatic reappraisal of cases.

While the Court's willingness to reconsider its own decisions introduces uncertainty into the law, from a practitioner's perspective it provides challenges and opportunities when appearing before the Supreme Court. Counsel who provide principled and creative arguments in favour of changes to the law may face a receptive Court.

Postscript: *R. v. Grant*—The Trend Continues

I delivered a previous version of this article at the Canadian Bar Association Constitutional Law and Human Rights Conference on 19 June 2009. A month later, the Court delivered a major case which provided another example of the Court reconsidering its earlier decisions: *R. v. Grant.*[130] A detailed review of the case is beyond the scope of this article, but the case is significant for its re-examination of three major *Charter* cases: *R. v. Therens,*[131] *R. v. Collins,*[132] and *R. v. Stillman.*[133] The majority decision by McLachlin C.J. and Charron J. maintained *Therens,* dealing with the test for detention under sections 9 and 10 of the *Charter,* but with some changes in emphasis. On the issue of the exclusion of evidence under section 24(2), they did not follow the long-standing principles set out in *Collins* and *Stillman,* instead crafting a new approach to the exclusion of evidence under section 24(2). In a concurring decision, Binnie J. agreed with the majority approach to section 24(2), but criticized them for continuing to apply *Therens.* Justice Deschamps agreed with the majority that *Collins* and *Stillman* should be disregarded and argued for a new test that was not based on *Collins.*

The practical implications of *Grant* are far-reaching, but one point that clearly emerges is the Court's continued willingness to re-examine its own decisions, even in such foundational cases as *Collins* which has been the standard approach to exclusion of evidence under section 24(2) for over twenty years. The trend identified in this paper continues.

---

130 *R. v. Grant,* 2009 SCC 32.

131 *R. v. Therens,* [1985] 1 S.C.R. 613.

132 *R. v. Collins,* [1987] 1 S.C.R. 265.

133 *R. v. Stillman,* [1997] 1 S.C.R. 607.

Les décisions de la juge McLachlin à la Cour suprême du Canada : une analyse statistique comparative

MARIE-CLAIRE BELLEAU, ANIK LAMONTAGNE, ET REBECCA JOHNSON*

La pratique de l'opinion dissidente fait partie intégrante de la tradition juridique canadienne. L'opinion dissidente est porteuse de mélodies nouvelles, de diverses avenues de justice possibles à une même problématique. En même temps, elle trouble la prévisibilité du droit en offrant de nouvelles perspectives et en remettant en question parfois le résultat, parfois le raisonnement de l'opinion majoritaire qui constitue le droit[1]. Dans ce texte, nous allons exposer des pistes de réflexion par le biais de quelques statistiques au sujet des décisions rendues par la Cour suprême du Canada entre 1982 et 2008 en portant une attention toute particulière à l'institution et au parcours de la juge en chef[2] Beverley McLachlin.

Nous allons d'abord cerner l'objet de notre étude afin d'identifier clairement les paramètres de notre projet de recherche (Partie 1). Nous allons ensuite examiner des statistiques concernant le nombre de décisions rendues par la Cour suprême du Canada depuis 1982. Nous allons également exposer d'autres statistiques au sujet non seulement du type de décisions rendues

* Les auteures souhaitent remercier le Conseil de recherches en sciences humaines du Canada pour son soutien à la recherche sur la pratique des opinions judiciaires dissidentes.

1 Marie-Claire Belleau et Rebecca Johnson, « La dissidence judiciaire : réflexions préliminaires sur les émotions, la raison et les passions du droit / Judicial Dissent: Early Reflections on Emotion, Reason and Passion in Law » dans Marie-Claire Belleau et Francois Lacasse, dir., *Claire L'Heureux-Dubé à la Cour suprême du Canada, 1987-2002*, Québec, Wilson & Lafleur, 2004, 699.

2 Le titre officiel de la juge en chef Beverley McLachlin est « la très honorable ». Afin de simplifier le présent texte, nous la désignerons « juge en chef ». Nous ferons de même pour les juges en chef Dickson et Lamer. Les juges puinés seront également désignés par le terme « juge ». Nous nous excusons pour cette entorse au protocole.

(unanime, majoritaire ou divisée), mais aussi des valeurs nominales et des pourcentages concernant les juges auteurs de ces opinions (Partie 2).

A. L'OBJET D'ÉTUDE

Plusieurs chercheurs produisent et analysent des données statistiques de la Cour suprême du Canada[3]. Selon l'objet d'étude, l'organisation des catégories, et donc des données, diffère d'un projet de recherche à l'autre. En conséquence, nos résultats ne correspondent pas toujours à ceux issus d'autres études et à ceux produits par la Cour suprême du Canada puisque les choix méthodologiques que nous avons faits sont propres à notre démarche. En effet, notre recherche porte principalement sur une étude qualitative et quantitative des opinions dissidentes rendues par la Cour suprême du Canada depuis 1982[4].

---

3 Peter James McCormick, *Supreme at last : the evolution of the Supreme Court of Canada*, Toronto, J. Lorimer, 2000; Peter James McCormick, « Second Thoughts: Supreme Court Citation of Dissents and Separate Concurrences, 1949-1996 » (2002) 81 Can. Bar Rev. 369-395; F.L Morton, Peter H. Russel et Troy Riddell, « *The Canadian Charter of Rights and Freedoms*: A Descriptive Analysis of the First Decade, 1982-1992 » (1994) 5:1 N.J.C.L. 1; Donald R. Songer, *The Transformation of the Supreme Court of Canada : An Empirical Examination*, Toronto, University of Toronto Press, 2008; Daved Muttart, *The Empirical Gap in Jurisprudence : A Comprehensive Study of the Supreme Court of Canada*, Toronto, University of Toronto Press, 2007.

4 *Supra* note 1; Marie-Claire Belleau et Rebecca Johnson, « Les femmes juges feront-elles véritablement une différence? Réflexions sur les décisions des femmes juges à la Cour suprême du Canada » (2005) 17 R.F.D. 27; Marie-Claire Belleau et Rebecca Johnson, « Les opinions dissidentes au Canada », CD-Rom : *Les méthodes de jugement*, Paris, Droit In-Situ, 2005; Marie-Claire Belleau et Rebecca Johnson, « Faces of Judicial Anger : Answering the Call » dans Myriam Jézéquel et Nicolas Kasirer, dir., *Les sept péchés capitaux et le droit privé*, Montréal, Thémis, 2007, 13; Marie-Claire Belleau, Rebecca Johnson et Valérie Bouchard, « Visages de la colère judiciaire : répondre à l'appel / Faces of Judicial Anger : Answering the Call », en ligne : (2007) 2 European Journal of Legal Studies www.ejls.eu; Marie-Claire Belleau et Rebecca Johnson. « Judging Gender: Difference and Dissent at the Supreme Court of Canada » (2008) 15 I.J.L.P. 57; Marie-Claire Belleau et Rebecca Johnson, « La diversité identitaire et les opinions dissidentes de la Cour suprême du Canada : conséquences sur la sécurité juridique? » (2008) 110 R. du N. 319; Marie-Claire Belleau et Rebecca Johnson, « I Beg to Differ : Interdisciplinary Questions about Law, Language and Dissent » dans Logan Atkinson et Diana Majury, dir., *Law, Mystery & the Humanities: Collected Essays*, Toronto, University of Toronto Press, 2008, 145; Marie-Claire Belleau, Rebecca Johnson et Christina Vinters, « Voicing an Opinion : Authorship, Collaboration and the Judgments of Justice Bertha Wilson » (2008) 41 Sup. Ct. Rev. 53; Marie-Claire Belleau *et al.*, « Appendix A : Supreme Court of Canada Cases Written by Justice Bertha Wilson 1982–1991 » (2008) 41 Sup. Ct. Rev. 409; Marie-Claire Belleau, Rebecca Johnson et Christina Vinters, « "I Agree/Disagree for the Following Reasons" : Convergence, Divergence, and Justice Wilson's "Modest Degree of Creativity » dans Kim Ruth Brooks, dir., *Looking Forward: The Contributions of Bertha Wilson*, Vancouver, UBC Press, 2009, 373;

ABSTRACT

With the use of statistics, this article reflects on and asks questions about how to best understand the opinions taken by Beverley McLachlin C.J. in the body of judgments rendered by the Supreme Court of Canada between 1982 and 2008. We pay particular attention to the voting patterns of the judges. There are parallels that can been seen in the judgments rendered under the last three chief justices. Of the three, McLachlin is the judge most frequently in dissent, while at the same time, her Court has produced a higher level of unanimity than her two predecessors. At base, this study focuses on certain indicators that are suggestive and yet limited by their nature, and sets out the groundwork for more detailed qualitative study.

Afin de réaliser cette recherche, nous avons fait plusieurs choix méthodologiques. Notre projet inclut les jugements pertinents rendus par écrit rapportés dans le Recueil de la Cour suprême du Canada. La norme de la pertinence se mesure en fonction de nos besoins pour mener à bien une étude qualitative des décisions. Pour qu'un arrêt fasse partie de notre projet, il doit contenir des motifs, suffisamment de motifs. Nous avons donc exclu de notre projet de recherche toutes les décisions dont les motifs se limitent à quelques lignes. Pour la même raison, notre étude exclut les requêtes ainsi que les jugements rendus oralement.

Notre recherche porte sur les années 1982 à aujourd'hui. L'année 1982 a été choisie parce qu'elle marque l'adoption de la *Charte canadienne des droits et libertés*[5]. De même, les données incluses dans le présent texte s'arrêtent au 31 décembre 2008 puisqu'au moment d'écrire ces lignes, les données statistiques de l'année 2009 n'étaient pas complètes et elles ne comptaient pas suffisamment de décisions pour être significatives. Par contre, il importe de remarquer que notre recherche est longitudinale car nous mettons nos banques de données à jour en y ajoutant périodiquement les décisions rendues par la Cour suprême du Canada.

Marie-Claire Belleau, Rebecca Johnson et Valérie Bouchard, « Rapport minoritaire : La dissidence fait juge » (2009) 21 R.F.D. 1-17; Marie-Claire Belleau , Rebecca Johnson et Valérie Bouchard, « Droit, cinéma et doute : Rapport minoritaire » (printemps 2009), en ligne : Lex Electronica www.lex-electronica.org/docs/articles_230.pdf.

5 *Loi constitutionnelle de 1982*, constituant l'annexe B de la *Loi de 1982 sur le Canada* (R.-U.), 1982, c. 11.

En somme, à la fin de l'année 2008, notre étude comprenait environ 2 850 décisions pertinentes rendues par écrit.

Il importe aussi de qualifier les décisions rendues par la Cour suprême du Canada afin d'identifier précisément les catégories de notre étude. Ainsi, la Cour peut se prononcer à l'unanimité. Dans les cas où les juges ne partagent pas tous la même opinion, les décisions sont rendues à la majorité. Les décisions rendues par la Cour suprême du Canada conduisent donc à différents types d'opinions. Les opinions majoritaires désignent celles qui sont écrites et signées par la majorité, c'est-à-dire avec un minimum de trois sur un banc de cinq juges, quatre sur un banc de sept et cinq sur un banc de neuf. L'opinion majoritaire détermine le droit applicable au Canada à un moment précis dans le temps.

Les autres opinions rendues dans le cas d'une décision divisée sont dissidentes. L'opinion dissidente sur les motifs signifie celle qui est écrite par une ou un juge qui n'arrive pas à rassembler la majorité des voix, où la ou le juge est d'accord avec le résultat de la décision majoritaire, mais pas avec les raisons qui l'ont motivée. L'opinion dissidente sur le résultat correspond plutôt à celle qui est écrite par la ou le juge qui n'est pas d'accord avec la majorité, ni sur les raisons de la décision, ni sur le résultat ou la conclusion de la décision[6].

Les opinions dissidentes ne constituent pas le droit. Elles ont par contre une certaine autorité de persuasion principalement parce qu'elles proviennent de la Cour suprême du Canada. De plus, ces opinions peuvent devenir le droit dans la mesure où des décisions majoritaires subséquentes reprendront l'argumentation qu'elles contenaient. De même, le législateur peut choisir de changer l'état du droit à la suite d'une décision rendue par la Cour suprême du Canada.

Enfin, deux précisions interreliées s'imposent : l'une d'ordre linguistique, l'autre relevant de l'établissement de catégories. Premièrement, comme nous venons de le voir, dans la langue française du Québec les opinions dissidentes se déclinent principalement en deux catégories : les dissidences sur le résultat et les dissidences sur les motifs. Dans ce dernier cas, l'expression met l'accent sur les distinctions fondées sur les motivations ou sur les raisons entre les argumentations minoritaires et majoritaires. Elles sont donc consi-

6 Aux fins de notre propos, les quelques catégories qui suivent suffiront. Par contre, la typologie des différents types d'opinions judiciaires est complexe. En effet, les opinions dissidentes peuvent se décliner de multiples façons telles que la dissidence sur le résultat, la dissidence sur les motifs alors que la décision contient une majorité, la dissidence sur les motifs alors que la décision ne contient pas de majorité et la dissidence partielle.

dérées toutes les deux comme relevant de la dissidence. Or, dans la langue anglaise le terme «*dissent*» désigne la dissidence sur les résultats alors que le mot «*concurrence*» signifie dissidence sur les motifs. Le mot «*concurrence*» provient du verbe «*to concur*» qui signifie «être d'accord, s'entendre ... ; [opinions] converger»[7]. Ainsi, par ces expressions, la langue anglaise insiste sur le résultat de la décision en associant la dissidence sur les motifs à la congruence au niveau de la conclusion similaire à celle de l'opinion majoritaire. Cette distinction est d'autant plus importante que la pratique de la publication de l'opinion dissidente, qu'elle porte sur le résultat ou sur les motifs, appartient à la tradition de la *common law*. En effet, en théorie et traditionnellement, la famille juridique romano-germanique rend des décisions unanimes et anonymes. Toutefois, dans les faits, la plupart des pays de tradition civiliste publient les opinions minoritaires judiciaires. En effet, même si le système juridique de la France constitue le modèle classique de tradition du droit civil et que ses tribunaux rendent des décisions unanimes et anonymes, les pays civilistes qui font exception à ce principe particulier sont légions[8].

Deuxièmement, notre projet de recherche plus général porte sur une étude qualitative et quantitative des opinions dissidentes rendues par la Cour suprême du Canada. Nous avons choisi de nous intéresser aux distinctions qui séparent non seulement les conclusions des juges lorsqu'ils rendent des décisions, mais d'analyser également les différences entre les motifs qu'ils font valoir pour justifier leurs opinions. En effet, surtout au niveau de la plus haute cour du Canada, l'argumentation détermine le droit. En conséquence, contrairement aux études de plusieurs politologues qui unissent opinions majoritaires et opinions dissidentes sur les motifs, nous avons choisi de traiter séparément ces deux catégories d'opinions. En ce sens, nous embrassons les choix linguistiques de la langue française plutôt que ceux de l'anglais en étudiant autant les dissidences sur les résultats que celles sur les motifs dans notre analyse des opinions minoritaires de la Cour suprême du Canada. Bref, dans notre projet de recherche et dans cet article, nous examinons la production des juges de la Cour suprême du Canada en considérant l'ensemble

---

7 Le Robert & Collins super senior : grand dictionnaire français-anglais, anglais-français, 2005, *s.v.* «concur».

8 Voir Wanda Mastor, *Les opinions séparées des juges constitutionnels*, Paris, ECONOMICA/PUAM, 2005, à la pg. 135 pour des exemples de pays civilistes qui publient les opinions judiciaires minoritaires. En effet, en 2005, Mastor énumérait seulement quatre pays d'Europe qui rendaient des décisions unanimes et anonymes : l'Autriche, l'Irlande, la France et l'Italie. De même, les pays colonisés par le Portugal et par l'Espagne qui appartiennent à la tradition civile suivent leurs exemples en publiant les opinions minoritaires rendues par leurs juges.

des décisions qu'ils rendent, mais en analysant les dissidences comme comprenant autant celles sur le résultat que celles sur les motifs.

B. QUELQUES STATISTIQUES SUR LES DÉCISIONS DE LA COUR SUPRÊME DU CANADA

Les études quantitatives révèlent des tendances générales méritant d'être mieux comprises par une approche comparative et longitudinale. Dans ce texte, notre objectif consiste à dégager certaines conclusions en offrant un éclairage quantitatif. Par contre, si ces statistiques permettent de considérer des éléments différents en présentant une vue d'ensemble, nous sommes conscientes des limites importantes de cette approche. Selon notre conception, les études quantitatives génèrent des questions. Les réponses à ces questions nécessitent des études qualitatives fouillées et nuancées qui dépassent le cadre du présent article. Ainsi, nous proposons un modeste portrait statistique accompagné d'hypothèses explicatives dont la démonstration et la validation restent à faire.

Dans la prochaine partie, nous allons examiner la quantité et l'unanimité des décisions rendues sous trois juges en chef (section B(1)), l'unanimité et la division des décisions (section B(2)) et qui sont les juges dissidents et à quelle fréquence (section B(3)). Enfin, dans la section B(4) nous allons analyser les statistiques plus particulières qui se dégagent du parcours de la juge en chef Beverley McLachlin.

1) La quantité et l'unanimité des décisions rendues sous trois juges en chef

Dans cette partie, nous mettons en parallèle le nombre de causes entendues par années en rapport avec les taux d'unanimité sous trois juges en chef soit les juges en chef Brian Dickson, Antonio Lamer et Beverley McLachlin. Au moment de produire ces statistiques, les années de transition nous posaient problème puisque certaines causes avaient été entendues sous un juge en chef, mais rendues sous le suivant. Nous avons donc choisi d'attribuer toutes les causes rendues sous un juge en chef à ce dernier plutôt qu'à celui qui présidait l'audience.

Les colonnes qui se trouvent sous l'appellation « quantité » contiennent le nombre de jugements rendus sous les trois juges en chef. Nous avons fait la moyenne du nombre de décisions rendues par années sous un juge en chef. Toutefois, pour mieux comprendre la situation, nous avons choisi d'inclure également le plus grand ainsi que le plus petit nombre de déci-

Tableau 1 *La quantité et l'unanimité des décisions sous trois juges en chef*

La Cour de:	*La quantité (nb)*		*L'unanimité (%)*	
Dickson (1984–1990)	+ ↑ 113 + ↓ 71	Moyenne 84,3	+ ↑ 70,7 + ↓ 40,7	Moyenne 56,6%
Lamer (1990–2000)	+ ↑ 93 + ↓ 57	Moyenne 71,3	+ ↑ 57,9 + ↓ 28,9	Moyenne 43,6%
McLachlin (2000–2008)	+ ↑ 77 + ↓ 46	Moyenne 65,4	+ ↑ 70,1 + ↓ 39,1	Moyenne 60,0%

sions rendues pour une année sous chacun des juges en chef. Les colonnes situées sous l'intitulé « unanimité » rendent compte des pourcentages de décisions unanimes rendues sous les trois juges en chef. Dans ce cas, nous avons inclus le plus grand ainsi que le plus petit pourcentage des décisions unanimes rendues pour une année sous un juge en chef. Enfin, la dernière colonne fait état de la moyenne des décisions unanimes rendues sous un juge en chef pendant toute la durée de son mandat.

Il est intéressant de noter l'importante diminution, en 24 ans, du nombre de jugements rendus par année. La Cour de la juge en chef McLachlin rend en moyenne une vingtaine de jugements de moins par année que celle du juge en chef Dickson. Notez aussi que le plus grand nombre de décisions rendues sous la juge en chef McLachlin, soit 77, est proche du plus faible nombre de décisions rendues sous le juge en chef Dickson, soit 71.

Quant à la question du pourcentage de décisions unanimes rendues par la Cour, les chiffres sont révélateurs. Remarquez la parenté frappante entre les pourcentages des juges en chef Dickson et McLachlin: 70%–40%, 70%–39%. Quant aux moyennes des décisions unanimes, si la Cour semble avoir été très divisée pendant le mandat du juge en chef Lamer, les juges en chef Dickson et McLachlin ont su conserver une moyenne élevée de décisions unanimes. Ce qui est notoire, mais non apparent dans ce tableau, c'est le contraste entre les pourcentages au moment de la transition entre la Cour du juge en chef Lamer et celle de McLachlin. À la fin des années 1990, les moyennes des décisions unanimes de la Cour sous le juge en chef Lamer sont d'environ 54%. Or, dès sa première année comme juge en chef, la Cour de la juge en chef McLachlin a atteint un taux de 70% de décisions unanimes soit plus de 15% de plus qu'au cours des dernières années de son prédécesseur[9].

9 De 1998 à 2000, la proportion des décisions unanimes rendues par la Cour suprême du Canada était respectivement de 54,8%, 49,2% et de 57,9% alors que dès 2001 elle a atteint un taux de 70,1 %.

2) L'unanimité et la division des décisions

Entre 1982 et 2008, 54% des décisions de la plus haute cour du Canada sont unanimes. La Cour de la juge en chef McLachlin porte ce pourcentage à 60%, ce qui est une augmentation non négligeable.

Tableau 2 *L'unanimité et la division des décisions*

	CSC 1982–2008	CSC 2000–2008
	Toutes les décisions rendues par écrit et rapportées	
Décisions unanimes	54%	60%
Décisions divisées	46%	40%
	Les décisions non unanimes	
Juges avec la majorité	61%	67%
Juges avec la dissidence	38%	33%

Depuis 1982, dans les causes où les juges ne sont pas unanimes, les juges sont en accord avec la majorité en moyenne dans 61% des cas. Or, sous la juge en chef McLachlin, les juges sont encore moins dissidents puisqu'ils se rallient dans 67% des cas à la majorité. En conséquence, les juges sont en désaccord (sur le résultat, sur les motifs ou sur les deux) dans 38% des décisions non unanimes entre 1982 et 2008, mais seulement dans 33% des cas sous la juge en chef McLachlin[10]. Les opinions dissidentes sont donc une partie intrinsèque de la pratique judiciaire au Canada et ne sont pas inhabituelles. Elles sont acceptées, par la communauté juridique et non juridique, comme appartenant à la tradition judiciaire canadienne.

3) Qui est dissident et à quelle fréquence?

Notre projet de recherche plus vaste porte sur la valeur constructive des opinions dissidentes. Nous avons ainsi porté plus particulièrement notre attention aux jugements divisés. Le tableau suivant révèle plusieurs dimensions de la différence dans les opinions judiciaires rendues par la Cour suprême du Canada :

10 Le fait que nous n'obtenions pas à 100% en additionnant 61% et 38% est dû à l'exclusion de certaines causes principalement pour deux motifs. Nous avons exclu les causes où des juges ont pris part à l'audition sans pour autant prendre part au jugement. Nous avons également éliminé les statistiques concernant les opinions multiples soit les cas où un même juge a pris part à plus d'une opinion dans un même jugement.

Tableau 3 *Qui est dissident et à quelle fréquence? Du moins au plus dissident.*

Décisions non unanimes rapportées de la Cour suprême du Canada 1982–2008 (31 décembre 2008)						
Juge	Non unanime (nominal)	A pris part par écrit (%)	Avec la majorité (%)	Avec la dissidence sur les motifs (%)	Avec la dissidence sur le résultat (%)	Avec la dissidence Total (%)
Iacobucci	420	24,8	72,9	14,3	10,2	26,4
Rothstein	**33**	**24,2**	**72,7**	**9,1**	**18,2**	**27,3**
Binnie	**252**	**26,2**	**72,2**	**7,9**	**19,9**	**27,8**
Le Dain	70	30,0	68,8	24,3	5,7	30,0
Abella	**95**	**34,7**	**68,4**	**8,7**	**22,1**	**30,8**
Cory	397	35,5	68,0	19,4	9,8	31,0
Arbour	108	37,0	67,6	10,2	14,8	32,4
Charron	**91**	**26,4**	**67,0**	**8,8**	**24,3**	**33,1**
Chouinard	86	16,3	65,1	20,9	12,8	34,9
Gonthier	506	17,2	62,6	21,3	12,5	35,2
Major	384	24,7	64,0	14,3	19,5	35,4
Fish	**110**	**29,1**	**62,7**	**10,9**	**24,5**	**35,4**
Estey	107	42,1	61,7	17,8	17,8	37,4
Bastarache	256	41,0	60,9	12,5	26,6	39,1
Dickson	229	39,3	59,4	27,9	12,2	40,5
Beetz	134	22,4	57,5	29,1	11,1	41,6
Deschamps	**141**	**31,9**	**58,2**	**11,3**	**30,5**	**41,8**
Stevenson	70	25,7	57,1	28,8	14,3	42,9
LeBel	**196**	**39,3**	**56,6**	**15,8**	**27,6**	**43,4**
McIntyre	183	37,2	55,8	23,5	16,4	43,7
Sopinka	382	46,1	54,2	25,7	17,3	44,8
Lamer	502	44,5	54,9	29,1	13,4	45,0
La Forest	467	38,8	54,8	30,4	12,0	45,2
McLachlin	**578**	**44,6**	**54,7**	**23,4**	**22,0**	**45,4**
Wilson	249	55,0	40,2	32,1	22,5	59,8
L'Heureux-Dubé	531	42,7	35,6	31,5	28,1	63,3
Moyenne	244,3 Total: 6596	33,8	61,0	19,2	17,8	38,0

Aux fins de ce tableau, nous avons classé les juges du moins au plus dissidents. La première colonne fait état du nombre total de causes non unanimes entendues par chaque juge. La deuxième colonne illustre les pratiques reliées à la rédaction en donnant la proportion en pourcentage des arrêts auxquels chaque juge a pris part par écrit par rapport au nombre de décisions non unanimes rendues. Il s'agit ici de toutes les opinions écrites par un juge qu'elles soient majoritaires, dissidentes sur les motifs ou sur le résultat. Les trois colonnes suivantes décrivent quantitativement les votes dans les décisions non unanimes rendues : la proportion des votes d'une ou d'un juge pour la majorité, pour la dissidence sur les motifs ou sur le résultat. La dernière colonne combine toutes les dissidences pour produire un indicateur permettant de connaître dans quelle mesure une ou un juge adopte une position qui diverge de celle de la majorité. Les données portant sur les juges qui siégeaient en décembre 2008 à la Cour suprême sont indiquées en caractère gras. Le juge Thomas Cromwell a été nominé à la Cour suprême du Canada le 22 décembre 2008. Nous n'avons donc pas inclus ses statistiques aux fins de la présente analyse.

Par exemple, le juge Fish a pris part à 110 décisions non unanimes. Il a écrit des motifs dans 29% de ces causes, ce qui le place près de la moyenne de la Cour qui est de 34%. Son profil général par rapport à la majorité est le suivant : il a voté avec la majorité dans 62,7% des cas (proche de la moyenne de la Cour de 61%); avec les dissidents sur les motifs dans 11% des cas (bien en dessous de la moyenne de près de 20%) et avec la dissidence sur le résultat dans 24,5% des cas (bien au-dessus de la moyenne de la Cour de 18%). Le juge Fish tend donc à être plus dissident sur le résultat que sur les motifs lorsqu'on le compare à la moyenne de la Cour entre 1982 et 2008. Au total, le juge Fish a été dissident dans 35% des causes non unanimes qu'il a entendues par rapport à une moyenne de 38% pour la Cour.

À la suite de l'analyse de ce tableau, il est juste de conclure que la juge en chef McLachlin est aujourd'hui la juge en exercice à la Cour suprême du Canada la plus dissidente (sur le résultat et sur les motifs), suivie par les trois juges du Québec, soit les juges LeBel, Deschamps et Fish.

4) Le parcours de la juge en chef McLachlin

Les chiffres ne révèlent toutefois qu'une partie de l'histoire. Si nous poursuivons l'analyse, il s'avère que le parcours de la juge McLachlin est plus complexe. En effet, si l'on examine les pourcentages d'opinions dissidentes de la juge McLachlin depuis son arrivée à la Cour suprême du Canada en 1989 jusqu'à la fin de l'année 2008, nous observons qu'elle était plus dissidente dans la première partie de sa carrière à la Cour suprême du Canada et que, depuis qu'elle est devenue juge en chef en 2000, ses taux de dissidences ont diminué de façon significative :

Figure 1 *La juge en chef Beverley McLachlin prend part à une opinion dissidente (%)*

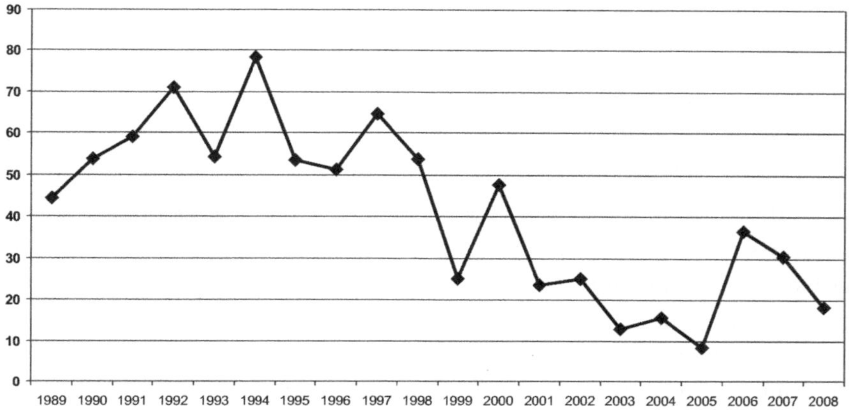

Plusieurs hypothèses permettraient d'expliquer la diminution des opinions dissidentes auxquelles la juge McLachlin a pris part. Par exemple, la juge en chef pourrait tout simplement être objectivement moins dissidente dans les causes pour lesquelles elle est appelée à trancher.

Une autre hypothèse réside dans le fait qu'elle pourrait réussir à rallier un plus grand nombre de juges à ses positions. En effet, nous avons remarqué que la juge McLachlin, contrairement à d'autres juges très dissidentes comme la juge L'Heureux-Dubé, tendait à signer des opinions dissidentes avec un ou deux autres collègues. Dans ces cas, le nombre de votes qu'elle obtenait la plaçait à la portée d'une opinion majoritaire. Ainsi, dans bien des cas, un ou deux votes de plus lui aurait permis de former une majorité. Peut-être a-t-elle réussi à rallier ces quelques votes supplémentaires depuis qu'elle est devenue juge en chef?

Aussi, la juge McLachlin pourrait exercer un ascendant sur ses collègues favorable à une plus grande unanimité. Lors d'une entrevue de la juge en chef parue dans le *Canadian Lawyer* en juin 2006, Christopher Guly écrivait[11] : « The Chief Justice is proud of the unanimity she and her colleagues reach on the 80 decisions they have rendered annually, on average, since 2000. In 2005, 89 judgements were delivered: 65 of them—73 per cent—were unanimous ». Si les propos de la juge en chef ont été bien rapportés, il se peut que l'unanimité soit l'un des objectifs qu'elle a fixé pour la Cour.

11 Cristophe Guly, « Beverley McLachlin : A model judge » (2006) 30 : 6 Can. Law. 22.

Il est aussi possible de penser que, puisque les juges ont actuellement moins de décisions à rendre, ils ont plus de temps pour parvenir à des compromis et à des consensus. Cette hypothèse pourrait expliquer, en partie, la diminution des opinions dissidentes de la juge en chef. Cependant, lors de la conférence du 19 juin 2009, l'honorable Michel Bastarache, juge retraité de la Cour suprême du Canada, remettait en question cette même hypothèse en notant, à juste titre, que sous la juge en chef McLachlin, la Cour siège plus souvent en banc de 9 juges alors que la pratique des bancs de 5 ou 7 juges était beaucoup fréquente sous le leadership de ses deux prédécesseurs. Nos statistiques confirment ce changement important dans la composition des bancs à la Cour suprême du Canada.[12] En conséquence, selon l'honorable Michel Bastarache, malgré la diminution du nombre de pourvois entendus par année, chaque juge de la Cour de la juge en chef McLachlin prendrait part à autant de décisions que sous les juges en chef Dickson et Lamer.

D'autres hypothèses à explorer résideraient dans les nouveaux modes d'attribution de la rédaction des opinions instituées par la juge en chef qui contrastent avec ceux des juges en chef Dickson et Lamer.

Enfin, il importerait d'analyser les changements dans la composition des membres de la Cour suprême du Canada. En effet, la juge en chef McLachlin est la seule juge toujours en exercice depuis 1989, année de sa nomination. Le juge Binnie, nommé en 1998, est le juge en fonction détenant le plus d'ancienneté après la juge en chef McLachlin. Avec un écart de près de 10 ans entre eux, il est possible d'imaginer que le visage de la Cour a tellement changé que la juge en chef McLachlin connaît une plus grande collégialité d'idées avec ses nouveaux collègues qu'avec celles et ceux qui y siégeaient à son arrivée sur le banc.

Ainsi, il appert de ce qui précède que si les nombres s'avèrent révélateurs, ils ne peuvent nous aider qu'à formuler des questions et à suggérer des hypothèses, d'où l'importance fondamentale d'études qualitatives pour trouver des réponses à ces interrogations.

Le tableau suivant permet de tirer un portrait plus général de la jurisprudence de la juge en chef depuis son arrivée à la Cour suprême du Canada:

12 En effet, nos analyses montrent qu'une formation de 9 juges entendait 11,9 % des causes sous le juge en chef Dickson, alors que cette proportion est passée à 25,3 % sous le juge en chef Lamer et a de nouveau augmenté à 34,6 % sous la juge en chef McLachlin.

Figure 2 *Les décisions de la juge en chef Beverley McLachlin (1989-2008)*

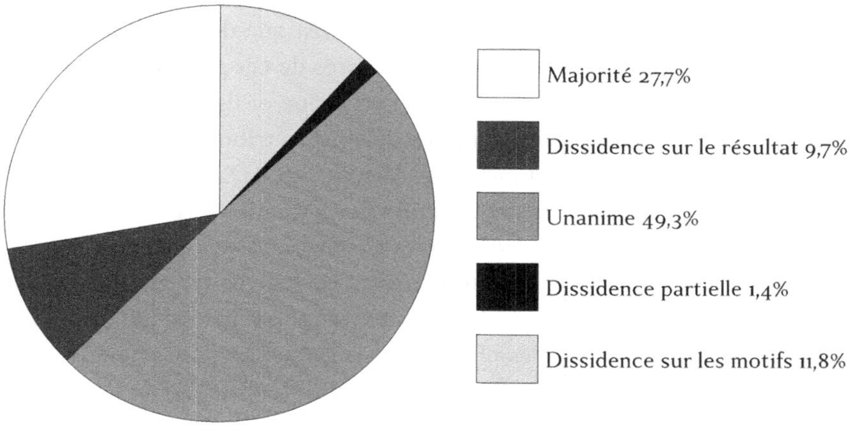

Entre 1989 et 2008, la juge en chef Beverley McLachlin a pris part dans 49,3% des cas à des décisions unanimes. Elle s'est jointe à la majorité dans 27,7% des cas. Ses opinions dissidentes constituent 22,9% de ses jugements soit 9,7% de dissidences sur le résultat, 11,8% de dissidences sur les motifs et 1,4% de dissidences partielles.

Dans le tableau 3, celui qui détaille les données sur chaque juge dans le cas des décisions non unanimes rapportées, il est frappant de remarquer qu'entre 1982 et 2008, les juges qui étaient les plus susceptibles d'être dissidents étaient les juges Claire L'Heureux-Dubé, Bertha Wilson et Beverley McLachlin, soit les trois premières femmes juges de la Cour suprême du Canada. Les nombres justifient de décerner à la juge Claire L'Heureux-Dubé le titre de la « grande dissidente » avec le record de 63,3% en moyenne!

Encore ici, les études qualitatives s'avèrent essentielles. En effet, il faut se garder de conclure que ces trois femmes étaient dissidentes ensemble. Dans leur analyse de la jurisprudence issue de la première décennie d'application de la *Charte canadienne des droits et libertés*, F.L. Morton et ses coauteurs ont noté la fréquence des opinions distinctes des femmes.[13] Toutefois, dans leur étude des décisions concernant la Charte uniquement, ils affirment que les similitudes s'arrêtent à cette constatation. Ils ont classé les décisions des juges de la Cour suprême du Canada dans des quadrants déterminés par deux axes. D'une part, l'axe vertical concerne la reconnaissance ou non des droits des groupes historiquement marginalisés (*court party claims*). L'expression

13 F.L. Morton, Peter H. Russel et Troy Riddell, *supra* note 3.

anglaise *court party claims* inclut les demandes des féministes, des Premières Nations, des minorités linguistiques et autres minorités, des environnementalistes, des homosexuels et des lesbiennes ainsi que des activistes pour la paix et le désarmement. Les intérêts prioritaires de ces groupes minoritaires qui recherchent l'égalité ont pour objet la réforme et ils tendent à défendre leurs projets politiques dans des litiges devant les tribunaux plutôt que par l'adoption de lois issues d'instances législatives élues. D'autre part, l'axe horizontal porte sur la reconnaissance ou non des garanties juridiques des accusés en matière criminelle (*criminal rights claims*). Classées de cette manière, les décisions des femmes qui portent le titre de juge se trouvent alors dans trois catégories distinctes. Les résultats mettent en relief les différences entre les trois juges mentionnées plus haut. Malgré un fort taux de dissidence, chacune exprime son opinion d'une façon fort différente. Selon ces auteurs, la juge Bertha Wilson le faisait en défendant à la fois les droits des groupes historiquement marginalisés et les garanties juridiques des accusés en matière criminelle; la juge Claire L'Heureux-Dubé, en appuyant les droits des groupes historiquement marginalisés, mais en s'opposant à ceux des criminels; et la juge en chef Beverley McLachlin, en manifestant une forte opposition aux droits des groupes historiquement marginalisés jumelée à un appui modéré aux garanties juridiques des accusés en matière criminelle.

Ces statistiques suggèrent que le genre de la personne qui siège à un tribunal ne peut permettre de prédire le résultat auquel elle arrivera, et que les premières femmes qui ont exercé cette fonction ne partageaient pas nécessairement une idéologie commune. Toutefois, les mêmes statistiques démontrent également que les trois premières femmes juges de la Cour suprême du Canada ont un point commun, soit le fait d'être dissidente par rapport à la majorité, peu importe la position de cette dernière.

CONCLUSION

En guise de conclusion, plusieurs constats se dégagent de nos études statistiques. La Cour suprême du Canada de la juge en chef McLachlin entend moins de décisions que celle de ses deux prédécesseurs. Elle rend en moyenne 65 jugements par année. De même, la Cour sous la juge en chef McLachlin dépasse les taux d'unanimité atteints par ses deux prédécesseurs avec un taux de 70% en moyenne depuis qu'elle est juge en chef. La pratique des opinions dissidentes fait partie intrinsèque de la tradition juridique du Canada puisqu'en moyenne, depuis 1982, 46% des décisions rendues par écrit de la Cour suprême du Canada sont divisées.

La juge en chef McLachlin demeure la juge en exercice la plus dissidente de la Cour suprême du Canada avec un taux de 45% dans les décisions non unanimes. Ces statistiques incluent tant les dissidences sur les motifs que celles sur le résultat. Par contre, les taux de dissidences de la juge McLachlin tendent à diminuer de façon significative depuis qu'elle est devenue juge en chef en janvier 2000. La juge McLachlin continue donc de faire partie du groupe des juges les plus dissidents de la Cour suprême du Canada parmi les juges qui y ont siégé depuis 1982. Ses deux compagnes dans l'expression d'opinions minoritaires divergentes demeurent les deux autres premières femmes juges nommées à la Cour suprême du Canada, les honorables Bertha Wilson et Claire L'Heureux-Dubé. Ces trois pionnières auront apporté une diversité dans les perspectives, les valeurs et les avenues d'une autre justice potentielle[14].

14 Claire L'Heureux-Dubé, « L'opinion dissidente : voix de l'avenir? » (2000) C. du Cons. Const. 85.

The McLachlin Court and the Promise of Procedural Justice

LORNE SOSSIN[*]

If we do things the right way, we are likely to do the right thing.

—Lon L. Fuller[1]

A. INTRODUCTION

As I often have to remind my administrative law students, people do not go to court for procedural rights. People do not think that it is fine that they are to be deported, or lose their claim over land, or end up with diminished benefits at work, so long as it is done fairly. Rather, people do not want to be deported. They want to have their land claim recognized and to receive better benefits at work. Parties seek to develop new procedural rights or apply existing rights to new situations so that it will be more likely that they will achieve successful outcomes, or alternatively, so that negative outcomes will be lessened, deferred, or delayed. Procedure, in other words, should never be viewed in isolation. That said, process is important for reasons other than the outcome of particular cases.[2]

---

* I am indebted to Danny Saposnik for his very helpful research assistance on this paper. This paper was originally prepared for the Canadian Bar Association conference *The McLachlin Court's First Ten Years: Reflections of the Past and Projections of the Future* held in Ottawa, Canada, 19 June 2009, and was subsequently revised for inclusion in the Asper Centre for Constitutional Rights' Working Paper Series.

1 Lon L. Fuller, "What the Law Schools Can Contribute to the Making of Lawyers" (1948) 1 J. Legal Educ. 189 at 204.

2 For a wide-ranging discussion of the justifications for procedural justice, see Lawrence Solum, "Procedural Justice" (2004) 78 S. Cal. L. Rev. 181.

All legal process both reflects and advances claims to legitimacy, fairness, and accountability. Further, some kinds of procedural requirements are difficult to disentangle from substantive requirements. For example, the duty to provide reasons and the substantive requirement of reasonableness are inextricably linked.[3] The debate about whether procedure is a means to an end, or an end in itself, or somewhere in between, defines much about the implications of law and, as I will suggest, characterizes some of the most significant contributions of the Supreme Court under the leadership of McLachlin C.J. (the McLachlin Court).

While procedural justice extends far beyond administrative law, it is fair to say that it is in administrative law that the Supreme Court first identified the potential, and the potential challenges, of procedural justice. In *Cardinal et al. v. Director of Kent Institution*,[4] it famously described fairness as an "independent, unqualified right" which arises whenever a person's rights, interests, or privileges are at stake in a public, non-legislative decision. That is to say, the right to fairness exists apart from the difference it might make in any individual case. To underscore this point, Le Dain J. wrote:

> [T]he denial of a right to a fair hearing must always render a decision invalid, whether or not it may appear to a reviewing court that the hearing would likely have resulted in a different decision. The right to a fair hearing must be regarded as an independent, unqualified right which finds its essential justification in the sense of procedural justice which any person affected by an administrative decision is entitled to have. It is not for a court to deny that right and sense of justice on the basis of speculation as to what the result might have been had there been a hearing.[5]

But does process really matter entirely unhinged from any focus on outcomes? Even the Supreme Court is not so sure. Subsequently, in *Mobil Oil Canada Ltd. v. Canada-Newfoundland Offshore Petroleum Board*,[6] for example, the Court accepted that in some settings, a procedural flaw is not sufficient to invalidate a public decision if it would have no conceivable impact on the outcome. In that case, the Supreme Court confirmed that "a court may

---

3 See David Dyzenhaus & Evan Fox-Decent, "Rethinking the Process/Substance Distinction: *Baker v. Canada*" (2001) 51 U.T.L.J. 193.

4 [1985] 2 S.C.R. 643.

5 *Ibid.* at 661.

6 [1994] 1 S.C.R. 202 [*Mobil Oil*].

RÉSUMÉ

Dans cette étude, l'auteur soutient que la Cour suprême du Canada s'est tourné vers des solutions aux différends de procédure de fond sur des droits constitutionnels d'une façon nouvelle et dramatique. Le chapitre examine des études de cas dans le domaine de la sécurité nationale, les droits ancestraux et les droits économiques, sociaux et de démontrer cette tendance et d'explorer ses implications. Il conclut que si la Cour traite de la justice procédurale défaite de résultats de fond qui amènent les parties à la Cour, en premier lieu, tourner à la procédure de la Cour sera semblent moins prudent et plus problématique.

exercise its discretion not to grant a remedy for a breach of procedural fairness where the result is *inevitable*."[7]

It is reasonable to say that fairness always matters, but what matters most is not always fairness. This is where prudential reasoning enters the picture. To the extent the Court has discretion as to how a problem or dispute should be resolved, when should the Court impose a substantive outcome and when is a procedural solution to a problem the better approach? In other words, when is process the prudent choice? Prudence has several meanings, but in this context, I use it generally to mean making decisions based on reason; a strategic or shrewd assessment of the implications of the decision; good judgment in the use of resources; and circumspection as to danger or risk. When applied to procedural justice, I would suggest that prudence means deploying or designing procedural solutions to problems based on a calculation of what is justified on reasoned grounds; what will create the most positive set of implications; what may be defended as an effective use of judicial resources and resources of the parties; and what will minimize downside risk (including risk to the credibility and effectiveness of the Court, and to public confidence in the administration of justice).

This debate over the purposes and ends of procedural rights, for many years internal to administrative law, has now spilled over into a wide range of public and private settings. The McLachlin Court has turned to procedural justice as a wellspring for solving difficult disputes in a variety of contexts. In this brief article, I examine three such contexts: (1) national security,

7 *Ibid.* at 228–29 [emphasis added].

(2) Aboriginal rights, and (3) social and economic rights. In each context, the Court has turned to creatively designed procedures to address difficult and potentially divisive substantive problems. I have chosen these three settings among many possibilities, in part, because the chief justice herself was instrumental in developing the Court's approach to procedural justice in each of these contexts. The trend is sufficiently prevalent in many disparate settings and I suggest that "prudential proceduralism" has become a defining hallmark of the Supreme Court during McLachlin C.J.'s tenure.

In each context I discuss below, however, the implications of the Court's procedural turn also may frustrate its intention. I argue that the Supreme Court of Canada has turned to procedural solutions to substantive disputes over constitutional rights in new and dramatic ways, and also that if the Court treats procedural justice unhinged from the substantive outcomes that bring parties to Court in the first place, the Court's procedural turn will, over time, seem less "prudent" and more problematic.

B. PART ONE: THE IDEA OF PROCEDURAL JUSTICE

Prudential proceduralism carries on a tradition of the "passive virtues" of judicial reasoning highlighted by Alexander Bickel's ground-breaking work on American constitutional interpretation, *The Least Dangerous Branch*.[8] Bickel argued that Courts should exercise prudence in deciding as little as needed to resolve a particular dispute, and to serve as a catalyst for problems to be worked out voluntarily where possible.

The Court has interpreted its public law mandate over the past decade with this prudential concern at the forefront of its agenda. It is manifest, for example, in the many cases in which the Court has affirmed that it should be reluctant to second-guess the wisdom of government action.[9] I suggest a related dynamic is at work when the Supreme Court declines an opportunity to impose an outcome on the parties, and instead tailors a contextual process designed to lead the parties to a just outcome.

The seeds of what I have termed *prudential proceduralism* were sown long before McLachlin C.J.C. assumed leadership of the Supreme Court a decade ago. For example, the notion of "dialogue" emerged as a central norm of Canadian constitutionalism in the 1999 decision in *Vriend v. Alberta* when

8 Alexander Bickel, *The Least Dangerous Branch* (New York: Bobbs-Merril, 1962).

9 See, for example, the Court's decision in *Newfoundland (Treasury Board) v. N.A.P.E.*, 2004 SCC 66 at para. 84.

the Court adopted "dialogue" as a metaphor for judicial review under the Constitution.[10] In *Vriend*, Iacobucci J. discussed the relationship between the legislatures and the courts under the *Charter*, specifically responding to those contesting the legitimacy of constitutional judicial review.[11] He characterized the courts as trustees and arbiters of the rights and freedoms conferred by the Constitution, acting in the interests of a democratically chosen social contract.[12] For Iacobucci J., judicial review represents a process marked by mutual respect, the maintenance of which requires the courts to be reluctant to second-guess the policy choices of legislatures and the executives.[13] Dialogue theory both justified judicial intervention and provided a rationale for limiting that intervention. Dialogue theory justified a procedural solution to the substantive problem of which branch of government is paramount where constitutional rights are engaged.

Some of the most significant decisions of the Dickson Court (like *Morgentaler*)[14] and of the Lamer Court (like the *Secession Reference*)[15] reflected a similar propensity for the Court to opt for proceduralism in the face of very difficult, highly divisive issues.

R. v. Morgentaler, a centrepiece of the Dickson Court's architecture of *Charter* rights, involved the constitutionality of the then section 251(1) of the *Criminal Code*.[16] Section 251 generally required women and their medical

10 [1998] 1 S.C.R. 493 [*Vriend*]. The Court adopted the "dialogue" metaphor from the article by Peter Hogg & Allison Bushell, "The Charter Dialogue between Courts and Legislatures" (1997) 35 Osgoode Hall L.J. 75; see also Peter Hogg & Allison Thornton, "The Charter Dialogue between Courts and Legislatures" (1999) 20 Policy Options 19.

11 *Vriend, ibid.* at paras. 129–43. Justice Iacobucci was dealing with s. 1 of the *Charter* after the Court had concluded that Alberta's human rights legislation violated s. 15 as it excluded protection against discrimination on grounds of sexual orientation.

12 *Ibid.* at para. 134.

13 *Ibid.* at para. 136.

14 [1988] 1 S.C.R. 30. In *Morgentaler*, the majority of the Supreme Court held that the process by which hospital committees determined when an abortion would be available violated the psychological security of the person under s. 7 of the *Charter*. In other words, the majority declined to find criminalizing abortion unconstitutional, and instead found the process to which the abortion provision in the *Criminal Code* had given rise was unconstitutional. Justice Wilson, concurring, would have decided the case based on a right of women to control their own bodies as a feature of the "liberty" aspect of s. 7.

15 *Reference re Secession of Quebec*, [1998] 2 S.C.R. 217. In the *Secession Reference*, the Court held that a "clear majority" vote in favour of secession based on a "clear question" would give rise to a "duty to negotiate" on the federal and Quebec governments. The Court found that the Constitution required a process rather than an outcome in relation to secession.

16 R.S.C. 1970, c. C-34.

practitioners to obtain a certificate from a therapeutic abortion committee of an accredited or approved hospital stating that in the committee's opinion, the continuation of the pregnancy would or would be likely to endanger the woman's life or health. In his judgment, Dickson C.J. observed that while "Parliament must be given room to design an appropriate administrative and procedural structure for bringing into operation a particular defence to criminal liability," that structure must be struck down if "it is so manifestly unfair, having regard to the decisions it is called upon to make, as to violate the principles of fundamental justice."[17]

With this principle of fair process in mind, Dickson C.J. found that the system regulating access to therapeutic abortions was manifestly unfair. Chief Justice Dickson returned to the principle of fairness in his section 1 analysis, drawing upon the second branch of the *Oakes* test, which requires that the means chosen to achieve an important objective should be rational, fair, and not arbitrary.[18] He found that these elements were not satisfied.[19] Justice Beetz, in his concurring reasons, provided an extended analysis of the shortcomings in the administration of the law, focusing on the delay inherent in the process.[20]

The *Secession Reference*, arguably the most significant decision of the Lamer Court, applied a procedural approach to the highly divisive context of national unity.[21] The questions posed by the government to the Supreme Court touched upon the rights of the National Assembly, legislature, or government of Quebec to effect the unilateral secession of Quebec from Canada under domestic and international law. The term "unilateral" was understood by the Court in this context as effecting secession without prior negotiation.[22] The Court held that four of Canada's foundational constitutional principles—federalism, democracy, constitutionalism, and the rule of law—and the protection of minorities, required a particular process to make secession legal. The unanimous Court found that secession would require (a) an amendment to the Constitution,[23] and (b) decisive support for an unambiguous referendum question, if it is to carry weight.[24] A clear

17 *Morgentaler*, above note 14 at para. 52, quoting [1986] 2 S.C.R. 284, 31 D.L.R. (4th) 569.
18 *Ibid.* at para. 54.
19 *Ibid.* at para. 57.
20 *Ibid.* at para. 138.
21 Above note 15.
22 *Ibid.* at para. 86.
23 *Ibid.* at para. 84.
24 *Ibid.* at para. 87.

repudiation of the existing order and a clear expression to pursue secession would then trigger a reciprocal obligation on all parties to Confederation to negotiate constitutional changes to respond to that desire.[25] That negotiation would have to occur in line with the four constitutional principles.[26] It would proceed without the assumption that a legal obligation existed to accede to the secession of a province, but with an understanding that some obligation existed toward the province.[27] The negotiation would have to be meaningful and real. As the Court notes, "the conduct of the parties assumes primary constitutional significance."[28]

In these and other cases, the Dickson and Lamer Courts established key precedents for procedural solutions in contexts where a substantive result imposed by the Court would have significantly alienated a large segment of the Canadian public. The McLachlin Court's procedural turn, I argue, is different. Both the degree of inventiveness of the procedures selected and the purposes of those procedures reflect a phenomenon of *prudential proceduralism*. In the cases discussed below, the Court not only has turned to process to solve problems, but has explored the content of process in new ways—the Court has focused not just on the requirement of a fair hearing, a consultation, or negotiations, but on the features that make such procedures meaningful.

By the term *prudential proceduralism,* I do not suggest that the Court engages in an explicit, strategic process to deal with substantive problems through procedural means (though I also do not preclude the possibility that this may occur from time to time in particular cases). Further, it is also important not to discount the impact of the arguments advocates have put before the Court, and the role of lower court decisions in shaping the Supreme Court's approach. That said, I suggest the Court has developed a collective orientation that is particularly inclined to procedural solutions.

As the Court develops creative procedural solutions to problems in one legal area, there is a greater likelihood that similar solutions will be drawn upon in other areas. For example, without the work in developing procedural fairness in administrative law, it might look quite different as a feature of the *Charter.* The adoption of a contextual approach to process under the *Charter,* in turn, represented the building blocks for the Court's development of the duty to consult and accommodate in the context of Aboriginal rights. There

25 *Ibid.* at para. 88.

26 *Ibid.* at para. 90.

27 *Ibid.* at paras. 90–92.

28 *Ibid.* at para. 94.

are elements of the duty to consult and accommodate, in turn, which resonate in the context of the right to collective bargaining, and so forth.

At root, prudential proceduralism is premised on the unshakeable belief that sensible and reasonable people of good faith will always work out their differences if given a fair and transparent process to do so—it may well be that there is no value more quintessentially Canadian. Similarly, prudential proceduralism is predicated on the belief that decision makers will come to a reasonable decision if only the affected parties are granted a fair shot at making their point to the decision maker. Finally, prudential proceduralism builds on the idea that innovative procedure may move forward otherwise intractable disputes. This approach is particularly important where solutions require compromise, and not the all-or-nothing substantive remedies available to courts.

If you do not share these beliefs, of course, prudential proceduralism might well worry you. To some, what I call the Court's procedural turn is simply an indication that the Court has avoided the hard questions at key junctures. Regardless, the Court's procedural turn is worthy of scrutiny. It is, I would suggest, the harbinger of the Court's second generation of engagement with the *Charter*. While the first generation jurists saw constitutional rights primarily as conferring rights on vulnerable parties, the second generation jurists are more likely to frame those guarantees as a means to structure the determination of solutions to problems. In other words, I believe the second generation approach will interfere with government choices less, but will more often compel government to consider, consult, talk, disclose, accommodate, reconsider, and justify the action taken in light of the process followed. This may be a sign of a weakening of the Court's commitment to the Constitution as a mechanism to constrain government action, or it just might signal a maturing of that commitment, and an evolution of the Court's role as a catalyst of compromise.

Prudential proceduralism has emerged as a central dynamic in Canadian law for at least five reasons:

- First, process builds on the distinctly Canadian norms of dialogue and reasoned engagement by disputing parties, and enjoys significant acceptance by the public;
- second, process is difficult to challenge or oppose, as the meaningful exchange of views and perspectives has inherent value and appeal;
- third, process defers difficult decisions and leaves open further opportunity for compromise, settlement, building trust, and improving

relations. In this way, process results in the parties taking "ownership" over the substantive resolutions which result from the process;

- fourth, a better process minimizes the risk of error in the substantive determination at issue; and
- fifth and finally, imposing a process tends not to be viewed as "judicial activism" in the same way as imposing a substantive result. Process implies respect for the parties, their positions, and the limits of the judicial role.

Below, I briefly discuss the implications of procedural justice in three contexts: first, I examine the national security context, where procedural guarantees have allowed the Court to reconcile the needs of government to take extraordinary measures to confront national threats and the rights of those individuals affected by these measures; second, I canvass the setting of Aboriginal rights and the Court's development of the duty to consult and accommodate; and third, I consider the sphere of social rights, and the Court's bold reversal on recognizing a constitutional right to bargain collectively.

In each of these settings, I suggest that proceduralism saved the Court from embarking on a divisive course which would have challenged the credibility of the Court, and the context therefore made compromise solutions more likely. In each case, the Court served as a catalyst for justice without determining the most just outcome in the circumstances.

C. PART TWO: PROCEDURAL JUSTICE IN ACTION

Procedural justice is a contextual dynamic. There is no *Oakes* framework or test to guide the Court in exercising prudential decision making of the kind I address in this paper. There are common principles and themes that emerge and give shape to the Court's procedural turn. For example, the principle that the Court should decide as little as possible to resolve the issue before it animates each of the prudential judgments discussed below.

I now turn to analyze three case studies (national security, Aboriginal rights, and social and economic rights) in an attempt to draw together these principles and themes.

1) National Security

One of the most difficult settings with which the McLachlin Court has had to grapple has been national security. At the time of the September 2001 terrorist attacks on the United States, the Supreme Court had under reserve the case of *Suresh v. Canada (Minister of Citizenship and Immigration)*.[29] *Suresh* involved the case of an alleged LTTE member, who as a "terrorist" was subject under the then *Immigration Act* to deportation to Sri Lanka, where he claimed he would be subject to torture.

When *Suresh* was released in January of 2002, it represented the first post-9/11 opportunity for the Court to chart a path through the competing demands of protecting collective security through state action and individual liberty.

In *Suresh*, the Court first considered the standard of review with respect to ministerial discretion under the *Immigration Act*, and the constitutionality of the minister's power to deport foreign nationals suspected of terrorist activity under section 7 of the *Charter*. The Court found that the exercise of ministerial discretion attracted the highest level of deference from the Court, and further that the deportation of an individual found to meet the definition of "terrorist" under the Act was not unconstitutional, even where a *prima facie* case had been met that torture would occur if the person were returned to his country of origin.

Having decided in favour of the Crown on two key substantive elements of the case, the Court concluded by deciding in favour of Suresh in his challenge of the procedure by which the deportation occurred.

The Court grafted its framework for analyzing procedural fairness at common law (developed in *Baker v. Canada (Citizenship and Immigration)*)[30] to the context of determining the requirements of procedural fairness under section 7 of the *Charter*. Applying this framework to the circumstances of *Suresh*, the Court held that in order for these requirements to be met, a person facing deportation under the *Immigration Act* to a country where he might be tortured had to be informed of the situation. This condition included further requirements of disclosure, the right to present evidence and test the evidence of the Crown, a right to be heard, and the provision of reasons.

The Court noted that while the minister had accepted written submissions from Suresh in this case, in the absence of access to the materials she was receiving from her staff and on which she based much of her decision, Suresh and his counsel had no knowledge of which factors they specifically needed to address, or any chance to correct any factual inaccuracies or mischaracterizations. In other words, while Suresh had received the right to make submissions, he had not been granted a *meaningful* opportunity to provide input into the decision affecting him.

---

29 2002 SCC 1 [*Suresh*].

30 [1999] 2 S.C.R. 819.

The Court concluded that the requirements of fairness had not been met in Suresh's case, and that the violation of section 7 of the *Charter* could not be saved under section 1 as a reasonable limit. I argue that *Suresh* represents an example of the Court engaging in prudential proceduralism. The Court could have invalidated the deportation order on procedural grounds and declined to deal with the substantive elements of the challenge. Instead, the Court intentionally, and I would suggest, tellingly, left the procedural issue for last. The Court first upheld the constitutionality of the deportation power, and indicated it was not prepared to second-guess the merits of the minister's exercise of discretion to apply that power to the facts and circumstances of *Suresh*. By invalidating the deportation on the ground that the process was unfair, however, the Court was able to locate an important and elusive middle ground. The focus on process allowed the Court to advance values of individual civil liberties and collective security.

Suresh was issued with a companion case, *Ahani v. Canada (Minister of Citizenship and Immigration*.[31] On the facts, the Court concluded that no *prima facie* case that there was a possibility of torture if Ahani were deported to Iran had been shown, and so the section 7 *Charter* issues did not arise as they had in *Suresh*. Even so, while the procedural requirements of section 7 did not apply, the Court nonetheless applied the *Suresh* framework. The Court concluded that the process followed in *Ahani* was consistent with section 7's principles of fundamental justice, as he was given a meaningful opportunity to make submissions. This result has a prudential dimension to it as well—it demonstrates that providing a minimum degree of fairness is not inconsistent with safeguarding national security.

The focus on proceduralism as a mechanism to balance individual liberty and national security was apparent in the Court's two judgments in the *Charkaoui* matter. First, in *Charkaoui v. Canada (Citizenship and Immigration)*,[32] the Court considered the constitutionality of the security certificate system by which foreign nationals could be held as suspected terrorists for an indefinite period of time. As in *Suresh*, the Court in *Charkaoui* found that Parliament's choice to provide for the deportation of foreign nationals on national security grounds did not violate the *Charter*, but that the process used by the government failed to meet the constitutional standards.

Again, the Court focused on the content of fairness, and in particular the defendant's right to know the case against her in order to participate

31 2002 SCC 2.

32 2007 SCC 9 [*Charkaoui (2007)*].

in a fair proceeding before an independent and impartial decision maker. While the *Immigration and Refugee Protection Act*[33] procedures reflect the exigencies of the national security context, McLachlin C.J., writing for the Court, held that such concerns could not be used to excuse procedures that do not conform to fundamental justice. She concluded that without knowledge of the information put against him, the person named in a certificate may not be in a position to raise legal objections relating to the evidence, or to develop legal arguments based on the evidence. If section 7 was to be satisfied, in other words, either the person would have to be given the necessary information, or a substantial substitute for that information must be found. Chief Justice McLachlin further held that the scheme could not be saved under section 1 as alternative options that would impair Charkaoui's procedural rights more minimally were available to government.

In the second case involving the same claimant, *Charkaoui v. Canada (Citizenship and Immigration)*,[34] the Court considered the duty of the government to retain and disclose documents underlying its decision to issue or maintain a security certificate. With its earlier decision in *Suresh* in mind, the Court was particularly concerned with the procedural shortcomings of how the scheme actually operated. Because of limitations in the disclosure provided, the Court found that Charkaoui had been denied the right to a fair hearing, since, without disclosure or inquisitorial judicial powers, judges could be making decisions based on incomplete information and only the government would know.[35] The focus of the Court in *Charkaoui (2008)* was not merely on identifying the requirement of fairness but also its content. As the Court observed, "It is not enough to say that there is a duty to disclose. We must determine exactly how that duty is to be discharged in the context of the procedures relating to the issuance of a security certificate and the review of its reasonableness, and to the detention review."[36] While the Court found the procedures employed by the government fell short of its *Charter* obligation, importantly, it concluded that this did not warrant a stay of proceedings, but rather mandated a better and fairer process.

Finally, in *Canada v. Khadr*,[37] the Court once again addressed issues of individual rights and collective interests through a procedural lens, con-

33 S.C. 2001, c. 27.

34 2008 SCC 38 [*Charkaoui (2008)*].

35 For a precursor McLachlin Court decision probing a similar issue in a similar way, see *Ruby v. Canada (Solicitor General)*, 2002 SCC 75.

36 *Charkaoui (2008)*, above note 34 at para. 59.

37 2008 SCC 28.

cluding that a Canadian held at the Guantanamo Bay facility was entitled to disclosure of relevant documents in the Canadian government's possession, subject to national security and other interests outlined in the *Canada Evidence Act*.

Khadr shows a different way in which the Court has engaged in prudential proceduralism. The Court held that Canada's participation in the "Guantanamo Bay process" itself was a violation of Canada's international human rights obligations.[38] That said, having chosen to participate in this process, the Government of Canada triggered its own procedural duties toward Khadr, including the obligation of disclosure. As the Court put it, "Canada has an obligation under s. 7 to provide disclosure to Mr. Khadr to mitigate the effect of Canada's participation by passing on the product of the interviews to U.S. authorities."

While the Court could do little to ensure the substantive outcome sought (that is, ensure the release of Khadr to Canada), its findings reflect the ways in which process has become the canvas on which rights in the national security context have been brought to life by the McLachlin Court.

While the national security cases considered above are a traditional venue for procedural justice (that is, the right to fairness), Aboriginal rights represent new terrain for the extension of procedural justice.

2) Aboriginal Rights: Duty to Consult and Accommodate[39]

Just as national security represented a divisive and intractable dispute in which the Supreme Court has used prudential proceduralism as a catalyst for compromise, the field of Aboriginal rights similarly does not lend itself to all-or-nothing solutions. In *R. v. Sparrow*,[40] the Court had interpreted section 35 of the *Constitution Act* as a remedial measure intended to serve as a constitutional basis on which to afford Aboriginal peoples a degree of control over government conduct affecting their rights. In *Van der Peet*,[41] the Court held that section 35 provides the constitutional framework for reconciling

38 *Ibid.* at para. 27.

39 Portions of this section draw upon Lorne Sossin, "Duty to Consult and Accommodate: Procedural Justice as Aboriginal Rights." Paper prepared for the International Political Science Association meeting in Santiago, Chile, 13 July 2009. I am indebted to Amanda Montague for her research assistance on that project, and to the Faculty of Law, University of Toronto, and the Social Science and Humanities Research Council for their generous support of that aspect of the project.

40 [1990] 1 S.C.R. 1075 [*Sparrow*].

41 [1996] 2 S.C.R. 507.

the sovereignty of the Crown with the reality that Aboriginal peoples lived on the land in distinctive societies, with their own practices, traditions, and cultures. Since then, as Arthur Pape has observed, "the promotion of reconciliation has been understood as the primary purpose of section 35, in all the Court's jurisprudence."[42]

Cases such as *Sparrow* and *Van der Peet* developed the fiduciary relationship between the Crown and Aboriginal peoples, and provided remedies against the application of laws which infringe that obligation without justification. In 2004, the Supreme Court introduced a new and distinctive framework for understanding the relationship between the Crown and Aboriginal peoples, one based not on negating laws or tree licenses, but on a process of consultation and accommodation. The contextual nature of the duty, which varied based on the particular circumstances, was developed from the Supreme Court's judgment in *Delgamuukw*, which dealt with a significant Aboriginal land claim in British Columbia and the scope of section 35 rights, and focused on the Crown's moral obligation to negotiate with Aboriginal communities in good faith.[43] As *Delgamuukw* demonstrated, the duty to consult and, consequently, to accommodate Aboriginal rights and interests, cannot be severed from the overall purpose of protecting the substance of section 35(1) rights, and of furthering reconciliation between the Aboriginal and non-Aboriginal Canadian societies."[44]

---

42 Arthur Pape, "Consultation, Accommodation and Beyond" (Lecture presented to the Aboriginal Law Conference, Pacific Business & Law Institute, 6 March 2008) [unpublished].

43 *Delgamuukw v. British Columbia*, [1997] 3 SCR 1010 at para. 168. *Delgamuukw* represented the longest trial in Canada's history (involving 318 days of testimony and resulting in a judgment 400 pages in length). The Supreme Court identified flaws in the conduct of that trial and ordered a new trial. Significantly, after ordering a new trial, Lamer C.J. observed,

> 186 Finally, this litigation has been both long and expensive, not only in economic but in human terms as well. By ordering a new trial, I do not necessarily encourage the parties to proceed to litigation and to settle their dispute through the courts. As was said in *Sparrow*, at p. 1105, s. 35(1) "provides a solid constitutional base upon which subsequent negotiations can take place." Those negotiations should also include other Aboriginal nations which have a stake in the territory claimed. Moreover, the Crown is under a moral, if not a legal, duty to enter into and conduct those negotiations in good faith. Ultimately, it is through negotiated settlements, with good faith and give and take on all sides, reinforced by the judgments of this Court, that we will achieve what I stated in *Van der Peet*, above, to be a basic purpose of s. 35(1)—"the reconciliation of the pre-existence of aboriginal societies with the sovereignty of the Crown." Let us face it, we are all here to stay.

44 See Veronica Potes, "The Duty to Accommodate Aboriginal Peoples Rights: Substantive Consultation?" (2006) 17 J. Envtl. L. & Prac. 27 at 29–30 [Potes].

The importance of consultation with Aboriginal communities is not new,[45] but in *Haida Nation v. British Columbia (Minister of Forests)*,[46] and *Taku River Tlingit First Nation v. British Columbia*,[47] McLachlin C.J., writing for the Court, developed a creative mix of procedural and substantive constraint on the Crown in dealing with contested resources. The duty to consult and accommodate is rooted in the "honour of the Crown" which requires the Crown to act "honourably" in its dealings with Aboriginal people.

In *Haida*, McLachlin C.J. summed up the relationship between the honour of the Crown and the duty to consult and accommodate in the following blunt terms:

> Put simply, Canada's Aboriginal peoples were here when Europeans came, and were never conquered. Many bands reconciled their claims with the sovereignty of the Crown through negotiated treaties. Others, notably in British Columbia, have yet to do so. The potential rights embedded in these claims are protected by s. 35 of the *Constitution Act, 1982*. The honour of the Crown requires that these rights be determined, recognized and respected. This, in turn, requires the Crown, acting honourably, to participate in processes of negotiation. While this process continues, the honour of the Crown may require it to consult and, where indicated, accommodate Aboriginal interests.[48]

The Haida challenged the replacement and transfer of tree farm licences on land subject to their Aboriginal title claim. Chief Justice McLachlin held that when the Crown has knowledge of potentially existing Aboriginal rights or title and considers activity that risks infringing upon them, the Crown's legal duty to consult and accommodate is engaged. This duty is proportionate to the *prima facie* strength of the Aboriginal case and the seriousness of the potential harm to that case.[49] This variability fits with the model of procedural fairness developed by the Court in administrative and constitutional law (and is discussed above in the context of national security caselaw). Chief Justice McLachlin also acknowledged this wellspring of

45 See *Sparrow*, above note 40 at 1105–106. See also Sonia Lawrence & Patrick Macklem, "From Consultation to Reconciliation: Aboriginal Rights and the Crown's Duty to Consult" (2000) 79 Can. Bar Rev. 252 [Lawrence & Macklem].

46 2004 SCC 73 [*Haida*].

47 2004 SCC 74 [*Taku River*].

48 *Haida*, above note 46 at para. 25.

49 In the Haida context, the trial judge had determined that the Haida claim to the forests in question, while unproven, was strong, and that there was a real risk that the forests would be gone by the time the Haida claim was eventually heard and adjudicated.

the duty to consult and accommodate, observing that in order to determine the content of the duty, regard may be had to the procedural safeguards developed by administrative law.[50]

In *Taku River*, an Aboriginal community challenged a proposed mining road passing through contested territory. Writing for the Court, McLachlin C.J. held that the duty to consult and accommodate guarantees attentiveness to Aboriginal concerns and provides for their participation. Nevertheless, once again, the Court reiterated that a duty to consult and accommodate does not compel a particular substantive outcome. Chief Justice McLachlin elaborated that so long as consultation is "meaningful," there is no duty to reach an agreement. This process is necessarily one of compromise between Aboriginal concerns and competing societal interests. Chief Justice McLachlin, highlighting a recurring theme of procedural justice, observed that the duty will vary with the circumstances, but always requires meaningful, good faith consultation and willingness on the part of the Crown to make changes based on information that emerges during the process.[51]

As in *Suresh* and *Ahani*, the use of companion cases in the *Haida* and *Taku River* decisions, involving what the Court found to be both an insufficient and a sufficient process, emphasizes that the Court's approach is balanced and principled, and reinforces the prudential rationale underlying the Court's procedural remedy. Unlike the national security cases, however, the duty to consult and accommodate goes beyond meaningful participation to require some connection between process and outcome. In *Taku River*, McLachlin C.J. captures this point by concluding, "Responsiveness is a key requirement of both consultation and accommodation."[52]

While consultation is a well-worn motif of Crown–Aboriginal relations, the focus of the Court in *Haida* and *Taku River* on accommodation seems to suggest something closer to a blurring of the boundary between procedural and substantive justice. Arthur Pape has contended that the central substance of the duty ought to be the accommodation, so that all consultation is viewed as a means to reaching suitable accommodation for the parties.[53] Veronica Potes has suggested that the standard of what constitutes

---

50 *Ibid.* at para. 41.

51 On the facts of *Taku River*, McLachlin C.J. held that the Crown's duty had been met. She found key facts supporting this finding, including that the Taku River Tlingit received financial support to help them participate, their concerns were identified in a government report made under the Act, and other mitigation strategies were adopted.

52 *Taku River*, above note 47 at para. 25.

53 Interview of Arthur Pape by the author (29 May 2009).

adequate accommodation should continue to be raised: she argues that the doctrine of justification should also be to inform the duty to consult and accommodate, such that "in deciding among the universe of accommodating measures only demonstrable, compelling, and substantial objectives should trump Aboriginal protected interests."[54]

As the idea of accommodation continues to be developed (including the ancillary question of the degree of deference the Court should show to the accommodation choices of government), the potential of the duty to consult and accommodate to serve as a route to reconciliation will become clear. As David Mullan observes, "the process and good faith elements are the ones that have to this point predominated in judicial articulation and assessment of the duty to accommodate. It remains to be seen whether there is any judicial disposition to push the limits further and engage in a fuller merits review of accommodation decisions."[55]

The key but often subtle distinction between a right to a process and a right to an outcome also lies at the centre of the debate over social and economic rights under the *Charter*, in particular, the right to collective bargaining.

3) Social and Economic Rights: Right to Collective Bargaining

In *Health Services and Support—Facilities Subsector Bargaining Assn. v. British Columbia*,[56] the Court affirmed that section 2(d) of the *Charter* encompasses a procedural right to collective bargaining. The *BC Health and Social Services Delivery Improvement Act* was held to infringe the procedural right to collectively bargain, and could not be saved by section 1. The constitutional right to

54 Potes, above note 44 at 44.

55 David Mullan, "The Duty to Consult Aboriginal Peoples—The Canadian Example" (2009) 22 Canadian Journal of Administrative Law and Practice 107 at 127. For additional discussion of the duty, see J. Timothy S. McCabe, *The Honour of the Crown and its Fiduciary Duties to Aboriginal Peoples* (Toronto: LexisNexis Canada, 2008); Monique Passelac-Ross & Veronica Potes, "Consultation with Aboriginal Peoples in the Athabasca Oil Sands Region: Is it Meeting the Crown's Legal Obligations?" (2007) 98 Resources 1; Potes, above note 44 at 27; Heather Treacy, Tara Campbell, & Jamie Dickson, "The Current State of the Law in Canada on Crown Obligations to Consult" (2007) 44 Alta. L. Rev. 571; Timothy Huyer, "Honour of the Crown: The New Approach to Crown–Aboriginal Reconciliation" (2006) 21 Windsor Rev. Legal & Soc. Issues 33; Thomas Isaac & Anthony Knox, "The Crown's Duty to Consult Aboriginal People" (2003) 41 Alta. L. Rev. 49; and Lawrence & Macklem, above note 45 at 252; Constance MacIntosh, "The Reconciliation Doctrine in Chief Justice McLachlin's Court: From a 'Final Legal Remedy' to a 'Just and Lasting' Process" (this volume).

56 2007 SCC 27.

collective bargaining, according to the Court, protects the ability of workers to engage in associational activities, and protects the capacity of workers to act together to reach shared goals related to workplace issues and terms of employment.

The Court held that determining whether legislation or government activity infringes upon the right to collective bargaining would involve an inquiry into whether the legislation or activity "substantially interferes" with the collective bargaining process. Specifically, the Court analyzed: (1) the importance of the matter affected to the process of collective bargaining; and (2) the manner in which the measure impacts on "the collective right to good faith negotiation and consultation."[57] If the matters affected do not substantially impact on the process of collective bargaining, the legislation or activity does not violate section 2(d) and the employer may be under no duty to discuss and consult. If, on the other hand, the changes substantially touch on collective bargaining, employers still do not violate section 2(d) if they preserve a process of consultation and good faith negotiation. Only where the matter is both important to the process of collective bargaining *and* has been imposed in violation of the duty of good faith negotiation will section 2(d) be breached.

Having established a right to a process, the Court here, as in the settings of national security and Aboriginal rights, confirmed that such a procedural entitlement entails no right to an outcome. In discussing the nature of the right at issue under section 2(d), McLachlin C.J. and Lebel J., writing for the majority, observe that, "In our view, it is entirely possible to protect the 'procedure' known as collective bargaining without mandating constitutional protection for the "fruits of that bargaining process."[58] Subsequently, they emphasize this point in the following terms:

> The right to collective bargaining thus conceived is a limited right. First, as the right is to a process, it does not guarantee a certain substantive or economic outcome. Moreover, the right is to a general process of collective bargaining, not to a particular model of labour relations, nor to a specific bargaining method.[59]

The Court turned to a procedural solution in the context of labour relations in order to advance rights in a potentially contentious setting, where

57 *Ibid.* at para. 93.

58 *Ibid.* at para. 29.

59 *Ibid.* at para. 91.

the Court could be vulnerable to the charge of activism. This context also demonstrates how the Court no longer simply invokes procedure, but also explores the purposes of process.

The majority views the right to collective bargaining as a right to expect bargaining in good faith. In elaborating on the duty to bargain in good faith, McLachlin C.J. and Lebel J. explain that the parties have a duty to engage in "meaningful dialogue" and that they must be "willing to exchange and explain their positions," and "must make a reasonable effort to arrive at an acceptable contract."[60] Subsequently, they reiterate, "the right to bargain collectively protects not just the act of making representations, but also the right of employees to have their views heard in the context of a meaningful process of consultation and discussion."[61]

In this way, the McLachlin Court has affirmed the core principles of prudential proceduralism. As in the national security and Aboriginal rights settings, the Court deployed procedural justice in the context of social and economic rights to serve as a catalyst for a just outcome, without imposing what the content of a just solution need be on the parties.

4) The Implications of Procedural Justice

In the wake of the recent trend toward procedural solutions to substantive problems in the areas of national security, Aboriginal rights, and social and economic rights discussed above, some important implications arise. I want to sketch the most salient of these implications.

a) More Litigation

One of the counterintuitive implications of the Court's direction in all three of the areas discussed for the parties to engage in a meaningful process is that this instead appears to have been the catalyst for still more litigation. For example, a number of claims to extend the right to bargain collectively are moving through the courts in the wake of the *Health Services* decision.[62] The Supreme Court heard another major "duty to consult and accommodate" case in the fall of 2009, exploring to what extent the duty survives

60 *Ibid.* at para. 101.

61 *Ibid.* at para. 114.

62 See, for example, *Mounted Police Association of Ontario v. Canada (Attorney General)* (2009), 96 O.R. (3d) 20 (S.C.J.).

treaty agreements.[63] In both cases, the courts are grappling with parties who cannot agree on the scope or limits of the procedural right that the Court first carved out. Rather than investing resources in the process into which the Court sought to divert disputes, parties instead are returning to litigation. Indeed, it is telling that the *Khadr* matter has now landed in the Supreme Court on three separate occasions.

b) More Uncertainty

A second and related concern is the level of greater uncertainty. While the Court provided general direction on the procedural approach to be followed, parties lacked specificity as to what would or would not comply with the Court's direction. Uncertainty is not an unexpected or inadvertent result of procedural justice; it is, rather, inherent in it. The classic example of this dynamic in Canadian law occurred after the *Secession Reference*.[64] The Court had indicated negotiations on secession would be required following a "clear majority" vote on a "clear question." What constituted a clear majority or a clear question remained intentionally uncertain. The very point of the Court's nuanced approach in the *Secession Reference* was to avoid determining the substantive (and, therefore, political) issues and instead to map out the procedural roadmap to secession. In the *Secession Reference* context, the government responded in 1999 with its well-known and aptly entitled *Clarity Act*.[65] Will similar legislation be needed to map out how the government will discharge its obligations under the duty to consult and accommodate? While uncertainty may be incidental to procedural solutions, that uncertainty may also be corrosive to the very trust and shared points of reference that procedural solutions depend on for success.

c) Frustrated Expectations

The third and most significant implication, in my view, is the inevitable frustration of the parties seeking redress if procedural solutions do not yield at least some substantive gains some of the time. For example, if Aboriginal groups see little change arising out of the process, there is a high likelihood that cynicism and a lack of faith in the courts could ensue. Similarly, if lawyers for terror suspects perceive no change in the culture of law enforce-

---

63 *Little Salmon/Carmacks First Nation v. Yukon (Minister of Energy, Mines and Resources)*, 2008 YKCA 13, appeal dismissed *Beckman v. Little Salmon/Carmacks First Nation*, 2010 SCC 53.

64 Above note 15.

65 S.C. 2000, c. 26.

ment and national security administration with respect to disclosure or the fairness of the process, then procedural justice will come to be seen as little more than formalism.

In other words, in the sphere of procedural justice (and perhaps especially in that sphere), results matter. Is there anything the Court can do to address the implications set out above? While more precision can mitigate the challenges of uncertainty and perhaps diminish the likelihood of subsequent litigation, the prospect of frustrated expectations strikes me as an endemic risk to the path of proceduralism. To this point, it is a risk the McLachlin Court appears willing to take.

D. CONCLUSION

In this brief study, I have explored the rationale for and some of the implications of the Court's "procedural turn." The Supreme Court under McLachlin C.J.'s leadership has built on a long-standing inclination toward prudential proceduralism and made it a defining feature of Canadian law. In a variety of contentious and divisive settings, the McLachlin Court has embraced the promise of procedural justice.

Where will this second-generation approach to procedural rights lead the Court? Ultimately, I believe that the distinction between process and substance itself may be called into question. Just as the Court emphasized in each of the three settings analyzed above that participation alone was insufficient to satisfy the right at issue, and rather, that *meaningful* participation was required, the next logical step for the Court may well be to articulate how meaningful participation leads to procedural justice. In other words, are just outcomes a corollary of meaningful participation? This is a question which can be answered only in context, and after one considers the process *and* the outcome to which it led.

As the substantive results of the McLachlin Court's procedural turn become clear, the Court's vision of procedural justice (or lack thereof) likely will come into view. To reach a conclusion regarding the promise of procedural justice, it may be helpful to keep in mind the words Lon Fuller wrote fifty years before McLachlin C.J. assumed leadership of the Supreme Court:

> Life is itself a process, and by making process the center of our attention we are getting closer to the most enduring part of reality. For that reason, I believe that the recommended emphasis on procedures for solving

conflicts will not tend simply to suppress those conflicts but will promote their just resolution.[66]

66 Fuller, above note 1 at 204.

PART TWO

Administrative Law

The McLachlin Court and the Public Law Standard of Review: A Major Irritant Soothed or a Significant Ongoing Problem?

DAVID J. MULLAN

A. INTRODUCTION

When Justice McLachlin became chief justice of Canada on 7 January 2000, there were few signs that the selection and application of a standard of review in the scrutiny of the decisions of statutory and prerogative authorities would be one of the major preoccupations of the Court's public law workload over the next decade. For a period of twenty years, the Court had struggled with developing an approach to judicial review of administrative action. Under that approach, the Court attempted to ensure that the competing competences of those responsible for the administrative process, on the one hand, and the courts, on the other, were reflected appropriately in the identification of the standard of review to be applied in any particular instance. This evolution took place against a complex constitutional backdrop that included the guaranteed jurisdiction of the section 96 courts,[1] appropriate recognition of legitimate legislative choice of instruments of governance, administration, and adjudication, and the limited though important intrusions in administrative processes of the *Canadian Charter of Rights and Freedoms*, as well as respect for the rule of law and other underlying principles of the Canadian

* I am indebted to Professor Alice Woolley of the University of Calgary for her assessment of an earlier version of this paper and her suggestions for clarification.

1 As recognized in *Crevier v. Quebec (Attorney General)*, [1981] 1 S.C.R. 220 and *MacMillan Bloedel Ltd. v. Simpson*, [1995] 4 S.C.R. 725.

RÉSUMÉ

Au cours des dix premières années du mandat de Beverley McLachlin en qualité de juge en chef à la Cour suprême du Canada, la norme de contrôle applicable pour la révision des décisions axées sur le pouvoir conféré par la loi ou découlant d'une prérogative a été l'une des préoccupations majeures de la Cour. La résolution finale adoptée par la Cour à la suite de ce qui était devenu un schéma insatisfaisant combinant des approches en apparence contradictoires pour régler cette question s'est traduite par l'arrêt *Dunsmuir* et par un important et nouveau calibrage de l'approche envers la norme de contrôle en droit public. Cet article retrace l'historique qui a mené à ce changement, il décrit la nature de cet ordre nouveau, évalue les difficultés potentielles découlant de cette nouvelle approche, pour finalement conclure que bon nombre des problèmes relatifs à la jurisprudence antérieure à l'arrêt *Dunsmuir* auraient été résolus. En bref, il y a matière à considérer avec un certain optimisme la prochaine décennie du mandat de la juge en chef de Beverley McLachlin.

Constitution,[2] recognized in *Reference re Secession of Quebec*,[3] and, latterly, Canada's international obligations.[4]

As will be seen, by the beginning of 2000, there was reason to believe that that task had, at long last, been accomplished. There was a sense that controversies over choice of the appropriate standard of review to be applied in particular situations would be minimized and the courts would be free to deal with the merits of applications for judicial review (and statutory appeals) on the basis of what would, in most instances, be an obvious and readily applied standard of scrutiny. However, the Court's administrative law caseload over the first eight years of the McLachlin Chief Justiceship made it abundantly clear that such sanguinity was by no means completely justified. During this period, the Court spent a great deal of time struggling

2 See the judgment of L'Heureux-Dubé J. in *Baker v. Canada (Minister of Citizenship and Immigration)*, [1999] 2 S.C.R. 817 at para. 56 [*Baker*]:

> [D]iscretion must be exercised in accordance with the boundaries established in the statute, the principles of the rule of law, the principles of administrative law, the fundamental values of Canadian society, and the principles of the *Charter*.

3 [1998] 2 S.C.R. 217.

4 As also recognized in *Baker*, above note 2.

with refinements to the tests for standard of review that were in place in 2000 as well as differentiating between the two deferential standards of review—unreasonableness and patent unreasonableness. In doing so, the Court provided ample warrant for the claim that there was no clear consensus among its members as to the precise contours of the criteria by which it was to settle upon the appropriate standard of review in any particular case and, thereafter, how to apply the selected standard. Indeed, behind the debate and inconsistency in the delineation and application of the detail of the standard tests may well have been fundamental disagreements over the principles on which those standard tests were founded.

In early 2008, to the surprise of few, in *Dunsmuir v. New Brunswick*[5] the Court conceded that elements of the law governing the selection and application of the standard of review needed recasting. It then set about doing so in a manner that at least the majority of the Court clearly hoped would remove many of the elements of controversy and dramatically decrease the significance of standard of review analysis that had become the tail that wagged the dog in so many judicial review applications and statutory appeals. Almost a year to the day later, in *Canada (Citizenship and Immigration) v. Khosa*,[6] the Court further refined the *Dunsmuir* approach in the context of a statutory codification of the grounds of judicial review in the *Federal Courts Act*.[7]

In this paper, I have two objectives. The first is to tease out what went wrong between the beginning of 2000 and the early part of 2008.[8] The second is to ask whether the Court's recasting of the approach to the delineation and application of the appropriate standard of review in both *Dunsmuir* and *Khosa* means that this sometimes tiresome and distracting issue will cease to be a major preoccupation in the second decade of Chief Justice McLachlin's stewardship of the Court. More generally, the project is analysis and diagnosis, not prescription.

---

5 2008 SCC 9, [2008] 1 S.C.R. 190 [*Dunsmuir*].

6 2009 SCC 12, [2009] 1 S.C.R. 339 [*Khosa*].

7 R.S.C. 1985, c. F-7 (as amended), s. 18.1(4).

8 In so doing, I should not be interpreted as, in any sense, making an assessment of the actual substantive outcomes in the cases discussed, whether they affirmed, set aside, or reversed the original decision of the statutory decision maker. The question of the extent to which those outcomes advanced the principles of general regulatory law or the substantive law of the particular regimes under scrutiny is beyond the scope of this paper. Of course, if, at the end of the day, a considered assessment would lead to the conclusion that, by and large, the Court has produced positive substantive results, the question whether standard of review makes any real difference would loom much larger!

B. POTTED HISTORY OF THE 1979–2000 EVOLUTION OF THE STANDARD OF REVIEW

In 1979, in *Canadian Union of Public Employees, Local 963 v. New Brunswick Liquor Corporation*,[9] the Court laid the foundations for an approach to judicial review of administrative action that recognized both the expertise of a wide range of statutory authorities and the legislature's intention that the role of the section 96 courts in the scrutiny of those authorities would be limited. The era of deference had begun. Thereafter, the Court, in *Union des employés de service, Local 298 v. Bibeault*,[10] advanced that cause by developing a methodology, the pragmatic and functional criteria, that would enable courts to determine whether deference under the rubric of a standard of patent unreasonableness was appropriate to the issue or issues on which the courts' judicial review authority was engaged.

While this approach and methodology evolved in the context of applications for judicial review for alleged errors of law in the case of tribunals protected by privative clauses, its tentacles eventually extended much further. It was applicable to review of not just questions of law but also the factual determinations of statutory and prerogative authorities, subsuming the previous "no evidence" test for judicial review of factual determinations.[11] More controversially,[12] the Court, in both *Pezim v. British Columbia (Superintendent of Brokers)*[13] and *Canada (Director of Investigation and Research) v. Southam Inc.*,[14] accepted that the deferential approach to review was not confined to situations where a privative clause–protected tribunal was the subject of the judicial review application. It could be appropriate in the absence of a privative clause and, indeed, even where there was a statutory right of appeal from the authority's decision to the courts. "Specialization of duties"[15] was a concept that had purchase across the range of tribunal decision making.

---

9 [1979] 2 S.C.R. 227.

10 [1988] 2 S.C.R. 1048 [*Bibeault*].

11 See, for example, *Lester (W.W.) (1978) Ltd. v. United Association of Journeymen and Apprentices of the Plumbing and Pipefitting Industry, Local 740*, [1990] 3 S.C.R. 644 and *Toronto (City) Board of Education v. O.S.S.T.F. District 15*, [1997] 1 S.C.R. 487.

12 The controversy persisted in *Khosa*, above note 6, where Rothstein J. argued (at paras. 90–91) for the position that deference had no role to play in statutory appeals on questions of law and jurisdiction, a proposition rejected by Binnie J., for the majority (at paras. 23–26).

13 [1994] 2 S.C.R. 557.

14 [1997] 1 S.C.R. 748 [*Southam*].

15 An expression coined by Gonthier J. in *Bell Canada v. Canada (Canadian Radio-Television and Telecommunications Commission)*, [1989] 1 S.C.R. 1722 at para. 32, a judgment that foreshadowed *Pezim* and *Southam*.

Southam did, however, recognize that the spread of deference necessitated a more nuanced regime. As a consequence, the Court accepted a calibrated approach to judicial review. Between correctness and patent unreasonableness review, there was now an intermediate standard of unreasonableness or unreasonableness *simpliciter.*

The seemingly final stanza came six months prior to the appointment of the chief justice. On 9 July 1999, the Court handed down its seminal judgment in *Baker v. Canada (Minister of Citizenship and Immigration).*[16] Among the contributions of that case to administrative law was the acceptance in L'Heureux-Dubé J.'s majority judgment that there was no bright line distinction between determining questions of law and exercising statutory or prerogative discretion. The principal consequence of this, as far as the standard of review was concerned, was that henceforth exercises of discretion were brought within the rubric of the pragmatic and functional approach. Depending on an appropriately modified application of the four factors that were the foundation of that approach, the courts were to review decisions of a discretionary character by reference to one of the three then accepted standards of review: correctness, unreasonableness, or patent unreasonableness.

Writing shortly thereafter, I expressed the following sentiment:

> [T]he Court has provided an overarching or unifying theory of review of the substantive decisions of all manner of statutory and prerogative authorities.[17]

In a sense, *Baker* had completed the circle, and, it appeared that, aside from a few details (and, principally the precise contours of some of the four pragmatic and functional factors), the Court had provided lower courts with a template for dealing with standard of review disputes across the entire spectrum of public law decision making. Life under the new chief justice seemed about to begin with one of the major irritants of the previous twenty years of the Court's history effectively marginalized.

C. 2000—THE CHIEF JUSTICE'S FIRST YEAR

On the surface, the first year of McLachlin C.J.'s tenure suggested an approach to judicial review of administrative action that was working satisfactorily. While it was not a year in which there were a great number of

---

16 *Baker,* above note 2.

17 David J. Mullan, *Administrative Law* (Toronto: Irwin Law, 2001) at 108.

administrative law appeals on substantive grounds,[18] there seemed little reason to quarrel with the Court's choice or application of the standard of review in those few cases.

In three of its decisions, the Court simply applied a correctness standard without conducting any standard of review analysis. While at first blush that might seem troubling, given the Court's general commitment to deference where appropriate, there was nothing startling about any of these three instances of the automatic use of correctness review.

Regina Police Association Inc. v. Regina (City) Board of Police Commissioners[19] involved a jurisdictional saw-off or duelling jurisdictions situation in which the Court was called upon to decide whether the right to grieve under a collective agreement was precluded by a statutory regime for police discipline. In *Global Securities Corporation v. British Columbia (Securities Commission)*,[20] the challenge to a decision or order of the Securities Commission was based on a claim that the provision under which the Commission acted was *ultra vires* in terms of the division of powers under sections 91 and 92 of the *Constitution Act, 1867*. Finally, in *Quebec (Commission des droits de la personne et des droits de la jeunesse) v. Montréal (City)*,[21] the context was an appeal from a decision of the Quebec Human Rights Tribunal interpreting the term *handicap* in the *Quebec Charter of Human Rights and Freedoms*.[22]

---

18 The most important administrative law case of the year was almost certainly *Blencoe v. British Columbia (Human Rights Commission)*, 2000 SCC 44, [2000] 2 S.C.R. 307, a case exploring the connections between the common law principles of natural justice and procedural fairness, the requirements of fundamental justice under section 7 of the *Canadian Charter of Rights and Freedoms*, and more particularly, the circumstances, if any, under which undue delay in the conduct of administrative processes might represent a threat to "life, liberty and security of the person" as guaranteed by s. 7. The issue of deference did not play any direct role in the proceedings because the application for judicial review was for relief in the nature of prohibition to prevent the British Columbia Human Rights Tribunal commencing a hearing. The Tribunal had not itself ruled on whether the hearing's fairness had been compromised by reason of excessive delay so no question arose as to whether there was any room for deference to that kind of procedural ruling. Indirectly, of course, to proceed with the hearing of the judicial review application before the Tribunal itself had had an opportunity to address the issue bespoke a lack of concern for the Tribunal's processes. However, this argument was raised and rejected by Lowry J., at first instance ((1998), 49 B.C.L.R. (3d) 201 at paras. 15–16 (S.C.)), and did not feature in the ultimate appeal to the Supreme Court of Canada, even in the recitation of the judicial history.

19 2000 SCC 14, [2000] 1 S.C.R. 360 [*Regina Police Association*].

20 2000 SCC 21, [2000] 1 S.C.R. 494.

21 2000 SCC 27, [2000] 1 S.C.R. 665 [*Montréal (City)*].

22 R.S.Q. 1977, c. C-12 (re-enacted S.Q. 1982, c. 61, s. 16), s. 10.

Save in those situations where the legislature has conferred authority on one of the duelists to deal with competing jurisdiction issues,[23] such matters are in a sense *a priori* jurisdictional questions demanding correctness review. Indeed, this was how the Court approached its task:

> The sole issue in this appeal is whether the arbitrator had jurisdiction to hear and decide the dispute . . . . In my view, the arbitrator was correct in deciding that she did not have jurisdiction to hear this dispute.[24]

Similarly, tribunal determination of constitutional issues (including the assignment of legislative competence under sections 91 and 92 of the *Constitution Act, 1867*), at least in so far as they involve questions of law as opposed to fact, has always been treated as subject to correctness review. Somewhat more controversial is whether human rights tribunals are entitled to deference in the interpretation of their constitutive or empowering statutes. However, at least in terms of precedent, the Court had already decided in *Canada (Attorney General) v. Mossop*[25] that human rights tribunals did not deserve deference in determining the meaning of the various categories of discrimination under human rights legislation. The Court justified this in part by reference to the role of "statutory interpretation and general legal reasoning" in the teasing out of the meaning of discrimination, on which the courts were as, if not more, competent than human rights tribunals.[26] In *Montréal (City)*, the Court reinforced this by reference to the similarity between the task of the courts when dealing with section 15, the equality provision in the *Canadian Charter of Rights and Freedoms*, and the issues posed by anti-discrimination provisions in human rights codes.[27]

In three other judgments rendered during 2000,[28] the Court did directly address issues respecting the standard of review. The only one in which the

---

23 See, for example, *Pasiechynk v. Saskatchewan (Workers' Compensation Board)*, [1997] 2 S.C.R. 890, where the Court applied a patent unreasonableness standard of review to a Board decision that the Workers' Compensation regime barred a civil action. In fact, on 20 January 2002, in two judgments rendered from the Bench, McLachlin C.J. (for the Court) sustained two Court of Appeal judgments to the same effect: *Kovach v. British Columbia (Workers' Compensation Board)*, 2000 SCC 3, [2000] 1 S.C.R. 55; and *Lindsay v. Saskatchewan (Workers' Compensation Board)*, 2000 SCC 4, [2000] 1 S.C.R. 59.

24 *Regina Police Association*, above note 19 at para. 40.

25 [1993] 1 S.C.R. 554.

26 *Ibid.* at para. 45 (La Forest and Iacobucci JJ. concurring) and see also paras. 25–26 (Lamer C.J., and Sopinka and Iacobucci JJ. concurring).

27 *Montréal (City)*, above note 21 at para. 42.

28 See also *Kovach* and *Lindsay*, above note 23.

Court engaged in a pragmatic and functional analysis was *Nanaimo (City) v. Rascal Trucking Ltd.*,[29] a case argued before the appointment of McLachlin J. as chief justice but in which she was a member of the hearing panel. In this instance, there were essentially two issues: whether the city had authority to declare a pile of soil a nuisance, and, assuming it could do so, the sustainability of the order that it made having made that declaration. Justice Major, delivering the judgment of the Court on the basis of a pragmatic and functional analysis, determined that the municipality's determination of the first question was subject to review for correctness. Having found that the municipality had correctly determined this issue of authority, he then sustained the actual order on the basis of a patently unreasonable standard of review.

The other two cases arose in a labour law setting. In *Syndicat de l'enseignement du Grand-Portage v. Morency*,[30] the issue essentially involved the interpretation of a collective agreement and the parties conceded that the standard of review was that of patent unreasonableness, a concession that LeBel J., delivering a short judgment of the Court sustaining the award, was prepared to accept. In *Ajax (Town) v. National Automobile, Aerospace and Agricultural Implement Workers Union of Canada (CAW-Canada), Local 222*,[31] the issue was a Labour Board's interpretation of the successor rights provisions in its home statute and, again, it had been conceded that the standard of review was that of patent unreasonableness. Here too, McLachlin C.J. accepted this concession, as did Bastarache J. in his solitary dissent. Thereafter, however, in a very short judgment,[32] she did little more than endorse the judgment delivered by Goudge J.A. in the Ontario Court of Appeal holding that the Board's conclusion was not "clearly irrational."[33]

Taken at face value, this limited body of caselaw augured well for the sustainability of the approach that the Court had been developing since 1979, especially for those who favoured the essential philosophy of *New Brunswick Liquor*: that courts should be hesitant to deny deference to tribunals and agencies and engage in correctness review.[34]

---

29 2000 SCC 13, [2000] 1 S.C.R. 342 [*Rascal Trucking*].

30 2000 SCC 62, [2000] 2 S.C.R. 913 [*Morency*].

31 2000 SCC 23, [2000] 1 S.C.R. 538 [*Ajax (Town)*].

32 *Ibid.* at para. 2.

33 (1998), 41 O.R. (3d) 426 at para. 30 (C.A.). In fact, shortly thereafter, faced with an amended successor rights provision in the Quebec *Labour Code*, the Court, in *Ivanhoe v. UFCW, Local 500*, 2001 SCC 47, [2001] 2 S.C.R. 565, distinguished *Bibeault* and applied the patent unreasonableness standard of *Ajax (Town)*, thereby marginalizing the actual outcome in *Bibeault*. See also *Sept-Îles (City) v. Quebec (Labour Court)*, 2001 SCC 48, [2001] 2 S.C.R. 670.

34 *Kovach* and *Lindsay*, above note 23, also provide supporting evidence.

Particularly significant in this regard was *Ajax (Town)*, where the Court affirmed that patent unreasonableness was the standard to be applied to the Board's decision whether there had been a "sale" of business such as to trigger successor rights. Despite the fact that the Court in *Bibeault* had developed the pragmatic and functional approach as the basis on which it would be determined whether a tribunal received deference, on the facts of that case, the Court determined that "correctness" was the standard to be applied to the particular issue that was before the Court: whether there had been an "alienation" such as to trigger the successor rights provision in the Quebec *Labour Code*. According to Beetz J., delivering the judgment of the Court, this was a term that had a well-known currency in general Quebec civil law and this was a strong indicator that the courts were more competent to determine it than the labour court.[35] In *Ajax (City)*, in the Ontario Court of Appeal, Goudge J.A. rejected the application of *Bibeault*, both distinguishing it on the facts and also holding that the "relevant legal provision did not have the expansive definition of 'sells'"[36] that appeared in the Ontario Act.

It is also noteworthy that, in *Morency*, the Court's short judgment actually reversed the Quebec Court of Appeal's sustaining of the holding of the Quebec Superior Court that the arbitral award was patently unreasonable. In the Quebec Court of Appeal,[37] the foundation for the judgment was the Court's sense that the arbitrator had failed to give effect to two previous Court of Appeal decisions that, while not exactly on the same point, were relevant and should have produced a different outcome. While LeBel J. does not elaborate, there is reason to assume that the Supreme Court was of the view that this was not the touchstone for patent unreasonableness, and that the arbitrator was entitled to form her own view as to the meaning of the relevant provision in the collective agreement as framed by her own assessment of the relevant statutory context. As long as this led to an outcome that was not irrational, there was no basis for intervention. Putting it another way, it was not appropriate for the courts to see irrationality as a way of imposing coherence or consistency on the whole body of arbitral jurisprudence.[38]

35 *Bibeault*, above note 10 at paras. 140 and 188–90.

36 *Ajax (Town)*, above note 31 at para. 29.

37 *Sub nom Syndicat de l'enseignement du Grand-Portage c. Commission scolaire de Rivière-du-Loup* (1998), 198 D.L.R. (4th) 423 at paras. 24–28 (Que. C.A.).

38 This is consistent with the Court's judgment in *Domtar Inc. v. Québec (Commission d'appel en matière de lésions professionnelles)*, [1993] 2 S.C.R. 756, that inconsistency is not a free-standing basis for judicial review of a tribunal's decision [*Domtar Inc.*].

At a more general level, *Rascal Trucking* can also be seen as answering one of the dangling questions about the comprehensive nature of the pragmatic and functional approach. How was it to be reconciled with the concept of *vires* applied traditionally to the regulation making capacity of the royal representatives in council and, more generally, to decision making by municipalities whether by way of bylaw or, as in *Rascal Trucking*, by resolution? In his judgment, Major J. used the pragmatic and functional analysis to determine the standard of review for both elements of the municipality's decision-making process and did so by reference to the language of and authorities based on *vires*. In so doing, he was clearly equating the concept of *vires* with that of jurisdiction, and deploying this mode of analysis to determine whether a question was one that went to *vires* or jurisdiction (and therefore indicated a correctness standard of review), as opposed to a decision that was within the municipality's *vires* or jurisdiction (and therefore normally subject to a deferential standard of review). In that sense, the Court had taken *Baker* one step further and, in doing so, again underscored the comprehensive or universal reach of the pragmatic and functional test for determining the standard of review.

Nonetheless, the judicial review jurisprudence of 2000 did contain some troubling elements. The judgment in *Rascal Trucking* was notable for the fact that Major J. held that the municipality had correctly determined the scope of its authority before conducting a pragmatic and functional analysis to establish a standard of review.[39] This was clearly putting the cart before the horse and was confusing. More problematic, however, is the Court's assessment of the nature of the first element of the municipality's decision-making process as jurisdictional in nature, yet treating this as simply part of the pragmatic and functional analysis and not as in and of itself decisive as to correctness review. While ultimately the Court concluded that this "jurisdictional" question or issue of *vires* was reviewable on a correctness basis, the clear implication was that there are some questions of jurisdiction or *vires* on which the courts should defer because of other elements of the pragmatic and functional analysis. As a matter of both principle and precedent, this was difficult to grasp and foreshadowed further uncertainty on this critical element of the whole standard of review enterprise.

As for the application of the patent unreasonableness standard, McLachlin C.J. emphasized in *Ajax (Town)* that, where that was the standard of re-

39 *Rascal Trucking*, above note 29 at paras. 14–26, which occur before the pragmatic and functional analysis at paras. 27–38.

view, it was not for the Court to assess the correctness of the Labour Board's findings on successor rights.[40] That seems obvious. However, it may be that the chief justice was indirectly taking issue with the approach of the dissenting judgment of Bastarache J., which was in effect a full-blown analysis from a correctness perspective of the Board's interpretation of the relevant provision, albeit under the umbrella of patent unreasonableness.[41] It is also a judgment in which the dissenting justice takes comfort from previous decisions of the Ontario Labour Relations Board, an approach that, as with the Quebec Court of Appeal in *Morency*, can be characterized as treating "patent unreasonableness" as at least in part concerned with jurisprudential consistency and coherence. At the very least, what the Bastarache judgment does anticipate is the Court's subsequent difficulties in developing an approach and vocabulary that reflects the objectives of confining review in certain situations to that which is patently unreasonable or "clearly irrational."[42]

What, however, was not to be anticipated was the extent to which, over the following seven years, the whole standard of review regime would begin to unravel and the consternation that it would produce in the Court itself and, more immediately, among lower court judges and practitioners involved in judicial review applications and statutory appeals.

D. HOW IT ALL CAME APART

1) Unwarranted Sanguinity

Between 2000 and the early 2008 judgment of the Court in *Dunsmuir*, McLachlin C.J. did not write frequently in judicial review cases.[43] However, in

40 *Ajax (Town)*, above note 31 at para. 2.

41 Despite some statements to the contrary by the Court itself, I do, however, recognize that it will sometimes be impossible (as perhaps in *Ajax (Town)*) to assess whether a decision is patently unreasonable in the sense of being irrational without engaging in a thorough analysis of the relevant provisions against the background of the controlling facts. To this extent, I have always favoured the approach of Gonthier J., over that adopted by Wilson J. in *National Corn Growers Assn. v. Canada (Import Tribunal)*, [1990] 2 S.C.R. 1324 [*National Corn Growers Assn.*], and have problems with accepting as a universal proposition that, in general, the difference between an unreasonable decision and a patently unreasonable one lay "in the immediacy or obviousness of the defect": Iacobucci J. in *Southam*, above note 14 at para. 57, though admittedly Iacobucci J. himself went on to qualify the general applicability of this by reference to Gonthier J.'s judgment.

42 This was the language deployed by Cory J. to characterize a patently unreasonable decision in *Canada (Attorney General) v. Public Service Alliance of Canada*, [1993] S.C.R. 941 at 963–64.

43 Aside from *Dr. Q.*, below note 44, McLachlin C.J.'s most significant substantive review judgment since assuming the Chief Justiceship was probably her majority judgment in

April 2003, in *Dr. Q. v. College of Physicians and Surgeons of British Columbia*,[44] she provided her own synthesis of the existing state of the standard of review principles and jurisprudence. The clear message of the judgment for lower courts was that the principles were established and that those principles pervaded every situation in which courts were called upon to review the decisions of statutory or prerogative authorities: "[T]he pragmatic and functional approach represents a principled conceptual model which the court has used consistently in judicial review."[45]

She therefore reiterated the message of *Pezim* and *Southam* that this was the case even where the matter was before the Court by way of statutory appeal,[46] and stated: "In every case where a stature delegates power to an administrative decision-maker, the reviewing judge must begin by determining the standard of review on the pragmatic and functional approach."[47]

By way of further clarification of *Baker* and its impact on the traditional stand-alone grounds for review of the exercise of discretionary power, she stated:

> Nor is it sufficient merely to identify a categorical or nominate error, such as bad faith, error on collateral or preliminary matters, ulterior or improper purpose, no evidence, or the consideration of an irrelevant factor. Rather the pragmatic and functional approach calls upon the court to weigh a series of factors in an effort to discern whether a particular issue before the administrative body should receive exacting review by a court, undergo "significant searching or testing" (*Southam*), or be left to the near exclusive determination of the decision-maker.[48]

Chamberlain v. Surrey School District No. 36, 2002 SCC 86, [2002] 4 S.C.R. 710 [*Chamberlain*], though she has written majority judgments in other administrative law cases, and, most notably, two judgments concerning the independence of tribunals and other statutory adjudicators: *Ocean Port Hotel Ltd. v. British Columbia (General Manager, Liquor Control and Licensing Branch)*, 2001 SCC 52, [2001] 2 S.C.R. 781, and *Bell Canada v. Canadian Telephone Employees Association*, 2003 SCC 36, [2003] 1 S.C.R. 884 (with Bastarache J.); the procedural fairness cases of *Congrégation des témoins de Jéhovah de St.-Jérôme-Lafontaine (Village)*, 2004 SCC 48, [2004] 2 S.C.R. 650, and *Canadian Pacific Railway Co. v. Vancouver (City)*, 2006 SCC 5, [2006] 1 S.C.R. 227; as well as *Haida Nation v. British Columbia (Minister of Forests)*, 2004 SCC 73, [2004] 3 S.C.R. 511, on the duty to consult and accommodate First Nations peoples as part of regulatory initiatives.

44 2003 SCC 19, [2003] 1 S.C.R. 226 [*Dr. Q.*].

45 *Ibid.* at para. 23.

46 *Ibid.* at para. 21.

47 *Ibid.*

48 *Ibid.* at para. 22.

She then underscored this in summarizing: "The nominate grounds, language of jurisdiction, and ossified interpretations of statutory formulae, while still useful as familiar landmarks, no longer dictate the journey."[49]

Thereafter, McLachlin C.J. provided a detailed elaboration of the four factors that constituted the content of the "pragmatic and functional" approach.[50]

The very same day, the Court, in *Law Society of New Brunswick v. Ryan*,[51] in a judgment delivered by Iacobucci J., rejected an argument that it should either expand the number of standards of review or recognize a sliding scale within the unreasonableness standard.[52] Three were enough! However, in doing so, Iacobucci J. provided a detailed and useful elaboration of the contours of unreasonableness review, and reiterated his conception in *Southam* of the distinction between unreasonableness and patent unreasonableness.[53]

The seemingly clear message of these two judgments was that the pragmatic and functional approach and its three standards of review were going to be part of the judicial review firmament for the foreseeable future, and that the role of lower courts was to be attentive to that imperative and to address the four factors in a way that was responsive to the detailed exposition of their content that McLachlin C.J. had provided in *Dr. Q.*, building on the Court's previous jurisprudence. In a sense, 3 April 2003 was the high watermark of the pragmatic and functional approach. The building blocks were now securely in place.

However, there had already been rumbling in the ranks. Four months previously, in his concurring judgment in *Chamberlain v. Surrey School District No. 36*,[54] LeBel J. had called into question the legitimacy of the pragmatic and functional approach as a comprehensive or all-inclusive modality. While supporting the legitimacy of the pragmatic and functional approach in the case of adjudicative tribunals, LeBel J. expressed the opinion that it was not appropriate to apply it to elected bodies required to make policy decisions such as the school board in *Chamberlain*.[55] The four pragmatic and functional factors did not transfer readily to this context. Here, the task

49 *Ibid.* at para. 24.

50 *Ibid.* at paras. 26–35.

51 2003 SCC 20, [2003] 1 S.C.R. 247.

52 *Ibid.* at paras. 24–26 and 43–47.

53 *Ibid.* at paras. 48–56.

54 *Chamberlain*, above note 43.

55 *Ibid.* at paras. 191–97. In contrast, the other members of the Court applied the pragmatic and functional approach to fix a standard of review for the school board's exercise of discretion. See also *C.U.P.E. v. Ontario (Minister of Labour)*, 2003 SCC 29, [2003] 1 S.C.R.

was determining whether the "body acted within the bounds of the authority conferred on it." In other words, the task of the reviewing court should continue to be the traditional *ultra vires* approach, unadorned by standard of review analysis. As for *Rascal Trucking*, LeBel J. both distinguished it as involving a municipality exercising an adjudicative function and invoked it in support of his position insofar as Major J. characterized the first step in that case as involving the authority of the municipality over a mound of soil under the relevant provision and assessing that determination on a correctness basis.[56]

While it might be thought that not much store could be placed on a single judgment of the then most junior judge on the Court, subsequent events proved that this was indeed the thin end of the wedge in terms of the viability of the existing standard of review principles. While the full story of the next seven years is a detailed and complex one, there were a number of crucial elements in the breakdown of the overarching pragmatic and functional approach.

Principal among them was the persistence of LeBel J. In November 2003, eleven months after his judgment in *Chamberlain*, he broadened the reach of his criticism of the existing contours of the pragmatic and functional approach in his lengthy concurring judgment in *Toronto (City) v. C.U.P.E., Local 79*,[57] a concurrence that found the support of Deschamps J. While repeating his concerns about the Court's use of the pragmatic and functional analysis as a one-size-fits-all test for the intensity of judicial scrutiny,[58] he then moved his attack to what he regarded as the problems that the Court had had in providing a satisfactory conceptual basis for describing, distinguishing among, and applying the three standards of review.[59] While his greatest concern was the lack of clear boundaries between unreasonableness and patent unreasonableness review, he also asserted that there was not necessarily a clear demarcation between correctness and patent unreasonableness review. He also wondered about the public perception of an approach

539, for another application of the pragmatic and functional standards to a ministerial discretionary power [*C.U.P.E.*].

56 *Chamberlain, ibid.* at paras. 198–99.

57 2003 SCC 63, [2003] 3 S.C.R. 77 [*Toronto (City)*]. In that case, Binnie J., for the majority, seemed comfortable working with the application of the pragmatic and functional approach to a ministerial exercise of discretion, as he had been earlier (with McLachlin C.J.'s concurrence), in his concurring (in the result) judgment in *Mount Sinai Hospital v. Quebec (Minister of Health and Social Services)*, 2001 SCC 41, [2001] 2 S.C.R. 281 at paras. 52–65.

58 *Toronto (City), ibid.* at para. 61.

59 *Ibid.* at paras. 62–134.

under which a decision that was unreasonable to the reviewing court could, nonetheless, be safe because the standard of review was that of patent unreasonableness, and that threshold had not been crossed.

Thereafter, he reiterated these concerns in another concurring judgment (in which he was again joined by Deschamps J.): *Voice Construction Ltd. v. Construction & General Workers' Union, Local 92.*[60] His apparent solution was to reduce the number of standards of review to two and, in doing so, to eliminate patent unreasonableness. He also made these same points in papers that he delivered at conferences, one of which appeared in the *Canadian Journal of Administrative Law & Practice.*[61] Indeed, the published paper was a preview of the judgment that he and Bastarache J. were to deliver for a majority of the Court in *Dunsmuir v. New Brunswick.*[62]

In this paper, I will not traverse the now well-known arguments that LeBel J. made against the then prevailing standard of review mode of analysis, or his criticisms of the Court's deployment of the pragmatic and functional test with its three standards of review. I will also refrain from reprising the various criticisms of the Court's treatment of expertise as one of the four components of the pragmatic and functional analysis; indeed, the most important factor, according to the Court.[63] However, I do want to draw particular attention to three very specific aspects of the Court's approach to the selection of the standard of review during the period of 2000 to early 2008, which, in my assessment, were as critical in the breakdown of the methodology as the Court's failure to adequately articulate the differences among the three standards of review and how exactly expertise was to be evaluated.

---

60 2004 SCC 23, [2004] 1 S.C.R. 609 at paras. 40–41.

61 See "Labour Adjudication, Deference and Rationality" (Paper presented to the annual CBA National Administrative Law and Labour and Employment Law Conference, 21 November 2003) [unpublished], and "Some Properly Deferential Thoughts on Deference" (2008) 21 *Canadian Journal of Administrative Law & Practice* 1. For other writings by members of the Court on the issue of standard of review, see The Honourable Madam Justice B. McLachlin, "The Role of Administrative Tribunals and Courts in Maintaining the Rule of Law" (1998–1999) 12 *Canadian Journal of Administrative Law & Practice* 171; The Honourable Frank Iacobucci, "Articulating a Rational Standard of Review Doctrine: A Tribute to John Willis" (2002) 27 Queen's L.J. 859; and Madame Justice L'Heureux-Dubé, "The 'Ebb' and 'Flow' of Administrative Law on the 'General Question of'Law'" in Michael Taggart, ed., *The Province of Administrative Law* (Oxford: Hart Publishing, 1997) at 331.

62 *Dunsmuir*, above note 5.

63 See the judgment of Iacobucci J., in *Southam*, above note 14 at para. 50, by reference to the judgment of Sopinka J. in *United Brotherhood of Carpenters and Joiners of America, Local 579 v. Bradco Construction Ltd.*, [1993] 2 S.C.R. 316 at 335.

2) A Failure to Come to Terms with the Concept of Jurisdictional Error

Both *New Brunswick Liquor*[64] and *Bibeault*[65] clearly contemplated a continuing, if limited, place for the concept of jurisdictional error. Indeed, it would have been difficult to have jettisoned the concept entirely given that, in 1981, in *Crevier v. Quebec (Attorney General)*,[66] the Court had held that judicial review for jurisdictional error was part of the constitutionally guaranteed jurisdiction of the provincial superior courts, a guarantee that arose by implication from sections 96–101 of the *Constitution Act, 1867*. However, the truth was that judicial review for jurisdictional error was marginalized in the rubric of the Supreme Court's judicial review jurisprudence in the period prior to the appointment of McLachlin C.J. as chief justice. Indeed, in 1998, Bastarache J. best captured the mood of the times in *Pushpanathan v. Canada (Minister of Citizenship and Immigration)*[67] (in a judgment concurred by then McLachlin J.). While accepting that it was still appropriate to state that a tribunal had to answer jurisdictional questions correctly in order to act in an *intra vires* fashion,[68] he continued:

> But it should be understood that a question which "goes to jurisdiction" is simply descriptive of a provision for which the proper standard of review is correctness, based upon the outcome of the pragmatic and functional analysis. In other words "jurisdictional error" is simply an error on an issue with respect to which, according to the outcome of the pragmatic and functional analysis, the tribunal must make a correct interpretation and to which no deference will be shown.[69]

In other words, at least in the case of adjudicative tribunals, the concept of jurisdiction had no independent existence. It was simply a way of describing one of the products of standard of review analysis: correctness scrutiny.

---

64 Above note 9.

65 Above note 10. Though as *Bibeault* makes clear, not in the previous sense of jurisdictional questions being of a "preliminary or collateral" nature. Rather, drawing on his earlier judgment in *Syndicat des employés de production du Québec et de l'Acadie v. Canada Labour Relations Board*, [1984] 2 S.C.R. 412 at 420–21, Beetz J. stated (at paras. 112–15) that jurisdiction was better understood in terms of a provision that "describes, lists and limits the powers of an administrative tribunal."

66 Above note 1.

67 [1998] 1 S.C.R. 982.

68 *Ibid.* at para. 28.

69 *Ibid.*

However, one does not have to look beyond the cases decided in 2000, the first year of the McLachlin Chief Justiceship, to realize that things were not quite this straightforward: recall the three instances from that year in which the Court engaged in automatic correctness review without conducting a pragmatic and functional analysis. Of course, it is quite possible that the Court's engaging in automatic correctness review in those three cases (involving the allocation of legislative powers in sections 91 and 92 of the *Constitution Act, 1867*, resolving a duelling jurisdictions issue, and the determination of what constituted discrimination on the basis of disability in a human rights code) was a product of the following three factors: the assumption of the parties that correctness review was the appropriate standard; precedent; and the obviousness of the conclusion that would be reached by a pragmatic and functional analysis.

Far more problematic, however, was the apparent acceptance by Major J. in *Rascal Trucking*[70] that there might be occasions on which a standard other than correctness review would be appropriate in the case of a jurisdictional question. This seemed completely contrary to the very concept of jurisdictional error and the Bastarache characterization in *Pushpanathan*. This notion that the status of an issue as a "jurisdictional question" was an element, but not necessarily a decisive one in the pragmatic and functional analysis, garnered further support in *Chieu v. Canada (Minister of Citizenship and Immigration)*.[71] At stake in this 2002 decision was a determination by an adjudicative tribunal, the Immigration Appeal Division of the Immigration and Refugee Board, that it did not have to take into account potential foreign hardship in deciding an appeal from a removal decision. Without elaboration, Iacobucci J., in delivering the judgment of the Court, described this as an issue of "jurisdiction."[72] As such, this was a type of issue "where little deference is given"[73] and where "[a]dministrative bodies generally must be correct in determining the scope of their delegated mandate"[74]—not "where no deference is given" and "where administrative bodies always must be correct." The confusion generated by this approach was exacerbated by the absence of any elaboration of the basis on which Iacobucci J. classified the critical question as one of jurisdiction. It scarcely partook of the almost *a*

70 *Rascal Trucking*, above note 29.

71 2002 SCC 3, [2002] 1 S.C.R. 84 [*Chieu*]. See also *Alberta Union of Public Employees v. Lethbridge Community College*, 2004 SCC 28, [2004] 1 S.C.R. 727 at para. 18.

72 *Chieu, ibid.* at para. 24.

73 *Ibid.*

74 *Ibid.*

priori jurisdictional character of the constitutional authority and duelling jurisdiction cases.

In 2004, it also became clear that there was some, if not total sympathy on the part of the Court for the position advocated by LeBel J. in *Chamberlain*. In *United Taxi Drivers' Fellowship of Southern Alberta v. Calgary (City)*,[75] Bastarache J., delivering a judgment in which McLachlin C.J. concurred and without reference to *Dr. Q.*, firmly repudiated the deployment of the "pragmatic and functional" approach when the issue concerned the *vires* of a municipal bylaw freezing the issuance of taxi plate licences. Correctness was the automatic standard in such cases. A pragmatic and functional analysis was necessary only "where a municipality's adjudicative or policy-making function is being exercised."[76] In *Chamberlain*, LeBel J. would also have put a municipality's policy-making function beyond the reach of the pragmatic and functional analysis, and, obviously, in not going that far, Bastarache J. left open the question of where the line is to be drawn in the case of municipalities between those questions that attract *vires* review and those that are of a policy-making variety.

Eventually, in 2006, the two problematic aspects of the Court's post-2000 jurisdictional error jurisprudence came together in the majority judgment (from which McLachlin C.J. dissented[77]) of Bastarache J. in *ATCO Gas & Pipelines Ltd. v. Alberta (Energy & Utilities Board)*.[78] Here, the question was a decision by the Board, exercising its public interest jurisdiction, to approve a sale of assets by a regulated utility subject to the condition that part of the proceeds of any sale flow through to the customers of the utility. Justice Bastarache commenced his standard of review analysis by indicating his agreement with the Alberta Court of Appeal that this raised an issue of jurisdiction on which no deference was warranted.[79] In aid of this conclusion, he invoked[80] both *Pushpanathan* and *United Taxi Drivers* before stating, seemingly in contradiction of *Dr. Q.*, that a full pragmatic and functional analysis was not necessary in a case such as this.[81] However, in deference to the dissenting judgment, he then proceeded to support his conclusion on the basis of an analysis of the four pragmatic and functional factors.

75 2004 SCC 19, [2004] 1 S.C.R. 485.

76 *Ibid.* at para. 5.

77 Concurring in a judgment delivered by Binnie J. (the Court split 5:4).

78 2006 SCC 4, [2006] 1 S.C.R. 140.

79 *Ibid.* at para. 21.

80 *Ibid.*

81 *Ibid.* at para. 22.

In this analysis, the question whether the Board's public interest powers entitled it to make an order with respect to the proceeds of a sale of assets is asserted to be not just the determination of a question of law, but "deciding the scope of its powers."[82] It is a question of "jurisdiction."[83] This bears a remarkable similarity to the analysis conducted by Major J. in *Rascal Trucking*, a similarity that is further evidenced by the majority's conclusion that unreasonableness or patent unreasonableness review would have been triggered in this case only if the Board had the power to deal with the proceeds. At that point, deference would have been appropriate to the method that it employed in allocating the funds.[84]

There is an additional confusion here, also paralleling the Major J. judgment in *Rascal Trucking*. Initially, Bastarache J. seems to be saying that the principal issue is a jurisdictional one for which the standard of review is automatically that of correctness. However, by then using the assumed jurisdictional character of the question as just one component (albeit, a very important one) of the pragmatic and functional analysis, the judgment seems to be conceding (as in *Rascal Trucking* and in *Chieu*) that at least on occasion the determination of jurisdictional questions may attract deference, even if not in that case. And, what has happened in all of this to Bastarache J.'s statement in *Pushpanathan* that the character of a question as jurisdictional is merely descriptive of a situation where the pragmatic and functional analysis results in a correctness standard of review?

In summary, in the post-2000 jurisprudence of the Court, jurisdictional error began to resurface but in a shadowy form. At times, the character of a question as jurisdictional in nature was simply assumed as obvious, and correctness review automatically followed. On other occasions, while the jurisdictional character of the question was again assumed, it became just one factor in the pragmatic and functional analysis. This was confusing, and the confusion was compounded by the Court's failure to articulate the criteria for labelling a question as jurisdictional or involving *vires*. While that might have been obvious where the issue related to the constitutional division of legislative authority or duelling jurisdictions, that does not extend to cases such as *Chieu* or *ATCO*, as the dissent in the latter case makes abundantly clear. Moreover, both of these approaches involve a modification, if not an

82 *Ibid.* at para. 27.

83 *Ibid.* at paras. 31–32.

84 *Ibid.* at para. 33.

outright repudiation, of the conception of jurisdictional error so recently endorsed by the Court in *Pushpanathan*.

3) Confusion over Tribunal Interpretation of Home and Related Statutes

By the beginning of 2000, the Supreme Court, building on the 1975 concurring judgment of Laskin C.J. in *McLeod v. Egan*,[85] appeared to have accepted, at least in the context of judicial review of decision makers protected by privative clauses, that there should usually be deference to those decision makers' interpretations of not only their home or constitutive statutes, but also closely related statutes or ones that they encountered frequently in the exercise of their mandate.[86]

However, as cases such as *ATCO* demonstrated, that entitlement to deference disappeared or, at the very least, diminished dramatically, if the issue arising out of the home, constitutive, or related statute was jurisdictional. But it was not just in the murky world of jurisdictional error that the Court regarded the right to deference as forfeited. In *Bibeault* itself,[87] as noted already, the fact that the Court saw the term "alienation" in a home statute as based on the *Quebec Civil Code* concept of the same name was a major factor in the application of correctness review in that case. Moreover, this persisted after 2000. Thus, in 2001, in *Canada (Deputy Minister of National Revenue—M.N.R.) v. Mattel*,[88] Major J., in delivering the judgment of the Court, justified correctness review of a Canadian International Trade Tribunal (CITT) decision partially on the basis that the relevant terminology in the Tribunal's home statute involved "concepts that are intrinsic to commercial law."[89] It is, however, by no means self-evident that the term "sale of goods for export to Canada" in the *Customs Act*[90] carries with it the same conception of what constitutes a sale of goods in general commercial law or the *Sale of Goods Act*.

Even more troubling in its open-endedness was the second reason that the Court gave for not giving the CITT any deference. The provisions that

85 [1975] 1 S.C.R. 517.

86 *Canadian Broadcasting Corp. v. Canada (Labour Relations Board)*, [1995] 1 S.C.R. 157 at para. 48; *Toronto (City) Board of Education*, above note 11 at para. 39.

87 *Bibeault*, above note 10.

88 2001 SCC 36, [2001] 2 S.C.R. 100.

89 *Ibid.* at para. 33.

90 R.S.C. 1985, c. 1 (2nd Supp.), s. 48.

the CITT had had to interpret were "pure questions of law that require the application of the principles of statutory interpretation."[91]

Taken literally, this statement meant that, as part of the "nature of the question" element of the pragmatic and functional analysis, the interpretation of pure questions of law arising out of the tribunal's home statute was a strong correctness indicator. This has the potential for drastically undercutting any presumption of tribunals having an entitlement to deference when interpreting their home or constitutive statute, let alone any related or frequently encountered statute.

Justice Bastarache made this point very forcefully in *Barrie Public Utilities v. Canadian Cable Television Ass'n*.[92] However, his was a lone dissent. The approach that prevailed in the majority's adoption of correctness review in setting aside a decision of the Canadian Radio-Television and Telecommunications Commission (CRTC) was expressed by Gonthier J., in the course of a pragmatic and functional assessment:

> Deference to the decision maker is called for only when it is in some way more expert than the court and the question under consideration is one that falls within the scope of its greater expertise . . . . In my view this is not such a case. The proper interpretation of the phrase "the supporting structure of a transmission line" in s. 43(5) is not a question that engages the CRTC's special expertise in the regulation of Canadian broadcasting and telecommunications. This is not a question of telecommunications policy, or one which requires the understanding of technical language. Rather, it is a purely legal question and is, therefore, . . . "ultimately within the province of the judiciary" . . . . This Court's expertise in matters of pure statutory interpretation is superior to that of the CRTC. This factor suggests a less deferential approach.[93]

Nonetheless, it is puzzling to see how the meaning of the term "the supporting structure of a transmission line" is anything other than an issue that is at the core of telecommunications regulation and the heartland of what the CRTC has been created to deal with.

Subsequently, in *ATCO*, the Court took even further the concept that on a pure question of law, the reviewing court was at least as competent as

---

91 Above note 88 at para. 33.

92 2003 SCC 28, [2003] 1 S.C.R. 476 at paras. 73–96 particularly.

93 *Ibid.* at para. 16 [references omitted]. See also the judgment of Deschamps J. in *Monsanto Canada Inc. v. Ontario (Superintendent of Financial Services)*, 2004 SCC 54, [2004] 3 S.C.R. 152.

the tribunal under review. There, Bastarache J. (for the majority), dealing with the authority of the Alberta Energy and Utilities Board to act by reference to the "public interest" and attach "conditions" to an order approving a sale of a regulated utility's assets, described "public interest" and "conditions" as "general concepts" and not matters over which the "the tribunal has been held to have greater expertise than the courts."[94] Putting it bluntly, the judgment seems to be asserting that the Court has superior expertise to that of the legislatively designated regulator in assessing the public interest in the highly specialized area of energy regulation.

In other cases, the Court further qualified its commitment to the presumption of deference in the domain of tribunal interpretation of their home or related statutes. In *Southam*'s context of a statutory appeal on law and jurisdiction, Iacobucci J. had referred to the precedential value of the decision under review as one of the factors pointing towards correctness review.[95] Subsequently, in *Chieu*, he reiterated this point in the context of an application for judicial review,[96] albeit where access to the Federal Court of Appeal from the Federal Court depended on the Federal Court certifying that the case raised a "serious question of general importance."[97] However, the proposition then assumed more general proportions in *Alberta Union of Public Employees v. Lethbridge Community College*,[98] an application for judicial review of a labour arbitration board.

While the Supreme Court had previously rejected an argument that inconsistency should be a ground for judicial review in at least some circumstances,[99] I suppose it might be argued that, in statutory appeal or certified question situations, the legislature has provided an indication that it is expecting the reviewing courts to have a role in ensuring the coherence of the relevant tribunal's jurisprudence or caselaw. However, the Court did not stop there. The precedential value of a tribunal's decision on a pure question of law became a factor that was relevant in all judicial review and statutory appeal situations, and seemingly irrespective of the presence of a privative clause. The prime example of this is the majority judgment of the Court in *Lévis (City) v. Fraternité des 2007 policiers de Lévis Inc.*[100]

---

94 Above note 78 at para. 31.

95 *Southam*, above note 14 at paras. 36–37.

96 *Chieu*, above note 71 at para. 23.

97 *Immigration Act*, R.S.C. 1985, c. I-2, s. 83.1.

98 Above note 71 at para. 19.

99 See *Domtar Inc.*, above note 38.

100 2007 SCC 14, [2007] 1 S.C.R. 591 at paras. 20–21 [*Lévis (City)*].

Save perhaps in situations where the tribunal's jurisprudence on a particular issue of law is in disarray, the treating of the precedential value of a decision as a factor indicating correctness review is highly problematic. In effect, it contradicts the basic notion that, particularly when the legislature chooses to protect the decision of a tribunal with a privative clause, it is entrusting that administrative tribunal to set the precedents. This is the tribunal's core task, not that of the courts.

This tendency towards greater interventionism gained further momentum in the 2004 judgment of the Court in *Voice Construction Ltd. v. Construction & General Workers' Union, Local 92*,[101] where the Court made an unusual decision to apply an unreasonableness rather than patent unreasonableness standard to the decision of a labour arbitrator. In the course of delivering the judgment of the Court, Major J. stated "[b]y its nature, the application of patent unreasonableness will be rare."[102] At the time, I interpreted that to mean that it would be rare or unusual for a court to set aside a decision as patently unreasonable, not that it would be a rare case in which patent unreasonableness was the applicable standard.[103] David Phillip Jones thought otherwise,[104] and he was correct and I was wrong. In *Lévis (City)*, the majority made it clear that Major J. had meant that patent unreasonableness would seldom be the appropriate standard against which to assess a statutory authority's decision.[105] Reasonableness was the preferred option whenever deference was required.

4) The Straw That Broke the Camel's Back?

In his concurring judgment in *Toronto (City) v. C.U.P.E., Local 79*, LeBel J. made it clear that he was in part motivated by the "sustained concerns coming from the legal community in relation to the state of Canadian jurisprudence in this important part of the law . . . . Given its broad application, the law governing the standards of review must be predictable, workable and coherent."[106] In considerable measure, the concerns of the legal community

101 Above note 60.

102 *Ibid.* at para. 18.

103 See "*Voice Construction*—One Swallow Does Not a Summer Make?" (2004) 11 C.L.E.L.J. 113 at 134.

104 See David Phillip Jones, "Standards of Review in Administrative Law" in Laverne A. Jacobs & Justice Anne L. Mactavish, eds., *Dialogues between Courts and Tribunals—Essays in Administrative Justice (2001–2007)* (Montréal: Les Éditions Thémis, 2008) 213 at 272.

105 *Lévis (City)*, above note 100 at para. 28.

106 Above note 57 at para. 64.

were the result of the Court's failure in the period under review to acknowledge, let alone explain, apparent inconsistencies in its standard of review jurisprudence. Three examples will suffice.

a) In *Baker*, L'Heureux-Dubé J. had identified respect for the procedural choices of tribunals as a factor to be taken into account in responding to allegations of procedural fairness.[107] However, in other cases,[108] the Court proclaimed that standard of review analysis had no role to play in procedural fairness cases. Procedural fairness claims were always adjudicated on a correctness basis. There was no place for deference.
b) In *Multani v. Marguerite-Bourgeoys (Commission Scolaire)*,[109] the Court was adamant that constitutional questions were also invariably subject to correctness review. In that case, the Court engaged in a full merits review of a decision that affected the *Charter* rights of the applicant. Yet, in other cases, such as *Suresh v. Canada (Minister of Citizenship and Immigration)*,[110] the Court was prepared to accord deference to executive decisions affecting the applicants' *Charter* rights and freedoms. How these examples of seemingly conflicting rules could be reconciled was hard to fathom, and the Court did not provide guidance.
c) Some of the Court's more important debates about the contours of the pragmatic and functional approach occurred in the context of an application for judicial review under the *Federal Courts Act*.[111] However, for example, there was never any question raised in either *Canada (Attorney General) v. Mossop* or *National Corn Growers Assn. v. Canada (Import Tribunal)*[112] as to whether standard of review analysis had any relevance at all in the face of the statutory codification of the grounds of review in the *Federal Courts Act*. Nonetheless, in *Mugesera v. Canada (Minister of Citizenship and Immigration)*, a unanimous Court stated that, under those provisions, "questions of law are reviewable on a standard of correctness."[113]

---

107 *Baker*, above note 2 at para. 27.

108 *C.U.P.E.*, above note 55 at para. 100, and *Moreau-Bérubé v. Judicial Council*, 2002 SCC 11, [2002] 1 S.C.R. 249 at paras. 74–75.

109 2006 SCC 6, [2006] 1 S.C.R. 256.

110 2002 SCC 1, [2002] 1 S.C.R. 3. See also *Pinet v. St. Thomas Psychiatric Hospital*, 2004 SCC 21, [2004] 1 S.C.R. 528, and *United States v. Lake*, 2008 SCC 23, [2008] 1 S.C.R. 761.

111 R.S.C. 1985, c. F-7 (as amended).

112 Above notes 25 and 41.

113 2005 SCC 40, [2005] 2 S.C.R. 100 at para. 37. In *Khosa*, above note 6 at para. 122, Rothstein J. relied on this statement in support of his position that deference had no role to play under the codified grounds of review in the *Federal Courts Act*. However, at para. 44, Binnie J. rejected that interpretation of para. 37. It had to be read in the context of the

A further dramatic manifestation of this apparent lack of concern about the impression of inconsistency occurred in March 2007 when on successive days the Court rendered judgment in *Lévis (City)*[114] and *Council of Canadians with Disabilities v. Via Rail Canada Inc.*[115] In the first, Bastarache J., delivering the judgment of the majority, segmented the decision of a labour arbitrator for standard of review purposes, applying correctness to one element of the decision and unreasonableness to the other. In the course of doing so, he addressed the issue of when segmentation was appropriate:

> Of course, it may not always be easy or necessary to separate individual questions from the decision taken as a whole. The possibility of multiple standards should not be taken as a licence to parse an administrative decision into myriad parts in order to subject it to heightened scrutiny. However, reviewing courts must be careful not to subsume distinct questions into one broad standard of review. Multiple standards of review should be adopted when there are clearly defined questions that engage different concerns under the pragmatic and functional approach.[116]

In a concurring judgment, Abella J. criticized the decision to segment the arbitrator's decision for standard of review purposes. In order to avoid an "unduly interventionist approach,"[117] the courts should avoid routine segmentation. Moreover, in this instance, "the labour arbitrator's mandate and expertise merge to entitle him to a single deferential standard of review both for his decision as to the scope of the relevant legislation and its application to the case."[118]

The very next day Abella J. delivered the judgment of the majority in *Via Rail Canada*. Here too, it had been argued that the decision of the Canadian Transportation Agency should be segmented for standard of review purposes and, in particular, the human rights dimensions of the agency's decision requiring Via Rail to refit carriages to make them accessible to the disabled. As in *Lévis (City)*, Abella J. held that the agency was entitled to a single undifferentiated standard of review:

---

questions of law raised in that case, questions involving both criminal and international law, and, as such, beyond the ken of the decision maker, and subject to correctness review by reference to normal common law principles.

114 *Lévis (City)*, above note 100.

115 2007 SCC 15, [2007] 1 S.C.R. 650.

116 *Lévis (City)*, above note 100 at para. 19.

117 *Ibid.* at para. 111.

118 *Ibid.* at para. 116.

> To engage in a wide-ranging review of a tribunal's specific conclusions when its interpretation of its constitutive statute cannot be said to be irrational, or unreasonable, would be an unwarranted trespass into the realm of reweighing and re-assessing evidence. Where an expert tribunal and specialized tribunal has charted an appropriate analytical course for itself, with reasons that serve as a rational guide, reviewing courts should not lightly interfere with its interpretation and application of its enabling legislation.[119]

It may very well be that there are sufficient differences between the two cases to justify segmentation in one but not the other. However, they are not self-evident. Thus, the failure of the Court to cross-reference the two judgments, let alone explain those differences explicitly was frustrating, especially given that they were released almost contemporaneously. As a consequence, counsel and lower courts were left without a road map for differentiating situations where segmentation was appropriate from those where it was not.[120] There was also the added dimension that in *Lévis (City)*, the Court deployed correctness and unreasonableness review on an application for judicial review of the decision of a labour arbitrator, where, until *Voice Construction*, patent unreasonableness had been the norm. In contrast, despite the statement in *Lévis (City)* that review on a patently unreasonableness basis would be "relatively rare," the Court in *Via Rail* applied an overall standard of patent unreasonableness on a statutory appeal on questions of law and jurisdiction. Both aspects of the judgment, segmentation and standard of review, provoked a joint dissent from Deschamps and Rothstein JJ.

Is it too much to claim that, from this moment, the days of the pragmatic and functional approach and the three standards of review were numbered, and in fact, as it turned out, fewer than 365?

---

119 Above note 115 at para. 104. In a very real sense, these two cases involved a replay of the contest that had taken place between Wilson and Gonthier JJ. in *National Corn Growers Assn.*, above note 41, and Abella J. acknowledges as much at paras. 103–4.

120 For contemporary criticism, see Freya Kristjanson, "Standards of Review: Are We There Yet?" (Paper presented to the Law Society of Upper Canada Conference: The New Administrative Law, 24 October 2007).

E. ON THE EVE OF THE SECOND DECADE

On 7 March 2008, the Court delivered its long-awaited[121] judgment in *Dunsmuir v. New Brunswick*.[122] Much has already been written[123] about the meaning and impact of the majority judgment of Bastarache and LeBel JJ., and the further implications to be drawn not only from the concurrence of Binnie J. but also from the joint concurrence of Deschamps J., joined by Charron and Rothstein JJ. Now is not the occasion to engage in a further detailed examination of this seminal judgment or, for that matter, the subsequent judgment of the Court in *Canada (Citizenship and Immigration) v. Khosa*.[124] The latter made it clear that the principles enunciated in *Dunsmuir* also applied to the statutory codification of grounds of review in the *Federal Courts Act*, and provided some elaboration and clarification of the judgment in *Dunsmuir*. However, at the end of the first decade of the McLachlin Chief Justiceship, it is appropriate to provide analysis of the extent to which these two judgments have brought closure to some of the issues that caused the unravelling of the pragmatic and functional approach to discerning the standard of review and that have featured in the earlier parts of this paper.

---

121 Argument in the case had taken place on 15 May 2007, and from the tenor of the Court's questioning, it seemed almost certain that the Court was going to take this opportunity to revisit in a significant way the whole issue of standard of review.

122 *Dunsmuir*, above note 5.

123 Besides the papers otherwise noted in this chapter, see David Phillip Jones, Q.C., "Recent Developments in Administrative Law" (Paper presented to the Canadian Bar Association National Administrative Law and Labour & Employment Law CLE Conference, "Beyond the Horizon: The Expanding and Overlapping Jurisdiction of Arbitrators & Tribunals," Ottawa, 21–22 November 2008) at 2–27; Gerald Heckman, "*Dunsmuir* and Substantive Review—Implications and Impact: A Preliminary Assessment" (Paper presented to the 2009 Canadian Institute for the Administration of Justice Roundtable on Administrative Law, 29 May 2009); Laverne Jacobs, "Developments in Administrative Law: The 2007–2008 Term—The Impact of *Dunsmuir*" (2008) 43 Sup. Ct. L. Rev. 1; Mark G. Underhill, "*Dunsmuir v. New Brunswick*: A Rose by Any Other Name?" (2008) 21 Can. J. Admin. L. & Prac. 247; Alice Woolley, "The Metaphysical Court: *Dunsmuir v. New Brunswick* and the Standard of Review" (2008) 21 Can. J. Admin. L. & Prac. 259; Ron Goltz, "'Patent Unreasonableness Is Dead. And We Have Killed It'—A Critique of the Supreme Court of Canada's Decision in *Dunsmuir*" (2008) 46 Alta. L. Rev. 253; Lorne Sossin, "*Dunsmuir*—Plus ça change" *The Court* (17 March 2008), online: www.thecourt.ca/2008/03/17/dunsmuir; and Gus Van Harten, "*Dunsmuir* and the Quixotic Quest for Certainty" *The Court* (27 March 2008), online: www.thecourt.ca/2008/03/27/. See also the website for a seminar held at the University of Toronto Faculty of Law, "Roundtable on *Dunsmuir*" (4 June 2008), online: www.law.utoronto.ca/faculty_content.asp?itemPath=1/13/1/0/08contentId=1743.

124 *Khosa*, above note 6.

To no one's surprise, once it was known that LeBel J. was one of the authors of the principal or majority judgment, the most immediately salient feature of the standard of review part of *Dunsmuir* was its compression of the number of standards of review from three into two with patent unreasonableness the victim of this reconceptualization.[125] In that context, the Court, presumably because of its now bad reputation, repudiated the terminology of "pragmatic and functional" and simply referred to the exercise as the standard of review analysis.[126]

As Binnie J. makes clear in his concurring judgment, the compression into just two standards does raise questions as to whether there will henceforth be a spectrum of deference within the single unreasonableness standard.[127] Indeed, that may well be an important question, though it remains to be seen whether Binnie J. himself has finessed the need for further refinements by his statement in *Khosa*—"Reasonableness is a single standard that takes its colour from the context."[128]

There are also questions about the majority's articulation of how courts should conduct review for unreasonableness:

> A court conducting a review for reasonableness inquires into the qualities that make a decision reasonable, referring both to the process of articulating the reasons and to outcomes. In judicial review, reasonableness is concerned mostly with the existence of justification, transparency and intelligibility within the decision-making process. But it is also concerned with whether the decision falls within a range of possible, acceptable outcomes which are defensible in respect of the facts and the law.[129]

What is puzzling here is the nature of the link between the reasons provided for a decision and the outcome. Should a court attend to arguments that the outcome was reasonable even when it is not supported by reasons or where those reasons are deficient in some way? A later reference to the reasons that "could be offered"[130] indicates as much, but in *Khosa*, Binnie J. states, "as long as the process *and* the outcome fit comfortably with

125 *Dunsmuir*, above note 5 at paras. 44–45 particularly.

126 *Ibid.* at para. 63.

127 *Ibid.* at para. 149.

128 *Khosa*, above note 6 at para. 59.

129 *Dunsmuir*, above note 5 at para. 47.

130 *Ibid.* at para. 48.

the principles of justification, transparency and intelligibility, it is not open to a reviewing court to substitute its own view of a preferable outcome."[131]

This suggests that, within the new order, the provision of reasons has attained a higher level of importance, and that possibly an absence of (or flawed) reasons has now become a free-standing test for unreasonableness. If so, to what extent does this apply beyond the world of tribunals and those situations where the common law would not have previously imposed a duty to give reasons?

With respect to the critical first stage of the process—selecting a standard of review—what is clear is that the replacement of the language of "pragmatic and functional" with the term "standard of review analysis" has not in itself changed the contours of the task of discerning the appropriate standard of review. The four factors still remain the same, though it may be questionable whether "expertise" as a stand-alone criterion remains the most important of the four.[132]

However, much of the meat of the judgment in *Dunsmuir* is found in the detail of the judgment's prescription for diminishing the time and energy spent on identification of the standard of review. Elsewhere,[133] I have tried to summarize that detail into the following propositions:

- There is no need to engage in a detailed standard of review analysis if that standard has already been settled satisfactorily by previous authority.
- Correctness is the automatic standard of review for constitutional questions, procedural fairness claims, and issues of jurisdiction (including the jurisdictional lines between two or more competing tribunals), though the Court cautions against any return to the broad conceptions of jurisdiction that prevailed in the jurisprudence prior to 1979 and *Canadian Union of Public Employees, Local 963 v. New Brunswick Liquor*.[134]
- Questions of fact, discretion, and policy, as well as mixed questions of law and fact from which the legal component is not readily extracted or isolated, should generally be reviewed on an unreasonableness basis.

---

131 *Khosa*, above note 6 at para. 59 [emphasis added].

132 In neither *Dunsmuir* nor *Khosa* does the majority refer to the primacy of expertise.

133 "Administrative Law and Energy Regulation" in Gordon Kaise & Bob Heggie, eds., *Energy Law and Policy* (Toronto: Carswell, 2011).

134 Above note 9.

- Decision makers are also normally entitled to deference with respect to their interpretation of their home or other frequently encountered statutes, as well as general common or civil law rules with which they will have expertise as a result of those rules' connection to the particular statutory context.
- However, correctness is the appropriate standard of review for questions of law that are general and that are "both of central importance to the legal system as a whole and outside the adjudicator's specialized area of expertise."[135]

In terms of the concerns that I have identified in the earlier parts of this paper, the most critical of these propositions, as far as clarity and an appropriately deferential approach are concerned, is the fourth. Justice John Evans of the Federal Court of Appeal has argued in his 2009 10th Heald Lecture delivered at the College of Law at the University of Saskatchewan that in *Dunsmuir* (reinforced by *Khosa*), the Court had now established (re-established?) a very strong presumption of deferential review when a statutory authority is interpreting its home, or constitutive, statute, or any other frequently encountered statute, or even common or civil law principle.[136] I too accept that and, for the moment, that may have taken care of most of the caselaw in which the Court appeared to trade in concepts such as pure questions of law or issues involving the principles of statutory interpretation as a basis for asserting a greater competence than the statutory authority notwithstanding that these questions arose out of the statutory authority's home or constitutive statute, or another frequently encountered piece of legislation.

However, one of two domains where the presumption gives way is where the provision in the home or related statute is jurisdictional in character. Admittedly, the judgment of Bastarache and LeBel JJ. eschews any intention of reinstating the broad concepts of jurisdictional error that bedevilled judicial review in Canada from the 1950s through to 1979 and the judgment in *New Brunswick Liquor*.[137] Justice Evans also takes comfort[138] from the fact

135 *Dunsmuir*, above note 5 at para. 60, by reference to LeBel J. in *Toronto (City)*, above note 57 at para. 62.

136 Justice John Evans, "The Most Vexed Question: The Standard of Review of Statutory Interpretation" (10th Heald Lecture, College of Law, University of Saskatchewan, 2 March 2009) [unpublished] (on file with author) at 10.

137 Dunsmuir, above note 5 at para. 59, citing *Rio Hotel Ltd. v. New Brunswick (Liquor Licensing Board)*, [1987] 2 S.C.R. 59.

138 Above note 136 at 16–17.

that the only example deployed by the judgment of jurisdictional error or assessment on the basis of *vires* is *United Taxi Drivers*.[139] Nonetheless, there is nothing in the terms of the judgment that provides a clarification of how precisely a question of jurisdiction or *vires* is to be identified. Indeed, I was bold enough to suggest[140] that the terminology used by the Court to describe such questions did not preclude the possibility of a conception of jurisdictional error that in 1970 allowed the Court, in *Bell v. Ontario Human Rights Commission*,[141] to label the issue of whether accommodation was a "self-contained dwelling unit" as a question of jurisdiction:

> "Jurisdiction" is intended in the narrow sense of whether or not the tribunal had the authority to make the inquiry. In other words, true jurisdiction questions arise where the tribunal must explicitly determine whether its statutory grant of power gives it the authority to decide a particular matter.[142]

In a very recent paper, newly retired Bastarache J. puts me on the right path on this, and I trust that this is vindicated in the post-*Dunsmuir* caselaw: "The question in *Bell* described above is clearly one of mixed fact and law and would thus not fall within the scope of what would be jurisdictional under *Dunsmuir*."[143]

However, I remain nervous. After all, it was in 2006 in *ATCO* that Bastarache J. described the critical issue in that case "as one of mixed law and fact"[144] in the course of reaching the conclusion that it was a jurisdictional question on which the Alberta Energy and Utilities Board had to be correct. Moreover, even if it is possible to logically confine the concept of true jurisdictional issues to pure questions of law, former Justice Bastarache's final sentence in this section of his paper describing his intentions in *Dunsmuir* is also troubling in terms of the concerns I expressed earlier. By reference

---

139 Above note 75.

140 In "*Dunsmuir v. New Brunswick*: Standard of Review and Procedural Fairness for Public Servants: Let's Try Again!" (2008), 21 Can. J. Admin. L. & Prac. 117 at 129–30. See also "The Year in Review: Key Developments in Administrative Law" (Paper presented to the Osgoode Hall Law School Professional Development CLE, 5th Annual National Forum on Administrative Law and Practice, 14 October 2009).

141 [1971] S.C.R. 756.

142 Above note 5 at para. 59.

143 In "Modernizing Judicial Review" (Paper presented to the Council of Canadian Administrative Tribunals 25th Annual Conference, 2 June 2009) at 6 [unpublished]. [Delivery version on file.]

144 Above note 78 at para. 31.

to McLachlin C.J.'s judgment in *Dr. Q*,[145] he reiterates that "decisions of a precedential value demanded a more searching review."[146]

It is also worth noting that in *Toronto Hydro-Electric System Ltd. v. Ontario Energy Board*[147] (which occurred after *Dunsmuir*), the Ontario Divisional Court saw *ATCO* as still satisfactorily determining the standard of review with respect to an Ontario Energy Board order ostensibly made as part of its responsibility to approve just and reasonable rates in the public interest. Whether that responsibility included requiring the approval of a majority of its independent directors before a regulated public utility could issue a dividend to its sole shareholder was a jurisdictional question on which the Board had to be correct.[148]

In short, I fear that the concept of jurisdictional error, as recognized in *Dunsmuir* (as opposed to *Pushpanathan*[149]), will continue to provide temptation to judges wishing to engage in correctness review of all manner of perceived "threshold" issues arising out of various statutory authorities' home or constitutive statutes.

I also see further work ahead for the Court in other aspects of the principles and law affecting identification of the standard of review. Neither *Dunsmuir* nor *Khosa* does anything to resolve the problematic nature of the Court's sometimes contradictory approaches to judicial review on procedural fairness grounds or of constitutional questions. Instead, in *Dunsmuir*, the Court simply repeats the statement that review of constitutional questions is always on a correctness basis.[150] In *Khosa*, Binnie J. states that the same holds true for procedural fairness issues.[151] Moreover, the Court does nothing in either case to resolve the uncertainties as to when decisions should be segmented for review purposes and when their correctness or reasonableness should be reviewed on the basis of the overall conclusion or outcome, which is the dilemma left following *Lévis (City)*[152] and *Via Rail*.[153]

145 *Dr. Q.*, above note 44.
146 Above note 135 at 6.
147 (2008), 93 O.R. (3d) 380 (Div. Ct.). Though, *cf Toronto Hydro-Electric System v. Ontario Energy Board*, [2009] O.J. No. 1872 (Div. Ct.), distinguishing both *ATCO* and the earlier decision on this point.
148 *Ibid.* at paras. 31–33 (despite a vigorous dissent by Lederman J.).
149 Above note 67.
150 *Dunsmuir*, above note 5 at para. 58.
151 *Khosa*, above note 6 at para. 43.
152 *Lévis (City)*, above note 100.
153 Above note 115.

It is also important to recall where LeBel J. started in *Chamberlain* in his concerns about the pragmatic and functional approach in establishing the standard of review. It was not an easy or comfortable fit where the application for review engaged a discretionary, policy-oriented determination by a statutory authority that was not adjudicative in character, such as a school board, municipality, or minister of the Crown.[154] In *Toronto (City)*, he also raised the dissonance that existed between unreasonableness and patent unreasonableness standards of review, and review on such traditional grounds as failing to take notice of relevant factors, taking account of irrelevant factors, or acting for an improper purpose.[155] As a consequence, he questioned McLachlin C.J.'s characterization of the pragmatic and functional approach as an overarching theory appropriate to all applications for judicial review on substantive (if not procedural) grounds.[156]

Ultimately, these are matters that the majority does not really address in *Dunsmuir*. The approach remains overarching for all types of substantive review and all contexts. Presumably, that assumes the continued applicability of McLachlin C.J.'s reconciliation in *Dr. Q.* of the nominate grounds of abuse of discretion review with unreasonableness review. They are now part of and have become subsumed within whatever standard is applicable, and, most commonly, unreasonableness review. That aside, under the continuing overarching approach the task remains that of sorting out those aspects of discretionary statutory authority that implicate *vires* or jurisdiction from those that are within the discretionary ambit where "deference will apply automatically."[157] In short, it is the perpetuation of the distinctions that prevailed in both *Rascal Trucking* and *ATCO* between the outer limits of discretionary power and the core of the regulatory responsibilities of the statutory authority. This remains a problematic distinction, but perhaps one that the courts remain destined to struggle with as an integral part of the tensions present in Canadian conceptions of the role of the courts in the review of discretionary exercises of statutory and prerogative power.[158]

---

154 *Chamberlain*, above note 43 at paras. 191–99.

155 *Toronto (City)*, above note 57 at paras. 86–89.

156 For a thorough canvassing of these problems, see Ann Chaplin, "The Unanswered Question of *Dunsmuir v. New Brunswick*: What Standard of Review Applies to Judicial Review of Ministers' Discretion?" (LL.M., Faculty of Law, University of Ottawa, Common Law, 2009) [unpublished]. [On file.]

157 *Dunsmuir*, above note 5 at para. 53, Bastarache and LeBel JJ.

158 For my account of the ebbs and flows since its creation in the Supreme Court's attitude towards the scope of judicial review of administrative action, see "The Supreme Court of Canada and Tribunals—Deference to the Administrative Process: A Recent Phenomenon

F. CONCLUSIONS

Defining and elaborating on the standard of judicial review that courts should apply to decisions of public bodies is at the core of judicial review of administrative action. These are tasks that almost inevitably are affected by changing conceptions of not only the nature of state power and the place of administrative processes within the state, but also the role of the judiciary in the policing of the various components of an ever-evolving administrative state. Therefore, it should not be surprising, particularly at a time when the Canadian courts are still coming to terms with the ramifications of the *Canadian Charter of Rights and Freedoms* for the relationship between the legislative and executive branches of government, that the terrain on which common law judicial review of administrative action is conducted is also subject to re-evaluation and evolution.

As a consequence, any confidence that at long last the struggle over standard of review had finally ended in all but a few details in 2000, the year McLachlin J. became chief justice, was misplaced. It paid insufficient regard to the lessons of history, and the continuing struggles over the forging of a coherent theory of judicial review in the age of the *Charter* and in the face of a re-emerging sense of the inherent relationship between basic constitutional norms and the common law of judicial review,[159] not to mention the emerging influence of Canada's international obligations as reflected in both treaties and norms of customary international law.

What is also clear is that, at the margins, there will be cases involving the appropriate posture to take in conducting review on which there will be disagreement even among judges committed to the same basic principles about the relationship between the courts and the administrative process. Sorting out the dividing line between issues going to the jurisdiction of a statutory or prerogative authority, and questions of law that are part of the core responsibilities of that authority, is an inherently difficult task and one over which there will frequently be understandable disagreement. The same is true if the proposition is recast in terms of delineating matters that go to the *vires* or authority of a statutory body to take action and exercises

---

or a Return to Basics?" (2001) 80:2 Can. Bar Rev. 399, a paper given at the conference celebrating the 125th anniversary of the Court.

159 A recognition that owes much to the work of David Dyzenhaus. See "The Politics of Deference: Judicial Review and Democracy" in Mike Taggart, ed., *The Province of Administrative Law* (Oxford: Hart Publications, 1997), cited with approval by Bastarache and LeBel JJ. in *Dunsmuir*, above note 5 at para. 48.

of discretion within the zone of that authority where deference to the judgment of the designated decision maker is appropriate.

All of this said, however, the first decade of the McLachlin Court has certainly produced more than its share of engagement and turmoil over the issue of standard of review. In part, the confusion that manifested itself and the time that was spent on this issue in the conduct of judicial review and statutory appeal cases was the result of the Court's ambivalence and vacillation. At times, the Court wanted to present a united front on what were the key elements of the test for an appropriate standard of review applicable across the whole range of statutory and prerogative decision making. However, very close to the surface were some profound disagreements among its various members as to important elements of both the nature and the detail of the criteria on which they should determine whether to defer and, if so, to what extent. Indeed, the disagreements extended beyond the criteria for the identification of a standard of review to the definition and application of the selected standard.

In the wake of this experience, there is once again reason for confidence that, at least in the short term, the Court, by its judgments in *Dunsmuir* and *Khosa*, has put some of the most troubling aspects of the recent controversy behind it. In the elimination of the patent unreasonableness standard and its replacement by a contextual concept of unreasonableness review, in which the reasons offered in support of the decision under review will generally play a critical role, the Court may have provided a framework that is easier to work with both in the choice between deferring and not deferring and, thereafter, in actually conducting review when that choice produces the deferential reasonableness standard. Moreover, for those who favour a framework in which deference is the norm, the recognition of a strong presumption of respect for statutory authorities' determination of questions of law arising out of their home or constitutive statutes, as well as other frequently encountered statutes and the common law, seems to indicate a genuine rededication to one of the key principles enunciated by Dickson J. (as he then was) in *New Brunswick Liquor* in 1979.

It would, however, be folly to see *Dunsmuir* as a complete panacea. Even with the additional layer of *Khosa*, it does not resolve all of the conceptual problems, let alone the questions of detail bearing upon standard of review analysis. Provided, however, there is explicit recognition of the continuing gaps in the theory and acknowledgment of disagreements over some of the detail in the form of genuine engagement among the members of the Court and a willingness to accept publicly that the Court's previous jurisprudence is by no means consistent on important aspects of the standard of review enterprise, there is reason for optimism in the second decade of the McLachlin Chief Justiceship.

Procedural Fairness at the McLachlin Court

FREYA KRISTJANSON

A. INTRODUCTION

In 1998, shortly before her elevation to the position of chief justice, McLachlin J. delivered a paper, "The Roles of Administrative Tribunals and Courts in Maintaining the Rule of Law."[1] She recognized the integral role of administrative tribunals in the maintenance of legal order, and spoke of the "ethos of justification," referring to the idea that the exercise of public power must be justified to citizens in terms of rationality and fairness. The chief justice stated:

> Fair procedures, equitable treatment, and responsiveness to the public are the cornerstones of a system of administrative tribunals built according to the Rule of Law. I suggest that, in many important ways, it falls to the members and support staff of those administrative boards to ensure that every person dealing with the state is treated fairly and with respect.[2]

The question that arises is whether and how the Supreme Court's procedural fairness jurisprudence has provided guidance to administrative tribunals, enabling them to justify, or legitimize, exercises of public power, by providing fair procedures, equitable treatment, and responsiveness to the public.

My short answer is that in the last decade, the Court has been distracted by the debate over the standard of review. My hope for the next decade

1 Beverley McLachlin, "The Roles of Administrative Tribunals and Courts in Maintaining the Rule of Law" (1999) 12 Can. J. Admin. L. & Prac. 171 at 174.

2 *Ibid.* at 186.

is that the Court will return to the basics of administrative law, providing guidance to tribunals and those who seek to assert rights before them.

Procedural fairness is the central concern for administrative decision makers, justice seekers, regulated parties, and lawyers involved in administrative law. The requisite level of procedural protection is considered every day, by a bewildering variety of decision makers: how much disclosure is required? How can I limit irrelevant cross-examination without breaching fairness? Will a written hearing suffice? Are my reasons sufficient? What consultation does a policy change require, if any? How do cutbacks affecting services affect tribunal independence? These are practical issues that are not particularly "sexy," but are of great importance in the daily dispensing of administrative justice across the nation.

The ability of administrative decision makers to provide "fair procedures, equitable treatment and responsiveness to the public" requires that the Supreme Court engage more directly in the practical issues facing tribunals, provide procedural appeals the same attention that historically standard of review and substantive appeals have received, and where possible, speak with one voice.

Another important element in improving the quality of administrative justice is potential tort liability. Administrative bodies must consider issues relating to regulatory negligence, and develop practices in response to the developing jurisprudence. The Supreme Court has considered regulatory negligence in a number of cases in the last decade. The jurisprudence, however, is in a "state of lamentable confusion." I suggest that a legislative solution might be preferable to the contemporary uncertainty in this area, and refer to a UK Law Commission consultation on redress for substandard administrative action.

B. *BAKER*: THE PERFECT CASE?

Is *Baker v. Canada (Minister of Citizenship and Immigration)*[3] the perfect administrative law case? Does it provide sufficient guidance to administrative decision makers on issues of procedural fairness? Is that why in the last decade the Supreme Court has spent so little time on issues of procedural fairness, and comparatively, so much time on issues of standard of review and jurisdiction?

In *Baker v. Canada (Minister of Citizenship and Immigration)*, L'Heureux-Dubé J. established the common law's modern approach to the duty of fair-

3 [1999] 2 S.C.R. 817, [1999] S.C.J. No. 39 [*Baker*].

RÉSUMÉ

Dans cet article, l'auteur se penche sur l'évolution de la jurisprudence de la Cour suprême dans deux secteurs en particulier, soit l'équité procédurale et la négligence réglementaire. L'auteur soutient que l'équité procédurale est une préoccupation cruciale pour les membres de la collectivité de la justice administrative. Dans cet article, l'auteur analyse la jurisprudence de la Cour en matière de procès équitable et d'indépendance judiciaire, et postule que la Cour, concentrée sur le débat entourant la norme de contrôle judiciaire, ne s'est pas penchée comme elle l'aurait dû sur l'évolution de la doctrine de l'équité procédurale au cours de la dernière décennie. Bien que la négligence réglementaire soit un aspect du droit de la responsabilité délictuelle, et non pas du droit administratif, cette forme de négligence a une incidence importante sur les pratiques en vigueur dans les instances administratives. L'auteur discute des développements jurisprudentiels survenus dans ce secteur, en soutenant qu'il se caractérise par une « nébulosité et une confusion déplorables ». L'auteur exhorte la Cour à examiner de manière plus approfondie la responsabilité de l'autorité réglementaire, ce qui comprend une réforme législative en vue d'établir un régime spécialisé relatif à la négligence lorsqu'elle découle d'une décision administrative.

ness. There is no longer any bright line between administrative decision makers subject to fairness duties and those that are not, nor is there any strict application of those rights once triggered. Administrative decision making is now seen as falling somewhere on a spectrum between quasi-judicial and legislative decision making, with procedural entitlements varying according to placement on the spectrum.

The decision in *Baker* has provided a flexible framework within which these practical issues may be addressed. In other words, fairness works. Administrative decision makers are able to assess the hearing-related requirements of procedural fairness in a stable framework. Lawyers can come reasonably close to predicting the outcome of a court challenge. This is in contrast to the last decade of standard of review jurisprudence, which until *Dunsmuir*[4] was wildly unpredictable.

4 2008 SCC 9, [2008] 1 S.C.R. 190 [*Dunsmuir*].

There are, however, concerns with the lack of engagement by the Supreme Court in procedural fairness issues, and these relate in part to the significant deference contained in the fifth *Baker* factor. The five "*Baker* factors" that are now the benchmark in assessing the level of procedural fairness to be afforded in any given proceeding are as follows:

1) the nature of the decision being made and the process followed in making it;
2) the nature of the statutory scheme and the terms of the statute pursuant to which the body operates;
3) the importance of the decision to the individual or individuals affected;
4) the legitimate expectations of the person challenging the decision; and
5) the choices of procedure made by the agency itself and its institutional constraints.

The fifth *Baker* factor causes concern with respect to maintaining the integrity of the concept of procedural fairness. In *Congrégation des témoins de Jéhovah de St-Jérôme-Lafontaine v. Lafontaine (Village)*, this factor was described as "the nature of the deference due to the decision maker."[5]

The fifth *Baker* factor may limit the procedural protections required to be afforded by administrative decision makers, tempering judicial review of agency processes which may be deficient or compromise fairness. There are no limits to the justifications an administrative body may offer when compromising procedural protections in the name of an agency's "choice of procedures." There is no *Oakes* test. There is no requirement to consider other measures more supportive of participatory rights, for example.[6]

The concept of "institutional constraints" built into the fifth *Baker* factor is of particular concern in an era of ever-increasing demands on an ever-decreasing public purse.[7] Government allocation of resources may be used to justify the failure to provide procedural protections—all in accordance with procedural

---

5 2004 SCC 48, [2004] 2 S.C.R. 650 at para. 11 [*Lafontaine*].

6 For a discussion of the application of the fifth *Baker* factor to the Ontario Labour Relations Board, see Leonard Marvy & David A. Wright, "'Master of Its Own House': Procedural Fairness and Deference to Ontario Labour Relations Board Procedure" (2008) 21 Can. J. Admin. L. & Prac. 361.

7 See *Thamotharem v. Canada (Minister of Citizenship and Immigration)*, [2008] 1 F.C. 385 and also *Benitez v. Canada (Minister of Citizenship and Immigration)*, [2008] 1 F.C. 155. These companion decisions affirmed the right of the Refugee Protection Division (RPD) to adopt a policy of denying counsel the right to conduct examination-in-chief during refugee claim hearings. The RPD maintained that this policy was necessary to address backlogs in the hearing and processing of claims. The court cited a variety of reports and studies

fairness. A good example is empirical work conducted by Professor Sossin into whether or not interviews are provided to individuals claiming immigration status on humanitarian and compassionate grounds.[8] The failure to provide such an interview, or an "oral hearing," was one of the grounds on which Mavis Baker unsuccessfully asserted a failure of procedural fairness in the *Baker* case. Professor Sossin's research suggests that interviews are afforded in smaller regional offices, but not in the busy urban offices of Citizenship and Immigration Canada. One has to ask whether "institutional constraints" built into the fifth *Baker* factor are being used to defend arbitrary decisions made on the basis of unjustifiable differences in regional resource allocation, for example.

In *Dunsmuir*,[9] the Court has reaffirmed the concept that we are entitled to procedural fairness in administrative decision making. The standard of review analysis does not apply to decisions involving procedural fairness. However, the fifth *Baker* factor creates a "back door," importing deference to institutional choice of procedures into the very test for common law procedural fairness. This is an area ripe for consideration by the Court in the future.

C. THE RIGHT TO A HEARING

There have been surprisingly few decisions involving the right to a hearing—the *audi alteram partem* aspect of procedural fairness—in the last decade. Disclosure is the only hearing-related procedural protection which has received any significant consideration by the Court in the past decade. On this point, I consider three decisions in the classic disclosure context: *May v. Ferndale Institution*;[10] *Charkaoui v. Canada (Citizenship and Immigration)*;[11] *Deloitte & Touche v. Ontario Securities Commission*;[12] and two disclosure decisions made in the context of solicitor–client privilege, in *Pritchard v. Ontario (Human Rights Commission)*[13] and *Canada (Privacy Commissioner) v. Blood Tribe Department of Health*.[14] I briefly review the requirement for reasons in the administrative context as well.

---

conducted by the government, one of which recommended dispensing with examination-in-chief in order to increase efficiency.

8 Lorne Sossin, "From Neutrality to Compassion: The Place of Civil Service Values and Legal Norms in the Exercise of Administrative Discretion" (2005) 55 U.T.L.J. 427.

9 Above note 4.

10 [2005] 3 S.C.R. 809, 2005 SCC 82 [*May*].

11 2007 SCC 9 [*Charkaoui* 2007]; 2008 SCC 38 [*Charkaoui* 2008].

12 [2003] 2 S.C.R. 713 [*Deloitte*].

13 [2004] 1 S.C.R. 809, 2004 SCC 31 [*Pritchard*].

14 2008 SCC 44 [*Blood Tribe*].

1) Disclosure: *Stinchcombe* or Not?

In *May v. Ferndale Institution*,[15] LeBel and Fish JJ. for the majority[16] considered the duty of disclosure in the context of the reclassification leading to transfer from minimum to medium security institutions. Justices LeBel and Fish held that "*Stinchcombe* principles do not apply in the administrative context,"[17] distinguishing such proceedings from the "innocence at stake" principle in the context of criminal law. In the administrative context, the procedural fairness requirement is that the individual know the case she has to meet, and the administrative decision maker must disclose the information he relied upon. Failure to provide adequate disclosure means that a decision will be void for lack of jurisdiction. Further, the Court confirmed that statutory obligations may impose an additional informational burden, which must also be met. In *May*, the Court held that correctional services officials had failed to disclose relevant information, and indeed had "concealed crucial information" in violation of their statutory duty.[18] The transfer decisions were held to be null and void; the applications for *habeas corpus* were granted.

What is interesting to note, however, is that despite this strong comment that *Stinchcombe* disclosure obligations do not apply in administrative proceedings, the Federal Court has been reluctant to follow. The Federal Court of Appeal almost immediately distinguished *May* in its 2006 decision in *Sheriff v. Canada (Attorney General)*[19] in the context of the professional conduct of a trustee in bankruptcy. The Court held, referring to *May*, that

> While the Court is unequivocal in stating that "[t]he *Stinchcombe* principles do not apply in the administrative context," it clearly is not referring to a licensing review hearing, where a loss of livelihood and damage to professional reputation are at stake. In contrast, in the present appeal, the innocence, i.e. the reputation of the Trustees, is under review. Accordingly, I would classify a review of a trustee in bankruptcy's licence by the OSB as an exception to the rule established in *May*.[20]

---

15 *May*, above note 10.

16 Major, Bastarache, and Charron JJ. dissenting.

17 *May*, above note 10 at para. 91.

18 *Ibid.* at para. 120.

19 2006 FCA 139 [*Sheriff*].

20 *Ibid.* at para. 29.

These cases are hard to reconcile. The Supreme Court was clear in *May*. The issue in that case was a restriction on liberty, a value typically protected at common law. The failure of the Federal Court of Appeal to follow one of the few clear, basic, and direct administrative law cases of the last decade certainly makes it harder for lawyers to advise their clients about the predictability of administrative decisions.

2) The *Charter* to the Rescue: *Charkaoui*

In two interesting decisions in the national security context, the *Charter* has been effectively used to supplement common law disclosure requirements. *Charkaoui v. Canada (Citizenship and Immigration)*[21] was a challenge to provisions in the *Immigration and Refugee Protection Act*[22] authorizing the minister to issue "security certificates." The issuance of a security certificate on national security or other grounds renders an individual inadmissible to Canada and subject to immediate detention in Canada. These certificates were reviewable by Federal Court judges, sitting in *ex parte, in camera* hearings. An individual named in a security certificate was not entitled to disclosure of the case against him.

In a unanimous decision in 2007, the Supreme Court found aspects of the security certificate regime contrary to section 7 of the *Charter*, insofar as it deprived individuals of liberty without providing for disclosure required by the principles of fundamental justice. Nor, the Court found, could it be saved under section 1 of the *Charter*, because less liberty-impairing alternatives were available. While the decision is to be lauded for establishing that the principles of fundamental justice require that individuals held in custody receive some form of disclosure, it can also be criticized for failing to establish when "the implications for liberty or security of the person will be sufficiently great that notice, full disclosure (at least to the individual's legal representative) and an opportunity to be heard will be constitutionally mandated." As noted by Professor Stribopoulos, simply stating that "when the stakes are great enough[,] the demands of procedural fairness increase, [telling] us very little."[23]

---

21 *Charkaoui* 2007, above note 11.

22 S.C. 2001, c. 27, ss. 33 and 77–85.

23 James Stribopoulos, "*Charkaoui*: Beyond Anti-terrorism, Procedural Fairness, and Section 7 of the *Charter*" (November 2007) 16 Const. Forum Const. 16.

The 2008 *Charkaoui* decision[24] dealt more specifically with disclosure issues which are potentially broadly relevant to a number of administrative decision makers. The issues include late disclosure of information, and the destruction of interview notes in accordance with Canadian Security Intelligence Service (CSIS) policy.

The *CSIS Act* directs that CSIS "shall collect, by investigation or otherwise . . . and analyse and retain information and intelligence" respecting potential threats to the security of Canada.[25] CSIS, however, developed an internal policy requiring that operational notes must be destroyed after they have been transcribed into a report by the employee who took them. The Court canvassed the practical purposes of notes, as a better source of evidence and to refresh memory when testifying. The Court determined that as a result of the Act and "for practical reasons," CSIS officers must retain their operational notes when investigating targeted individuals or groups.[26] This finding is of broad application to all administrative bodies conducting investigations. The Court cautioned, however, that requiring CSIS officers to retain their notes will not always fully guarantee procedural fairness, since some notes must remain secret for national security or other reasons.

The Court also found a duty to disclose based on section 7 of the *Charter*, as a result of the severity of the possible consequences (liberty, security, and potentially the right to life). The Court determined that procedural fairness requires that CSIS retain all the information in its possession, and disclose it to the ministers and the designated judge. The designated judge will be responsible to filter the evidence for threats to national security and summarize the remaining evidence, checked for accuracy and reliability, to the person named in the security certificate. The Court also held that the remedy for late disclosure was an adjournment.

3) Third Party Privacy Interests and Disclosure

The Court dealt with the issue of third party privacy interests and disclosure in the decision of *Deloitte & Touche v. Ontario Securities Commission*.[27] In the course of an investigation into Philip Services Corporation, the Ontario Securities Commission (OSC) compelled the provision of information

24 *Charkaoui* 2008, above note 11.

25 *Canadian Security Intelligence Service Act*, R.S.C. 1985, c. C-23, s. 12.

26 *Charkaoui* 2008, above note 11 at para. 43.

27 *Deloitte*, above note 12.

from Deloitte & Touche, who acted as auditors for Philip Services Corporation. The OSC subsequently commenced a Commission proceeding against Philip Services Corporation and its officers, and determined that it was in the public interest to disclose all of the compelled information and material to Philip Services Corporation and its officers. The OSC used the *Stinchcombe* relevance standard, which Iacobucci J. for the Court determined was reasonable in the circumstances.[28] The Supreme Court noted the statutory basis for the OSC's duty to protect third party privacy interests and confidences, and the appropriate balancing of interests to allow Philip Services Corporation and its officers to make "full answer and defence."[29]

In holding that it was reasonable (from a standard of review perspective) for the OSC to apply the *Stinchcombe* relevance standard in assessing its disclosure obligations, the Court should not be taken as requiring the *Stinchcombe* standard. However, this is the kind of confusion that sometimes does arise as a result of misconstruing the standard of review analysis in the context of procedural fairness requirements.

4) Disclosure and Solicitor–Client Privilege: The Administrative Realm

One of the notable features of the McLachlin Court has been the expansion, constitutionalization, and protection of solicitor–client privilege in all its applications in decisions such as *R. v. McClure*,[30] *R. v. Brown*,[31] *Lavallee, Rackel & Heintz v. Canada (Attorney General)*,[32] *Blank v. Canada (Minister of Justice)*,[33] and *Goodis v. Ontario (Ministry of Correctional Services)*.[34] There have been two significant decisions in the administrative realm.

In *Pritchard v. Ontario (Human Rights Commission)*,[35] the Supreme Court held that solicitor–client privilege "appl[ies] with equal force in the context of advice given to an administrative board by in-house counsel as it does to advice given in the realm of private law."[36] As a shield against disclosure, it

28 *Ibid.* at paras. 26–27.

29 *Ibid.* at para. 1.

30 [2001] 1 S.C.R. 445 [*McClure*].

31 [2002] 2 S.C.R. 185, 2002 SCC 32 [*Brown*].

32 [2002] 3 S.C.R. 209, 2002 SCC 61 [*Lavallee*].

33 [2006] 2 S.C.R. 319, 2006 SCC 39 [*Blank*].

34 [2006] 2 S.C.R. 32, 2006 SCC 31 [*Goodis*].

35 *Pritchard*, above note 13.

36 *Ibid.* at para. 21.

is "nearly absolute," and "exceptions to it will be rare."[37] The policy rationale supporting expansive protection of solicitor–client privilege generally applies equally in the administrative realm.

In *Canada (Privacy Commissioner) v. Blood Tribe Department of Health*,[38] the Court held that the Privacy Commissioner's statutory authority under the *Personal Information Protection and Electronic Documents Act* (*PIPEDA*) to compel the production of records in the course of an investigation did not confer a right of access to solicitor–client privileged documents. Like many other administrative tribunals, the Privacy Commissioner has the statutory power to compel production of "any records and things that the Commissioner considers necessary to investigate the complaint, in the same manner and to the same extent as a superior court of record."[39] She argued that since a superior court of record has the power to compel the production of privileged documents, interpreting this provision to give her the power to review privilege claims would be consistent with Parliament's objective of creating an inexpensive and expeditious process to "ensure the integrity and proper functioning of the legislative scheme protecting fundamental privacy rights."[40] The Court held, following *Pritchard*, that a general production provision that does not specifically indicate that production must include records subject to solicitor–client privilege is not sufficient to compel production. The Court also held that

> In any event, a court's power to review a privileged document in order to determine a disputed claim for privilege does not flow from its power to compel production. Rather, the court's power to review a document in such circumstances derives from its power to adjudicate disputed claims over legal rights. The Privacy Commissioner has no such power. [41]

The use of the term "legal rights" is important in this passage, and has caused concern in the administrative tribunal community. Procedural fairness has been the common law's attempt to provide fairness to those whose privileges and interests are affected by administrative conduct, not just legal rights. All adjudicative tribunals are called upon to resolve privilege disputes and production issues. Counsel and parties cannot, except at great cost and with delay, proceed to a superior court for a ruling on privilege.

37 *Ibid.* at para. 18.

38 *Blood Tribe*, above note 14.

39 *Personal Information Protection and Electronic Documents Act*, S.C. 2000, c. 5, s. 12.

40 *Blood Tribe*, above note 14 at para. 19.

41 *Ibid.* at para. 22.

Whether or not the *Blood Tribe* decision will undermine the power of adjudicative tribunals is an open question at the present time.

Peter Ruby and Lauren McLeod make a similar argument in their article, "Solicitor–Client Privilege and Administrative Agencies."[42] They note that as a result of the decision in *Blood Tribe* "reaffirming the importance and strength of solicitor–client privilege, the power of administrative tribunals was arguably weakened." They argue that a number of the advantages and purposes of administrative tribunals, in particular the efficiency of less formal rules of procedure, may have been undermined by the Supreme Court insofar as administrative bodies "will no longer be able to make informal decisions about evidence and whether it is protected from disclosure."[43] To the extent that the decision in *Blood Tribe* undermines some of the very advantages administrative tribunals were designed to offer, the purpose of these bodies has also been undermined. One issue that remains unresolved as a result of this decision is whether it will be extended and applied to other forms of privilege.[44] This will obviously have a bearing on the ultimate ramifications of the Court's findings on administrative tribunals.

5) Reasons and Procedural Fairness

Baker established that in some circumstances, procedural fairness will require administrative decision makers to provide reasons. While there has not been significant jurisprudential development regarding when procedural fairness will require reasons, since the Court's decision in *R. v. Sheppard*,[45] there has been a significant trend by administrative decision makers to provide reasons.

The chief justice wrote the majority decision in *Lafontaine*,[46] finding that the municipality, in refusing a number of rezoning applications to build a place of worship, breached its duty of procedural fairness in failing to give reasons for its denial. The conduct of the municipality was rather puzzling. In refusing the third rezoning application, the municipality staked out the position (essentially) that it had an untrammelled discretion, informing the Congregation that

42 Peter Ruby & Lauren MacLeod, "Solicitor–Client Privilege and Administrative Agencies" (2009) 22 Can. J. Admin. L. & Prac. 91.

43 *Ibid.* at 103.

44 *Ibid.* at 105.

45 2002 SCC 26.

46 *Lafontaine*, above note 5 at para. 11, Major, Bastarache, LeBel, and Deschamps JJ. dissenting.

> You have made a number of applications to amend the zoning by-law. *The Legislature has given the municipal council the responsibility for exercising this power, which is discretionary.* Upon careful consideration, the municipality of Lafontaine has decided not to take action in respect of your applications. *The municipal council of Lafontaine is not required to provide you with a justification and we therefore have no intention of giving reasons for the council's decision.*[47]

The chief justice turned to policy justifications for the requirement for reasons in this case, stating:

> Giving reasons for refusing to rezone in a case such as this serves the values of fair and transparent decision-making, reduces the chances of arbitrary or capricious decisions, and cultivates the confidence of citizens in public officials.

The chief justice commented that the municipality acted in an arbitrary manner and "straddled the boundary separating good from bad faith."[48]

D. THE RIGHT TO AN UNBIASED AND (POSSIBLY) INDEPENDENT DECISION MAKER

The second rule of procedural fairness is generally expressed as the right to an impartial and independent decision maker. In the last decade the Court has been significantly more active in the realm of administrative independence and impartiality than it has in relation to hearing-related procedural protections. It is notable, however, that the Court has not established a "bright line" test for the requisite level of administrative independence, even in adjudicative situations. Professor Sossin has noted that

> The Canadian case law on administrative independence is mostly unsatisfying. These cases do not explore the structural relationship between independent bodies and the government which matter most (e.g. budgetary and staffing autonomy, etc.), or the issue of politically motivated interference with the decision-making of administrative bodies. Much of the appellate case law has concerned the issue of government attempts to remove or not reappoint members or leaders of independent administrative bodies. As in the *Keen* case, these disputes reflect the tension between

47 *Ibid.* at para. 27 [emphasis in original].

48 *Ibid.* at para. 30.

the legitimate government direction for administrative tribunals on the one hand and illegitimate political interference on the other.[49]

Independence is a central focus of concern within the tribunal community. The removal of Linda Keen as president of the Canadian Nuclear Safety Commission on the day before she was scheduled to appear before a House of Commons committee to testify on events leading to the shutdown of the medical isotope producing Chalk River reactor, and the subsequent failure of her judicial review application in light of *Dunsmuir*,[50] have caused a chill in the regulatory community.

Other issues include appointments, failures to appoint, the federal government's new position on the role of Department of Justice counsel seconded to administrative agencies,[51] and judicial review applications by governments against their own boards and tribunals. Is this a direct result of *Ocean Port*? Or, perhaps, the result of *Ocean Port* combined with *Dunsmuir*? According to Professor Sossin, the Court's "reluctance in *Keen* to explore the obligations of government to refrain from dismissing 'at pleasure' appointments for improper reasons, or in an improper way, represents the fulfilment of an unsettling implication of the Supreme Court's landmark 2008 *Dunsmuir* decision."[52] He goes on to note that the position of "members of adjudicative, oversight and accountability positions is even more precarious" in light of *Dunsmuir*.[53] Institutional independence has been a central focus of the Court's attention, with some development in adjudicative independence and impartiality.

1) The Significance of *Ocean Port*: 2001

In *Valente v. The Queen*,[54] Le Dain J. established the structural preconditions for judicial independence: security of tenure, financial security, and institutional independence with respect to matters of administration bearing directly on the judicial function. In 2001, the chief justice wrote the seminal decision regarding of administrative independence in *Ocean Port*,

49 Lorne Sossin. "The Puzzle of Independence for Administrative Bodies" (2009) 26:1 N.J.C.L. at 19 [Sossin. "Puzzle of Independence"].

50 *Keen v. Canada (Attorney General)*, 2009 FC 353.

51 See Lorne Sossin, "Administrative Law at Pleasure: *Keen v. Canada*" (2009) 10 Regulatory Boards and Administrative Law Litigation 628.

52 Sossin, "Puzzle of Independence," above note 49 at 19.

53 *Ibid.* at 20.

54 S.C.J. No. 77, [1985] 2 S.C.R. 673 at 685 [*Valente*].

which established that there is no constitutional right to institutional independence for administrative decision makers in Canada.[55] In this case, the challenge was to the independence of the Liquor Control and Licensing Board. The respondent had been found liable for violations of liquor licence laws and received a penalty following a hearing. The respondent appealed to the Liquor Appeal Board by way of hearing *de novo*, where four of five allegations were upheld and the penalty was confirmed. The respondent challenged the independence of the Board. The members served "at the pleasure of the Lieutenant Governor in Council," were appointed for one-year terms, served on a part-time basis, and all of whom—except for the Chair—were paid on a *per diem* basis. The Court of Appeal had held that the Board lacked the requisite guarantees of independence required of administrative decision makers with the power to impose penalties. The Supreme Court allowed the appeal.

Chief Justice McLachlin held that superior courts and provincial courts are constitutionally required to possess "objective guarantees" of both individual and institutional independence, to demarcate the "fundamental division between the judiciary and the executive," thus protecting the impartiality of judges from external influence, particularly that of the executive.[56] Chief Justice McLachlin went on to state:

> Administrative tribunals, by contrast, lack this constitutional distinction from the Executive. They are, in fact, created precisely for the purpose of implementing government policy. Implementation of that policy may require them to make quasi-judicial decisions. They thus may be seen as spanning the constitutional divide between the executive and judicial branches of government. However, given their primary policy-making function, it is properly the role and responsibility of Parliament and the legislatures to determine the composition and structure required by a tribunal to discharge the responsibilities bestowed upon it. While tribunals may sometimes attract *Charter* requirements of independence, as a general rule they do not. Thus, the degree of independence required of a particular tribunal is a matter of discerning the intention of Parliament or the legislature and, absent constitutional constraints, this choice must be respected.[57]

---

55 *Ocean Port Hotel Ltd. v. British Columbia (General Manager, Liquor Control and Licensing Branch)*, 2001 SCC 52 at para. 31 [*Ocean Port*].

56 *Ibid.* at para. 23.

57 *Ibid.* at para. 24.

Just as importantly, the chief justice held that "like all principles of natural justice, the degree of independence may be ousted by express statutory language or necessary implication."[58] Oddly, the decision in *Ocean Port* left open the possibility that a tribunal member, appointed at the pleasure of the cabinet, faced with a *Charter* issue, could be terminated if the government did not approve of the decision, while a judge deciding the same issue would be protected from interference.[59] At the outset of the decade, then, we were left in an awkward position. Independence was part of the common law of procedural fairness, as established in cases such as *Consolidated-Bathurst* and *Matsqui Indian Band*. It became clear that there was no constitutional protection, except that apparently sometimes the *Charter* might apply, and the issue would be to discern the will of Parliament in any given circumstance. As noted by Professor Lorne Sossin, "[a]s a legal matter, independence remains, importantly, a right owed to those affected by administrative decision-makers, not a right enjoyed *by* those decision-makers."[60] Ron Ellis has referred to this as the "hope and a prayer" theory of institutional independence, since there are no objective structural guarantees required.[61]

2) *Bell Canada*: 2003

In 2003, the Court dealt with two significant issues relating to tribunal independence in *Bell Canada v. Canadian Telephone Employees Association*.[62] In the course of a pay equity complaint heard by the Canadian Human Rights Tribunal, Bell Canada argued that the independence of the Tribunal was compromised because the applicable guidelines issued by the Canadian Human Rights Commission and by statute were binding on the Tribunal, thus limiting its ability to interpret the Act. There was a further concern raised because the Commission appeared before the Tribunal as a party to pay equity complaints. Bell also argued that the Tribunal chair's power to extend the terms of members for ongoing inquiries undermined the security

58 *Ibid.* at para. 22.

59 Gerald Heckman & Lorne Sossin, "How Do Canadian Administrative Law Protections Measure Up to International Human Rights Standards?" (2005) 50 McGill L.J. 245.

60 Sossin, "Puzzle of Independence," above note 49 at 16.

61 Ron Ellis, "The Future of Administrative Justice: Current Issues in Tribunal Independence" (Paper delivered at "The Future of Administrative Justice," University of Toronto, 17–18 January 2008), online: www.law.utoronto.ca/documents/conferences/adminjustice08_Ellis.pdf.

62 [2003] SCC 36 [*Bell Canada*].

of tenure of members and hence their independence. Impartiality arguments were raised as well.

The Chief Justice and Bastarache J. emphasized the statutory scheme and the nature of the tribunal, holding that

> A tribunal may have a number of different functions, one of which is to conduct fair and impartial hearings in a manner similar to that of the courts, and yet another of which is to see that certain government policies are furthered. In ascertaining the content of the requirements of procedural fairness that bind a particular tribunal, consideration must be given to *all* of the functions of that tribunal. It is not adequate to characterize a tribunal as "quasi-judicial" on the basis of one of its functions, while treating another aspect of the legislative scheme creating this tribunal—such as the requirement that the tribunal follow interpretive guidelines that are laid down by a specialized body with expertise in that area of law—as though this second aspect of the legislative scheme were external to the true purpose of the tribunal. All aspects of the tribunal's structure, as laid out in its enabling statute, must be examined, and an attempt must be made to determine precisely what combination of functions the legislature intended that tribunal to serve, and what procedural protections are appropriate for a body that has these particular functions.[63]

The Court concluded that the Tribunal had a high degree of independence from the executive, which was appropriate both in light of the adjudicative nature of the decision-making process, and the nature of the interests affected by Tribunal proceedings which include "the dignity interests of the complainant, the interests of the public in eradicating discrimination, and the reputation of the party that is alleged to have engaged in discriminatory practices."[64]

The Court held that even though the Tribunal was entitled to a high degree of independence, the power of the Commission to issue binding guidelines did not undermine the Tribunal's independence or impartiality, but was instead "Parliament's way of ensuring that the Act would be interpreted in a manner that was sensitive to the needs of the public and to developments across the country, and hence that it would be interpreted by the Tribunal in the manner that best furthered the aims of the Act as a whole."[65]

63 *Ibid.* at para. 22 [emphasis in original].

64 *Ibid.* at para. 24.

65 *Ibid.* at para. 41.

Clearly there are echoes of *Ocean Port* in this decision. The Court has continued the trend of not establishing a bright line test upon which a tribunal's independence can be gauged. As in the *Ocean Port* decision, McLachlin C.J. and Bastarache J. emphasized the multiple roles played by an administrative tribunal as a justification for curtailing its independence. Of the multiple roles administrative tribunals are assigned, the Court has consistently pointed to the policy implementation role as being one that is particularly important. Unfortunately this role is one that does not sit comfortably alongside a robust level of independence.

3) *C.U.P.E.* (Retired Judges Case): 2003

C.U.P.E. v. Ontario (Minister of Labour)[66] (the retired judges case) needs no introduction, given its prominence in the "patently unreasonable" debate. From an institutional independence perspective, the issue was whether the minister compromised the independence of arbitration boards under the *Hospital Labour Disputes Arbitration Act* by appointing four retired judges to chair arbitration boards. The minister had the power to appoint arbitrators, although historically the unions and the hospitals had mutually agreed on arbitrators, or they had been appointed from an agreed list.

C.U.P.E. took the position that the indicia of independence (based on the *Valente* criteria) were absent, and hence the boards could not be independent. Justice Binnie, writing for the majority, rejected this argument:

> However, as explained above, the Court cannot substitute a different tribunal for the one designed by the legislature. An *ad hoc* tribunal is by definition constituted on a case-by-case basis. Security of tenure does not survive the termination of the arbitration, and financial security is similarly circumscribed. Administrative independence has little formal protection. Professional labour arbitrators (including those on the s. 49(10) list) function successfully in such a structure even though there may be no guarantee of continuing work from any particular employer or union.[67]

The Court also considered impartiality concerns, that retired judges (as a class) might be seen as "inimical to labour," at least in the eyes of the unions. Justice Binnie held, however, that the test for impartiality cannot be directed to the subjective perspective of a party, but to the reasonable, detached, and informed observer. He held that allegations of individual bias

66 2003 SCC 29 [*C.U.P.E.*].

67 *Ibid.* at para. 190.

must be dealt with on a case-by-case basis, but that the "fully informed, reasonable person" would not "tar the entire class of presently retired judges with the stigma of an anti-labour bias."[68]

As was the case in *Ocean Port* and *Bell Canada*, in *C.U.P.E.* the Supreme Court emphasized the importance of deference to the will of the legislature (as determined by the wording of the statute). And, as per the decisions cited above, it did so at the expense of institutional independence. This decision seems to exemplify Professor Sossin's lament that the decisions of the Court have failed to "explore the structural relationship between independent bodies and the government which matter most (e.g. budgetary and staffing autonomy, etc.)."[69]

4) Discretion and Impartiality: *Imperial Oil*, 2003

Imperial Oil Ltd. v. Quebec (Minister of the Environment)[70] explored the issue of impartiality in relation to a minister's discretionary decision to direct Imperial Oil to prepare an environmental decontamination study for review by the minister. Imperial Oil instead sought to quash the order, on the ground that the minister was not impartial or had a conflict of interest because the minister had been involved in an earlier remediation project, was presently being sued as a result, and thus had a personal interest.

The Supreme Court held that the minister had to comply with precise procedural obligations. However, when exercising his discretion to make decisions implementing legislative policy in a mainly political role, the minister is not expected to have the same degree of impartiality as a "judge or administrative decision-maker whose primary function is adjudication."[71] He was acting in the public interest, which can legitimately include saving the public money. Thus, here too, deference was paid to implementing government policy, as expressed in the legislation, while issues of institutional independence were left essentially unanswered.

E. ADJUDICATIVE INDEPENDENCE

Adjudicative independence in Canada is established through the common law, including "the rule against dictation, the presumption against sub-dele-

68 *Ibid.* at para. 202.

69 See Sossin, "Puzzle of Independence," above note 49.

70 2003 SCC 58, [2003] 2 S.C.R. 624 [*Imperial Oil*].

71 *Ibid.* at para. 34.

gation of quasi-judicial decision-making authority, and the rule that only those tribunal members who were actually present throughout the hearing may participate in the decision."[72]

An issue for Canadian administrative decision-makers is how to ensure consistency in decision making, particularly where there are a number of part-time members or decision makers are regionally dispersed. An important decision on the role of full board consultation is *Ellis-Don Ltd. v. Ontario (Labour Relations Board)*, [73] which built on the seminal decision of Gonthier J. in *Consolidated-Bathurst*.[74]

In *Ellis-Don*, a panel of the Labour Relations Board prepared a draft decision following a hearing of a grievance for violation of a provincial collective agreement. The panel's draft decision dismissed the grievance. Following a meeting of the full Board at which the decision was discussed, the panel's final decision upheld the grievance. The issue in the case involved the appropriateness of institutional consultations, and the tension between deliberative secrecy, the independence of adjudicators, and fair process. Justice LeBel for the majority[75] held that institutional consultation ensures consistency in administrative decision making, and will not constitute an apprehension of bias or lack of independence, so long as

(a) the consultation proceeding is not imposed by a superior level authority within the administrative hierarchy;
(b) the consultation is limited to questions of policy and law, rather than findings of fact;
(c) even on questions of law and policy, the decision makers must remain free to make their own decision; and
(d) if new issues arise in the full Board discussion, the parties should be notified and allowed an opportunity to respond.[76]

Justice LeBel further held that

> Deliberative secrecy also favours administrative consistency by granting protection to a consultative process that involves interaction between the adjudicators who have heard the case and the members who have

72 Professor Philip Bryden, "A Canadian Perspective on Tribunal Independence" (Paper presented to the Conference of the Canadian Council of Administrative Tribunals, May 2007).

73 2001 SCC 4, [2001] 1 S.C.R. 221 [*Ellis-Don*].

74 *IWA v. Consolidated-Bathurst Packaging Ltd.*, [1990] 1 S.C.R. 282, [1990] S.C.J. No. 20.

75 Major and Binnie JJ. dissenting.

76 *Ellis-Don*, above note 73 at para. 29.

> not, within the rules set down in *Consolidated-Bathurst* . . . . Without such protection, there could be a chilling effect on institutional consultations, thereby depriving administrative tribunals of a critically important means of achieving consistency.[77]

This decision goes further than most in terms of establishing some concrete tests which can be used to determine if rules of procedural fairness have been violated with respect to consultation amongst administrative decision makers. Unfortunately it is not entirely clear how these tests could be either enforced or monitored. Parties to hearings where such consultations take place are essentially operating in the dark with respect to what is said during the consultation and the ultimate impact it has on the decision rendered. This is, in and of itself, sufficient to cast the independence and impartiality of the process into doubt. To the extent that the decision of the Court leaves the fairness of the decision-making process in doubt, it has failed to adequately address the issues that arise out of board-wide consultations.

F. REGULATORY NEGLIGENCE—THE NEXT FRONTIER

Regulatory negligence is an aspect of tort law, not administrative law. However, the prospect of regulatory negligence has an effect on the environment and practices of administrative bodies. Further, there has been significant development in this area by the Supreme Court in the past decade. The starting point is 1940 and the decision in *East Suffolk Rivers Catchment Board v. Kent* where McKinnon L.J. stated: "The case law as to the duties and liabilities of a statutory body to members of the public is in a state of lamentable obscurity and confusion."[78] The "lamentable obscurity and confusion" as to the duties and liabilities of a statutory body to members of the public was equally applicable in 2011.[79] Administrative decision makers and persons harmed by substandard administrative action both deserve greater predictability as to the prospect of tort liability.

Most of the jurisprudence to date involves motions to strike rather than decisions on the merits, and a significant number of claims do not pass even this minimal threshold. Even where the courts find no liability, however,

77 *Ibid.* at para. 53.

78 *East Suffolk Rivers Catchment Board v. Kent*, [1940] 1 KB 319 at 322.

79 This is an abbreviated discussion based on a paper I delivered, "Regulatory Liability of Public Authorities" (Paper presented to The Six-Minute Administrative Lawyer 2009, Law Society of Upper Canada, 24 February 2009).

there are significant reputational risks for regulators. The commencement of a lawsuit may also significantly harm stakeholder relations. On the other hand, regulators and governments create and manage risks, citizens rely upon governments and regulators to protect us from harm, and understandably look for compensation when public authorities fail to deliver.

1) *Cooper v. Hobart*

The chief justice and Major J. wrote the Supreme Court of Canada's 2001 decision in *Cooper v. Hobart*.[80] *Cooper* determined that the factors giving rise to proximity for the purposes of the private law duty of care owed by a public body must be found in the governing statute. The case involved the Registrar of Mortgage Brokers, a statutory regulator which suspended a mortgage broker's licence and issued a freeze order over assets provided by investors which were allegedly used by the broker for unauthorized purposes. The plaintiff in the proposed class proceeding was an investor who had advanced money to the broker. The allegations against the Registrar were that the Registrar was aware and should have acted earlier to suspend the broker's licence and notify investors that the broker was under investigation, thereby avoiding or reducing the loss to investors. The Supreme Court held there was no duty of care owed by the Registrar to the investors.

The Court held specifically that when dealing with a public authority, in this case the Registrar of Mortgage Brokers,

> *The factors giving rise to proximity, if they exist, must arise from the statute under which the Registrar is appointed.* That statute is the only source of his duties, private or public. Apart from that statute, he is in no different position than the ordinary man or woman on the street. If a duty to investors with regulated mortgage brokers is to be found, it must be in the statute.[81]

The Court reviewed relevant statutory provisions, determining that the statute did not impose a duty of care on the Registrar to investors; rather, the Registrar's duty is to the public as a whole. Since a duty to individual investors would potentially conflict with the Registrar's overarching duty to the public, the Court found that there was insufficient proximity between the investors and the Registrar to ground a *prima facie* duty of care.

---

80 2001 SCC 79, [2001] 3 S.C.R. 537 [*Cooper*].

81 *Ibid.* at para. 43 [emphasis added].

The Court held that even if there had been sufficient proximity, the duty would have been negatived at the second stage for overriding policy reasons. These included the following:

- The determination to suspend a mortgage broker involves both policy and quasi-judicial elements, which require balancing public and private interests.
- The Registrar is deciding, as an agent of the executive branch of government, what the policy should be.
- In the regulatory quasi-judicial role (decision to suspend or revoke a licence), the Registrar owes duties of fairness to the broker which are inconsistent with a duty of care to investors.
- The Registrar makes discretionary policy decisions.
- The spectre of indeterminate liability—there is no limit in the Act, and the Registrar has no means of controlling the number of investors or the amount of money invested in the mortgage brokerage system.
- To impose a duty of care would be to effectively create an insurance scheme for investors at great cost to the taxpaying public.

2) *Edwards v. Law Society of Upper Canada*

Edwards v. Law Society of Upper Canada[82] was released as a companion case to *Cooper*, and was also written by the chief justice and Major J. This case was a proposed class action by individual investors allegedly victimized by a gold delivery fraud in which the investors deposited money to a lawyer's trust account pursuant to a "Gold Delivery Contract." No gold was delivered, the investors were out $9 million, and they claimed against the Law Society for damages. The solicitor had written to the Law Society with respect to the trust account improprieties, and the Law Society commenced an investigation. The investors claimed the Law Society had a duty to ensure the solicitor operated his trust account according to regulations once it became aware of the improprieties or, alternatively, to warn the investors that it had "chosen to abandon its supervisory jurisdiction."[83] Again, the Court found there was insufficient proximity, no *prima facie* duty of care, and even if there had been a *prima facie* duty it would have been negated by residual policy considerations.

82 2001 SCC 80, [2001] 3 S.C.R. 562 [*Edwards*].

83 *Ibid.* at para. 3.

Once again, the Court held that the *Law Society Act* did not reveal any "legislative intent to expressly or by implication impose a private law duty on the Law Society on the facts of this case."[84] The Law Society's investigative and disciplinary powers over its members is geared to the protection of clients and thereby the public as a whole; it does not owe a private law duty of care to members of the public who deposit funds into a solicitor's trust account.

The Court noted that clients are protected and compensated through the Compensation Fund and Lawyers' Professional Indemnity Company insurance, which were means chosen to compensate for economic loss in lieu of the private tort duty.

The Court placed great weight on the statutory immunity clause, a typical clause providing that no action or other proceedings for damages shall be instituted "for any act done in good faith in the performance or intended performance of any duty or in the exercise or in the intended exercise of any power" or "any neglect or default in the performance or exercise in good faith of any such duty or power."[85] The Court held that the good faith immunity clause "precludes any inference of an intention to provide compensation in circumstances that fall outside the lawyers' professional indemnity insurance and the lawyers' fund for client compensation."[86]

3) *Finney v. Barreau du Quebec*

The Supreme Court's 2004 decision in *Finney v. Barreau du Quebec*[87] involved a different Law Society, and a very different result. Notwithstanding a good faith statutory immunity clause, the Barreau was found liable for what was essentially gross regulatory negligence in failing to act with diligence to suspend a rogue lawyer from practice. The significant facts were the delay by the Barreau in responding to the lawyer's incompetence, egregious conduct issues brought to the Barreau's attention regarding his performance, and complaints made by the individual plaintiff to whom damages were awarded.

A brief chronology of the Law Society's relations with the lawyer and the plaintiff help illustrate the factors that led the Court to find the Barreau liable to pay damages in this case:

---

84 *Ibid.* at para. 13.

85 *Law Society Act*, R.S.O. 1990, c. L.8, s. 9; *Edwards*, above note 82 at para. 16.

86 *Edwards, ibid.* at para. 17.

87 2004 SCC 36 [*Finney*].

1978	B. called to the bar of Quebec
1981–87	Barreau finds B. guilty on three occasions of disciplinary offences.
1985	Inspection Committee initiates investigation into B.'s competence (five years to complete investigation).
1990	Inspection Committee report to the Executive Committee that B. is incompetent; recommends that B.'s right to practise be suspended, and he be required to redo his bar training.
1992	Executive Committee does not suspend B. After a hearing, it instead directs he take a refresher course and practise law under a tutor (supervising lawyer).
1991–93	Christina Finney, a schoolteacher, and her lawyer file several complaints against B. with Barreau, and complain to oversight body re delay of Barreau.
1993	Due to B.'s flurry of unmeritorious litigation, Superior Court in Quebec summons all parties including a Barreau representative, and Court orders any proceeding brought by B. to be subject to a special review.
1993	B's tutor (supervising lawyer) resigns.
1993	Oversight body asks Barreau about the delay in dealing with complaints.
1994	Lawyer acting for Finney's son complains to Barreau about B.'s actions; the son is not interviewed until 1996.
1994	B. is provisionally struck off the rolls in relation to twenty-three counts.
1996	Finney commences action in damages against Barreau for breach of its obligation to protect the public in handling of complaints against B.
1998	B. is struck off the rolls for five years (retroactively to 1994) after being found guilty on seventeen counts by Discipline Committee.

The Court of Appeal found that the lawyer, Belhassen, posed a "grave and imminent danger to the public" and the Barreau was aware of this danger. The Court found the delay between the complaints in early 1993 and striking him provisionally off the rolls in 1994 was "unacceptable and inexcusable."

The Barreau was protected by a good faith immunity clause. The Supreme Court of Canada held that "gross or serious carelessness is incompatible with good faith"[88] and that an immunity provision is intended to give

88 *Ibid.* at para. 40.

professional regulators the scope, latitude, and discretion they need in order to perform their duties. It is not meant to exclude liability for gross carelessness or serious negligence, the standard it found the Barreau to have met. The "virtually complete absence of the diligence" required in the situation meant the Barreau did not meet the standards of its fundamental mandate, which is to protect the public.

Justice LeBel for the Court held:

> The attitude exhibited by the Barreau, in a clearly urgent situation in which a practising lawyer represented a real danger to the public, was one of such negligence and indifference that it cannot claim the immunity conferred by s. 193. The serious carelessness it displayed amounts to bad faith, and it is liable for the results. [89]

The Supreme Court emphasized that the case was not restricted to the Quebec *Civil Code*, stating that the Barreau would have been liable under the analysis set out in *Cooper* and *Edwards*. The Court concluded by stating:

> The decisions made by the Barreau were operational decisions and were made in a relationship of proximity with a clearly identified complainant, where the harm was foreseeable. The common law would have been no less exacting than Quebec law on this point.[90]

In the result, the Court awarded Ms. Finney damages for moral injury, assessed at $25,000, together with costs on a solicitor–client basis.

4) *Syl Apps Secure Treatment Centre v. B.D.*

In *Syl Apps Secure Treatment Centre v. B.D.*,[91] Abella J. for the Court upheld the striking out of a negligence claim against a treatment centre and a social worker on the grounds of proximity, statutory immunity, and residual policy considerations. A teenager was removed from the home and placed in a treatment centre because of alleged parental abuse. The family sued the Children's Aid Society, the treatment centre, and the social worker for wrongly depriving them of their relationship with their child, in part based on the relevant statute which recognized the importance of family relationships.

The Supreme Court found that there was insufficient proximity given the governing statute. The primary objective of the legislation is protection

89 *Ibid.* at para. 43.
90 *Ibid.* at para. 46.
91 2007 SCC 38, [2007] 3 S.C.R. 83 [*Syl Apps*].

of the best interests of the child. Recognition of the private law duty of care to the parents raised a potential for conflicting duties, and the legislative intent embodied in the statutory scheme had primacy. The Court states:

> The deciding factor for me, as in *Cooper* and *Edwards*, is the potential for conflicting duties: imposing a duty of care on the relationship between the family of a child in care and that child's court-ordered service providers, creates a genuine potential for "serious and significant" conflict with the service providers' transcendent statutory duty to promote the best interests, protection and well-being of the children in their care.[92]

Other relevant factors negating a duty were administrative remedies available to the family and the statutory immunity provisions.

5) *Hill v. Hamilton-Wentworth Regional Police Services Board*

The chief justice's majority decision in 2007 in *Hill v. Hamilton-Wentworth Regional Police Services Board*[93] is significant in that the Court recognized a new category of relationship sufficiently proximate to give rise to a duty of care—police officer/suspect under investigation—and a new tort: the tort of negligent investigation.

In the proximity analysis, the Court identified a "personal, close and direct" relationship between an officer and a specific suspect. Another important consideration was the interest of the suspect; there was no personal representation or reliance at issue. Rather, the Court emphasized that the targeted suspect's interests at stake included "his freedom, his reputation and how he may spend a good portion of his life," noting that these "high interests" support a finding of proximate relationship.[94]

Other factors included the lack of existing alternative remedies, the public interest in ensuring that appropriate investigations are undertaken given the serious problems of wrongful convictions and institutionalized racism, and the expectation that the duty would be consistent with the values underlying the *Charter of Rights and Freedoms*.

The Court carefully considered a number of arguments raised to negate the duty of care, including the argument that a duty of care to an individual suspect conflicted with the police's overarching public duty to prevent crime. The Court limited the scope of the conflict argument as follows:

---

92 *Ibid.* at para. 41.

93 2007 SCC 41, [2007] 3 S.C.R. 129 [*Hill*].

94 *Ibid.* at para. 34.

> A *prima facie* duty of care will be negated only when the conflict, considered together with other relevant policy considerations, gives rise to a real potential for negative policy consequences. This reflects the view that a duty of care in tort law should not be denied on speculative grounds.[95]

The Court considered and rejected a number of policy arguments raised to negate the duty of care at Stage 2 of the *Anns* test:

- the "quasi-judicial" nature of police duties;
- the potential for conflict with other police duties;
- the discretion inherent in police work;
- the potential for a chilling effect on the investigation of crime; and
- flood of litigation.

The standard of care was held to be that of a reasonable police officer in similar circumstances, applied in a manner that gives due recognition to the discretion inherent in police investigation. The Court found that the investigation met the standard in light of police practices at the time. This case is of obvious concern to all agencies that perform investigations.

6) *Holland v. Saskatchewan*

The chief justice's 2008 decision in *Holland v. Saskatchewan*[96] is of particular interest to administrative law lawyers, illustrating the relationship between administrative law remedies and civil liability. A group of game farmers refused to register in a federal program aimed at preventing chronic wasting disease (CWD), because they objected to a broadly worded indemnification and release clause in the registration form. As a result of their refusal to sign the form, the game farmers lost the CWD-free herd certification level previously obtained by them under provincial rules, before the merging of the federal and provincial programs. As a result of the downgrading of certification, both their ability to market their game and the price of their product was reduced, causing a financial loss to the farmers.

The farmers initially commenced an application for judicial review, and established that the impugned indemnification and release clauses had been invalidly included on the registration form. The Queen's Bench judge on judicial review found that the minister had no legislative authority to make acceptance of these clauses a condition to participate in the CWD program.

95 *Ibid.* at para. 43.

96 2008 SCC 42 [*Holland*].

The applications judge declared that if the applicants otherwise met the certification program conditions, the court's declarations would "serve to remove the earlier impediments," that is, the offending indemnification and release provisions. The government did not appeal from the judicial review decision.

However, even though the applications judge had declared that the government's reduction of the herd status was invalid, the government did not take steps to reconsider the farmers' certification or compensate the farmers for lost revenue. The farmers commenced a class action; at the Supreme Court of Canada the issue was whether the negligence claim could proceed.

To the extent that the claim alleged failure to comply with a statutory duty—that the government and its employees were under a duty of care to ensure the statute and regulations were administered in accordance with law and not to operate in breach of them—the Court held that there is no cause of action in tort, citing *Saskatchewan Wheat Pool*.[97] However, the Court upheld the claim to the extent that it was a claim for "negligent failure to implement an adjudicative decree."[98] The chief justice held:

> Policy decisions about what acts to perform under a statute do not give rise to liability in negligence. On the other hand, once a decision to act has been made, the government may be liable in negligence for the manner in which it *implements* that decision . . . . Public authorities are expected to implement a judicial decision. Consequently, implementation of a judicial decision is an "operational" act. It is therefore not clear that an action in negligence cannot succeed on the breach of a duty to implement a judicial decree.[99]

Whether the citizens of Canada would agree that it makes sense that there will be no tort liability where the government decides not to operate in accordance with laws, but there be will for failure to implement a Court order, is best left to another day.

A review of this jurisprudence highlights the state of "lamentable confusion" of this area of the law. While the Court appears to refer to a consistent set of principles in their analysis, the application of those principles to the facts has been inconsistent. The governing legislation will normally feature prominently in the analysis, as will any potential for conflicting duties. What remains unclear, and therefore leads to uncertainty, is the weight

97 *Ibid.* at paras. 8–9.

98 *Ibid.* at para. 12.

99 *Ibid.* at para. 14.

that will be accorded to these factors. The somewhat murky area of "residual policy considerations" further adds to the unpredictability of this area of the law. As was the case with respect to the Court's treatment of issues of procedural fairness, here too the Court has been reluctant to establish bright line tests that would give an element of stability and clarity to an area that is currently lacking in both.

G. THE UNITED KINGDOM: POTENTIAL LEGISLATIVE SOLUTIONS

It is interesting to note that in the United Kingdom, the Law Commission engaged in an extensive consultation process with respect to "Administrative Redress: Public Bodies and the Citizen."[100] The consultation paper addresses the question of when and how should an individual be able to obtain redress from a public body that has acted in a substandard manner.

The consultation starts from the premise that "in principle, claimants should be entitled to obtain redress for loss caused by clearly substandard administrative action," with special consideration given to the role played by public bodies in considering when and on what terms they should be liable. The consultation encompasses the "four pillars" of redress:

- internal mechanisms of redress (complaint procedures);
- external non-court avenues of redress (public inquiries, tribunals);
- public sector ombudsmen; and
- remedies available in public and private law by way of court action.

What is particularly interesting is the Law Commission's approach to negligence. They start from the premise that

> In private law, we consider that the current situation is unsustainable. The uncertain and unprincipled nature of negligence in relation to public bodies, coupled with the unpredictable expansion of liability over recent years, has led to a situation that serves neither claimants nor public bodies.[101]

The United Kingdom has encountered problems similar to those now evident in Canada. The Law Commission suggests a specialized scheme for negligence in "truly public" activities that would require a showing of

100 The Law Commission, *Consultation Paper No. 187, Administrative Redress: Public Bodies and the Citizen* (17 June 2008). The response to the Consultation Paper was "overwhelmingly negative," and the Law Commission did not pursue the project.

101 *Ibid.* at 3.

serious substandard administrative action, and would recognize the wide range of competing demands on public bodies. They also suggested a modification of joint and several liability in public law as it applies to public bodies. The failure in regulatory oversight is usually not the direct cause of the claimant's loss (see Bernie Madoff, for example), but the public body may have to bear the loss in its entirety. The Law Commission encountered significant opposition by many parties, particularly the government. Given the opposition and lack of evidence, the Law Commission ultimately decided not to pursue legislative reform.

It may be that rather than the hit and miss of litigation, a more principled and comprehensive approach such as that presented in the United Kingdom would be beneficial, both for plaintiffs and for regulated bodies increasingly uncertain as to the potential for exposure to liability.

H. CONCLUSION

The Supreme Court has spent much of the last decade grappling with the standard of review, to the detriment of the development of procedural fairness jurisprudence. However, administrative tribunals and justice seekers will benefit from a return to procedural fairness and a focus on the foundation of the administrative justice system.

The chief justice has challenged administrative decision makers to provide "fair procedures, equitable treatment, and responsiveness to the public." Liability for regulatory negligence may well assist in achieving this goal. However, the present state of the law is confusing. It is difficult to find the right balance in the modern regulatory state between protecting the rights of citizens and providing the necessary scope for government action. Predictability as to the outcome will assist administrative bodies in establishing procedures to avoid liability (and benefit the regulated public). Legislative reforms which would provide a principled systemic basis for redress for substandard administrative action, such as those proposed in the UK Law Commission consultation, should be considered in Canada in the future if the courts are unable to establish a clear and predictable standard for regulatory negligence.

In Search of Coherence: The *Charter* and Administrative Law under the McLachlin Court

SUSAN L. GRATTON AND LORNE SOSSIN*

With her appointment as chief justice, Madame Justice McLachlin inherited one of the most exasperating analytical tangles in modern public law. When an alleged *Charter* violation occurs as a result of an administrative decision, should the judicial review analysis proceed on *Charter* principles or administrative law principles? Both analytical avenues engage rich bodies of jurisprudence designed to check government action where it impairs individual interests. Both number among the Supreme Court's most celebrated doctrinal innovations of the last three decades. And both have strong purchase for legal experts of each field examining public law problems through the lens of their respective traditions. However, these two analytical avenues sit uncomfortably alongside one another.[1] Whenever administrative decision making is involved in the alleged breach of *Charter* rights, the Court must make a preliminary choice as to the analysis to be pursued and this choice, in turn, determines the range of public law remedies available.[2]

---

* This paper is based, in part, on a presentation by Lorne Sossin, prepared for the Canadian Bar Association conference, *The McLachlin Court's First Ten Years: Reflections of the Past and Projections of the Future*, held in Ottawa, Canada, 19 June 2009.

1 While a number of constitutional law and administrative law scholars have discussed the relationship between administrative law and *Charter* principles as an issue incidental to their field, few scholars have focused on the relationship itself as their area of scholarly inquiry. For a notable exception, see Nicolas Lambert, *The Impact of the Charter of Rights and Freedoms on Canadian Administrative Law* (D.C.L. Dissertation, McGill University, 2004).

2 For example, should the Court approach the case first through administrative law with its attendant remedies and examine the *Charter* only if the matter cannot be resolved by administrative law (as occurred in *Baker v. Canada (Minister of Citizenship and Immigration),*

This uneasy relationship between administrative law and the *Charter* has surfaced more frequently in recent years as *Charter* jurisprudence has matured and possible *Charter* violations are weeded out of proposed legislation and regulations before they are ever enacted.[3] *Charter* violations are more likely to arise as a result of discretionary administrative action rather than appearing explicitly in the wording of a legislative or regulatory enactment.

The analytical tension between *Charter* review and administrative law review gives rise, in turn, to more fundamental questions about the values informing public law. Was the introduction of the *Charter* intended to nourish administrative law values? During the McLachlin Court's tenure, a strong argument for the coordination and, ultimately, the unity of public law values has taken hold in the scholarly literature.[4] According to this theory, both areas of law are gradually merging into a unified concern for protecting individual interests from the abuse of public power.[5] Or, alternatively, is administrative law restricted to matters of statutory authority and jurisdiction, with the *Charter* alone devoted to the protection of substantive rights and freedoms?[6] The McLachlin Court inherited an ongoing search for coherence on both these levels: analytical coherence in administrative review versus *Charter* review, as well as coherence in the underlying values that inform public law in the post-*Charter* era.

In their decisions up to and including *Multani v. Commission scolaire Marguerite-Bourgeoys*, the judges of the McLachlin Court engaged in ongoing dissension over both the analytical relationship between administrative law review and *Charter* review, and the unity of public law thesis.[7] In its most recent decision on point, *Canadian Federation of Students v. Greater Vancouver Transportation Authority*, the Court has adopted a new approach to the

---

[1999] 2 S.C.R. 817 [*Baker*]), or should it adopt a *Charter* analysis with its attendant remedies and only examine administrative law if the matter cannot be resolved under the *Charter* (as occurred in *Blencoe v. British Columbia (Human Rights Commission)*, [2000] 2 S.C.R. 307 [*Blencoe*])?

3 See Lori Sterling, "The *Charter*'s Impact on the Legislative Process: Where the Real 'Dialogue' Takes Place" (2007–8) 23 N.J.C.L. 139.

4 See, for example, David Dyzenhaus, ed., *The Unity of Public Law* (Oxford: Hart, 2004).

5 This is the prevailing view of administrative law scholars. See, for example, Genevieve Cartier, "The *Baker* Effect: A New Interface between the *Canadian Charter of Rights and Freedoms* and Administrative Law—The Case of Discretion" in David Dyzenhaus, ed., *The Unity of Public Law* (Oxford: Hart, 2004) [Cartier, "The *Baker* Effect"].

6 This latter position is articulated in Susan L. Gratton, "Standing at the Divide: The Relationship between Administrative Law and the *Charter* Post-*Multani*" (2008) 53 McGill L.J. 477 [Gratton, "Standing at the Divide"].

7 *Multani v. Commission scolaire Marguerite-Bourgeoys*, 2006 SCC 6 [*Multani*].

RÉSUMÉ

Les auteurs examinent les efforts déployés par la Cour de madame le juge McLachlin en vue d'élaborer une approche fondée sur des principes pour analyser les relations entre le droit administratif et la *Charte* à deux niveaux distincts : soit l'analyse applicable à l'examen judiciaire des décisions administratives qui soulèvent des questions relatives à la *Charte* et les valeurs sous-jacentes engagées par ces deux branches du droit public. Les auteurs concluent que, bien que les efforts précédemment déployés en vue d'élaborer une cohérence analytique et conceptuelle n'aient pas réussi à susciter une adhésion durable parmi une majorité des membres de la Cour, des causes plus récentes démontrent que l'on met la priorité sur le consensus au détriment d'une cohérence conceptuelle à long terme.

problem and, in so doing, has achieved unanimity among all of its members.[8] Chief Justice McLachlin has a well-earned reputation as a talented consensus-builder and the Court has set the stage for a fundamental shift in our understanding of the relationship between the *Charter* and administrative law. However, it remains to be seen whether this latest approach is capable of achieving true coherence within modern public law.

Our analysis is divided into two parts. The first part tracks the Supreme Court's approach to the relationship between administrative law and the *Charter* prior to the McLachlin Court, while the second part examines the approach of the McLachlin Court. We conclude that the Court has yet to develop a workable and coherent approach to the relationship between the *Charter* and administrative law. The seeds of a possible solution have been sown with the *Vancouver Transit* decision but we suggest that, although this new approach has won short-term acceptance among the members of the McLachlin Court, it is unlikely to succeed in reconciling public law analysis and values over the long term.

8 *Canadian Federation of Students v. Greater Vancouver Transportation Authority*, 2009 SCC 31 [*Vancouver Transit*].

A. THE PRE-McLACHLIN COURT YEARS

In the early days of *Charter* jurisprudence, the Dickson Court staked out administrative discretion, exercised both by administrative tribunals and ministerial officials, as the site where the relationship between *Charter* and administrative law principles would have to be reconciled.[9] The *Charter* may justify intervention in administrative decisions in at least four different circumstances involving different degrees of discretion.[10]

First, a law granting discretion may be facially unconstitutional. For example, a law authorizing a tribunal to grant a benefit to a defined group creates a discretion which, by its very terms, might violate section 15 of the *Charter* if it necessarily excludes another group from the benefit based on one of the enumerated grounds. This is analogous to *M. v. H.*, in which a provision of the *Ontario Family Law Act* was held to be discriminatory since it granted courts the discretion to award spousal support only to heterosexual spouses and not to same-sex couples.[11]

The second circumstance involves a law granting discretion which is not facially unconstitutional, but might nevertheless be applied in an unconstitutional manner. For example, in *Eldridge v. British Columbia (A.G.).*, a law authorizing the Medical Services Commission to fund certain health services was found not to violate the *Charter*, but the exercise of discretion by that Commission, deciding not to fund interpreters for deaf patients, was found to be unconstitutional.[12]

In the third circumstance, a law granting wide discretionary authority without sufficient guidance as to its application, or without safeguards against arbitrary conduct, might violate the procedural component of section 7 of the *Charter*. This basis for challenging discretion was relied upon by the majority of the Supreme Court in *R. v. Morgentaler*.[13] In *Morgentaler*, the impugned provision was a law prohibiting abortion unless a physician determined that the life or health of a woman was endangered. The pro-

9 See, in particular, *Slaight Communications Inc. v. Davidson*, [1989] 1 S.C.R. 1038 [*Slaight*] and *Ross v. New Brunswick School District No. 15*, [1996] 1 S.C.R. 825 [*Ross*]. Portions of this analysis are drawn from Lorne Sossin, "Discretion Unbound: Reconciling the *Charter* and Soft Law" (2003) 45 Canadian Public Administration 465–89.

10 In most cases, the grounds for a *Charter* challenge in administrative discretion cases are provided by violations of ss. 2, 7, or 15 but the unconstitutional exercise of discretion might also be located elsewhere under the *Charter*.

11 *M. v. H.*, [1999] 2 S.C.R. 3.

12 *Eldridge v. British Columbia (A.G.)*, [1997] 3 S.C.R. 624.

13 *R. v. Morgentaler*, [1988] 1 S.C.R. 30.

cedures which therapeutic abortion committees established in hospitals to decide whether this threshold was met in individual cases were found by the majority to lack coherence, predictability, and fairness.

Fourth, a law granting a discretion that is too vague to provide sufficient notice to those who might infringe it might violate the substantive component of section 7.[14] As David Mullan has observed, "Where the line is actually to be drawn between overly broad discretionary power and permissible undefined discretion, nonetheless, remains a highly speculative exercise."[15] In *R. v. Morales*, for example, the Court held that a provision granting pre-trial detention where it was justified in "the public interest" was unconstitutionally vague.[16]

These four bases on which administrative discretion may be attacked under the *Charter* are by no means exhaustive. Further, the line dividing a vague discretion from a precise one is by no means clear. The difficulty in distinguishing among laws authorizing varying degrees of discretion has, itself, caused much confusion in the caselaw.[17]

The Supreme Court's first detailed examination of the relationship between the *Charter* and administrative discretion was in *Slaight Communications Inc. v. Davidson*.[18] At issue in that case was a remedial discretion in the *Canada Labour Code*.[19] The grievance in *Slaight* concerned an allegation of wrongful dismissal. The adjudicator found that the dismissal had been wrongful and ordered the company to first, provide the employee with a factual reference and, second, to refrain from expressing any other views about the employee. Chief Justice Dickson for the majority of the Court chose to conduct a *Charter* analysis and held that neither aspect of the adjudicator's order violated the *Charter*. Justice Lamer (as he then was) dissented in part in the case. He reasoned that recourse to the *Charter* was unnecessary since the impugned order preventing the company from expressing an opinion beyond that contained in the reference letter was patently unreasonable and therefore should be quashed on administrative law grounds. However, Lamer J. wrote for the Court on the issue of the proper

---

14 See generally *R. v. Nova Scotia Pharmaceutical Society*, [1992] 2 S.C.R. 606.

15 David Mullan, *Administrative Law* (Toronto: Irwin Law , 2001) at 127.

16 *R. v. Morales*, [1992] 3 S.C.R. 711.

17 Gratton, "Standing at the Divide," above note 6.

18 *Slaight*, above note 9. On the significance of *Slaight*, see June Ross, "Applying the *Charter* to Discretionary Authority" (1991) 29:2 Alta. L. Rev. 382.

19 R.S.C. 1985, c. L-2.

approach to discretionary decision making under the *Charter*. He identified two kinds of discretion, each of which led to different remedies under the *Charter*:

1. The exercise of discretion was made pursuant to legislation which confers, either expressly or by necessary implication, the power to infringe a protected *Charter* right.
   - It is then necessary to subject the legislation to the test set out in s. 1 by ascertaining whether it constitutes a reasonable limit that can be demonstrably justified in a free and democratic society.
2. The legislation pursuant to which the exercise of administrative discretion was made confers an imprecise discretion and does not confer, either expressly or by necessary implication, the power to limit the rights guaranteed by the *Charter*.
   - It is then necessary to subject the order made to the test set out in s. 1 by ascertaining whether it constitutes a reasonable limit that can be demonstrably justified in a free and democratic society.[20]

In the circumstances of *Slaight*, the Court found that the *Code* did not require expressly or by necessary implication that a *Charter* right be infringed; therefore the *Code* created an imprecise discretion which permitted a *Charter* right to be limited. Thus, it was the order, and not the legislation, which must be subject to *Charter* scrutiny.[21]

The central holding of *Slaight* was that no public official could be authorized by a statute to breach the *Charter* and therefore, all discretionary authority had to be read down to authorize only decision making that is consistent with *Charter* rights and guarantees. Justice Lamer explained this reasoning in the following terms:

> The adjudicator is a statutory creature: he is appointed pursuant to a legislative provision and derives all his powers from the statute. As the Constitution is the supreme law of Canada and any law that is inconsistent with its provisions is, to the extent of the inconsistency, of no force or effect, it is impossible to interpret legislation conferring discretion as conferring a power to infringe the *Charter*, unless, of course, that power is expressly conferred or necessarily implied. Such an interpretation would

20 *Slaight*, above note 9 at para. 91.

21 The majority found that, while both the positive and the negative order violated the freedom of expression under s. 2(b) of the *Charter*, each was a reasonable limit under s. 1 and therefore the orders were upheld.

> require us to declare the legislation to be of no force or effect, unless it could be justified under s. 1. Although this court must not add anything to legislation or delete anything from it, in order to make it consistent with the *Charter*, there is no doubt in my mind that it should also not interpret legislation that is open to more than one interpretation so as to make it inconsistent with the *Charter* and hence of no force or effect. Legislation conferring an imprecise discretion must therefore be interpreted as not allowing the *Charter* rights to be infringed. Accordingly, an adjudicator exercising delegated powers does not have the power to make an order that would result in an infringement of the *Charter* and he exceeds his jurisdiction if he does so.[22]

Thus, discretionary authority always comes with an implied condition, which is that it be exercised in a manner consistent with all applicable *Charter* rights.

Beyond the articulation of this inaugural principle, *Slaight* left a great deal of work to be done in developing coherent approaches to the various points at which the *Charter* and administrative law may intersect. Chief Justice Dickson remarked that the "precise relationship" between the *Charter* and administrative law would be worked out in future cases, in the incremental tradition of the common law.

The principle in *Slaight* was applied by the Lamer Court in *Ross v. New Brunswick School District No. 15*.[23] In *Ross*, the Supreme Court upheld certain remedial orders made by a Human Rights Tribunal against a school board which had failed to discipline a teacher for his discriminatory behaviour. The Court responded both to administrative law and *Charter* challenges by noting that, while the two types of review differed (principally in the application of section 1 to *Charter* breaches), there was significant overlap in the analyses. Applying *Slaight*, the Court held that if a discretionary act was upheld as reasonable under section 1, it was inconceivable that it could also be held to be patently unreasonable.[24]

The Lamer Court took the *Slaight* principle one step further in *Eaton v. Brant County Board of Education*.[25] In that case, Arbour J.A. (as she then was), writing for the Ontario Court of Appeal, held a provision of the *Ontario Education Act* to be unconstitutional because it failed to prohibit certain

---

22 *Ibid.* at 1077–78.

23 *Ross*, above note 9.

24 *Ibid.* at paras. 31–32.

25 *Eaton v. Brant County of Education*, [1997] 1 S.C.R. 241.

exercises of a statutory discretion relating to the placement of special needs children in public schools. Chief Justice Lamer, concurring with the disposition of the majority on the *Charter* issue, took issue with Arbour J.A.'s application of *Slaight*.[26] Chief Justice Lamer reiterated that a legislative provision could not be invalidated for failing to proscribe certain kinds of discretionary decision making, since any legislative silence had to be interpreted in a fashion consistent with the *Charter*. Therefore, discretionary authority is not required to expressly prohibit unconstitutional conduct in order to comply with the *Charter*.

This was the state of affairs when McLachlin C.J. was appointed to head up the Court in January 2000. The relationship between the *Charter* and administrative law had been dealt with mainly on an *ad hoc* basis, in response to issues raised by the particular cases before the Court. Little progress had been made in developing a comprehensive approach to the analytical choice to be made in these cases. Certainly, no consensus had developed on the proper relationship among administrative law values and those of the *Charter*. The McLachlin Court assumed the burden of taking the next step in the search for coherence.

B. THE McLACHLIN COURT

The McLachlin Court was exposed to the *Charter*-administrative law quandary early in its tenure with its decision in *Little Sisters Book and Art Emporium v. Canada (Minister of Justice)*.[27] At issue was the discretionary authority of customs officials to seize imported goods which met the obscenity test under section 163 of the *Criminal Code*.[28] Parliament simply incorporated the

---

26 *Ibid.* at paras. 1–4.

27 *Little Sisters Book and Art Emporium v. Canada (Minister of Justice)*, [2000] 2 S.C.R. 1120 [*Little Sisters*]. The McLachlin Court had an even earlier taste of the problem in *Blencoe*. The majority chose not to deal with it in any depth but simply adopted a *Charter* analysis without explanation. In contrast, a four member minority, led by LeBel J., did address the analytical issue. The minority argued, instead, in favour of an administrative law analysis, stating: "Assuming that the *Charter* must solve every legal problem would be a recipe for freezing and sterilizing the natural and necessary evolution of the common law and of the civil law in this country" (at para. 189).

28 This section of the *Criminal Code* states, "(8) For the purposes of this Act, any publication a dominant characteristic of which is the undue exploitation of sex, or of sex and any one or more of the following subjects, namely, crime, horror, cruelty and violence, shall be deemed to be obscene."

term "obscenity" from the *Criminal Code* and left it up to customs officials to elaborate, refine, and apply the term in the context of imported material.[29]

Little Sisters is a lesbian and gay bookshop in Vancouver. Its owners claimed that their *Charter* rights were violated by the targeting actions of customs officers in seizing material which Little Sisters sought to import across the border. Justice Binnie, writing for the majority, characterized the administration of the *Customs Act* by customs officers as oppressive and dismissive of the appellants' freedom of expression. He concluded that the effect—whether intended or not—was to isolate and disparage the appellants on the basis of their sexual orientation.

The Court recognized that a source of the targeting of Little Sisters lay in the Operations Manual (Memorandum D9-1-1) relied upon by customs officials. Notwithstanding the evidence that customs officers followed the manual in virtually every instance, Binnie J. was unwilling to subject this non-legislative instrument to *Charter* scrutiny. He reasoned:

> the trial judge put too much weight on the Memorandum, which was nothing more than an internal administrative aid to Customs inspectors. It was not law . . . . It is the statutory decision . . . , not the manual, that constituted the denial. It is simply not feasible for the courts to review for *Charter* compliance the vast array of manuals and guides prepared by the public service for the internal guidance of officials. The courts are concerned with the legality of the decisions, not the quality of the guidebooks, although of course the fate of the two are not unrelated.[30]

The Court also held that, although the exercise of discretion by customs officers violated the *Charter*, the *Customs Act* provision authorizing this conduct did not. Following the *Slaight* approach, the majority of the Court characterized the discretion contained in the customs legislation as capable of being applied in a fashion consistent with the *Charter*. Therefore, the majority saw no basis to strike down the authority of customs officials to seize material on the grounds of obscenity.

Justice Iacobucci, writing for himself and two other members of the Court, dissented on this point. He held that the legislation itself was unconstitutional since it did not contain sufficient safeguards against un-

29 Section 99 of the *Customs Act* empowers officials to seize material set out in Customs Tariff, S.C. 1987, c. 49, Schedule VII, which includes, *inter alia*, 9,956 books, printed paper, drawings, paintings, prints, photographs or representations of any kind that are deemed to be obscene under s. 163(8) of the *Criminal Code*.

30 *Little Sisters*, above note 27 at para. 85.

constitutional enforcement. For the minority, simply trusting the customs bureaucracy to improve its administration of the Act was not enough. Justice Iacobucci argued contrary to the philosophy of *Slaight*:

> This Court's precedents demand sufficient safeguards in the legislative scheme itself to ensure that government action will not infringe constitutional rights. In the face of an extensive record of unconstitutional application, it is not enough merely to provide a structure that could be applied in a constitutional manner. This is particularly the case where fundamental *Charter* rights, such as the right to free expression, are at stake. The legislation itself must provide an adequate process to ensure that *Charter* rights are respected when the legislation is applied at the administrative level.[31]

With the dichotomous reasons of the majority and minority in *Little Sisters*, the McLachlin Court assumed responsibility for the analytical and conceptual tension created by the *Charter*'s arrival within modern public law. The complexity of the problem and the diversity of opinions held by Court members may well have dissuaded the Court from tackling the issue too early in its tenure. Whatever the case, the Court shied away from expressly considering the issue in spite of the opportunity offered by *Suresh v. Canada (Minister of Citizenship and Immigration)*.[32]

Suresh concerned the discretionary authority of the minister to deport refugees in circumstances where they faced the possibility of torture.[33] Suresh challenged the minister's deportation order on both *Charter* and administrative law grounds. A unanimous Court conducted both a *Charter* review of the enabling provision and an administrative review of the minister's decision pursuant to that provision, in turn, without enquiring whether these two analyses were internally coherent. This two-pronged approach led the Court into conceptual contradiction. On the one hand, the Court held that, under administrative law principles, the minister's decision was entitled to judicial deference. On the other hand, applying *Charter*

---

31 *Ibid.* at para. 204.

32 *Suresh v. Canada (Minister of Citizenship and Immigration)*, [2002] 1 S.C.R. 3 [*Suresh*]; see, generally, David W. Elliott, "*Suresh* and the Common Borders of Administrative Law: Time for the Tailor?" (2002) 65 Sask. L.R. 469.

33 Paragraph 53(1)(b) of the *Immigration Act* gave the minister limited discretion to deport where the refugee's "life or freedom would be threatened" if she was returned to her country; and the minister's belief that the refugee constituted "a danger to the security of Canada."

principles, the Court undertook its own interpretation of the legislation in the abstract to determine its constitutionality. If the minister, as statutory decision maker, is truly entitled to judicial deference, why should this deferential attitude not extend to the minister's own interpretation of her enabling authority? Furthermore, should not this interpretation be informed by the particular facts before the minister, rather than being carried out by the Court in a factual vacuum? The Court reasoned simply that "[t]he issues of the constitutionality of the deportation provisions of the *Immigration Act* do not involve review of ministerial decision-making."[34] But, surely, the constitutionality of her enabling authority *was* one of the matters that the minister was obliged to consider in making her decision, particularly post-*Slaight* where she was required to interpret her authority consistently with the *Charter.*

This conceptual confusion in the Court's reasoning is further illustrated by the Court's comments about the respective roles of the minister and the reviewing court in such cases:

> The Minister's task is to make a decision that conforms to Parliament's criteria and procedures as well as the Constitution. The court's task, if called upon to review the Minister's decision, is to determine whether the Minister has exercised her decision-making power within the constraints imposed by Parliament's legislation and the Constitution. If the Minister has considered the appropriate factors in conformity with these constraints, the court must uphold her decision.[35]

In this passage, the Court clearly recognized that its reviewing role should be carried out *in relation to* the minister's decision. But given the holistic nature of the exercise of ministerial discretion, and the inherent difficulty in parsing such a decision into its constituent factors, the Court's review risked becoming an artificial exercise driven by the result which the Court wished to find.

In 2006 with its decision in *Multani,* the McLachlin Court made its first effort to develop a more comprehensive approach to this dilemma.[36] *Multani* involved the discretionary decision of a school board to prohibit a Sikh stu-

34 *Suresh,* above note 32 at para. 27.

35 *Ibid.* at para. 38.

36 Other earlier judgments by the McLachlin Court raised the problematic relationship between administrative law and the *Charter,* but the Court did not expressly address the issue: *Trinity Western University v. British Columbia College of Teachers,* [2001] 1 S.C.R. 772 and *Chamberlain v. Surrey School District No. 36,* 2002 SCC 86, [2002] 4 S.C.R. 710.

dent from wearing his kirpan, a ceremonial dagger, to school. The student and his family challenged the decision as an infringement of his freedom of religion. The Supreme Court was unanimous in allowing the challenge and striking down the board's decision but it split 6:2 on whether a *Charter* or administrative law analysis should be applied in reaching this result.

Madame Justice Charron for the majority adopted a *Charter* analysis since the central issue in the case was whether or not the board's decision complied with the requirements of the *Charter*. Her approach was a pragmatic one:

> [I]t is of little importance to Gurbaj Singh—who wants to exercise his freedom of religion—whether the absolute prohibition against wearing a kirpan in his school derives from the actual wording of a normative rule or merely from the application of such a rule.[37]

In contrast, Deschamps and Abella JJ. for the minority argued that an administrative law analysis should be conducted instead of a *Charter* analysis because the instrument being assessed by the Court was an administrative decision rather than a "norm of general application" such as "a law, regulation, or other similar rule of general application."[38]

Although the result in *Multani* was unanimous, the stark divide in the majority and concurring minority opinions revealed that the McLachlin Court was engaged in rethinking earlier efforts towards analytical coherence. The opinions did, however, serve to crystallize two clear choices to the dilemma.[39] The majority approach, authored by Charon J., was a purposive one—the choice between administrative law review and *Charter* review would be made according to the purpose of the judicial review exercise before the court. Cases calling into question the statutory authority of an administrative decision maker would be analyzed under administrative law principles but cases

37 *Multani*, above note 7 at para. 21. The majority (Charron, McLachlin C.J., Bastarache, Binnie, and Fish JJ.) held that the board's decision infringed the student's freedom of religion under s. 2(a) of the *Charter* and that the infringement could not be justified under s. 1. Justice LeBel wrote a separate opinion agreeing with the majority that a *Charter* analysis was appropriate but proposing that the s. 1 analysis should be modified in cases involving administrative discretion (at paras. 140–55).

38 *Multani, ibid.* at paras. 103 and 85. The minority would have reviewed the board's decision on a standard of reasonableness and would have concluded that the decision was unreasonable in disregarding the student's freedom of religion.

39 These two approaches and an argument in favour of the purposive approach are developed in Gratton, "Standing at the Divide," above note 6.

alleging the violation of fundamental rights and freedoms would be subject to *Charter* analysis.[40]

At the level of public law values, the majority approach was a clear rejection of the unity of public law thesis which posits a substantive value-laden role for administrative law. For example, according to Genevieve Cartier, an administrative standard of review of reasonableness is "not limited to sanctioning formal legal limits to the exercise of discretion," but has a role to play "in the protection of rights and the consideration of values."[41] In contrast, the majority in *Multani* seemed determined to maintain the separate existence of administrative law and *Charter* values, as articulated in *Slaight*, and, more significantly, persisted in ascribing a formal role to the former. The majority defined the role of administrative law solely in terms of jurisdiction and warned against allowing the fundamental values protected by the *Charter* to be "dissolved" into "mere" administrative law principles.[42] The majority position appears either to be unaware of or to discount the significant substantive role of administrative law in supervising the exercise of discretion, and the exercise of public authority more broadly. It is difficult to reconcile the *Multani* majority's thin and one-dimensional view of administrative law with the robust view of administrative law animating earlier Supreme Court judgments, such as *Baker*.[43]

The concurring minority decision in *Multani*, authored by Deschamps and Abella JJ., took a dramatically different approach to the problem. Deschamps and Abella JJ. applied a categorical basis for choosing between a *Charter* or administrative law analysis—the determination of whether an administrative law or *Charter* analysis should be applied should be based on the type of governing instrument at play in the dispute. Administrative decisions should be subject to administrative law review, while the validity of laws should be subject to *Charter* review. At first glance, this approach is attractive from the point of view of coherence, and it would further the unity of public law thesis in the sense that administrative decisions would

40 Evan Fox-Decent refers to this as the orthodox approach in "The *Charter* and Administrative Law: Cross-Fertilization in Public Law" in Colleen M. Flood & Lorne Sossin, eds., *Administrative Law in Context* (Toronto: Emond Montgomery, 2008) at 182 [Fox-Decent, "The *Charter*"].

41 Cartier, "The *Baker* Effect," above note 5 at 73 and 75.

42 *Multani*, above note 7 at para. 16.

43 *Baker*, above note 2.

be dealt with through an administrative law analysis, but informed by substantive *Charter* values.[44]

Although the purposive approach carried the day in *Multani*, the strong minority opinion, along with scholarly critiques of the majority decision, meant that the McLachlin Court's search for coherence was not over.[45] How would it reconcile two such polarized approaches to the relationship between the *Charter* and administrative law? Furthermore, how could *Multani* be reconciled with *Suresh*? The decision in *Multani* to adopt a *Charter* analysis meant that no deference was accorded to the school board's decision that the kirpan was a "weapon or dangerous object" and, therefore, prohibited by the board's *Code de vie*. But, in *Suresh*, the Court's segmented approach allowed the court to apply a deferential administrative law standard of review to the more fact-intensive aspects of the minister's discretion.

The McLachlin Court tackled the relationship between the *Charter* and administrative law once more in *Vancouver Transit*. This time, some deft analytical moves succeeded in bringing the Court together in a new unified approach to the problem. The Court asserted the primacy of *Charter* review over administrative law review as preferred by the majority in *Multani*, while, at the same time, the Court shifted to the categorical analytical approach preferred by the minority in *Multani*. The result was unanimous agreement among the judges that the case should be decided by the application of *Charter* principles.[46] However, we suggest that the McLachlin Court may well have achieved this unanimity at the expense of analytical and conceptual coherence over the long term.

Vancouver Transit involved the refusal of transit authorities to post election advertisements on the side of their buses in accordance with their advertising policies. The students' federation alleged that these policies violated their right to freedom of expression under section 2(b) of the *Charter*. Madame Justice Deschamps, writing for a seven member majority, essentially side-stepped the quandary over the analytical path to be applied by characterizing the challenge as one directed at law rather than at the transit

44 Fox-Decent refers to this as the administrative law approach in "The *Charter*," above note 40 at 187.

45 See David Mullan, "Administrative Tribunals and Judicial Review of *Charter* Issues after *Multani*" (2006–2007) 21 N.J.C.L. 127 [Mullan, "After *Multani*"]; and Robert Leckey, "Prescribed by Law/Une règle de droit" (2007) 45 Osgoode Hall L.J. 571.

46 Justice Fish wrote a minority opinion but agreed with the majority decision to apply a *Charter* analysis.

authorities' decisions.[47] With this move, the Court proceeded directly to a *Charter* analysis, and found the restriction on advertising to violate section 2(b) of the *Charter*. The "laws" in issue were the transit authorities' advertising policies. Discussing whether the measures at issue were "prescribed by law" for purposes of the section 1 analysis, Deschamps J. reasoned that the policies deserved legal status since the transportation authorities were acting within their statutory authority in enacting them and they were binding rules of general application. She found that the restrictions could not be justified under section 1 and that a remedy under section 52(1) of the *Constitution Act, 1982*, was appropriate.

Vancouver Transit is a fascinating move in the McLachlin Court's search for coherence in public law. At first glance, the decision simply adds to the inconsistency in the Court's jurisprudence on the relationship between administrative and *Charter* review. But looking beyond this inconsistency, it is possible to see the beginnings of a new approach to their analytical relationship as well as to the coordination of public law values.

First the areas of inconsistency must be acknowledged. The Court chose not to acknowledge the dilemma that was raised by the opposing opinions in *Multani* but proceeded directly to a *Charter* analysis.[48] Tellingly, *Multani* was not mentioned by either the majority or minority in *Vancouver Transit*. And yet, the discrepancies between the two decisions are significant.

In *Multani*, the Court reasoned that Gurbaj Singh did not care (and should not have to care) whether or not the refusal to allow him to wear his kirpan derived from a normative rule or a decision applying that rule. Why, then, should it have been instrumental to the students' challenge in *Vancouver Transit* that the transit authorities' prohibition against election advertising was contained in a policy rather than in their decision to apply that policy? Presumably, the relevant factual distinction in these two decisions is that the school board policy in *Multani* did not explicitly prohibit kirpans but merely prohibited weapons or dangerous objects. Therefore,

---

47 Although the Court approached the issue through an analysis of the scope of the "prescribed by law" condition in s. 1 of the *Charter*, there is little doubt that the characterization of the transit authorities' policies as "laws" for this purpose will also impact the initial choice as to whether administrative law review or *Charter* review is appropriate in such cases. For a similar approach, see *Canadian Broadcasting Corp. v. Canada (Attorney General)*, 2011 SCC 2, where the Court held that a directive setting out rules for the use of public areas within courthouses was a "law" for the purposes of *Charter* analysis.

48 This is reminiscent of the McLachlin Court's earlier decisions in *Trinity Western* and *Chamberlain* where, again without acknowledging that there was any choice to be made, the Court proceeded directly to an administrative law analysis.

the board was required to do some interpretive work in applying the policy to the particular circumstances of the case before it. In this sense, the *Charter* limit in *Multani* was located in the decision rather than in the policy. On the other hand, in *Vancouver Transit* the transit authorities' policies explicitly prohibited political advertising. Therefore, the *Charter* limit was located within the policy itself and the transit authorities' decision to apply it was straightforward. However, even if this distinction reconciles the facts in *Vancouver Transit* with those in *Multani*, the reason *why* the McLachlin Court chose a *Charter* analysis in *Vancouver Transit* remains inconsistent with the reason why it did so in *Multani*.[49]

The Court presumably chose a *Charter* analysis in *Vancouver Transit* because it located the *Charter* limit in a "law" rather than in an administrative decision. But in *Multani*, the Court reasoned that this categorical distinction should not matter to the analysis chosen. Rather, the decision to pursue a *Charter* analysis should be based on the purpose of the judicial review exercise before the Court.

Nor did the Court in *Vancouver Transit* explain the sharp divergence in its reasoning from earlier decisions such as *Slaight* and *Little Sisters*. In *Slaight*, discussed above, the Court had held that a section 1 analysis under the *Charter* should be directed at legislation rather than an administrative decision made pursuant to the legislation only where the *Charter* limit was necessarily implicit in the legislation itself. Although the majority in *Vancouver Transit* purported to rely on *Slaight*, it was able to do so only by replacing the word "legislation," used by the Court in *Slaight*, with the word "law" in quotation marks. In point of fact, the legislation authorizing the policies in *Vancouver Transit* conferred broad discretion on the transportation authorities—a circumstance which, under the reasoning in *Slaight*, should have led the Court to focus on the authorities' decision, which arguably could have been read down to authorize only *Charter*-compliant interpretations and applications of the policy. Nevertheless, the *Slaight* case did not involve policy guidelines, and was not conceived with soft law instruments in mind.[50]

More significant was the Court's departure from the reasoning of the majority in *Little Sisters*. There, the majority refused to recognize as "law" the internal policy guidelines used by customs officials in carrying out

49 It is significant that the majority opinion in *Vancouver Transit* was written by Deschamps J. who was in the minority in *Multani*.

50 Laura Pottie & Lorne Sossin, "Demystifying the Boundaries of Public Law: Policy, Discretion, and Social Welfare" (2005) 38 U.B.C. L. Rev. 147 [Pottie & Sossin].

what was held to be their discriminatory behaviour.[51] However, the Court in *Vancouver Transit* reconciled its position with *Little Sisters* by drawing a distinction between "indoor management" policies not intended to create entitlements, as in *Little Sisters*, and legislative rules establishing rights and obligations of general rather than specific application.[52]

The Court's decision in *Vancouver Transit* to expand the concept of "law" to include some forms of administrative policy was an unprecedented move, although one which resonates with the need for legal accountability over discretionary decision making.[53] However, the Court's attempt to parse policy into formalist categories risks frustrating the goal of accountability and is potentially dangerous. Any policy with a meaningful influence over a discretionary decision should comply with the *Charter*—whether it is categorized as internal or external should not be relevant to the analysis. The Court must be alive to the reality of decision making from the vantage of the decision maker and the affected party. Where a decision maker relies on law, the Court's focus should be on the law. Where a decision maker relies on law and policy, the Court's focus should be on law and policy. Where the decision maker relies on internal directives, or ingrained practices, then those should be the focus. The search for clear, bright line distinctions in the context of discretion is ultimately not tenable.

The decision in *Vancouver Transit* to devote relatively little attention to the existing authorities may well be a signal that the McLachlin Court has decided to start from ground zero in building coherence in public law.[54] It has done so by structuring the relationship between the *Charter* and administrative law around two novel public law principles: first, elasticity in the concept of "law" (arguably long overdue in a state increasingly governed through administrative action); and, second, a simpler, categorical approach to the choice between conducting administrative law review and *Charter* review.[55] It remains to be seen how these principles will be developed by the

51 *Little Sisters*, above note 27 at para. 85.

52 *Vancouver Transit*, above note 8 at para. 63.

53 See Pottie & Sossin, above note 50, and Lorne Sossin, "Discretion Unbound: Reconciling the *Charter* and Soft Law" (2002) 45 Can. Public Admin. 465.

54 The Court does cite much of the "prescribed by law" condition jurisprudence but applies it in a novel fashion by using it to support the characterization of the transit authorities' polices as "laws" rather than as decisions made pursuant to law.

55 This latter principle is in line with the McLachlin Court's decision in *Dunsmuir v. New Brunswick*, 2008 SCC 9, where it attempted to simplify the standard of review analysis in administrative law by reducing the standards of review from three to two and by adopting a categorical approach to the kinds of issues that would attract each standard.

McLachlin Court in future jurisprudence. In particular, it is doubtful that the Court will be able to develop a consistent and predictable test for distinguishing between administrative rules and legislative rules.[56] Nevertheless, the impact of these two novel public law principles is already being felt in the Court's section 1 jurisprudence as well as in its choice of *Charter* remedies.[57]

Two other collateral public law issues are likely to be influenced by the decision in *Vancouver Transit*. First is the relationship between procedural fairness in administrative law and the procedural content of fundamental justice under section 7 of the *Charter*.[58] In *Suresh*, the McLachlin Court, while adopting an administrative law approach to determining the degree of fairness appropriate to the circumstances under section 7,[59] chose to maintain a conceptual distinction between these two principles while acknowledging that the same values and objectives underlay both: "At the end of the day, the common law is not constitutionalized; it is used to inform the constitutional principles that apply to this case."[60]

Second is the continuing controversy over whether deference should be extended to expert administrative decision makers who make decisions affecting human rights.[61] Although *Vancouver Transit* is silent on both these issues, the majority's categorical approach to the distinction between law and administrative decision making suggests that the Court may moving incrementally towards the unity of public law thesis. Where administrative decision making is concerned, it seems very possible that the Court will rethink its majority position in *Multani* and preserve for that category an administrative law analysis informed by *Charter* values.[62]

---

56 Gratton, "Standing at the Divide," above note 6, argues that this distinction may be more problematic than the McLachlin Court has acknowledged.

57 In *Alberta v. Hutterian Brethren of Wilson Colony*, 2009 SCC 37 at paras. 66–71, McLachlin C.J., writing for the majority, drew a sharp distinction between *Charter* violations arising from law and those arising from administrative action for the purpose of applying the minimal impairment branch of the s. 1 *Oakes* test. She held that a reasonable accommodation analysis was appropriate only in respect of the latter. Earlier, in *R. v. Ferguson*, 2008 SCC 6 at paras. 58–66, McLachlin C.J. had again distinguished between law and administrative action, this time in attributing different *Charter* remedies to each.

58 See Freya Kristjanson & Morgana Kellythorne, "*Charter* Cases before Administrative Tribunals and on Judicial Review" (2009) 25 N.J.C.L. 217.

59 The five-part test developed in *Baker*, above note 2, was applied as the s. 7 test in *Suresh*, above note 32 at para. 115.

60 *Suresh*, *ibid.* at para. 114.

61 Mullan, "After *Multani*," above note 45.

62 Most recently, the McLachlin Court has extended its search for coherence to another problem area in the relationship between the *Charter* and administrative law—that is, determining the circumstances in which administrative tribunals have jurisdiction to

C. CONCLUSION

The McLachlin Court's decision in *Vancouver Transit* represents a new direction in the Supreme Court's approach to the relationship between administrative law and the *Charter*. Earlier efforts at building analytical and conceptual coherence in *Slaight* and *Multani* have proved unsuccessful and have perpetuated the confusion and uncertainty in how to deal with these cases. With *Vancouver Transit*, the McLachlin Court seems to have abandoned the search for conceptual coherence in favour of the predictability and relative simplicity of a categorical approach to the analytical choice between *Charter* review and administrative review. Unfortunately, this attempt to carve out watertight doctrinal categories is likely to distort as much as it might clarify. The ill-conceived distinction between indoor and outdoor policies cited in *Vancouver Transit* is just one example.

We believe the Court ought to more clearly elaborate the ways in which administrative law informs *Charter* principles (for example, with respect to the contextual nature of fairness) and the ways in which administrative law principles may be inappropriate for *Charter* analysis (for example, the standard of review, which is predicated on deference to the preferences of Parliament, is not an appropriate lens through which to test the constitutional sufficiency of statutes). An approach to the relationship between administrative law and the *Charter* that is both purposive and functional has far more promise to achieve coherence, in our view, than a formalist or categorical approach.

---

grant *Charter* remedies. In *R. v. Conway*, [2010] 1 S.C.R. 765, the Court reviewed twenty-five years of caselaw, including the *Slaight* decision and subsequent cases on the exercise of statutory discretion, and developed a new test consolidating three distinct lines of authority. The result was to affirm the importance of *Charter* values in the exercise of statutory discretion by administrative decision makers, and more specifically, to expand the jurisdiction of tribunals to grant all *Charter* remedies where those tribunals have the express or implied authority to decide questions of law, and where the jurisdiction has not otherwise been excluded by statute.

PART THREE

Federalism and Aboriginal Law

The Busy Harbours of Canadian Federalism: The Division of Powers and Its Doctrines in the McLachlin Court

PETER C. OLIVER*

A. INTRODUCTION

The first century of Canadian legal federalism was largely about heads of power and how they should be interpreted. Canadian constitutional commentators have tracked the ebb and flow of this process, noting the generally pro-provincial bias of the early Privy Council decisions and, later, the restoration of federal powers by the Supreme Court of Canada. By way of example, the federal trade and commerce power was significantly constrained by the Privy Council and later resuscitated by the Supreme Court of Canada.[1] The same could be said of the peace, order, and good government power.[2]

Were one to have become mesmerized by the cyclical interpretive flow of these and other powers, one might have predicted further significant movement in the cycle in Canada's second century, and on into the twenty-first century. However, while important developments still occur,[3] for all

---

* The author would like to thank the SSHRC for ongoing research support. The views expressed in this chapter are the author's own and should not be taken to represent the views of the Intergovernmental Affairs Secretariat or of the Government of Canada. The author would like to thank Professor Fabien Gélinas and an anonymous reviewer for exceptionally helpful comments and suggestions on an earlier draft. This chapter discusses the first decade of federalism in the McLachlin Court. It analyzes caselaw through the end of 2009.

1 See, for example, *Toronto Electric Commissioners v. Snider*, [1925] A.C. 396 [*Snider*], and *Ontario Farm Products Marketing Reference*, [1957] S.C.R. 198.

2 See, for example, *Snider*, *ibid*. and *Munro v. National Capital Commission*, [1966] S.C.R. 663.

3 See the recent Supreme Court of Canada decision in *Fastfrate* interpreting narrowly the transport aspect of federal jurisdiction over federal works and undertakings. (*Consolidated Fastfrate Inc. v. Western Canada Council of Teamsters*, [2009] 3 S.C.R. 407); and the decision

RÉSUMÉ

Depuis au moins 50 ans les tribunaux canadiens traitent des approches méthodologiques—le caractère véritable, le double aspect, la compétence accessoire, la prépondérance, l'exclusivité des compétences—beaucoup plus du renouvellement de notre compréhension du partage des compétences législatives. Cette tendance est encore plus marquée depuis l'arrivée de la *Loi constitutionnelle de 1982*, vu l'importance de la *Charte* et des droits protégés par l'art. 35. La Cour suprême du Canada fait des efforts afin d'encourager un fédéralisme flexible et coopératif, selon lequel on invalide des lois infréquemment et l'on gère les désaccords au niveau intergouvernemental. Cette tendance persiste sous la direction de la juge en chef McLachlin; la Cour suprême a aussi fait des ajustements importants aux approches méthodologiques afin d'encourager ce genre de fédéralisme coopératif.

intents and purposes, as of approximately 1982, the interpretation of heads of power stabilized. Also as of that year, the Supreme Court of Canada began to take the opportunity to set out clear tests for some of the most important heads of power, rather than to rely on case-by-case determinations. One thinks, once again, of the highest court's treatment of the (general regulation of) trade and commerce power (*General Motors* (1989))[4] and the peace, order, and good government power (*Crown Zellerbach* (1988)),[5] in which the Supreme Court of Canada virtually codified the criteria by which these powers should be judged. The emphasis this time was on stability and predictability. If one thinks of the other business which was preoccupying the Supreme Court of Canada at this time—principally the *Charter of Rights and Freedoms* and section 35 Aboriginal rights—it would not be surprising if, in federalism cases, the Court was essentially attempting to put matters on autopilot, sending a message along the lines of "here are the rules; they are pretty clear; sort things out amongst yourselves intergovernmentally rather than come to court; we are busy with other more pressing matters."

in the *EI Reference* indicating that s. 91(2A) is capable of growth and expansion consistent with changing times (*Reference re Employment Insurance Act (Can.)*, ss. 22 & 23, [2005] 2 S.C.R. 669, 2005 SCC 56).

4 *General Motors of Canada Ltd. v. City National Leasing*, [1989] 1 S.C.R. 641 [*General Motors*].

5 *R. v. Crown Zellerbach Canada Ltd*, [1988] 1 S.C.R. 401.

Furthermore, if one thinks of the wide range of constitutional change that was being proposed in the 1980s and 1990s at a political level, the Court's reluctance to weigh in dramatically on one side or the other in federalism cases was even more understandable.[6]

If I am right about this, we have witnessed in the past twenty-five or so years a stabilization in the interpretation of the federal heads of powers, whether because of the advent of the *Charter*, or because of the intensity of constitutional discussion that was occurring for much of this period at a political level, or simply because, after a century of constitutional interpretation devoted principally to the federal division of powers, we were starting to get the hang of it. Does this mean that legal federalism is no longer where the action is? In one sense, relative to the *Charter* and section 35, the answer is clearly yes. Is legal federalism the constitutional equivalent of medieval history, in which new discoveries and new developments are few and far between? It turns out that, despite the relative stability in the interpretation of the division of power, there is still a good deal of important activity in the field of legal federalism. How can this be?

The answer is that, while interpretation of heads of powers is, relatively speaking, steady, there has been and continues to be considerable movement regarding the *doctrines* of Canadian legal federalism. By "doctrines" I mean, generally speaking, the various rules which govern the way courts analyze federalism cases, above and beyond the interpretation of the various heads of power. One thinks, for example, of pith and substance analysis, "the double aspect doctrine," "the ancillary powers doctrine," "the paramountcy doctrine," and of "the interjurisdictional immunity doctrine." And, here, regarding these doctrines, there has been considerable movement in the past twenty-five years, and notably during the first ten years of the McLachlin Court. It should be noted, however, that the aim of this development appears to be, as with interpretation of heads of power, the encouragement of co-operative federalism.

I propose to focus on the evolution of these key constitutional doctrines and methods of analysis in the McLachlin era.[7] However, I would not want

---

6 It is relevant to point out that, prior to 1982, legal federalism arguments represented the only means of invalidating federal and provincial legislation. Accordingly, federalism arguments were used even if the main objective was to ensure respect for rights and freedoms. One thinks, for example, of *Union Colliery Co. of British Columbia v. Bryden*, [1899] A.C. 580, and *Switzman v. Elbling*, [1957] S.C.R. 285.

7 The analysis which follows is an attempt to determine the direction which the McLachlin Court appears to be taking in division of powers cases. With rare exceptions, it does not

to give the impression that this is the full extent of action in the federalism field. One could add the following to the list: the rules regarding standing, evidence, and justiciability; the increasing importance of international law; the interaction between federalism and the *Charter*; the interaction between federalism and Aboriginal peoples; and the operation of the federal spending power, just to name a few. The doctrines of legal federalism will undoubtedly play an important part in Canadian governments' political decisions regarding such weighty matters as health, the environment, and the management of a competitive economy.

B. STAGES OF ANALYSIS IN LEGAL FEDERALISM CASES

Legal analysis in federalism cases proceeds in three stages, the order of which has become somewhat controversial in recent years.[8] On any view, however, the first stage involves the characterization of any relevant federal or provincial legislation in order to determine its *validity*.[9] Characterization involves a two-step process: first, determination of the pith and substance or dominant feature of the relevant legislation; and second, assignment to the appropriate head of power by virtue of that pith and substance.

Given the recent downgrading of interjurisdictional immunity (the former second stage),[10] it is now appropriate in most legal federalism cases involving a challenge to a provincial legislative measure to analyze second the issue of paramountcy, that is, the existence of conflict with federal provisions, in order to determine whether the provincial measure, though valid, remains operative. Even if a valid provincial measure is inoperative due to federal paramountcy, repeal of the inconsistent federal provisions would render the inoperative provincial measure operative once again.

---

attempt to summarize the academic literature regarding the relevant cases.

8 The order of analysis was discussed by the Supreme Court of Canada in *Canadian Western Bank*, a case which will be discussed in detail below.: *Canadian Western Bank v. Alberta*, [2007] 2 S.C.R. 3 [*Canadian Western Bank*].

9 In the case of municipal bylaws, for example, these cannot exceed the powers of the provincial legislature, so the analysis regarding validity has a similar basis. See, for example, *114957 Canada Ltée (Spraytech, Société d'arrosage) v. Hudson (Town)*, [2001] 2 S.C.R. 241.

10 The order of division of powers analysis is still controversial, notably in cases involving established situations where interjurisdictional immunity applies; however, where interjurisdictional immunity has not been recognized in the past, it seems clear that paramountcy should now follow on the characterization stage. Given that interjurisdictional immunity situations are the exception rather than the rule, it seems appropriate to state that the stages of legal federalism analysis are now characterization, paramountcy, and interjurisdictional immunity.

The final stage of federalism analysis brings the doctrine of interjurisdictional immunity into play. It is important to remember that interjurisdictional immunity can be relevant even where there is no federal legislation at issue (though federal legislation often is present). The issue with respect to interjurisdictional immunity is not whether federal and provincial law conflict, but whether a valid provincial law of general application should be deemed to apply to federal things (for example, Aboriginal lands), persons (for example, Aboriginal peoples), or undertakings (for example, transportation and communication extending beyond provincial borders).[11]

With these legal federalism fundamentals now set out, I can locate the areas in which the Court made important moves in the past ten years. The first group of these—pith and substance, the double aspect doctrine, and the ancillary powers doctrine—have knock-on effects at all three stages of analysis. The second and third distinct doctrines are the paramountcy and interjurisdictional immunity doctrines themselves. I begin therefore with pith and substance, the double aspect doctrine, and the ancillary powers doctrine.

C. CHARACTERIZATION OF LEGISLATION: PITH AND SUBSTANCE, THE DOUBLE ASPECT DOCTRINE, AND THE ANCILLARY POWERS DOCTRINE

Sections 91 and 92 have an orderly look about them. The reference to "exclusive" jurisdiction, which appears in both sections, gives the impression

11 I have used only examples of interjurisdictional immunity benefitting *federal* things, persons, or undertakings despite the fact that the Supreme Court of Canada confirmed in *Canadian Western Bank* that the doctrine in theory assists the provinces. I have done this for two reasons: first, other than caselaw regarding reading down, there is a dearth of Supreme Court of Canada precedents regarding this type of provincial interjurisdictional immunity; and second, because the Court in *Canadian Western Bank* appeared to have mentioned the point about provincial interjurisdictional immunity as a theoretical point only to discount it as a practical way forward. The Court seemed to be saying that while interjurisdictional immunity was theoretically available to protect both federal and provincial powers, the better way was to reduce the role of the doctrine altogether. The British Columbia Court of Appeal has recently applied interjurisdictional immunity in a manner which appears, with respect, to miss this point: *PHS Community Services Society v. Canada (A.G.)*, 2010 BCCA 15 [*Insite*]. I expect the Supreme Court of Canada to remind us of the point it was trying to make in *Canadian Western Bank* when the appeal from British Columbia is heard. See *Attorney General of Canada et al. v. PHS Community Services Society et al.* (BC), leave to appeal to SCC granted 24 June 2010, SCC File Number 33556. The Court may nonetheless find another way to protect PHS Community Services.

of discrete subject matters. To use a nautical analogy, it is as if each head of power is the anchor which confirms exclusive ownership of a discrete set of marine allotments on which legislation of a particular type could be safely moored. The harbour is divided in two, the provincial anchorages on one side, the federal ones on the other. This was the early understanding of the division of powers, an understanding which is often conveyed using another nautical term: each head of power was said to be a "watertight compartment."

However, it was soon realized that exclusive heads of power, or exclusive anchors, do not necessarily mean exclusivity with regarding to moorings—that is, to the notional surface of water on which legislation was deemed to reside for constitutional purposes. Legislation that was deemed to be, in pith and substance, provincial, could have secondary or incidental effects on federal waters, and vice versa.[12] Pursuing the nautical analogy even further, it became clear that legislation regarding certain subject matters could have multiple potential anchors, whether more than one provincial, more than one federal or, most interestingly, one federal and one provincial. Taking the first two scenarios, provincial legislation can often be anchored, for example, under both section 92(13) (property and civil rights) *and* section 92(16) (local and private matters), and federal legislation can be anchored to both, say, trade and commerce *and* criminal law.

However, the most interesting case, as I have just indicated, is where the same piece of legislation can be anchored to either a federal head of power *or* a provincial head of power. In *Hodge v. The Queen*,[13] the Privy Council recognized that one and the same patch of water—in this case, the subject matter "regulation of taverns"—could be covered by measures anchored in section 91(2) (trade and commerce) and by measures anchored in section 92(16) (local and private matters). As the Privy Council famously stated, "subjects which in one aspect and for one purpose fall within sect. 92, may in another aspect and for another purpose fall within sect. 91."[14] All depends on the pith and substance analysis.

Now it should be easy to see that if exclusivity lies at the level of heads of power (anchors under water) but not necessarily at the level of subject

12 The law regarding pith and substance analysis and secondary or incidental effects is an important part of federalism analysis. The law regarding secondary or incidental effects did not undergo a significant transition in the first ten years of the McLachlin Court. This explains the emphasis in this chapter on other more fluid parts of the first stage of legal federalism analysis: double aspect and the ancillary powers doctrine.

13 (1883) 9 A.C. 117.

14 *Ibid*. at 130.

matters (moorings at the surface), and if the same patch of water could occasionally be covered by measures secured either using section 91 anchors *or* using section 92 anchors (the "double aspect" doctrine), then it was theoretically possible for federal and provincial measures to simultaneously occupy the same subject matter space. For a time, it was assumed that if Parliament had not yet legislated, the mooring must remain reserved for it; however, that assumption was eventually rejected.[15] By the early 1960s, the courts had come to assume that even if Parliament had already legislated, it should not be assumed to have intended to have the mooring to itself.[16] The "double aspect" doctrine was by that stage in full swing.

How then does the "double aspect" doctrine differ from concurrency? Immigration and agriculture are concurrent powers according to section 95 of the *Constitution Act, 1867*. Section 95 allows both the federal Parliament and the provincial legislatures to legislate regarding these measures (subject to federal paramountcy). Parliament and the provincial legislatures share not just the same mooring but also the same anchor. In the case of the "double aspect" doctrine, both the federal Parliament and the provincial legislatures can legislate regarding the same matter—say, the regulation of taverns or highways—but the anchors are different. At the level of anchors there is an important distinction between concurrency and double aspect, but in terms of surface appearances, double aspect and concurrency are substantially the same. They both result in federal and provincial measures occupying the same patch of water.

We will see in a moment that, whether as a result of concurrency or double aspect, collisions between federal and provincial measures are regulated principally by means of the doctrine of paramountcy, stage two in division of powers analysis. But let us remain with stage one, the characterization stage, for now.

We have seen thus far that the validity of legislation is determined according to its pith and substance; that, once characterized, that same legislation must be anchored to a head of power; and that a single subject matter can be simultaneously governed by federal and provincial legislation, differently anchored. As long as legislation is properly anchored using the two-stage characterization process (pith and substance analysis followed

15 This doctrine was referred to using a land-based analogy: "the doctrine of the unoccupied field." Canadian constitutional analysts cannot agree on whether nautical or land-based analogies are most appropriate. The mixing of metaphors is therefore inevitable.

16 That is to say, even "the doctrine of the occupied field" was rejected by the Supreme Court of Canada.

by assignment to the appropriate head of power), it is, generally speaking, no matter that legislation attached to one head of power incidentally affects heads of power based on the other side of the division of powers.[17] However, all of this assumes that pith and substance of the legislation is uniform. What happens if certain parts of the federal legislation are very different in nature from the rest and, if considered on their own, would be deemed in pith and substance in relation to a provincial subject matter. Or vice versa? One approach would be to nonetheless view the pith and substance of legislation as a whole and to deem "incidental" the admitted effects of certain parts on provincial jurisdiction.[18] Another approach, favoured by litigants determined to find a way past the Supreme Court of Canada's post-1982 tendency to uphold legislation on division of powers grounds, was to target not the legislation as a whole, but particularly egregious parts.

Pursuing still further our nautical analogy, it is as if we cease to view a piece of legislation as a series of barges tethered together and anchored appropriately, and focus instead on any of the tethered barges whose subject matter seems egregiously *hors compétence*.

According to Dickson C.J. in the *General Motors* case, if provisions in a federal Act are in pith and substance in relation to a provincial matter, the provisions can nonetheless be saved if they are part of a federal scheme, and sufficiently integrated into (that is, sufficiently well tethered to) that federal scheme. This will be referred to as the ancillary powers doctrine. The status of the ancillary powers doctrine is controversial, and this is principally for the following reason. As stated above, in the case of legislation (as opposed to tethered barges), there is a fine line between (a) a judge looking at a legislative measure as a whole and deciding that it in pith and substance relates to a federal matter despite "incidental" effects on provincial matters, and (b) a judge isolating the provisions which produce these "incidental effects" and declaring instead that their pith and substance relates to a provincial matter, and as such requires analysis along the lines of the ancillary powers doctrine. It can be confusing to determine which approach is appropriate. However, to my mind, both the double aspect doctrine and the ancillary powers doctrine should be viewed as different aspects of the general trend of upholding legislation where possible.

---

17 One exception to this rule will be discussed under the doctrine of interjurisdictional immunity, below.

18 See Peter W. Hogg, *Constitutional Law of Canada*, 5th ed. supp. (Toronto: Carswell, 2007) at 15.9(c).

Given the fundamental natures of these doctrines and methods of analysis, it may be instructive to see how the McLachlin Court has handled issues regarding pith and substance, especially in relation to double aspect and the ancillary powers doctrine. Has it been inclined, for example, to view legislation as a whole, or to separate it into its more or less controversial parts?

In one of the first cases under the leadership of McLachlin C.J., *Global Securities*,[19] the Supreme Court of Canada was faced with a question regarding the constitutionality of a new provision in the British Columbia *Securities Act*. The new provision authorized the BC Securities Commission to order a registrant to produce records "to assist in the administration of the securities laws of another jurisdiction." Justice Iacobucci set out the structure of the ancillary powers doctrine, but then proceeded to find that the provincial provision in question was *intra vires* the province. Given the strong interprovincial and international commercial aspects of the section in question, it would have been possible for the Court to isolate that provision from the otherwise valid provincial Act, and to run the ancillary powers doctrine analysis discussed above in order to determine whether it was sufficiently integrated into a provincial scheme. Justice Iacobucci, for a unanimous court, preferred to say that the pith and substance of the new provision related to provincial security law, using arguments that might otherwise have been deployed in a *General Motors* analysis to establish the sufficiency of the integration. Justice Iacobucci later confirmed that securities law is furthermore a matter to which the "double aspect" doctrine applies.[20]

In *Mangat*,[21] the Court had to determine whether provisions of the federal *Immigration Act* allowing non-lawyers to represent aliens before the Immigration and Refugee Board (IRB) were valid, and whether BC provisions regarding the qualifications of legal advisors were operative or applicable. Justice Gonthier, for a unanimous court, observed that representation of aliens by counsel before the IRB was a subject matter about which both Parliament and the provinces could legislate, thereby confirming the "double aspect."[22] Justice Gonthier not only confirmed the existence of this "double aspect," but listed other instances of the same phenomenon: highway traffic; securities regulations; insolvency; temperance; interest rates; maintenance of spouses and children, and custody of children; entertainment in

19 *Global Securities Corp. v. British Columbia (Securities Commission)*, [2000] 1 S.C.R. 494 [*Global Securities*].

20 *Ibid.* at para. 46.

21 *Law Society of British Columbia v. Mangat*, [2001] 3 S.C.R. 113 [*Mangat*].

22 *Ibid.* at paras. 47 & 48.

taverns and gaming;[23] and provided a further reference to Hogg's work, *Constitutional Law of Canada*,[24] on the matter.[25] In listing double aspects in this way, the Court appeared to be in no way backing off from continuing to recognize them. With the finding of a double aspect even with respect to representation by counsel, Gonthier J. concluded that it was not necessary to pursue the ancillary powers doctrine approach.[26]

In the *Kitkatla* case,[27] the distinction between an ancillary powers doctrine approach isolating the impugned provisions, and a pith and substance approach applied to the whole Act, was squarely identified by the Court. The measure at issue was the British Columbia *Heritage Conservation Act*. Sections 12(2)(a) and 13(2)(c) and (d) of the Act granted a provincial minister discretion to allow alteration or removal of Aboriginal heritage objects in the province, in this case, culturally modified trees. All the parties agreed that the province had jurisdiction to protect heritage or cultural property, but the appellants argued that the above-noted provisions related instead to Aboriginal affairs, a matter of federal jurisdiction. Justice LeBel observed that the parties disagreed fundamentally as to how the characterization stage, and especially the pith and substance analysis, should be conducted:

> The appellants tend to emphasize the characterization of the impugned provisions outside the context of the Act as a whole. The respondents and interveners take the opposite view, placing greater emphasis on the pith and substance of the Act as a whole. The parties also disagree as to the order in which the analysis should take place: the appellants favour looking at the impugned provisions first, while the respondents and interveners tend to prefer to look at the Act first.[28]

Justice LeBel stated that the proper approach was to first look to the challenged provision, and he cited Dickson C.J. in *General Motors* by way of authority.[29] Justice LeBel restated Dickson C.J.'s test as follows:

---

23 A double aspect in "gaming" was confirmed by the McLachlin Court in *Siemens v. Manitoba (Attorney General)*, [2003] 1 S.C.R. 6.

24 Above note 18.

25 *Mangat*, above note 21 at para. 49.

26 *Ibid.* at para. 50.

27 *Kitkatla Band v. British Columbia (Minister of Small Business, Tourism and Culture)*, [2002] 2 S.C.R. 146 [*Kitkatla*].

28 *Ibid.* at para. 55.

29 *Ibid.* at para. 56. It is submitted that this is still the correct approach despite the difference of approach in *Reference re Assisted Human Reproduction Act*, 2010 SCC 61 [*Re Assisted*

1) Do the impugned provisions intrude into a federal head of power, and to what extent?
2) If the impugned provisions intrude into a federal head of power, are they nevertheless part of a valid provincial legislative scheme?
3) If the impugned provisions are part of a valid provincial legislative scheme, are they sufficiently integrated with the scheme?[30]

According to LeBel J., "the first stage of the analysis requires a characterization of the impugned provision in isolation, looking at both their purpose and effect."[31] This is the "pith and substance" stage. Justice LeBel concluded that the measures were essentially aimed at heritage conservation within the province, despite the admittedly disproportionate effects on Aboriginal people and their cultural artifacts. As in *Global Securities*, arguments that were used to establish the provincial nature of the provisions could have been deployed at a later stage of the ancillary powers doctrine analysis, even if the provincial provisions had been declared *prima facie* federal in nature. The Court seemed keen to cite the ancillary powers doctrine but equally keen to avoid having to proceed beyond the first stage of the *General Motors* test. That was to change in the 2005 *Kirkbi* case.[32]

In *Kirkbi*, the appellants were the holders of the trademark for LEGO construction sets. Ritvik Holding, a Canadian competitor company producing similar sets, challenged the constitutionality of section 7(b) of the federal *Trade-marks Act* which created a civil cause of action, deployed by the appellants, essentially codifying the common law tort of passing off. Justice LeBel, for a unanimous Court, restated the ancillary powers doctrine, noting that "it is necessary to consider both the impugned provision and the Act as a whole when undertaking constitutional analysis."[33] After analyzing the pith and substance of section 7(b) he concluded that the provision truly encroached on an important aspect of provincial jurisdiction over property and civil rights, but that the extent of the encroachment was minimal.[34] That is, unlike in *Global Securities* and *Kitkatla*, the impugned provision was in pith and substance an intrusion, so it was necessary here to proceed to stages

Human Reproduction Act]. Difficulties arise, as there were multiple provisions requiring ancillary powers doctrine analysis; however to date, this has not been the most common scenario.

30 *Ibid.* at para. 58.

31 *Ibid.* at para. 59.

32 *Kirkbi AG v. Ritvik Holdings Inc.*, [2005] 3 S.C.R. 302 [*Kirkbi*].

33 *Ibid.* at para. 21.

34 *Ibid.* at para. 27.

two and three of the ancillary powers doctrine analysis. Justice LeBel confirmed the validity of the federal *Trade-Marks Act* (stage two of the ancillary powers doctrine) and then proceeded to assess the extent of the integration of section 7(b) into the otherwise valid federal Act. Given that the encroachment on provincial jurisdiction was minimal, it was necessary to show only that there was a "functional relationship" between the impugned provision and the Act as a whole (stage three of the ancillary powers doctrine).[35] Justice LeBel concluded that section 7(b) played a clear role in the federal scheme and was therefore "sufficiently integrated."[36] In this case, one can easily imagine the arguments regarding sufficiency of integration being redeployed as reasons why the Act as a whole was in pith and substance federal, the effects of section 7(b) being regarded in the normal way as "merely incidental."

In the seminal 2007 case, *Canadian Western Bank*, the Supreme Court of Canada returned to the subject of the double aspect doctrine. Whereas the doctrine began in *Hodge* and in the early 1960s as an acknowledgment that some legislation has both a federal and provincial aspect, the Court in *Canadian Western Bank* presented it in its contemporary form as a frank acknowledgment that numerous "matters" are, by their very nature, impossible to categorize under one head of power. The importance of the double aspect doctrine was no longer limited to findings of validity regarding a single piece of legislation; it was part of a philosophy of federalism:

> The double aspect doctrine, as it is known, which applies in the course of a pith and substance analysis, ensures that the policies of the elected legislators of both levels of government are respected . . . . The double aspect doctrine recognizes that both Parliament and the provincial legislatures can adopt valid legislation on a single subject depending on the perspective from which the legislation is considered, that is, depending on the various "aspects" of the "matter" in question.[37]

It is easy to get lost in the intricacies of pith and substance, "double aspects," the ancillary powers doctrine analysis, and nautical analogies of dubious utility. But the bottom line is that the Supreme Court of Canada is obviously inclined not to put obstacles in the way of federal and provincial legislative intentions, provided that they comply with *Charter* and section 35 requirements. The double aspect doctrine allows for federal and provin-

35 *Ibid.* at para. 33. If the provision had been "highly intrusive," it would have had to qualify as "truly necessary" or "integral" in order to pass muster at stage three.

36 *Ibid.* at para. 36.

37 *Canadian Western Bank*, above note 8 at para. 30.

cial legislation regarding an ever-increasing list of subject matters. And even where no double aspect exists and a certain provision appears to offend the division of powers, the ancillary powers doctrine allows such provisions to remain valid as a result of their integration into an otherwise valid legislative scheme, rather than face severance or, worse, bringing down the whole Act. While there are sure to be cases in the future where legislators exceed even these generous jurisdictional terms, the broad trend is highly facilitative. As I stated earlier, the courts' general willingness to uphold legislation on federalism grounds means that there is considerable pressure on the intergovernmental process to ensure the smooth running of the federation.[38]

One of the potential consequences of recognizing double aspects and of providing means via the ancillary powers doctrine of saving provisions which would be *ultra vires* on their own but for that analysis, is that there are, so to speak, many legislative boats and barges moored in Canadian waters. The doctrines of paramountcy and interjurisdictional immunity provide the courts with means of policing the jurisdictional overlaps inevitably caused by the Supreme Court of Canada's approach to the first stage of division of powers analysis. However, we will see that the Court has been reluctant to set out doctrines that would necessitate frequent court intervention. Paramountcy and, more recently, interjurisdictional immunity have both been weakened. The general rule in Canadian federalism waters is to keep a keen watch and to maintain bumpers in place.

D. THE PARAMOUNTCY DOCTRINE

Assuming that we are presented with one or more valid federal laws and one or more valid provincial laws, collisions may occur. Collisions between federal and provincial laws are governed by the paramountcy doctrine, with priority given to federal law where true conflict has been identified. The difficulty regarding paramountcy lies in identifying when true conflicts exist, justifying application of the paramountcy doctrine, and resulting inoperability.

---

38 As the Binnie and LeBel JJ. stated in *Canadian Western Bank*: "the task of maintaining the balance of powers in practice falls primarily to governments, and constitutional doctrine must facilitate, not undermine what this Court has called 'co-operative federalism.'" *Ibid.* at para. 24. See also *ibid.* at para. 37: "The 'dominant tide' finds its principled underpinning in the concern that a court should favour, where possible, the ordinary operation of statutes enacted by *both* levels of government."

As indicated, "there are sure to be cases . . . where legislators exceed even these generous jurisdictional terms." See, for example, *Re Assisted Human Reproduction Act*, above note 29.

The modern law regarding paramountcy was set out in yet another key case from the 1980s, this one decided just months after the arrival of the *Constitution Act, 1982* coming into force, and no doubt in awareness of powerful new grounds (based in the *Charter* and in section 35 Aboriginal rights) for challenging federal and provincial legislation. In *Multiple Access v. McCutcheon*,[39] Dickson J. (as he then was) set out the test for paramountcy as follows:

> In principle, there would seem to be no good reasons to speak of paramountcy and preclusion except where there is actual conflict in operation as where one enactment says "yes" and the other says "no"; "the same citizens are being told to do inconsistent things"; compliance with one is defiance of the other.[40]

By wording the test for paramountcy in this way, Dickson J. seemed to be reserving paramountcy and resulting inoperability only for cases where Canadian citizens (and courts, though this point was not yet emphasized) are effectively being given contradictory messages. The *Multiple Access* test seemed to leave plenty of room for provincial provisions which duplicated or supplemented federal provisions dealing with the same subject matter.

While this test gave the courts little reason to intervene in legal federalism disputes, as was probably intended, it may have overlooked one particularly problematic scenario. We have already seen that the existence of a federal statute dealing with a particular matter does not preclude the province from legislating regarding that same matter if it has a section 92 anchor—there is no longer a "doctrine of the occupied field." However, what happens if Parliament legislates so as to regulate an area minimally because it believes that minimal regulation is a good legislative choice, and the province then takes advantage of the free regulatory space to impose its own (less-than-minimal) choices? The citizen is arguably not being given a contradictory message, but there is clearly tension between the federal and provincial legislative aims. This is essentially what occurred in the 1990 case of *Bank of Montreal v. Hall*.[41] While attempting to remain within the ratio of *Multiple Access*, La Forest J. resolved this question in the following way:

> A showing that conflict can be avoided if a provincial Act is followed to the exclusion of a federal Act can hardly be determinative of the question

39 [1982] 2 SCR 161 [*Multiple Access*].

40 *Ibid*. at 191.

41 [1990] 1 S.C.R. 12.

> whether the provincial and federal acts are in conflict, and, hence, repugnant. That conclusion, in my view, would simply beg the question. The focus of the inquiry, rather, must be on the broader question whether operation of the provincial Act is compatible with the federal legislative purpose.[42]

Multiple Access and *Hall* were clearly the leading cases regarding paramountcy as the McLachlin Court took Canada into the twenty-first century. The former justified a *laissez-faire* approach by the courts, while the latter justified what had become rare interventionism. The question for the McLachlin Court, therefore, was which leading case would truly lead: were they equal branches of a broad paramountcy doctrine, or was *Hall* merely an exception to the general *Multiple Access* rule?

The first case to deal with the question, though in fairly brief terms, was *Spraytech*[43] in which landscaping and lawn care companies operating in the suburbs of Montreal challenged a municipal bylaw prohibiting the use of certain pesticides. The pesticides in question had been approved by the federal *Pest Control Products Act* (*PCPA*). In dealing with the claim that the bylaw was inoperative by reason of federal paramountcy, L'Heureux-Dubé J. noted that the *PCPA* regulated which pesticides can be registered for manufacture and distribution in Canada, and that the Act was permissive rather than exhaustive. Accordingly she found no operational conflict on the terms of *Multiple Access*. She added, with reference to *Hall*, that there was "no concern in this case that application of [the] By-law . . . displaces or frustrates 'the legislative purpose of Parliament.'" If anything the *Multiple Access* and *Hall* cases seemed to have equal relevance.

The next, more significant, case dealing with paramountcy was *Mangat*,[44] a case discussed earlier under the heading of "double aspect." As we have already seen, Mangat was an immigration consultant carrying on work in the province of British Columbia, including appearances as counsel or advocate for "aliens" before the Immigration and Refugee Board (IRB) for a fee. The Law Society of British Columbia applied for an injunction preventing Mangat from engaging in what it viewed as the practice of law in contravention of section 26 of the BC *Legal Profession Act*. Mangat claimed in turn that his work was justified under sections 30 and 69(1) of the federal *Immigration Act* which permitted non-lawyers to appear on behalf of clients before the IRB.

---

42 *Ibid.* at 155.

43 *114957 Canada Ltée (Spraytech, Société d'arrosage) v. Hudson (Town)*, [2001] 2 S.C.R. 241.

44 *Mangat*, above note 21.

The relevant question before the court was whether section 26 of the BC Act was inoperative with respect to persons acting by virtue of sections 30 and 69(1) of the federal Act.

Regarding the paramountcy argument, Gonthier J. began by saying that sections 30 and 69(1) demonstrated Parliament's intention to regulate immigration counsel who are not members of the provincial bar. Justice Gonthier summarized the *Multiple Access* test by quoting from the earlier case where Dickson J. referred to a scenario in which "one enactment says 'yes' and the other says 'no'; 'the same citizens are being told to do inconsistent things'; compliance with one is defiance of the other."[45] He then cited La Forest J. in *Hall*, referring to it as "a gloss"[46] on the implications of *Multiple Access*. Following the "expanded version"[47] of *Multiple Access* afforded by *Hall*, Gonthier J. concluded that compliance with both the provincial and federal Acts was not possible and stated, "To require 'other counsel' to be a member in good standing of the bar of the province or to refuse the payment of a fee would go contrary to Parliament's purpose in enacting ss. 30 and 69(1) of the *Immigration Act*."[48] Justice Gonthier distinguished *Spraytech* where compliance with the municipal bylaw did not frustrate Parliament's purpose. *Mangat* reaffirmed the importance of *Hall*, but left its status in relation to *Multiple Access* unclear. This status was resolved in the *Rothmans* case, and even more authoritatively so in *Canadian Western Bank* and *Lafarge*.[49]

In *Rothmans*, a manufacturer of cigarettes sought a declaration that section 6 of the Saskatchewan *Tobacco Control Act* was inoperative by virtue of the fact that it was inconsistent with section 30 of the federal *Tobacco Act*. Section 30 allowed retailers to display tobacco and tobacco product–related brand elements and post signs indicating the availability and price of tobacco products, while section 6 of the Saskatchewan Act banned all advertising, display, and promotion of tobacco or tobacco-related products in any premises in which persons under eighteen years of age were permitted. Justice Major, for a unanimous Court, made it clear that the doctrine of paramountcy had two distinct branches, based respectively in *Multiple Access* and *Hall*:

> The doctrine of federal legislative paramountcy dictates that where there is an inconsistency between validly enacted but overlapping provincial

45 *Multiple Access*, above note 39 at 191, cited in *Mangat*, *ibid.* at para. 69.

46 *Multiple Access*, *ibid.* at para. 70.

47 *Ibid.* at para. 72.

48 *Ibid.*

49 *Rothmans, Benson & Hedges Inc. v. Saskatchewan*, [2005] 1 S.C.R. 188.

> and federal legislation, the provincial legislation is inoperative to the extent of the inconsistency. *Multiple Access Ltd. v. McCutcheon*, [1982] 2 S.C.R. 161, is often cited for the proposition that there is an inconsistency for the purposes of the doctrine if it is impossible to comply simultaneously with both provincial and federal enactments . . . .
>
> However, subsequent cases indicate that impossibility of dual compliance is not the sole mark of inconsistency. Provincial legislation that displaces or frustrates Parliament's legislative purpose is also inconsistent for the purposes of the doctrine. In *Bank of Montreal v. Hall*, [1990] 1 S.C.R. 121, at p. 155, La Forest J wrote . . . . See also *Spraytech*, at para. 35, and *Law Society of British Columbia v. Mangat*, [2001] 3 S.C.R. 113, 2001 SCC 67, at paras. 69–70.
>
> . . .
>
> It follows that in determining whether s. 6 of *The Tobacco Control Act* is sufficiently inconsistent with s. 30 of the *Tobacco Act* so as to be rendered inoperative through the paramountcy doctrine, two questions arise. First, *can a person simultaneously comply* with s. 6 of *The Tobacco Control Act* and s. 30 of the *Tobacco Act*? Second, does s. 6 of *The Tobacco Control Act frustrate Parliament's purpose* in enacting s. 30 of the *Tobacco Act*?[50]

While emphasizing both the *Multiple Access* and *Hall* aspects of paramountcy, Major J. took one further step, identifying the *Hall* principle as effectively acting as the common denominator: "In my view, the overarching principle to be derived from *McCutcheon* and later cases is that *a provincial enactment must not frustrate the purpose of a federal enactment*, whether by making it impossible to comply with the latter or by some other means."[51] In *Rothmans* itself, Major J. concluded that neither branch of the paramountcy doctrine was engaged; however, by emphasizing "frustration of federal purpose" he made available a powerful weapon for litigants seeking to render provincial enactments inoperative, and this, seemingly, against the general tendency of the Court since 1982. Subsequent cases brought *Rothmans* back into line, however, as we will see.

We will study the facts of *Canadian Western Bank* and *Lafarge* more closely in a moment, under the heading of interjurisdictional immunity, but for present purposes it is important to note that these cases solidify a two-branch paramountcy doctrine based around *Multiple Access*, first, and *Hall*, second.

---

50 *Ibid.* at paras. 12–13 and 15 [emphasis added].

51 *Ibid.* at para. 14 [emphasis added].

In *Canadian Western Bank* we see a rendition of the paramountcy doctrine that sets out its two branches clearly and distinctly. Justices Binnie and LeBel further emphasized that the burden of proof is on the party alleging paramountcy:

> To sum up, the onus is on the party relying on the doctrine of federal paramountcy to demonstrate that the federal and provincial laws are in fact incompatible by establishing *either* that it is *impossible to comply* with both laws *or* that to apply the provincial law would *frustrate the purpose* of the federal law.[52]

However, the majority judges were also intent in making sure that the second (or *Hall*) branch was not allowed to overwhelm the general *laissez-faire* nature of the *Multiple Access*–inspired rule. They did so in fairly emphatic terms, stating that "care must be taken not to give too broad a scope to *Hall, Mangat* and *Rothmans*."[53] They underlined the point by affirming that "frustration of federal purpose" was never intended to affect a return to the "doctrine of the occupied field" that had been rejected in the early 1960s. In the words of Binnie and LeBel JJ., "the fact that Parliament has legislated in respect of a matter does not lead to the presumption that in so doing it intended to rule out any possible provincial action in respect of that subject."[54] Rather, the presumption worked in the opposite direction: the coexistence of federal and provincial laws was to be expected. The majority reasons were intent on encouraging a flexible version of federalism: "To interpret incompatibility broadly has the effect of expanding the powers of the central government, whereas a narrower interpretation tends to give provincial governments more latitude."[55]

Justices Binnie and LeBel also attempted to clarify a few smaller points regarding paramountcy. A point that will reappear in the discussion of interjurisdictional immunity but which is also relevant here is that the Court is in favour of a "firm application of pith and substance analysis," including reading down, in order to resolve some of the problems that arise as a result of some of the more troublesome incidental effects of legislation: "The flexible nature of the pith and substance analysis makes it perfectly suited to the modern views of federalism in our constitutional jurisprudence."[56] A further

52 *Canadian Western Bank*, above note 8 at para. 75 [emphasis added].

53 *Ibid.* at para. 74.

54 *Ibid.*

55 *Ibid.* at para. 70.

56 *Ibid.* at para. 31.

point was that the Court appeared to be emphasizing that incompatibilities justifying paramountcy can occur between any provisions in federal and provincial legislation, whether those provisions are justified by global pith and substance analysis or by the ancillary powers doctrine.[57]

The Court found no reason to apply the paramountcy doctrine in *Canadian Western Bank*. The doctrine was applied, however, in the companion case, *Lafarge*,[58] though in circumstances which made its application somewhat unconvincing. The question at issue in the case was essentially whether the City of Vancouver should have insisted that Lafarge Canada obtain a city development permit in advance of building an integrated ship offloading/concrete batching facility on waterfront lands owned by the Vancouver Port Authority (VPA). In their defence, Lafarge, the city, and the VPA argued that VPA lands enjoyed interjurisdictional immunity (as federal public property or as a federal undertaking) and, in the alternative, that the inconsistency between federal and provincial building rules regarding this land should be resolved in favour of the former by application of the doctrine of paramountcy. The province claimed that dual compliance was clearly possible: Lafarge simply needed to obtain building permits from both the VPA and the city. The problem with this argument was that city bylaws imposed a 30-foot height restriction which the Lafarge project clearly breached. At this stage, the fact that Lafarge had not applied for a city permit became important. Apparently, it was possible for the city to waive the 30-foot height requirement, but no request to exercise this discretion had been made. On the federal side, the *Canadian Marine Act*, section 48, authorized land use controls and procedure for uses related to shipping. Such controls and procedures had been set out in a document entitled Port 2010, and these, rather than the city bylaws, were deemed to apply to Lafarge. Despite the fact that the city's discretion had not been tested, the Supreme Court of Canada took the view that federal paramountcy applied. The Court described the inconsistency in the conditional:

> It *would* be within the City's discretion to waive the height limit up to 100 feet, but that *would* impose the condition precedent of an exercise of discretion by the City to approve a project that has already been approved by the VPA. This *would* create an operational conflict that *would* flout the federal purpose, by depriving the VPA of its final decisional authority on

57 *Ibid.* at para. 69.

58 *British Columbia (Attorney General) v. Lafarge Canada Inc.*, [2007] 2 S.C.R. 86 [*Lafarge*].

> the development of the port, in respect of matters which fall within the legislative authority of Parliament.[59]

The test for paramountcy which the Court applied was that which had been set out in *Canadian Western Bank*: "The party raising the issue must establish the existence of valid federal and provincial laws and the impossibility of their simultaneous application by reason of an operational conflict or because such application would frustrate the purpose of the enactment."[60] The Court found both an operational conflict and frustration of the federal purpose. It may be significant that, regarding the operational conflict, the Court cited *M & D Farm Ltd. v. Manitoba Agricultural Credit Corp.*,[61] and in so doing emphasized the conflicted position a judge would be in on this issue, given the existence of the federal and municipal rules.

It is also important to read *Lafarge* in the context of its partner case, *Canadian Western Bank*. As we will see, the latter case significantly reduced the protection which federal undertakings received as a result of interjurisdictional immunity. In that case, the Court reminded the federal authorities that they retain the option of clearly setting out their preferences and in so doing attempting to invoke federal paramountcy. The partner case, *Lafarge*, then became an example of just that.

The final case which should be mentioned in this discussion of paramountcy is the Court's 2009 decision in *Chatterjee*.[62] In the first paragraphs of the judgment, before reciting the facts, Binnie J. set out a reminder of the understanding of federalism which animates the McLachlin Court, quoting from his own judgment in *Canadian Western Bank*:[63] "a court should favour, where possible, the ordinary operation of statutes enacted by *both* levels of government."[64] The Ontario *Remedies for Organized Crime and Other Unlawful Activities Act, 2001 (Civil Remedies Act)* (CRA) was enacted to deter crime and compensate victims. Its main instrument was an *in rem* civil action to effect forfeiture of the proceeds of crime. As summarized by Binnie J.:

> In essence, therefore, the *CRA* creates a property-based authority to seize money and other things shown on a balance of probabilities to be tainted by crime and thereafter to allocate the proceeds to compensating victims

59 *Ibid*,. at para. 75 [emphasis added].

60 *Ibid*. at para. 77.

61 [1999] 2 S.C.R. 961.

62 *Chatterjee v. Ontario (Attorney General)*, [2009] 1 S.C.R. 624 [*Chatterjee*].

63 Above note 8 at para. 37.

64 *Chatterjee*, above note 62 at para. 2 [emphasis in the original].

> of and remedying the societal effects of criminality. The practical (and intended) effect is also to take the profit out of crime and to deter its present and would-be perpetrators.[65]

After noting both the criminal and property aspects of the legislation, Binnie J. concluded that the CRA was in pith and substance in relation to property and therefore properly anchored in section 92(13) "property and civil rights." In the spirit of flexible, co-operative federalism, he issued a by now familiar reminder that the assignment to a section 92 anchor did not mean that section 91 was unaffected: "I agree that the *CRA* was enacted 'in relation to' property and civil rights and may incidentally 'affect' criminal law and procedure without doing violence to the division of powers."[66]

However, even if the provincial law was valid, and even if incidental effects on the federal criminal law power were thereby permitted, it was still necessary to consider whether any of the CRA provisions should be declared "inoperative" by virtue of either of the two branches of paramountcy so clearly laid out in *Canadian Western Bank* and *Lafarge*, a paramountcy doctrine which Binnie J. pointedly referred to as "restrained."[67] Justice Binnie could find neither operational conflict nor frustration of federal purpose. Without purporting to set out a new test, he identified the common denominator between the two branches in terms of compromising the proper functioning of federal legislation: "The Constitution permits a province to enact measures to deter criminality and to deal with its financial consequences so long as those measures are taken in relation to a head of provincial competence and do not *compromise the proper functioning* of the *Criminal Code* including the sentencing provisions."[68]

If we return to the image of the crowded harbour of Canadian federalism imagined earlier, it seems clear that the Supreme Court of Canada is not intent on policing these waters. In the spirit of what is now a refrain in this chapter, it would appear that the onus is on federal and provincial actors to steer carefully, communicate frequently, and maintain a good set of bumpers.

---

65 *Ibid.* at para. 23.

66 *Ibid.* at para. 30. See also para. 32: "Co-operative federalism recognizes that overlaps between provincial and federal laws are inevitable."

67 *Ibid.* at para. 36.

68 *Ibid.* at para. 40 [emphasis added].

E. THE INTERJURISDICTIONAL IMMUNITY DOCTRINE

As described earlier, the issue with respect to interjurisdictional immunity is not whether federal and provincial law conflict, but whether, to take the most familiar examples, a valid provincial law of apparently general application should be deemed to apply to federal things, persons, or undertakings. In the case of the best-known instances of interjurisdictional immunity—banks, interprovincial transportation and communication undertakings, and Aboriginal lands and peoples, the federal thing, person, or undertaking is present and active in the province and ostensibly subject to the multiple provincial measures that have been enacted over the years to regulate land, individuals, and companies existing, living, and operating within the province. And yet if, for example, the plentiful, validly anchored provincial laws of a general nature regarding hunting and land use applied to Aboriginal peoples and lands,[69] and if provincial laws regarding key labour relations matters applied to airlines, television companies, and banks, then federal jurisdiction over Aboriginals and Aboriginal lands, interprovincial undertakings, and banks would not be exclusive either at the level of anchors or at the surface level. Interjurisdictional immunity protects these things, persons, and undertakings from the direct and the incidental effects of legislation anchored on the other side of the division of powers, without the need for Parliament to assert its exclusive jurisdiction by means of the paramountcy doctrine. It should now be possible to see why interjurisdictional immunity is such a useful protection for federal things, persons, and undertakings which would otherwise be overwhelmed with provincial regulation in the natural course of events, and why, as a doctrine of general application to sections 91 and 92 of the *Constitution Act, 1867*,[70] it runs counter to the contemporary current of legal federalism as articulated by the McLachlin Court.

In fact, the "problem" with an interjurisdictional immunity doctrine of general application ran deeper than this. For historical and even for logical reasons (from one perspective), interjurisdictional immunity analysis was

69 By virtue of s. 88 of the *Indian Act*, a number of these provincial laws are incorporated by reference by Parliament, but this is a federal choice rather than an inevitability of the division of powers.

70 If interjurisdictional immunity is a doctrine of general application to ss. 91 and 92 then this amounts to saying that each head of power has a basic, minimum, and unassailable content upon which legislation from across the division of powers may not encroach, whether directly or incidentally. See, for example, the doctrine as described by Braidwood J.A. in *Kitkatla*, above note 27 at para. 19.

the second stage in division of powers cases, ahead of paramountcy. The logic behind this, as explained by Bastarache J. in his separate reasons in *Canadian Western Bank* and *Lafarge,* is that interjurisdictional analysis can dictate that a law not apply in a particular context, and thereby avoid what would otherwise have been an operational conflict between the two laws. For example, if interjurisdictional immunity makes it clear that provincial health and safety laws regulating pregnant employees who work in front of certain types of computer screens do not apply to bank employees, then there is no need to consider whether the provincial law and the *Canada Labour Code* provisions regarding the same subject matter are inconsistent. However, the logic which has just been described in a classic interjurisdictional immunity case breaks down when the doctrine can be argued in any and all division of powers cases. In all but the exceptional classical instances of interjurisdictional immunity, the doctrine can be said to amount to a life raft deployed by litigants to resist the implications of the sort of flexible, co-operative federalism that is described already and, most emphatically, in *Canadian Western Bank.*

A problem related to the prominent position of interjurisdictional immunity in the various stages of legal federalism analysis was that the test for the doctrine was famously difficult for the Supreme Court to pin down and for the lower courts and legal advisors to apply.[71] Accordingly it was an infamous generator of constitutional litigation and instigator of lengthy, convoluted argument. Indeed, interjurisdictional immunity was an obvious target for a Court concerned with developing the doctrines of legal federalism so as to favour flexibility, co-operation, and increased legal certainty. Let us now look at the McLachlin Court's caselaw in this area.

The first McLachlin Court encounter with the interjurisdictional immunity doctrine was the *Mangat* case, described earlier. That which was not described earlier was that the British Columbia Court of Appeal, unanimous as to the result in allowing the appeal, had divided on whether it should do so on the basis of interjurisdictional immunity or paramountcy. Justice Gonthier, for a unanimous Supreme Court of Canada, agreed that paramountcy was the preferable basis on which to decide the appeal, but his comments regarding the order and preferability of the interjurisdictional immunity and paramountcy doctrines were of particular interest. Justice

71 The test shifted even at the Supreme Court of Canada level, often in lengthy, complicated judgments: see *Commission du Salaire Minimum v. Bell Telephone Co.*, [1966] S.C.R. 767; *Bell Canada v. Quebec*, [1988] 1 S.C.R. 749 [*Bell (1988)*]; and *Irwin Toy v. Quebec*, [1989] 1 S.C.R. 927.

Gonthier argued that the existence of a double aspect favoured the application of paramountcy rather than interjurisdictional immunity. The latter doctrine would have had the result of excluding provincial jurisdiction regarding representation of aliens before the IRB, whereas paramountcy safeguarded parliamentary control over the tribunal it had created, while preserving the principle of general provincial control over the legal profession. In this respect, the paramountcy doctrine was more "supple" than interjurisdictional immunity.[72] It was not clear at this stage whether the order of division of powers analysis depended on the facts of the case, but clearly it was no longer obligatory to consider interjurisdictional immunity second, following immediately after the characterization of the legislation.

The second McLachlin Court case regarding interjurisdictional immunity was *Kitkatla*, another case that has already been discussed. Once again, it is important to note that the British Columbia Court of Appeal had been considerably preoccupied with issues regarding interjurisdictional immunity. It should also be noted, however, that "Indians and Indian lands" is a long-standing category of interjurisdictional immunity analysis. In *Kitkatla*, LeBel J. appeared to discuss interjurisdictional immunity issues ahead of paramountcy—issues such as "impairment" of the "core" of the Aboriginal identity appeared to be rolled into an exploration of the effects of provincial legislation on federal powers (that is, question 1 of the ancillary powers doctrine analysis)—but then interjurisdictional immunity received its formal discussion and rapid disposition after paramountcy. Thus *Kitkatla* perpetuated the uncertainty about what the McLachlin Court was doing with the order, preferability, and substance of the interjurisdictional immunity doctrine.

Kitkatla was yet another unanimous decision by the McLachlin Court, but it may be important to point out that the future dissenter on interjurisdictional immunity, Bastarache J., did not sit on the case. In *Canadian Western Bank* and *Lafarge* it became apparent that the majority of the Court had different views than Bastarache J. regarding numerous aspects of the interjurisdictional immunity doctrine.

The facts of *Lafarge* have already been set out, but *Canadian Western Bank* has not yet been introduced. It is important, first of all, to know that banking,[73] like incorporation of companies with other-than-provincial objects more generally, is an established category of interjurisdictional

72 *Mangat*, above note 21 at paras. 52–54.

73 This despite the fact the definition of banking was, for a time, in doubt: see *Canadian Pioneer Management v. Labour Relations Board of Saskatchewan*, [1980] 1 S.C.R. 433.

immunity. It should be easy to see that if the vast range of provincial legislation regulating companies applied to banks, it would be difficult for Parliament to have real control over banking (section 91(15)) unless it filled all the gaps in its jurisdiction by means of paramountcy legislation. Interjurisdictional immunity preserves banking jurisdiction without Parliament having to legislate to protect that jurisdiction, but important questions remained regarding the extent of that protection. *Canadian Western Bank* began to answer those questions.

The relevant facts of the case are as follows. The federal *Bank Act* defines who is a bank and in what activities banks are free to engage. Canadian Western Bank qualified as a bank and, ever since the early 1990s, in addition to the familiar activities of banking, banks were allowed to offer a range of insurance products, including mortgage protection insurance, personal accident insurance, and travel insurance. The Alberta *Insurance Act* of 2000 in turn regulated the sale of insurance, including the sort of credit-related insurance now permitted by the federal *Bank Act*. There was no question regarding the validity of the Alberta *Insurance Act*. Insurance has been a proper subject of provincial legislation since the nineteenth century. The constitutional questions in the case related, first, to whether the *Insurance Act* and its regulations were applicable to the promotion of authorized insurance in banks (the interjurisdictional immunity argument) and, second, to whether the Alberta Act and regulations were inoperative in relation to the federal legislation (the paramountcy argument).

The Court in *Canadian Western Bank* was not content to answer the questions in the traditional way. From the outset, it was determined to delineate, or at least confirm, the new approach to legal federalism that first appeared in the early 1960s but which consolidated as of 1982. As already noted, the Court wished to facilitate co-operative federalism, not by intervening on a case-by-case basis, but by affirming clear guiding principles, and allowing governments to get on with things:

> As the final arbiters of the division of powers, the courts have developed certain constitutional doctrines, which, like the interpretations of the powers to which they apply, are based on the guiding principles of our constitutional order. The constitutional doctrines permit an appropriate balance to be struck in the recognition and management of the inevitable overlaps in rules made at the two levels of legislative power, while recognizing the need to preserve sufficient predictability in the operation of the division of powers. The doctrines must also be designed to reconcile

> the legitimate diversity of regional experimentation with the need for national unity. Finally, they must include a recognition that the task of maintaining the balance of powers in practice falls primarily to governments, and constitutional doctrine must facilitate, not undermine what this Court has called "co-operative federalism."[74]

With these principles in mind, the Court then analyzed the key doctrines and methods of analysis of legal federalism—pith and substance, paramountcy, and interjurisdictional immunity. The case is, in many ways, a complete course in the fundamentals of the Canadian division of powers. We have already seen what the Court said regarding pith and substance and paramountcy. The real importance of the case is with respect to interjurisdictional immunity. Here, the Court innovated in at least three ways: (1) the test for interjurisdictional immunity was clarified in terms which make its successful invocation less likely; (2) interjurisdictional immunity was confined to contexts in which it has already been applied, to cases where precedents already exist; and (3) in jurisdictional contexts where interjurisdictional immunity has not already been recognized, it was appropriate to move from characterization (validity) to paramountcy (operability) rather than attempting to carve out new contexts for interjurisdictional immunity. Of course, this summary of the importance of the case is too brief and lacks subtlety, so it may be helpful to look more closely at what the Court actually said.

We have already noted in *Kitkatla* that LeBel J. discussed interjurisdictional immunity issues at the characterization stage in considering the effect of provincial legislation on federal aspects before returning more formally to interjurisdictional immunity later on in his analysis. In *Canadian Western Bank*, Binnie and LeBel JJ. spoke first of the normal interaction of provincial and federal legislation given "double aspects" and "incidental effects." Where problems arise due to incidental effects (and here one can easily have in mind interjurisdictional immunity scenarios) they recommended "a firm application of the pith and substance analysis."[75] They acknowledge that "the scale of the alleged incidental effects may indeed put a law in a different light so as to place it in another constitutional power," but they then observe that "the usual interpretation techniques of constitutional interpretation, such as reading down, may then play a useful role."[76] This sounds

74 *Canadian Western Bank*, above note 8 at para. 24.

75 *Ibid.* at para. 31.

76 *Ibid.*

a good deal like interjurisdictional immunity. So even though the doctrine is downgraded at least in terms of the stages in division of powers litigation, some of the effects of the doctrine may be accomplished earlier in the analytical process when discussing pith and substance. This observation was perhaps intended to address some of Bastarache J.'s concern regarding the logical need to discuss interjurisdictional immunity ahead of paramountcy. However, reading down is normally available only where two interpretations of a law (say, provincial) are possible and where one would result in the law being characterized as in relation to a matter that cannot be attributed to a provincial head of power. It is not usually used where the "incidental effects" on federal powers are read out of the provincial statutory instrument. Accordingly, the Court has some future work to do in explaining the nature of "a firm application of the pith and substance doctrine."

It is also important to remember that the value of interjurisdictional immunity is not exhausted by the sort of weak reading down that has just been noted. At its full deployment, the doctrine operates to deflect all intrusions, whether frontal or incidental.[77] Accordingly, it is still important to discuss the contemporary nature of the doctrine and to determine the point at which it should be considered in division of powers analysis.

On one view of interjurisdictional immunity, it is a doctrine which applies to some extent to each and every head of power in sections 91 and 92. Justices Binnie and LeBel are clearly not of this view. They refer to the doctrine as one "of limited application."[78] Though they cite broader elaborations of the doctrine, such as that expressed by Beetz J. in *Bell Canada (1988)*,[79] they seem to view the doctrine as a relic of the "watertight compartments" approach to the division of powers.[80] In their view, the tide of constitutional analysis has turned and no longer favours interjurisdictional immunity. They cite Dickson C.J. who first expressed the idea that interjurisdictional immunity was increasingly out of favour:

---

77 Justices Binnie and LeBel make this point clear at para. 32:

> That being said, it must also be acknowledged that, in certain circumstances, the powers of one level of government must be protected against *intrusions*, even incidental ones, by the other level. For this purpose, the courts have developed two doctrines. The first, the doctrine of interjurisdictional immunity, recognizes that our Constitution is based on an allocation of exclusive powers to both levels of government, not concurrent powers, although these powers are bound to interact in the realities of the life of our Constitution. [Emphasis added.]

78 *Canadian Western Bank*, above note 8 at para. 33.

79 *Bell (1988)*, above note 71.

80 They cite Lord Atkin's famous metaphor at *Canadian Western Bank*, above note 8 at para. 34.

> The history of Canadian constitutional law has been to allow for a fair amount of interplay and indeed overlap between federal and provincial power. It is true that doctrines like interjurisdictional immunity . . . and concepts like "watertight compartments" qualify the extent of that interplay. But it must be recognized that these doctrines and concepts have not been the dominant tide of constitutional doctrines; rather they have been an undertow against the strong pull of pith and substance, the aspect doctrine and, in recent years, a very restrained approach to concurrency and paramountcy issues.[81]

The contemporary dominant tide "finds its principled underpinning in the concern that a court should favour, where possible, the ordinary operation of statutes enacted by *both* levels of government."[82] Accordingly, Binnie and LeBel JJ. rejected "the sweeping immunity"[83] argued for by the banks in this case.

Given the general downgrading of interjurisdictional immunity by the Supreme Court of Canada, it is surprising to see that the British Columbia Court of Appeal has recently carved out a *new* role for the doctrine in the provincial health sphere.[84] The Court of Appeal noted that Binnie and LeBel JJ. confirm that the doctrine is "reciprocal," applying "to protect provincial heads of power and provincially regulated undertakings from federal encroachment" in the same way as it does so for federal equivalents. However, it is important to point out that Binnie and LeBel JJ. were simply making a theoretical point here; they were certainly not recommending the development of a new range of provincial interjurisdictional immunity precedents. Instead, in mentioning that interjurisdictional immunity is "in theory . . . reciprocal,"[85] Binnie and LeBel JJ.'s intention was to point out that the doctrine was "in reality" available, at least in its strong form, only for the federal powers, and that this was yet a further reason for downgrading the doctrine. "For all these reasons . . . the Court does not favour an intensive reliance on the doctrine, nor should we . . . turn it into a doctrine of first recourse in a division of powers dispute."[86] Given that there are only three major stages in division of powers analysis, was the Court saying in so many words that it was a doctrine of last resort?

---

81 *OPSEU v. Ontario (A-G)*, [1987] 2 S.C.R. 17, cited with approval in *General Motors*, above note 4 at 669.

82 *Canadian Western Bank*, above note 8 at para. 37.

83 *Ibid.* at para. 38.

84 *Insite*, above note 11.

85 *Canadian Western Bank*, above note 8 at para. 35.

86 *Ibid.* at para. 47.

After making very clear that the interjurisdictional immunity is out of step with the contemporary trend towards coexistence of federal and provincial laws, Binnie and LeBel JJ. then addressed the flip side of the question: when and how does the doctrine apply? At this point, the judges surveyed the range of situations in which the doctrine has been deployed in the past. They observed that the doctrine has always required some level of impact on "a vital or essential part"[87] of the federal thing, person, or undertaking, but Binnie and LeBel JJ. emphasized the narrowness of this concept by underlining Beetz J.'s limitation of its scope in *Bell (1988)* to the "basic, minimum and unassailable content"[88] or "core" of the legislative power in question. By "minimum," the justices understood Beetz J. to have been referring to "the minimum content necessary to make the power effective for the purpose for which it was conferred."[89] On the facts of *Canadian Western Bank*, this meant that the banks would have to convince the Court that promotion of "peace of mind" insurance was at the "core" of banking.

Having confirmed the narrowest interpretation of the concept of "core," the Court then went on to determine what the interjurisdictional immunity doctrine required in terms of the impact on that "core" from the other side of the division of powers. The caselaw effectively laid out a spectrum of impacts, ranging from "sterilize" at one end, through "impair" in the middle, to "affect" at the other end. Whereas the test had been pitched at "affect" by Beetz J. in *Bell (1988)*, Binnie and LeBel JJ. preferred the stricter "impair," noting that "the difference between 'affects' and 'impairs' is that the former does not imply any adverse consequences whereas the latter does."[90] Therefore, even if the Alberta Act had reached the core of banking, it would have had to adversely impact on that core rather than merely affect it. Therefore, the banks' claim failed.

We have seen thus far how interjurisdictional immunity is out of line with the contemporary currents in Canadian legal federalism, and how the Court in *Canadian Western Bank* tapered the doctrine so as to reduce its sphere of application. But the Court went further. It set down strict terms for further deployment of the doctrine:

> *Interjurisdictional immunity is of limited application and should in general be reserved for situations already covered by precedent.* This means, in practice,

87 *Bell (1988)*, above note 71 at 859–60.

88 *Ibid.* at 839.

89 *Canadian Western Bank*, above note 8 at para. 50.

90 *Ibid.* at para. 48.

> that it will be largely reserved for those heads of power that deal with federal things, persons or undertakings, or where in the past its application has been considered absolutely indispensable or necessary to enable Parliament or a provincial legislature to achieve the purpose for which exclusive legislative jurisdiction was conferred, as discerned from the constitutional division of power as a whole, or what is absolutely indispensable or necessary to enable an undertaking to carry out its mandate in what makes it specifically of federal (or provincial) jurisdiction.[91]

This passage appeared after Binnie and LeBel JJ. had just completed a survey of interjurisdictional immunity precedents under these headings: "federal transportation," "federal communication," "maritime law" (navigation and shipping), "Indian cases," "management of federal institutions" (such as the post office, the RCMP), and "federal companies and undertakings" (such as banking).

The final adjustment to the interjurisdictional immunity doctrine came in the downgrading of that doctrine *vis-à-vis* the doctrine of paramountcy. This occurred in two ways, the second of which is arguably the most important. The first way that this occurred was in the Court's assertion that paramountcy provides the federal way of doing things with sufficient protection for any matter that interjurisdictional immunity can no longer protect.[92] Thus, for example, if Parliament is not happy with provincial environmental regulations affecting the transport of hazardous materials in interprovincial vehicles, then it can legislate clearly so as to contradict the provincial rules and federal paramountcy should allow the federal preferences to prevail.[93]

The second way that interjurisdictional immunity was downgraded *vis-à-vis* paramountcy was that the order of division of powers argumentation had been adjusted, placing paramountcy ahead of interjurisdictional immunity as a general rule. If we take the previous point seriously, that interjurisdictional immunity is, practically speaking, limited to situations covered by a limited range of precedents, then the interjurisdictional immunity argument should not even appear outside that range of precedents. However, even within that

---

91 *Ibid.* at para. 77 [emphasis added].

92 *Ibid.* at para. 46:

> Finally, the doctrine would seem as a general rule to be superfluous in that Parliament can always, if it sees fit to do so, make its legislation sufficiently precise to leave those subject to it with no doubt as to the residual or incidental application of provincial legislation. As we shall see, sufficient confirmation of this can be found in the history and operation of the doctrine of federal paramountcy.

93 See, for example, *R. v. TNT Canada Inc.* (1986), 37 D.L.R. (4th) 297 (Ont. C.A.).

range of precedents it appears that interjurisdictional immunity may only follow the characterization and paramountcy stages. Justice Bastarache objected to this alteration in the order of constitutional argumentation, but as we have seen, the majority attempted to take care of his objections by other means. The sort of weak reading down that interjurisdictional immunity offered is to be accomplished by statutory interpretation and by firm pith and substance analysis. The stronger effects of the interjurisdictional immunity doctrine—inapplicability of provincial legislation clearly applicable on its terms to federal entities operating in the province—could not be easily resolved by interpretation and firm pith and substance analysis. However, this was where the Court's reminder regarding paramountcy kicked in. Perhaps the Court had in mind that in the twenty-first century, unlike the turn of the previous century when interjurisdictional immunity was developed, there was greater likelihood that federal legislation would have already contradicted the provincial legislation at issue. And if this were the case, as it was in *Mangat*, the Supreme Court of Canada would apparently rather hear a relatively straightforward paramountcy argument ahead of the traditionally convoluted interjurisdictional immunity analyses.

Therefore, as Binnie and LeBel JJ. said by way of conclusion to their discussion of the doctrines of division of powers analysis, "in most cases, a pith and substance analysis and the application of the doctrine of paramountcy have resolved difficulties in a satisfactory manner,"[94] without the need for interjurisdictional immunity. The judges specifically addressed "the order of application of the constitutional doctrines" later in the judgment, and there it was also clear that interjurisdictional immunity is now third fiddle, though not inflexibly so:

> The above review of constitutional doctrines inevitably raises questions about the logical order in which they should be applied. It would be difficult to avoid beginning with the 'pith and substance' analysis . . . Although our colleague Bastarache J takes a different view on this point, we do not think it appropriate to *always* begin by considering the doctrine of interjurisdictional immunity. To do so could mire the Court in a rather abstract discussion of 'cores' and 'vital and essential' parts to little practical effect. As we have already noted, interjurisdictional immunity is of limited application and should in general be reserved for situations already covered by precedent. This means, in practice, that it will be largely reserved for

94 *Canadian Western Bank*, above note 8 at para. 67.

> those heads of power that deal with federal things, persons or undertakings . . . . If a case can be resolved by the application of pith and substance analysis, and federal paramountcy where necessary, it would be preferable to take that approach.[95]

Given that many division of powers cases do not involve federal things, persons, or undertakings, Binnie and LeBel JJ.'s statement that "we do not think it appropriate to *always* begin by considering the doctrine of interjurisdictional immunity" should be taken with a grain of salt. The judges acknowledged as much in concluding that "while in theory a consideration of interjurisdictional immunity is apt for consideration after the pith and substance analysis, in practice the absence of prior case law favouring its application to the subject matter at hand will generally justify a court proceeding directly to the consideration of federal paramountcy."[96] In cases where prior caselaw favours the application of interjurisdictional immunity, it is probable that courts will choose the order of doctrines that suits efficient treatment of the facts. For example, in a case where the issue is whether federal legislation regarding safe transport of hazardous materials is valid, and such federal legislation is clearly in contradiction with provincial legislation dealing with the same matter, then it will be appropriate to move to paramountcy after concluding the characterization stage. However, if paramountcy is uncertain, and the applicant potentially a cross-border transportation undertaking, it may be more efficient to deal with the interjurisdictional immunity question ahead of paramountcy.

In any event, with three new lines of argument against interjurisdictional immunity set out in *Canadian Western Bank*, the result was hardly at issue. Given that the Alberta legislation did not reach the core of banking, much less impair it, the banks' appeal failed.

The final case dealing with interjurisdictional immunity in the McLachlin era was the companion case to *Canadian Western Bank*, *Lafarge*, a case that was already discussed in some detail under the heading of paramountcy. As noted in that discussion, *Lafarge* may be best understood as an illustration by the Court of the advantages of using paramountcy rather than interjurisdictional immunity, even in a case involving a traditional context for interjurisdictional immunity. Otherwise, we find in *Lafarge* numerous echoes of points made in *Canadian Western Bank*: that interjurisdictional immunity

95 *Ibid.* at para. 77 [emphasis in original].

96 *Ibid.* at para. 78.

runs against "the dominant tide of Canadian constitutional jurisprudence"[97] and that it is "an exception to the ordinary rule."[98] And, not surprisingly, Binnie and LeBel JJ. would have found no interjurisdictional immunity in the case in any event.

Ironically, although the Court went to great lengths in *Canadian Western Bank* and *Lafarge* to dissuade litigants from making complex interjurisdictional immunity arguments, some of the most important Supreme Court of Canada decisions in coming years will involve precisely this issue.[99]

F. CONCLUSION

The past fifty years of division of powers jurisprudence has been more about the doctrines and methods of analysis of legal federalism—pith and substance, double aspect, ancillary powers, paramountcy, and interjurisdictional immunity—than about new understandings of sections 91 and 92 powers. This trend only intensified with the arrival of the *Constitution Act, 1982*, the courts' focus largely diverted to the *Charter* and Aboriginal rights. The Supreme Court of Canada has been intent on encouraging flexible, co-operative federalism whereby legislation is generally upheld and disputes allocated to the intergovernmental process. The McLachlin Court has continued the trend of upholding legislation; it has also made important adjustments to constitutional doctrines and methods of analysis to promote this sort of co-operative federalism. As Binnie and LeBel JJ. stated in *Lafarge*: "Federal-provincial-municipal co-operation . . . is not unconstitutional. It is essential."[100] *Lafarge* dealt with the crowded waters of Vancouver harbour. As a result of the Supreme Court's (including the McLachlin Court's) adjustments to key division of powers doctrines, Canadian federal waters are also crowded. Federal, provincial, territorial, municipal, and other actors must remember that the exclusive anchors of sections 91 and 92 attach long anchor lines to boats and barges carrying highly varied legislative cargo, and that consequently the surface waters are a busy place where a watchful eye, a good radio, and thick bumpers are essential to the job of ensuring mutually beneficial coexistence.

---

97 *Lafarge*, above note 58 at para. 4.

98 *Ibid.* at para. 41.

99 See *Quebec (Attorney General) v. Canadian Owners and Pilots Association*, 2010 SCC 39, [2010] 2 S.C.R. 536; *Quebec (Attorney General) v. Lacombe*, 2010 SCC 38, [2010] 2 S.C.R. 453; and *Insite*, above note 11.

100 *Lafarge*, above note 58 at para. 38.

The Reconciliation Doctrine in the McLachlin Court: From a "Final Legal Remedy" to a "Just and Lasting" Process

CONSTANCE MACINTOSH*

A. INTRODUCTION

Our current chief justice, Beverley McLachlin, was appointed to sit on the bench of the Supreme Court of Canada in 1989. At that time, section 35(1) of the *Constitution Act, 1982*, a provision which recognizes and affirms existing Aboriginal and treaty rights, was fairly freshly minted. Although "born in the political arena, it was left to the judiciary to flesh out how these rights would be defined and protected."[1] By 1989, the Court had heard arguments on section 35(1), but had not yet delivered its first set of reasons interpreting it.[2] The situation was considerably different by the time Beverley McLachlin was appointed chief justice, in 2000, as during those eleven years the Court released a number of foundational decisions that interpreted section 35(1) in terms of Aboriginal rights,[3] title rights,[4] and treaty rights.[5] During its

* I would like to thank and acknowledge Michael Asch, John Borrows, Kent McNeil, and Brian Noble for their comments, insights, and helpful conversations on earlier drafts of this paper. I would also like to thank Hamar Foster for conversations on aspects of this paper. Errors are, of course, my own. A draft of this paper was prepared for "The McLachlin Court's First Decade: Reflections on the Past and Projections for the Future," Canadian Bar Association conference, 19 June 2009.

1 Gordon Christie, "Judicial Justification of Recent Developments in Aboriginal Law" (2002) 17:2 C.J.L.S. 41 at 41 [Christie, "Judicial Justification"].

2 The case of *R. v. Sparrow*, [1990] 1 S.C.R 1075, was argued in 1988 [*Sparrow*].

3 See *ibid.*; *R. v. Van der Peet*, [1996] S.C.J. 77, [1996] 2 S.C.R. 507 [*Van der Peet*]; and *R. v. Gladstone*, [1996] 2 S.C.R. 723, [1996] S.C.J. No. 79 [*Gladstone*].

4 *Delgamuukw v. British Columbia*, [1997] 3 S.C.R. 1010 [*Delgamuukw*].

5 See *R. v. Marshall*, [1999] 3 S.C.R. 456; *R. v. Marshall*, [1999] 3 S.C.R. 533 [*Marshall (No. 2)*]; *R. v. Sundown*, [1999] 1 S.C.R. 393; and *R. v. Sioui*, [1990] 1 S.C.R. 1025.

first decade, McLachlin's Court has rendered decisions addressing a broad scope of matters where section 35(1) has been squarely at issue. These have included decisions regarding what section 35(1) means for the rights of Métis people[6] and for the Crown's obligations to Aboriginal peoples, whether as a fiduciary or as a matter of Crown honour.[7] The Court has also spoken to how section 35(1) interacts with the division of powers under the *Constitution Act, 1867*,[8] and with how statutory rights or provisions engage with constitutional and *Charter* rights.[9]

The issue upon which this paper focuses is one that runs through much of the Aboriginal jurisprudence over the last ten years: the idea of "reconciliation."[10] This term is evoked as a norm in Aboriginal rights cases. However, the way in which the term is deployed, the values that inform it, the logic that drives it, and the conclusions that it supports have shifted and are continuing to shift. There are considerable differences between how this term was used at the time of Lamer C.J., its earlier meaning for the bench under McLachlin C.J., and the new role it has evolved to take on most recently. In particular, reconciliation has come to be understood as requiring dynamic processes of negotiation, instead of just serving as a normative justification for infringing Aboriginal rights. This article does not analyze whether the Court's understanding of reconciliation resonates with that of scholars nor does it substantively address what scholars have argued ought to be included in trying to affect reconciliation.[11] Rather, the paper seeks

6 *R. v. Powley*, 2003 SCC 43, [2003] 2 S.C.R. 207 [*Powley*], and *R. v. Blais*, 2003 SCC 44.

7 See *Wewaykum Indian Band v. Canada*, 2002 SCC 79, [2002] 4 S.C.R. 245 [*Wewaykum*], and *Mikisew Cree First Nation v. Canada (Minister of Canadian Heritage)*, [2005] 3 S.C.R. 388 [*Mikisew Cree*].

8 See *R. v. Morris*, 2006 SCC 59 [*Morris*].

9 See *Ermineskin Indian Band and Nations v. Canada*, 2009 SCC 9, [2009] S.C.J. 9 [*Ermineskin*], and *R. v. Kapp*, 2008 SCC 41, [2008] S.C.J. No. 42 [*Kapp*].

10 See Dwight Newman & Danielle Schweitzer, "Between Reconciliation and the Rule(s) of Law: *Tsilhqot'in Nation v British Columbia*" (2008) 41 U.B.C.L. Rev. 249 at para. 3.

11 There is a large and thoughtful body of writing on this matter which offers a variety of perspectives. See, for example, James Tully, *Public Philosophy in a New Key: Volume II: Democracy and Civic Freedom* (Cambridge: Cambridge University Press, 2008) at 223–56 [Tully]; Mark Walters, "Constitutionalism and Political Morality: A Tribute to John D. Whyte, the Morality of Aboriginal Law" (2006) 31 Queen's L.J. 470, esp. at paras. 54–83 [Walters, "Constitutionalism"]; Newman & Schweitzer, *ibid.*; Christie, "Judicial Justification," above note 1; John Borrows, "Sovereignty's Alchemy: An Analysis of *Delgamuukw v. British Columbia*" (1997) 37 Osgoode Hall L.J. 537 [Borrows, "Sovereignty's Alchemy"]; and John Borrows, "Domesticating Doctrines: Aboriginal Peoples after the Royal Commission" (2001) 46 McGill L.J. 615 at para. 64 [Borrows, "Domesticating"], where Borrows writes: "Courts have read Aboriginal rights to land and resources as requiring a reconciliation that asks much more of Aboriginal

RÉSUMÉ

On réfère constamment à la « doctrine de la réconciliation » lorsqu'il est question de décisions relatives à des revendications de droits ancestraux autochtones. Cependant, la manière dont cette doctrine est appliquée a considérablement évolué, en particulier depuis la nomination de Beverley McLachlin en qualité de juge en chef. Dans cet article, on fait le recensement de ces transformations en illustrant la manière dont cette doctrine est de moins en moins invoquée à titre de justification normative pour violer les droits ancestraux. À l'heure actuelle, elle joue plutôt le rôle de processus dynamique pour négocier des relations empreintes de respect, et a démontré son bien-fondé lorsqu'il s'agit d'étayer ce type de relations en tant que relations continues. Par conséquent, la doctrine de réconciliation remaniée modifie la centralité de l'analyse de la violation justifiée à titre de lieu de la surveillance judiciaire du pouvoir discrétionnaire de la Couronne. Dans ce chapitre, on analyse en outre les tensions entre la doctrine et le principe de la primauté du droit, de même que la manière dont la Cour de madame le juge McLachlin a laissé entendre que la doctrine de la réconciliation constitue une pratique qui s'infiltre dans une vaste gamme d'interactions entre la Couronne et les Autochtones, et pas seulement celles qui sont visées par le paragraphe 35(1).

to explore what the Court is signalling or intends when it draws upon the language of reconciliation. As such, the article tracks a complex storyline which is marked with both internal debate and change, as well as with our current chief justice promoting a fairly consistent trajectory.

The flow of this chapter is as follows. The substantive analysis begins in the second section, which identifies the early deployments of the term "reconciliation" and in particular draws attention to distinctions between Lamer C.J.'s understanding and use of "reconciliation," and those of McLachlin C.J. in the years before she was named chief justice. These distinctions set a

---

peoples than it does of Canadians. Reconciliation should not be a front for assimilation." See also Brian Slattery, "The Generative Structure of Aboriginal Rights" (2007) S.C.L.R. (2d) 595 [Slattery, "Generative Structure"]; Dwight Newman, "Reconciliation: Legal Conception(s) and Faces of Justice" in John Whyte, ed., *Moving Toward Justice: Legal Traditions and Aboriginal Justice* (Saskatoon: Purich Publishing, 2008) at 80–87 [Newman, "Reconciliation"]; and Kent McNeil, "Reconciliation and the Supreme Court: The Opposing Views of Chief Justices Lamer and McLachlin" (2003) 2 Indigenous L.J. 1–25 [McNeil, "Reconciliation"].

comparative baseline for the rest of the paper. The third section then turns to the decisions rendered by the Court during Beverley McLachlin's first ten years as chief justice. The third section is divided into two subsections. The first subsection considers whether Lamer C.J.'s approach to reconciliation, as a state of compromise where Aboriginal rights may need to yield to the common good, has been embraced by the current bench. It also identifies how elements of McLachlin C.J.'s formerly articulated approach to reconciliation from when she sat on Lamer C.J.'s bench, surface in various forms, either in her reasons or those of other members of the Court. The second subsection considers how the McLachlin Court casts "reconciliation" as a dynamic process, demanding the establishing of relationships that, like all relationships, must both be founded in mutual respect and be renewed if they are to flourish. The fourth section of the paper considers tensions that arise due to reconciliation interests being largely absent from judicial considerations of non-section 35(1) matters (such as when legal claims turn on statutory interpretation). The fifth section suggests that McLachlin's Court has created some room for reconciliation interests to infuse Aboriginal-Crown law more generally.

B. ORIGIN STORIES: EARLY DIFFERENCES REGARDING THE MEANING OF RECONCILIATION AND THE JUDICIAL ROLE IN ENABLING IT

I begin this analysis of "reconciliation" by briefly sketching out its judicial history. In 1990, Dickson C.J., writing with LaForest J., first drew upon the term "reconciliation" in the context of section 35(1) in *Sparrow*. Here the term was mobilized to explain what section 35(1) called upon the federal government to do:

> [Section 35(1) requires that] federal power be reconciled with federal duty and the best way to achieve that reconciliation is to demand the justification of any government regulation that infringes upon or denies aboriginal rights.[12]

Thus section 35(1) mandated governmental restraint. Previously discretionary exercises of power now had to be reconciled with governmental duties or obligations.[13] When Dickson C.J.'s successor, Lamer C.J., addressed

12 *Sparrow*, above note 2 at para. 62.

13 For a careful discussion of the *Sparrow* decision and its theoretical logic, see Michael Asch & Patrick Macklem, "Aboriginal Rights and Canadian Sovereignty: An Essay on *R. v. Sparrow*" (1991) 29 Alta. L. Rev. 498 [Asch & Macklem]. For a discussion of how the content

section 35(1) some six years later in 1996,[14] he too identified its purpose as being realized through reconciliation. His interpretation, although adopted by the majority of the Court, developed the reconciliation doctrine in a fashion that sparked disagreement. As discussed below, McLachlin J. (as she then was) interpreted the directions in *Sparrow* quite differently in terms of what they authorized and required, and also identified a more clear division between the legitimate scope of judicial versus political decision making.

In an oft-cited passage in *R. v. Van der Peet*, Lamer C.J. wrote the following:

> [W]hat s. 35(1) does is provide the constitutional framework through which the fact that aboriginals lived on the land in distinctive societies, with their own practices, traditions and cultures, is acknowledged and reconciled with the sovereignty of the Crown. The substantive rights which fall within the provision must be defined in light of this purpose; the aboriginal rights recognized and affirmed by s. 35(1) must be directed towards the reconciliation of the pre-existence of aboriginal societies with the sovereignty of the Crown.[15]

This passage affirms that section 35(1) is interpreted to mandate reconciliation, but suggests a changed emphasis on who must undertake accommodations to enable that reconciliation. Chief Justice Lamer further clarified his interpretation when he wrote that when adjudicating claims, courts must "be sensitive to the aboriginal perspective, but they must also be aware that aboriginal rights exist within the general legal system of Canada."[16] That is, the majority position saw a clear hierarchy. Section 35(1)'s promise of reconciliation was interpreted to take place against the backdrop of the existing Canadian legal order.

Former Chief Justice Lamer's position on what reconciliation requires of Aboriginal people was perhaps most clearly articulated when he delineated interests that the state could legitimately call upon to limit Aboriginal rights, so as to enable this "reconciliation of the pre-existence of aboriginal societies with the sovereignty of the Crown."[17] He addressed this matter

---

of s. 35(1) was originally intended to be determined, see Kent McNeil, "The Decolonization of Canada: Moving toward Recognition of Aboriginal Governments" (1994) 7:1 Western Legal History 113.

14 *Van der Peet* and *Gladstone*, above note 3.

15 *Van der Peet*, *ibid.* at para. 31, Lamer C.J.C.

16 *Ibid.* at para. 49, Lamer C.J.C.

17 *Ibid.* at para. 31, Lamer C.J.C.

in one of the companion cases to *Van der Peet*—*R. v. Gladstone*.[18] After first asserting that "limits" on Aboriginal rights in furtherance of objectives "of sufficient importance to the broader community" are "a necessary part of reconciliation,"[19] the then chief justice elaborated as follows:

> with regards to the distribution of the fisheries resource after conservation goals have been met, objectives such as the pursuit of economic and regional fairness, and the recognition of the historical reliance upon, and participation in, the fishery by non-aboriginal groups, are the type of objectives which can (at least in the right circumstances) satisfy this standard [for justified infringement]. In the right circumstances, such objectives are in the interest of all Canadians and, more importantly, the *reconciliation* of aboriginal societies with the rest of Canadian society may well *depend* on their successful attainment.[20]

As recently observed by Dwight Newman, "[i]nstead of reconciliation functioning as a concept that calls for limits on federal power in light of federal duties, it becomes a concept that limits the scope of section 35."[21] Interpreting section 35(1)'s mandate of reconciliation as requiring Aboriginal people to accept the unilateral diminution of their rights has been subjected to considerable scholarly critique.[22] Of relevance for this article is the fact that McLachlin J. (as she then was) expressed disagreement with the approach to section 35(1) which Lamer C.J. had articulated.[23] In *Van der Peet*, she voiced an interpretation of section 35(1), and an understanding of what

18 *Gladstone*, above note 3. The reasons in *Gladstone* and *Van der Peet* were delivered on the same day, 21 August 1996.

19 *Ibid.* at para. 73.

20 *Ibid.* at para. 75 [emphasis added].

21 Newman, "Reconciliation," above note 11 at 82.

22 The core critique relates to the fact that the non-Aboriginal reliance or interest is in some instances the direct consequence of Aboriginal rights having historically been denied or ignored. Conceptual and logical concerns are thus raised by historic denial being used to justify the lawfulness of contemporary erosion. See, for example, Asch & Macklem, above note 13; Christie, "Judicial Justification," above note 1; Borrows, "Sovereignty's Alchemy," above note 11; and Borrows, "Domesticating," above note 11 at para. 64. See also Russell Barsh & James Sakej Youngblood Henderson, "The Supreme Court *Van der Peet* Trilogy: Native Imperialism and Ropes of Sand" (1997) 42 McGill L.J. 993, and Kent McNeil, "How Can Infringements of the Constitutional Rights of Aboriginal Peoples Be Justified?" (1997) 8:2 Const. Forum Const. 33.

23 For a detailed analysis of the contrasting approaches to reconciliation of former Chief Justice Lamer and current Chief Justice McLachlin, focusing upon cases prior to 2000, see McNeil, "Reconciliation," above note 11.

reconciliation means and requires of the Crown and Aboriginal peoples, which was quite different in several respects.

In particular she found that reconciliation did not require Aboriginal people to cede their rights without consent. She found that both this demand, and the role Lamer C.J. articulated for courts in approving such decisions in the name of societal reconciliation, were contrary to the goal of reconciliation. She wrote:

> As *Sparrow* recognized, one of the two fundamental purposes of s. 35(1) was the achievement of a just and lasting settlement of aboriginal claims. The Chief Justice . . . correctly notes that such a settlement must be founded on the reconciliation of aboriginal rights with the larger non-aboriginal culture in which they must . . . find their exercise. The question is how this reconciliation of the different legal cultures of aboriginal and non-aboriginal peoples is to be accomplished. More particularly, *does the goal of reconciliation of aboriginal and non-aboriginal interests require that we permit the Crown to require a judicially authorized transfer of the aboriginal right to non-aboriginals without the consent of the aboriginal people, without treaty, and without compensation? I cannot think it does.*[24]

Justice McLachlin argued that the only lawful limitations on section 35(1) rights were internal (for example, as defined by the inherent scope or nature of the right) or external ones that "any property owner or rights user would reasonably expect . . . if the resource is to be used now and in the future."[25] She then asked, "[h]ow, without amending the Constitution, can the Crown cut down the aboriginal right? . . . [Rights] can be diminished only through treaty and constitutional amendment."[26] On this interpretation, aside from limitations that went to the one external exception of reasonable use, any unilateral act which diminished section 35(1) rights would violate the Constitution, and so could not be endorsed by a court.

Not only did McLachlin J. argue that Lamer C.J.'s approach was constitutionally problematic, she was also very clear that the sort of concessions that Lamer C.J. believed were necessary to effect reconciliation were not practically necessary:

---

24 *Van der Peet*, above note 3 at para. 310, McLachlin J. in dissent [emphasis added].

25 *Ibid.* at para. 306, McLachlin J. in dissent. Then Justice McLachlin also noted that "future cases may endorse limitation of aboriginal rights on other bases" (at para. 306).

26 *Ibid.* at para. 315, McLachlin J. in dissent.

> [T]he right imposes its own internal limit . . . The government may impose additional limits under the rubric of justification to ensure that the right is exercised responsibly . . . There is no need to impose further limits on it to effect reconciliation between aboriginal and non-aboriginal peoples.[27]

Therefore, prior to being appointed chief justice, McLachlin J. arguably held a clear theory of how section 35(1) operated to enable reconciliation. She positioned the judiciary's key contribution to reconciliation, as mandated by section 35(1), as that of "recognizing the aboriginal legal entitlement." She wrote:

> The second reason why it is unnecessary to adopt the broad doctrine of justification proposed by the Chief Justice is that other means, yet unexploited, exist for resolving the different legal perspectives of aboriginal and non-aboriginal people. In my view, a just calibration of the two perspectives starts from the premise that full value must be accorded to such aboriginal rights as may be established on the facts of the particular case. Only by fully recognizing the aboriginal legal entitlement can the aboriginal legal perspective be satisfied. At this stage of the process—the stage of defining aboriginal rights—the courts have an important role to play.

The manner in which these legal rights and two legal perspectives would then be reconciled with political and social interests was to be through treaty negotiations. To this end, McLachlin J. wrote:

> The process must go on to consider the non-aboriginal perspective—how the aboriginal right can be legally accommodated within the framework of non-aboriginal law. Traditionally, this has been done through the treaty process, based on the concept of the aboriginal people and the Crown negotiating and concluding a just solution to their divergent interests, given the historical fact that they are irretrievably compelled to live together. *At this stage, the stage of reconciliation, the courts play a less important role. It is for the aboriginal peoples and the other peoples of Canada to work out a just accommodation of the recognized aboriginal rights.* This process—definition of the rights guaranteed by s. 35(1) followed by negotiated settlements—is the means envisioned in *Sparrow*, as I perceive it, for reconciling the aboriginal and non-aboriginal legal perspectives.[28]

---

27 *Ibid.* at para. 312, McLachlin J. in dissent.

28 *Ibid.* at para. 313, McLachlin J. in dissent [emphasis added].

To summarize these key passages, McLachlin J. did not see the role of the Court as affecting or creating a state of reconciliation. Rather, the Court's powers under section 35(1) were to recognize the legal entitlements which would inform political negotiations about mutual accommodation, which would in turn support reconciliation through "a just and lasting settlement." Effectively, the judiciary would oversee the reconciliation process, while the substance of how interests and rights were reconciled was a matter of political negotiation and balancing.[29] Thus, her perspective at this time was that the accommodation of non-Aboriginal interests and any recognition that reconciliation may require eroding Aboriginal rights was a *political matter* to be assessed in a *negotiation process.* Aside from the reasonable use restraint described above, infringements could not be unilaterally imposed by the state.

This theory, so strongly expressed in 1996, was arguably absent by 1997, when in *Delgamuukw v. British Columbia* McLachlin J. simply wrote that she concurred with the chief justice's set of reasons.[30] Chief Justice Lamer had found in *Delgamuukw* that the process of reconciliation could justify state infringement of Aboriginal title for a vast array of activities, including the "settlement of foreign populations," the creation of infrastructure, and the exploitation of various resources,[31] a rather overwhelming list that suggested that section 35(1) supported a relationship of power and priorities only modestly different than how it was when Aboriginal rights were ignored.[32] The whole bench appeared to have endorsed the same approach. There was also a unanimous decision from the Court in *Marshall (No. 2)*[33] that further extended Lamer C.J.'s approach to infringement as a route for enabling the reconciliation of Aboriginal and treaty rights and interests with those of the general Canadian public. Notably, in all these cases, including both Lamer C.J. and McLachlin J.'s reasons in *Van der Peet*, the Court has been unanimous in stating that reconciliation will come about only through negotiations. The core distinction arising from *Van der Peet* was differing interpretations of what section 35(1) authorized or required the state to do.

29 I specifically thank John Borrows for engaging me in conversations on this point.

30 *Delgamuukw*, above note 4 at para. 109.

31 *Ibid.* at para. 161.

32 On this point, see James Tully, "The Struggles of Indigneous Peoples for and of Freedom" in Ardith Walkem & Halie Bruce, eds., *Box of Treasures or Empty Box: Twenty Years of Section 35* (Penticton, BC: Theytus Publishing, 2003) 272 at 287. See also Christie, "Judicial Justification," above note 1 at 51–52, where he questions "what constitutionalization has amounted to."

33 *Marshall (No. 2)*, above note 5.

C. THE COURT UNDER CHIEF JUSTICE McLACHLIN AND RECONCILIATION

The first subsection below considers whether former Chief Justice Lamer's approach to infringement, as a necessary corollary to reconciliation, has been endorsed or perpetuated by the McLachlin Court. It does so by examining cases where Aboriginal rights were proven and there was cause to consider if an infringing regulation or law was justified. This examination is effectively inconclusive on this point. The second subsection proposes that McLachlin's Court has developed a theory of reconciliation which essentially displaces the practical relevance of Lamer C.J.'s approach.

1) Reconciliation and Infringement

During the first ten years following Beverley McLachlin's appointment as chief justice, there were only three cases in which Aboriginal or treaty rights were found to exist—*R. v. Powley*,[34] *R. v. Morris*,[35] and *R. v. Sappier; R. v. Gray*,[36]—resulting in situations where the Court turned to a justification analysis. Some members of the Court also took the opportunity to speak to justification in *R. v. Mitchell*.[37] These cases reveal little about whether the Court under McLachlin C.J. will continue to adhere to the approach endorsed by the Lamer Court of interpreting the reconciliation mandate as sometimes requiring and authorizing the erosion of Aboriginal rights for the general social good. As will be discussed in subsection C(2), the answer to this question may have come to bear rather reduced significance, given other developments in the reconciliation jurisprudence. Intriguingly, in several instances these decisions resonate in various ways with the interpretation of section 35(1) that McLachlin C.J. proposed in her dissent in *Van der Peet*. These cases are discussed chronologically.

Mitchell involved a claimed right to be exempt from paying taxes when crossing international borders with goods intended for personal consumption or sale to other Aboriginal people. In this case, both the majority and the minority decisions found that the claimed right was not made out. This finding was a matter of evidence for the majority. However, the minority set of reasons, written by Binnie J., was founded on the claimed right not

34 *Powley*, above note 6.

35 *Morris*, above note 8.

36 *R. v. Sappier; R. v. Gray*, 2006 SCC 54 [*Sappier*].

37 *Mitchell v. M.N.R.*, 2001 SCC 33, [2001] S.C.J. No. 33 [*Mitchell*].

having survived the assertion of Crown sovereignty, because it was ousted pursuant to the rules of sovereign succession.[38] Justice Binnie found that this conclusion was consistent with enabling reconciliation because

> [the claimed right] relates to national interests that all of us have in common rather than to distinctive interests that for some purposes differentiate an aboriginal community. In my view, reconciliation of these interests in this particular case favours an affirmation of our collective sovereignty.[39]

This sense of reconciliation resonates with that of former Chief Justice Lamer in *Van der Peet*, given its emphasis upon reconciliation through identifying and promoting what are assumed to be common interests. As noted above, McLachlin C.J., writing for the majority in *Mitchell*, found that the claimed right was not made out, and so did not engage in a justification analysis. However, McLachlin C.J. did respond briefly to Binnie J.'s deployment of the doctrine of sovereign succession.

Although stating that she was refraining from commenting upon whether the doctrine of sovereign succession was relevant for defining Aboriginal rights, she pointed out that the jurisprudence of the Court had already "affirmed the doctrines of extinguishment, infringement, and justification as the appropriate framework for resolving conflicts between aboriginal rights and competing claims, including claims based on Crown sovereignty."[40] This statement could be taken to endorse the jurisprudence of her predecessor, with which she had once so vigorously taken issue. Alternately it could be read as merely stating a fact—that the jurisprudence exists and so there is already a route for dealing with the sorts of issues raised in the litigation, without bringing in another doctrine.

Two years after *Mitchell*, in *R. v. Powley*, the Crown attempted to justify legislation which infringed Métis Aboriginal rights on the basis of conservation[41] and administrative complexity.[42] However, the conservation argument was based upon a rather scanty factual foundation and so merited little discussion by the Court, except the observation that if conservation was indeed an issue, "the Métis would still be entitled to a priority allocation to

38 *Ibid.* at para. 172, Binnie J. for Major J.

39 *Ibid.* at para. 164, Binnie J. for Major J.

40 *Ibid.* at para. 63 [emphasis added], McLachlin C.J. for Gonthier, Iacobucci, Arbour, and LeBel JJ.

41 *Powley*, above note 6 at para. 48.

42 *Ibid.* at para. 49.

satisfy their subsistence needs."[43] Although there is no suggestion here that the Court would moderate the right for the benefit of the Canadian public, no argument on this point was actually made, so it would be inappropriate to read much into this. The administrative burden argument was, not surprisingly, dismissed as an inappropriate "basis for defeating . . . rights under the Constitution of Canada."[44] Having found in this case that there was no lawful ground for denying Métis people the right to hunt, the Court gestured briefly to the work which lay ahead: "In the longer term, a combination of negotiation and judicial settlement will more clearly define the contours of the Métis right to hunt."[45] We see here something of an echo of McLachlin C.J.'s earlier writing—that the court will identify the legal rights, but only negotiation will enable a full understanding of what those rights mean in the contemporary setting.

In *R. v. Morris*,[46] however, the question of whether public interests justify infringement in the name of reconciling Aboriginal rights with public safety concerns was aggressively argued. This case concerned whether a provincial prohibition on night hunting unlawfully infringed a treaty right to hunt "as formerly," given that the Aboriginal party's ancestors who had signed the treaty had engaged in night hunting. Unfortunately for the purposes of this paper, the majority judgment did not consider the arguments on justified infringement because they found that the provincial law in question was rendered jurisdictionally inoperative, pursuant to the division of powers.[47] The dissenting judgment, authored by McLachlin C.J. and Fish J., also did not address the justification analysis. However, we do see the resurgence of some of McLachlin J.'s (as she then was) reasoning in dissent in *Van der Peet*.

Chief Justice McLachlin and Fish J. found against the Aboriginal claimants not on the basis that a legislated infringement was justified in the name of reconciliation, but because they found that the constitutionally protected right did not extend to the practice at issue, which they had defined as hunting in an unsafe manner.[48] They based their decision on an interpretation of the right's own internal limits, as defined by the understandings that both the Aboriginal and European signatories would have brought to the

---

43 *Ibid.* at para. 48.

44 *Ibid.* at para. 49.

45 *Ibid.* at para. 50.

46 *Morris*, above note 8.

47 *Ibid.* at paras. 53–55, Deschamps and Abella JJ. for Binnie and Charron JJ.

48 *Ibid.* at paras. 110, 119, and 132, McLachlin C.J. and Fish J. for Bastarache J.

treaty table. This approach, of focusing foremost on defining legal entitlement, is the same approach that McLachlin C.J. had said would clearly pass constitutional muster in her dissent in *Van der Peet.* It is not insignificant for the objective of reconciliation that this approach also implicitly supports a robust role for indigenous self-regulation and laws in defining the scope of Aboriginal and treaty rights.

The only other case in which a right was proven was *R. v. Sappier; R. v. Gray.*[49] As the Crown did not attempt to argue that its infringing legislation was justified, the Court does not discuss its approach to infringement,[50] although it does bring up the matter of reconciliation. In a situationally nuanced phrasing of the purpose of section 35(1), Bastarache J. wrote that that section

> is to provide a constitutional framework for the protection of the distinctive cultures of aboriginal peoples, so that their prior occupation of North America can be recognized and reconciled with the sovereignty of the Crown.[51]

Under this approach, the purpose of section 35(1) is still about reconciliation, but the manner in which it enables this purpose is framed in terms of granting protection, not sanctioning erosion. Once again, given the brevity of the comment in *Sappier,* it is important not to speculate too much about what was intended. However, further insight may arise through the fact that the Court was effectively unanimous in this case in finding that the proper interpretation of the *Van der Peet* test, for identifying Aboriginal rights, had evolved to more closely resemble the approach that had been advocated for by McLachlin J. and L'Heureux-Dubé J. in their dissenting reasons in *Van der Peet.*[52] This could suggest that more is indeed at play here.

The case also stands out for the robust manner in which the Court defines the claimed right. The scope of the right—to harvest timber from Crown lands for domestic purposes such as home building—will almost definitely result in conflicts with existing Crown practices.[53] Given the consequences

---

49 *Sappier,* above note 36.

50 *Ibid.* at paras. 54–55, Bastarache J. for McLachlin C.J and LeBel, Deschamps, Fish, Abella, Charron, and Rothstein JJ. Justice Binnie concurred except on one aspect of how the right in question ought to be defined (at para. 74).

51 *Ibid.* at para. 22.

52 *Ibid.* at paras. 33–47.

53 Constance MacIntosh, "Developments in Aboriginal Law: The 2006–2007 Term" (2007) 38 S.C.L.R. (2d) 1 at 36–37 [MacIntosh, "2006–2007"].

of this definition for industry tree farm licence holders and others, governments were effectively put on alert that they cannot let negotiations about the contemporary manifestations of Aboriginal legal entitlements languish.

There is little to be specifically gleaned from the rights cases discussed above regarding how the current Court links governmental authority to infringe upon Aboriginal rights to its vision of what is required to enable reconciliation, although it has cast considerable doubts on provincial authority to infringe upon Aboriginal rights.[54] We do, however, see considerable development of the concept of reconciliation in a series of other cases that were released in 2004 and 2005. These cases follow a different line and deploy the concept of reconciliation to signal a dynamic process.[55]

2) Foregrounding Reconciliation as a Process

The theory of reconciliation to which the members of McLachlin's Court subscribe, and the role of the judiciary in enabling reconciliation, emerge strongly in a pair of decisions written by McLachlin C.J.: *Taku River Tlingit First Nation v. British Columbia*[56] and *Haida Nation v. British Columbia*.[57] The theory subsequently guides the analysis in the reasons authored by Binnie J. in *Mikisew Cree First Nation v. Canada*.[58] There is thematic unity regarding the notion of reconciliation in all three of these decisions. Notably, they are all decisions where one judge wrote for the full court. Given this level of unity, it becomes appropriate to speak of McLachlin's Court as sharing a theory of reconciliation. As discussed below, the evolved notion of reconciliation *moderates the centrality* of the justified infringement analysis as the location for judicial oversight of whether the Crown has acted in a manner consistent with the reconciliation process.

In *Haida Nation*, the Court was asked to decide whether Crown obligations arose in the context of claimed rights which had not been recognized

54 See, for example, Kent McNeil, "Reconciliation and Third Party Interests: *Tsilhqot'in Nation v. British Columbia*" (2010) 8 Indigeous L.J. 7 [McNeil, "Third Party Interests"], and Kent McNeil, "The Métis and the Doctrine of Interjurisdictional Immunity: A Commentary" in Frederica Wilson & Melanie Mallet, eds., *Métis-Crown Relations: Rights, Identity, Jurisdiction and Governance* (Toronto: Irwin Law, 2008) 289–322.

55 See Newman, "Reconciliation," above note 11 at 85.

56 *Taku River First Nation v. British Columbia (Project Assessment Director)*, [2004] 3 S.C.R. 550, 2004 SCC 74 [*Taku River*].

57 *Haida Nation v. British Columbia (Minister of Forests)*, [2004] 3 S.C.R. 511, 2004 SCC 73 [*Haida Nation*].

58 *Mikisew Cree First Nation v. Canada (Minister of Canadian Heritage)*, [2005] 3 S.C.R. 388, 2005 SCC 69.

by the Canadian state or pursuant to a judicial process. (The Court gives such claimed rights the rather problematic label "unproven rights."[59]) The specific question was whether, in such situations, the Crown was under any unique obligation to acknowledge or address those claims through a process of consultation and accommodation.[60] The Court's answer, in brief, was that sometimes such procedural and potentially substantive obligations *had* to arise, because, if they did not, reconciliation would not be possible.[61] Writing for the Court, McLachlin C.J. observed that consultation was likely a necessary precondition for reconciliation, because it could "preserve . . . the Aboriginal interest pending claims resolution and foster . . . a relationship between the parties that makes possible negotiations, the preferred process for achieving ultimate reconciliation."[62]

This approach, to be adopted when claimed rights or "proven" rights[63] may be at odds with actual or proposed state decisions or laws, has the effect of *displacing* the *practical relevance* of the justified infringement analysis. Whereas in the face of conflict, the *Van der Peet* (and *Sparrow*) approach would ask whether a law is justified in infringing an Aboriginal right given competing public interests, this approach asks whether the law-making or decision-making process which makes infringement a possibility was lawful given the claimed Aboriginal interests. The Court thus interprets section 35(1)'s reconciliation mandate as requiring the state to engage in negotiation about the terms under which a right can potentially be impaired in the name of social, economic, or other interests *before* it can expect any judicial endorsement that its ultimate assessment is constitutionally sound. The *significance* of the state objective—as the litmus test for whether infringements are constitutional—consequently fades as the judicial focus on constitu-

59 See discussion in Constance MacIntosh, "On Obligations and Contamination: The Crown–Aboriginal Relationship in the Context of Internationally-sourced Infringements" (2009) 72:2 Sask. L. Rev. 187 [MacIntosh, "On Obligations"].

60 *Haida Nation*, above note 57 at para. 6, McLachlin C.J.

61 *Ibid.* at para. 33, McLachlin C.J. She wrote that unless obligations arose prior to proof, then when "the distant goal of proof is finally reached, the Aboriginal peoples may find their land and resources changed and denuded. This is not reconciliation. Nor is it honourable" (at para. 33).

62 *Ibid.* at para. 38, McLachlin C.J.

63 In *Mikisew Cree*, above note 7 at para. 59, Binnie J. observes that in the case of a proposed "taking up" under a treaty, that "it is not correct . . . to move directly to a *Sparrow* analysis." Rather, the consultation process must be assessed. The Court offered further clarification on this point when it heard *Beckman v. Little Salmon/Carmacks First Nation*, [2010] 3 S.C.R. 103 [*Little Salmon*]. This case considers the duty to consult in the context of a modern treaty.

tionality shifts to scrutinizing the consistency of the process with what is *necessary* to foster respectful relations. Presumably, when the process meets constitutional standards and is consistent with the honour of the Crown, then the ultimate Crown decision about how to balance interests will likely pass muster.[64] In this way, the Court robustly shifted the role that the state and Aboriginal parties can expect it to play in overseeing the reconciliation process.

Chief Justice McLachlin's discussion of reconciliation in *Haida Nation* and *Taku River* resonates somewhat with her reasons in dissent in *Van der Peet,* where she stressed that Aboriginal people's constitutionalized rights could, in most instances, be lawfully abrogated only by consent—that is, by treaty. In *Haida Nation,* she brings a consonant position forward, reminding the parties that "[t]reaties serve to reconcile pre-existing Aboriginal sovereignty with assumed Crown sovereignty."[65] By implication, incident-specific judicial decisions about whether or not certain statutes or regulations can lawfully infringe upon a certain right are positioned as playing a marginal role in the reconciliation process. Writing on recent jurisprudence, Mark Walters made this point in a very simple fashion. He wrote: "By 'reconciliation,' the Court does not mean a technical process of fitting disparate parts together—it is not like reconciling financial accounts."[66]

Having foregrounded negotiated and consensual agreements, as opposed to judicial findings, as the key routes to reconciliation, McLachlin C.J. resurrected one of her objections to former Chief Justice Lamer's approach to infringement in *Van der Peet.* As noted above, she had objected to his approach to infringement because it permitted the Crown to unilaterally erode section 35(1) rights in the name of reconciling those rights with public interests. In *Haida,* the Court unanimously endorsed the conclusion that consultation pending resolution of a claim may be required because "[t]o unilaterally exploit a claimed resource during the process of proving and resolving the Aboriginal claim to that resource, may be to deprive the Aboriginal claimants of some or all of the benefit of the resource. That is not honourable."[67] Returning to this practical reading in *Mikisew Cree,* Binnie J. described consultation as "key to [the] achievement of the overall objective

64 See *Mikisew Cree,* above note 7.

65 *Haida Nation,* above note 57 at para. 20, McLachlin C.J.

66 Walters, "Constitutionalism," above note 11 at para. 54.

67 *Haida Nation,* above note 57 at para. 27, McLachlin C.J.

of the modern law of treaty and aboriginal rights, namely, reconciliation."[68] Reconciliation is centrally achieved *not* by determining how Aboriginal rights may need to be infringed in the name of the public good, but by *negotiating* how to respect the various legal and social interests.

Although the McLachlin Court's vision of reconciliation would, in some instances, restrain the Crown from acting unilaterally in a way that affected "unproven" Aboriginal rights, this vision does not suggest that the Crown must yield to Aboriginal perspectives on the appropriate outcome of the consultation process. Instead, the Court indicates at many points in *Haida Nation* and *Taku River* that the ultimate decision about how to proceed in situations of "unproven rights" rests with the Crown, and that the Crown is required to balance societal and Aboriginal interests, which may result in decisions that do not meet the approval of the Aboriginal parties.[69]

Arguably, the McLachlin Court is exercising caution here, to carefully carve out the territory of judicial versus political roles in enabling reconciliation. Once again, this resonates with then Justice McLachlin's approach to the court's proper role in the reconciliation process as articulated in her dissent in *Van der Peet*. As discussed in *Haida Nation*, this approach preserves a robust role for treaties, and ensures that the obligation to consult does not result in Aboriginal parties experiencing as fulsome an outcome as they potentially could through treaty negotiations. Such an outcome would be undesirable to the McLachlin Court, because it would be too close to enabling a situation where courts—and not consensual political processes—impose terms for reconciliation (which, of course, would not be a reconciliation at all!).[70] Nonetheless, the judicial push to define rights

---

68 *Mikisew Cree*, above note 7 at para. 63, Binnie J. [emphasis added].

69 *Haida Nation*, above note 57 at paras. 45, 48, and 50; *Taku River*, above note 56 at para. 42. This outcome has been critiqued, as has the pair of decisions, for setting up a complicated task with inadequate guidance. For a critique that the cases assert an assimilative pressure upon Aboriginal peoples to accede to Canadian law's categories (and thus deny their own), see Gordon Christie, "A Colonial Reading of Recent Jurisprudence: *Sparrow, Delgamuukw* and *Haida Nation*" (2005) 23 Windsor Y.B. Access Just. 17. For a general discussion of advantages and "pitfalls" of this jurisprudence, see Timothy Huyer, "Honour of the Crown: The New Approach to Crown–Aboriginal Reconciliation" (March 2006) 21 Windsor Rev. Legal Soc. Issues 33. For a discussion of how the cases were applied in the first few years after they were rendered, see Gordon Christie, "Developing Case Law: The Future of Consultation and Accommodation" (2006) 39 U.B.C.L. Rev. 139 at paras. 66–129.

70 See McNeil, "Third Party Interests," above note 54, where he observes that such decisions have the effect of recognizing rights, but not reconciling them. On the importance of distinguishing between recognition and reconciliation, see Slattery, "Generative Structure," above note 11.

through treaties has been critiqued as a form of neocolonial consensual entailment—as the outcome of treaties seems to be Aboriginal people ceding some rights so as to have other rights affirmed, instead of having all existing rights affirmed.[71] The newly conceptualized reconciliation process may modestly assuage this critique.

The McLachlin Court identifies the reconciliation process—which on a practical level is only marginally about resolving specific clashes, and centrally about enabling processes for finding ways to agree to live together—as perpetual or ongoing. This aspect of the Court's understanding of "reconciliation" is raised as part of a general discussion in *Haida,* and then explicitly applied in *Mikisew Cree.* In *Haida Nation,* McLachlin C.J. wrote:

> the duty to consult and accommodate is part of a process of fair dealing and reconciliation that begins with the assertion of sovereignty and continues beyond formal claims resolution. Reconciliation is not a final legal remedy in the usual sense. Rather it is a process flowing from rights guaranteed by s. 35(1) of the *Constitution Act, 1982.*[72]

The Court could not have been clearer in signalling that political energies will need to go into reconciling the consequences of how "pre-existing Aboriginal sovereignty" articulate with "assumed Crown sovereignty"[73] for as long as there are Aboriginal peoples and a Crown in Canada. Writing on how the Court used "reconciliation" in its decisions in *Haida Nation* and *Taku River,* Dwight Newman describes the jurisprudence as transforming section 35(1) "from a static guarantee into a bulwark of a dynamic constitutional process" and "transform[ing] the conception of reconciliation from a description of an end state into a concept that . . . shapes a creationary constitutional process."[74] This approach is resonant with that advocated by such political philosophers as James Tully, who writes:

> [R]econciliation is neither a form of recognition handed down to Indigenous peoples from the state nor a final settlement of some kind. It is an on-going partnership negotiated by free peoples based on principles they can both endorse and open to modification *en passant.*[75]

71 See Tully, above note 11 at 278.

72 *Haida Nation,* above note 57 at para. 32.

73 This phrasing is drawn from *ibid.* at para. 20.

74 Newman, "Reconciliation," above note 11 at 85.

75 Tully, above note 11 at 223. I thank John Borrows for introducing me to this volume.

The interpretation of reconciliation which is articulated in *Haida Nation*, that it is a process with certain tangible markers along the way (like treaties), is aggressively put into play in the reasons for judgment in *Mikisew Cree*. Here the litigation concerned a treaty term which precluded the exercise of certain rights on tracts of land "as may be required or taken up" by the Crown for various purposes.[76] The Crown decided to take up land for what the Court observed was likely an appropriate purpose given the terms of the treaty.[77] It wanted to build a winter road that would cross over treaty land and join various communities. One group of treaty beneficiaries objected on the ground that they held rights to be consulted and accommodated, due to likely impacts upon their rights to hunt and trap under the treaty, and that the consultation about these impacts had been inadequate. Among other arguments, the minister took the position that consultation and accommodation had already taken place, prior to the treaty being signed in 1899, and were reflected in the terms of the treaty itself.[78] In short, the Crown argued that it had already fulfilled its obligations to honourably effect a reconciliation, and that it could act upon its treaty right to take up land without further consultation. The Court disagreed.

In response to the Crown's argument, Binnie J. wrote:

> [The Crown's position] is not correct . . . Treaty making is an important stage in the long process of reconciliation, but it is only a stage. What occurred at Fort Chilewyan in 1899 was not the complete discharge of the duty arising from the honour of the Crown, but a rededication of it.
>
> In summary, the 1899 negotiations were the first step in a long journey that is unlikely to end any time soon.[79]

This decision represents a fine-tuning and clarification of the relationship between reconciliation and treaty-making.[80] What can fairly be observed thus far is that in the early jurisprudence, as described above, the process of negotiating treaties was described as "the stage of reconciliation."[81] Here the process of negotiating a treaty is no longer recognized as "*the*

76 *Mikisew Cree*, above note 7 at para. 3, Binnie J.

77 *Ibid.* at para. 60, Binnie J.

78 *Ibid.* at para. 53, Binnie J.

79 *Ibid.* at paras. 54–55, Binnie J.

80 This relationship is further developed in the context of a modern treaty in *Little Salmon*, above note 63. As this decision was delivered during McLachlin C.J.'s second decade as chief justice, it is not discussed here.

81 *Van der Peet*, above note 3 at para. 313, McLachlin J. in dissent.

stage." Instead, it is an "important stage . . . but it is only a stage." The consequences of this evolved understanding of the relationship between treaties and reconciliation are considerable. This shift illustrates a close attentiveness on the part of the Court to what their prior formulations did or did not effectively signal or clearly enable.

The ability to add nuance, responsiveness, and incremental change—in novel situations, or based upon the experience of how reasons have been applied and interpreted (and their practical outcomes)—is key for enabling the common law system to produce just outcomes. Such revisiting and revisionism is highly desirable in this area of law, "given the complexity and sensitivity of the task"[82] required by section 35(1).

In his recent writings about specific aspects of the *Van der Peet* test, and how the Court "has quietly initiated the process of reshaping the test's basic tenets,"[83] Brian Slattery makes the following observation:

> This evolution in the jurisprudence should come as no surprise. It is a distinctive feature of common law systems to shun absolute principles conceived *a priori* in favour of flexible principles fleshed out in concrete cases. The *Van der Peet* decision was handed down at a time when there was a dearth of judicial authority on the Aboriginal rights recognized in section 35(1) . . . . While the test served its purpose at the time, inevitably it has needed revision and amendment.[84]

So, just over a year after the reasons in *Haida Nation* and *Taku River* were released, with their emphasis upon reconciliation as an ongoing process, we have a concrete example in *Mikisew Cree* of what the Court meant when it wrote that reconciliation is a process that continues "beyond formal claims resolution." A treaty is not a final accommodation of Aboriginal and Crown interests, but rather a rededication that the Crown will continue to reconcile conflicting interests when its activities or interests may impinge upon those of Aboriginal peoples (moderated, of course, by the actual terms of the treaty). The promise of "reconciliation" of section 35(1) is a promise to engage in processes of attempting to come to consensual agreements about how to live together, where those agreements are not final but rather a template for managing good relations, which is to be revisited as circumstances

82 Slattery, "Generative Structure," above note 11 at 628.

83 *Ibid.* at 598.

84 *Ibid.* at 628.

change. However, jurisprudential findings do not always support the formation of such positive processes or relationships of respect.

D. UNRECONCILED TENSIONS

Several of the decisions rendered by the McLachlin Court in its first decade have, in various ways, referred to the need to enable a "just and lasting settlement," a phrase which, following *Mikisew Cree*, could fairly be recast as a "just and lasting process." Decisions such as *Haida Nation*, *Taku River*, and *Mikisew Cree* clearly indicate that the Court contemplates the formation of relationships of mutual respect, as well as processes for maintaining and refreshing those relationships, as pivotal to realizing this goal.[85] The jurisprudence discussed above supports this goal in several ways. One core means is by requiring the Crown and Aboriginal peoples to engage in political dialogue through the consultation and accommodation process. As a result, neither party should take the other party by surprise, and neither party should experience a sense of its interests being denigrated or ignored. This is a very challenging objective that the Court has set out to achieve, given the history of relationships and power differentials between the parties.

The challenge is made all the harder by the fact that not every matter that impacts upon the Crown–Aboriginal relationship in a significant way is embraced by the scope of section 35(1). The filter for identifying what falls under section 35(1)—and so the content which Aboriginal people are deemed to *a priori* have the legal right to carry into negotiations, or be consulted about—is fairly narrow. For example, rights to the land (for example, what falls from Aboriginal title) only attract section 35(1)'s reconciliation imperative if Aboriginal claimants can show, or have a chance of showing pursuant to the *Haida Nation* spectrum,[86] exclusive occupation at the time of Crown sovereignty.[87] For other Aboriginal interests to be embraced within the reconciliation framework, the rights must be shown to be (or shown likely to be) "integral to the distinctive culture" of the Aboriginal people in question.[88]

This creates tension, as many matters of vital importance to fostering Aboriginal–Crown relations and remedying past and ongoing injustices, fall

85 Reconciliation and practices of mutual respect are explicitly tied together by Binnie J. in *Mikisew Cree*, above note 7 at para. 49.

86 *Haida Nation*, above note 57 at paras. 35–38.

87 *Delgamuukw*, above note 4 at para. 143.

88 *Van der Peet*, above note 3.

outside of this framework. This is not to suggest that the courts should be everywhere—their role is restrained to when they are asked to adjudicate, and even then the courts may determine that their powers do not extend to resolving the matter at issue. Reconciliation is ultimately a political relationship, and turns on governmental, not judicial action.[89] However, when these instances arise in the courtroom, and the court finds it has jurisdiction to adjudicate, the rule of law may in practice *undermine, and not facilitate*, the relationships of historically responsive mutual respect which logically must be co-constituted with relationships of reconciliation.

This tension is illustrated in two recent decisions of the McLachlin Court, *Ermineskin Indian Band and Nation v. Canada*[90] and *McDiarmid Lumber Ltd. v. God's Lake First Nation*.[91] Both cases turned, in part, on the interpretation of the *Indian Act*. This statute controls many facets of Aboriginal peoples' lives, and dictates aspects of their relationship with the federal government, both in its executive and legislative capacities.[92] However, its terms have largely been imposed unilaterally by the federal government. This creates considerable practical problems for relationship-building. These cases, and what they represent for enabling reconciliation, are described below. In the following section, the paper will address how the Court has identified sources of authority for the judiciary to legitimately extend reconciliation practices, without overstepping the judicial/political divide, to try to ensure that we are not left with an untenable situation.

In *God's Lake First Nation*, an Aboriginal community had entered into an agreement (known as a CFA) with the federal government to transfer to them the responsibility for administering and delivering some specific social services and community health programming. CFAs are a common element of the current federal initiative to enable self-government through devolution protocols. Under CFAs, the federal government continues to finance, to some degree, the devolved programming.[93] God's Lake First Na-

89 I am particularly grateful to Michael Asch for conversations on the distinctions between the governmental and judicial role in reconciliation.

90 *Ermineskin*, above note 9.

91 *McDiarmid Lumber Ltd. v. God's Lake First Nation* 2006 SCC 58, [2006] 2 S.C.R. 846.

92 For a careful discussion of the distinctions between the executive and legislative branches of the government, and how these branches are pulled into relationships with Aboriginal peoples in different ways, see Kent McNeil, *Emerging Justice: Essays on Indigenous Rights in Canada and Australia* (Saskatoon: Native Law Centre, 2001) at 316–22 [McNeil, *Emerging Justice*].

93 For specific details on funding programming which has been devolved under a health transfer initiative, see Constance MacIntosh, "Envisioning the Future of Aboriginal

tion also had a large debt to a construction supply company. This company brought an action to seize most of the funds that Canada had provided to the First Nation for it to administer its programming.

The Crown and the First Nation together argued that the CFA funding was shielded from garnishment pursuant to section 90(1)(b) of the *Indian Act* which embraces "personal property" that is "given" to "a band under a treaty or an agreement between a band and Her Majesty."[94] Based upon her reading of section 90(1)(b), and the 1990 precedent of *Mitchell v. Peguis Indian Band*,[95] the chief justice found the CFA funding was not shielded. Rather, writing for a 6:3 majority, she concluded that when these statutory provisions were drafted in 1951, Parliament had intended to shield only treaty property and property rendered under an agreement which was ancillary to a treaty.[96] Justice Binnie, writing the dissenting judgment, would have interpreted section 90(1)(b)'s reference to "agreement" to embrace the property provided under any Crown–Aboriginal agreement which "reflects the responsibilities assumed by the Crown" under section 91(24).[97] That is, he interpreted the statute with close attention to the role it plays, and responsibilities it recognizes, in the Crown–Aboriginal relationship.

The chief justice's interpretation was based on Parliamentary intention at the time the statutory terms were enacted in 1951 to promote "greater self-government and participation in economic enterprise,"[98] and a close reading of statutory language as guided by the *ejusdem generis* rule. The dissenting interpretation was driven by a concern with what Binnie J. described as "the realities of life on most reserves."[99] In particular, Binnie J. argued that any band facing debts "would be better off letting the government provide services directly to the reserve rather than attempting to provide the public services themselves through . . . funding" to prevent the funds from being

---

Health under the Health Transfer Process" (2008) Health L.J. 67. For details on funding capital projects, such as water treatment facilities, see Constance MacIntosh, "Testing the Waters: Jurisdictional and Policy Aspects of the Continuing Failure to Remedy Drinking Water Quality on First Nation Reserves" (2008) 39 Ottawa L.R. 63.

94 *Indian Act*, RSC 1985, c. I-5, s. 90(1)(b).

95 [1990] 2 S.C.R. 85.

96 *God's Lake*, above note 91 at paras. 26, 28, and 46–68, McLachlin C.J. for Bastarache, LeBel, Deschamps, Charron, and Rothstein JJ.

97 *Ibid.* at para. 87, Binnie J. for Fish and Abella JJ.

98 *Ibid.* at para. 51, McLachlin C.J.C. for Bastarache, LeBel, Deschamps, Charron, and Rothstein JJ.

99 *Ibid.* at para. 82, Binnie J. for Fish and Abella JJ.

intercepted by creditors.[100] And so, Binnie J. argued that in practical terms the chief justice's interpretation may ironically result in only the bands that are already prosperous and solvent being able to participate. This division arguably continues the divergence in approaches between these two justices that was evidenced in their contrary sets of reasons in 1998 in *Union of New Brunswick Indians v. New Brunswick (Minister of Finance).*[101] The split in that case could similarly be characterized as focusing on the question of whether courts must interpret statutory terms according to original Parliamentary intent, or if courts are to interpret terms in accordance with what is practically required to currently enable the background Parliamentary purpose.

This case is not discussed here to suggest that the matters under consideration ought to have fallen under section 35(1), or to offer an analysis about whether the case was properly decided.[102] Rather, it is raised because it may impact upon possibilities for reconciliation. This decision rendered funding arrangements highly vulnerable across the country, and resulted in the federal government paying off the private debt of God's Lake First Nation and then likely having to provide the CFA funding a second time.

According to the majority, core principles of statutory interpretation—adhering to the rule of law—demand this outcome. However, this outcome effectively erodes the work that the federal government and First Nations had done themselves towards figuring out how to reconcile Aboriginal interests in self-governing given their various economic situations. The Court can tell the government and Aboriginal parties the effect of the law, but it (rightfully) does not have the power to enact the legislation to enable redress or to overcome adverse consequences to Crown–Aboriginal relationships.

The *Ermineskin* case is far more problematic in terms of eroding the relationships which are required between Aboriginal peoples and the Crown if the reconciliation process is to be supported.[103] This decision, released in the spring of 2009, largely turned on the interpretation of the interplay of several statutes, both with themselves and with the common law. One question the Court had to address was what responsibilities the Crown had

---

100 *Ibid.* at para. 94, Binnie J. for Fish and Abella JJ.

101 *Union of New Brunswick Indians v. New Brunswick (Minister of Finance),* [1998] 1 S.C.R. 1161, [1998] S.C.J. No 50.

102 For an analysis of this case, see MacIntosh, "2006–2007," above note 53 at 5–18.

103 For a more fulsome discussion of *Ermineskin*, above note 9, see Constance MacIntosh, "Developments in Aboriginal Law: The 2008–2009 Term" (2009) 48 Sup. Ct. L. Rev. (2d) 1 [MacIntosh, "2008–2009"].

when accruing and holding royalties on behalf of First Nations following the surrender of treaty-based reserve lands for oil and gas production. Among other points, the First Nations argued that the Crown had a fiduciary duty to invest the royalties on their behalf. The Crown maintained that although it may be a fiduciary, its duties were restricted by legislation to protecting the funds from erosion and paying a reasonable rate of interest.[104] The Court concluded that federal legislation (the *Financial Administration Act* and the *Indian Act*) required the Crown to borrow against the royalties and invest them for its own benefit,[105] while the *Indian Act* made it unlawful for the Crown to invest the funds for First Nations benefit.[106] The Court thus determined that the federal legislation in question exonerated the Crown, finding:

> A fiduciary that acts in accordance with legislation cannot be said to be breaching its fiduciary duty. The situation which the bands characterize as a conflict of interest is an inherent and inevitable consequence of the statutory scheme.[107]

Although clearly not its intention, the outcome of this decision effectively undermines the development of conciliatory relationships through its finding that Parliament can legitimately and unilaterally set terms for Crown responsibilities to First Nations which are far below that of a fiduciary or trustee at common law, and that Parliament can create what would otherwise be an explicit conflict of interest between the Crown and First Nations as long as it passes laws that sanction that conflict.[108] There is a striking contrast here between the nature of the relationship which Aboriginal peoples can expect to have with the Crown and the Crown in Parliament when section 35(1) is clearly at play, and the relationship when it is not. The legal justification for such a distinction can be easily laid out, but that is not the point. The point, rather, is that the separation between the executive and legislative branches of government may not be perceived as legitimate by Aboriginal peoples who seek to be involved in a relationship with the government. One cannot realistically expect Aboriginal peoples to trust in a relationship when the other party is expected to show respect or

104 *Ermineskin, ibid.*

105 *Ibid.* at para. 127.

106 *Ibid.* at para. 122.

107 *Ibid.* at para. 128.

108 I thank Kent McNeil for his insights on thinking through the consequences for these matters of the government being divided into an executive and legislative branch. All erroneous comments remain, of course, my own.

recognize that a relationship is at play only when acting with one hat on, and not the other.

Most painfully in terms of the broader reconciliation agenda, although the *Indian Act* authorizes the expenditure of funds held on behalf of a band "for the benefit of the band," there is no suggestion in this decision that the meaning of that legislated phrase would best be determined in consultation with a band. Certainly such consultation was not the norm in 1951 when it was assumed that the Crown best knew how to take care of its ward. But the ward relationship has long since been officially discarded.

In the opening passage of *Mikisew Cree First Nation*, Binnie J. wrote the following about the relationship between reconciliation and the general context in which reconciliation must take place:

> The fundamental objective of the modern law of aboriginal and treaty rights is the reconciliation of aboriginal peoples and non-aboriginal peoples and their respective claims, interests and ambitions. The management of these relationships takes place in the shadow of a long history of grievances and misunderstanding. The multitude of smaller grievances created by the indifference of some government officials to aboriginal people's concerns, and the lack of respect inherent in that indifference has been as destructive of the process of reconciliation as some of the larger and more explosive controversies.[109]

The decisions in *God's Lake First Nation* and in *Ermineskin* about the consequences of legislation for defining the terms of relationships and responsibilities—between the Crown and First Nations, between the Crown and First Nations and private parties—will likely increase the size of the shadow which Binnie J. was referring to. Such decisions and relationships are part of the context which fuels grievances and which—to borrow Binnie J.'s phrasing—may be as destructive of the process of reconciliation as the denial of the obligations clearly arising out of section 35(1). Justice Binnie further observed that "unilateral Crown action . . . is the *antithesis* of reconciliation and mutual respect."[110] Although softened by rules of interpretation,[111] the *Indian Act*, as the product of unilateral Parliamentary action, is presumably open to the same critique. Justice Binnie's comment,

109 *Mikisew Cree*, above note 7 at para. 1, Binnie J.

110 *Ibid.* at para. 49, Binnie J. [emphasis added].

111 The *Indian Act*'s terms are to be "liberally construed and doubtful expressions resolved in favour of the Indians": *Nowegijick v. The Queen*, [1983] 1 S.C.R. 29 at 36, affirmed in *Mitchell*, above note 37 at 142–43, La Forest J., and 107–8, Dickson C.J.

once again, conceptually resonates with one of the core principles that animated McLachlin C.J.'s rejection of former Chief Justice Lamer's approach in her dissenting reasons in *Van der Peet*.[112] Although Binnie J. was writing in the context of a treaty claim, and then Justice McLachlin was writing about a claimed section 35(1) Aboriginal right, the conclusion about the impact of unilateral Crown action for the Crown–Aboriginal relationship—as a matter of fact—holds true in other contexts as well.

What is the judiciary's role in this? It cannot—and must not—do violence to statutory law or otherwise appropriate legislative jurisdiction by reading statutes to say something which they do not. Writing about the limited role of courts in enabling reconciliation, Vickers J. observed:

> In an ideal world, the process of reconciliation would take place outside the adversarial milieu of a courtroom. This case demonstrates how the Court, confined by the issues raised in the pleadings and the jurisprudence on Aboriginal rights and title, is ill equipped to effect a reconciliation of competing interests. That must be reserved for a treaty negotiation process. Despite this fact, the question remains: how can this Court participate in the process of reconciliation between Tsilhqot'in people, Canada and British Columbia in these proceedings?[113]

The McLachlin Court has signalled awareness of this complex situation and of the broader context in which the judiciary is being asked to make its decisions.

The next section shows how the McLachlin Court has drawn upon reconciliation practices as practices that support relationship building in cases where section 35(1) was not at play. Her Court has signalled that the reconciliation mandate is not contained by section 35(1), but exists more broadly. As a result, in some instances, the Court has identified room for legitimately allowing the judiciary to provide some relief to the tensions described above without transgressing the judicial-political divide.

---

112 *Van der Peet*, above note 3 at para. 310, McLachlin J. (in dissent).

113 *Tsilhqot'in Nation v. British Columbia* 2007 BCSC 1700, [2008] 1 CNLR 112 at para. 5 [*Tsilhqot'in Nation*]. For a careful analysis of how Vickers J. defines judicial versus political roles and how they play out in addressing complex interests, see McNeil, "Third Party Interests," above note 54.

E. RECONCILIATION PRACTICES OUTSIDE OF SECTION 35(1) SITUATIONS

This section will illustrate that the Court has left somewhat open-ended the question of whether and how the goal of reconciliation is legally relevant in situations which do not directly engage section 35(1). In the two cases discussed above, the fact that there is a relationship which needs to be advanced is simply not raised (except in Binnie J.'s dissenting reasons in *God's Lake*), and the outcome is arguably potentially destructive of the reconciliation process. However, in a few decisions, the Court's reasons have indicated that reconciliation is a *more general requirement*, and is not contained by situations where section 35(1) rights are squarely at issue. A level of open-endedness is evident here because we do not yet know the extent of such situations.

A hint of this position arises in *Mitchell*, where in her set of reasons the chief justice observed that out of the Crown assertion that "sovereignty over the land, and ownership of its underlying title were vested in the Crown . . . [there] arose an obligation to treat aboriginal peoples fairly and honourably . . ."[114] Although the context was the assessment of a section 35(1) claim, this statement does not suggest that the obligation to act honourably arises only when rights claims are at issue. Rather, it comes out of the fact that the Crown asserted it was sovereign. The chief justice is more explicit in *Haida Nation*. Here she invoked a principle that has been articulated in a number of decisions, going back to at least 1996.[115] She wrote that "the honour of the Crown is always at stake in its dealings with Aboriginal peoples."[116] She then describes how acting with honour is a *precondition* for reconciliation:

> The historical roots of the principle of the honour of the Crown suggest that it must be understood generously in order to reflect the underlying realities from which it stems. In all its dealings with Aboriginal peoples, from the assertion of sovereignty to the resolution of claims and the implementation of treaties, the Crown must act honourably. Nothing less is required if we are to achieve "the reconciliation of the pre-existence of aboriginal societies with the sovereignty of the Crown."[117]

---

114 *Mitchell*, above note 37 at para. 9.

115 Chief Justice McLachlin specifically cites *R. v. Badger*, [1996] 1 S.C.R. 771 at para. 41, and *R. v. Marshall*, [1999] 3 S.C.R. 456.

116 *Haida Nation*, above note 57 at para. 16.

117 *Ibid.* at para. 17.

Once again, although these comments are made in a case about a claim based on section 35(1), it is clear that this requirement to act with honour so as to enable reconciled and respectful relationships does not arise exclusively as a result of section 35(1) being enacted, nor is it contained by matters recognized by section 35(1). This is expressly indicated by the example McLachlin C.J. draws upon to elucidate her point. Making reference to a non-section 35(1) case in her next paragraph, McLachlin C.J. writes:

> The honour of the Crown gives rise to different duties in different circumstances. Where the Crown has assumed discretionary control over specific Aboriginal interests, the honour of the Crown gives rise to a fiduciary duty: *Weywaykum Indian Band v Canada*, 2002 SCC 79 . . .[118]

Thus the requirement to act with honour clearly extends reconciliation practices beyond the ambit of section 35(1) cases. Sometimes these actions will take the form of duties which, although having nothing to do with defining or accommodating Aboriginal or treaty rights, are nonetheless part of ensuring that reconciliation does not become "a distant legalistic goal."[119] What we do not know is the scope of "different circumstances" in which "duties" will arise, nor what those "different duties" may look like.

Reflecting back upon the complex litigation and multiple issues that were brought up in *Ermineskin*, one is left wondering what this Court would have decided if it was squarely asked to contemplate the relationship between the obligations of honour and the legislation that drove the result. In particular, whether in enacting the series of statutes that drove the Court's findings, was Parliament's unilateral exercise of control over the interests of Aboriginal peoples sufficient to invoke fiduciary responsibilities regarding permissible terms?[120] Alternatively, was the unilateral exercise of legislative power sufficient to raise concerns about Parliamentary enactments eroding the possibility of the Crown being able, on a practical level, to act with honour? The Court may be pressed to speak to such questions in the future, about what normative doctrines may restrain or guide Parliamentary authority when acting pursuant to the powers recognized by section 91(24). It would not be inconsistent with existing jurisprudence to find that the constitutional imperative to strive toward reconciliation practices permeates

118 *Ibid.* at para. 18.

119 *Ibid.* at para. 33.

120 For example, under the terms of *Wewaykum*, above note 7. For an analysis of when Parliament became subject to fiduciary obligations, see McNeil, *Emerging Justice*, above note 92 at 316–22.

and guides most aspects of Crown–Aboriginal relationships, and so introduces, at the least, *elements of restraint* into how this power is legitimately exercised whenever it is exercised.

There is one clear example of what it could mean to broadly infuse the reconciliation mandate into Crown–Aboriginal relations in the minority decision in *R. v. Kapp*,[121] written by Bastarache J. His reasons radiate with concern about how the judiciary can support the broader reconciliation project, and particularly reflect the fact that, at the end of the day, reconciliation depends upon a negotiated political relationship that is supported by Canadian and Aboriginal governments. Although concurring with the majority that the federal government could issue commercial fishing permits to First Nation organizations to engage in exclusive fishing openings without offending the *Charter* rights of non-Aboriginal fishers, Bastarache J.'s path of reasoning was novel.[122] He resolved the claim by mobilizing section 25 of the *Charter*. His reasons were not endorsed by the majority, which signalled that it may have interpreted section 25 quite differently,[123] and so we see a potential fissuring of the Court on the reconciliation mandate.

Nonetheless, Bastarache J.'s decision provides the first fulsome treatment of section 25 by a justice of the Supreme Court of Canada—and so will be an important touchstone for subsequent decisions.[124] This provision states that *Charter* rights guarantees "shall not be construed to abrogate or derogate from any aboriginal, treaty or other rights and freedoms that pertain to the aboriginal people of Canada," including those recognized by the Royal Proclamation of 1763 and those that exist or may be acquired by way of land claims agreements. Justice Bastarache concluded that this provision "protects federal, provincial and aboriginal initiatives that seek to further interests associated with indigenous difference from *Charter* scrutiny."[125] These sorts of initiatives include "[l]egislation that distinguishes between aboriginal and non-aboriginal people in order to protect interests associated with aboriginal culture, territory, sovereignty, or the treaty process."[126] That is, legislation which would most likely be enacted pursuant to the authority of section 91(24).

Justice Bastarache's conclusion bears repeating. He found the constitutional intention was that legislation that protected Aboriginal interests (not

121 *Kapp*, above note 9.

122 *Ibid.* at paras. 76–77, Bastarache J.

123 *Ibid.* at paras. 62–65, McLachlin C.J. and Abella J.

124 For commentary on *Kapp*, see MacIntosh, "2008-2009," above note 103.

125 *Kapp*, above note 9 at para. 103, Bastarache J.

126 *Ibid.* at para. 103, Bastarache J.

just matters which fit through section 35(1)'s filter) was shielded from *Charter* scrutiny. There is an intriguing resonance here with Binnie J.'s dissent in *God's Lake*, where he would have found that all agreements that reflected section 91(24) responsibilities would have been shielded from garnishment and taxation.[127]

Justice Bastarache's interpretation of section 25 came from his reading of the Court's unanimous reconciliation jurisprudence: *Haida Nation* and *Taku River*. It also follows from Bastarache J.'s reasons in *Sappier*, writing for the Court on this point, that section 35(1) requires Aboriginal cultures to be protected if reconciliation is to be achieved. Justice Bastarache also found support for this outcome in the admonitions in *Delgamuukw* and *Sparrow* that the Crown must negotiate in good faith.[128] His reasoning is persuasive on a variety of levels. On a practical level, *Haida Nation* and *Taku River* require the Crown to accommodate Aboriginal claims prior to rights being proven. Logically, if such accommodation agreements are subject to private challenges on *Charter* grounds, then the Aboriginal party could be forced by a third party to formally prove its right for the accommodation to remain in place, and the reconciliation that the negotiated accommodation represents would likely be undermined.

Note that Bastarache J.'s approach would shield not just agreements that address matters that could be proven to be Aboriginal rights under section 35(1), but would embrace other, broader issues which need to be addressed in agreements which are not just preliminary to a treaty, but are part of forming a treaty relationship. In Bastarache J.'s words, "[section] 25 reflects this imperative need to accommodate and reconcile aboriginal interests."[129] In finding that section 25 operates not unlike a "notwithstanding clause," Bastarache J. is arguing for judicial deference to negotiated political decisions in this complex arena of working through political, legal, social, and economic interests.

It is in the third last paragraph of Bastarache J.'s reasons that he most explicitly ties all the threads together. He writes that "Section 25 is a necessary partner to s. 35(1); it protects s. 35(1)['s] purposes and enlarges the reach of measures needed to fulfill the promise of reconciliation."[130]

It is this final argument, with its call to practical necessity, which may prove to be the most persuasive to his colleagues on McLachlin C.J.'s bench,

127 *God's Lake*, above note 91 at para. 87, Binnie J. for Fish and Abella JJ. (in dissent).

128 *Ibid.* at para. 106, Bastarache J.

129 *Ibid.*, Bastarache J.

130 *Ibid.* at para. 121, Bastarache J.

and so may enable his position to come to be endorsed by the McLachlin Court. The Court has demanded that parties adopt a practical and meaningful approach to section 35(1)'s manifestations. It has taken the position that if one fails to contemplate practical outcomes, then reconciliation will arise only in theory, not in lived relationships, and that this outcome is not an acceptable one.[131] This approach was perhaps most strongly articulated in *Sappier*,[132] but was also present in *Marshall*[133] and *Haida Nation*,[134] as well as in Lamer C.J.'s Court in *Delgamuukw*.[135] Justice Bastarache's observations in *Kapp* are immensely practical ones, given the complexities involved in enabling a consensual and treaty-based relationship between Aboriginal peoples and the Crown. In reasons that are not unlike those of then Justice McLachlin in *Van der Peet* in terms of their passion, clarity, and emphasis upon legal principle, Bastarache J. has pointed to another key route for the judiciary to enable and support the process of reconciliation and the political development of relationships of mutual respect.

F. CONCLUSION

The current Court, under the guidance of McLachlin C.J., has drawn upon the purpose of section 35(1)—reconciliation—to transform many aspects of Crown–Aboriginal relations, bringing in changes and challenges which have brought the parties into conversation in a manner which has likely not been experienced for centuries in some parts of the country. Reviving McLachin C.J.'s basic premises in *Van der Peet*, her Court has uniformly endorsed the position that the reconciliation process largely takes place outside of the courtroom, and that judicial decisions cannot be expected to create the terms of reconciliation for the parties, although courts will marshal this creationary constitutional process to some degree when asked to do so.[136]

Although the purpose of 35(1) "is to facilitate the ultimate reconciliation of prior Aboriginal occupation with *de facto* Crown sovereignty,"[137] given

131 For a discussion of the Court's emphasis upon interpreting rights to be meaningful in their contemporary form, and to approaching the adjudication process with an eye to practicalities, see MacIntosh, "On Obligations," above note 59.

132 *Sappier*, above note 36 at para. 49.

133 *Marshall (No. 2)*, above note 5 at para. 52.

134 *Haida Nation*, above note 57 at paras. 31 and 63.

135 *Delgamuukw*, above note 4 at paras. 90–108.

136 These conclusions are clearly present in the recent decision of Vickers J. in *Tsilhqot'in Nation*, above note 113. See, in particular, paras. 1357–368.

137 *Taku River*, above note 56 at para. 42, McLachlin C.J.

the broader context in which Crown–Aboriginal relations take place, this purpose likely needs bolstering from outside the spectrum of section 35(1) rights considerations if it is to be realistically attainable. The Court has signalled a certain level of sensitivity to this matter, and it has—unanimously—identified somewhat open-ended conceptual points that potentially grant the judiciary considerable room to bring in the norm of reconciliation, while simultaneously taking care not to overstep the political-judicial divide. Undoubtedly, the Court will continue to develop its reconciliation jurisprudence in response to changing situations, experiences, and practical imperatives.

The Duty to Consult Aboriginal Peoples: Government Approaches to Unresolved Issues

LORI STERLING AND PETER LANDMANN*

In a unanimous judgment delivered by Beverley McLachlin C.J. in 2004, the Supreme Court determined in *Haida Nation v. British Columbia (Minister of Forests)*[1] that the Crown has a duty to consult Aboriginal peoples when it acts in a manner that may adversely affect Aboriginal or treaty rights guaranteed by section 35 of the *Constitution Act, 1982*. The existence of the rights need not be proven but only credibly asserted in order to trigger the duty.[2] Where potential adverse impacts on asserted rights are identified, the objective of such consultation is to accommodate legitimate Aboriginal concerns.

From the perspective of governments, this is one of the most significant decisions of the Supreme Court of Canada in the last ten years.[3] For

---

* The views expressed herein are those of the authors and not of the Government of Ontario. The authors wish to thank Tanya Nayler, Andrea McGarry, and Justin Lim, students at the Ministry of Energy, Legal Services Branch, for their assistance with the research.

1 *Haida Nation v. British Columbia (Minister of Forests)*, 2004 SCC 73, 3 S.C.R. 511 at para. 35 [*Haida*].

2 *Ibid.* at 37.

3 There have been several decisions of the Supreme Court contributing to the Aboriginal jurisprudence during the first decade of McLachlin C.J.'s tenure including *R. v. Powley*, below note 33, dealing with Métis Aboriginal rights; *Paul v. British Columbia (Forest Appeals Commission)*, [2003] 2 S.C.R. 585, 2003 SCC 55, dealing with the jurisdiction of administrative tribunals to determine s. 35 issues; *Taku River Tlingit First Nation v. British Columbia (Project Assessment Director)*, below note 5; *R. v. Marshall; R. v. Bernard*, 2005 SCC 43, 2 S.C.R. 220, dealing with the admissibility of oral evidence; *R. v. Van der Peet*, [1996] 2 S.C.R. 507, [1996] S.C.J. No. 77, dealing with the s. 35-protected practices of First Nations [*Van der Peet*]; *Mikisew Cree First Nation v. Canada (Minister of Canadian Heritage)*,

Aboriginal peoples, it may be the most significant judgment since the seminal *Sparrow*[4] decision established the framework for analyzing alleged infringements of Aboriginal and treaty rights.

Prior to *Haida* and its companion case *Taku River Tlingit First Nation v. British Columbia (Project Assessment Director)*,[5] the consultation obligation of the Crown was limited to instances where it sought to justify demonstrated infringements of Aboriginal or treaty rights under the *Sparrow* test—a fairly narrow and contained set of circumstances. In order to obtain Crown consultation and accommodation of adverse impacts, the onus was on the First Nation to first prove both the existence of the right and its infringement. The difficulty under *Sparrow* was that proving rights takes a long time; Aboriginal rights litigation can require a detailed evidentiary record, a lengthy trial, and possibly subsequent appeals—or alternatively, claims may be addressed in negotiations, which sometimes last many years. The question left unanswered by *Sparrow* was whether projects could proceed unconstrained in the interim.

The specific problem dealt with by McLachlin C.J. in *Haida* was relatively straightforward: what are the obligations of the Crown when a proposed decision affects lands against which a First Nation has asserted—but not yet proven—a claim?[6] It would, according to the chief justice, render the section 35 right illusory if governments could proceed with projects that affect

---

below note 13, which follows *Haida* in the treaty context and is discussed below; *Quebec (Attorney General) v. Moses*, 2010 SCC 17, [2010] S.C.J. No. 17 [*Moses*]; *Rio Tinto Alcan v. Carrier Sekani Tribal Council*, 2010 SCC 43, [2010] S.C.J. No. 43 [*Rio Tinto*] and *Beckman v. Little Salmon/Carmacks First Nation*, 2010 SCC 53 [*Little Salmon*], dealing with various consultation issues discussed below. See also the following: *Lovelace v. Ontario*, 2000 SCC 37, 1 S.C.R. 950; *Mitchell v. Canada (Minister of National Revenue—M.N.R.)*, 2001 SCC 33, 1. S.C.R. 911; *Osoyoos Indian Band v. Oliver (Town)*, 2001 SCC 85, 3 S.C.R. 746; *Kitkatla Band v. British Columbia (Minister of Small Business, Tourism and Culture)*, 2002 SCC 31, 2 S.C.R. 146; *Ross River Dena Council Band v. Canada*, 2002 SCC 54, 2 S.C.R. 816; *Wewaykum Indian Band v. Canada*, 2002 SCC 79, 4 S.C.R. 245; *R. v. Blais*, 2003 SCC 44, 2 S.C.R. 236; *British Columbia (Minister of Forests) v. Okanagan Indian Band*, 2003 SCC 71, 3 S.C.R. 371; *R. v. Sappier; R. v. Gray*, 2006 SCC 54, 2 S.C.R. 686 [*Sappier*]; *McDiarmid Lumber Ltd. v. God's Lake First Nation*, 2006 SCC 58, 2 S.C.R. 846; *R. v. Morris*, 2006 SCC 59, 2 S.C.R. 915; *Canada (Attorney General) v. Lameman*, 2008 SCC 14, 1 S.C.R. 372; *R. v. Kapp*, 2008 SCC 41, 2 S.C.R. 483; and *Ermineskin Indian Band and Nation v. Canada*, 2009 SCC 9, 384 N.R. 20.

4 *R. v. Sparrow*, [1990] 1 S.C.R. 1075, [1990] S.C.J. No. 49 [*Sparrow*].

5 *Taku River Tlingit First Nation v. British Columbia (Project Assessment Director)*, 2004 SCC 74, 3 S.C.R. 550 [*Taku River*].

6 *Haida*, above note 1 at para. 26.

such lands without regard to credible claims to those lands.[7] The Court has determined that the fundamental objective of Aboriginal law is the reconciliation of "prior aboriginal occupation of the land with the reality of Crown sovereignty,"[8] and the Court recognized in *Haida* that limiting such reconciliation to the post-proof period was inconsistent with this intent.[9] What, then, was the best approach to protecting Aboriginal peoples from the effects of projects undertaken during the period between the assertion of a right and the determination of the right? The chief justice rejected resorting to traditional interim injunctions[10] and instead relied upon the concept of honourable Crown conduct first introduced as part of the justification analysis in *Sparrow*.[11] She held that honourable conduct entails a constitutional duty to consult Aboriginal communities where they have a credibly asserted right and there are potential adverse impacts of the project on the right.[12]

Making the trigger for consultation a potential impact on an asserted right represents a vastly broadened Crown obligation as compared with the previous state of the law. The result has been an exponential increase in the volume of consultation activity undertaken prior to proceeding with projects and approvals, and a profound change in the importance of Aboriginal concerns in government decision making.

The application of the duty to consult was extended from the context of asserted Aboriginal rights or title (common issues in British Columbia) to the treaty interpretation context in the subsequent decision in *Mikisew Cree First Nation v. Canada (Minister of Canadian Heritage)*.[13] As a result, the duty also applies in those parts of Canada subject to historic treaties. In addition, the decision in *Little Salmon* indicates that the duty applies in parts of the country subject to modern land claim settlements.[14]

---

7 *Ibid.* at para. 33.

8 See, for example, *R. v. Van der Peet*, above note 3 at para. 31.

9 *Haida*, above note 1 at paras. 17 and 33.

10 *Ibid.* at paras. 12–15.

11 *Sparrow*, above note 4 at paras. 64 and 75.

12 *Haida*, above note 1 at para. 35. In *Rio Tinto*, above note 3 at para. 63, the Court indicated that the duty to consult is of a constitutional character.

13 *Mikisew Cree First Nation v. Canada (Minister of Canadian Heritage)*, 2005 SCC 69, 3 S.C.R. 388 [*Mikisew*].

14 See also *Moses*, above note 3 at para. 45. The Court held that where a federal environmental assessment process pursuant to the *Canadian Environmental Assessment Act* applied to a proposed project on *James Bay and Northern Quebec Agreement* territory, the process must be undertaken in a way that respects the Crown's duty to consult on matters affecting treaty rights in accordance with the principles established in *Haida*.

Since *Haida* and *Taku River* were decided, the expanded Crown duty to consult has had a profound impact on the activities of governments across Canada and affects the day-to-day operations of ministries responsible for the mining, forestry, energy, transportation, and land development sectors. Since the Crown activity that triggers consultation includes not only Crown-sponsored projects[15] but also regulatory approvals of private sector projects,[16] there is a particular impact on ministries responsible for land tenure issues and for regulation of land use including environmental assessment, natural resource permitting, and municipal planning. In addition, there have been important implications for ministries responsible for Aboriginal policy and for the legal advice–giving and litigation functions of the federal and provincial attorneys general.

For governments, a failure to consult appropriately can lead to judicial review, injunctions, orders to carry out consultation with the affected Aboriginal community, and other relief possibly including damages.[17] For proponents whose projects are affected by a Crown failure to meet its duty, the potential consequences are serious. In such circumstances governments face the possibility of lawsuits not only from Aboriginal communities but also from proponents, who need fair and timely regulatory decisions.[18]

Among the challenges for governments are the sheer volume of projects and the need to deploy significant human and financial resources in order to comply with this new constitutional imperative. Government regulatory tribunals are now dealing for the first time with complex Aboriginal consultation issues (where they have statutory authority to do so[19]) before issuing approvals. Aboriginal communities have likewise faced significant new demands on their far more limited resources and have had to develop technical expertise or retain experts to respond to numerous offers of consultation. As well, where the Crown delegates some of the process to third party proponents, concerns have been raised by proponents about the cost of Aboriginal consultation and delay of projects.

Also challenging for the Crown, Aboriginal communities, and proponents is the number of outstanding questions regarding the interpretation of the duty that create uncertainty in determining the respective obligations

15 For example, public roads and highways.

16 For example, mines, housing developments, and private sector energy projects.

17 *Rio Tinto*, above note 3 at para. 37.

18 *Little Salmon*, above note 3 at paras. 12 and 33–35.

19 See *Rio Tinto*, above note 3; and *Fond du Lac et al. v. Canada (Attorney General) and Areva Resources* 2010 FC 948, [2010] F.C.J. No. 1182 [*Fond du Lac*].

of the participants in consultation. Indeed, despite a growing body of jurisprudence interpreting the duty, fundamental issues remain unresolved by the courts.

The Supreme Court has spoken of a dialogue between the Court and legislatures in developing the law.[20] Since the release of *Haida* in 2004, governments across the country, including the Ontario government, have attempted to comply with the duty through a variety of approaches and tools including legislation,[21] regulations,[22] guidelines,[23] and other instruments.[24] Whereas governments speak through such policy instruments, the Court speaks through its judgments and remedies. In 2010, the Supreme Court released judgments in the cases of *Rio Tinto, Little Salmon,* and *Moses.* These address some of the outstanding legal questions, but other critical issues remain unresolved. In future years, continued active dialogue between the Supreme Court and government, in which the Court considers government approaches to the duty and clarifies outstanding questions, can be anticipated.

---

20 See, for example, *Vriend v. Alberta*, [1998] 1 S.C.R. 493, 156 D.L.R. (4th) 385 at paras. 129–42.

21 See, for example, *Green Energy and Green Economy Act, 2009*, S.O. 2009, c. 12, Schedule B, and *Electricity Act, 1998*, S.O. 1998, c. 15, s. 5(1) amending s. 25.32 by adding s. 4.4:

> The Minister may direct the OPA to implement procedures for consulting Aboriginal peoples and other persons or groups as may be specified in the direction, on the planning, development or procurement of electricity supply, capacity, transmission systems and distribution systems and the direction may specify the manner or method by which such consultations shall occur and the timing within which such consultations shall occur.

See also *Mining Act*, R.S.O. 1990, c. M.14, s. 2.

22 See, for example, Ontario Regulation 231/08 under the *Environmental Assessment Act, Transit Projects and Greater Toronto Transportation Authority Undertakings*, s. 8; Ontario Regulation 359/09 under the *Environmental Protection Act*, ss. 14–18, which address Aboriginal consultation with respect to the approvals process for renewable energy projects.

23 See, for example, Ontario Regulation 101/07 under the *Environmental Assessment Act*, Guide to Environmental Assessment Requirements for Waste Management Projects (15 March 2007), online: Ontario Ministry of the Environment www.ene.gov.on.ca/en/publications/forms/6168e.pdf at A.3.3.

24 See Ontario Power Authority, Request for Proposals for approximately 500MW of Renewable Energy Supply, online: Ontario Power Authority www.powerauthority.on.ca/gp/Page.asp?PageID=122&ContentID=713&SiteNodeID=180&BL_ExpandID= at file 05 at 1.2, 3.3.1, and 4.11, and files 10, 11, 12, & 13 [RES III RFP]. See also *Government of Saskatchewan First Nation and Métis Consultation Policy Framework* (June 2010), online: Government of Saskatchewan First Nations and Métis Relations www.fnmr.gov.sk.ca/Consult-Policy/Framework.pdf. More recently, Ontario's Long-Term Energy Plan sets out not just the proposed sources of future energy but also refers to the need to consult with Aboriginal communities: *Ontario's Long-Term Energy Plan: Building Our Clean Future* (Queen's Printer for Ontario, 2010), online: Ministry of Energy www.mei.gov.on.ca/en/pdf/MEI_LTEP_en.pdf.

Some of the outstanding issues are dealt with below. These issues may be categorized under the broad questions of *who*, *when*, *how*, and *on what* to consult.

A. WHO SHOULD BE CONSULTED

The question of who must be consulted is not yet fully resolved. It seems clear from the section 35 jurisprudence that, for First Nations at least, it is the local communities that hold section 35 rights[25] as distinct, for example, from the provincial chiefs, a provincial/territorial organization (PTO), or tribal council.[26] The communities are, therefore, the entities entitled to be consulted while umbrella organizations can exercise that right only if it is delegated to them by one or more communities.[27]

It is always open to individual communities to be represented in consultations by a tribal council, PTO, or similar corporate entity,[28] or to put in place a process whereby an umbrella organization is the point of entry for consultations. For example, the communities that form part of Treaty No. 3 have requested that rather than consult individually with each community, Ontario should begin the process with the Office of the Grand Chief or Ogichidaakwe. The grand chief will consult with the affected communities and then return to the Crown with a response.[29] Similarly, in eastern Ontario where there is an outstanding Algonquin land claim, the Algonquins of Ontario (AOO), which includes both recognized and unrecognized First Nations, have negotiated with Canada and Ontario the establishment of a one-window consultation office for the purpose of making more efficient the process of giving notice and the internal review of projects.

Other models that promote efficiencies in the consultation process exist as well, including regional networks that enable First Nations to share

---

25 See *R. v. Van der Peet*, above note 3; *R. v. Sappier; R. v. Gray*, above note 3; *R. v. Powley*, below note 33; and *R. v. Marshall*, [1999] 3 S.C.R. 533, [1999] S.C.J. No. 66.

26 Examples of umbrella organizations include the Chiefs of Ontario, Grand Council of Treaty #3, Nishnawbe Aski Nation, Association of Iroquois and Allied Indians, Union of Ontario Indians, Mushkegowuk Tribal Council, Wabun Tribal Council, North Shore Tribal Council, United Chiefs and Councils of Manitoulin, and others.

27 But see *Nlaka'pamux Nation Tribal Council v. British Columbia (Project Assessment Director, Environmental Assessment Office)*, 2009 BCSC 1275, [2009] B.C.J. No. 1863 [*Nlaka'pamux*].

28 See *Labrador Métis Nation v. Newfoundland and Labrador*, 2007 NLCA 75, [2007] N.J. No. 421 [*Labrador Métis Nation*].

29 Grand Council Treaty #3, Manito Aki Inakonigaawin (the Great Earth Law), 9 October 2008.

community knowledge and consult more effectively and cohesively. Four communities including the Chapleau Cree, Michipicoten, Hornepayne, and Pic Mobert developed a regional "centre of excellence" approach to consultation wherein each community builds technical capacity within a particular resource-related field and provides support to the other communities on a reciprocal basis.

The *Mikisew Cree* case tells us that for communities that are beneficiaries of treaties covering vast treaty areas (such as the Robinson and post-Confederation numbered treaties), the communities to be consulted do not include every First Nation that is a beneficiary of the treaty or is located within the treaty lands in question no matter how remote from the project. Rather, it is only communities whose traditional territories or traditional activities might be affected that are entitled to be consulted.[30]

Of course, the determination of whether a particular First Nation or Métis community has interests in a particular territory can be a matter of debate, and a matter on which governments, Aboriginal communities, and proponents may disagree. On occasion, community assertions overlap, leading to disputes among them. In identifying which First Nations to consult, governments typically try to be inclusive in identifying communities to be notified of a project, leaving the harder choices regarding the nature of the consultation and accommodation to later in the consultation process. Given the low threshold for triggering the duty—a potential adverse impact on a credibly asserted claim—governments expect that the courts will be more deferential to Crown choices regarding how to consult than to a failure to notify altogether. Following *Haida*, it is understood that the standard of review for the former is reasonableness while for the latter, it is correctness.[31]

While the law on who to consult seems reasonably clear for reserve-based First Nations, what of Métis and other Aboriginal communities not recognized as bands? In Ontario, there are a number of communities populated by status Indians who may have elected a chief and assert rights as independent First Nations despite a lack of recognition of their community under the *Indian Act*. The possibility that a duty to consult is owing to such

30 *Mikisew*, above note 13 at para. 48.

31 *Haida*, above note 1; *Fond du Lac*, above note 19; *Brokenhead Ojibway Nation v. Canada (Attorney General)*, 2009 FC 484, [2009] F.C.J. No. 608 at paras. 17–18 [*Brokenhead*]; and *Tzeachen First Nation v. Canada (Attorney General)*, 2008 FC 928, [2008] F.C.J. No. 1207 at paras. 23–24. Note that in *Little Salmon*, above note 3 at para. 48, the Court states that the adequacy of consultation will also be reviewed on a standard of correctness.

communities cannot be ruled out and it is necessary to consider claims to community-based Aboriginal or treaty rights on a case-by-case basis.[32]

As for the Métis, the *Powley*[33] decision of the Supreme Court of Canada recognized the section 35 Aboriginal rights of the Métis peoples of Canada and it seems straightforward that credible Métis assertions can also therefore trigger the Crown duty to consult and accommodate.[34] Governments are beginning to systematically consult organizations representing asserted Métis rights-holding communities. What is less obvious for governments is which Métis organizations to consult. There is no legislated recognition of Métis communities analogous to the band system under the *Indian Act*. Furthermore, Métis communities are often comprised of Métis individuals interspersed within larger non-Aboriginal communities. In such circumstances, the Crown will require some familiarity with the organizations asserting rights on behalf of Métis. The need to be satisfied in respect of the legitimacy of such organizations is necessary particularly given that consultation is typically accompanied by requests for capacity funding and governments are responsible to ensure careful stewardship of public funds.

Should the Crown consult local Métis groups or larger province-wide entities? To date, governments have largely assumed that the local community rights model applies equally to Métis as it does to First Nations, and have sought out local Métis partners with whom to consult, with the assistance of the larger province-wide Métis organizations. However, certain Métis spokespersons now assert that the Métis people were historically more mobile than First Nations and, therefore, the rights-holding entity for Métis is a larger regional community or even a nation of considerable geographic extent,[35] as distinct from a local community as is the case for First Nations. Were this view to be accepted by the courts, there would arguably be a larger role for the Métis regional and umbrella organizations such as the Métis Nation of Ontario (MNO). For governments, consulting with larger, better-resourced entities with offices in urban centres can be more efficient, and therefore an attractive proposition, but it remains unclear whether this will

32 See also *John Voortman & Associates Ltd. v. Haudenosaunee Confederacy Chiefs Council*, [2009] O.J. No. 1350, [2009] 3 C.N.L.R. 117 at paras. 72–73 where the Court was dealing with the types of organizations that have the authority to speak for Aboriginal communities.

33 *R. v. Powley*, 2003 SCC 43, 2 S.C.R. 207 [*Powley*].

34 See, for example, *Labrador Métis Nation*, above note 28.

35 See *R. v. Goodon*, 2008 MBPC 59, [2009] M.J. No. 3 at 46–48, in which the court recognized a large regional Métis community in Manitoba, the extent of which it contrasted with the Sault Ste. Marie Métis community recognized in *Powley*.

meet the legal imperative. Views on the question of regional versus local community rights remain divided among the Métis, and it is an issue which has yet to be resolved by the Supreme Court.

Another open question is who is the Crown for the purposes of the Crown duty to consult? The question of who bears and can fulfill the duty is a significant area of uncertainty with important practical implications. Chief Justice McLachlin ruled definitively in *Haida* that the Crown bears the duty while private sector proponents do not.[36] Although proponents may be delegated procedural aspects of consultation, the duty itself is that of the Crown and cannot be delegated. Unfortunately, this leaves unresolved the status of quasi-governmental entities such as agencies, boards, and commissions (ABCs), municipalities, universities, schools, and hospitals (the MUSH sector), and Crown corporations. Can a municipality ignore the Crown duty on the basis that it is not the Crown, or to the contrary, as a government that makes decisions potentially affecting constitutionally protected rights, does it bear a "Crown-like" duty?[37]

This issue points to the tension between the express rationale for the duty set out by the chief justice in *Haida* and practical considerations in achieving broader reconciliation objectives. *Haida* is premised on an obligation of honourable Crown conduct in its dealings with Aboriginal peoples,[38] which itself finds its origins in the long-standing historical relationship between the Crown and First Nations and the need to reconcile Crown sovereignty with prior Aboriginal occupation of the land.[39] As indicated by McLachlin C.J., this underlying premise provides no support for imposing a duty to consult on non-Crown actors: the honour of the Crown cannot be delegated.[40] However entities such as municipalities and other non-Crown governmental authorities routinely issue regulatory decisions and permits having potentially significant adverse impact on asserted Aboriginal or treaty rights.

Some governments have applied a test of "Crown agency" to determine whether an entity bears and can fulfill the duty to consult. This test arguably

36 *Haida*, above note 1 at para. 53.

37 The issue has been raised in Ontario litigation but the decision leaves the issue open: *City of Brantford v. Montour et. al*, 2010 ONSC 6253. The province of Saskatchewan has also addressed this issue in its *First Nation and Métis Consultation Policy Framework*, but, similarly, the province does not take a conclusive position on whether there is a municipal duty to consult.

38 *Haida*, above note 1 at para. 16.

39 *Ibid.* at para. 17.

40 *Ibid.* at para. 53.

corresponds well with the legal theory underlying *Haida*. Under this test government bodies that are Crown agents bear the duty to consult, while non-Crown agents do not. This approach, however, can raise practical difficulties because of the range of bodies it excludes. The Supreme Court will have to consider whether to allow significant land use decisions to be made by municipalities, conservation authorities, and other government-created entities without triggering the consultation duty even though those decisions can affect treaty and Aboriginal rights. Under the Crown agency test it is also possible that such entities are not subject to any duty to consult but provincial ministries are responsible for consulting and accommodating in respect of any potential adverse effects of their decisions. This could create a gap between the decision-making activities of front line regulatory bodies and the locus of constitutional responsibility for the duty in provincial ministries. Might this make it difficult to meet the duty to consult at the operational level?

A possible alternative—and a broader approach—is to impose the duty to consult on the category of entities defined as "government" for the purposes of the application of the *Charter of Rights and Freedoms* in cases such as *Eldridge v. British Columbia (Attorney General)*.[41] If this broader approach were to apply, the legal obligation to consult would fall on those entities that exercise government-like functions and are obliged through statutory delegation to exercise Crown duties.

B. WHEN IS CONSULTATION REQUIRED

The Supreme Court has indicated that consultation should occur early in the strategic planning stages of projects, and certainly not be left so late that the project is fully defined, rendering any accommodation difficult to implement.[42] Some have suggested that consultation is required at the earliest possible stage, for example, when considering general policy or legislative initiatives which may lead to projects.[43] Under this approach, the duty would arise when governments develop broad long-term plans such as exist in the areas of land use planning (for example, Ontario's Greenbelt Plan), energy (for example, Ontario's twenty-year Integrated Power System Plan (IPSP)), and transportation (Ontario's five-year Southern Ontario Highway

41 *Eldridge v. British Columbia (Attorney General)*, [1997] 3 S.C.R. 624, 151 D.L.R. (4th) 577.

42 *Haida*, above note 1 at para. 76; *Rio Tinto*, above note 3 at para. 44.

43 See *Tsuu T'ina Nation v. Alberta (Minister of Environment)*, 2010 ABCA 137, [2010] A.J. No. 479.

Program (SOHP)). Certainly including Aboriginal people in the development of policies—including legislation[44]—that affects them makes for a more informed policy. The *Haida* decision suggests that, at the very least, consultation should take place at the stage in planning when decisions begin to significantly narrow the opportunities for accommodation of adverse impacts on rights.

It can be difficult for some standard government processes to include early consultation. For example, competitive procurements entailing requests for proposals (RFPs) require sealed bids and strict confidentiality to ensure fair processes and competitive bidding. This means that focused Crown consultation is not possible prior to bid selection, even though the choice made by governments to select certain projects over others could theoretically narrow the options for addressing Aboriginal concerns. For such processes, it is suggested that the extent of prior engagement with Aboriginal communities by bidders could be a relevant consideration in the selection process, and further, that Crown consultation should begin as soon as practicable after the bids are selected and the successful projects are announced. This was the model followed in the Renewable Energy Supply III (RES III) procurement process completed in 2009 by the Ontario Power Authority.[45]

One of the key steps in consultation is for the Crown to satisfy itself as to the sufficiency of Crown consultation and of any necessary accommodation of Aboriginal interests. It seems clear that the Crown must satisfy itself that it has fulfilled its duty before issuing permits or approvals allowing the project to proceed.[46] What, however, is the requirement in terms of assessing consultation when multiple regulatory approvals are required, as is typically the case for large energy projects such as major generating stations and high tension transmission lines? Do the different policy concerns dealt with by each regulator at each regulatory step require distinct consultation processes and separate decisions by each regulator on the sufficiency of Crown consultation?

In its decision in *Kwikwetlem First Nation v. British Columbia (Utilities Commission)*,[47] the British Columbia Court of Appeal ruled in the affirmative, requiring both the British Columbia Utilities Commission (responsible for

44 The question of whether there is a duty in relation to legislation was left open in *Rio Tinto*, above note 3 at para. 44.

45 RES III RFP, above note 24.

46 *Haida*, above note 1 at para. 76.

47 *Kwikwetlem First Nation v. British Columbia (Utilities Commission)*, 2009 BCCA 68, [2009] B.C.J. No. 260.

issuing a certificate of public convenience and necessity (CPCN)) and the British Columbia Ministry of the Environment (responsible for issuing an environmental assessment certificate (EAC)) to determine whether Aboriginal consultation on a transmission line was sufficient.[48] Such a requirement of multiple consultations and determinations of sufficiency of consultation on the same project can, however, become duplicative and burdensome. An alternative approach is the one adopted by the Ontario Energy Board in its decision on a leave to construct application for the Bruce to Milton transmission reinforcement where it deferred the main decision on Aboriginal consultation to the subsequent environmental assessment:

> There is only one Crown. The requirement is that the Crown ensure that Aboriginal consultation takes place for all aspects of the project. It is not necessary that each actor that is involved with an approval for the project take on the responsibility to ensure that consultation for the entire project has been completed; such an approach would be unworkable. It would lead to confusion and uncertainty and the potential for duplication and inconsistency.
>
> . . .
>
> In fulfilling its responsibility to assess the adequacy of consultation, the Board must necessarily take responsibility for the aspects of the consultation that relate to the matter before it, but should do so with a recognition of any other forum in which consultation issues related to the project are being addressed.
>
> . . .
>
> The EA [Environmental Assessment] process . . . is an entirely appropriate and logical means by which the Crown can assure itself that consultation has been adequate.[49]

A similar issue arises in major projects involving both federal and provincial Crown actors, such as major transportation routes and hydroelectric generation projects. Is each level of government required to consult independently and make an independent determination of whether the Crown duty is fulfilled? Would it be possible to permit a single consultation and determination by one Crown so long as the full range of potential effects on traditional activities and culturally significant sites is considered, and appropriate ac-

48 But see *Standing Buffalo Dakota First Nation v. Enbridge Pipelines Inc.*, 2008 FCA 222, [2008] F.C.J. No. 1124, application for leave to appeal dismissed, 2 December 2010.

49 Decision and Order of the Ontario Energy Board, dated 15 September 2008.

commodation is implemented? Such co-operative government approaches could be encouraged by the courts in order to reduce duplication and relieve the consultation burden on Aboriginal communities, governments, and proponents—so long as such approaches do not diminish the ability of Aboriginal peoples to be appropriately consulted and accommodated.

Equally, in order to avoid over burdening Aboriginal communities with requests for consultation from multiple ministries of the same government, or on matters on which the communities have no interest, governments should consider methods for easing the administrative burden. This could be done by having consultations on different matters at a consolidated event. For example, communities might be offered Crown–community forums where representatives from multiple ministries and proponents can meet and discuss projects with community representatives. Similarly, project proponents could be offered one window sources of government information and assistance in relation to Aboriginal consultation.[50] Where multiple ministries and agencies must be involved, governments can co-ordinate their consultation approaches and activities through internal co-ordinating mechanisms that ensure consistency and avoid duplication of consultation efforts.[51]

C. HOW TO UNDERTAKE CONSULTATIONS

In *Haida*, the Court stated that the Crown should be guided by the twin principles of "balance" and "compromise" in order to achieve the overriding goal of reconciliation.[52] By way of example of a consultation process, the chief justice referred to the New Zealand Ministry of Justice consultation guide.[53] It refers to consultation as a process by which both parties become better informed through open and transparent information gathering and a willingness to alter a proposed plan of action. It also provides for feedback not just during the consultation process but also after a decision has been made.[54]

The chief justice further indicated that the depth of consultation required for a particular project falls on a spectrum and it is necessary to

50 RES III RFP, above note 24.

51 For example, a single provincial government official has been appointed to coordinate mineral development in the "Ring of Fire" in far-northern Ontario.

52 *Haida*, above note 1 at para. 45.

53 *Ibid.* at para. 46.

54 *Ibid.*

carry out a preliminary assessment and determine case-by-case where on this spectrum a particular consultation process should fall.[55] The preliminary assessment entails both a "project impact assessment" and a "strength of claims assessment." While the former assessment is largely a matter of engineering and science, including social science, the latter is a legal issue. Crown lawyers are able to provide advice on the strength of particular claims including whether an assertion meets the minimum standard of a "credible" claim and the likelihood it will succeed.

What is not known is whether the Aboriginal communities are entitled to know the basis for the Crown's decision regarding the depth of consultation afforded or whether this remains solicitor–client privileged legal advice. Also unclear is whether the assessment can be informal or need always be a written document. Governments make thousands of decisions potentially engaging the duty to consult and already invest considerable legal resources in carrying out assessments. Where the Crown has dealt with similar projects in the same area, or intends to consult fully whether or not required to do so, it might be possible to avoid preparing a new written assessment on the same subject.[56]

In preparing and implementing the preliminary assessment, it is important to avoid inadequate consultation. While the methods used to consult need only be reasonable, *Little Salmon* states expressly that the adequacy of consultation will be reviewed on a standard of correctness.[57]

In situations where the required depth of consultation is at the medium or lower end of the spectrum,[58] existing approval procedures including environmental assessment requirements may offer sufficient opportunities for Aboriginal input and be suitable for fulfilling the constitutional duty.[59] By contrast, for large projects entailing potentially significant impacts, the creation of special consultation mechanisms may be required to supplement consultation carried out as part of the existing regulatory process. In the case of the Bruce to Milton transmission line, for example, the proponent consulted on behalf of the Crown in the course of the leave to construct

---

55 *Ibid.* at paras. 37 and 43–45.

56 But see *Wii'litswx v. B.C. (Minister of Forests)*, 2008 BCSC 1139, [2008] 4 C.N.L.R. 315 at paras. 143, 147, 205; and *Brown v. Sunshine Coast Forest District (District Manager)*, 2008 BCSC 1642, [2009] 1 C.N.L.R. 110 at para. 18.

57 *Little Salmon*, above note 3 at para. 48.

58 *Little Salmon, ibid.*, is an example of the required depth on consultation falling on the lower end of the spectrum.

59 See, for example, *Taku River*, above note 5; *Hiawatha First Nation v. Ontario (Minister of the Environment)*, [2007] O.J. No. 506, 221 O.A.C. 113; and *Brokenhead*, above note 31.

application and the environmental assessment, but the Ontario Crown also opened direct dialogue with certain communities.

In practice, once notice is given and a community chooses to engage, the consultations take on a life of their own and the extent and type of consultation can be driven as much by community expectations as the legal assessment of the extent of consultation to which the community is entitled. With longer-term relationship building, governments do not typically restrict interaction to the minimum legally required.

In instances where deep consultation is required, capacity funding has become a key part of consultation as Aboriginal communities typically have limited ability to pay for needed expertise to respond to consultation requests. In Ontario, a fund has been established through which every Aboriginal community can create a consultation office and officer.[60] Funding has also been made available for consultation on larger projects requiring specific expertise and for participation in legislative reform on matters related to treaty and Aboriginal rights.

An interesting procedural question regarding how consultation should be undertaken is the extent to which the Crown can delegate aspects of consultation to private proponents, and the appropriate mechanism for doing so. As a practical matter, many ministries of the Crown must rely, to some extent, on delegating to private proponents, while retaining legal responsibility for fulfilling the duty. Chief Justice McLachlin indicated in *Haida* that only procedural aspects of consultation can be delegated but did not spell out what is procedural and what is substantive.[61]

A possible approach to determining which aspects of consultation are "substantive" and cannot be delegated is to restrict to the Crown those decisions involving the application of the legal standards identified in this paper to determine "who, when, how, and on what" to consult. Accordingly the Crown should (1) identify the Aboriginal communities to consult and at what stage of the project to do so; (2) determine the depth of consultation required for the particular project; (3) satisfy itself that the consultation carried out was sufficient; and (4) satisfy itself that any necessary accommodation is appropriate.[62] Some ministries of the Ontario government have negotiated project-specific memoranda of understanding, setting out the

60 This fund is called the New Relationship Fund and was created in 2008.

61 *Haida*, above note 1 at para. 53.

62 The Crown should be able to consider proposals from proponents and Aboriginal communities regarding these matters, but should make the identification or determination itself.

respective roles of proponents and the Crown in consultation.[63] The chief justice indicated her preference for express delegation of procedural aspects of consultation.[64] In addition to MOUs, Ontario has attempted to comply through legislation,[65] regulations,[66] directions,[67] and guidelines.[68]

A further outstanding issue is the extent to which the Aboriginal communities' own consultation processes and guidelines should be followed by the Crown and proponents. The chief justice in *Haida* did not go so far as to suggest that there is a duty to consult on how to consult[69] or a duty to consult only in the manner preferred by Aboriginal communities. Nonetheless, it is certainly consistent with reconciliation between the Crown and Aboriginal people to respect reasonable processes established by the communities themselves. Some Ontario Aboriginal communities have crafted processes to allow them to manage multiple consultation requests in an efficient manner and these should be respected to the extent possible.[70]

The Supreme Court has clarified that Aboriginal communities must not obstruct or frustrate the consultation process[71] or claim a failure by the Crown to consult if they do not make themselves available for meetings or otherwise respond to invitations within a reasonable time frame.[72] Similarly, if community representatives insist on using the consultation opportunity exclusively to discuss matters other than potential adverse impacts on rights, they cannot thereafter claim that the Crown failed to consult on the substantive impacts of the project.[73]

---

63 The Ministry of Energy has entered into MOUs with Hydro One, the Ontario Power Authority, and several private proponents. Binding consultation agreements between the Crown and proponents were required by RES III RFP, above note 24.

64 *Haida*, above note 1 at paras. 44, 51, and 55.

65 See, for example, *Electricity Act*, above note 21, s. 25.32 (4.4).

66 See, for example, O.Reg. 231/08. s. 8; O.Reg. 359/09, ss. 14–18.

67 See, for example, Direction to the Ontario Power Authority dated 27 August 2007.

68 See, for example, O.Reg. 101/07, *Guide to Environmental Assessment Requirements for Waste Management Projects*, s. A.3.3. Guidelines are also to be issued on the Aboriginal consultation process for renewable energy projects under O.Reg. 359/09.

69 But see *Dene Tha' First Nation v. Canada (Minister of the Environment)*, 2006 FC 1354, [2006] F.C.J. No. 1677, aff'd 2008 FCA 20, [2008] F.C.J. No. 444, in which the court ruled that the planning of an environmental assessment, where the assessment is to be relied upon to fulfill the duty to consult, required the input of all affected First Nations.

70 For example, Great Earth Law, above note 29.

71 *Haida*, above note 1 at para. 42.

72 *Nlaka'pamux*, above note 27 at para. 97; see also *Little Salmon*, above note 3.

73 *Ahousaht Indian Band v. Canada (Minister of Fisheries and Oceans)*, 2008 FCA 212, [2008] F.C.J. No. 946; *R. v. Tommy*, 2008 BCSC 1095, [2008] B.C.J. No. 1543; and *R. v. Aleck et al.*, 2008 BCSC 1096, [2008] 4 C.N.L.R. 102.

Immediately after the *Haida* decision, governments across the country attempted to develop general guidelines for the numerous ministries involved in consultation. Some of these guidelines essentially involved repeating and interpreting the *Haida* decision itself. Many provincial guidelines were not agreed to by Aboriginal communities. Since then, different communities and treaty organizations have made it clear that they wish to be consulted differently, in accordance with their particular needs. The diverse group of Aboriginal communities in Canada have different perceptions, experiences, and history, all of which influence the way in which they wish to be consulted by the Crown.

D. ON WHAT ISSUES TO CONSULT

On what claims should the Crown consult? In *Haida* the chief justice indicated that there is a very low threshold for triggering the duty to consult—Aboriginal communities need merely make a credible claim of a potential infringement of an asserted treaty or Aboriginal right or title.[74] What amounts to a claim (or "assertion") of section 35 rights? Is the Crown on notice where a person belonging to a First Nation or Métis community alleges in correspondence that he or she has certain rights? At the very least, where any kind of solemn written assertion is made by a person representing the collective interests of the Aboriginal community, be it in a letter, land claim, or notice of proceeding, the Crown is on notice that the community has made a claim potentially requiring consultation and accommodation.

Note also that the Court has referred to "constructive" knowledge which presumably means that once an assertion is made to any representative of the Crown, the entire government is deemed to be aware.[75] As a result, it is now incumbent on governments to know what assertions it has received, a very complex task given the range of distinct interactions ministries and agencies have with Aboriginal communities.

Determining what constitutes a potential adverse impact has also proved problematic. It had been assumed by governments that some new legal encumbrance or physical impact of a decision is required in order for an Aboriginal community to allege adverse impacts on rights.[76] There have

74 *Haida*, above note 1 at para. 37.

75 *Taku River*, above note 5 at para. 25.

76 Generally, adverse impacts are those that affect traditional harvesting of plants or animals, and likely archaeological or burial sites, and possibly the disposition or encumbrance of Crown land where this could compromise Aboriginal title claims.

been cases where the triggering event was the mere transfer of a permit or licence, such as *Haida* itself,[77] but there was the prospect of subsequent activity affecting the land and claims to land.[78] In its 2010 decision in *Rio Tinto*, the Supreme Court of Canada addressed this issue in holding that the duty is not triggered by an agreement to purchase power that would result in no appreciable new impact on water levels or the fishery. As there had never been consultation on the original 1950s-era hydroelectric diversion project, the Court of Appeal had assumed that the facility constituted a continuing infringement. This would be perpetuated by the power purchase, which could not therefore proceed absent consultation.[79] The Supreme Court rejected this reasoning and ruled that the duty to consult is confined to situations where a current decision will have a new adverse impact on the future exercise of a right. Past impacts should be addressed through other means such as bringing an action for damages.[80]

Some projects, such as high tension transmission lines, may be built for the purposes of enabling or facilitating other projects, such as new generating facilities. It has been argued that the duty to consult requires consideration of subsequent projects enabled by the line, including projects that may not yet have been proposed or even contemplated. The *Rio Tinto* decision, however, confines the duty to consult to adverse effects flowing from the specific decision in issue, not to larger impacts of a project of which it may be a part: "The subject of the consultation is the impact . . . of the *current* decision under consideration."[81] This reasoning suggests that the duty does not require consideration of secondary development enabled by a project in circumstances where consultation will occur on the subsequent projects once they are better defined.[82]

In practice, regulatory approval procedures, such as the environmental assessment process and applications to the Ontario Energy Board, may not be able to effectively consider all of the potential secondary impacts of development. With that said, and irrespective of the limits of the duty

---

77 *Haida*, above note 1 at para. 4.

78 In *Haida*, there was the prospect of forest harvesting subsequent to the transfer of the licence.

79 *Carrier Sekani Tribal Council v. British Columbia (Utilities Commission)*, 2009 BCCA 67, [2009] B.C.J. No. 259.

80 *Rio Tinto*, above note 3 at paras. 46–54.

81 *Ibid.* at para. 53 [emphasis by McLachlin C.J.].

82 See *Brokenhead*, above note 31 at paras. 24–37; and Ontario Energy Board Decision and Order RP-2005-0022, EB-2005-0441, EB-2005-0442, EB-2005-0443, EB-2005-0473 (6 January 2006), online: www.oeb.gov.on.ca/documents/cases/RP-2005-0022/decision_060106.pdf.

to consult and of existing regulatory approval processes, Crown efforts to understand and incorporate Aboriginal perspectives into long-term planning will assist with later consultations. A beneficial effect of intensive consultation on the original project can be to improve relationships and establish forums that remain available to facilitate early consultation on subsequent development.

Is it necessary to consult on economic impacts and financial benefits from projects outside the ambit of section 35 guaranteed rights? To date, the jurisprudence requires consultation on potential adverse impacts on Aboriginal and treaty rights and is therefore limited (based on the scope of section 35 rights recognized to date) to consultations on hunting, fishing, trapping, plant harvesting, and other traditional or ceremonial activities, as well as possibly the potential disturbance of culturally significant burial and other archaeological sites.[83] However, communities often have different objectives in the consultations and may prefer to discuss economic benefits from the project through an impact-benefit agreement (IBA) or other mechanism. Statutory environmental assessment regimes provide a further incentive for proponents to consult on economic and other matters beyond the scope of the constitutional duty, since such regimes may require consulting a broadly defined category of "interested parties" which embraces those with economic interests. In practice, project schedules and the costs of delay provide a strong incentive for proponents to reach agreement with Aboriginal communities on pragmatic solutions that allow projects to move forward.

To some proponents, the need to discuss economic benefits from projects including IBAs may seem a distortion of the purpose of *Haida*, especially when no obvious impacts on rights are demonstrated. There may, however, be benefits to the proponents, who gain access to the Aboriginal labour force and to local business partners with economic interests allied with their own. Further, unemployment among Aboriginal people is, at present, significantly higher, while education attainment levels are lower, health outcomes are worse, and housing is often substandard. When the Crown and private proponents consult on large and potentially profitable initiatives, it is not surprising that they are being asked not only for capacity funding for consultation, but also for economic benefits from the project. In *Haida*, the Court required the Crown to consult with local Aboriginal communities on the adverse impacts of projects on harvesting and other rights: was the Court

83 But see British Columbia Utilities Commission, *Reconsideration of the Interior to Lower Mainland Transmission Project* (3 February 2011) at 91–95.

hoping that by bringing the communities closer to government and business decision-making processes an opportunity would be created for them to seek improvement of their often deplorable economic and social conditions?

E. ACCOMMODATION

Accommodation is the second half and an integral part of the duty.[84] What accommodation is required where there is a potential adverse impact on treaty or Aboriginal rights? Easy examples include restoring the habitat of a harvested species or adjusting the route of a roadway to avoid a culturally significant archaeological site. More complicated accommodation includes financial compensation for adverse impacts on rights. Such agreements can include cash payments, profit sharing, trusts, agreements to hire, and provide skills training, or preferential treatment for contracted services such as catering or trucking.

In *Little Salmon*, the Court stated that there is no Crown duty to accommodate to the point of undue hardship for the non-Aboriginal population.[85] Following *Haida*, the Court reiterated that accommodation does not include a community's right to approve or veto projects or government decisions.[86] (An exception may be decisions that would have a very serious adverse impact on an Aboriginal title claim.[87]) In *Little Salmon*, the Court also applied a deferential standard in reviewing the substance of accommodation, making reference to the reasonableness of the decision, using the term "palpable error," and stating that it was not relevant whether a court would have reached a different conclusion on the facts.[88]

The Government of Ontario is increasingly focused on addressing the needs of Aboriginal communities by creating opportunities for economic participation and business partnerships. The issues of rights-driven accommodation, settlement of past grievances, and socio-economic policy objectives merge in arrangements such as the agreement by Ontario Power

84 *Haida*, above note 1 at paras. 46–50.

85 *Little Salmon*, above note 3 at para. 81.

86 *Ibid.* at para. 14; *Haida*, above note 1 at paras. 42 and 48–49. It will be interesting to see whether Canada's recent endorsement of the UN Declaration on Indigenous Rights, which refers to "free, prior and informed consent" will influence this jurisprudence. UN General Assembly, *United Nations Declaration on the Rights of Indigenous Peoples* resolution adopted by the General Assembly, 13 September 2007, A/RES/61/295, online: www.unhcr.org/refworld/docid/471355a82.html.

87 *Haida, ibid.* at para. 24.

88 *Little Salmon*, above note 3 at paras. 81–88.

Generation to include an equity stake for Lac Seul First Nation in the recently opened Lac Seul hydroelectric project, and a similar arrangement with the Moose Cree First Nation on the Lower Mattagami project, currently under construction. Additional similar arrangements are being concluded in relation to renewable energy projects under Ontario's *Green Energy and Economy Act*, supported by special legislative and regulatory provisions,[89] a capacity-building fund to assist Aboriginal community-owned enterprises to enter the field, higher prices per kilowatt/hour for Aboriginal generation projects, and government loan guarantees.

F. BROADER IMPLICATIONS

The Aboriginal jurisprudence of the McLachlin Court encourages governments and Aboriginal communities to reach negotiated solutions to land and harvesting disputes without resort to litigation. The resolution of Aboriginal rights and treaty interpretation issues through adversarial judicial proceedings can be difficult for all parties, and the Supreme Court has encouraged negotiations through the requirement that the Crown engage in dialogue with Aboriginal communities. The establishment of the duty has also removed an incentive to litigation arguably created by the Supreme Court itself in *Sparrow*, since it is no longer necessary to prove claims in court in order to obtain Crown consultation and accommodation. In effect, the convergence of the government justification for breaches under the *Sparrow* test with the new duty to consult, combined with the opening of opportunities to address the very significant non-rights based needs of Aboriginal communities, may help the process of negotiated resolution and reduce the volume of Aboriginal litigation.

Disputes over broader government policy may also be reduced. Whether or not the duty to consult applies to legislative initiatives,[90] the *Haida* decision has altered the way in which governments ensure meaningful

---

89 See *Green Energy and Green Economy Act*, above note 21, Schedule B, and *Electricity Act*, above note 21, s. 5(1) amending s. 25.32 by adding s. 4.5:

> The Minister may direct the OPA to establish measures to facilitate the participation of aboriginal peoples in the development of renewable energy generation facilities, transmission systems and distribution systems and such measures may include programs or funding for, or associated with, aboriginal participation in the development of such facilities or systems.

90 See *Rio Tinto*, above note 3 at para. 44, and *R. v. Lefthand*, 2007 ABCA 206, [2007] A.J. No. 681.

input of the Aboriginal community into broader policy making. Examples include the 2009 amendments to Ontario's *Mining Act* that modernized the mining regime, and Ontario's legislation enacted in 2010 regarding land use planning in the far north of the province. As part of the process of legislative reform of the mining legislation, Aboriginal leaders from across the province met regularly over several weeks to discuss provisions for notice, consultation, and accommodation. In addition, community-level information sessions were organized by both the Ministry and the PTOs to discuss the reforms. Among the changes to the legislation made as a result of the process was the inclusion of a purpose clause that expressly recognizes the constitutional duty to consult.[91]

The impact on governments of the duty to consult has been enormous. Moving forward, governments need further clarification from the Supreme Court of Canada on the issues of "who, when, how, and on what" to consult. A continued active dialogue between the Court and governments on the unresolved legal issues will allow the *Haida* case to achieve its purpose more efficiently. From the McLachlin Court, governments can anticipate consensual and pragmatic decisions of the type for which the chief justice of the Supreme Court has become known—decisions that promote recognition of section 35-protected treaty and Aboriginal rights, reconciliation with the Crown, negotiated solutions, and new economic opportunities for Aboriginal communities.

91 *Mining Act*, above note 21, s. 2. The *Green Energy and Green Economy Act*, above note 21, s. 1(2), also includes an interpretation section that explicitly recognizes s. 35 and the duty to consult, as does the *Far North Act, 2010*, S.O. 2010, c. 18, s. 1.

PART FOUR

Equality and Fundamental Freedoms

Le poids de l'histoire : les années McLachlin et la liberté de religion

NATHALIE DES ROSIERS*

> We have just enough religion to make us hate, but not enough to make us love another.[1]

> Ce qu'il faudrait, c'est toujours concéder à son prochain qu'il a une parcelle de vérité et non pas de dire que toute la vérité est à moi, à mon pays, à ma race, à ma religion.[2]

Beaucoup a déjà été écrit sur le thème de la liberté de religion au cours des dernières années[3]. Les décisions majeures rendues par la Cour suprême[4]

---

* Mes remerciements au commentateur–évaluateur du texte dont les suggestions ont été grandement appréciées. Mes remerciements également à Christian Pearce pour son appui à la recherche pour le présent texte, dont les conclusions n'engagent que moi.

1 Jonathan Swift, « Thoughts on Various Subjects ».

2 *Dictionnaire des citations, s.v.* « Amadou Hampâté Bâ » en ligne : 100.000 citations [du monde] www.evene.fr/citations (consulté le 28 mai 2009).

3 La liberté de religion et les arrêts discutés dans le présent texte ont été discutés dans la doctrine. Voir les travaux de Iain Benson, Benjamin Berger, Jeremy Webber, David Brown, Jean-François Gaudreault-Desbiens, Pascale Fournier, Richard Moon, Bruce Ryder et Shauna Van Praagh.

4 Les décisions étudiées incluent : *Syndicat Northcrest c. Amselem*, 2004 CSC 47, [2004] 2 R.C.S. 551 [*Amselem*]; *Congrégation des témoins de Jéhovah de St-Jérôme-Lafontaine c. Lafontaine (Village)*, 2004 CSC 48, [2004] 2 R.C.S. 650 [*Congrégation St-Jérôme*]; *Multani c. Commission scolaire Marguerite-Bourgeoys*, 2006 CSC 6, [2006] 1 R.C.S. 256 [*Multani*]; *Bruker c. Marcovitz*, 2007 CSC 54, [2007] 3 R.C.S. 607 [*Bruker*]; *Université Trinity Western c. British Columbia College of Teachers*, 2001 CSC 31, [2001] 1 R.C.S. 772 [*Trinity Western*]; *Chamberlain c. Surrey School District No. 36*, 2002 CSC 86, [2002] 4 R.C.S. 710 [*Chamberlain*]; *A.C. c. Manitoba (Directeur des services à l'enfant et à la famille)*, 2009 CSC 30, [2009] 2 R.C.S. 181 [*A.C.*]; *Alberta c. Hutterian Brethren of Wilson Colony*, 2009 CSC 37, [2009] 2 R.C.S. 567 [*Hutterian Brethren*].

ayant trait à la liberté de religion[5], au cours des derniers dix ans, ont été analysées sous plusieurs angles. J'avance l'hypothèse que, contrairement peut-être à d'autres secteurs, nous sommes en présence d'un domaine où il y a continuité. Ma réflexion fait donc place en première partie à l'héritage historique canadien en matière de traitement des religions (A). Je développe cette idée de la continuité et du poids de cet héritage dans la deuxième partie (B) où j'analyse comment la liberté de religion doit être comprise dans un contexte de relations inégalitaires entre majorité et minorités (1), où les tribunaux se montrent plus ou moins sceptiques face aux justifications étatiques (2) et où il faudra éventuellement intervenir pour minimiser les abus causés par les relations de pouvoir qui pourraient exister au sein même des minorités religieuses (3).

La première partie du texte explique donc le contexte historique dans lequel la liberté de religion se présente : contexte historique qui, selon moi, milite pour une analyse de la liberté de religion sous l'angle de l'égalité et de la lutte contre la discrimination. Non pas qu'une analyse « liberté » soit désuète, mais je pense que l'éclairage « égalité » peut permettre d'expliquer les résultats et le raisonnement dans les diverses décisions étudiées[6]. Malgré les critiques du professeur Woehrling[7] sur la confusion que cette approche « égalité » crée, et en réponse donc aux questions posées par Richard Moon[8] dans son article percutant, je répondrai que la liberté de religion possède certainement des aspects de dignité de la personne, certainement de liberté d'expression et qu'elle s'analyse techniquement dans le cadre des considérations données à l'article 2 de la *Charte canadienne des droits et libertés*. Cependant, le contexte canadien présuppose une sensibilité à l'égalité dans le contexte de l'appréciation des libertés religieuses. Le Canada a, d'une part,

5 Toutes ne sont pas des décisions de droit constitutionnel : *Congregation St-Jérôme* et *Trinity Western*, *ibid.*, sont particulièrement davantage des décisions de droit administratif.

6 Les décisions traitant de la liberté de religion peuvent aussi être analysées sous l'angle des droits individuels et collectifs : Nathalie Des Rosiers, « Free Religions or Freedom from Religion? Canada, Federalism and Religion » dans Josep Maria Castellà Andreu et Sébastien Grammond, dir., *Diversidad, derechos fundamentales y federalismo : un diálogo entre Canadá y España*, Barcelona, Atelier, 2010. Mes excuses auprès de David Brown pour les rapprochements avec un titre qu'il a utilisé dans un article dont je n'étais pas au courant au moment du colloque espagnol.

7 José Woehrling, « La place de la religion dans les écoles publiques du Québec » (2007) 41 : 3 R.J.T. 651, à la p. 655.

8 Richard Moon, « Religious Commitment and Identity: *Syndicat Northcrest v. Amselem* » (2005) 29 Sup. Ct. L. Rev. (2d) 201; Richard Moon, « Liberty, Neutrality, and Inclusion: Religious Freedom under the *Canadian Charter of Rights and Freedoms* » (2003) 41 : 3 Brandeis L.J. 563.

ABSTRACT

The thesis defended here is that during the McLachlin years, the Supreme Court has conceptualized freedom of religion very much as its predecessors did—that is, an idea shaped by its history. In the first part of the paper, I describe our complex history: its measure of aspirations for religious toleration confronted by the reality of religious discrimination; its stated hope for the neutrality of the state marked by a certain hypocrisy; and its general support and acceptance of religious life, spirituality, and religious communities destabilized by the recognition of abuse of power and inequality within religion itself. In the second part of the paper, I argue that, like its predecessors, the McLachlin Court has articulated the concept of freedom of religion with strong anti-discrimination concerns. The Court is concerned with monitoring majority/minority conflicts, views suspiciously (although recently less so) the majority rationales, and attempts to empower the minority, while becoming more and more cognizant of the reality of inequality and the potential for abuse of power within religious communities.

tenté de développer un modèle de tolérance religieuse et a, d'autre part, vécu et reproduit la discrimination religieuse. Cette dimension complexe et ambivalente continue de hanter toute analyse de la liberté de religion. La dimension égalitaire de l'analyse de la liberté de religion au Canada doit donc continuer de s'imposer, c'est l'héritage des précédents historiques. Plusieurs des arrêts marquants pour la liberté de religion étaient issus du Québec des années 1950, entre autres, *Saumur c. la Ville de Québec*[9]. Ces décisions me semblent avoir tracé une approche qui continue d'animer la pensée juridique contemporaine. Il se peut que les tensions les plus récentes qui mettent en cause les relations de pouvoir au sein même des communautés religieuses et la valeur de leur contribution à la société, c'est-à-dire les questions de sécularité ou la neutralité de l'État; de la liberté de religion comme droit collectif, du traitement inégal des femmes au sein des religions requièrent de nouveaux concepts. Jusqu'à présent, je suggère que le modèle adopté issu des années 50 n'est pas dépassé et est conforme à l'héritage historique canadien.

9 *Saumur c. la Ville de Québec*, [1953] 2 R.C.S. 299 [*Saumur*].

A. LE POIDS DE L'HISTOIRE

L'histoire du Canada est marquée par des conflits religieux, et ce comme partout ailleurs: l'opposition entre catholiques et protestants motivent en partie la déportation des Acadiens[10], l'Acte de Québec peut s'apparenter à un premier geste d'accommodement religieux[11] où le roi d'Angleterre accepte qu'au Canada et seulement au Canada, les catholiques n'auront pas à prêter le Serment d'allégeance[12]. L'histoire constitutionnelle sera influencée par cet aménagement religieux : l'article 93 de la Loi constitutionnelle de 1867, si porteur de difficultés, en est la preuve[13]. Malgré le désir d'avoir une constitution à l'image de la Grande-Bretagne[14], il y aura dès le début une tolérance pragmatique[15] de la religion catholique.[16] Notons que les alliances entre les communautés chrétiennes et les élites gouvernementales servent des fins bien définies, entre autres, l'assimilation des populations autochtones par la voie des pensionnats et écoles résidentielles et le développement de la colonisation.[17] Les églises et communautés religieuses auront le pouvoir délégué de célébrer les mariages et feront souvent office de bureau d'enregistrement des naissances et des décès, et s'occuperont de l'éducation des enfants et du soin des malades[18], des fonctions maintenant assumées en partie par l'État.

Par la suite, le processus visera l'élargissement des privilèges accordés aux groupes chrétiens aux autres religions. La liberté de religion comme

10 Maurice A. Léger, « La déportation et la religion » dans Ronnie-Gilles LeBlanc, dir., *Du grand dérangement à la déportation : Nouvelles perspectives historiques*, Moncton, Chaire d'études acadiennes, Université de Moncton, 2005, 105 à la p. 129. James Laxer, *The Acadians: In Search of a Homeland*, Toronto, Doubleday Canada, 2006, 89 à la p. 96.

11 Hilda Neatby, *Quebec: The Revolutionary Age, 1760–1791*, Toronto, McClelland et Stewart, 1966 aux pp. 125–141, cité par John McLaren, « The Doukhobor Belief in Individual Faith and Conscience and the Demands of the Secular State » dans John McLaren et Harold Coward, dir., *Religious Conscience, the State, and the Law: Historical Contexts and Contemporary Significance*, Albany, State University of New York Press, 1999, 117 à la p. 134, n. 60.

12 Micheline Milot, « Les principes de laïcité politique au Québec et au Canada » (2005) 13 Bulletin d'histoire politique 13.

13 Voir le recours devant le Comité des droits de la personne des Nations Unies et sa conclusion que l'Ontario serait en violation des droits de la personne internationaux en raison de son financement limité aux écoles catholiques : *Waldman v. Canada*, 5 novembre, 1999, N.U. Doc. No. CCPR/C/67/D/694/1996, en ligne: www.unhchr.ch/tbs/doc.nsf/0/b3bfc541589cc30f802568690052e5d6?.

14 Préambule au *Loi Constitutionnelle de 1867* 30 & 31 Vict., c. 3 (R.-U.).

15 Milot, *supra* note 12 à la p. 16.

16 *Ibid.*

17 James S. Frideres et René R. Gadacz, *Aboriginal Peoples in Canada*, 8e éd., Toronto, Pearson/Prentice Hall, 2008, aux pp. 3 et 111.

18 Milot, *supra* note 12 à la p. 18.

concept sera associée à la nécessité de contrôler le monopole des traditions chrétiennes et de corriger le traitement injuste qu'elles imposent à l'occasion aux minorités religieuses[19]. La liberté de religion sera donc associée dès le début au désir et à la vision d'une coexistence marqués par la tolérance, et donc liée à des valeurs de respect de la dignité humaine. La neutralité de l'État sera perçue, dans ce contexte, comme un traitement délibérément égalitaire de toutes les religions. Jacques Zylberberg et Pauline Côté résument ainsi : « La tolérance, plus que la liberté de conscience, facilitera l'établissement, dans la colonie puis dans les dominions, de différentes autres collectivités, par exemple juives, baptistes et mormones »[20].

Ce lien entre tolérance religieuse et liberté de religion me semble évident dans les premières expressions juridiques. D'une certaine façon, la présence et le désir de vivre « avec » une minorité canadienne française fortement liée à la religion catholique, incitent à concevoir la religion comme intimement liée à l'idée de la tolérance culturelle et du vivre ensemble. Cependant, le contexte d'inégalité est bien connu : l'antisémitisme canadien devra être dénoncé[21] ainsi que la discrimination contre les minorités religieuses comme les Doukhobors[22] et les Témoins de Jéhovah. Ces deux derniers groupes sont perçus comme menaçants pour les valeurs majoritaires de capitalisme, de patriotisme, du rôle prépondérant des religions majoritaires. Les deux congrégations sont donc vilipendées et devront se tourner vers les tribunaux pour chercher une protection[23].

Il n'est donc pas surprenant que les premières itérations de notre régime de primauté du droit dans *Roncarelli c. Duplessis* aient été articulées dans un contexte de discrimination religieuse, déjà dénoncé dans *Saumur c. La Ville*

---

19 *Roncarelli c. Duplessis*, [1959] R.C.S. 121.

20 Jacques Zylberberg et Pauline Côté, « Les balises étatiques de la religion au Canada » (1993) 40 : 4 Social Compass 529.

21 Irving Abella et Harold Troper, *None Is Too Many: Canada and the Jews of Europe, 1933–1948*, 3e éd., Toronto, Key Porter, 2000, à la p. 340; *Noble c. Alley*, [1951] S.C.R. 64; William W. Black, « Religion and the Right of Equality » dans Anne Bayefsky et Mary Eberts, dir., *Equality Rights and the Canadian Charter of Rights and Freedoms*, Toronto, Carswell, 1985, à la p. 131 [Black].

22 Tel que les Doukhobors, voir John McLaren, « The Doukhobor Belief in Individual Faith and Conscience and the Demands of the Secular State » dans John McLaren et Harold Coward, dir., *Religious Conscience, the State, and the Law: Historical Contexts and Contemporary Significance*, Albany, State University of New York Press, 1999; William Janzen, *Limits on Liberty: the Experience of Mennonite, Hutterite and Doukhobor Communities in Canada*, Toronto, University of Toronto Press, 1990.

23 Les Hutterites seront également l'objet de lois abusives en Alberta : Black, *supra* note 21 à la p. 132.

de Québec,[24] où la légalité d'un règlement municipal interdisant la distribution de brochures sans obtenir la permission au préalable des autorités a été contestée. Les paroles du juge Rand sont encore porteuses de sens :

> From 1760, therefore, to the present moment, religious freedom has, in our legal system, been recognized as a principle of fundamental character; and although we have nothing in the nature of an established church, that the untrammelled affirmations of religious belief and its propagation, personal or institutional, remain as of the greatest constitutional significance throughout the Dominion is unquestionable[25].

L'arrêt *Chaput c. Romain*,[26] suivra *Saumur*, dénonçant le traitement des Témoins de Jéhovah et dans lequel le juge Taschereau prononcera ces paroles maintenant célèbres:

> Dans notre pays, il n'existe pas de religion d'État. Personne n'est tenu d'adhérer à une croyance quelconque. Toutes les religions sont sur un pied d'égalité, et tous les catholiques comme d'ailleurs tous les protestants, les juifs, ou les autres adhérents des diverses dénominations religieuses, ont la plus entière liberté de penser comme ils le désirent. La conscience de chacun est une affaire personnelle, et l'affaire de nul autre. Il serait désolant de penser qu'une majorité puisse imposer ses vues religieuses à une minorité. Ce serait une erreur fâcheuse de croire qu'on sert son pays ou sa religion, en refusant dans une province, à une minorité, les mêmes droits que l'on revendique soi-même avec raison, dans une autre province[27].

Les « accommodements » suivront et permettront des adaptations aux horaires de travail[28] qui n'entravent pas trop les pratiques des employeurs[29], des repas spéciaux dans les hôpitaux ou les prisons[30]. On se rappellera également la question épineuse des turbans pour les officiers de la gendarmerie royale[31]. Dès le début, on anticipe que la question des « accommodements »

24 *Saumur, supra* note 9.

25 *Ibid.* à la p. 327.

26 *Chaput c. Romain*, [1955] R.C.S. 834.

27 *Ibid.* à la p. 840.

28 *Ontario (Commission ontarienne des droits de la personne) c. Simpsons-Sears Ltd.*., [1985] 2 S.C.R. 536, 2 R.C.S. 536.

29 *Central Okanagan School District No. 23 c. Renaud*, [1992] 2 S.C.R. 970, 2 R.C.S. 970.

30 Pierre Bosset, *Le régime alimentaire des détenus de foi hébraïque : obligations des autorités carcérales, Commission des droits de la personne et des droits de la jeunesse Québec*, 1991, en ligne: www.cdpdj.qc.ca/fr/publications/docs/aliments_hebraique.pdf.

31 *Grant c. Canada (Procureur général)*, [1995] A.C.F. no 830, 125 D.L.R. (4e) 556, autorisation de pourvoi à la C.S.C. refusée, [1995] S.C.C.A. No. 394.

pourra présenter des difficultés : le juge McIntyre, dans *Comm. Ont. des Droits de la Personne c. Simpsons-Sears*, le dit bien :

> La question n'est pas exempte de difficultés. La thèse selon laquelle chaque personne devrait être libre d'adopter la religion de son choix et d'en observer les préceptes ne pose aucun problème. Cette notion générale de la liberté religieuse est bien établie dans notre société et constituait un droit reconnu et protégé bien avant que ne soient adoptés les codes des droits de la personne qu'on a vu apparaître récemment. Le problème se pose lorsqu'on se demande jusqu'où peut aller une personne dans l'exercice de sa liberté religieuse? À quel moment, dans la profession de sa foi et l'observance de ses règles, outrepasse-t-elle le simple exercice de ses droits et cherche-t-elle à imposer à autrui le respect de ses croyances? Dans quelle mesure, s'il y a lieu, une personne peut-elle, en pratiquant sa religion, obliger autrui à accomplir un acte ou à accepter une obligation qu'elle n'aurait pas autrement accomplie ou acceptée selon le cas[32]?

Puis viendront les énoncés classiques du juge Dickson dans *Big M Drug Mart* :

> Une société vraiment libre peut accepter une grande diversité de croyances, de goûts, de visées, de coutumes et de normes de conduite. Une société libre vise à assurer à tous l'égalité quant à la jouissance des libertés fondamentales et j'affirme cela sans m'appuyer sur l'art. 15 de la *Charte*. La liberté doit sûrement reposer sur le respect de la dignité et des droits inviolables de l'être humain. Le concept de la liberté de religion se définit essentiellement comme le droit de croire ce que l'on veut en matière religieuse, le droit de professer ouvertement des croyances religieuses sans crainte d'empêchement ou de représailles et le droit de manifester ses croyances religieuses par leur mise en pratique et par le culte ou par leur enseignement et leur propagation. Toutefois, ce concept signifie beaucoup plus que cela. La liberté peut se caractériser essentiellement par l'absence de coercition ou de contrainte. Si une personne est astreinte par l'état ou par la volonté d'autrui à une conduite que, sans cela, elle n'aurait pas choisi d'adopter, cette personne n'agit pas de son propre gré et on ne peut pas dire qu'elle est vraiment libre. L'un des objectifs importants de la *Charte* est de protéger, dans des limites raisonnables, contre la coercition et la contrainte. La coercition comprend non seulement la contrainte flagrante exercée, par exemple, sous forme d'ordres directs d'agir ou de s'abstenir

32 *Simpsons-Sears. supra* n. 28.

> d'agir sous peine de sanction, mais également les formes indirectes de contrôle qui permettent de déterminer ou de restreindre les possibilités d'action d'autrui. La liberté au sens large comporte l'absence de coercition et de contrainte et le droit de manifester ses croyances et pratiques. La liberté signifie que, sous réserve des restrictions qui sont nécessaires pour préserver la sécurité, l'ordre, la santé ou les mœurs publics ou les libertés et droits fondamentaux d'autrui, nul ne peut être forcé d'agir contrairement à ses croyances ou à sa conscience.
>
> Une majorité religieuse, ou l'État à sa demande, ne peut, pour des motifs religieux, imposer sa propre conception de ce qui est bon et vrai aux citoyens qui ne partagent pas le même point de vue. La *Charte* protège les minorités religieuses contre la menace de "tyrannie de la majorité"[33].

On note que cet énoncé est présenté dans un contexte où la Cour Dickson est malgré tout prête à accepter la justification de la violation du droit à la liberté de religion en déterminant un jour de congé plus pratique pour tous (le dimanche), et a défini une sphère de manœuvre relativement large pour les gouvernements. Selon moi, la Cour McLachlin continuera dans la même veine : elle voudra protéger les minorités religieuses, avec cette différence qu'elle prendra jusqu'en 2009 une attitude plus sévère à l'égard des justifications majoritaires : refusant les objectifs d'esthétique dans *Amselem*, de sécurité dans *Multani*, de discrétion dans le zonage urbain dans *Congrégation St-Jérôme*. On notera cependant un resserrement dans *Hutterian Brethren* où la Cour, par un vote serré, acceptera une justification d'intégrité d'un système de reconnaissance des traits faciaux et de prévention de la falsification d'identité pour obliger les membres de la communauté huttérite à se faire photographier pour obtenir un permis de conduite et ce, malgré leurs convictions religieuses et les exemptions qui protégeaient leur mode de vie depuis trente-cinq ans[34].

Donc, à l'heure où les questions soulevées par la place de la religion dans notre société resurgissent[35] et que certains disent embrasser un concept de

---

33 *R. c. Big M Drug Mart Ltd.*, [1985] 1 R.C.S. 295 aux paras. 94–96.

34 Voir pour une analyse plus détaillée de la décision, Nathalie Des Rosiers, *Freedom of Religion, What Is the Strategy after Hutterian Brethren?,* disponible sur le site de l'Association des libertés civiles du Canada, http://ccla.org/resources/ebulletin-3/ebulletin; Mahmud Jamal, « Recent Developments in Freedom of Religion » dans 8th Annual *Charter* Conference, Ontario Bar Association, 2009 (disponsible auprès de l'auteur).

35 Voir entre autres les travaux de Paul Bramadat et David Seljak, dir., *Christianity and Ethnicity in Canada*, Toronto, University of Toronto Press, 2008.

sécularité absolue[36] plutôt que la neutralité bienveillante, assez souple, « à la canadienne », il faut demeurer sensible à la façon dont le concept de liberté de religion a évolué jusqu'à présent. La neutralité n'a pas toujours été bienveillante et s'est présentée dans un contexte marqué par des inégalités et du racisme.[37] C'est en raison de ces discriminations qu'il m'apparaît essentiel de lier les développements récents à cette histoire tumultueuse : c'est le poids de l'histoire.

B. LE POIDS DE L'HISTOIRE

Il y a trois aspects de cet héritage historique dont je veux traiter : la liberté de religion dans un contexte de gestion des conflits majorité/minorités, la question du scepticisme à l'égard des raisons avancées par la majorité pour rejeter la prétention de la minorité et finalement la question de l'abus de pouvoir ou de la discrimination au sein même des religions.

1) Une gestion des conflits majorité/minorités

Presque toutes les décisions touchant la liberté de religion durant la période étudiée mettent en cause une religion « minoritaire » au Canada : il s'agit des religions juive[38], sikh[39], de la congrégation des Témoins de Jéhovah[40] et de la communauté huttérite[41].

---

36 Voir Martin Geoffroy, « Le Québec et la gestion du pluralisme religieux : Une société de plus en plus distincte », *Le Devoir [de Montréal]* (2 février 2007), en ligne : Le Devoir.com www.ledevoir.com/non-classe/129564/le-quebec-et-la-gestion-du-pluralisme-religieux-une-societe-de-plus-en-plus-distincte; online: http://classiques.uqac.ca/contemporains/geoffroy_martin/geoffroy_martin.html. Suggérant un modèle séculaire de religiosité au Québec en contraste avec le modèle émergeant dans le reste du Canada.

37 Voir Pierre Bosset et Paul Eid, « Droit et religion : de l'accommodement raisonnable à un dialogue internormatif ? » (2007) 41 : 2 R.J.T. 513, ainsi que le célèbre rapport de la Commission Bouchard-Taylor : Gérard Bouchard et Charles Taylor, *Building the Future : A Time for Reconciliation*, Gouvernement du Québec, Commission de consultation sur les pratiques d'accommodement reliées aux différences culturelles, 2008, en ligne : www.accommodements.qc.ca/documentation/rapports/rapport-final-integral-en.pdf.

38 Voir *Amselem, supra* note 4, qui discute le droit d'ériger une souccah pendant les fêtes juives malgré l'interdiction d'installer des ornements sur les balcons dans la convention de copropriété. Voir aussi *Bruker, supra* note 4, concernant le droit à un dédommagement pour avoir refusé de demander l'annulation d'un mariage selon les préceptes religieux et ainsi empêché le remariage et la légitimité d'enfants à venir.

39 *Multani, supra* note 4, est une affaire qui traite du droit de garder un petit couteau sacré à l'école même dans le contexte d'une interdiction totale de tout instrument de violence.

40 *Congrégation St-Jérôme, supra* note 4, met en cause l'annulation d'une décision municipale de refuser un changement au règlement de zonage pour permettre l'érection d'un temple.

41 *Hutterian Brethren, supra* note 4.

Comme on pourrait s'y attendre, les décisions traitant de la minorité chrétienne sont plus complexes à comprendre dans le présent contexte mais, selon moi, leur analyse confirme mon hypothèse. La décision dans l'affaire *Trinity* met en cause l'annulation d'une décision administrative qui visait à refuser la reconnaissance du diplôme de Trinity Western, un établissement chrétien fondamentaliste en raison du code de conduite qui interdisait les pratiques homosexuelles. La Cour suprême refusera de confirmer ce qui aurait été une discrimination à l'égard des diplômés d'un collège religieux dont le Code de conduite interdisait l'homosexualité. La Cour justifie sa décision en soulignant que des préjugés contre les gens religieux ou les chrétiens semblent avoir animé les décideurs. La décision aurait pu aller dans l'autre sens, mais, selon moi, il s'agit d'une analyse du rapport de pouvoir entre les minorités religieuses et une majorité qui s'associe à des valeurs civiques plutôt que religieuses. L'analyse majorité/minorité est donc une majorité à valeurs laïques qui développe des préjugés à l'endroit d'une minorité plus religieuse. La Colombie-Britannique est d'ailleurs une des provinces qui comptent le plus de personnes se disant sans religion[42].

L'arrêt *Chamberlain*, sur lequel je reviendrai dans la troisième partie, met aussi en cause des chrétiens fondamentalistes et leur tentative de définir le curriculum dans les écoles et d'interdire certains livres présentant de façon non discriminatoire les parents de même sexe. Selon moi, la Cour, même en rejetant la demande de la minorité religieuse pour des raisons de discrimination au sein de la religion, démontre également un respect pour leur conception religieuse de la vie et de l'éducation avec lesquelles cette minorité s'identifie. Le juge en chef McLachlin :

> Le fait que la *School Act* insiste sur la stricte laïcité ne signifie pas que les considérations religieuses n'ont aucune place dans les débats et les décisions du conseil scolaire. Les conseillers scolaires ont le droit et, en fait, le devoir, aux réunions du conseil, de faire valoir les points de vue des parents et de la collectivité qu'ils représentent. *La religion jouant un rôle important dans de nombreux milieux, ces points de vue seront souvent dictés par des considérations religieuses. La religion est un aspect fondamental de la vie des gens, et le conseil scolaire ne peut en faire abstraction dans ses délibérations.* Toutefois, l'exigence de laïcité fait en sorte que nul ne peut invoquer les convictions religieuses des uns pour écarter les valeurs des autres. Bien que le conseil scolaire puisse tenir compte des préoccupations religieuses des parents, l'exigence de laïcité l'oblige à accorder une même recon-

42 Voir les analyses de Zylberberg et Côté, *supra* note 20.

> naissance et un même respect aux autres membres de la collectivité. Les convictions religieuses qui interdisent la reconnaissance et le respect des membres d'un groupe minoritaire ne peuvent être invoquées pour exclure le point de vue minoritaire. Ce principe est juste envers les deux groupes, en ce qu'il garantit à chacun autant de reconnaissance qu'il peut logiquement exiger tout en accordant aux autres la même reconnaissance.[43]
>
> (C'est moi qui ajoute les italiques.)

J'estime que définir une analyse des rapports majorité-minorités est utile pour comprendre les enjeux entourant la liberté de religion. Entre autres, cette analyse explique un des aspects les plus controversés des décisions en matière de la liberté de religion, soit le refus de définir le contenu de la religion. En effet, la décision *Amselem* a donné lieu à passablement de critiques parce qu'elle ouvre la porte à des conceptions même marginales des obligations religieuses. On se souviendra qu'en l'espèce, la pratique d'installer une souccah n'était pas obligatoire pour les juifs et qu'il était possible donc de maintenir son appartenance religieuse tout en obéissant aux prescriptions du contrat de copropriété. Néanmoins, la Cour suprême reconnaît une grande liberté aux croyants de définir le contenu de leur foi et de leurs obligations religieuses. Le juge Iacobucci s'exprime ainsi : « la personne qui présente un argument fondé sur cette liberté doit démontrer (1) qu'elle possède une pratique ou une croyance qui est liée à la religion et requiert une conduite particulière, soit parce qu'elle est objectivement ou subjectivement obligatoire ou coutumière, soit parce que, subjectivement, elle crée de façon générale un lien personnel avec le divin ou avec le sujet ou l'objet de sa foi spirituelle, que cette pratique ou croyance soit ou non requise par un dogme religieux officiel ou conforme à la position de représentants religieux; (2) que sa croyance est sincère. »[44]

La reconnaissance de cette conception subjective du lien avec le divin et des obligations s'y accordant fait craindre l'émergence de croyances et pratiques farfelues qui deviendraient constitutionnalisées parce que proposées comme étant sincèrement liées à la spiritualité. Cette décision de maintenir la conception plus subjective de la liberté de religion s'explique de plusieurs façons : c'est la conception qui s'apparente le mieux à l'aspect « liberté » de la liberté de religion. En effet, de la même façon que les tribunaux s'efforcent de reconnaître une interprétation large de la liberté d'expression et d'analyser

---

43 *Chamberlain, supra* note 4 au para. 19.

44 *Amselem, supra* note 4 au para. 56.

ses limites dans le cadre de l'article 1 plutôt que dans le cadre d'une définition ontologique de ce qu'est ou non l'expression, on peut penser que la liberté de religion doit éviter de demander une définition limitative de ce qu'est la religion. D'autant plus, comme le souligne le juge Iacobucci, que cet exercice définitionnel demanderait aux tribunaux de résoudre des débats ecclésiastiques difficiles. Je pense également que cette interprétation subjective et large permet une habilitation de la minorité à exprimer ses attentes et ses façons de voir sans être assujettie à la nécessité d'une objectivation externe. En quelque sorte, il s'agit de permettre l'expression par le groupe minoritaire de sa différence sans devoir justifier outre mesure la nature de cette différence, ses origines ou ses ramifications. Selon moi, une telle interprétation de la liberté de religion se comprend bien dans un cadre de rapports minorités-majorité où il importe de permettre à la minorité de définir elle-même le mode d'interaction qu'elle veut avec la majorité avant que ce mode ne soit modelé, circonscrit ou approprié par les justifications majoritaires. Il ne s'agit pas de donner carte blanche aux minorités ou d'accepter toutes leurs revendications mais de créer un espace d'écoute où les échanges sont possibles. Je tire ces réflexions de l'étude des rapports politiques d'échanges entre minorités-majorité peu importe le type de minorité, culturelle, politique, linguistique ou religieuse. Selon moi, lorsque la majorité parle au nom de la minorité, lorsque les membres des religions majoritaires ou laïcs définissent le contenu obligatoire des religions minoritaires, le risque de stéréotype est toujours présent.

En conclusion, bien qu'un contenu subjectif de la religion puisse donner lieu à des interprétations individuelles exagérées ou marginales qui dépassent largement les façons de vivre d'un groupe minoritaire particulier, il est préférable d'opter pour cette interprétation large plutôt que pour une interprétation étroite exigeant une validation extérieure au groupe. Le vrai débat ne devrait pas se tenir dans le cadre de la définition de la liberté de religion mais bien dans le cadre des justifications proposées pour en limiter l'exercice, soit dans le cadre de l'article 1 de la *Charte* canadienne ou de l'article 9.1 de la Charte québécoise des droits et libertés de la personne.

2) Le scepticisme à l'égard des raisons offertes par la majorité

Multani est certainement la décision la plus controversée de cette décennie bien qu'elle semble techniquement banale et se situe carrément dans la lignée de *Simpson Sears*. Certains ont suggéré que la décision avait été l'élément déclencheur du tollé médiatique entourant les accommodements raisonnables au Québec et la création, par la suite, de la Commission Bouchard

Taylor. Pourtant, la décision bien que complexe à lire ne dévie pas de l'héritage *Saumur / Chaput c. Romain*. En fait, les conclusions de la juge de première instance étaient assez claires quant à la nécessité d'une approche de tolérance et de résolution pratique des appréhensions de la majorité quant à la sécurité des élèves, c'est-à-dire coudre le couteau sacré dans la poche de l'élève. Selon moi, la Cour suprême s'exprime sans équivoque quant à la nécessité de présenter des preuves convaincantes de danger, et non simplement de projeter ses préjugés ou son ignorance pour justifier les demandes des groupes majoritaires. On voit dans ce scepticisme face à l'argumentaire majoritaire une reconnaissance d'une hypocrisie qui peut exister dans certaines délibérations qui excluent le point de vue d'autres groupes.

Amselem peut se lire de la même façon. Tel que discuté plus haut, c'est une décision certes intéressante à plusieurs égards, dans son traitement du contrat de copropriété et de la suprématie de la liberté de religion sur les clauses contractuelles. On y note le même scepticisme face aux prétentions esthétiques. Le juge Iacobucci est assez sévère à cet égard :

> De même, il est impossible de concilier le fait de protéger la jouissance par les copropriétaires de leur bien en préservant l'apparence esthétique des balcons et en rehaussant ainsi l'harmonie externe de l'immeuble avec l'interdiction totale frappant l'exercice par les appelants de leur liberté de religion. Bien que les copropriétaires puissent préférer vivre dans un immeuble présentant toute l'année une apparence extérieure uniforme et harmonieuse, la contrariété que pourrait causer l'installation de quelques souccahs pendant neuf jours chaque année serait sans doute bien insignifiante.
>
> Dans un pays multiethnique et multiculturel comme le nôtre, qui souligne et fait connaître ses réalisations en matière de respect de la diversité culturelle et des droits de la personne, ainsi qu'en matière de promotion de la tolérance envers les minorités religieuses et culturelles—et qui constitue de bien des manières un exemple pour d'autres sociétés—, l'argument de l'intimé selon lequel le fait que de négligeables intérêts d'ordre esthétique subissant une atteinte minime devraient l'emporter sur l'exercice de la liberté de religion des appelants est inacceptable. De fait, la tolérance mutuelle constitue l'une des pierres d'assise de toute société démocratique. Vivre au sein d'une communauté qui s'efforce de maximiser l'étendue des droits de la personne requiert immanquablement l'ouverture aux droits d'autrui et la reconnaissance de ces droits.[45]

45 *Amselem, ibid.* au paras. 86–87.

Une comparaison avec *Edwards Books and Art* est intéressante à cet égard : on se souviendra que le juge Dickson s'était servi de l'article 1 pour justifier la constitutionnalité de la législation ontarienne[46]—suggérant que le législateur pouvait décider quel jour de congé était le plus pratique en autant qu'il accommodait, même parcimonieusement, la minorité. Évidemment, une association de propriétaires de condo comme dans *Amselem*, une commission scolaire comme dans *Multani* n'ont pas le même statut qu'un gouvernement provincial et il n'est pas surprenant qu'on leur accorde moins de déférence. À cet égard, notons le rejet du modèle d'accommodement raisonnable comme modèle dialogique entre le gouvernement et ses minorités religieuses dans *Hutterian Brethren*. Le modèle de l'accommodement raisonnable a certes ses torts mais il permet un dialogue entre le gouvernement et la minorité, un échange et une considération obligatoire du point de vue de la minorité. On comprend la préférence de la Cour pour le modèle de l'article 1 qui évite la négociation avec la minorité et permet une approche pus générale. Néanmoins, il ne faudrait pas perdre l'idée de consulter, écouter et inviter la minorité à définir les conditions de sa coexistence. Un modèle qui invite la participation, la consultation est davantage susceptible de créer des occasions de participation démocratique des membres de la minorité concernée. L'article 1 devra éventuellement permettre une évaluation non seulement de la substance des arguments des gouvernements, mais également de la procédure suivie par les gouvernements pour arriver à la conclusion que la loi enfreint aussi peu que possible les droits de la minorités. Dans l'affaire *Hutterian Brethren*, le gouvernement de l'Alberta avait certainement engagé un dialogue avec la communauté huttérite. Il serait dommage que le résultat de l'affaire *Hutterian Brethren* soit interprété trop largement et donne lieu à des refus d'engager de tels dialogues.

Dans l'affaire *Edward Books and Art*, le gouvernement de l'Ontario bénéficiait du rapport de sa Commission de réforme du droit sur la question et on peut se demander si des gouvernements ou autres acteurs publics ou privés devront s'appuyer sur des études approfondies pour pouvoir répondre à ce scepticisme. Par exemple, est-ce qu'un rapport semblable à celui de la Commission Stasi[47] en France pourrait justifier l'interdiction du Hijab dans les écoles

46 Voir la *Retail Business Holidays Amendment Act (Sunday Shopping)*, R.S.O. 1993, c. 14, s. 1.

47 La Commission Stasi a fait plusieurs recommandations au gouvernement français. Une, celle interdisant le port de signes religieux, a rapidement été mise en oeuvre : *Loi n° 2004-228 du 15 mars 2004 encadrant, en application du principe de laïcité, le port de signes ou de tenues manifestant une appartenance religieuse dans les écoles, collèges et lycées publics* D'autres recommandations , en particulier l'ajout des fêtes juives et musulmanes au calen-

publiques[48]? Quel genre de preuve, quel genre d'études préliminaires seront nécessaires pour prouver l'absence de préjugés, la reconnaissance de l'ouverture vers l'autre et la considération de son point de vue? Selon moi, des approches consultatives et participatives où les groupes affectés ont été consultés et ont participé à la décision devraient être valorisées par la Cour pour y trouver une justification à la déférence envers les justifications majoritaires.

3) Le contrôle de l'abus de pouvoir au sein des religions

Déjà les tribunaux ont reconnu que la religion des parents ne peut mettre en péril la vie ou la santé[49] ou même l'éducation[50]de leurs enfants, que les propos religieux haineux[51] peuvent être contrôlés et que la religion ne peut justifier d'infliger des punitions corporelles à ses enfants[52].

En effet, si le tribunal est intéressé à protéger la minorité religieuse dans l'articulation de ses rapports avec la majorité, il intervient aussi dans le contexte de la discrimination au sein même de la religion. On peut penser entre autres que les questions de l'inégalité sur la base du genre seront particulièrement difficiles[53]. L'arrêt *Bruker* s'explique certainement ainsi.

On doit noter le développement d'une perspective axée sur les rapports de genre dans la religion juive et une protection des droits de la femme juive, dans son accès au mariage religieux au sein de la religion juive. Il s'agit en quelque sorte de reconnaître les droits à la liberté de religion et à l'exercice de sa spiritualité par l'épouse.

Selon moi, l'arrêt *Chamberlain* est aussi un excellent exemple de cette analyse : dans *Chamberlain*, il s'agit d'une organisation de parents chrétiens qui tentent de définir le contenu du curriculum scolaire. La Cour se voit

---

drier scolaire n'ont pas été mises en œuvre. Bernard Stasi, *Rapport 2003 au Président de la République et au Parlement*, Paris, La Documentation française, 2004., en ligne : http://lesrapports.ladocumentationfrancaise.fr/BRP/044000099/0000.pdf.

48 Woehrling, *supra* note 7 à la p. 703, suggère que les pressions sur les jeunes Françaises sont peut-être différentes de celles exercées sur les jeunes Québécoises de foi musulmane.

49 *R.B. c. Children's Aid Society of Metropolitan Toronto*, [1995] 1 R.C.S. 315; *B.H. c. Alberta (Director of Child Welfare)*, 2002 ABQB 371, 302 A.R. 201, 7 W.W.R. 616.

50 *R. c. Jones*, [1986] 2 R.C.S. 284, juge Wilson.

51 *Ross c. Conseil scolaire du district no 15 du Nouveau-Brunswick*, [1996] 1 R.C.S. 825.

52 *Children's Aid Society of the District of Thunder Bay c. T.T.*, [1992] O.J. No. 2975 (Ct. J. Ont.); *Family and Children's Services of St. Thomas and Elgin c. W.F.*, [2003] O.J. No. 717, 36 R.F.L. (5th) 310 (Ct. J. Ont.) (QL); *Canadian Foundation for Children, Youth and the Law c. Canada (Procureur général)*, 2004 CSC 4, [2004] 1 R.C.S. 76.

53 Anne Saris, "Les tribunaux religieux dans les contextes canadien et québécois" (2006) 40 : 2 R.J.T. 353.

dans la position de devoir tenter de limiter le côté abusif et discriminatoire de certaines religions à l'égard de l'homosexualité. Il ne fait aucun doute que dans ce contexte, les prochaines années révéleront des tensions et inviteront des débats houleux : que ce soit dans le cadre des contestations de la polygamie ou du port du niqab ou de la burqa, la question de l'inégalité au sein même des pratiques religieuses sera le prochain terrain de questionnement du rôle des tribunaux dans la définition de la liberté de religion.

C. CONCLUSION

J'aimerais suggérer que même s'il peut y avoir des erreurs de parcours, la Cour a développé une vision assez cohérente de son rôle dans le cadre de la liberté de religion. Depuis Alexis de Tocqueville jusqu'à John Ely, les préoccupations entourant les relations entre majorité/minorités soutiennent un rôle des tribunaux dans la protection et la gestion des rapports de pouvoirs entre la majorité et les minorités.

Nous savons que tout groupe peut ostraciser ses dissidents, politiques, culturels ou religieux. Nous nous devons d'exercer une vigilance à cet égard. Il n'est pas étonnant que la Cour suprême se sente à l'aise dans une définition de son rôle de « protecteur des minorités », surtout depuis le *Renvoi relatif à la sécession du Québec*.[54] C'est un rôle qui, même dans le cadre de la dénonciation du trop grand pouvoir des juges, continue d'être généralement accepté. Beaucoup ont noté que la Cour McLachlin a peut-être été déstabilisée par les critiques virulentes du « gouvernement par les juges », qu'elle s'est peut-être retranchée dans une vision plus minimaliste de son rôle en particulier dans le cadre des droits économiques et sociaux. Cependant la protection des minorités, principe sous-jacent à la constitution canadienne, continuait d'animer la pensée de la cour certainement jusqu'à l'affaire *Hutterian Brethren* qui sera peut-être vue et reçue comme une anomalie.

On doit conclure que les questions soulevées ici ne s'estomperont pas et qu'elles continueront de préoccuper nos concitoyens pour les prochaines décennies. Nous connaissons encore mal comment gérer les conflits interreligieux, l'oppression religieuse, la ghettoïsation possible des familles de religions minoritaires, le développement de sectes ou du fanatisme religieux, ou d'autre part, le rôle souvent positif que l'appartenance religieuse peut jouer dans le développement de la cohésion sociale ou du développement communautaire. Tous ces enjeux demandent à être explorés davantage par

54 [1998] 2 R.C.S. 217.

les chercheurs parce que la justification de politiques publiques nécessaire en vertu de l'article 1 devra se faire de façon éclairée et en l'absence d'hypocrisie. Les décideurs devront s'acquitter honnêtement et sans subterfuges de leurs tâches, puisque la primauté du droit demande des décideurs qui s'abstiennent d'abuser de leur pouvoir et d'imposer à la minorité la « tyrannie de la majorité ». C'est le poids de l'histoire.

L'arrêt *Kapp* : L'interprétation du paragraphe 15(1) de la *Charte* (enfin) recentrée sur son objet égalitaire de non-discrimination

DANIEL PROULX

Si on veut évaluer l'influence de la « Cour McLachlin » sur l'interprétation du droit à l'égalité au cours des dix dernières années, l'analyse des jugements de la juge en chef elle-même me paraît incontournable. En effet, cette dernière s'est toujours vivement intéressée à ce droit et a indéniablement joué un rôle-clé dans son évolution. Elle a, par exemple, rendu la décision de la Cour d'appel de Colombie-Britannique dans le fameux arrêt *Andrews*[1] qui, en 1989, devint le premier arrêt de principe de la Cour suprême en matière d'égalité. Elle a par la suite joué un rôle déterminant dans la reformulation de l'objet et du cadre d'analyse de l'article 15 dans l'arrêt *Law*[2] de 1999 par sa décision marquante rendue quatre ans plus tôt dans l'arrêt *Miron c. Trudel*[3]. C'est dans ce dernier arrêt en effet qu'elle avait introduit la notion de dignité qui a fait son chemin jusqu'à l'arrêt *Law*. Puis, en 2008, elle cosigne le jugement de la majorité dans l'arrêt *Kapp*[4] qui tente à nouveau de corriger le tir de la Cour sur l'approche interprétative qu'il convient d'adopter en matière d'égalité.

C'est ainsi qu'avec le concours de sa collègue Rosalie Abella, la juge en chef Beverley McLachlin ne propose rien de moins dans l'arrêt *Kapp* que d'abandonner le critère de la dignité comme élément et objet essentiels de l'égalité constitutionnelle. Elle rendrait donc les armes, au nom de la Cour, face aux critiques nombreuses et constantes auxquelles a donné lieu ce fameux

1 *Andrews c. Law Society of British Columbia*, [1989] 1 R.C.S. 143 [*Andrews*].

2 *Law c. Canada (Ministre de l'Emploi et de l'Immigration)*, [1999] 1 R.C.S. 497 [*Law*].

3 *Miron c. Trudel*, [1995] 2 R.C.S. 418 [*Miron*].

4 *R. c. Kapp*, 2008 CSC 41, [2008] 2 R.C.S. 483 [*Kapp*].

critère de la dignité en doctrine[5]. Voilà, à première vue, une excellente nouvelle qui montre l'ouverture d'esprit et l'attitude d'écoute qui ont caractérisé la « Cour McLachlin » au cours des dix dernières années.

En revanche, dans ce même arrêt, la Cour a choisi de conserver certains éléments de l'arrêt *Law*, dont l'exigence d'une preuve de préjugés ou de stéréotypes, ainsi que ses facteurs contextuels de détermination de l'effet discriminatoire[6]. Or, ces éléments d'analyse demeurent problématiques puisqu'ils étaient étroitement associés au concept décrié de l'atteinte à la dignité.

La question est donc la suivante : l'arrêt *Kapp* marque-t-il un changement d'orientation réel en matière d'égalité constitutionnelle ou, au contraire, le repositionnement de la Cour ne constitue-t-il qu'une illusion? La réponse à cette question est loin d'être évidente. Afin d'y voir plus clair, il importe tout d'abord de rappeler à grands traits les principaux éléments de l'évolution de cet important droit constitutionnel.[7]

A. L'ÉGALITÉ FORMELLE

Avant l'avènement de la *Charte*, c'est-à-dire sous l'empire de la *Déclaration canadienne des droits*[8] de 1960, la Cour suprême avait adopté une conception plutôt formelle de l'égalité qui faisait de ce droit une protection sans grand

5 Pour une liste des « détracteurs » de la Cour, selon les termes mêmes des juges McLachlin et Abella, voir la note 1 de l'arrêt *Kapp, ibid.* Voir aussi ma récidive, en tant que « détracteur » : Daniel Proulx, « La dignité : élément essentiel de l'égalité ou cheval de Troie? » dans Barreau du Québec, dir., *Les 25 ans de la Charte canadienne des droits et libertés*, Cowansville (Qc), Yvon Blais, 2007, à la p. 95.

6 Il s'agit: (1) de la préexistence d'un désavantage; (2) de la correspondance aux besoins; (3) de l'objet ou de l'effet améliorateur de la loi; (4) de la nature du droit touché. Voir *Law, supra* note 2, aux para. 62–70, 88 (points 7–9).

7 Sur les notions d'égalité formelle et réelle, voir Daniel Proulx, « L'objet des droits constitutionnels à l'égalité » (1988) 29 C. de D. 567; Christian Brunelle, *Discrimination et obligation d'accommodement en milieu de travail syndiqué*, Cowansville (Qc), Yvon Blais, 2001 aux pp. 142–149; Leon E. Trakman, « Substantive Equality in Constitutional Jurisprudence : Meaning without Meaning » (1994) 7 Can. J.-L. & Jur. 27; Beverley Baines, « Is Substantive Equality a Constitutional Doctrine? » dans Y. Gendreau, dir., *La doctrine et le développement du droit*, Montréal, Les Editions Thémis, 2005, 59; Fay Faraday, Margaret Denike et M. Kate Stephenson, « Introduction : In Pursuit of Substantive Equality » dans Fay Faraday, Margaret Denike et M. Kate Stephenson, dir., *Making Equality Rights Real*, Toronto, Irwin Law, 2006, 9; William Black et Lynn Smith, « The Equality Rights » dans Gérald A. Beaudoin et Errol Mendes, dir., *Charte canadienne des droits et libertés*, Markham (On), LexisNexis Butterworths, 2005, 969.

8 *Déclaration canadienne des droits*, L.R.C. 1985, App. III.

ABSTRACT

The *Law* case has been highly criticized by numerous legal academics for requiring plaintiffs to prove a breach of human dignity in section 15 equality rights cases under the *Charter*. In *Kapp*, McLachlin C.J.C. finally decided to drop that requirement. Does *Kapp* constitute a real change in the orientation of the Supreme Court of Canada in constitutional equality cases? After placing the debate in its larger context and in the evolution of constitutional equality rights in Canadian caselaw, the author tries to demonstrate that *Kapp* is a step in the right direction. Putting aside the concept of human dignity will allow the courts to focus on the true anti-discriminatory purpose of section 15 and to eliminate the confusion that has prevailed since *Law* between two discrete types of legal distinctions: those required by section 15 to achieve more equality, and those justified under section 1 of the *Charter* by public interest considerations.

intérêt ni efficacité contre l'action gouvernementale. L'égalité était limitée au concept de la *rule of law* selon laquelle on ne peut pas remettre en question les catégorisations faites par le législateur, mais simplement vérifier si, à l'intérieur de ses catégorisations, les personnes ciblées sont traitées de la même façon.

Cette approche dite de « la situation analogue » faisait en sorte que le traitement discriminatoire fait aux femmes indiennes n'a pu être déclaré discriminatoire dans l'arrêt *Lavell*[9] puisque, en étant « également » privées de leurs droits lorsqu'elles épousaient un non-Indien, toutes les femmes indiennes étaient traitées de la même façon. La conclusion fut au même effet à l'égard des femmes enceintes dans l'arrêt *Bliss*[10] puisque, même si la loi avait un effet discriminatoire à leur égard, elle leur était appliquée « également » ! Cependant, la disparité de traitement discriminatoire entre femmes et hommes ne pouvait alors être remise en question puisque, d'une part, les hommes et les femmes n'étaient pas dans une situation analogue et que, d'autre part, la loi, souveraine, demeurait à l'abri de toute contestation.

Rompant graduellement avec cette vision fondée sur le principe cardinal de la souveraineté du parlement, la *Charte* a prévu à son paragraphe 15(1)

9 *Lavell c. Canada (Procureur géneral)*, [1974] R.C.S. 1349.

10 *Bliss c. Canada (Procureur géneral)*, [1979] 1 R.C.S. 183.

que l'égalité doit être respectée par la loi (« La loi ne fait acception de personne ») et que son contenu même peut être scruté et invalidé pour cause de discrimination. C'est ce qu'exprimait le juge McIntyre dans l'arrêt *Andrews*[11] lorsqu'il opposait le droit à l'égalité substantielle *dans* la loi, nouvellement enchâssé au paragraphe 15(1) de la *Charte*, au droit à l'égalité procédurale *devant* la loi reconnu à l'alinéa 1(*b*) de la *Déclaration canadienne* et découlant de la *rule of law*.

Par ailleurs, la conception substantielle de l'égalité retenue par les tribunaux canadiens dans l'interprétation du paragraphe 15(1) de la *Charte* jusqu'à l'arrêt *Andrews* fut principalement (mais non exclusivement) celle de l'interdiction des distinctions arbitraires, non pertinentes ou injustifiées[12]. La conséquence pratique de cette approche s'est avéré énorme: le plaignant se retrouvait avec le fardeau de démontrer qu'il était non seulement victime d'une distinction de traitement lui causant un préjudice sur la base d'une caractéristique personnelle, mais que cette distinction était irrationnelle, injustifiée ou dénuée de pertinence dans le contexte de la loi. L'imposition d'un fardeau de preuve aussi lourd, compte tenu qu'il s'agit de faire une démonstration négative, à savoir que la loi *n'est pas* justifiée ou que la distinction qu'il conteste *n'est pas* pertinente, a produit des résultats prévisibles : un droit à l'égalité factice, rhétorique et sans efficacité. Il va sans dire que cette approche protectrice davantage de l'action gouvernementale que des droits fondamentaux était peu compatible avec l'objet réparateur de la *Charte* et de son article 15 en particulier, comme l'a rappelé le juge McIntyre pour la Cour dans l'arrêt *Andrews*.[13]

B. L'ÉGALITÉ RÉELLE[14]

1) L'arrêt *Andrews* : la recherche de l'effet discriminatoire

Afin de parvenir à donner au droit à l'égalité une portée véritable et une protection efficace contre l'action gouvernementale inégalitaire, la Cour su-

---

11 *Andrews*, *supra* note 1 à la p. 165.

12 Ce fut, du reste, la position adoptée par la juge McLachlin lorsqu'elle siégeait à la Cour d'appel de Colombie-Britannique dans l'arrêt *Andrews*. Pour un exposé complet du droit antérieur à *Andrews*, voir Daniel Proulx, « Le défi de l'égalité et la Charte canadienne des droits » (1988) 48 R. du B. 633.

13 *Andrews*, *supra* note 1 à la p. 169.

14 Pour une analyse détaillée de l'évolution jurisprudentielle des tribunaux en matière d'égalité à partir de l'arrêt *Andrews*, voir Daniel Proulx, « Les droits à l'égalité revus et corrigés par la Cour suprême du Canada dans l'arrêt *Law* : un pas en avant ou un pas en arrière? »

prême a donné un coup de barre majeur dans l'arrêt *Andrews*[15]. Prenant acte de l'encadrement constitutionnel du droit à l'égalité par une interdiction, au paragraphe 15(1) de la *Charte*, de certaines formes particulières de discrimination reposant sur des caractéristiques personnelles fondamentales non pertinentes *a priori* pour l'exercice d'un droit, la Cour a opté pour une interprétation axée sur le principe de non-discrimination.

En sorte que le droit constitutionnel à l'égalité a alors été déclaré comme ne constituant pas un droit général et indéfini à l'égalité, selon le modèle du XIVe Amendement de la Constitution américaine, mais comme étant un droit spécifique à la protection contre certaines formes de discrimination, à savoir celles qui sont fondées sur les motifs illicites ou suspects énumérés au paragraphe 15(1) et sur ceux qui leur sont analogues.

D'autre part, la Cour a clairement rejeté la conception formelle et procédurale de l'égalité prévalant jusqu'alors, pour adopter la perspective dite de l'égalité réelle et effective. Qu'est-ce à dire? Cela signifie trois choses : en premier lieu, que l'égalité passe non seulement par l'interdiction des distinctions de traitement évidentes et manifestes, par exemple lorsque la loi utilise ouvertement la race, le sexe ou la religion pour parvenir à ses fins, mais qu'il faut aller au-delà du texte de la loi et en vérifier, en tenant compte de l'ensemble du contexte, les effets indirects mais bien réels sur un groupe d'individus. C'est ainsi qu'une loi de Colombie-Britannique sur l'assurance-santé et l'assurance-hospitalisation a pu être déclarée discriminatoire à l'endroit des personnes sourdes dans l'arrêt *Eldridge*[16] en 1997 parce que, bien qu'elle prévoyait la gratuité des services de santé à tous les résidents de la province, elle imposait indirectement aux assurés sourds et malentendants la charge de frais importants de services d'interprète[17].

En second lieu, et en corollaire de la recherche des effets préjudiciables indirects, le concept d'égalité réelle reconnaît que la véritable égalité ne passe pas toujours par l'application du même traitement pour tous, mais par un traitement différencié et adapté aux circonstances. Lorsqu'une mesure uni-

---

(2001) 61 R. du B. 185; P. Blache, « Étude comparative de l'évolution des normes antidiscriminatoires ou égalitaires des articles 15 de la *Charte canadienne des droits et libertés* et 10 de la *Charte des droits et libertés de la personne* : convergences et divergences » (2003) R. du B. 151.

15 *Andrews, supra* note 1 aux pp. 163-176 pour l'ensemble des motifs du jugement du juge McIntyre sur l'interprétation du para. 15(1) auxquels se rallieront les juges La Forest et Wilson pour l'essentiel dans leurs motifs séparés.

16 *Eldridge c. Colombie-Britannique (Procureur géneral)*, [1997] 3 R.C.S. 624 [*Eldridge*].

17 Voir aussi : *Vriend c. Alberta*, [1998] 1 R.C.S. 493. Dans le contexte de la Charte québécoise, voir: *Commission scolaire régionale de Chambly c. Bergevin*, [1994] 2 R.C.S. 525.

forme produit des effets d'exclusion ou des effets négatifs sur un groupe de personnes en fonction de sa race, de son sexe ou de sa déficience par exemple, l'égalité réelle ne peut émerger que par la prise en compte des caractéristiques des membres de ce groupe, c'est-à-dire par la création d'une obligation dite d'accommodement raisonnable à la charge de l'auteur de la mesure discriminatoire. Le traitement différencié s'avère également conforme au principe d'égalité réelle lorsque, dans le but de corriger des inégalités sociales criantes, le gouvernement décide de s'y attaquer par des mesures correctives au moyen de programmes sociaux généraux (l'assurance-emploi ou l'aide sociale) ou ciblés (aide aux handicapés, aux personnes âgées, aux autochtones, etc.). C'est ce que reconnaît du reste le paragraphe 15(2) de la *Charte*.

En troisième lieu, la Cour reconnaît dès l'arrêt *Andrews* que l'égalité réelle exige le respect de la structure analytique prévue par l'article premier de la *Charte*. Ce faisant, la charge de démontrer qu'une distinction de traitement fondée sur un motif de discrimination énuméré ou analogue se justifie dans une société libre et démocratique relève du gouvernement et augmente considérablement la protection contre la discrimination. En effet, ne pas respecter cette structure analytique en exigeant du plaignant qu'il fasse la preuve, souvent insurmontable, que la mesure législative est injustifiée, non pertinente ou déraisonnable eu égard aux objectifs poursuivis par la loi, conduit inévitablement à réduire la protection anti-discrimination à un vœu pieu.

En conséquence, le juge McIntyre définit la discrimination, au nom de la Cour, comme étant « une distinction, intentionnelle ou non, mais fondée sur les motifs relatifs à des caractéristiques personnelles d'un individu ou d'un groupe d'individus, qui a pour effet d'imposer à cet individu ou à ce groupe d'individus, des fardeaux, des obligations ou des désavantages non imposés à d'autres ou d'empêcher ou de restreindre l'accès aux possibilités, aux bénéfices et aux avantages offerts à d'autres membres de la société »[18].

En d'autres termes, la preuve de la discrimination se composait de trois éléments : (1) une distinction de traitement, intentionnelle ou non; (2) un lien avec un motif de discrimination énuméré au paragraphe 15(1) ou analogue; (3) un effet préjudiciable (imposition de désavantages ou privation d'avantages). Toute autre considération devait être reportée à l'étape de l'article premier et être à la charge du gouvernement.

C'est ainsi que Monsieur Andrews aura gain de cause sur la seule preuve que la *Loi sur le barreau* établissait (1) une distinction de traitement, (2) fon-

18 *Andrews*, *supra* note 1 à la p. 174.

dée sur la citoyenneté (motif jugé analogue), (3) ayant pour effet de retarder son admission à la profession pendant trois ans (effet préjudiciable). Aucun autre élément de preuve ne sera exigé de lui dans le cadre du paragraphe 15(1). Puis, à l'étape des justifications raisonnables de la loi, la majorité de la Cour jugera que le gouvernement n'a pas fait la preuve que l'exclusion des non-citoyens constitue une limite raisonnable dans une société libre et démocratique et déclarera la disposition contestée inconstitutionnelle.

2) L'arrêt *Law* : la recherche de l'atteinte à la dignité

Bien qu'il y ait eu, du moins en apparence, unanimité dans l'arrêt *Andrews* sur la nouvelle conception de l'égalité réelle et sur le respect de la structure analytique de la *Charte* imposée par son article premier, la Cour suprême s'est rapidement divisée par la suite lorsque mise à l'épreuve des faits et circonstances d'autres affaires[19]. Voilà pourquoi, elle a choisi dix ans plus tard de modifier les éléments de l'analyse de la discrimination fixés dans cet arrêt de principe en en ajoutant un nouveau : l'atteinte à la dignité.

a) L'ajout de l'élément de la dignité

En effet, plusieurs mesures sociales ont été mises à rude épreuve devant la Cour pendant ces dix années, et les juges ont senti le besoin de se porter à la rescousse du législateur. Le défi était le suivant : comment déterminer l'effet discriminatoire sans menacer l'ensemble des lois, règlements et programmes sociaux qui font de nombreuses distinctions fondées sur les motifs de discrimination énumérés dans la *Charte*?

C'est ainsi qu'est né le fameux critère de l'atteinte à la dignité humaine. D'abord proposé par la juge McLachlin en 1995 dans l'arrêt *Miron c. Trudel*[20] dans un jugement minoritaire, il fut adopté par une cour unanime dans l'arrêt *Law*[21] quatre ans plus tard. Il semble bien que, pour les juges de la Cour, les trois éléments de preuve exigés par un plaignant pour faire la preuve d'un effet discriminatoire contraire au paragraphe 15(1) de la *Charte* dans l'arrêt

19 Comparer par exemple ces arrêts (ainsi que les disparités manifestes entre juges de la majorité et juges dissidents dans chacun d'eux) dont les cadres d'analyse de l'art. 15 sont nettement contradictoires, voire irréconciliables : *R. c. Turpin*, [1989] 1 R.C.S. 1296; *R. c. Hess; R. c. Nguyen*, [1990] 2 R.C.S. 906 [*Hess*]; *Weatherall c. Canada (Procureur géneral)*, [1993] 2 R.C.S. 872 [*Weatherall*]; *Miron*, *supra* note 3.

20 *Miron*, *ibid*. Les juges Cory et L'Heureux-Dubé l'avaient également proposé dans *Egan c. Canada*, [1995] 2 R.C.S. 513 rendu le même jour et partie de la «trilogie de 1995».

21 *Law*, *supra* note 2.

Andrews permettaient trop facilement de contester des acquis sociaux mis sur pied par les gouvernements et, partant, de les fragiliser.

La « solution *Law* » consistait donc à alourdir le fardeau de preuve du plaignant en lui imposant la charge de démontrer que la loi porte atteinte à la dignité humaine du groupe dont il fait partie. Pour la Cour, non seulement l'objet essentiel de l'article 15 devait dorénavant être considéré comme étant le respect de la dignité humaine, mais aucune distinction de traitement ne devait désormais être jugée discriminatoire sans une démonstration qu'elle allait à l'encontre de l'objet de l'article 15. Le juge Iacobucci affirmait en effet qu'il « doit absolument y avoir un conflit entre l'objet ou les effets de la loi contestée et l'objet du paragraphe 15(1) pour fonder une allégation de discrimination » et en concluait qu'une « différence de traitement ne constituera vraisemblablement pas de la discrimination au sens du paragraphe 15(1) si elle ne viole pas la dignité ou la liberté d'une personne ou d'un groupe »[22]. Dans cette perspective, même si elle a pour effet de causer un préjudice sérieux à un individu ou à un groupe d'individus sur la base d'un motif de discrimination énuméré ou analogue, une différence de traitement n'est plus nécessairement considérée comme discriminatoire.

C'est ainsi que Madame Law sera déboutée, à l'étape de l'article 15, parce qu'elle a été incapable de prouver que le *Régime de pensions du Canada*—qui l'excluait de la protection offerte à titre de conjoint survivant sur la base de son âge—portait atteinte à la dignité humaine des gens de moins de trente-cinq ans.

Mais en quoi consiste cet élément de la dignité et que signifie-t-il du point de vue de la preuve exigée du demandeur? La notion de dignité s'entend philosophiquement de la valeur intrinsèque inhérente à chaque être humain et du respect dû à soi-même et aux autres[23]. En droit, cette idée sera transposée dans *Law* par l'obligation d'établir qu'une distinction de traitement a pour effet soit de dévaloriser un groupe d'individus protégé par l'énumération de l'article 15, soit de véhiculer des préjugés ou des stéréotypes négatifs à son endroit[24]. La question de savoir si une distinction

22 *Ibid.* aux para. 51, 88. Voir point 4.

23 Daniel Proulx, « Le concept de dignité et son usage en contexte de discrimination : deux Chartes, deux modèles » (2003) numéro spécial R. du B. 485 à la p. 497 et s.; C. Brunelle, « La dignité dans la Charte des droits et libertés de la personne : de l'ubiquité à l'ambiguïté d'une notion fondamentale » (2006) numéro spécial R. du B. 143.

24 *Law, supra* note 2 au para. 51: « On pourrait affirmer que le par. 15(1) a pour objet d'empêcher toute atteinte à la dignité . . . par l'imposition de désavantages, de stéréotypes et de préjugés politiques ou sociaux . . . ».

repose sur des préjugés ou si elle a pour effet d'entretenir des préjugés ou des opinions négatives à l'égard d'un groupe devient donc dorénavant « la question primordiale »[25] à toute analyse du caractère discriminatoire d'une mesure gouvernementale puisque, il importe de le répéter, sans une preuve de violation de la dignité humaine, il n'y a aucune discrimination au sens du paragraphe 15(1).

De plus, afin d'éviter l'arbitraire total dans la détermination de ce qui constitue ou non une atteinte à la dignité humaine, la Cour a proposé de procéder à l'analyse de la mesure contestée à l'aide de quatre facteurs contextuels, à savoir : (1) la préexistence d'un désavantage chez un groupe donné (celui du plaignant); (2) la correspondance de la mesure aux besoins d'un groupe; (3) l'objet ou l'effet réparateur de la mesure contestée; (4) l'importance ou la nature du droit touché. Je reviendrai plus loin sur le rôle et le sens donné à chacun de ces facteurs.

b) Les conséquences de l'ajout de l'élément de la dignité

Comme elle l'a admis dans l'arrêt *Kapp*, la Cour a pratiquement fait l'unanimité contre elle en doctrine[26]. C'est que, bien que fondé sur de bonnes intentions, l'ajout de l'élément de l'atteinte à la dignité humaine a soulevé une série de problèmes majeurs remettant en cause le principe même de l'égalité réelle pourtant promu par la Cour.

Tout d'abord, l'atteinte à la dignité apparaît comme un critère philosophique flou, subjectif et ambigu qui, au surplus, n'est aucunement propre au droit à l'égalité[27]. La dignité constitue en effet le fondement de la *Charte*

25 *Lavoie c. Canada*, [2002] 1 R.C.S. 769 au para. 46, juge Bastarache. Voir dans le même sens *Nouvelle-Écosse (Procureur géneral) c. Walsh*, [2002] 4 R.C.S. 325 au para. 62, juge Bastarache [*Nouvelle-Écosse*]; *Gosselin c. Québec (Procureur géneral)*, [2002] 4 R.C.S. 429 aux para. 18–27, juge en chef McLachlin [*Gosselin*]; *Trociuk c. Colombie-Britannique (Procureur géneral)*, [2003] 1 R.C.S. 835 au para. 133, juge Deschamps [*Trociuk*]; *Nouvelle-Écosse (Workers' Compensation Board) c. Martin; Nouvelle-Écosse (Workers' Compensation Board) c. Laseur*, [2003] 2 R.C.S. 504 aux para. 84–85; *Canadian Foundation for Children, Youth and the Law (Procureur géneral) c. Canada*, [2004] 1 R.C.S. 76 aux para. 54, 68, juge en chef McLachlin [*Canadian Foundation for Children*].

26 *Kapp, supra* note 4 aux para. 21–22.

27 En ce sens, voir Peter W. Hogg, « What Is Equality? The Winding Course of Judicial Interpretation » (2005) 29 Sup. Ct. L. Rev. 39 à la p. 56 pour qui le critère de la dignité est « vague, confusing and burdensome »; Sheilah Martin, « Balancing Individual Rights to Equality and Social Goals » (2001) 80 R. du B. can. 319 aux pp. 329–32; Dianne Pothier, « Connecting Grounds of Discrimination to Real People's Real Experiences » (2001) 13: 1 C.J.W.L. 37 à la p. 56 : « Human dignity is a concept that is malleable enough that it can mean whatever the judges want it to mean ». J'ai pour ma part eu l'occasion de qualifier

dans son ensemble et de chacun des droits et libertés qu'elle garantit. La Cour n'a pourtant jamais exigé, pour aucun d'eux, qu'un plaignant démontre que leur restriction passe par une atteinte à la dignité.

Ensuite, le fardeau de preuve imposé au plaignant via ce critère est vite devenu insurmontable. Comment, en effet, faire la preuve qu'une mesure législative dévalorise un groupe de personnes? Faut-il présenter des études sociologiques? Faut-il avoir recours à des experts de diverses disciplines du domaine des sciences humaines? La connaissance d'office et le raisonnement logique peuvent-ils suppléer au manque de données, et s'il y a lieu, dans quelle mesure? Et, à défaut de preuves par experts de disciplines exogènes au droit, ne risque-t-on pas d'aboutir à des décisions elles-mêmes fondées sur des préjugés à l'endroit des groupes qui sont censés être protégés contre ce fléau par l'article 15? La Cour consacre un long développement à ces questions de preuve dans *Law* sans en arriver à clarifier vraiment les choses[28].

La question s'est présentée dans plusieurs arrêts depuis 1999, à commencer par l'arrêt *Law* lui-même. Madame Law a été déboutée parce qu'elle a été incapable de faire une telle preuve, de nature sociologique, sur la situation des jeunes en général, du point de vue des préjugés sociaux, et en particulier sur l'effet, de nature psychologique, politique ou économique, que peut avoir une loi qui exclut de ses bénéfices les conjoints d'un bénéficiaire décédé du régime de pensions en raison de son jeune âge.[29]

Enfin, le critère de l'atteinte à la dignité et, surtout, le fait d'avoir statué que la dignité constitue dorénavant l'objet essentiel de l'article 15 comporte, à mon sens, une erreur fatale dans l'analyse puisque cette détermination fait perdre de vue le véritable objet de l'article 15. Celui-ci ne réside pas tant dans le respect de la dignité humaine que dans la lutte contre les inégalités et exclusions injustes et arbitraires, l'intégration ou l'inclusion de tous dans la société, la jouissance des mêmes droits pour tous, le droit d'être traité sur le même pied, avec le même respect et la même considération[30]. Voilà, à mon

---

l'atteinte à la dignité de « critère impressionniste et non distinctif » : Proulx, *supra* note 14 à la p. 273.

28 *Law, supra* note 2 aux para. 76–87.

29 Voir aussi *Gosselin, supra* note 25, où la juge en chef McLachlin a conclu que l'appelante n'avait pas réussi à faire la preuve que le *Règlement sur l'aide sociale*, R.R.Q. 1981, c. A-16, r. 1, art. 29(a), réduisant les prestations des bénéficiaires de moins de 30 ans portait atteinte à la dignité des jeunes assistés sociaux malgré une preuve accablante, selon les quatre juges dissidents, à l'effet contraire.

30 Ces objets spécifiques ont d'ailleurs été relevés par le juge Iacobucci, mais ce dernier les a ensuite occultés au profit du nouvel objet de la dignité qui a obtenu la préférence de la Cour. Voir *Law, supra* note 2 au para. 51.

sens, des objets à la fois spécifiques à l'article 15 et susceptibles d'éclairer l'analyse du droit à la non-discrimination.

En mettant l'accent sur la dignité comme objet essentiel et primordial de l'article 15, la Cour suprême a ensuite provoqué une erreur magistrale de perspective dans la signification de deux facteurs contextuels-clés (la « correspondance aux besoins » et « l'objet ou l'effet réparateur ») et fait en sorte que l'analyse en vertu de l'article premier soit intégrée au paragraphe 15(1) avec la conséquence suivante : souvent confondus entre eux[31], ces deux facteurs contextuels d'atteinte à la dignité sont la plupart du temps assimilés au critère de pertinence ou de justification générale liée à des considérations d'intérêt public. Comme c'était le cas avant *Andrews*, le plaignant se retrouve donc, sous l'empire du critère de l'atteinte à la dignité, avec un fardeau de preuve négatif impossible à relever. En plus d'avoir à démontrer le caractère préjudiciable d'une mesure législative, il doit faire la preuve qu'elle n'est *pas* justifiée, *pas* pertinente ou *pas* raisonnable. Voilà le drame identifié par la doctrine et auquel la juge en chef McLachlin et la juge Abella tentent aujourd'hui de remédier dans l'arrêt *Kapp*.

L'arrêt *Canadian Foundation for Children*[32] (ou « l'affaire de la fessée ») qu'a rendu la juge en chef McLachlin en 2004 illustre on ne peut mieux cette malheureuse confusion. Dans cette affaire, il s'agissait de la contestation de l'article 43 du *Code criminel* autorisant les enseignants et les parents à employer la force pour corriger un enfant «pourvu que la force ne dépasse pas la mesure raisonnable dans les circonstances».

Écrivant pour la majorité, la juge en chef observe tout d'abord que l'article 43 traite de façon différente et désavantageuse les enfants de moins de 18 ans. Toute autre personne âgée de 18 ans ou plus bénéficie en effet de la protection du *Code criminel* contre l'usage de la force à son endroit via les dispositions interdisant les voies de fait. Il y a donc, à l'encontre des enfants mineurs, distinction de traitement préjudiciable fondé sur l'âge, un motif expressément énuméré à l'article 15. En vertu de l'arrêt *Andrews*, la preuve de discrimination aurait été complète. Cependant, depuis l'arrêt *Law*, la juge en chef doit se demander si une telle distinction de traitement est contraire à la dignité des enfants.

---

31 Quoique distincts, les facteurs de la « correspondance aux besoins » et de « l'objet ou l'effet améliorateur » sont fréquemment confondus en jurisprudence en raison de l'exigence suivant laquelle, selon l'arrêt *Law*, *supra* note 2, un programme améliorateur doit, à l'instar d'une mesure d'accommodement (facteur contextuel de la correspondance aux besoins), « correspondre aux besoins » du groupe ciblé par le programme.

32 *Supra* note 25.

Elle en conclura qu'il n'en est rien. Bien qu'elle admette que les enfants forment un groupe très vulnérable[33] et que le droit touché, l'intégrité physique, revêt une grande importance pour l'être humain[34], elle estime que l'article 43 ne porte pas atteinte à la dignité des enfants parce qu'il répond adéquatement à leurs besoins et à leur situation[35]! À son avis, l'article 43 correspond aux besoins qu'ont les enfants d'être guidés et disciplinés, d'une part, et de pouvoir jouir d'un milieu familial et scolaire stable et sûr, d'autre part. En autorisant les parents et enseignants à faire usage d'une force raisonnable à leur endroit, l'article 43 permet ainsi à ces derniers d'éduquer raisonnablement les enfants sans encourir de sanctions pénales et favorise la stabilité du milieu familial et scolaire nécessaire à l'épanouissement de l'enfant. Pour elle, en effet, « l'intervention du droit criminel dans le milieu familial et scolaire des enfants leur causerait plus de tort que de bien » puisque le droit criminel est « un instrument radical dont la puissance peut aussi détruire les rapports au sein de la famille et à l'école »[36]. Par conséquent, le paragraphe 15(1) n'est nullement violé par l'article 43 du *Code criminel* et le gouvernement n'a pas à justifier cette mesure législative en vertu de l'article premier.

Comme le fait voir avec raison le juge Binnie (avec l'appui de la juge Deschamps), en intégrant dans l'analyse du paragraphe 15(1) des considérations sociales qui n'ont rien à voir avec le droit à l'égalité des enfants, la majorité des juges de la Cour prive en réalité ces derniers de la protection que leur garantit la *Charte* contre la discrimination[37]. En effet, le raisonnement de la juge en chef revient à dire que l'article 43 n'est pas discriminatoire, au sens et à l'étape de l'article 15, parce qu'il met à la disposition des parents et des éducateurs un moyen (la force physique) qui se justifie par un objectif général d'intérêt public ou par des considérations sociales qui n'ont pas de lien avec l'égalité : préserver la stabilité de la famille et de l'école dans notre société. En effet, ce n'est pas pour protéger les enfants que l'article 43 a été adopté, mais bien pour immuniser les parents et les instituteurs contre les poursuites pénales lorsqu'ils utilisent la force pour corriger un enfant.

Indiscutablement donc, le juge Binnie a parfaitement raison et cela n'est pas sans conséquence, tant s'en faut. Attentif aux facteurs contextuels de la vulnérabilité des enfants et de l'importance du droit (la protection du *Code criminel*) dont ils sont privés avec l'article 43, le savant juge ne peut qu'en

33 En vertu du facteur contextuel du désavantage préexistant.

34 En vertu du facteur contextuel de la nature ou de l'importance du droit touché.

35 En vertu du facteur contextuel de la correspondance aux besoins.

36 *Canadian Foundation for Children, supra* note 25 aux para. 58–60.

37 *Ibid.* aux para. 74, 104–105.

arriver à une seule conclusion : cette disposition viole à première vue le paragraphe 15(1). Puis, passant à l'article premier, il estime que l'article 43 se justifie uniquement à l'égard des parents d'un enfant. Selon lui, l'objectif de préserver la stabilité du milieu familial pour l'enfant ne peut être atteint autrement que par l'exonération des parents qui utilisent une «force raisonnable» pour le corriger. Toutefois, cette considération s'avère beaucoup moins capitale en milieu scolaire puisque les enseignants jouent un rôle très différent des parents dans la vie d'un enfant. Selon lui, accorder une immunité contre les voies de fait à des personnes extérieures à la famille ne peut être considéré comme une mesure législative raisonnable et proportionnée à l'objectif d'éducation des enfants. En effet, cela ne constitue en aucune façon une atteinte minimale aux droits à l'égalité de l'enfant ni une réponse proportionnée au problème de l'ordre et de la discipline dans les écoles[38].

Comme on le voit, en utilisant le facteur contextuel de la correspondance aux besoins des enfants avec un but égalitaire pour en faire un facteur de correspondance de l'article 43 avec les objectifs d'intérêt public général que poursuit le législateur, la juge en chef a télescopé un élément de l'article premier, soit celui du lien rationnel entre les moyens et l'objectif législatif, à l'intérieur même de l'analyse de la discrimination et a complètement dénaturé celle-ci. Elle a ainsi empêché la Cour de vérifier, comme a pu le faire le juge Binnie, si une telle disposition est justifiée et raisonnable en vertu de l'ensemble des critères distincts de l'article premier.

Le drame de cette confusion, bien sûr, c'est qu'elle a pour effet concret de diminuer très considérablement la garantie d'égalité prévue par le paragraphe 15(1) de la *Charte*. Par son manque de spécificité, l'objet du respect de la dignité humaine fait entrer, avec ses facteurs contextuels, des éléments de pertinence aux objectifs généraux du gouvernement dans l'analyse de la discrimination et fait dévier le paragraphe 15(1) de son véritable but : garantir à tous l'égalité réelle et effective des chances par une lutte efficace contre la discrimination. Cette confusion serait sans incidence si elle était rare, mais tel n'est pas le cas. On la retrouve partout en jurisprudence et ce, jusque dans les arrêts de la Cour suprême du Canada elle-même.[39]

---

38 *Ibid.* au para. 112 et s.

39 Voir par ex. *Delisle c. Canada*, [1999] 2 R.C.S 989 au para. 45; *Little Sisters Book and Art Emporium c. Canada (ministre de la Justice)*, [2000] 2 R.C.S. 1120 [*Little Sisters*]; *Therrien (Re)*, [2001] 2 R.C.S. 3; *Trociuk*, *supra* note 25.

3) L'arrêt *Kapp* : le retour nuancé à l'effet discriminatoire

Dans leur brève mise au point sur l'analyse du paragraphe 15(1), les juges McLachlin et Abella commencent par faire des aveux importants. D'une part, « plusieurs difficultés ont découlé de la tentative . . . de faire de la dignité humaine un critère juridique » et, concèdent-elles, « en fait, la protection de tous les droits garantis par la Charte est guidée par la promotion de la dignité de l'être humain »[40]. D'autre part, elles admettent que non seulement la dignité humaine constitue une notion «abstraite et subjective», mais encore qu'elle s'est avérée un «fardeau additionnel» pour les plaignants et qu'elle « a permis au formalisme . . . de ressurgir sous la forme d'une analyse comparative artificielle »[41].

Les juges McLachlin et Abella proposent ensuite une reformulation de l'objet du paragraphe 15(1) qui exclut toute référence à la notion de dignité. Pour elles, l'article 15 dans son ensemble promeut l'idée d'égalité réelle et le paragraphe 15(1) « vise à empêcher les distinctions discriminatoires ayant un effet négatif sur les membres des groupes caractérisés par les motifs énumérés à l'art. 15 ou par des motifs analogues »[42]. Elles ajoutent, et c'est là, je crois, l'élément-clé de leur remise en question, qu'il faut recentrer l'analyse du paragraphe 15(1) sur son « principal enjeu », lequel a été identifié dans l'arrêt *Andrews* : la lutte contre la discrimination. Celle-ci est alors qualifiée comme étant « l'objectif primordial » de l'article 15 et l'objet spécifique du paragraphe 15(1) consiste dorénavant à « empêcher les gouvernements d'établir des distinctions fondées sur des motifs énumérés ou analogues qui ont pour effet de perpétuer un désavantage ou un préjugé dont un groupe est victime, ou qui imposent un désavantage fondé sur l'application de stéréotypes ».[43]

Enfin, les juges McLachlin et Abella estiment que les facteurs contextuels développés dans l'arrêt *Law* pour déterminer si une distinction de traitement porte atteinte à la dignité humaine demeurent pertinents à condition de les interpréter comme « des facteurs qui permettent de reconnaître l'effet discriminatoire » dans la perspective de l'arrêt *Andrews*, à savoir celle « de la perpétuation d'un désavantage et de l'application de stéréotypes comme étant les principaux indices de discrimination »[44].

---

40 *Kapp, supra* note 4 au para. 21.

41 *Ibid.* au para. 22.

42 *Ibid.* au para. 16.

43 *Ibid.* aux para. 24–25.

44 *Ibid.* au para. 23.

Ces aveux, concessions et mises au point suscitent plusieurs questions légitimes, à commencer par celles-ci : l'arrêt *Kapp* a-t-il réglé quoi que ce soit à l'égard du paragraphe 15(1)? La mise au rencart de la dignité correspond-elle à un changement d'orientation réel par rapport à *Law*? A-t-on vraiment voulu régler les difficultés causées par l'arrêt *Law* avec sa consécration de la dignité[45] comme objet du paragraphe 15(1) et son imposition du critère de l'atteinte à la dignité comme élément de preuve indispensable mis à la charge du plaignant?

Malheureusement, rien n'est moins sûr pour trois raisons bien simples. Tout d'abord, la mise au point des juges McLachlin et Abella constitue à proprement parler un *obiter dictum* puisque le paragraphe 15(1) sera en définitive jugé non pertinent dans cet arrêt. La Cour estime en fin de compte qu'il s'agit d'un cas où c'est uniquement le paragraphe 15(2), considéré dorénavant comme ayant une existence et un rôle indépendants du paragraphe 15(1), qui trouve application[46]. On ne peut donc avoir aucun indice, dans l'arrêt *Kapp*, de l'impact concret de cette mise au point qui reste, somme toute, assez théorique. Ensuite, les juges McLachlin et Abella insistent à nouveau, comme dans l'arrêt *Law*, pour faire dire à l'arrêt *Andrews* des choses que le juge McIntyre, son auteur principal, n'a jamais dites, notamment en ce qui concerne le critère des préjugés et des stéréotypes. Enfin, la conservation des facteurs contextuels de discrimination développés dans l'arrêt *Law* permettent évidemment de douter des véritables intentions de la Cour dans cet arrêt *Kapp* et de craindre que la jurisprudence continue de s'en remettre à l'approche de l'arrêt *Law*, bien que les juges McLachlin et Abella reconnaissent clairement son caractère problématique en matière d'égalité constitutionnelle.

J'examinerai l'impact possible des motifs de jugement des juges McLachlin et Abella relatifs au paragraphe 15(1) sous deux angles : celui du fardeau de preuve du plaignant et celui des rapports entre les articles 15 et premier.

a) Le fardeau de preuve du plaignant

Le maintien du premier facteur contextuel de la préexistence d'un désavantage ou, si l'on préfère, de l'appartenance à un groupe désavantagé ou vulnérable aux préjugés sociaux, continue d'entretenir une ambivalence. D'une part, on pose qu'en principe, le fait de désavantager un groupe défavorisé

45 Il s'agissait bien de consacrer dans l'arrêt *Law*, *supra* note 2, la dignité comme objet du par. 15(1) et non de créer cet objet puisque, comme on l'a vu, ce sont les juge McLachlin, Cory et L'Heureux-Dubé qui sont à l'origine de cette idée dans la trilogie de 1995. Voir *supra* note 20.

46 *Kapp*, *supra* note 4 aux para. 37–41.

milite en faveur d'une conclusion d'effet discriminatoire. D'autre part, on affirme avec raison que la protection contre la discrimination est reconnue à tous, c'est-à-dire tant aux hommes qu'aux femmes, aux blancs qu'aux gens de couleur, aux hétérosexuels qu'aux homosexuels. C'est ainsi que la Cour a reconnu qu'un homme avait été victime de discrimination fondée sur le sexe au sens du paragraphe 15(1) dans l'arrêt *Trociuk*[47]. Dans cette affaire, un père contestait une loi qui réservait aux mères le droit de déclarer leur enfant aux autorités de l'état civil et leur octroyait au surplus le droit unilatéral d'exclure de la déclaration de naissance les renseignements concernant l'identité du père de l'enfant. Puisqu'on trouve par ailleurs plusieurs cas où la Cour a jugé non discriminatoire une mesure défavorable aux membres d'un groupe vulnérable ou défavorisé[48], ce facteur contextuel paraît peu probant. C'est ailleurs, manifestement, que la partie se joue.

Le fardeau de preuve du plaignant est-il modifié au regard du facteur contextuel de l'importance ou de la nature du droit dont le plaignant est privé dans une affaire de discrimination? Ce facteur postule que plus le droit dont on prive le plaignant est important, plus l'effet discriminatoire ressort clairement. Dans la mesure où, en matière constitutionnelle, ce sont le plus souvent des droits prévus par la loi qui sont soumis au crible de l'article 15, comment leur privation peut-elle s'avérer mineure puisque le paragraphe 15(1) n'interdit au départ, par l'identification de motifs *a priori* illicites ou suspects, que les discriminations les plus injustes (et non toutes les distinctions arbitraires comme aux États-Unis en vertu du XIVe Amendement)? En effet, comment un traitement préjudiciable causé par la loi et fondé sur la race, l'orientation sexuelle, la religion ou le handicap peut-il être sans importance pour un individu et, partant, non discriminatoire?

Si le paragraphe 15(1) garantit vraiment un droit à l'égalité réelle et effective, il y aurait lieu d'opter, comme dans l'arrêt *Andrews*, pour la cohérence et la rigueur en admettant que le seul critère pertinent en matière de discrimination est celui de l'effet préjudiciable, à savoir:

> une distinction, intentionnelle ou non, mais fondée sur des motifs relatifs à des caractéristiques personnelles d'un individu ou d'un groupe d'indivi-

---

47 *Trociuk, supra* note 25.

48 Voir par ex. *Canadian Foundation for Children, supra* note 25; *Auton (Tutrice à l'instance de) c. Colombie-Britannique (Procureur géneral)*, [2004] 3 R.C.S. 657; *Nouvelle-Écosse, supra* note 25; *Gosselin, supra* note 25; *Lovelace c. Ontario*, [2000] 1 R.C.S. 950; *Granovsky c. Canada (Ministre de l'Emploi et de l'Immigration)*, [2000] 1 R.C.S. 703; *Little Sisters, supra* note 39; *Eaton c. Conseil scolaire du comté de Brant*, [1997] 1 R.C.S. 241 [*Eaton*]; *Thibaudeau c. Canada*, [1995] 2 R.C.S. 627.

> dus, qui a pour effet d'imposer à cet individu ou à ce groupe *des fardeaux, des obligations ou des désavantages* non imposés à d'autres ou d'empêcher ou de restreindre l'accès aux possibilités, aux bénéfices et aux avantages offerts à d'autres membres de la société.[49]

Cela dit, en plus du préjudice matériel exigé dans l'arrêt *Andrews*, à savoir la privation d'un droit ou l'imposition de fardeaux ou d'obligations non imposés aux autres, faut-il exiger du plaignant la preuve *supplémentaire* qu'une norme perpétue des stéréotypes ou des préjugés? Si la réponse à cette question était négative, l'arrêt *Kapp* constituerait un changement d'orientation majeur par un retour à l'approche adoptée dans l'arrêt *Andrews* en matière d'effet préjudiciable.

Cependant, il y a lieu d'être sceptique à cet égard. On note tout d'abord une certaine ambivalence, voire une confusion marquée dans le texte du jugement McLachlin/Abella. Tantôt, les savantes juges affirment que la discrimination s'entend de « la perpétuation d'un préjugé *ou* d'un désavantage »[50], tantôt elles parlent de « la lutte contre la discrimination au sens de la perpétuation d'un désavantage *et* de l'application de stéréotypes »[51].

Pour une raison obscure, la Cour suprême insiste depuis la trilogie de 1995 pour faire dire au juge McIntyre dans l'arrêt *Andrews* ce qu'il n'a jamais dit ni même écrit dans son analyse, en vertu du paragraphe 15(1), du caractère discriminatoire de la loi de Colombie-Britannique fermant les portes du Barreau de Colombie-Britannique aux non-citoyens. La Cour prétend donc dans *Kapp* que le juge McIntyre a conclu au caractère discriminatoire de l'exclusion en question en raison du fait qu'elle reposait sur un stéréotype[52]. Elle va même plus loin : à son avis, « le modèle établi dans l'arrêt *Andrews* . . . établissait un critère à deux volets . . . : 1) la loi crée-t-elle une distinction fondée sur un motif énuméré ou analogue? 2) la distinction crée-t-elle un *désavantage par la perpétuation d'un préjugé ou l'application de stéréotypes*? »[53]

Or, le juge McIntyre n'a jamais rien exigé de tel dans le cadre du paragraphe 15(1), s'en tenant à la définition de la discrimination citée ci-dessus. Et cette définition, on l'a vu, ne traite strictement que de la privation de droits ou l'imposition de fardeaux pour certains et non pour d'autres. On n'y trouve nulle mention ni même allusion à une exigence obligatoire de preuve de pré-

49 *Andrews, supra* note 1 à la p. 174.

50 *Kapp, supra* note 4 aux para. 18, 25.

51 *Ibid.* aux para. 24–25.

52 *Supra* note 4 au para. 18.

53 *Ibid.* au para. 17 (les italiques sont ajoutées).

jugé ou de stéréotype qui, il faudrait bien que nos savants juges l'admettent une fois pour toutes, est une création postérieure à l'arrêt *Andrews*.[54]

Certes, le juge McIntyre a affirmé dans le cadre du paragraphe 15(1), et cela est bien différent, que la discrimination résulte de distinctions qui entraînent un préjugé *ou* un désavantage[55], mais jamais il n'a exigé que ces deux conditions soient réunies et prouvées pour pouvoir conclure au caractère discriminatoire d'une mesure. De fait, il n'a rien requis de tel de la part de Monsieur Andrews puisque la seule constatation que la loi le privait d'un droit sur la base de sa non-citoyenneté a amené la Cour à conclure que cette mesure législative était discriminatoire au sens du paragraphe 15(1). *Res ipsa loquitur* aurait dit mon vieux professeur de latin !

Le juge McIntyre avait raison de statuer que la discrimination peut résulter d'un désavantage matériel *ou encore*, en l'absence de celui-ci, de l'application d'un préjugé. Il peut arriver en effet qu'une mesure n'impose pas de fardeaux matériels ou de désavantages tangibles à un certain groupe de personnes, mais qu'elle soit discriminatoire parce qu'elle repose sur des préjugés. Il en serait ainsi d'une loi qui, appliquant la théorie «*separate but equal*», prévoirait la ségrégation des élèves «immigrés», mais qui, par ailleurs, ferait en sorte que les écoles accueillant ces enfants bénéficient des mêmes services que ceux de la majorité. Le caractère discriminatoire d'une telle ségrégation ressortirait alors non pas d'un préjudice matériel comme tel, chaque groupe ayant un droit sensiblement «égal» à l'éducation du point de vue des moyens et des services, mais bien d'un préjudice moral. Celui-ci résulterait du préjugé que les élèves issus de l'immigration ne sont pas égaux devant la loi et ne méritent pas de fréquenter les mêmes écoles que celles de la majorité établie au pays depuis longtemps.

Par ailleurs, cette exigence de preuve de préjugés et de stéréotypes est incompatible avec le concept de la discrimination indirecte. Puisqu'une

---

54 À noter la similarité du para. 17 de l'arrêt *Kapp* avec le para. 51 de l'arrêt *Law, supra* note 2, ainsi libellé: «On pourrait affirmer que le par. 15(1) a pour objet d'empêcher toute atteinte à la dignité . . . *par l'imposition de désavantages, de stéréotypes et de préjugés politiques ou sociaux*».

55 *Andrews, supra* note 1 aux pp. 180–181 : «. . . l'analyse de la discrimination doit se faire en fonction des motifs énumérés et de ceux qui leur sont analogues. L'expression «indépendamment de toute discrimination» exige davantage qu'une simple constatation de distinction dans le traitement de groupes ou d'individus. Cette expression est une forme de réserve incorporée dans l'art. 15 lui-même qui limite les distinctions prohibées par la disposition à celles qui entraînent un préjudice [*sic*] ou un désavantage». (N.B.: les cinq derniers mots de la version française auraient dû se lire «un préjugé ou un désavantage» puisque, dans la version anglaise originale, le juge McIntyre parle de «prejudice or disadvantage»).

telle discrimination découle d'une mesure uniforme conçue pour s'appliquer à tous de la même façon tout en affectant négativement un groupe de personnes en raison d'une caractéristique personnelle visée par le paragraphe 15(1) de la *Charte*, il va de soi que cet effet préjudiciable ne peut pas reposer sur des préjugés ni sur l'application de stéréotypes[56]. C'est ainsi que dans l'arrêt *Eldridge*[57] où des personnes sourdes contestaient le régime d'assurance-santé universel et gratuit pour tous les habitants de la Colombie-Britannique au motif qu'il ne s'avérait pas vraiment gratuit pour elles en raison du fait qu'elles devaient se payer un interprète pour pouvoir communiquer avec le médecin traitant, la Cour n'aurait jamais pu parvenir à la conclusion que la loi était discriminatoire si les plaignants avaient dû démontrer que la loi sur l'assurance-santé de la province reposait sur des préjugés ou des stéréotypes ou perpétuait ceux-ci.

Si mes craintes s'avéraient fondées et que le retrait du critère de l'atteinte à la dignité n'entraînait pas le retrait du fardeau de prouver l'existence de préjugés ou de stéréotypes, les difficultés reliées à l'administration de la preuve auxquelles j'ai déjà fait allusion demeureront, à savoir : comment fait-on une telle preuve? Faut-il déposer des documents à caractère sociologique et faire témoigner des experts dans ce domaine? Compte tenu de la lourdeur, voire du caractère souvent inaccessible d'une telle preuve, la réponse ne reposera-t-elle pas en définitive sur la vision subjective et personnelle du juge?

D'autre part, lorsque le gouvernement veut contrer les allégations de stéréotype, il faut bien réaliser qu'il est souvent amené à le faire en faisant valoir les justifications d'intérêt public qui sous-tendent la loi. C'est ce qui s'est produit par exemple dans le récent arrêt de la Cour d'appel fédérale *Singh Gill c. Canada*[58]. Dans cette affaire, deux fonctionnaires contestaient des dispositions du régime de retraite des employés de la fonction publique qui les empêchaient d'obtenir une pleine pension en fonction de leur âge. Après avoir indiqué que le facteur d'analyse le plus important dans le cadre

---

56 Voir *Eaton*, *supra* note 48 au para. 67, J. Sopinka:

> Qu'il s'agisse de l'impossibilité pour une personne aveugle de réussir un examen écrit ou du besoin d'une rampe pour avoir accès à une bibliothèque, la discrimination ne consiste pas dans l'attribution de caractéristiques fausses à la personne handicapée. . . . L'enquête sur la discrimination qui recourt au raisonnement fondé sur « l'attribution de caractéristiques stéréotypées », dans son acception courante, est tout simplement inappropriée dans le cas présent.

57 *Eldridge*, *supra* note 16.

58 *Singh Gill c. Canada*, 2009 CAF 56, [2009] A.C.F. no 240 [*Singh Gill*].

du paragraphe 15(1) consistait dans la preuve que la loi « causes or perpetuates an adverse effect over the age of 71 on the basis of any negative stereotyping of older people »[59], la Cour d'appel a rejeté la prétention des appelants à ce sujet par les objectifs généraux du législateur, à savoir faire en sorte que le régime de retraite des fonctionnaires se conforme aux lois fédérales, notamment à la *Loi de l'impôt sur le revenu*. Comme on le voit, la Cour a télescopé l'analyse de l'article premier au cœur de l'analyse du paragraphe 15(1), ce qui a eu pour effet de nier aux appelants la garantie d'une protection effective contre la discrimination qu'est censée leur procurer justement la nécessaire séparation entre ces deux étapes distinctes dans tout examen d'une mesure contestée pour cause de discrimination.

De plus, la preuve de stéréotypes ou de préjugés équivaut parfois en pratique à exiger la preuve de l'intention discriminatoire du gouvernement, souvent impossible à faire puisque ce dernier a toujours une panoplie d'excellentes raisons *a priori* non discriminatoires pour traiter des catégories de gens de façon différente. C'est ainsi que dans l'affaire *Gosselin*[60], le traitement gravement préjudiciable infligé aux bénéficiaires de l'aide sociale sur la base de leur âge, à savoir la coupure des *deux tiers* de leur maigre prestation, a été nié par la Cour au motif que le gouvernement avait de bonnes intentions d'agir ainsi, à savoir les inciter à retourner au travail ou en formation. Pourtant, cette législation ne pouvait qu'entretenir des stéréotypes très tenaces sur l'absence de volonté réelle des jeunes bénéficiaires de l'aide sociale de retourner sur le marché de l'emploi.

Quoi qu'il en soit, sous le régime des diverses lois sur les droits de la personne en vigueur partout au Canada, le critère de l'intention discriminatoire a justement été mis au rencart depuis plus de trente ans parce que ce critère constituait auparavant le principal obstacle à une protection réelle et effective contre la discrimination[61]. La Cour suprême s'était clairement inspirée de sa jurisprudence portant sur cette législation quasi constitutionnelle dans l'arrêt *Andrews* pour en arriver à une définition de la discrimination qui n'exige aucune preuve d'intention discriminatoire, de préjugés, de stéréotypes ou d'arbitraire. Il fut décevant d'assister à la renaissance de cette exigence de preuve dans le cadre du paragraphe 15(1) de la *Charte*, via le critère de l'atteinte à la dignité humaine imposée dans l'arrêt *Law*. Il est encore plus déconcertant de constater que la Cour tient apparemment, dans

59 *Ibid.* aux para. 9–10.

60 *Gosselin, supra* note 25.

61 Proulx, *supra* note 23 aux pp. 525–33.

l'arrêt *Kapp*, à confirmer cette malheureuse exigence de preuve de préjugés ou de stéréotypes compte tenu de son apparente volonté d'éliminer le critère de la dignité.

Du reste, sauf pour quelques précieux arrêts[62] où les éléments de désavantage et de préjugés sont dissociés au lieu d'être imbriqués, il ressort de la jurisprudence postérieure à l'arrêt *Kapp* que c'est bien ce message de la preuve d'un désavantage *par* la perpétuation de préjugés ou l'application de stéréotypes qui est retenu et appliqué par la plupart des tribunaux[63]. La Cour suprême elle-même a eu l'occasion de réaffirmer cette position dans le récents arrêts *Bande et nation indiennes d'Ermineskin* et *Withler*[64]. De ce côté, donc, *Kapp* ne marque donc aucun progrès par rapport à *Law*.

b) Les rapports entre les articles 15 et premier

Il y a plus d'espoir d'un renouveau jurisprudentiel avec l'arrêt *Kapp* en ce qui concerne la clarification des rapports très stratégiques entre les articles 15 et premier. Les juges McLachlin et Abella insistent en effet sur l'idée qu'il faut abandonner le critère de la dignité pour « mettre l'accent sur le principal enjeu de l'art. 15 qui a été décrit dans l'arrêt *Andrews* [comme étant] la lutte contre la discrimination »[65]. Voilà qui est franchement rafraîchissant!

C'est donc dans cette perspective nouvelle qu'il faut recentrer les facteurs contextuels de discrimination que constituent la « correspondance

---

62 Voir par ex. *McIvor c. Canada (Registrar, Indian and Northern Affairs)*, 2009 BCCA 153, 306 D.L.R. (4e) 193 [*McIvor*]; *Plesner c. British Columbia (Hydro and Power Authority)*, 2009 BCCA 188, 308 D.L.R. (4e) 624; *Marshall Estate (Re)*, 2009 NSCA 25, 309 D.L.R. (4th) 459. À noter également ces deux décisions où les tribunaux, prenant acte de la position de la Cour suprême dans *Kapp, supra* note 4, essaie de faire des distinctions afin d'éviter l'application de l'exigence des préjugés et stéréotypes dans le cadre de lois anti-discrimination provinciales : *Van der Smit c. Alberta (Human Rights and Citizenship Commission)*, 2009 ABQB 121, 470 A.R. 325; *Ontario (Director, Disability Support Program) c. Tranchemontagne*, [2009] 95 O.R. (3e) 327, 99 Admin. L.R. (4e) 99 (C. Div.); *Commission des droits de la personne et des droits de la jeunesse c. Laval (Ville de) (Service de sécurité d'incendies)*, 2009 QCTDP 4, [2009] J.T.D.P.Q. no 4 (QL).

63 Voir par ex. *Downey c. Nova Scotia (Workers' Compensation Appeals Tribunal)*, 2008 NSCA 65, [2008] 267 N.S.R. (2e) 364 (QL); *Boulter c. Nova Scotia Power Inc.*, 2009 NSCA 17, 307 D.L.R. (4e) 293; *Harris c. Canada (Ministre des Ressources humaines et du Développement des compétences)*, 2009 CAF 22, 305 D.L.R. (4e) 498; *Hartling c. Nova Scotia (A.G.)*, 2009 NSSC 2, 278 N.S.R. (2e) 112 (QL); *Confédération des syndicats nationaux c. Québec (Procureur général)*, 2008 QCCS 5076, [2008] J.Q. no 10735 (QL); C.C.-W. *(Litigation Guardian of) c. Ontario (Health Insurance Plan, General Manager)*, 95 O.R. (3e) 48, 305 D.L.R. (4e) 538 (C.S.); *Vilven c. Air Canada*, 2009 CF 367, 191 C.R.R. (2d) 66 (QL); *supra* note 58.

64 *Bande et nation indiennes d'Ermineskin c. Canada*, [2009] 1 R.C.S. 222 aux para. 185–202; *Withler c. Canada (Procureur général)*, 2011 CSC 12 aux para. 30–40.

65 *Kapp, supra* note 4 au para. 24.

aux besoins» et «l'objet ou l'effet améliorateur». Comme on l'a vu, ces facteurs ont été utilisés jusqu'ici pour introduire dans l'analyse du caractère discriminatoire d'une mesure des considérations étrangères à l'objet égalitaire de l'article 15, à savoir des questions générales d'intérêt public relevant de l'article premier (ex.: les besoins de la société, les moyens financiers limités de l'État, une saine gestion administrative, la paix sociale, l'ordre public, la santé ou la sécurité publique, etc.).

À partir du moment où la Cour suprême indique clairement dans l'arrêt *Kapp* que le «principal enjeu»[66] et «l'objectif primordial»[67] de l'article 15 est de lutter contre la discrimination, c'est donc dire contre les inégalités et les traitements préjudiciables dont sont victimes les membres des groupes identifiables et identifiés par l'énumération ouverte de motifs du paragraphe 15(1), les facteurs contextuels de la correspondance aux besoins et de l'objet ou de l'effet réparateur pourront enfin viser des *enjeux proprement égalitaires ou anti-discrimination* par opposition aux enjeux d'intérêt public qui n'ont rien à voir avec l'objet de l'article 15, c'est-à-dire la recherche d'une égalité réelle et effective pour tous.

En sorte que le gouvernement, à l'étape du paragraphe 15(1), ne pourra dorénavant faire appel à ces facteurs contextuels en défense à une attaque constitutionnelle que s'il est en mesure de démontrer que sa distinction de traitement a pour objet de lutter contre la discrimination, à savoir protéger une catégorie de personnes contre l'exclusion, assurer la jouissance de ses droits en pleine égalité et autonomie ou encore alléger les fardeaux dont elle est affligée. Cela semble d'ailleurs avoir été bien compris par la jurisprudence récente[68]. C'est ainsi, par exemple, qu'après avoir analysé l'arrêt *Kapp*, la Cour d'appel de Colombie-Britannique en arrive à la conclusion suivante dans l'arrêt *McIvor*[69]:

> *Kapp* serves as a reminder that the third factor in *Law* is not directed at broad societal goals, but as the question of whether distinctions in impugned legislation are, themselves, designed to alleviate discrimination or are, rather, distinctions that tend to perpetuate disadvantage. . . .
>
> While there was, particularly after the *Law* decision, a tendency to treat all justifications as issues to be considered in determining whether differential treatment is "discriminatory", *Kapp*, in my view, serves as a

66 *Ibid.*

67 *Ibid.* au para. 25.

68 Voir la jurisprudence citée aux notes 62 et 63.

69 *McIvor, supra* note 62 aux para. 110, 116.

reminder that the discrimination analysis is more narrow, and that policy justifications for unequal treatment under the law will normaly be matters that must be treated outside of s. 15 itself.

Dès lors, un traitement différent pourrait être jugé non discriminatoire à l'aide des facteurs contextuels propres au paragraphe 15(1) dans certains cas de figure, notamment ceux-ci:

1) Un traitement différent conçu (au moins en partie) dans le but d'éviter l'exclusion, la privation de droits reconnus aux autres, le fardeau additionnel non imposé aux autres ou encore pour faire en sorte qu'un groupe puisse jouir de ses droits en pleine égalité. Ce serait par exemple le cas d'aménagements ou d'accommodements raisonnables sans lesquels un groupe d'individus se trouve privé de droits ou d'avantages consentis aux autres. Du reste, il s'agit du corollaire obligé de la théorie de l'effet discriminatoire découlant d'une mesure uniforme et qui se trouve au cœur du concept de l'égalité réelle et effective[70].
2) Une mesure conçue pour lever les obstacles empêchant des groupes défavorisés par l'âge, le sexe, le handicap ou la condition sociale de jouir en pleine égalité des droits et libertés ou pour diminuer les désavantages subis par ces groupes[71].

Les programmes dits d'accès à l'égalité ou de promotion sociale, dont le but est « de combattre de façon proactive la discrimination »[72] et d'améliorer la situation des groupes défavorisés visés par l'article 15, soit en corrigeant une situation discriminatoire, soit en refaisant les équilibres dans la représentation des groupes défavorisés, soit encore en favorisant temporairement de tels groupes pour leur donner une chance d'exercer leurs droits, sont évidemment conformes à l'objet égalitaire de l'article 15 et peuvent être invoqués par le gouvernement en défense. Toutefois, ce type de programmes et ce type de défense relèvent du seul paragraphe 15(2) qui joue désor-

70 Voir à ce sujet *Eldridge, supra* note 16; *Eaton, supra* note 48.

71 Voir par ex.: *Law, supra* note 2 (mesure sociale pour diminuer le fardeau des veuves âgées, celles ayant une déficience ou charge de famille); *Winko c. Colombie-Britannique* (*Forensic Psychiatric Institute*), [1999] 2 R.C.S. 625 (mesure évitant l'emprisonnement régulier aux individus non criminellement responsables en raison de leur déficience mentale); *Hess, supra* note 19 (traitement différent entre hommes et femmes afin de lutter contre les grossesses précoces); *Weatherall, supra* note 19 (traitement différent entre hommes et femmes afin de protéger les détenues contre les agressions sexuelles).

72 *Kapp, supra* note 4 au para. 37.

mais, nous dit la Cour dans l'arrêt *Kapp*, un rôle indépendant du paragraphe 15(1) et permet même de court-circuiter celui-ci.[73]

Dans ces cas de figure, la mesure législative destinée à contrer l'exclusion ou le désavantage n'est pas discriminatoire au sens de l'article 15 parce que, dans la perspective d'un droit à l'égalité réelle bien compris, elle répond directement à l'objectif d'égalité véritable recherché par cette garantie.

Cela dit, pour que la politique ou la mesure gouvernementale soit jugée non discriminatoire tant au sens du paragraphe 15(1) que du paragraphe 15(2), elle devra « correspondre aux besoins » de ceux à qui elle s'adresse. *A contrario*, comme le rappelle l'arrêt *Kapp*, elle sera jugée discriminatoire si elle s'avère irrationnelle et sans rapport suffisant avec la situation des personnes visées[74]. Il va de soi, en effet, qu'un traitement différencié constitue un accommodement raisonnable requis par le droit à l'égalité réelle s'il répond aux besoins particuliers d'un handicapé (ex.: prendre l'ascenseur pour un élève circulant en fauteuil roulant), mais qu'il constitue un privilège indu si ce n'est pas le cas (ex.: faire passer un handicapé en fauteuil roulant avant les autres élèves pour obtenir un relevé de notes alors que sa situation ne justifie nullement un traitement différent dans ce contexte).

On trouve dans la jurisprudence de la Cour suprême tant des cas d'application conformes à l'objet égalitaire de l'article 15 que des cas confondant les considérations égalitaires de cette garantie avec des considérations d'intérêt public relevant de l'article premier. Pour des exemples respectant l'objet de l'article 15, on consultera les arrêts *Law*, *Winko*, *Eaton*, *Hess* et *Weatherall*.[75] Pour des exemples de confusion, on peut lire *Gosselin*, *Canadian Foundation for Children*, *Delisle*, *Little Sisters*, *Trociuk*, et *Therrien*.[76]

Le récent arrêt *Bande et nation indiennes d'Ermineskin*[77] semble respecter la consigne de rigueur développée dans l'arrêt *Kapp*. À l'argument de la bande indienne selon laquelle les Indiens sont désavantagés par une série de lois et un traité qui empêchent le gouvernement fédéral de placer les redevances tirées de l'exploitation des ressources pétrolières et gazières situées dans le sous-sol de leurs réserves afin d'en tirer le maximum de revenus, le juge Rothstein répond que la politique gouvernementale correspond à leurs besoins d'autonomie et d'autodétermination tels qu'ils ont été exprimés par les autorités indiennes elles-mêmes et que, contrairement aux

---

73 *Ibid.* aux para. 37–40.

74 *Ibid.* au para. 48.

75 Voir les références aux notes 1, 20, 48, et 71.

76 Voir les références aux notes 25 et 39.

77 *Supra* note 64.

apparences, ladite politique n'a pas pour effet de les désavantager. Dans la mesure où il évite de confondre des justifications générales d'intérêt public avec les véritables besoins des groupes appelants, le juge Rothstein a donc respecté la structure analytique de la *Charte* en analysant l'allégation de discrimination sous le seul angle de l'égalité dans le cadre du paragraphe 15(1) de la *Charte*. Dans l'arrêt *Withler*[78], la Cour suprême souffle le chaud et le froid. Elle annonce d'entrée de jeu que l'analyse du caractère discriminatoire doit être centrée sur la situation et les besoins des demandeurs, mais elle accepte malgré tout de prendre en considération des arguments relatifs à « l'affection des ressources » et aux « objectifs particuliers d'intérêt public visés par le législateur »[79]. Cependant, comme ces objectifs consistent à assurer des prestations convenables à tous les employés retraités de l'État en tenant compte de leurs besoins à chaque étape de leur vie, on peut probablement en conclure qu'il s'agit de considérations de nature égalitaire (visés par l'article 15) et non d'objectifs d'intérêt public général relevant de l'article premier de la *Charte*.

C. CONCLUSION

J'aimerais, en terminant, dresser la liste des enseignements que m'inspire la mise au point de la juge en chef McLachlin et de la juge Abella dans l'arrêt *Kapp* :

1) Lors d'une attaque constitutionnelle fondée sur le paragraphe 15(1) de la Charte, les tribunaux doivent dorénavant recentrer leur examen des normes législatives et des politiques gouvernementales contestées pour le placer dans la seule perspective de l'égalité réelle, à savoir celle de la lutte contre les exclusions et les effets préjudiciables liés aux caractéristiques personnelles identifiées à l'article 15.
2) Dans ce contexte clarifié, les questions qu'il faut se poser pour vérifier le caractère discriminatoire ou non d'une loi ou d'une politique sont les suivantes :
   a) Y a-t-il différence de traitement apparente ou cachée?
   b) Cette différence de traitement a-t-elle un lien avec un motif énuméré ou analogue?
   c) En découle-t-il un préjudice (privation de droits; bénéfice non accordé; désavantage créé, etc.) par application d'un préjugé ou d'un

78 *Supra* note 64.

79 *Ibid.* Comparer les para. 38–40 avec les para. 67, 71, 76, et 78.

stéréotype?[80] À noter que les facteurs contextuels du désavantage préexistant ou de l'importance du droit peuvent jouer un rôle utile à ce stade-ci.

d) La mesure contestée est-elle destinée à réduire les inégalités? A-t-elle été adoptée dans le but d'éviter une exclusion discriminatoire? Favorise-t-elle l'autonomie d'un groupe identifiable? Dans l'affirmative, est-elle rationnelle par rapport avec ses objectifs égalitaires de manière à correspondre aux besoins de ceux qu'elle vise[81]?

3) On ne doit valider, dans le cadre de l'article 15, que les différences de traitement qui ont été édictées dans un but égalitaire : éviter les exclusions ou traitements préjudiciables fondés sur un motif interdit (énuméré ou analogue), assurer la pleine jouissance des droits pour tous et réduire les inégalités sociales.

4) Il faut rejeter comme non pertinente, au stade de l'article 15, toute considération sociale ou d'intérêt public qui n'a aucun objectif de promotion de l'égalité ou de réduction des inégalités parce que ces justifications sont totalement étrangères au droit à l'égalité réelle et effective garanti par cette disposition constitutionnelle. Les justifications d'une disparité de traitement tenant à des considérations légitimes d'intérêt public doivent être réservées à la seconde étape de l'analyse à effectuer sous l'égide de l'article premier.

---

80 Comme j'ai tenté de le démontrer dans ce texte, l'obligation de faire la preuve qu'une différence de traitement fondée sur un motif énuméré ou analogue perpétue un préjugé ou applique un stéréotype *en plus* de causer un préjudice matériel au plaignant (ex.: perte d'un emploi, refus d'une prestation, etc.) n'est ni requise, ni souhaitable dans la perspective d'un droit à l'égalité réelle et effective. Force est toutefois de constater que la Cour suprême s'en tient toujours, sur ce point, à la position arrêtée dans l'arrêt *Law*, *supra* note 2.

81 Il importe de ne pas confondre, comme je le rappelle au point 4 ci-dessous, la nécessaire rationalité liée aux objectifs proprement égalitaires de l'art. 15 (éviter l'exclusion de groupes défavorisés visés par la garantie constitutionnelle d'égalité) avec des considérations de rationalité liées à des objectifs externes à l'égalité (efficacité administrative, saine gestion des finances publiques, santé publique, sécurité ou ordre public, etc.). Ces dernières relèvent de l'article premier et n'ont donc aucune pertinence à l'étape de l'art. 15.

Collective Bargaining and Freedom of Association: Pondering *B.C. Health Services*

THOMAS KUTTNER, Q.C.*

A. INTRODUCTION

In the British Columbia *Health Services* case,[1] the Supreme Court of Canada surprised the labour law community by dramatically reversing twenty years of entrenched jurisprudence. Ever since the 1987 *Labour Trilogy*[2] the Court had consistently excluded the institution of collective bargaining from the protective embrace of the *Charter*[3] section 2(d) guarantee of freedom of

* This is a revised and expanded version of a paper originally given at a conference sponsored by the Canadian Bar Association in Ottawa, ON (June 2009) entitled "The McLachlin Court's First Decade: Reflections on the Past and Projections for the Future." As I was developing this piece, I benefitted from the many helpful comments, observations, and insights of Aloke Chatterjee and Jula Hughes of the University of New Brunswick; Roy Adams and John Whyte of the University of Saskatchewan; Brian Etherington and Laverne Jacobs of the University of Windsor; as well as those of the anonymous reviewer.

1 *Health Services and Support-Facilities Subsector Bargaining Assn. v. British Columbia*, [2007] 2 S.C.R. 391, [2007] S.C.J. No. 27 [*Health Services*].

2 *Reference re Public Service Employee Relations Act (Alta.)*, [1987] 1 S.C.R. 313, 38 D.L.R. (4th) 161 [*Reference re PSERA*]; *PSAC v. Canada*, [1987] 1 S.C.R. 424; *RWDSU v. Saskatchewan*, [1987] 1 S.C.R. 460 [collectively, the *Labour Trilogy*]. The immediate focus of the *Labour Trilogy* was the right to strike which the majority (4:2) refused to acknowledge as an exercise of freedom of association under *Charter* s. 2(d); arguably, the Court was ambivalent on the right to collective bargaining, only three of the majority explicitly excluding it from the *Charter*'s embrace. Any doubt in this regard was quieted by the decision of the Court in *Professional Institute of the Public Service of Canada v. Northwest Territories (Comm'r)*, [1990] 2 S.C.R. 367 [*PIPS v. NWT*], the majority there (4:3) categorically denying to collective bargaining protection under the *Charter*.

3 *Canadian Charter of Rights and Freedoms*, Part I of the *Constitution Act, 1982* being Schedule B to the *Canada Act, 1982*, (U.K.) 1982, c. 11.

association.[4] In *Health Services* it included collective bargaining within the reach of that embrace. *Health Services*, then, joins that constellation of recent public law decisions of the Court in which it has reversed (although admittedly not quite so dramatically) what had been heretofore understood to be settled law.

These include its rejection of *Cooper*[5] in *Martin*,[6] thereby expanding the class of administrative tribunals possessed of *Charter* jurisdiction; its resiling from *Kindler*[7] and *Ng*[8] in *Burns*,[9] thereby narrowing the discretion of the Minister of Justice to extradite to a death penalty state; its abandonment of *Law*[10] in *Kapp*,[11] thereby refashioning the legal test for determining discrimination in its equality jurisprudence; its double rejection in *Dunsmuir*[12]—first of *Knight*,[13] thereby banishing public servants from entitlement to procedural fairness on dismissal,[14] second, of *Southam*[15] and its progeny, thereby reverting to a two-tiered from a three-tiered standard of judicial review, but in the context abandoning that of patent unreasonableness as first conceived in the *NB Liquor Board* case,[16] the *fons et origo* of the modern jurisprudence.

Is there a jurisprudential force which draws these several cases into a single constellation and so explains a commonality of outcome? If so, will it assist us in predicting what else of the Supreme Court's settled doctrine will succumb to its pull, and another reversal be added to that constellation? Or are we better off rejecting the idea of such a unified theory and concluding

---

4 *Ibid.*, s. 2(d):

> 2. Everyone has the following fundamental freedoms:
>
> . . .
>
> (d) freedom of association.

5 *Cooper v. Canada (Human Rights Commission)*, [1996] 3 S.C.R. 854.

6 *Nova Scotia (Workers' Compensation Board) v. Martin; Nova Scotia (Workers' Compensation Board) v. Laseur*, [2003] 2 S.C.R. 504.

7 *Kindler v. Canada (Minister of Justice)*, [1991] 2 S.C.R. 779.

8 *Reference re Ng Extradition (Can.)*, [1991] 2 S.C.R. 858.

9 *United States v. Burns*, [2001] 1 S.C.R. 283.

10 *Law v. Canada (Minister of Employment and Immigration)*, [1999] 1 S.C.R. 497.

11 *R. v. Kapp*, [2008] 1 S.C.R. 483.

12 *Dunsmuir v. New Brunswick*, [2008] 1 S.C.R. 190.

13 *Knight v. Indian Head School Division No. 19*, [1990] 1 S.C.R. 653.

14 Indeed, in the public employment context, it severely constricts the application of the momentous English decision in *Ridge v. Baldwin*, [1963] 2 All E.R. 66. Quite shocking.

15 *Canada (Director of Investigation and Research) v. Southam Inc.*, [1997] 1 S.C.R. 748.

16 *Canadian Union of Public Employees, Local 963 v. New Brunswick Liquor Corp.*, [1979] 2 S.C.R. 227.

that each reversal is a singularity? Like astronomers who search for order in the firmament of the stars, we adepts of the law seek order in the firmament of the law.

Perhaps what we are witnessing is a maturing of our *Charter* jurisprudence as the Court gradually and ever more boldly departs from the dominant mode of deontological jurisprudential inquiry which characterized the common law and its narrow focus on the parties before the court; and more consciously espouses an openly instrumentalist or consequentialist mode of jurisprudential inquiry, one which looks beyond the immediate parties before the court to the broader sociological implications of the disputes it is called upon to determine.[17]

Such a critical analysis of the broad sweep of the *Charter* jurisprudence is not without analogous precedent. "There are statutes and there are statutes," Lord Chancellor Sankey reminded us, and the interpretation of "[a]n Imperial Act which creates a constitution for a new country" should be given "[a] large and liberal interpretation" he continued, chiding the Supreme Court of Canada for its timid interpretation of the *Constitution Act, 1867*,[18] in the celebrated *Persons* case.[19] If that is so in the interpretation of our original charter of federal union, then how much the more so in the interpretation of our new *Charter of Rights and Freedoms.*

Viewed from this perspective, *Health Services* becomes then a necessary—dare one say, inevitable—corrective to the jurisprudential deformity which was the *Labour Trilogy.* In the first two parts of this paper, I explore *Health Services* from this perspective. In the third, I then frame the place of the strike in our pre-*Charter* jurisprudence, and prognosticate on whether it too is swept under the protective umbrella of the *Charter*, section 2(d), freedom of association; I believe it can only be so. Finally, I explore the intriguing question whether in *Health Services* the Supreme Court has conferred constitutional status upon trade unions. Underlying the whole inquiry is the far-reaching question: whether broad-sweeping caselaw such as *Health Services*, which consciously considers normative outcomes as its justificatory criterion, has the necessary staying power to ensure that stability, predictability, and uniformity of result so central to the rule of law.

---

17 I wish to acknowledge here in particular the contribution of my colleague Aloke Chatterjee at the University of New Brunswick Faculty of Law, who has enhanced my understanding of these underlying jurisprudential currents.

18 30 & 31 Victoria, c. 1 (U.K.).

19 *Reference re Section 24 of the B.N.A. Act*, [1930] 1 D.L.R. 98 (P.C.), Sankey, L.C. at 107.

RÉSUMÉ

Dans cet article, l'auteur analyse la doctrine de la liberté d'association que la Cour suprême du Canada a révisée dans le cadre de sa décision rendue à propos de l'affaire *Health Services and Support—Facilities Subsector Bargaining Assn.* c. *Colombie-Britannique*, [2007] S.C.J. No. 27; [2007] 2 S.C.R. 391 et ses répercussions sur l'institution qu'est la négociation collective. Il entame son analyse en plaçant la décision au sein de la constellation des jugements récemment rendus par la Cour en matière de droit public et dans lesquels elle avait renversé ce qui était jusqu'alors considéré comme le droit constitutionnel établi. Toutefois, selon l'auteur, si l'on examine la décision selon une perspective historique, il est possible de ne pas la considérer comme une nouvelle direction, dans la mesure où elle vient corriger la jurisprudence antérieure relative à la *Charte*, laquelle avait cassé la tendance du droit du travail déjà fermement ancrée dans la jurisprudence antérieure à la *Charte*. L'auteur entreprend d'évaluer la vraisemblance d'une future décision de la Cour qui, de la même manière, placerait la grève sous la protection de la *Charte*, et examine dans quelle mesure, au regard de sa jurisprudence encore en évolution, on peut affirmer que la Cour a conféré un statut d'acteurs constitutionnels aux syndicats des travailleurs. Il conclut en observant que la nouvelle doctrine de la liberté d'association constitue une lueur d'espoir dans la jurisprudence de la Cour relative à la *Charte*.

B. PARSING THE TEXT OF THE JUDGMENT

Early on in the judgment, the Supreme Court stated baldly its rationale for disavowing the *Labour Trilogy*:

> We conclude that the grounds advanced in the earlier decisions for the exclusion of collective bargaining from the *Charter*'s protection of freedom of association do not withstand principled scrutiny and should be rejected.[20]

20 *Health Services*, above note 1 at para. 22. At para. 20 the Court sets out four propositions in support of its conclusion that the *Charter*, s. 2(d), shelters the institution of collective bargaining: first, the earlier reasoning to the contrary is faulty and cannot be sustained; second, the earlier jurisprudence is inconsistent with the historical record of recognition of collective bargaining as a fundamental value to the Canadian polity; third, collective bargaining enjoys status at international law as integral to freedom of association; and fourth, the inclusion of collective bargaining within the embrace of freedom of asso-

A harsh criticism indeed of the capacity of the judicial cohort which had first addressed the issue, to undergird with logic those earlier penned decisions.

For my purposes here, the decision needs require no painstaking elucidation. Suffice to say, the Court has vindicated fully the view which Dickson C.J., dissenting in the *Labour Trilogy*, so eloquently expressed that "[t]he profoundly social nature of human endeavours" must inform our understanding of the *Charter* section 2(d), for "[o]ur freedom to act with others is a primary condition of community life, human progress and civilized society."[21] The philosophical underpinnings of Dickson C.J.'s dissent are well captured in these words:

> Work is one of the most fundamental aspects in a person's life, providing the individual with a means of financial support and, as importantly, a contributory role in society. A person's employment is an essential component of his or her sense of identity, self-worth and emotional well-being. Accordingly, the conditions in which a person works are highly significant in shaping the whole compendium of psychological, emotional and physical elements of a person's dignity and self respect.[22]

In sharp contrast, McIntyre J., in a concurring opinion which, up until the *Health Services* case, came to represent the Court's pinched analysis of *Charter* section 2(d) in the context of collective bargaining, had characterized trade unions as "[o]verwhelmingly . . . concerned with the economic interests of their members,"[23] and belittled the right to strike as "[o]f relatively recent vintage."[24] All this is swept aside in *Health Services*, the Court opting to realign itself with the humane vision of the dignity of labour which had driven Dickson C.J.'s dissent in the *Labour Trilogy*, rather than the utilitarian characterization of work by McIntyre J., and therefore the worker, as simply an economic construct.

---

ciation is compatible with and furthers other *Charter* rights, freedoms and values. My remarks here touch principally on the first, second, and fourth of these propositions.

21 *Reference re PSERA* above note 2 at para. 86.

22 *Ibid.* at para. 91.

23 *Ibid.* at para. 178. To which Dickson C.J. retorted at para. 97: "I am satisfied, in sum, that whether or not freedom of association generally extends to protecting associational activity for the pursuit of exclusively pecuniary ends—a question on which I express no opinion--collective bargaining protects important employee interests which cannot be characterized as merely pecuniary in nature."

24 *Ibid.* at para. 181. To which Dickson C.J. retorted at para. 96: "The necessity and lawfulness of strikes has also been acknowledged by this Court: *Perrault v. Gauthier* (1898) 28 S.C.R. 241 at 256; *Canadian Pacific Railway Co. v. Zambri*, [1962] S.C.R. 609 at 618 and 621."

The Court speaks of the right to collective bargaining as one which "[e]nhances the human dignity, liberty and autonomy of workers,"[25] one which "reaffirms" fundamental informing values of the *Charter*, including equality and democracy.[26] However, there are anomalies in the analysis. Principal among these is the Court's insistence throughout the judgment that only the *process* of collective bargaining comes under the *Charter* rubric of freedom of association.[27] In the face of the Court's own labour law jurisprudence which has affirmed that the duty to bargain in good faith may require assent by an employer to "basic and standard terms" in a collective agreement,[28] this dichotomy between process and substance will prove difficult to sustain in a principled manner.[29]

25 *Health Services*, above note 1 at para. 82.

26 *Ibid.* at paras. 84–86.

27 *Ibid.* at paras. 19, 91–92, 128–29, and throughout.

28 *Royal Oak Mines Inc. v. Canada (Labour Relations Board)*, [1996] 1 S.C.R. 369. Justice Cory gave as examples of such terms a just cause clause, a grievance arbitration clause, and a pension plan (at para. 44), and indeed any term that is "[a]cceptable and included in other collective agreements in comparable industries throughout the country" (at para. 45). In *Allsco Bldg Products Ltd. v. U.F.C.W. Local 1288P* (2000), 223 N.B.R. (2d) 202, the New Brunswick Court of Appeal upheld the decision of the New Brunswick Labour and Employment Board in *Re Allsco Bldg Products Ltd* (1998), 50 C.L.R.B.R. (2d) 48, which had determined a seniority clause to be such a basic and standard term. On a Rand formula union security clause as such a term, see note 29 below. An appeal by the U.F.C.W. was allowed; see 2011 ABCA 93. The Alberta Court of Appeal set aside the order of the Queen's Bench judge which had granted intervenor status to a group of employees opposed to the consent order originally sought, and stated that no live constitutional issue remained to be addressed. In the interim, the Attorney General of Alberta brought parallel proceedings, which were not opposed by the U.F.C.W., before the Court of Queen's Bench; see 2010 ABQB 777. In that matter, the court quashed the original order of the A.L.R.B. to the extent that it purported to issue a formal declaration of invalidity of its constating legislation on *Charter* grounds for failure to include a provision mandating the Rand Formula. That decision was not appealed. The result? Whether s. 2(d) of the *Charter* entitles a trade union to have the Rand formula included in a collective agreement it negotiates on behalf of the employees it represents, remains an open question.

29 See Binnie J.'s comments in *Mount Sinai Hospital Center v. Quebec (Minister of Health and Social Services)*, [2001] 2 S.C.R. 281 [*Mount Sinai Hospital*] in the context of legitimate expectation doctrine, that "[i]t must be acknowledged that in some cases it is difficult to distinguish the procedural from the substantive . . . An undue focus on formal classification and categorization of powers at the expense of broad principles flexibly applied may do a disservice here" (at para. 35). For a recent analysis of the process/substance divide posited by the Court in *Health Services*, see the decision of the Alberta Labour Relations Board in *United Food and Commercial Workers Union, Local No. 401 v. Old Dutch Foods Ltd. and Minister of Justice and Attorney General of Alberta* (File No. GE-05611 (9 November 2009). It declared the Rand formula (mandatory dues shop) to be a matter going to the *process* of collective bargaining and not its substantive outcome, thereby entitling a trade

The Court also insists on treating Bastarache J.'s reasons for judgment in *Dunmore*[30] as the jurisprudential source for its embrace of collective bargaining as a *Charter* protected activity. To be sure, it is in *Dunmore* that the Court, through Bastarache J., acknowledged that there is a universe of activities which can only be exercised in association, for which there is no analogue exercisable by the individual, and that these may be embraced by freedom of association.[31] This is in contradistinction to its *Labour Trilogy* jurisprudence, where an anodyne conceptualization of associational rights had been articulated, one restricted to such as could be exercised by the individual acting alone.[32] Yet, notwithstanding Bastarache J.'s articulation of this (previously) heterodox doctrine, one which allowed for the recognition of purely associational activities, he continued to profess the received orthodoxy as to a right to collective bargaining, reiterating forcefully that such was excluded from the *Charter*'s reach.[33]

It is only with the decision in *Health Services* that the old orthodoxy was denounced as heretical, and a new orthodoxy proclaimed, namely that the institution of collective bargaining falls within the ambit of *Charter* section 2(d). In short, the Court embraced the robust (but until then rejected)

---

union to its inclusion in a collective agreement in exercise of the *Charter* s. 2(d) freedom of association; and as well requiring its legislative enactment. The subsequent procedural history of this decision is somewhat convoluted: the Attorney General for Alberta seeking judicial review in the face of employer compliance with the Board Order to agree to the Rand formula in the proposed collective agreement; the Respondent Union agreeing in those proceedings to the proposed issuance of a Consent Order striking down solely on s. 96 grounds the Board's declaration of constitutional invalidity; the Court of Queen's Bench Judge, however, demurring while granting intervenor status to a group of employees seeking to strike down the original Board Order *in toto*. See *Alberta (Attorney General) v. United Food and Commercial Workers Union Local No.401*, 2010 ABQB 455.

30 *Dunmore v. Ontario (Attorney General)*, [2001] 3 S.C.R. 1016 [*Dunmore*].

31 *Ibid.* at paras. 16–17.

32 The propositions underlying that jurisprudence are summarized by Sopinka J. in *PIPS v. NWT*, above note 2 at 402: "[f]irst, that s. 2(d) protects the freedom to establish, belong to and maintain an association; second, that s. 2(d) does not protect an activity solely on the ground that the activity is a foundational or essential purpose of an association; third, that s. 2(d) protects the exercise in association of the constitutional rights and freedoms of individuals; and fourth, that s. 2(d) protects the exercise in association of the lawful rights of individuals."

33 *Ibid.* at para. 17. That Bastarache J. could be prevailed upon to abandon the old doctrine in favour of the new is perhaps the most surprising aspect of the judicial *volte-face* in *Health Services*. Of the seven members of the Bench seized, he was most closely associated with the received orthodoxy, having penned two decisions in which it was articulated in absolute terms: *Dunmore*, *ibid.*, and earlier that of the plurality in *Delisle v. Canada (Deputy Attorney General)*, [1999] 2 S.C.R. 989 at para. 11.

conceptualization of associational activities earlier articulated by Dickson C.J. in his trenchant dissent in the *Labour Trilogy*.

C. THE NARRATIVE ARC OF THE LAW

The Court commences its fulsome excursus on the history of collective bargaining with the bold assertion:

> Association for purposes of collective bargaining has long been recognized as a fundamental Canadian right which predated the *Charter*. This suggests that the framers of the *Charter* intended to include it in the protection of freedom of association found in s. 2(*d*) of the *Charter*.[34]

Reiterating the theme that "[l]ong before the present statutory regimes were put in place, collective bargaining was recognized as a fundamental aspect of Canadian society,"[35] the Court then launches into an analysis of the historical record which it frames as follows: "The development of labour relations law in Canada may be divided into three major eras: repression, toleration and recognition."[36] Having sketched out the contours of each, it concludes some twenty paragraphs later:

> In summary, workers in Canada began forming collectives to bargain over working conditions with their employers as early as the 18th century. However, the common law cast a shadow over the rights of workers to act collectively. When Parliament first began recognizing workers' rights, trade unions had no express statutory right to negotiate collectively with employers. Employers could simply ignore them. However, workers used the powerful economic weapon of strikes to gradually force employers to recognize unions and to bargain collectively with them. By adopting the *Wagner Act* model, governments across Canada recognized the fundamental need for workers to participate in the regulation of their work environment. This legislation confirmed what the labour movement had been fighting for over centuries and what it had access to in the laissez-faire era through the use of strikes—the right to collective bargaining with employers.[37]

Here we have the well-known industrial pluralism school of labour history brought into service of the Court's newly articulated *Charter* section

34 *Health Services* above note 1 at para. 40.

35 *Ibid.* at para. 41.

36 *Ibid.* at para. 44.

37 *Ibid.* at para. 63.

2(d) exegesis.[38] Several commentators have criticized the Court for what they perceive to be a misreading, even a distortion, of the historical record, one which privileges the peculiar structure of collective bargaining in North America, characterized as it is by majoritarian exclusivity in the granting of bargaining rights to trade unions, and the concomitant duty to bargain imposed upon employers.[39] They take the Court to task for doing precisely that which it claims not to be doing: constitutionally entrenching a particular model of labour relations and a specific bargaining method—the *Wagner Act* model.[40]

My sense is that the criticism is misplaced. When Clio, the muse of history, enters the halls of justice it is not to engage in the discourse of historians nor to further the historian's craft in mastery of the past. Rather, it is

38 In support of its reading of the history of trade unionism and labour law, the Court draws upon the writings of several Canadian scholars from the industrial pluralism tradition, including these: George W. Adams, *Canadian Labour Law*, 2d ed. looseleaf (Aurora, ON: Canada Law Book, 1993); A.W.R. Carrothers, E.E. Palmer, & W.B. Rayner, *Collective Bargaining Law in Canada*, 2d ed. (Toronto: Butterworths, 1986); Robert P. Gagnon, Louis LeBel, et Pierre Verge, *Droit du travail*, 2e éd. (Sainte-Foy: Presses de l'Université Laval, 1991); and *Canadian Industrial Relations: The Report of Task Force on Labour Relations* (Ottawa: Privy Council Office, 1968) [*Woods Task Force Report*].

39 The major scholarly critiques have been reviewed recently by Brian Etherington in his study, "The *B.C. Health Services and Support* Decision—The Constitutionalization of a Right to Bargain Collectively in Canada: Where Did It Come From and Where Will It Lead?" (2009) 30 Comp. Lab. L. & Pol'y J. 715. They include Judy Fudge, "The Supreme Court of Canada and the Right to Bargain Collectively: The Implications of the *Health Services and Support* Case in Canada and Beyond" (2008) 37 Indus. L.J. 25, and Eric Tucker, "The Constitutional Right to Bargain Collectively: The Ironies of Labour History in the Supreme Court of Canada" (2008) 61 Labour/Le Travail 151. Also included are three articles by Brian Langille: "Can We Rely on the ILO?" (2008) 13 C.L.E.L.J. 363; "The Freedom of Association Mess—How We Got Into It and How We Can Get Out of It" (2009) 54 McGill L.J. 177; and most recently, "Why Are Canadian Judges Drafting Labour Codes—And Constitutionalizing the *Wagner Act* Model?" (2009–10) 15:1 C.L.E.L.J. 101. Also included: Roy Adams, "The Supreme Court, Collective Bargaining and International Law: A Reply to Brian Langille" (2008) 14 C.L.E.L.J. 317; and also see his article "Prospects for Labour's Right to Bargain Collectively after *B.C. Health Services*" (2009) 59 U.N.B.L.J. 85. Professors Fudge, Tucker, and Langille in the works cited are particularly critical of the Court's reading of history.

40 "The right to collective bargaining is a limited right . . . to a general process of collective bargaining, not to a particular model of labour relations, nor to a specific bargaining method.": *Health Services* above note 1 at para. 91. In "Conceptualizing Collective Bargaining under the *Charter*: The Enduring Problem of Substantive Equality" (2008) 42 S.C.L.R. (2d) 213, Professor Fudge is critical of the Court's espousal of the American *Wagner Act* model as "the apotheosis of the right to bargain collectively" (at 222). Professor Adams cautions against reading *Health Services* as entrenching the *Wagner Act* majoritarian exclusivity model of collective bargaining as the sole model enjoying *Charter* protection in his critical case comment: "*Fraser v. Ontario* and International Human Rights: A Comment" (2008) C.L.E.L.J. 379.

to serve in the pursuit of justice and its demands into the future. The Court uses one version of the history of collective bargaining and the law as a heuristic device in support of its principal normative objective: to establish that "[t]he protection enshrined in s. 2(d) of the *Charter* may properly be seen as the culmination of an historical movement towards the recognition of a procedural right to collective bargaining."[41] On this reading then, the *Labour Trilogy* has been marginalized as an irredentist, atavistic jurisprudence of an almost pre-industrial mindset. It interrupted the arc of the law of labour relations as it tracked the trajectory of the institution of collective bargaining, long recognized as "a fundamental aspect of Canadian society,"[42] through the eras of repression and tolerance, and into that of recognition; but only now rightfully, if somewhat belatedly, on into the *Charter* era from which it improperly had been barred.

That the Court is well aware that the historical record can be read differently is readily apparent in its remarks immediately following its espousal of the triple era thesis:

> We are aware that such categorization may not necessarily draw a perfectly accurate picture of the evolution of labour law in our country (see, e.g., E. Tucker, "The Faces of Coercion: The Legal Regulation of Labor Conflict in Ontario, 1880–1889" (1994), 12 *Law & Hist. Rev.* 277). However, for present purpose, such categorization provides a sufficient historical framework in which to summarize the evolution of our law and to underline the flourishing of labour unions and collective bargaining as well as the historic openness of government and society to those organizations over the past century.[43]

Indeed throughout its discussion of the history of labour law, the Court is careful to reference the work of those scholars critical of the industrial pluralism thesis, whether from a critical legal studies or feminist perspective, including the writings of Professors Tucker and Fudge, as well as the American scholar Karl Klare.[44] Nevertheless, it is clear that its primary objective—to give constitutional status to the institution of collective bargaining

41 *Health Services*, above note 1 at para. 68.

42 *Ibid.* at para. 41.

43 *Ibid.* at para. 44.

44 Close to forty scholarly works are referenced, including the sustained critique of the industrial pluralist model by Professors Judy Fudge and Eric Tucker in their highly acclaimed study *Labour before the Law: The Regulation of Workers' Collective Action in Canada, 1900–1948* (Oxford: Oxford University Press, 2001); and the classic critique of the *Wagner Act* model by Karl Klare: "Judicial Deradicalization of the Wagner Act and the Origins of Modern Legal Consciousness, 1937–1941" (1978) 62 Minn. L. Rev. 265.

as it has developed within the Canadian polity—is jurisprudential, rather than historical.[45] And therein also lies the answer to the charge that the Court has entrenched a particular model of labour relations and a specific bargaining method. To the contrary, the majoritarian exclusivist model coupled with a duty to bargain, broadly characteristic of Canadian labour law, is recognized as a legitimate instantiation of collective bargaining, without any hindrance to the development of other models in the future. Realistically, could the Court have determined otherwise without falling afoul of its judicial role and slipping into that of legislator?[46]

D. THE RIGHT TO STRIKE[47]

Early in its judgment the Court was swift to excise the right to strike from any consideration. It observed rather cryptically:

> We note that the present case does not concern the right to strike, which was considered in earlier litigation on the scope of the guarantee of freedom of association.[48]

But is that not the same line of litigation flowing from the *Labour Trilogy* which the Court considers unprincipled? Is the right to strike as a necessary incident of the right to bargain collectively so conceptually complex as to defy

45 The criticism of the Court's historical acumen brings to mind the wry comments of the historian H.E. Carr in his classic study *What Is History?* (New York: Random House Vintage Book, 1961). To the "common-sense view" that history comprises "a corpus of ascertained facts" available to the historian "like fish on the fishmonger's slab" which one takes away and cooks up "in whatever style appeals" (at 6), he retorts: "The facts are really not at all like fish on a fishmonger's slab. They are like fish swimming about in a vast and sometimes inaccessible ocean; and what the historian catches will depend partly on chance, but mainly on what part of the ocean he chooses to fish in and what tackle he chooses to use—these two factors being, of course, determined by the kind of fish he wants to catch. By and large, the historian will get the kind of facts he wants. History means interpretation." (at 26). So too law.

46 Indeed, earlier in *R. v. Advanced Cutting & Coring*, [2001] 3 S.C.R. 209, the Court upheld the constitutional integrity of a non-exclusivist, multi-bargaining agent model of collective bargaining statutorily entrenched in the Quebec construction industry.

47 In this section I draw on earlier studies: "Is the Collective Agreement a Contract" (Paper presented to the Viscount Bennett Seminar, University of New Brunswick, October 1984) [unpublished]; "Constitution as Covenant: Labour Law, Labour Boards and the Courts from the Old to the New Dispensation" in *Labour Law under the Charter* (Kingston: Queen's Law Journal and Industrial Relations Centre, 1988) 43; and my decision as vice-chair, New Brunswick Industrial Relations Board, in *Re Moncton Northeast Construction Association* (1986) 12 C.L.R.B.R. (NS) 203; 86 CLLC, Case No. 16,005.

48 *Health Services*, above note 1 at para. 19.

the Court's ability to take a principled approach to the place of the strike in our constitutional order? To pose the question is to answer it. Rather, its hesitation to address the strike in this, its first articulation of collective bargaining as a constitutional value, must be understood as strategic. In a reversal of the Court's jurisprudence of this magnitude, unanimity among the cohort of judges seized guarantees its entrenchment; it is probable that were the strike to have been included in the Court's consideration at this time, the cost would have been loss of that unanimity. A cost too great; rather, postpone to another day integration of the right to strike into our constitutional order.

That day is fast approaching. In *Fraser*,[49] on appeal from the Ontario Court of Appeal, the Court will address the requirement imposed upon the provincial legislature by that Court, to provide third-party compulsory binding arbitration for the resolution of interest disputes in its agricultural sector labour legislation. Implicit in such an imposed condition for constitutional integrity is recognition of the strike as an exercise of *Charter* section 2(d) freedom of association; or, as I have written elsewhere, the right to strike is entering *Charter* territory "by the backdoor."[50]

This is not surprising. To speak of collective bargaining is to speak of the strike. The two are inextricably linked, and neither has anything at all to do with the individual contract of employment, a socio-economic and political reality recognized even by McIntyre J. in his distorted analysis of the right to strike in the *Labour Trilogy*.[51] Both have everything to do with

---

49 *Fraser v. Ontario (Attorney General)*, (2008) 92 O.R. (3d) 481; leave to appeal granted, 3 April 2009, (2009) O.R. (3d) xvi. The case was argued before the Supreme Court on 17 December 2009, the Court reserving judgment.

50 *The Lawyer's Weekly* (6 March 2009) 8. The section 1 analysis of compulsory binding interest arbitration as a reasonable limit on the right to strike in the exercise of *Charter* s. 2(d), was fully laid out by Dickson C.J. in *Reference re PSERA* above note 2 at para. 101ff. The scholarly consensus is that the right to strike will be swept into the Court's *Health Services* revised freedom of association doctrine and its acceptance of the statutory process of collective bargaining as an instantiation of that freedom. See the papers originally presented at the Symposium: Is There a Constitutional Right to Strike in Canada?, University of Toronto, Faculty of Law, 5 December 2009), now edited and collected in (2009–2010) 15:2 C.L.E.L.J. 129–387; see, in particular, the following papers: Jamie Cameron: "The Labour Trilogy's Last Rites: *B.C. Health* and a Constitutional Right to Strike"; Brian Etherington, "Does Freedom of Association under the *Charter* Include the Right to Strike after *B.C. Health*? Prognosis, Problems and Concerns"; Judy Fudge & Eric Tucker, "The Freedom to Strike in Canada: A Brief Legal History"; Brian Langille, "What Is a Strike?"; Harry Arthurs, " Constitutionalizing the Right of Workers to Organize, Bargain and Strike: The Sight of One Shoulder Shrugging."

51 *Reference re PSERA*, above note 2 at para. 177ff. The distortion lies in his conclusion that, because there is no analogy between cessation of work by a single employee in breach

the solidarity of workers and their relationship to capital, and both are tolerated at common law, even as it denies contractual status to the collective agreement. This was recognized on the highest authority already by the end of the first quarter of the last century, long before statutory collective bargaining regimes had been enacted in Canada. As Lord Russell stated in *Young v. CNR*:

> By itself, it [the collective agreement] constitutes no contract between any individual employee and the company which employs him. If an employer refused to observe the rules, the effective sequel would be, not an action by any employee, not even an action by [the trade union] against the employer for specific performance or damages, but the calling of a strike until the grievance was remedied.[52]

That was on a *per saltem* appeal from Manitoba.[53] A decade later, in the *Harris Tweed* case, Lord Wright could state:

> The right of workmen to strike is an essential element in the principle of collective bargaining.[54]

And in Canada? Here is the view of our own Rand J. in *Newall v. Barker*, several years into a statutory collective bargaining regime in Canada:

> It is now established beyond controversy that in the competition between workmen and employers and between groups of workmen, concerted abstention from work for the purpose of serving the interest of organized labour is justifiable conduct.[55]

---

of a contract of employment and a refusal to work by many (a strike), it therefore follows that freedom of association does not extend to the strike (at para. 178). This is a reading which improperly allows the old law of master and servant to trump the reality of worker solidarity which, as recognized by the Court in *Health Services*, took root in the early- to mid-nineteenth century, was eventually buttressed by legislatures and tolerated by courts, and became fully entrenched in our legal order by the mid-twentieth century.

52 [1931] 1 D.L.R. 645 at 650 (PC) [*Young*].

53 [1930] 3 D.L.R. 352 (Man. CA).

54 *Crofter Hand Woven Harris Tweed Co. v. Veitch*, [1942] 1 All E.R. 142 at 158–59 (HL). In his dissent in the *Labour Trilogy*, above note 2, Dickson C.J. cited this passage (at para. 96) in support of his conclusion: "Under our existing system of industrial relations, effective constitutional protection of the associational interests of employees in the collective bargaining process requires concomitant protection of their freedom to withdraw collectively their services, subject to s. 1 of the *Charter*." [at para. 97].

55 [1950] S.C.R. 385, at p. 397. And see Dickson C.J.'s tracing back of the right to strike to the pre-statutory era in his dissent in the *Labour Trilogy*, cited above at note 2.

The strike itself had been fully developed during the period when collective bargaining fell outside the ken of the law and comprised its own order of mutual promise, one autonomous of the law and its institutions. The strike served three distinct, although inter-related remedial objectives within the dynamic of that regime.

First, the strike was used as an *instrument of persuasion* to induce recognition by the employer of the status of the trade union as the sole voice of its employees, their freely chosen representative, entitled as such to bargain on their behalf. Workers often found their solidarity frustrated by a stubborn refusal on the part of their employers to deal with the trade union chosen by them to be their sole representative. The strike could be a powerful disincentive to such employer recalcitrance.

Second, the strike was used as an *instrument of negotiation* once employer recognition of the trade union as sole representative of its workers had been attained and the process of collective bargaining to determine the terms and conditions of labour at the workplace had commenced. Where reason and hard bargaining had failed to birth a collective agreement, the full weight of worker bargaining power could be brought to bear and worker solidarity manifested to obtain a collective agreement setting out those terms and conditions of labour mutually agreed to be binding.

Third, the strike was used as an *instrument of relief* in the resolution of disputes arising under the terms of an extant collective agreement.[56] Workers dissatisfied with the manner in which the employer was managing the workplace in the face of collective agreement restraints, would often down their tools and refuse to work until the employer had been brought to heel and the breach of the collective agreement curbed.

Under the statutory regimes common to all Canadian jurisdictions for over half a century now, the first and the third of these uses of the strike weapon have been rendered illegal. In the first instance, as an instrument of persuasion, the strike has been replaced by the process of certification whereby a trade union becomes statutorily recognized as the sole voice of an employer's workers; in the latter instance, as an instrument of relief, the strike has been replaced by compulsory binding rights arbitration of all disputes arising between parties to a collective agreement. Only in the instance of its use as an instrument of negotiation does the strike remain lawful, and even then it is subject to stringent regulation as to the time and manner of recourse to its defensive thrust.

---

56 This was the situation addressed by Lord Russell in *Young*, above note 52.

Little wonder then that the celebrated *Woods Task Force Report* (1968) considered the strike to be "[a]n indispensible part of the Canadian industrial relations system" and "[l]ikely to remain so in our present socio-economic-political society."[57] Driving that system is the theory that in a free market economy, industrial democracy must underpin governance of the workplace, such as free collective bargaining "[f]or which there is no substitute in a free society."[58]

And the requirements of an effective system of collective bargaining?

> From the point of view of employees, such a system requires that they be free to engage in three kinds of activity: to form themselves into associations, to engage employers in bargaining with the associations, and to invoke meaningful economic sanctions in support of the bargaining.[59]

Of the three requirements, a reluctant Supreme Court gave to the first grudging recognition as a constitutional value in the *Labour Trilogy* and buttressed this bare essential some fifteen years later in *Dunmore.* The second, which had been so forcefully rejected as a constitutional value in the *Labour Trilogy*, was resoundingly affirmed to enjoy constitutional status in the *Health Services* case. With anticipation, workers await affirmation by the Supreme Court of the strike as an essential element of collective bargaining, and as such, an exercise of *Charter* section 2(d) freedom of association.[60]

---

57 *Woods Task Force Report*, above note 38 at 129.

58 *Ibid.* at 138.

59 *Ibid.* at 3–4.

60 In *British Columbia Teachers' Federation v. British Columbia Public School Employers' Association*, [2009] B.C.J. No. 155, leave to appeal dismissed, [2009] S.C.C.A. No. 160, the BC Court of Appeal found the prohibition of politically motivated strikes during the term of a collective agreement (as opposed to those directed against the employer) to be a violation of *Charter* section 2(b) freedom of expression, but justifiable under *Charter* section 1. Although the Court declined to address the challenge under *Charter* section 2(d) freedom of association, in doing so it commented: "Strikes remain an integral feature of systems of collective bargaining in the private sector and they have also become a feature of public sector bargaining in British Columbia. In the light of *Health Services*, it is an open question whether a right to strike is within the ambit of the freedom of association guarantee. For the purposes of these reasons, I assume that a right to strike is included within the *Charter* guarantee in principle. The question then is whether the statutory restriction on the right to strike consequent on the 1984 [BC *Labour Code*] redefinition is within reasonable limits." (MacKenzie J. at para. 41.) Even more intriguing is his assertion at para. 40 that

> [i]n *Health Services* (at para. 75) McLachlin C.J. endorsed the principle, taken from the dissenting reasons of Dickson C.J. in . . . [the *Alberta Reference*], that the ability "[t]o form and organize unions, even in the public sector, must include freedom to pursue the essential activities of unions, such as collective bargaining and strikes, subject to

E. FROM DUTY TO BARGAIN TO DUTY TO CONSULT: ARE TRADE UNIONS CONSTITUTIONAL ACTORS?

Near the very outset of its judgment in the several paragraphs summarizing the legislation under attack, the Court makes the following observation:

> There was no meaningful consultation with unions before it became law. The government was aware that some of the areas affected by Bill 29 were of great concern to the unions and had expressed a willingness to consult. However, in the end, consultation was minimal. A few meetings were held between representatives of the unions and the government on general issues relating to health care. These did not deal specifically with Bill 29 and the changes that it proposed. Union representatives expressed their desire to be further consulted. The Minister of Health Services telephoned a union representative 20 minutes before Bill 29 was introduced in the legislative assembly to inform the union that the government would be introducing legislation dealing with employment security and other provisions of existing collective agreements. This was the only consultation with unions before the Act was passed . . .[61]

Was there a duty to consult, and if so, where was it rooted—in labour law or in constitutional law?

The concept of consultation as a facet of the employer's duty to bargain in good faith, even if not explicitly so framed, is not altogether alien to Canadian labour law. Indeed the duty to bargain has come a fair distance from its original conceptualization as an empty procedural vessel, epitomized in the land of its origin by Senator Walsh's folksy quip to a somewhat dubious Congress:

> When employees have chosen their organization, when they have selected their representatives, all the bill proposes to do is to escort them to the door of the Employer and say, "Here they are, the legal representatives of your employees." What happens behind those doors is not enquired into, and the bill does not inquire into it.[62]

---

reasonable limits." Without doubt this is an overly expansive reading of the current chief justice's reference to that earlier dissent—but indicative of the position an appellate jurist anticipates the Supreme Court will take on the right to strike as an exercise of *Charter* section 2(d).

61 *Health Services*, above note 1 at para. 7.

62 (1935) 79 Congressional Record 7660, referenced in Bernard Adell, "The Duty to Bargain in Good Faith" (Kingston: Queen's University Industrial Relations Centre, 1980) and cited in part in *Health Services* above note 1 at para. 99.

In a now classic exposition of the duty to bargain in good faith, Archibald Cox discerned four purposes propelling its enactment: first, to reduce industrial conflict and the incidence of strike action; second, to enhance the employer's legal duty to recognize the union as representative of its employees; third, to implement the "basic philosophy" of the Act to further collective over against individual bargaining and so elevate labour to the status of an equal partner with the employer in determining conditions and terms of work at the workplace; fourth, to enhance the institution of collective bargaining as "a rational process of persuasion."[63] As Cox noted, of these purposes, only the first two were formally enacted into law, and although he was dubious whether the last two could be assimilated into the culture of a free market economy, later developments in American labour law went far to buttress the statutory duty.[64]

Despite some false starts,[65] Canadian labour boards too have infused the duty to bargain in good faith with robustness, and even substantive content. Although they may not yet have gone so far as to formally espouse the principle of "equal partnership,"[66] they have firmly entrenched the concept of "a rational process of persuasion" as the footing upon which the collective bargaining superstructure rests.[67] Most tellingly, they have imposed upon the employer a positive obligation arising during the negotiation process, to disclose to the union any corporate decision or near-decision taken in the boardroom which would affect the structure of the bargaining unit and alter the bargaining rights of the union.[68] A duty to consult by another name? Perhaps.

---

63 Archibald Cox, "The Duty to Bargain in Good Faith" (1958) 71 Harv. L. Rev. 1401, excerpted in Bernard Adell *et al.*, *Labour and Employment Law, Cases, Materials and Commentary*, 7th ed. (Toronto: Irwin Law, 2004) at 394–76.

64 In *Re Noranda Metal Industries Ltd.*, [1975] 1 Can. LRBR 145 BCLRB, Chair Paul Weiler summarizes the American doctrine as follows: "Negotiation nourished by full and informal discussion stands a better chance of bringing forth the fruit of a collective bargaining agreement than negotiation based on ignorance and deception" (at 162).

65 See Earl Palmer, "The Myth of Good Faith in Collective Bargaining" (1966) 4 Alta. L. Rev. 409.

66 See Brian Langille's critical assessment in "Equal Partnership in Canadian Labour Law" (1983) 21 Osgoode Hall L.J. 496; and Brian Langille & Patick Macklem, "Beyond Belief: Labour Law's Duty to Bargain" (1988) 13 Queen's L.J. 62.

67 "The duty reinforces the obligation of an employer to recognize the bargaining agent, and beyond this somewhat primitive though important purpose, it can be said that the duty is intended to foster rational, informed discussion thereby minimizing the potential for "'unnecessary' industrial conflict . . ." *Re DeVilbiss (Canada) Ltd.* (1976), 76 CLLC, No. 1609 [OLRB], Vice-Chair Adams at 405.

68 *Re Consolidated Bathurst Packaging Ltd.*, [1983] O.L.R.B. Rep. 1411.

In *Health Services*, the Court endorses this labour law doctrine without question but under the rubric of "consultation," speaking as it does of "[t]he fundamental precept of collective bargaining—the duty to consult and negotiate in good faith[69] . . . which lies at the heart of collective bargaining."[70] This is a duty which lies upon all employers, *ergo* upon the government *qua* employer. Although in formulation novel, this is pure labour law. Yet, the Court had made the point earlier that the case before it was one against the government *qua* legislator, not employer.[71] So, how did the language of "consultation," a term not native to Canadian labour law, come into the Court's labour law analysis, and what is its source? It can only be from its constitutional jurisprudence.

I began my discussion of this issue by referencing the Court's evident disapprobation early on in its judgment of the government's failure to consult the aggrieved trade unions in any meaningful sense prior to the introduction of legislation which severely impinged on their collective bargaining rights. The Court returns to this failing at the conclusion of its judgment. It acknowledges that the principle of parliamentary sovereignty admits of no such stricture upon the Legislature's law making authority,[72] but hastens to add that it is upon government that such an obligation lies in the pre-legislative ramping up process leading to legislative enactment.

It does so by reframing the obligation as a factor going to the minimal impairment inquiry under the *Oakes*[73] test. The government is criticized for presenting no evidence whatsoever "[w]hy there was no consultation with the unions about the range of options open to it."[74] There was "[n]o meaningful bargaining or consultation" prior to passage of the legislation despite the desire "[r]epeatedly expressed" by trade union representatives to consult the government, yet "[c]onsultation never took place."[75] This failing on the part of government in orchestrating the speedy passage[76] of "[a]n important and significant piece of labour legislation" with "[t]he potential

69 *Health Services*, above note 1 at para. 97.

70 *Ibid.* at para. 98. And see also para. 107: "[T]he collective right to good faith negotiations and consultation."

71 *Ibid.* at para. 88.

72 *Ibid.* at para. 157: "Legislators are not bound to consult with affected parties before passing legislation."

73 *R. v. Oakes*, [1986] 1 S.C.R. 791.

74 *Health Services*, above note 1 at para. 158.

75 *Ibid.* at para. 159.

76 The Act came into force three days after receiving first reading in the Legislature. *Ibid.* at para. 160.

to affect the rights of employees dramatically and unusually"[77] was central to the Court's ultimate conclusion. The government had failed the minimal impairment test, leading inexorably to the conclusion that the offending provisions of the Act could not meet the justificatory demands of *Charter* section 1.[78] This is pure constitutional law. And its origins?

One has to turn to another historically disenfranchised and vulnerable minority—and government's relationship to it—to discover the seedbed of a duty to consult: the Aboriginal peoples of Canada. In a trilogy of judgments handed down in 2004 and 2005,[79] the Supreme Court confirmed as a principle of constitutional law that a duty lies upon the Crown to consult Aboriginal peoples whenever the Crown or its licensee purports to take up or otherwise interfere with the use and enjoyment of lands subject to existing Aboriginal and treaty rights.[80] This duty is rooted in the Crown's assertion of exclusive jurisdiction over Aboriginal peoples and their lands under the *Constitution Act, 1867*,[81] a jurisdiction which engages the "honour of the Crown" in all its dealings with the Aboriginal peoples. The duty requires of the Crown "[m]eaningful good faith consultation" and a willingness to be accommodative following such consultation before taking action contrary to Aboriginal treaty or other existing rights.[82] Here we see the language of "consultation" which has crept into *Health Services* both as a restraint upon government as legislator in the constitutional sense, and as a restraint upon government as employer in the labour law sense.

This interrelationship of the two bodies of jurisprudence can be confusing, but need not be so when properly grasped. As a general principle, "[t]here subsists a requirement that the provisions of the Act preserve the process of good faith consultation fundamental to collective bargaining. That is the bottom line."[83] This is a directive to government as legislator, and it will be brought up short whether the scrutinized legislation, which is found to be lacking, governs labour relations in the private sector, where

77 *Ibid.* at para. 160.

78 *Ibid.* at para. 161.

79 *Haida Nation v. British Columbia (Minister of Forests)*, [2004] 3 S.C.R. 511 [*Haida Nation*]; *Taku River Tlingit First Nation v. British Columbia (Project Assessment Director)*,[2004] 3 S.C.R. 550; and *Mikisew Cree First Nation v. Canada (Minister of Canadian Heritage)*, [2004] 3 S.C.R. 550.

80 Such rights are constitutionally entrenched in Part II of the *Constitution Act, 1982*, above note 3 (Rights of the Aboriginal Peoples of Canada at s. 35(1)).

81 Above note 18 at s. 91(27)—Indians, and Lands reserved for the Indians.

82 See in particular, *Haida Nation*, above note 79 at paras. 17–19, 27, 39, and 53.

83 *Health Services*, above note 1 at para. 107.

employers are not themselves directly subject to *Charter* restraint in their collective bargaining relationships; or as here where it governs the public sector, where government itself acts as employer.

In the latter instance though, the two bodies of jurisprudence are conflated, for whenever the government as employer fails "[t]o consult and negotiate in good faith"[84] in the labour law sense, then *pace* the Court,[85] in its capacity as State actor it can only be said simultaneously to have engaged in conduct violative of *Charter* section 2(d), which now conclusively embraces the institution of collective bargaining.

However, in whichever capacity the government is acting, the Court will thrust upon it the duty to consult trade unions as the chosen representatives of workers whenever the process of bargaining collectively in good faith with the objective of entering into a collective agreement "[h]as been, or is likely to be, significantly and adversely affected"[86] in a manner

> [s]o substantial that it interferes not only with the attainment of the union members' objectives (which is not protected), but with the very process that enables them to pursue these objectives by engaging in meaningful negotiations with the employer.[87]

Granted, the political science physiology of the duty to consult is not identical to that in the case of the Aboriginal peoples which, as we have noted, is rooted in the honour of the Crown. By way of contrast, in the collective bargaining context it rests upon the executive branch of our tripartite constitutional structure. Yet, given the political reality of the party system which dominates our polity—a system of government best described as executive parliamentarianism—imposition of such a duty upon the executive has the practical effect of hobbling the legislative branch in the exercise of its sovereign right to legislate.[88]

---

84 *Health Services*, above note 1 at para. 97.

85 *Ibid.* at para. 88. "This case is concerned with an attack on government legislation, there is no allegation that the government of British Columbia, *qua* employer, violated s. 2(d) of the *Charter*."

86 *Ibid.* at para. 92.

87 *Ibid.* at para. 91.

88 Indeed, this is the rationale given by Charron J. for rejecting the concept of a duty to consult lying upon government. *Ibid.* at para. 179. And compare to *Reference Re Canada Assistance Plan (B.C.)*, [1991] 2 S.C.R. 3 where, on the same reasoning, Sopinka J., speaking for the Court, shielded the federal Cabinet from the attempt by British Columbia to bridle it with the administrative law legitimate expectations doctrine.

There is an alternative way of viewing the consultation directive. One could read the judgment as a restraint upon the undoubted discretion of the executive to shape governmental policy. Read in that light, one could draw upon that developing body of jurisprudence in which the Court has resurrected the theory of robust curial restraint of executive abuse of discretion, famously articulated by Rand J. in *Roncarelli v. Duplessis*.[89] Justice Binnie has been the catalyst here, and in two ingeniously crafted judgments[90] has breathed new life into this iconic, but hitherto neglected pillar of our public law jurisprudence. His first foray was in the *Mount Sinai Hospital* case where, in reaffirming that the administrative law doctrine of legitimate expectations is limited to procedural relief,[91] he noted parenthetically that the English jurisprudence, which allows for substantive relief, comprises "[t]he greatest intrusion by the courts into public administration" and represents

> [a] level of judicial intervention in government policy that our courts, to date, have considered inappropriate in the absence of a successful challenge under the *Canadian Charter of Rights and Freedoms*.[92]

The passage clearly hints at bridging the divide between procedural and substantive relief in the administrative law legitimate expectations jurisprudence by recasting the challenge to governmental action in *Charter* language where legitimate expectations may well attract substantive relief. There was no *Charter* issue in *Mount Sinai Hospital*. Yet, Binnie J. was able to see to it that the underlying facts were "[r]ecycled in the abuse of discretion analysis"[93] and so granted substantive relief to the legitimate expectations of the aggrieved hospital center. Only McLachlin C.J. endorsed Binnie J.'s analysis and creative disposition—the other five judges on the panel arrived at the same result in a more pedestrian manner.

In the *CUPE* case, Binnie J. was able to attract the support of five members of the Court in an even more daring application of the abuse of discretion doctrine.[94] There, he determined that in declining "[t]o select

89 [1959] S.C.R. 121.

90 *Mount Sinai Hospital*, above note 29; and *CUPE v. Ontario (Minister of Labour)*, [2003] 1 S.C.R. 539 [*CUPE*].

91 *Mount Sinai Hospital*, *ibid.* at paras. 22–38.

92 *Ibid.* at paras. 26–27.

93 *Ibid.* at para. 52.

94 The five members were Gonthier, Iacobucci, Arbour, LeBel, and Deschamps JJ. Chief Justice McLachlin and Major and Bastarache JJ. dissented. Of the Court, the chief justice and Gonthier, Iacobucci, Major, and Bastarache JJ. had also sat with Binnie J. on *Mount Sinai Hospital*, as had L'Heureux-Dubé J., who has since retired.

arbitrators from candidates who were qualified not only by their impartiality, but by their expertise and general acceptance in the labour relations community," the minister had failed "[t]o exercise his power of appointment in a manner consistent with the purpose and objects of the statute"[95] or in Rand's phraseology, outside of "[t]he perspective within which a statute is intended to operate,"[96] namely, "[t]hat of a legislative measure that seeks to achieve industrial peace."[97] Is it that much of a leap from failure to exercise a ministerial discretion in accord with a legislative mandate so as to attract substantive relief, to failure to exercise the power of governance within the bounds of the *Charter* so as to attract substantive relief? I think not. In each case, abuse of discretion analysis drives the outcome.

Are trade unions constitutional actors, then? In all probability they are, although the Court has not fully worked out such status conceptually. The constitutional status of trade unions may not be entrenched explicitly in the Constitution itself as is the case with the Aboriginal peoples,[98] but it is a necessary concomitant of the Court's determination to welcome the institution of collective bargaining into the *Charter* tent. There were already hints in its earlier jurisprudence that the Court would accord to trade unions a "most favoured nation" status under the *Charter*. In *Dunmore*, Bastarache J. had adverted to "[t]he dynamic and evolving role of the trade union in Canadian society,"[99] observing that in *Delisle*, L'Heureux Dubé J. had noted that

> [t]he right to freedom of association must take into account the nature and importance of *labour* associations as institutions that work for the betterment of working conditions and the protection of the dignity and collective interests of workers in a fundamental aspect of their lives: employment.[100]

From these earlier appreciations of the centrality of trade unions to freedom of association, it is but a small step to vest them with a consultative constitutional role where the institution of collective bargaining, now

95 *CUPE*, above note 90 at para. 49.

96 *Roncarelli v. Duplessis*, above note 89 at 140.

97 *CUPE*, above note 90 at para. 94.

98 See the *Constitution Act, 1982*, Part II, Rights of the Aboriginal Peoples of Canada; and contrast the *Constitution Act, 1867*, s. 91.24, where "Indians" are a passive constitutional "class of subjects."

99 *Dunmore*, above note 30 at para. 38.

100 *Ibid.* at para. 37, citing *Delisle v. Canada (Deputy Attorney General)*, [1999] 2 S.C.R. 989 at para. 6 [emphasis in the original].

Charter protected, is at risk. Yet, a caveat. Grant of such status presumes maturity in its exercise. Trade unions must act at the standard expected in the exercise of their consultative function, lest by overreaching they lose the trust which the Court has placed in them, and with it, any meaningful consultative role in shaping the institution of collective bargaining as a constitutional artifact.

F. CONCLUSION

Does broad-sweeping caselaw, such as *Health Services*, which consciously considers normative outcomes as its justificatory criterion, have the necessary staying power to ensure the stability, predictability, and uniformity of result so central to the rule of law? I think so, and I look forward with anticipation to the Supreme Court of Canada's continuing exegetical encounter with the *Charter* section 2(d) freedom of association as it considers the raft of cases certain to follow in the wake of *Health Services.* [101]

I commenced my paper with a simple observation: that the *Health Services* case joins "that constellation of recent public law decisions of the

101 Apart from the decision of the Ontario Court of Appeal in *Fraser*, above note 49, currently under reserve by the Court on appeal, to date these include two decisions of the Quebec Superior Court in *Confédération des syndicats nationaux v. Québec (Procureur général)*, [2007] QCCS 5513 (declaring legislation which unilaterally reconfigures public sector bargaining units unconstitutional) and in *Confédération des syndicats nationaux v. Québec (Procureur général)*, [2008] QCCS 5076 (declaring public sector legislation which deprives certain classes of workers of their employee status unconstitutional); the decision of the Ontario Superior Court in *Mounted Police Association of Ontario v. Canada (Att. Gen.)* (2009), 96 O.R. (3d) 20 (declaring unconstitutional provisions of the RCMP regulations which impose upon members a management-dominated entity to represent their interests in collective bargaining) [appeal adjourned *sine die* until thirty days after the Supreme Court of Canada releases its decision in *Fraser*, above note 49, in order to allow Parliament to address the declaration of invalidity; see 2010 ONCA 635]; the decision of the New Brunswick Court of Queen's Bench in *C.U.P.E. et al. v. New Brunswick*, 2009 NBQB 164 (declaring the exclusion of casual workers from public sector legislation unconstitutional); the decision of the Alberta Labour Relations Board in *Old Dutch Foods*, above note 29 (declaring the absence of a compulsory dues shop union security provision (Rand formula) in the governing legislation unconstitutional); the decision of the Ontario Labour Relations Board in *Re Independent Electricity Market Operator*, OLRB File nos. 3322-03-R and 2118-04-R, November 2009 (declaring provisions of the governing legislation which unilaterally terminate construction industry bargaining rights and collective agreements unconstitutional); and the decision of the Quebec Labour Relations Board in *Travailleurs et travailleuses unis de l'alimentation et du commerce Section locale 501 c. Johanne L'Écuyer & Pierre Locas et Procureur général du Québec*, 2010 QCCRT 0191 (16 April 2010) (declaring statutory limitations on the right of farm workers to bargain collectively unconstitutional). Doubtless, there will be others.

Court in which it quite dramatically has reversed what had been heretofore understood to be settled law." I conclude by observing that, happily, it is a constellation which burns brightly in the galaxy of the *Canadian Charter of Rights and Freedoms*.[102]

Addendum

As this volume was going to press, the Supreme Court of Canada released its decision in *Ontario (Attorney General) v. Fraser*, 2011 SCC 20. The Court reversed the Ontario Court of Appeal and upheld the constitutional validity of the legislation there in dispute. However, in doing so, contrary to my expectation, it eschewed discussion of the right to strike which I address in this article at section D.

102 Not all commentators consider the Court deserving of kudos for its revised freedom of association doctrine laid down in *Health Services*. Particularly harsh in his criticism is Professor Brian Langille, who takes the Court to task for what he perceives to be its failure to appreciate not only the history of domestic labour law and its interaction with trade unionism and the institution of collective bargaining and the international labour law regime; but also fundamental jurisprudential concepts underlying and contained within the *Charter*, in particular the distinction between "rights" and "freedoms." His sustained critique (see his papers cited above at notes 39 and 50) is premised largely on the proposition that in grounding the right to collective bargaining in *Charter*, s. 2(d), rather than in *Charter*, s. 15 (equality rights), the Court's analysis is deeply flawed. That proposition is, to say the least, contentious and has failed to gain widespread acceptance amongst commentators. See the other papers cited above at notes 39 and 50.

PART FIVE

The Old and the New: Criminal Law and International Law

Criminal Justice in the McLachlin Court: Many More Kudos Than Brickbats

DON STUART*

A. INTRODUCTION: THE COURT IS MORE BALANCED THAN PARLIAMENT

It is invidious and somewhat presumptuous for one individual to be assessing ten years of jurisprudence of the McLachlin Court in a field where the Court is so active and there is clearly room for difference of opinion. The Court itself has often been deeply divided on key rulings. This is not surprising given the Court's daunting docket and the difficulty of the issues that come before it. I also bear in mind Dickson C.J.'s view on a visit to Queen's University that academics are very good at criticizing but less impressive at making constructive suggestions as to how the law should be developed.

Any review of the Court's record in criminal law must be contrasted to the ever insatiable appetite for law and order politics by politicians of all stripes and the consequent unremitting legislative trend to toughen the criminal law. There are no votes in being soft on crime. Politicians fall over each other to be tough even though crime rates are falling and criminologists have made it very clear that stiffer and fixed penalties in the United States and elsewhere have had no effect on reducing crime.[1] Parliament has in the past decade produced a torrent of overly complex and unnecessarily

* Many of the views expressed in this paper first appeared in articles or annotations in the Criminal Reports or one of the following books: Don Stuart, *Canadian Criminal Law: A Treatise*, 5th ed. (Toronto: Carswell, 2007); Don Stuart, *Charter Justice in Canadian Criminal Law*, 5th ed. (Toronto: Carswell, 2010).

1 Tony Doob & Cheryl Webster, "Sentence Severity and Crime: Accepting the Null Hypothesis" in Michael Tonry, ed., *Crime and Justice Research: A Review of Research* (Chicago: University of Chicago Press, 2003) at 45–195 [Doob & Webster].

RÉSUMÉ

Cet article passe en revue les principales décisions de la Cour en matière de droit substantif, de pouvoirs policiers, de procédure et de preuve. La conclusion est à l'effet que la Cour a généralement opté pour une approche beaucoup plus équilibrée comparativement à la loi qui demeure inflexible et à l'ordre du jour des politiciens visant à rendre le système de justice criminelle de plus en plus rigide et plus complexe. La Cour a adopté des normes spécifiques d'application de la *Charte* exigeant la preuve de la faute et de son caractère volontaire, et a par ailleurs insisté sur les droits procéduraux et à la tenue d'un procès juste et équitable. Contrairement aux tendances récentes de la Cour suprême des États-Unis rejetant la règle d'exclusion, notre plus haut tribunal a récemment adopté des mesures réparatrices au caractère fortement discrétionnaire excluant la preuve obtenue, aux fins du maintien de l'ordre, par violation marquée des normes établies par la *Charte*, et ce, nonobstant la gravité du crime. L'auteur plaide pour le ré-examen des décisions en matière du droit de corriger un enfant, de la notion de détention donnant ouverture à la protection de la *Charte*, du manque de balises lors d'interrogatoires menés par les services policiers, du refus de permettre la remise en liberté sur parole afin de conserver le soutien du public et, finalement, le ré-examen des décisions appliquant les lois sur la protection des victimes du viol concernant les antécédents sexuels entre la victime et l'accusé.

pro-state amendments to the *Criminal Code*. Had I been reviewing the legislative record, I would have been mostly critical.

In contrast, our highest Court has followed a much more balanced approach. What follows is a review of the Court's major rulings on substantive law, police powers, trial procedure, and evidence. Many are the Court's major pronouncements as guardians of the *Canadian Charter of Rights and Freedoms*. However there are also many important non-*Charter* decisions. My conclusion will be that Canadians should be generally proud of our highest Court's often quite distinctive jurisprudence. Our justices are all serious, hard-working, and thoughtful. Some justices, particularly McLachlin C.J. and Binnie and Charron JJ., are especially clear and eloquent in their expression. The Court has helped ensure that we have a criminal justice system that tries to protect the procedural and fair trial rights of the accused against the tyranny of the majority. Procedural and fair trial rights of those accused of crime tend to be unpopular until the moment you, or someone you care about, gets charged. It will be suggested that there is, in some cases, a need for clarification, and in other cases, that law and order politics have crept into several key rulings of the McLachlin Court which ought to be reconsidered. I will express strong criticism of the Court's rulings in the following areas:

- the right to discipline children;
- the meaning of detention for section 9 and 10 *Charter* purposes;
- limits on police interrogation;
- denying bail to maintain public confidence; and
- rape shield laws.

B. SUBSTANTIVE LAW

1) Objective Fault for Crimes—Marked Departure but No Individual Factors: *Beatty*

In its major ruling in *R. v. Beatty*[2] on dangerous driving,[3] the Court held that, in contrast to civil liability for negligence, principles of fundamental justice under section 7 of the *Charter* require proof of a marked departure from the objective norm. The majority judgment of Charron J. is written in language which applies to any crime requiring objective fault where there is a risk of imprisonment. A uniquely and welcome Canadian constitutional standard is now firmly in place for *Criminal Code* crimes based on objective fault. Fault for the criminal sanction can sometimes be justified on the reasonable person standard but the marked departure standard provides a vehicle for restraint. Both Charron J. for the majority and McLachlin C.J. in her concurring opinion expressly call for restraint, a voice so seldom heard in Parliament. Justice Charron also breaks new ground in determining that sometimes it may be necessary to consider the accused's mental state to decide whether the reasonable person would have been aware of the risk.

The decision in *Beatty* on the facts seems, however, startlingly lenient. The accused veered off into the wrong lane and killed three persons in the oncoming lane. He had no explanation for his conduct other than that he had been working in the sun and may have lost consciousness or fallen

---

2 (2008), 54 C.R. (6th) 1 (S.C.C.).

3 *Criminal Code*, R.S.C. 1985, c. C-46, s. 249.

asleep. The Court held that a momentary lack of attention was not a marked departure from the objective norm. Given *Beatty*, expect defences of momentary inattention to be frequently advanced against dangerous driving charges. In *Beatty* there was no evidence of any other bad driving. However most major vehicle accidents happen in a flash and proof of a pattern of bad driving that day will often be hard to come by with witnesses long gone down the highway. Given the lenient ruling on the facts, one can expect that many serious accidents on highways, even those involving fatalities, will now almost always have to be dealt with by charges of careless driving under provincial laws, which usually[4] require proof only of ordinary negligence. The maximum penalties are typically as low as six months.

Beatty should lead to new arguments and welcome change in other contexts. If a marked departure from the objective norm is the minimum *Charter* standard for criminal offences resulting in imprisonment this should also govern all so-called crimes based on predicate offences. It is regrettable that the Court ever invented the complex analysis of offences based on predicate offences. The list of such crimes is, according to the Supreme Court, unlawful act manslaughter (section 22(5)(a)),[5] unlawfully causing bodily harm (section 269),[6] aggravated assault (section 268)[7] and, in lower court rulings, assault causing bodily harm (section 267).[8] These crimes presently require, in addition to proof of the fault for the underlying crime, only proof of dangerousness in the form of objective foresight of non-trivial bodily harm. There is no marked departure test unless the predicate offence is based on negligence.[9] What of a momentary lapse of attention in a hunting accident where a hunter accidentally shoots his best friend, who has taken off his red hunting jacket, and is charged with unlawful act manslaughter? Consistent with the reasoning in *Beatty*, the trier of fact should also not leap from a consequence of death or harm to the conclusion that there was a marked departure from the objective norm deserving of punishment as a crime.

It is disappointing that in *Beatty*, the Court would decide that no personal factors short of incapacity can be considered on an objective fault test

---

4 In Ontario, however, there has long been a requirement of proof of conduct deserving of punishment: *R. v. Beauchamp*, [1953] 16 C.R. 270 (Ont. C.A.), not followed in *R. v. Jacobsen* (1964), 44 C.R. 24 (B.C.C.A.).

5 *R. v. Creighton*, [1993] 3 S.C.R. 3.

6 *R. v. DeSousa*, [1992] 2 S.C.R. 944.

7 *R. v. Godin*, [1994] 2 S.C.R. 484.

8 See, for example, *R. v. Dewey* (1998), 2 C.R. (5th) 232 (Alta. C.A.), and *R. v. Emans* (2000), 35 C.R. 386 (Ont. C.A.).

9 *R. v. Gossett*, [1993] 3 S.C.R. 76.

on the basis that this had been determined in *R. v. Creighton*.[10] *Creighton* was a narrow 5:4 decision. Chief Justice Lamer in dissent argued for inclusion of personal factors the accused could not control (thereby excluding intoxication as a factor). The Lamer type of approach has been favoured by most scholars[11] since the insight of Professor H.L.A. Hart that punishment can sometimes be justified on an objective standard but only where the accused had the capacity and ability to conform to the norm. The Court itself has consistently decided since *Creighton* that the reasonable person standard for defences—those such as self-defence,[12] duress,[13] and necessity,[14] and long before *Creighton*, provocation as a partial defence to murder[15]—should be modified to require that some individual factors be considered. Here the reasonable person is usually considered in the context of the accused's real situation and experience. In the law of the tort of negligence, the Court has had no problem taking personal factors into account. In establishing the tort of negligent investigation in *Hill v. Hamilton-Wentworth Regional Police Services Board*,[16] McLachlin C.J., writing for the 6:3 majority, observes that

> The general rule is that the standard of care in negligence is that of the reasonable person in similar circumstances. In cases of professional negligence, this rule is qualified by an additional principle: the defendant must "live up to the standards possessed by persons of reasonable skill and experience in that calling."[17]

---

10 [1993] 3 S.C.R. 3.

11 See, for example, Eric Colvin & Sanjeev Anand, *Principles of Criminal Liability*, 3d ed. (Toronto: Thomson Carswell, 2007) at 65–68 and 221–22.

12 *R. v. Lavallee*, [1990] 1 S.C.R. 852 at para. 51 ("what the accused reasonably perceived, given her situation and experience" as a battered wife).

13 *R. v. Hibbert*, [1995] 2 S.C.R. 973 at para. 60 ("particular circumstances and human frailties of the accused").

14 *R. v. Latimer*, [2001] 1 S.C.R. 3 at para. 32 ("situation and characteristics of the particular accused" although, surprisingly, not when considering the proportionality requirement). In *R. v. Ruzic*, [2001] 1 S.C.R. 687, the Court thankfully adopts the modified approach to proportionality for duress but does not address the inconsistency with *Latimer*. The distinction is suspect. In *R. v. Kong* (2006), 40 C.R. (6th) 231 (S.C.C.), the Supreme Court, in adopting the conclusion of the dissenting Wittmann J., implicitly rejected the fully articulated view of Fraser C.J.A. in the Alberta Court of Appeal in the Court below that the strictly objective proportionality test of *Latimer* should also be adopted for self-defence. It is thus clear that the *Latimer* ruling is the anomaly in need of reconsideration.

15 *R. v. Hill*, [1986] 1 S.C.R. 313 at 331 ("ordinary factors" such as "sex, age or race" but not "idiosyncratic characteristics" such as "exceptionally excitable, pugnacious or in a state of drunkenness").

16 (2007), 50 C.R. (6th) 279 (S.C.C.).

17 *Ibid*. at para. 69.

Why then are we not to take into account the abilities, experience, and real situation of the driver in assessing objective fault in a dangerous driving case? Are we, for example, to hold a driver of a large transport truck, or a police officer at the wheel of a cruiser, criminally responsible for bad driving only on the standard of the average, reasonable driver? The current approach appears quite unrealistic and will likely continue to be ignored in trial courts with live witnesses. Can a trier of fact really overlook such obvious factors as age and experience?

2) Marked and Substantial Departure for Criminal Negligence (section 216): *R. v. J.F.*

For a stunning period of some twenty years since *R. v. Tutton*,[18] the Court was equally divided on what to make of the special fault element of "criminal negligence" as defined in section 216 ("shows wanton or reckless disregard for the lives or safety of other persons"). This is the fault required for those charged with criminal negligence causing bodily harm (section 220), criminal negligence causing death (section 221), or manslaughter by criminal negligence (section 222(5)(b)). The McIntyre group called for a marked departure from the objective norm test. The Wilson cohort asserted an approach of minimal subjective awareness with heavy reliance placed on the concept of wilful blindness. Most provincial courts before and after *Tutton* have applied the marked departure from the objective norm test. Yet some courts have insisted that this is a form of fault higher than that required for dangerous driving.[19]

In *R. v. J.F.*[20] Fish J., speaking for the Court,[21] resolved the *Tutton* issue in favour of an objective approach but he added a new wrinkle. Criminal negligence under section 219 is held to require a marked *and substantial* departure from the objective norm rather than just the marked departure required as a *Charter* standard for other objective crimes.

This new normative distinction between degrees of gross negligence seems likely to confuse lawyers, judges, and jurors. Be that as it may, until otherwise advised, there are now three degrees of objective fault requirements:

18 [1989] 1 S.C.R. 1392.

19 See, for example, *R. v. Palin* (1999), 135 C.C.C. (3d) 119 (QC C.A.) and *R. v. J.L* (2006), 204 C.C.C. (3d) 324 (Ont. C.A.).

20 2008 SCC 60.

21 The issue involved inconsistent verdicts and there was a dissent on the issue of remedy.

1) due diligence with the onus reversed for regulatory offences as a matter of common law presumption under *R. v. City of Sault Ste. Marie*[22] or as a *Charter* standard where there is a risk of imprisonment.[23] This is a standard of simple negligence like that long applied for the tort of negligence;
2) a marked departure from the objective norm as a *Charter* standard for crimes with objective fault requirements (*Beatty*) (gross negligence); and
3) a marked and substantial departure from the objective norm for offences based on criminal negligence under section 219 (*J.F.*) (apparently worse than gross negligence).

It would have been preferable for the Court in *J.F.* to have stuck with the notion that the fault requirements for the underlying crimes in question in a manslaughter case of criminal negligence and failing to provide necessities of life are essentially the same—a marked departure from the objective norm—and then to have pointed to the higher stigma, and especially the higher penalties declared by Parliament for criminal negligence. This way, future jurors could be advised that criminal negligence is the more serious offence carrying a larger penalty. The standard of fault for criminal negligence under section 216 should not be different from the Supreme Court's approach to dangerous driving in *Beatty*. The Court should avoid undue subtlety and rest content with the standard of a marked departure from the objective norm. In the case of bad driving there is no need to have two overlapping crimes of dangerous driving with one based on criminal negligence causing death or bodily harm. The Court should hold that they involve substantially the same elements such that the rule against multiple convictions should be applied. So too with manslaughter by unlawful act and manslaughter by criminal negligence.[24]

Justice Fish in *J.F.* confirms, as did Charron J. earlier for the majority in *Beatty*, that negligence is a form of fault and not part of the *actus reus*. That is clarifying and consistent with the definition of forms of fault in modern criminal codes, and also with the *Charter* standard in *Martineau*[25] that intentional conduct must be punished more than negligent conduct.[26]

---

22 [1978] 2 S.C.R. 1299.

23 *Re B.C. Motor Vehicle Act*, [1985] 2 S.C.R. 486.

24 See too Larry Wilson, "Too Many Manslaughters" (2007) 52 Crim. L.Q. 433, and *R. v. Tschetter*, 2009 ABPC 125 (this case involved a cement truck driver going through red light and killing five. He was guilty of manslaughter by unlawful act of dangerous driving; other charges stayed as overlapping).

25 [1990] 2 S.C.R. 633.

26 Professor Hamish Stewart, "*Beatty*: Towards a Coherent Law of Penal Negligence" (2008) 54 C.R. (6th) 45, would, however, prefer the marked departure test to be considered as

3) Using Criminal Sanction with Restraint: *Labaye, Boulanger, Dery*

Chief Justice McLachlin has led the Supreme Court in asserting a meaningful act requirement in two high profile contexts.

The first was the Court's startling decision in *R. v. Labaye* (2005)[27] that under section 210(1) of the *Criminal Code*, the operator of a Montreal swingers club was not guilty of keeping a common bawdy house for the practice of indecency. Chief Justice McLachlin, for a 7:2 majority,[28] held that in order to establish indecent criminal conduct, the Crown must prove beyond a reasonable doubt that two requirements have been met. The first is

> that, by its nature, the conduct at issue causes harm or presents a significant risk of harm to individuals or society in a way that undermines or threatens to undermine a value reflected in and thus formally endorsed through the Constitution or similar fundamental laws by . . . (a) confronting members of the public with conduct that significantly interferes with their autonomy and liberty, (b) predisposing others to anti-social behaviour, or (c) physically or psychologically harming persons involved in the conduct.

The second requirement is "that the harm or risk of harm is of a degree that is incompatible with the proper functioning of society." This two-branch test had, the Court held, to be "applied objectively and on the basis of evidence . . . In this way the basic criminal law requirements of fair notice to potential offenders and clear enforcement standards to police would, it was hoped, be satisfied."[29]

Clarity is a noble and commendable goal when our courts review the exercise of massive state power against the individual. Whether this deliberate shift from the test of the community standard of tolerance[30] to objectively defined harm has, or will, achieve greater clarity or better law is however debatable. The dissenters, LeBel and Bastarache JJ., were clearly not convinced.

---

part of the *actus reus* but concedes that this position is now water under the bridge.

27 (2005), 34 C.R. (6th) 1 (S.C.C.) [*Labaye*]. See too the companion case of *R. v. Kouri* (2005), 34 C.R. (6th) 86 (S.C.C.) (group sex on a dance floor behind a plastic curtain).

28 Major, Binnie, Deschamps, Fish, Abella, and Charron JJ. concurred. LeBel and Bastarache JJ. dissented.

29 Labaye, above note 27 at paras. 62–63.

30 *R. v. Butler*, [1992] 1 S.C.R. 452, *R. v. Tremblay*, [1993] 2 S.C.R. 932, and *R. v. Mara*, [1997] 2 S.C.R. 630.

Under the community standard of tolerance test, the Supreme Court has previously decided that strippers dancing for men while the men masturbate is not indecent,[31] whereas lap dancing in strip clubs is indecent.[32] Presumably these decisions should now be revisited under the objective harm criteria. Given the new approach in *Labaye* there is now a strong argument that charges for keeping a common bawdy house can no longer be sustained based on acts of prostitution in private. The majority in *Labaye* stress that no one paid for the group sex. But what about the membership fee?

The emphasis on evidence of objective harms appears, as the dissenters point out, to be at odds with the Court's earlier decision in *R. v. Malmo-Levine; R. v. Caine*[33] in rejecting *Charter* challenges to marijuana laws. Justices Gonthier and Binnie held for the majority that the principle that a criminal sanction could be validly imposed only where there is a reasonable risk of harm could not be elevated to a principle of fundamental justice guaranteed by section 7 of the *Charter*. The majority reasoned, over the sole dissent of Arbour J., that there was no societal consensus that criminal law should always be based on harm and that the harm principle could not be identified with sufficient precision to yield a manageable standard. Of course, the ruling in *Labaye* is not a declaration of a *Charter* standard. Parliament is therefore free to change it, but has not yet moved to do so.

The second restraint decision occurs in *R. v. Boulanger* (2003).[34] The Supreme Court was unanimous in holding that the crime of breach of trust by a public officer in section 122 of the *Criminal Code* required use of public office for a purpose other than public good and also conduct representing a serious and marked departure from standards expected of an individual in the accused's position of public trust. Neither requirement was met where an official had asked for a full police accident report involving his daughter.

This is an intriguing judgment capable of application in contexts other than the offence of breach of trust by a public official. The most startling aspect of the judgment is the Court's further determination that the accused should have been acquitted because the conduct lacked the level of seriousness required for the offence. The chief justice invokes in aid her remark for the majority in *Creighton*[35] that the "law does not lightly brand a person as a criminal." That was the basis on which the Court in *Creighton* required crimes

---

31 *Tremblay, ibid.*

32 *Mara*, above note 30.

33 [2003] 3 S.C.R. 571.

34 (2006), 39 C.R. (6th) 1 (S.C.C.).

35 [1993] 3 S.C.R. 3.

based on objective fault requirements to involve a marked departure from the norm. The problem here is that the Court in *Boulanger* had just determined that the breach of trust offence requires subjective *mens rea*. The *Creighton* dictum was not really germane. The *Boulanger* decision nevertheless applies this principle of restraint to the *actus reus* component. It appears to be saying that judges can acquit if they decide that the conduct was trivial. This has the look of the doctrine of *de minimis non curat lex* not previously fully endorsed by the Supreme Court.[36] The chief justice is certainly and commendably on a roll in leading the Court to interpreting criminal offences with restraint.

In *R. v. Déry* (2006),[37] the Supreme Court decided that there is no offence of attempting to conspire to commit a substantive offence. For the Court, Fish J. indicated that the Crown had proposed an *actus reus* for attempted conspiracy that, if not open-ended, was much broader than the *actus reus* of counselling. There was no conspiracy, which requires actual agreement and genuine intent. According to Fish J., "it has never been the goal of the criminal law to catch all crime 'in the egg' as Canada's Attorney General had put it. In this sense, conspiracies are criminalized when hatched, and they can only be hatched by agreement." Indeed,

> by its very nature, an agreement to commit a crime in concert with others enhances the risk of its commission. Early intervention through the criminalization of conspiracy was therefore both principled and practical. Likewise the criminalization of attempt was warranted because its purpose is to prevent harm by punishing behaviour that demonstrates a substantial risk of harm. When applied to conspiracy, the justification for criminalizing attempt is lost, since an attempt to conspire amounts, at best, to a risk that a risk will materialize.

Justice Fish held that "the criminal law does not punish bad thoughts that were abandoned before an agreement was reached, or an attempt made, to act upon them."[38]

4) Vagueness, Overbreadth, and Arbitrariness: *Clay, Canadian Foundation*

In two high profile cases, the Supreme Court of Canada has confirmed that criminal laws can be challenged under section 7 of the *Charter* as vague,

36 But see Arbour J. dissenting in *Canadian Foundation for Children*, below note 42.

37 (2006), 43 C.R. (6th) 94 (S.C.C.).

38 *Ibid.* at paras. 47–51.

overbroad, or arbitrary. However, the rejection of these challenges in these cases shows once again that the Supreme Court has set such high thresholds for such challenges that the doctrines are toothless.[39]

In *R. v. Clay*,[40] a 6:3 majority[41] of the highest Court quickly rejected arguments that marijuana laws offended section 7 of the *Charter* on the ground they are too broad or arbitrary in criminalizing marijuana possession but not the smoking of carcinogenic tobacco. The effects on the accused of enforcement were not grossly disproportionate. Two of the trio of dissenting judges, Lebel and Deschamps JJ., were of the view in short separate opinions that the offence of marijuana possession should be struck down because the criminal law in question was an arbitrary and disproportionate response to this social problem.

In the other controversial ruling a slightly differently composed majority of the Court in *Canadian Foundation for Children* (2004)[42] rejected vagueness, overbreadth, and equality challenges to section 43 of the *Criminal Code* (often referred to as the "spanking law") justifying reasonable force by parents and teachers in correction of children. Chief Justice McLachlin, who wrote for the 6:3 majority,[43] did so by radically reading down section 43 so that it now authorizes only minor physical correction by parents, but not by teachers, of children between the ages of two and twelve.

In her persuasive dissent, Arbour J. engaged in a comprehensive review of existing section 43 jurisprudence, emphasizing the number of acquittals. She decided that the phrase "reasonable under the circumstances" in section 43 violated children's security of the person interest under section 7 of the *Charter* and that the principle was too vague to be in accordance with fundamental justice.

According to the majority, "reasonableness" is an objective standard commonly used by the criminal law and a matter of interpretation by judges.

---

39 A rare Supreme Court acceptance of an overbreadth argument occurred in *R. v. Demers*, [2004] 2 S.C.R. 489. *Criminal Code* provisions respecting those found unfit to stand trial were struck down as overbroad since they did not allow an absolute discharge for people deemed to be permanently unfit who did not pose a significant threat to public safety.

40 [2003] 3 S.C.R. 735.

41 Gonthier and Binnie JJ., McLachlin C.J., Iacobucci, Major, Bastarache JJ. concurred.

42 *Canadian Foundation for Children, Youth and the Law et al. v. Attorney General of Canada et al.* (2004), 16 C.R. (6th) 203 (S.C.C.) [*Canadian Foundation for Children*]. See critical comments by Tim Quigley, "Correction of Children: The Supreme Court Divided" (2004) 16 C.R. (6th) 286, and Sanjeev Anand, "Reasonable Chastisement: A Critique of the Supreme Court's Decision in the Spanking Case" (2003) 42 Alta. L. Rev. 871.

43 Gonthier, Iacobucci, Major, Bastarache, and LeBel JJ. concurred.

In this case regard had to be paid to expert evidence before the trial court by way of affidavit, strong social consensus as to what should be permitted, and international treaty obligations against corporal punishment of children. The chief justice found a solid core of meaning sufficient to establish a zone in which discipline risked criminal sanction. To arrive at this conclusion the majority read in the following limits:

- Section 43 exempts from criminal sanction only minor corrective force of a transitory and trifling nature;
- it does not apply to corporal punishment of children under two or teenagers as children must be capable of learning from correction;
- degrading, inhuman, or harmful conduct is not protected;
- discipline by the use of objects or blows or slaps to the head is unreasonable;
- teachers may reasonably apply force to remove a child from a classroom or secure compliance with instructions, but not merely as corporal punishment;
- conduct must be corrective, which rules out conduct stemming from the caregiver's frustration, loss of temper, or abusive personality;
- it is wrong for law enforcement officers or judges to apply their own subjective views of what is "reasonable under the circumstances": the test is objective;
- the question must be considered in context and in light of all the circumstances of the case; and
- the gravity of the precipitating event is not relevant as that would be focusing on punishment not correction.[44]

Although this defence was interpreted by McLachlin C.J. for the majority to allow minor corrective force against children between the ages of two and twelve, this was not considered to amount to age discrimination. The dignity of those children had not been offended in the manner contemplated by section 15(1) as interpreted in *Law*.[45] Although children often experience disempowerment and vulnerability, when balanced against the limited amount of force permitted and the consequences for the family and educational settings if there were prosecutions, section 43 was neither arbitrarily demeaning nor discriminatory. The power was firmly grounded in the actual needs and circumstances of the children.

---

44 *Canadian Foundation for Children*, above note 42 at para. 40.

45 *Law v. Canada*, [1999] 1 S.C.R. 497.

In dissent, Binnie and Deschamps JJ. found that section 43 violated equality protections under section 15. Justice Binnie was of the view that the violation could be saved under section 1 for parents and those standing in the place of parents, but not for teachers. Justice Deschamps found that the violation could not be demonstrably justified in either case. She was also concerned about the vagueness of the defence.

There are significant problems with the majority's interpretation of section 43. Why should parents have a right to assault, within the majority's parameters, children between the ages of two and twelve, giving parents a defence not available to any other accused charged with assault? Clinicians working with highly disturbed and potentially dangerous children have, for example, no such special protection. The age limit amounts, as does any age-based line, to arbitrary demarcation especially for children close to those ages. It is arbitrary to decide that a minor slap to the head is criminal, but a minor slap to the bottom is not. The majority's criteria are full of uncertainty. What is a parent, a social worker, a prosecutor, or a judge to make of tests such as "capable of correction"? Fundamentally problematic is that, unlike normal defences to assault—such as self-defence—the Court allows no consideration of proportionality given that the gravity of the precipitating event is stated to be irrelevant. It doesn't matter whether the child spat or burned down the barn. Additionally, the assaulter also cannot be acting out of frustration or anger, so we are left with justifying coolly premeditated minor physical correction without reference to context. Trial judges will surely have difficulty in not considering the precipitating event. Explaining all this to the public is daunting. It is dangerous to advise parents and those standing in their place that they can lightly hit young children with impunity.[46]

The Supreme Court is certainly in disarray in protecting *Charter* rights for children. In *Canadian Foundation for Children*, the Court holds that the well known "best interests of the child" principle is not a principle of fundamental justice under section 7. Yet very recently in *R. v. D.B.*,[47] respecting sentencing of young offenders as adults, Abella J. held for a 5:4 majority

---

46 Early indications are that the tougher criteria read in by the majority are not always being faithfully applied, so judicial subjectivity and acquittals are still a major problem. See, for example, *R. v. Kaur* (2004), 27 C.R. (6th) 224 (where a mother lightly tapped cheek of her twelve-year-old daughter because of her silent treatment), criticized by Drew Mitchell, "*R. v. Kaur*: Child Assault and Children's Rights after *Foundation for Children*" (2005) 27 C.R. (6th) 230, *R. v. Plummer* (6 June 2006), (Ont. Ct. J.) (involving the use of a belt to correct, but causing no pain), and *R. v. Swan* (13 March 2008), (Ont. S.C.J.) (involving throwing a teenager into a truck to rescue her from a party and from her boyfriend).

47 2008 SCC 25, [2008] 2 S.C.R. 3.

(that included McLachlin C.J.) that section 7 guarantees a "principle of a presumption of diminished moral capacity in young persons . . . fundamental to our notions of how a legal system ought to operate."[48]

The majority constitutionalized a presumption of lower sentences for young offenders. This new *Charter* standard could be utilized to mount a new *Charter* challenge to section 43. The strongest *Charter* challenge is that of age discrimination, especially now that the Court has backed away from the stringent *Law* test for section 15 in *R. v. Kapp*.[49]

Parliament should repeal section 43 so that Canada can catch up to the worldwide trend to abolish the right to physically discipline children.[50] Canada is in breach of our obligations under the Convention on the Rights of the Child.[51] Section 43 is an embarrassment to Canada in the United Nations and to our reputation as human rights leaders. By 2008, twenty-six countries, including almost all those in Europe and New Zealand, had enacted laws prohibiting corporal punishment of children. If Canada followed this trend, defences available to parents, caregivers, and teachers would be those available to anyone charged with assault, include the defences of self-defence, duress, and necessity, and the emerging doctrine of *de minimis non curat lex*. The power of physical restraint would be limited to that presently authorized in section 27, which allows physical force where reasonably necessary to prevent crime or harm to others, and which involves an assessment of what the child actually did. I suspect that Parliament will not touch this controversial issue. All the more pity that the Supreme Court missed its privileged opportunity under the *Charter*.

5) Presumption of Strict Liability for Regulatory Offences and Stays for Officially Induced Error of Law: *City of Levis v. Tetreault*

According to LeBel J. for a unanimous court of seven in *City of Levis v. Tetreault*,[52] the provincial offences in question in the case did not place the burden of proving *mens rea* on the prosecution and included no expression

---

48 *Ibid.* at para. 68.

49 (2008), 58 C.R. (6th) 1 (S.C.C.).

50 Corinne Robertshaw, co-ordinator of the Repeal 43 Committee, has long campaigned for this result, supported by groups who work with children across the country. See online: www.repeal43.org.

51 As pointed out by Arbour J. in *Canadian Foundation for Children*, above note 42 at paras. 186–88.

52 *Lévis (City) v. Tétreault; Lévis (City) v. 2629-4470 Québec Inc.*, [2006] 1 S.C.R. 420 [*Lévis*].

of the legislature's intent to create an absolute liability offence. There was common law presumption under *Sault Ste Marie* that they should be characterized as strict rather than absolute, thereby affording the accused the chance of proving a due diligence defence. Absolute liability offences still exist, but they have, confirmed LeBel J., become an exception requiring clear proof of legislative intent. In deciding between strict and absolute liability, LeBel J. expressly rejected the inquiry added by Cory J. in *R. v. Pontes* (1995)[53] of asking whether the legislature intended to make a due diligence defence available. According to LeBel J., this made the approach harder to apply and it was better to return to the clear framework of *Sault Ste Marie.*[54] This is an important clarification and also emphasizes that the Supreme Court's presumption of strict liability for regulatory offences is alive and well.

Justice LeBel also accepted the Lamer view[55] that this defence should be recognized as a limited but necessary exception to the rule that ignorance of the law cannot excuse the commission of an offence for both regulatory and true crimes, and even where the offence is one of absolute or strict liability.[56] It operated as an excuse similar to entrapment: "The wrongfulness of the act is established. However, because of the circumstances leading up to the act, the person who committed it is not held liable for the act in criminal law. The accused is thus entitled to a stay."[57]

The Supreme Court's full acceptance of the defence of officially induced errors of law to any offence is welcome as a just exception to the rigid rule that ignorance of the law is no excuse. The criteria laid out bring welcome clarity. However, lingering doubts[58] remain as to whether the full Court was wise to accept the Lamer remedy of a stay rather than a full defence. A full defence was the choice of remedy of all courts below and in the United States where the defence developed. The analogy drawn to entrapment is not convincing. Is an act in reasonable reliance on erroneous official advice not lacking in culpability and entitled to an acquittal like other substantive defences?

---

53 [1995] 3 S.C.R. 44.

54 *Lévis*, above note 52 at para. 19.

55 Chief Justice Lamer was the only justice to address this issue in *R. v. Jorgenson*, [1995] 4 S.C.R. 55.

56 *Lévis*, above note 52 at paras. 22–24.

57 *Ibid.* at para. 25.

58 Christine Boyle & Sam de Groot, "The Responsible Citizen in the City of Levis: Due Diligence and Officially Induced Error of Law" (2006) 36 C.R. (6th) 249 at 254, see the Court as having otherwise attempted to reinforce the principle that ignorance of law is no excuse despite its "relatively weak policy rationales" and also having an onerous view of civic obligation to know the law.

6) Physical Involuntariness: *Daviault, Stone, Ruzic*

The constitutional requirement of voluntariness was established in *R. v. Daviault*[59] to allow for a defence of extreme intoxication akin to automatism and insanity for so-called general intent crimes. This *Charter* standard of voluntariness presently appears to apply, contrary to well established common law, even where there was negligence in getting into that state. That should be a matter for reconsideration if and when the Supreme Court gets to hear a *Charter* challenge to Parliament's attempt in section 33.1 of the *Criminal Code* to remove the *Daviault* defence from crimes of general intent involving bodily integrity, including sexual assault. Section 33.1 is presently considered to be unconstitutional in the Ontario Superior Court.[60]

A most disappointing decision of the Supreme Court occurred in *R. v. Stone*[61] where for a 5:4 majority, Bastarache J. reversed the full onus of proof for automatism. The majority simply asserted a new common law presumption of voluntariness. In dissent, Binnie J. pointed out that no Crown counsel had argued for this reversal of the presumption of innocence. Justice Lebel in *R. v. Ruzic*[62] later made it clear in *obiter* that there is no reverse onus in normal physical involuntariness cases, such as a motorist sliding on black ice, and that *R. v. Stone* applies only to that subset of voluntariness cases arising from dissociated states.

The majority in *Stone* also asserted a presumption that automatism cases are normally to be treated as cases of no criminal responsibility on account of mental disorder. The harshness of that ruling which makes automatism acquittals now highly unlikely is softened by the revised *Criminal Code* regime for disposition hearings following findings of no criminal responsibility on account of mental disorder, and especially by McLachlin C.J.'s ruling in *Winko v. Forensic Psychiatric Institute*[63] that the least restrictive alternative must be considered.

---

59 [1994] 3 S.C.R. 63.

60 *R. v. Jensen*, [2000] O.J. No. 4870 (S.C.J.), with the *Charter* matter unfortunately ducked on the further appeal: (2005), 27 C.R. (6th) 240 (Ont. C.A.). Concerns as to the fairness of the law where both parties were very drunk were expressed by Duncan J. in *R. v. Polo Cedano* (2005), 27 C.R. (6th) 251 (S.C.J.).

61 [1999] 2 S.C.R. 290.

62 [2001] 1 S.C.R. 687. See too *R. v. Swaby* (2001), 44 C.R. (5th) 1 (Ont. C.A.), and *R. v. Luedecke* (2009), 61 C.R. (6th) 139 (Ont. C.A.) (sexsomnia to result in NCRMD finding).

63 [1999] 2 S.C.R. 625.

7) Moral Involuntariness as *Charter* Standard for Defences: *Ruzic*

Canada has had one of the most restrictive defences of duress since 1892. It took the power of the *Charter* and the important judgment of LeBel J. in *R. v. Ruzic*[64] to widen section 7 by striking down the requirements in section 17 that the threats be immediate and by someone present. The Court declared a new *Charter* standard for defences for those acting in a situation of "moral involuntariness." That test, taken from George Fletcher's writings, is confusing, especially as morality is not in issue when dealing with an excuse and the accused cannot really be said to have been acting without exercising choice. Nevertheless it is salutary that the Supreme Court has erected a *Charter* standard to strike down laws which deny the accused a defence in a situation of truly agonizing choice. The standard ought to be applied in other cases—for example, to extend the *Criminal Code* section 37 defence of preventing force being applied to one under one's protection to a defence of preventing force against any third party.

Section 17 still denies a duress defence to a long list of offences. When the Court gets to consider such a *Charter* challenge to such limits, it may well be advised to turn to the *Charter* standard that the law cannot be arbitrary, as suggested by Laskin J. in the Ontario Court of Appeal in *Ruzic*.[65]

8) Significant Contributing Cause Test: *Nette*

In *R. v. Nette* (2001),[66] the Supreme Court unanimously decided for the first time that the *Smithers*[67] test of "a contributing cause outside the *de minimis* range" applies not only to manslaughter, but also to second-degree murder. Justice Arbour, writing for a 5:4 majority,[68] sought to further clarify the *Smithers* approach. Her preference was to avoid Latin and to phrase the test positively as a test of "a significant contributing cause," which is seen to be the same standard as that in *Smithers*. However, she gave trial judges discretion as to terminology in explaining the standard. Justice L'Heureux-Dubé for the minority[69] objected that the language of a significant contributing

64 [2001] 1 S.C.R. 687.

65 (1998), 41 O.R. (3d) 1 (C.A.)

66 (2001), 48 C.R. (5th) 197 (S.C.C.). See Sanjeev Anand, "Determining Causal Standards for First Degree Murder in the Wake of *Nette*: When Does the Substantial Cause Test Apply?" (2002) 46 Crim. L.Q. 282.

67 *Smithers v. The Queen* (1977), [1978] 1 S.C.R. 506.

68 Iacobucci, Major, Binnie, and LeBel JJ. concurred.

69 McLachlin C.J., Gonthier and Bastarache JJ. concurred.

cause would raise the standard and saw no reason for doing so. In *Nette* there is no mention of *Charter* standards for causation. The *Charter* issues were not argued and thus remain open in the highest court.

A 5:4 majority normally determines the legal issue. Here the majority preference is for "a significant contributing cause." However in *Nette*, Arbour J.'s ruling that the causation terminology is to be left to the trial judge to decide sets the scene for considerable confusion. This would appear to allow trial judges to instruct on the majority formulation of "a significant contributing cause" or the minority *Smithers* test of a not insignificant contributing cause.

Justice L'Heureux-Dubé was compelling in suggesting that the test of a significant cause *is* a higher standard than the *Smithers* test. However, she was not persuasive in seeing no reason to change the *Smithers* test which had "stood the test of time." A unanimous Supreme Court decision is hard to get reconsidered. There has been substantial criticism of the approach which the Court has chosen to ignore. The *Smithers* test throws the net far too wide in cases of multiple causation, independent cause, and even thin skull cases.

The Court should unambiguously decide, as has Doherty J. for the Ontario Court of Appeal,[70] that a meaningful test of causation in criminal law requires that there be at least proof of a significant cause. Regrettably, the decision in *Nette*, where causation was not a viable issue, has muddied rather than clarified. It will not be the last word on causation.

C. PROCEDURE

1) Police Powers to Stop, Search, and Question: *Mann, Clayton, Kang-Brown*

I recently published a lengthy paper on these controversial topics.[71] I will not repeat the detailed case analyses here but will stick to major themes and more recent developments.

Chief Justice Dickson was at pains in *Hunter v. Southam*[72] to declare that the Courts were "the guardians of the Constitution" and that the *Charter* "is intended to constrain governmental action inconsistent with those rights; it is not itself an authorisation for governmental action."[73]

70 *R. v. Talbot* (2007), 44 C.R. (6th) 176 (Ont. C.A.).

71 "*Charter* Standards for Investigative Powers: Have the Courts Got the Balance Right?" (2008) 40 Sup. Ct. L. Rev. 3–53.

72 [1984] 2 S.C.R. 145 [*Hunter*].

73 *Ibid.* at 110–11.

Collins confirmed that an illegal search was a violation of section 8 of the *Charter*. Yet ever since the majority *Dedman* decision,[74] various majorities of the Supreme Court have decided that RIDE stop programs could be authorized by the courts without enabling legislation, thereby doing an end-run around that vision by using the so-called ancillary powers doctrine to create a number of carefully limited new police powers, such as those of entry to investigate a 911 call,[75] strip searches,[76] investigative detention,[77] and roadblock stops.[78]

When Abella J. turned to ancillary powers doctrine to authorize roadblock stops for a 6:3 majority of the Supreme Court in *Clayton*, she adopted the following statement of Doherty J. in the court below:

> Where the prosecution relies on the ancillary power doctrine to justify police conduct that interferes with individual liberties, a two-pronged case specific inquiry must be made. First, the prosecution must demonstrate that the police were acting in the exercise of a lawful duty when they engaged in the conduct in issue. Second, and in addition to showing that the police were acting in the course of their duty, the prosecution must demonstrate that the impugned conduct amounted to a justifiable use of police powers associated with that duty.[79]

The key issue is almost always that of the second test of justifiability which, according to *Dedman*, is that of "reasonably necessary" given the liberty interest involved.

Many writers[80] argue that the problem with the ancillary powers doctrine is that it is a fact-specific *ex post facto* inquiry that is vague and speculative and contrary to the rule of law. It should be left to Parliament to allow for full democratic processes to come up with "clear, prospective and comprehensive rules that will serve to confine and structure the exercise of police discretion."[81]

---

74 [1985] 2 S.C.R. 2. Chief Justice Dickson registered a strong dissent, expressing concerns about the rule of law and the supremacy of Parliament.

75 *R. v. Godoy*, [1999] 1 S.C.R. 311.

76 *R. v. Golden*, [2001] 3 S.C.R. 679.

77 *R. v. Mann*, [2004] 3 S.C.R. 59.

78 *R. v. Clayton* (2007), 47 C.R. (6th) 219 (S.C.C.).

79 *Ibid.* at para. 22.

80 See, for example, Stephen Coughlan, "Common Law Police Powers and the Rule of Law," Annotation to *Clayton* (2007), 47 C.R. (6th) 222, and James Stribopoulos, "The Limits of Judicially Created Police Powers: Investigative Detention after Mann" (2007) 52 Crim. L.Q. 299.

81 Stribopoulos, *ibid.*, at 326.

Both citizens and the police officer need to know what state powers are in advance. But what of Parliament's inaction on the many recommendations by the Law Reform Commission of Canada in the 1980s to clarify police powers? And what of Parliament's record of the past fifteen years of almost always favouring arguments of law and order expediency and listening to like-minded lobby groups—in this context, police and prosecutors? There is now a significant body of caselaw since the *Charter* to suggest that, in applying the ancillary powers doctrine, our independent judges do a much better job than Parliament in balancing minority rights of accused against the interests of law enforcement and public safety. This reality has caused me to change flags on this issue.

In its rulings on police powers to use dog sniffers in *R. v. Kang-Brown*[82] and *R. v. A.M.*,[83] the Supreme Court of Canada, after reserving for eleven months, was deeply divided with four sets of reasons delivered in each case. In the result, a 6:3 majority holds that the police use of a sniffer dog in *Kang-Brown* to find drugs in the bag of someone getting off a bus and in *A.M.* in a knapsack after a search of an entire school violated section 8 of the *Charter* and should be excluded.

In terms of establishing *Charter* standards for future cases, the decisions in *Kang-Brown* and *A.M.* are unclear. All justices agree that a dog sniff is a search for section 8 purposes. A further *ratio* may be distilled by compiling a box score of the views of each justice on the law and on the facts. On the law four justices—LeBel J., with Fish, Abella, and Charron JJ. concurring—hold that there is no common law power to use sniffer dogs on buses and in schools and that any departure from the *Hunter v. Southam*[84] reasonable and probable and warrant standards should be left to Parliament with subsequent *Charter* review by courts. Four justices—Binnie J., with McLachlin C.J., Deschamps and Rothstein JJ. concurring—resort to the ancillary powers doctrine to hold that the police have a common law power to conduct a warrantless search using sniffer dogs on the basis of individualized reasonable suspicion. They also hold that this standard complies with section 8 although less than the *Hunter* standard. Justice Bastarache agrees but, expressly *obiter*, is of the view that a generalized reasonable suspicion standard will sometimes be sufficient. On the facts, Deschamps and Rothstein JJ., and Bastarache J. separately, dissented in both cases and found no violations.

82 2008 SCC 18.

83 2008 SCC 19.

84 *Hunter*, above note 72.

It would appear that five justices are already on record as favouring a reasonable suspicion standard for the use of dog sniffers on buses and in schools but there is regrettably no clear agreement as to what the test means. Since the LeBel cohort was concerned about departing from the reasonable and probable test it is clear that, with the retirement of Bastarache J., eight justices favour a *Charter* standard of at least individualized reasonable suspicion.

The Binnie test of individualized reasonable suspicion to limit the use of police sniffer dogs in routine criminal investigations is a well justified and pragmatically sound solution to making such a police power *Charter* compliant. Parliament has not bothered to attempt any regulation before. I also agree with Binnie J. that it seems far too late for the Court to now reject the use of the ancillary powers doctrine. The horse is well out of the barn.

The difference between reasonable and probable grounds and reasonable suspicion may be exaggerated and involve some dancing on a pin. The important and key aspect of the focus of all but one of the justices on an individualized standard is that police cannot just rely on police hunches which may mask arbitrariness and discriminatory behaviour, as long ago pointed out by Doherty J.A. in *R. v. Simpson.*[85]

The detailed determination by Binnie J. that there was no reasonable suspicion on the facts in *Kang-Brown* is much more persuasive than the view of Deschamps J. that suspicion was reasonably based on such cues as stares and rubbernecking. The Jetway program is a Royal Canadian Mounted Police (RCMP) adaptation of the Operation Pipeline program in the United States to use such profiling techniques in traffic stops to detect those carrying drugs. In Canada it has sometimes been justified as part of the law enforcement effort to find terrorists carrying explosives on buses, trains, and in airports, but it has clearly emerged as mostly a tool to go after young persons carrying illegal drugs. The US program was and is controversial because it is avowedly based on profiling techniques which encourage reliance on unreliable social cues (as in *Kang-Brown*) and in practice such invidious factors as race.[86] Here Kang-Brown was identified as East Indian. The police officer's assurance that racial profiling was not involved was meekly accepted.

---

85 (1993), 20 C.R. (4th) 1 (Ont. C.A.).

86 See especially David Tanovich, *The Colour of Justice. Policing Race in Canada* (Toronto: Irwin Law, 2006) at 91–95, and "A Powerful Blow against Police Use of Drug Courier Profiles" (2008) 55 C.R. (6th) 379.

2) Reasonable Expectation of Privacy (section 8): *Tessling, Patrick*

Reasonable expectation of privacy is of course the triggering device for *Charter* section 8 protection. Without this expectation, section 8 cannot be considered at all. I have been critical of earlier decisions of the Supreme Court in *R. v. Edwards*,[87] where the Court unduly favoured those with property interests, and *R. v. Tessling*.[88] In *Tessling*, Binnie J., for the Court, held that there was no reasonable expectation of privacy against rudimentary forward looking infrared (FLIR)[89] imaging of the outside of houses as this did not go to the biographical core or lifestyle and was simple information. The Court distanced Canada from the decision of Scalia J. for the United States Supreme Court in *Kyllo v. U.S.* (2000)[90] that FLIR imaging of the outside of houses is unconstitutional. Our highest Court does expressly enter two caveats: (1) FLIR information alone is insufficient ground to obtain a search warrant, and (2) if, as the Court expects, FLIR technology improves,[91] the constitutional issue will have to be reconsidered.

Judging from a recent Canadian Forces' video which shows FLIR technology swooping down to highlight details of an individual's conduct otherwise completely out of human sight, *Tessling* already looks to be obsolete. In any event, Binnie J., in his judgments in *Kang-Brown* and *R. v. Patrick*,[92] has fortunately significantly de-emphasized his approach in *Tessling*. The vitality of section 8 has been restored.

In *Patrick*, Binnie J., for a 6:1 majority, reached a carefully reasoned and justified compromise on the issue of police searches of garbage. There is no reasonable expectation of privacy and therefore no section 8 protection for garbage placed for collection. There are careful caveats. Section 8 still protects against searches of garbage where the public has no access to it or where the garbage disposer shows an intent to limit access, for example by locking up the garbage. These limits are likely to be relied on in the future by defence counsel attempting to distinguish the reach of *Patrick*. The Court was clear that nothing in *Patrick* is to be read as affecting the section 8 protection as it has previously put in place for perimeter searches[93]

87 [1996] 1 S.C.R. 128.

88 [2004] 3 S.C.R. 432.

89 FLIR stands for "forward looking infrared." It is an imaging technology that senses infrared radiation.

90 533 U.S. 27 (2000).

91 See online: www.gs.flir.com/videos/Land_TV3000.wmv.

92 [2009] 1 S.C.R. 579.

93 *R. v. Kokesch*, [1990] 3 S.C.R. 3.

and "knock on" searches.[94] This is important as some lower courts have appeared reluctant to apply the full rigour of such rulings. The Supreme Court implicitly returned to the approach of La Forest J. in *R. v. Wong*[95] who required the question of whether there was a reasonable expectation of privacy to be asked in a neutral way. In *Patrick* the majority of the Alberta Court of Appeal was rebuked for simply asserting that drug dealers can have no reasonable expectation of privacy. The proper question was whether householders putting out garbage for collection have a reasonable expectation of privacy in the contents of those bags. The majority did not accept the more generous compromise of Abella J. that there is a reduced reasonable expectation of privacy in garbage placed out for collection and that there should be a reduced section 8 standard of reasonable suspicion. The majority approach leaves no *Charter* protection against random searches by police of garbage set out for collection. Since the *Charter* does not apply in this context, presumably the police could use sniffer dogs for such searches (in marked contrast to the Court's reasonable suspicion standard for police dog sniffers in buses and schools).

3) Detention (sections 9 and 10): *Mann, Grant, Suberu*

Courts have had difficulty with the *Therens* notion of psychological detention where police are questioning a person short of arrest or physical detention. Decisions, including those of the Supreme Court, have been inconsistent. In *R. v. Mann*,[96] Iacobucci J. for the Court pronounced *obiter* that

> The police cannot be said to "detain" within the meaning of ss. 9 and 10 of the *Charter*, every suspect they stop for purposes of identification, or even interview. The person who is stopped will in all cases be "detained" in the sense of "delayed" or "kept waiting." But the constitutional rights recognized by ss. 9 and 10 of the *Charter* are not engaged by delays that involve no significant physical or psychological restraint.[97]

This remark resulted in disarray in lower court decisions.[98]

---

94 *R. v Evans*, [1996] 1 S.C.R. 8.

95 (1990), 1 C.R. (4th) 1 (S.C.C.).

96 (2004), 21 C.R. (6th) 1 (S.C.C.).

97 *Ibid.* at para. 19.

98 See Don Stuart, "The Ontario Court of Appeal Blinks and Flutters: Less Exclusion and Inconsistency in Stop Cases" (2007) 49 C.R. (6th) 282; Ken Lockhart, "The Urgent Need for the Supreme Court to Reconsider the Meaning of Detention for *Charter* Purposes" (2008)

In *R. v. Grant*,[99] handed down on 17 July 2009 after having reserved for fifteen months, the Supreme Court revised its approach to psychological detention. A lengthy and detailed joint opinion of McLachlin C.J. and Charron J. (LeBel, Fish, and Abella JJ. concurring, but with Binnie and Deschamps JJ. dissenting), concluded that the following should be the approach to detention:

> 1. Detention under ss. 9 and 10 of the *Charter* refers to a suspension of the individual's liberty interest by a significant physical or psychological restraint. Psychological detention is established either where the individual has a legal obligation to comply with the restrictive request or demand, or a reasonable person would conclude by reason of the state conduct that he or she had no choice but to comply.
> 2. In cases where there is no physical restraint or legal obligation, it may not be clear whether a person has been detained. To determine whether the reasonable person in the individual's circumstances would conclude that he or she had been deprived by the state of the liberty of choice, the court may consider, inter alia, the following factors:
>   (a) The circumstances giving rise to the encounter as would reasonably be perceived by the individual: whether the police were providing general assistance; maintaining general order; making general inquiries regarding a particular occurrence; or, singling out the individual for focussed investigation.
>   (b) The nature of the police conduct, including the language used; the use of physical contact; the place where the interaction occurred; the presence of others; and the duration of the encounter.
>   (c) The particular characteristics or circumstances of the individual where relevant, including age; physical stature; minority status; level of sophistication.[100]

According to the majority, the inquiry into whether there was psychological detention is objective:

> the focus must be on the state conduct in the context of the surrounding legal and factual situation, and how that conduct would be perceived by a reasonable person in the situation as it develops. The objective nature of this inquiry recognizes that the police must be able to know when a

---

58 C.R. (6th) 222; and Matthew Oleynik, "What Makes or Breaks a *Charter* Argument on a Pedestrian Stop" (2008) 54 Crim. L.Q. 79.

99 [2009] 2 S.C.R. 353 [*Grant*].

100 *Ibid*. at para. 44.

> detention occurs, in order to allow them to fulfill their attendant obligations under the *Charter* and afford the individual its added protections. However, the subjective intentions of the police are not determinative. While the test is objective, the individual's particular circumstances and perceptions at the time may be relevant in assessing the reasonableness of any perceived power imbalance between the individual and the police, and thus the reasonableness of any perception that she had no choice but to comply with the police directive.[101]

The majority noted that effective law enforcement is highly dependent on the co-operation of members of the public.

> Section 9 of the *Charter* does not require that police abstain from interacting with members of the public until they have specific grounds to connect the individual to the commission of a crime. Nor does section 10 require that the police advise everyone at the outset of any encounter that they have no obligation to speak to them and are entitled to legal counsel.

However, the Court also determined that there are *Charter* limits.

> The notion of psychological detention recognizes the reality that police tactics, even in the absence of exercising actual physical restraint, may be coercive enough to effectively remove the individual's choice to walk away from the police. This creates the risk that the person may reasonably feel compelled to incriminate himself or herself. Where that is the case, the police are no longer entitled simply to expect cooperation from an individual. Unless . . . the police inform the person that he or she is under no obligation to answer questions and is free to go, a detention may well crystallize and, when it does, the police must provide the subject with his or her section 10(b) *Charter* rights.[102]

In this case, the majority held that Grant was detained within the meaning of sections 9 and 10 of the *Charter*. Three officers were on patrol at midday in an area in Toronto where four schools had a history of student assaults, robberies, and drug offences occurring over the lunch hour. Two plainclothes officers driving an unmarked car noticed the accused, an eighteen-year-old black man, walk by them in a manner they considered suspicious. He stared at them and fidgeted with his coat and pants. They asked

101 *Ibid.* at paras. 31–32.

102 *Ibid.* at paras. 38–39.

a uniformed officer to have a chat with him. That officer was on directed patrol to maintain high visibility presence to provide student reassurance and to deter crime. The uniformed officer stood in his path, told him to keep his hands in front, and began to question him. He was first asked "what was going on" and for his name and address. The plainclothes officers arrived and stood behind the uniformed officer. The questioning turned to whether or not he had ever been arrested and whether "he had anything on him he that he shouldn't." He responded that he had a small amount of marijuana. When the officer asked if there was anything else, he admitted he had a firearm. The officer arrested him and searched him, finding marijuana and a loaded revolver.

The Court held the preliminary questioning was a legitimate exercise of police powers. However, while the act of telling the accused to keep his hands in front of him might not, in isolation, be sufficient to indicate detention, consideration of the entire context of what transpired from that point forward led to the conclusion that the accused was detained: "The sustained and restrictive tenor of the conduct after the direction to [the accused] to keep his hands in front of him reasonably supported the conclusion that the officers were putting him under their control and depriving him of his choice as to how to respond." Earlier,

> the encounter took on the character of an interrogation, going from general neighbourhood policing to a situation where the police had effectively taken control over the accused and were attempting to elicit incriminating information . . . Although [the] questioning was respectful, the encounter was inherently intimidating. The power imbalance was obviously exacerbated by [the accused's] youth and inexperience."

The police had engaged in a pointed line of questioning, his liberty was constrained, and he was in need of *Charter* protection associated with detention.[103]

The majority further found that the detention was arbitrary contrary to section 9 because the officers did not have legal grounds or reasonable suspicion to detain the accused prior to his incriminating statements. For first time, the Court thereby held that a detention without lawful authority is necessarily arbitrary contrary to section 9. This interpretation reflecting the rule of law is welcome in bringing section 9 jurisprudence in line with that under section 8.

---

103 *Ibid.* at paras. 45–52.

The majority in *Grant* also found a breach of Grant's right to counsel under section 10(b). As determined in the companion case of *R. v. Suberu*,[104] the section 10(b) right to counsel was held to arise immediately upon detention, whether or not the detention was solely for investigative purposes. The officers had not complied with section 10(b) as they did not believe they had detained him.

In dissent in *Grant*, Binnie J. voiced concerns as to the majority's approach to detention under sections 9 and 10 of the *Charter*. They had laid too much emphasis on the claimant's perception of psychological pressure, albeit as filtered through the eyes of the hypothetical reasonable person in the claimant's situation. As stated in *Grant*:

> A better and broader approach to detention would explicitly take into account (i) the objective facts of such encounters, whether or not evident to the person stopped . . . (ii) the perception of the police in initiating the encounter, whether or not evident to the person stopped, and (iii) whatever information the police possess[ed] at the time, which may or may not be known to the person stopped, as well as whatever change in the police perception occurs as the encounter develops.[105]

Justice Binnie identified a number of problems with the Court's reasonable person test for the purpose of determining when a simple interaction crystallizes into a detention. A problem in calibrating the "reasonable person" is to define exactly what information this fictional person possesses and what experience she brings to the assessment of the encounter. This was "of particular relevance to visible minorities who may, because of their background and experience, feel especially unable to disregard police directions, and feel that assertion of their right to walk away will itself be taken as evasive and subsequently argued by the police to be sufficient grounds of suspicion to justify a *Mann* detention."[106]

There is considerable force in Binnie J.'s arguments[107] and it is disappointing they did not carry the day. On the plus side it is salutary that the

---

104 [2009] 2 S.C.R. 460.

105 *Grant*, above note 99 at para. 180.

106 *Ibid.* at para. 169.

107 Tim Quigley, "Was It Worth the Wait? The Supreme Court's New Approaches to Detention and Exclusion of Evidence" (2009) C.R. (6th) 88 [Quigley, "Worth the Wait"]. This paper also prefers the Binnie position but see Stephen Coughlan, "Great Strides in Section 9 Jurisprudence" (2009) C.R. (6th) 75, who, on balance, favours the majority approach.

majority confirmed the Ontario Court of Appeal's ruling in *Grant* that the concept of psychological detention applies to both vehicle and pedestrian stops where there is a reasonable belief that there is no choice but to comply with a police request. Courts should not play down the coercive realities of all exchanges with police.

The problem with a sole focus on physical or psychological detention is, however, that this leaves one who naively or ignorantly thinks he is free to go without *Charter* protection. The test also encourages police to avoid section 9 and 10 rights by delaying arrest, and resorting to such strategies as telling the detainee she is free to leave when she is not and is suspected of criminal activity. These concerns would been addressed had the majority adopted as an alternative test that detention also occurs where police have a suspicion which has reached the point that they are attempting to obtain incriminating evidence, whether or not the person was aware of this reality. That was the compromise test carefully articulated by a majority of the Newfoundland Court of Appeal in *R. v. Hawkins*.[108] The Supreme Court certainly gives little justification for rejecting the wisdom of lower courts such as the Ontario Court of Appeal in *Moran*[109] that the perceptions of the police are important factors. It is doubtful whether the perceptions of the police will, as a practical matter, be able to be kept out of the *Grant* inquiry, especially as one of the stated factors to be considered is whether the individual has been singled out for focused investigation.

These general concerns about the revised *Grant* approach to detention are exacerbated by the majority ruling of the Supreme Court in the companion case of *Suberu* that in the circumstances Suberu was not detained. The police received a call that a man was attempting to use a stolen credit card at a liquor store in Cobourg and that the clerk was trying to stall the suspect. Officer R. arrived on the scene and saw that another officer was speaking to an individual at the cash register. Another individual, the accused, walked by him saying, "he did this, not me, so I guess I can go." The officer replied, "wait a minute, I need to talk to you before you go anywhere," and followed the accused outside to a parking lot. The accused sat in the driver's seat of a minivan and the officer engaged him in conversation, asking him questions about his connection to the events in the store. The accused indicated that the man in the shop was his friend and that the van belonged to the accused's girlfriend. Officer R. then received information

108 (1992), 14 C.R. (4th) 286 (Nfld. C.A.), rev'd in brief reasons [1993] 2 S.C.R. 1257.

109 (1987), 36 C.C.C. (3d) 225 (Ont. C.A.).

over the radio that two suspects who had used a stolen credit card in Belleville were driving a van. The description of the van and licence number matched the van in the parking lot and the officer saw shopping bags in the van. Officer R. arrested the accused, advised him of his right to counsel, questioned him, and searched his person and his purse. The accused was found guilty of possession of property obtained by crime and possession of stolen credit and debit cards.

It is hard to accept that Suberu was not detained as was the consensus in the courts below. The discrepancy between the ruling on the facts in *Grant* and that in *Suberu* will undoubtedly lead to uncertainty and protracted litigation. The concern about *Suberu* is that since the Court has determined that section 10(b) rights apply immediately to investigative detention, some courts will bend over backwards to find that there was no detention, as in *Suberu*. On the other hand, the ruling in *Grant* seems to find that detention arises the moment aggressive police questioning has crystallized into trying to obtain incrimination evidence. Surely, contrary to some recent pre-*Grant* rulings,[110] suspects are detained when police start to ask a person for identification to facilitate a criminal records search or search backpacks, whether the person is in a vehicle, place of public transit, or in the street.

4) Police Interrogation: *Oickle, Singh*

The principle of protection against self-incrimination once described by Lamer C.J. for the Supreme Court as the "organizing principle" of criminal law capable of growth[111] was later reduced to a principle of "limited application"[112] in a judgment written by Arbour J. The Court understandably came to realize that it could not be that the state can never compel an accused to incriminate herself as is the case with breathalyzer and DNA warrant laws.

---

110 See *R. v. Rajaratnam* (2006), 43 C.R. (6th) 280 (Alta. C.A.); *R. v. Lewis* (2007), 217 C.C.C. (3d) 82 (N.S.C.A.); and *R. v. L.B.*, (2007), 49 C.R. (6th) 245 (Ont. C.A.). Compare *R. v. Harris* (2007), 49 C.R. (6th) 220 (Ont. C.A.), with the majority holding no power to compel identification other than for traffic offences leading to a s. 8 breach. See also the persuasive analyses of Lane J. in *R. v. Powell* (2000), 35 C.R. (5th) 89 (pedestrian stopped for identification and records check arbitrarily detained), LaForme J. (as he then was) in *R. v. Ferdinand* (2004), 21 C.R. (6th) 65 (S.C.J.), and Jones J. in *R. v. D.(J.)* (2007), C.R. (6th) 292 (Ont. Ct. J.).

111 *R. v. P.(M.B.)*, [1994] 1 S.C.R. 555.

112 *R. v. S.(A..B.)*, [2003] 2 S.C.R. 678.

However, the Court's current jurisprudence allowing ever more leeway for police interrogation is deeply disturbing. The section 7 pretrial right to silence was recognized by McLachlin J. with very strong justificatory language in *R. v. Hebert*.[113] There was a need in the *Charter* era to move beyond the old common law's focus on reliability to allow judicial control of police interrogation, abuses, and tricks. The detainee had a fundamental right to choose whether to speak to police. However, the Court in *Hebert* was concerned about the implications of this new right for the use of undercover agents. So the majority imposed pragmatic limits:

> The accused need not be advised of the right; it applies only on detention; prohibits active elicitation "functionally equivalent to interrogation"[114]; does not apply to non state agents; and allows for questioning after counsel has been consulted.

In *R. v. Oickle*,[115] Iacobucci J. for the Court voiced heartfelt concerns about the emerging evidence that coerced confessions were a major factor in wrongful convictions. Yet the revised common law voluntary confession rule he stated for the 8:1 majority, with only Arbour J. dissenting on the facts, is only that a statement to a person in authority is inadmissible if it is the product of a threat or inducement, not of an operating mind, where oppressive conditions have resulted in involuntariness, or if the police conduct would shock the conscience of the community. I have elsewhere argued that the majority ruling in *Oickle*, especially that on the facts, reads like a manual for coercive interrogations.[116] The disturbing reality is that our Supreme Court has now clearly given the police huge authority to use tricks and inducements in interrogation. *Oickle* and the majority's later ruling in *R. v. Spencer*[117] will encourage police questioning to exploit emotions about possible prosecution against partners. *Oickle* says police may use polygraphs and lie about their accuracy and offer spiritual and other inducements. In *R. v. Osmar*,[118] the Ontario Court of Appeal found nothing in the *Charter* or *Oickle* to prevent police from pretending to be members of organized crime (the "Mr. Big" strategy) in their undercover investigations to obtain confessions.

---

113 [1990] 2 S.C.R. 151.

114 *R. v. Broyles*, [1991] 3 S.C.R. 595.

115 [2000] 2 S.C.R. 3.

116 See Don Stuart, *Charter Justice in Canadian Criminal Law*, 5th ed. (Toronto: Carswell, 2010), at 145–52.

117 (2007), 44 C.R. (6th) 199 (S.C.C.).

118 (2007), 44 C.R. (6th) 276 (Ont. C.A.).

Furthermore, in its especially disappointing ruling in *R. v. Singh*,[119] a 5:4[120] majority of the Supreme Court did not follow *Hebert*, or *obiter* by respected Doherty and Proulx JJ.[121] The majority held that the section 7 pretrial right to silence is subsumed by the voluntary confession rule. A confession can now be admitted if it is voluntary even if the interrogation goes on for hours, and over the accused's protests that he does not wish to talk. Singh asserted his right to silence eighteen times. In this context, the right no longer exists.

The problem is that even *Oickle* is not just about voluntariness. Under *Oickle* there is a freestanding discretion to exclude confessions obtained by tricks that shock the community. Why wasn't such a sustained effort by the police to override an assertion of the right to silence shocking? Justice Abella held for the Supreme Court in *R. v. Turcotte*[122] that adverse inferences should not be drawn against someone who is silent at the pretrial stage as it would be a "snare and delusion" to advise about the right to silence and then to turn around and use silence as a sign of guilt. Why isn't it a snare and delusion to say a suspect has the right to silence, but allow police to ignore its exercise? *Singh* has suddenly reduced this to the very little section 7 right that an undercover agent cannot elicit statements from a detainee by the functional equivalent of an interrogation. Certainly in *Singh* there is no mention of any section 7 right to be advised of the right to silence where police are not undercover. Whether the accused receives advice from the police or a lawyer (if there was one) is just a factor to be considered on the voluntariness inquiry.

The community shock test is a very high hurdle for accused and does not apply to the section 24(2) remedy of exclusion for *Charter* breaches. In the United Kingdom, judges under section 76(2) of the *Evidence Act* of 1984[123] have discretion to exclude a confession where police interrogation methods are considered oppressive, and not just where they shock the community. Under section 76(5), oppression "includes torture, inhuman or degrading treatment or the use or threatened use of violence (whether or not amounting to torture)."

---

119 [2007] 3 S.C.R. 405. A 5:4 majority declined to reconsider this ruling in the context of a major section 10(b) decision in *R. v. Sinclair* (2010), 7 C.R. (6th) 303 (S.C.C.).

120 Charron J. (McLachlin C.J., Bastarache, Deschamps, and Rothstein JJ. concurring). Justice Fish wrote a stinging dissent, with Binnie, LeBel, and Abella JJ. concurring.

121 *R. v. Roy* (2004), 15 C.R. (6th) 282 (Ont. C.A.), and *R. v. Otis* (2000), 37 C.R. (5th) 320 (Ont. C.A.).

122 (2006), 31 C.R. (6th) 197 (S.C.C.).

123 (U.K.), 1984, c. 60.

Trial judges in Canada who have relied on *Oickle* to exclude confessions on the basis that oppression has resulted in involuntariness have often felt it necessary to buttress their rulings by also finding a section 7 breach.[124] The resort to section 7 analysis is clearly no longer available given *Singh*.

Regulation of police interrogation is one area where Parliament may have achieved a better balance than the courts. Under section 269.1 of the *Criminal Code*, torture is an indictable offence punishable to a maximum of fourteen years. Torture is widely defined in section 269.1(2) as "any act or omission by which severe pain or suffering, whether physical or mental, is intentionally inflicted on a person."

Further, under subsection 4, a statement obtained by torture is inadmissible in any proceedings over which Parliament has jurisdiction. This may be a vehicle for further judicial checks on police interrogation. It is also of note that the newest member of the Court, Tom Cromwell J., wrote in his lengthy opinion for the Nova Scotia Court of Appeal in *Oickle* that the confession had been obtained by oppressive methods and ought to be excluded.

5) *Charter* Remedy of Exclusion of Evidence (section 24(2)): *Grant, Harrison*[125]

The ruling of the Canadian Supreme Court in *R. v. Grant*,[126] and the companion ruling in *R. v. Harrison*[127] are bellwether rulings on the approach to remedy of exclusion of evidence under section 24(2) of the *Charter*.

In *Grant*, a 6:1 majority asserted a discretionary approach with revised criteria and emphasis. Much of the voluminous prior jurisprudence on sec-

---

124 See, for example, *R. v. Hammerstrom* (2006), 43 C.R. (6th) 346 (B.C.S.C.) (police tricking the accused by claiming they had the crime videotaped on a store surveillance tape), and *R. v. N.* (2005), 28 C.R. (6th) 149 (Ont. S.C.J.) (five hour polygraph, hostile interrogation, and shocking number of tricks). Prior to *Oickle*, Fradsham J. in *R. v. S. (M.J.)* (2000), 32 C.R. (5th) 378 (Alta. P.C.), excluded a confession in part because the videotape revealed that the Calgary police were using the Reid method, pioneered in the United States, which created an oppressive atmosphere and used psychological brainwashing, which should not, he held, be accepted in Canada. Some judges appear to be excluding confessions since *Oickle* by giving a very wide meaning to the category of oppression resulting in involuntariness: *R. v. Taylor* (2008), 63 C.R. (6th) 142 (N.B.Q.B.), and *R. v. Choy* (2008), 239 C.C.C. (3d) 207 (Alta. Q.B.).

125 This section is a revised and updated version of part of a paper presented to the Law Journal Symposium on The Future of the Exclusionary Rule: American and International Perspectives, Southwestern Law School, Los Angeles, California, 9 October 2009.

126 *Grant*, above note 99.

127 [2009] 2 S.C.R. 494 [*Harrison*].

tion 24(2) over the past twenty-seven years will now be of little importance. The Court has arrived at a revised discretionary approach to section 24(2) free of rigid rules, but placing special emphasis on the factor of seriousness of the breach, rather than the seriousness of the offence or the reliability of the evidence. The same criteria are to be applied to all cases of *Charter* breach.

In my view,[128] the Court has adopted a more sensible, carefully balanced and distinctive approach to the exclusion of unconstitutionally obtained evidence of which Canadians should be proud[129] and which ought to be considered in the development of the remedy in other jurisdictions.

a) *Grant* Principles

In a joint judgment McLachlin C.J. and Charron J. (Binnie, LeBel, Fish, and Abella JJ. concurring) settled on the following revised template:

> When faced with an application for exclusion under s. 24(2), a court must assess and balance the effect of admitting the evidence on society's confidence in the justice system having regard to:
>
> (1) the seriousness of the *Charter*-infringing state conduct (admission may send the message the justice system condones serious state misconduct),
>
> (2) the impact of the breach on the *Charter*-protected interests of the accused (admission may send the message that individual rights count for little), and
>
> (3) society's interest in the adjudication of the case on its merits.
>
> The court's role on a s. 24(2) application is to balance the assessments under each of these lines of inquiry to determine whether, considering all the circumstances, admission of the evidence would bring the administration of justice into disrepute.[130]

---

128 I disclose a bias in that I appeared as counsel for an intervenor in *R. v. Grant*, representing the Canadian Civil Liberties Association. Several of our submissions were accepted by the Court.

129 Other early Canadian commentary has been largely favourable: see especially, David Paciocco & Lee Stuesser, *The Law of Evidence*, rev. 5th ed. (Toronto: Irwin Law, 2010) [Paciocco], and Quigley, "Worth the Wait," above note 107. Hamish Stewart, "The *Grant* Trilogy and the Right against Self-incrimination" (2009) 67 C.R. (6th) 97, however, expresses concern that the Court has unduly lessened the right against self-incrimination.

130 *Grant*, above note 99 at para. 71.

According to the chief justice and Charron J., "the words of section 24(2) capture its purpose: to maintain the good repute of the administration of justice." Viewed broadly, "the term 'administration of justice' . . . embraces maintaining the rule of law and upholding *Charter* rights in the justice system as a whole. The phrase 'bring the administration of justice into disrepute' must be understood in the long-term sense of maintaining the integrity of, and public confidence in, the justice system." While "exclusion of evidence resulting in an acquittal may provoke immediate criticism," section 24(2)

> does not focus on immediate reaction to the individual case. Rather, it looks to whether the overall repute of the justice system, viewed in the long term, will be adversely affected by admission of the evidence. The inquiry is objective. It asks whether a reasonable person, informed of all relevant circumstances and the values underlying the *Charter*, would conclude that the admission of the evidence would bring the administration of justice into disrepute.[131]

The majority elaborates on its three revised factors of seriousness of the violation, impact on *Charter* protected interests and society's interest in adjudication on the merits. At the first stage, the court considers the seriousness of the offending conduct by state authorities that infringed the *Charter* and led to the discovery of the evidence. As stated in *Grant*:

> The more severe or deliberate the state conduct that led to the *Charter* violation, the greater the need for the courts to dissociate themselves from that conduct, by excluding evidence linked to that conduct, in order to preserve public confidence in, and ensure state adherence to, the rule of law . . . The concern of this inquiry is not to punish the police or to deter *Charter* breaches, although deterrence of *Charter* breaches may be a happy consequence . . . Extenuating circumstances, such as the need to prevent the disappearance of evidence, may attenuate the seriousness of police conduct that results in a *Charter* breach . . . "Good faith" on the part of the police will also reduce the need for the court to disassociate itself from the police conduct.[132]

The majority added that

> ignorance of *Charter* standards must not be rewarded or encouraged and negligence or wilful blindness cannot be equated with good faith: *R. v.*

131 *Ibid.* at paras. 66–70.

132 *Ibid.* at paras. 72–75.

> *Genest*, [1989] 1 S.C.R. 59, at p. 87, per Dickson C.J.; *R. v. Kokesch*, [1990] 3 S.C.R. 3, at pp. 32–33, per Sopinka J.; *R. v. Buhay*, 2003 SCC 30, [2003] 1 S.C.R. 631, at para. 59. Wilful or flagrant disregard of the *Charter* by those very persons who are charged with upholding the right in question may require that the court dissociate itself from such conduct. It follows that deliberate police conduct in violation of established *Charter* standards tends to support exclusion of the evidence.[133]

The second stage of the inquiry

> calls for an evaluation of the extent to which the breach actually undermined the interests protected by the infringed right. The impact of a *Charter* breach may range from fleeting and technical to profoundly intrusive. The more serious the impact on these interests, the greater the risk that admission of the evidence may signal to the public that *Charter* rights, however high-sounding, are of little avail to the citizen, breeding public cynicism and bringing the administration of justice into disrepute.[134]

At the third stage, according to the majority, a court is to ask "whether the truth-seeking function of the criminal trial process would be better served by admission of the evidence or by its exclusion." The reliability of the evidence and its importance to the Crown's case are factors to be considered. "If a breach (such as one that effectively compels the suspect to talk) undermines the reliability of evidence, this points in the direction of exclusion." Section 24(2) operates independently of the seriousness of the offence.[135]

According to the Court, "section 24(2) of the *Charter* implicitly overruled the common law practice of always admitting reliable derivative evidence. Instead, the judge is required to consider the three lines of inquiry as to whether admission of derivative evidence obtained through a *Charter* breach would bring the administration of justice into disrepute."[136] Indeed, "[t]he weighing process and the balancing of these concerns is," held the majority, a matter "for the trial judge in each case." Where the trial judge has considered the proper factors, appellate courts should accord considerable deference to her ultimate determination. However,

> [a]s a general rule . . . where reliable evidence is discovered as a result of a good faith infringement that did not greatly undermine the accused's

133 *Ibid.* at para. 75.
134 *Ibid.* at para. 76.
135 *Ibid.* at paras. 79 and 81.
136 *Ibid.* at para. 118.

> protected interests, the trial judge may conclude that it should be admitted under section 24(2). On the other hand, deliberate and egregious police conduct that severely impacted the accused's protected interests may result in exclusion, notwithstanding that the evidence may be reliable.[137]

In lonely dissent, Deschamps J. expresses vigorous opposition to the majority's approach to section 24(2). It was inconsistent with the purpose of section 24(2) of the *Charter*, which she saw as to maintain public confidence in the administration of justice. The proposed test, by focusing the "analysis on the conduct of the police in the first branch and on the interest of the accused in the second, and by attaching less importance to the seriousness of the offence in the third, [did] not give sufficient consideration to the long-term societal interest that must guide the judge in reaching a decision." Whether the evidence is reliable and whether it is essential or peripheral were, in her view, factors crucial to the maintenance of public confidence, as was the seriousness of the offence.[138]

b) Canadian and US Supreme Courts: Rowing in Opposite Directions

The biggest blow against the exclusionary rule in the United States to date came in January 2009 in *Herring v. U.S.*[139] Chief Justice Roberts, writing for a 5:4 majority, confirmed that exclusion is not a necessary consequence of a Fourth Amendment violation and that the benefits of deterrence must outweigh the costs of letting guilty and possibly dangerous defendants go free. He held that

> To trigger the exclusionary rule, police conduct must be sufficiently deliberate that exclusion can meaningfully deter it, and sufficiently culpable that such deterrence is worth the price paid by the justice system . . . [The] exclusionary rule serves to deter deliberate, reckless, or grossly negligent conduct, or in some circumstances recurring or systemic negligence.

The majority ruled that the standard for exclusion had not been reached in this case of State carelessness. The accused had been arrested on a warrant because county officials had negligently not updated computer records to show that the warrant had actually been rescinded.

In marked contrast, we have seen in *Grant* that the Supreme Court of Canada (although the majority paid no attention to United States jurispru-

137 *Ibid.* at para. 127.

138 *Ibid.* at paras. 202 and 223–26.

139 555 U.S. 135 (2009).

dence) implicitly embraced what Ginsberg J., dissenting in *Herring*, described as the more "majestic" rationale of the remedy of exclusion: to preserve the rule of law and the integrity of the justice system. Our Supreme Court sees deterrence as merely a happy windfall of exclusion. There is some double-speak here in that when the Court speaks of not wishing to condone unconstitutional behaviour by the police it seems really to be saying that it wishes to punish police and deter them from continuing to commit such breaches. In any event, as a practical matter, it will be much easier to argue for exclusion in Canada in that there is no impossible burden of establishing that exclusion will in fact deter police in the future.[140]

There are two other dramatic points of contrast. The Canadian remedy is expressly discretionary. The Supreme Court sees no wisdom in an automatic rule of exclusion, however minor the violation. This approach also means that the constitutional standard developed for each *Charter* right does not have to be watered down by judges for fear of an overreaching exclusionary rule.

Finally the Supreme Court of Canada sees the need to encourage exclusion where police have deliberately or reckless violated the *Charter*, but also where they have been ignorant or merely careless in disregarding those rights. The Supreme Court of the United States is now clearly far more tolerant of unconstitutionality in putting the good faith bar as low as gross negligence or systemic or recurrent negligence.

c) Abandoning Conscripted/Non-conscripted Distinction

The 6:1 majority in *Grant* decided that it was time to abandon the *Collins/Stillman* framework for discretion. In *R. v. Collins*,[141] Lamer C.J. identified as a "matter of personal taste" three groups of factors to be considered. Under the first grouping where an accused had been conscripted against himself, the trial would be rendered unfair and the evidence should generally be excluded. The second factor was the seriousness of the breach, and the third the effect of admission or exclusion on the administration of justice. Ten years later, Cory J., speaking for a 5:4 majority in *R. v. Stillman*,[142] refused to change course and held that conscriptive evidence is generally

---

140 Courts in Canada and the United States routinely send people who have been accused to prison in the interests of general deterrence, although respected criminologists see no convincing evidence that increasing the severity of the sentence deters crime: Doob & Webster, above note 1.

141 [1987] 1 S.C.R. 265 at para. 36.

142 [1997] 1 S.C.R. 607 at para. 80.

inadmissible—because of its presumed impact on trial fairness—unless it is independently discovered. For several years, the effect of *Stillman* was the drawing of a bright line: conscripted evidence was almost always excluded and non-conscripted evidence almost always included. A satisfactory definition of conscription also proved elusive. In *Stillman*, Cory J. described conscription broadly as a process in which the accused is "compelled to participate in the creation or discovery of the evidence," and also as a narrow category approach of compelled incrimination "by means of a statement, the use of the body or the production of bodily samples." Courts tended to rely on the category test when defining conscription. Especially in the case of statements, this led to strange results. Where a statement by the accused to the police was obtained in violation of the right to counsel guarantee in section 10(b), but there was no issue of voluntariness, in what sense could the accused be said to have been compelled?

According to the majority in *Grant*, as interpreted and applied in subsequent decisions, the conscripted/non-conscripted dichotomy had brought a measure of certainty to the section 24(2) inquiry. However the analytical method it imposed, and the results it sometimes produced, had been justifiably criticized as inconsistent with the discretionary language and objectives of section 24(2). As *Grant* states:

> Despite reminders that "all the circumstances" must always be considered under section 24(2) . . . *Stillman* had generally been read as creating an all-but-automatic exclusionary rule for non-discoverable conscriptive evidence, broadening the category of conscriptive evidence, and increasing its importance to the ultimate decision on admissibility.
>
> This general rule of inadmissibility of all non-discoverable conscriptive evidence, whether intended by *Stillman* or not, [went] against the requirement of section 24(2) that the court determining admissibility must consider "all the circumstances." The underlying assumption that the use of conscriptive evidence always, or almost always, render[ed] the trial unfair was also open to challenge . . . . It [was] difficult to reconcile trial fairness as a multifaceted and contextual concept with a near-automatic presumption that admission of a broad class of evidence will render a trial unfair, regardless of the circumstances in which it was obtained . . . . [T]rial fairness [was] better conceived as an overarching systemic goal than as a distinct stage of the section 24(2) analysis.[143]

143 *Grant*, above note 99 at paras. 64–65.

Most Canadian academics[144] and many judges will welcome the abandonment of the distinction between conscripted and non-conscripted evidence. It is overly complex, arbitrary, and rigid. Apart from the difficult issue of definition, different approaches had to be followed when considering conscripted and non-conscripted evidence, even in the same trial. Furthermore a breach relating to conscripted evidence is not necessarily more serious than a breach relating to non-conscripted evidence. There was no presumption of exclusion, for example, where a drug squad ransacks a private dwelling without bothering to get a warrant in deliberate violation of section 8. Exclusion should not be based on artificial categories or inflexible rules. Instead, what should be at stake, as the majority held in *Grant*, is the integrity of the justice system in admitting evidence obtained in breach of the *Charter* where the breach was serious.

d) Seriousness of Violation Rather Than Seriousness of Offence Is Key

Whether there will be more or less exclusion in future will likely only become evident after several years of applying *Grant*. The first six months of post-*Grant* section 24(2) rulings point to a robust remedy of exclusion.[145] The Court has clearly decided that evidence can no longer be excluded simply because it was conscripted—which may well result in less exclusion in breathalyzer cases, for example. However, favouring exclusion is the Court's important rulings that the seriousness of *Charter* violation is the first consideration and that the same analysis is to be applied whatever the seriousness of the offence. This is made especially clear by McLachlin C.J., speaking for the 6:1 majority, in *R. v. Harrison*:

> As Cronk J.A. [dissenting in the Ontario Court of Appeal in the Court below] put it, allowing the seriousness of the offence and the reliability of the evidence to overwhelm the s. 24(2) analysis "would deprive those

---

144 See Paciocco, above note 129, and Quigley, "Worth the Wait," above note 107. See also Ron Delisle, "Collins: An Unjustified Distinction" (1987) 56 C.R. (3d) 216; Stephen Coughlan, "Developments in Criminal Procedure" (1998) 9 Sup. Ct. L. Rev. (2d) 272 at 303–22; Michael Davies, "Alternative Approaches to the Exclusion of Evidence under s. 24(2) of the *Charter*" (2002) 46 Crim. L.Q. 21; Steven Penney, "Taking Deterrence Seriously: Excluding Unconstitutionally Obtained Evidence under Section 24(2) of the *Charter*" (2004) 49 McGill L.J. 105. But see Hamish Stewart, above note 129 and Kent Roach, "The Evolving Fair Trial Test under Section 24(2) of the *Charter*" (1996) 1 Can. Crim. L. Rev. 117.

145 A recent Quicklaw survey of the first 100 section 24(2) decisions in 2010 by a Dalhousie LL.M. student showed that a robust remedy of exclusion is in place, especially at the trial court level, for all *Charter* violations. The Ontario exclusion rate was 78 percent. See Mike Madden, "Empirical Data on Section 24(2) under *Grant*" (2011) 78 C.R. (6th) 278.

> charged with serious crimes of the protection of the individual freedoms afforded to all Canadians under the *Charter* and, in effect, declare that in the administration of the criminal law 'the ends justify the means'" (para. 150). *Charter* protections must be construed so as to apply to everyone, even those alleged to have committed the most serious criminal offences. [The] . . . trial judge seemed to imply that where the evidence is reliable and the charge is serious, admission will always be the result. As *Grant* makes clear, this is not the law.[146]
>
> Additionally, the trial judge's observation that the *Charter* breaches "pale in comparison to the criminality involved" in drug trafficking risked the appearance of turning the s. 24(2) inquiry into a contest between the misdeeds of the police and those of the accused.
>
> The fact that a *Charter* breach is less heinous than the offence charged does not advance the inquiry mandated by s. 24(2). We expect police to adhere to higher standards than alleged criminals.[147]

There were indeed dangers in softening the exclusion remedy by adopting a test of "proportionality"[148] between the seriousness of the violation and the seriousness of the offence. A criminal trial under a system of entrenched *Charter* rights for the accused has to concern itself with the truth of police abuse and disregard of *Charter* standards, not just the truth of the accused's guilt. Without the remedy of exclusion in cases where the Court considers the crime serious, there would be a large number of criminal trials where the *Charter* will cease to provide protection. This could create public cynicism regarding the integrity of our system of law enforcement. There cannot be a *de facto* two-tier system where one zone is *Charter*-free and the police ends always justify the means. There must be a real risk of exclusion for serious *Charter* breaches even in cases of serious crimes, as the Supreme Court has now emphatically determined.

The first *Grant* factor of seriousness of the violation, and the second factor of impact on *Charter*-protected interests overlap in that the second factor also addresses the seriousness of the violation. The Court seemed to anticipate problems with its new second step and gives extensive advice about how its three-part inquiry might be approached regarding statements by

146 *Harrison*, above note 127 at para. 40.

147 *Ibid.* at para 41.

148 As suggested in David Paciocco, "*Stillman*, Disproportion and the Fair Trial Dichotomy under Section 24(2)" (1997) 2 Can. Crim. L. Rev. 163. In his careful review of *Grant* and *Harrison*, Paciocco wonders, "why the seriousness of the offence is recognized as a valid consideration if it will in fact have no material bearing on the outcome": above note 129 at 45.

the accused, bodily evidence, non-bodily physical evidence, and derivative evidence.[149] However, the Court was at pains to emphasize that the three *Grant* factors have to be applied to any type of evidence.

e) Reliability and Importance of Evidence Not Determinative

Exclusion is also favoured by the Court in cases where the *Charter* has been breached, even when the evidence is reliable and essential to the Crown's case. This is very evident in the Court's decision in *Harrison* to exclude thirty-five kilograms of cocaine found in a vehicle search in violation of sections 8 and 9. This is welcome. There must be a sanction for serious *Charter* breaches, even if the evidence is reliable and crucial to the Crown's case.

f) Police "Good Faith"

On the important issue of whether police good faith can mitigate the seriousness of the breach, the *Grant* majority held that intentional or reckless disregard of *Charter* rights should normally lead to exclusion, that ignorance of *Charter* standards must not be rewarded or encouraged, and negligence or wilful blindness cannot be equated with good faith.[150]

Unfortunately, it is not clear how demanding the Court is on this point, given the finding in *Grant* that the police officer's mistake was understandable given "considerable legal uncertainty" as to the meaning of the triggering concept of detention and did not amount to bad faith. Surely Grant was psychologically detained under existing Supreme Court law by the three police officers, who were clearly trying to obtain incriminating evidence. Furthermore, there is agreement in *Grant* that there was no reasonable suspicion for investigative detention required in *R. v. Mann*.[151] It is true that there was authority in Ontario[152] that the concept of psychological detention did not apply equally to pedestrian stops. That view is now clearly overruled. The Supreme Court in *Grant* also made it clear that aggressive police questioning on the street to gain incriminating evidence in violation

149 *Grant*, above note 99 at paras. 88–128.

150 *Ibid.* at para. 75, citing *R. v. Buhay*, [2003] 1 S.C.R. 631, and other authority.

151 [2004] 3 S.C.R. 59.

152 *R.* v. *B.(L.)* (2007), 49 C.R. (6th) 245 (Ont. C.A.). Justice Moldaver did not have to consider s. 24(2), since he found no *Charter* violation, but he indicated that exclusion should only be for egregious police behaviour and that "most Canadians" would not countenance not having a trial on the merits for a person found with a gun. Under this test, exclusion should be rare where the evidence is reliable and the offence serious, and should occur only when the community would be shocked. This view has now been clearly rejected by the Supreme Court.

of the *Mann* limits on investigative detention as in *Grant* should, in the future, result in exclusion:

> We add that the Court's decision in this case will be to render similar conduct less justifiable going forward. While police are not expected to engage in judicial reflection on conflicting precedents, they are rightly expected to know what the law is.[153]

The majority in *Harrison* also suggests courts should exclude to dis-associate from police misconduct "where the departure from *Charter* standards was major in degree, or where the police knew (or should have known) that their conduct was not *Charter*-compliant."[154]

It would have been preferable had the Court expressly disavowed the utility of the politically- and emotionally-charged labels of good or bad faith, which have produced uncertainty and inconsistency.[155] Judges are very familiar with deciding whether conduct was intentional or negligent. A *Charter* breach should be considered especially serious where the police have intentionally breached a *Charter* standard and serious where the breach was negligent. Police misperception or ignorance of *Charter* standards should only mitigate a *Charter* breach where the Crown has shown due diligence by the police in their attempt to comply with *Charter* standards. We should expect police not to be careless about *Charter* rights.[156] As in the case of the tort of negligent investigation, the standard should be that "police act professionally and carefully, not just to avoid gross negligence."[157]

g) Ineffectiveness of Other Remedies

In Canada, the remedy of exclusion for *Charter* breaches has proved to be an important vehicle to hold agents of the state indirectly and publicly ac-

---

153 *Grant*, above note 99 at para. 133. This is now a clear trend in lower court rulings. See especially the powerful judgment of Frankel J.A. for the majority in *R. v. Reddy*, 2010 BCCA 11, and Ontario Court of Justice rulings in *R. v. Osolky*, 2009 ONCJ 445, *R. v. Lee*, 2009 ONCJ 434, and *R. v. Peacock*, 2009 ONCJ 479.

154 *Harrison*, above note 127 at para. 22.

155 Justice Doherty of the Ontario Court of Appeal has pointed to dangers of labels such as good or bad faith in *R. v. Kitaitchuk* (2002), 4 C.R. (6th) 38 at para. 41 (Ont. C.A.), relying on C. Hill, "The Role of Fault in Section 24(2) of the *Charter*" in J. Cameron, ed., *The Charter's Impact on the Criminal Justice System* (Toronto: Carswell, 1996) 57.

156 Stephen Coughlan, "Good Faith and Exclusion of Evidence under the *Charter*" (1992) 11 C.R. (4th) 304.

157 *Hill v. Hamilton-Wentworth Regional Police Services Board*, 2007 SCC 41 at para. 70, McLachlin C.J. for the majority.

countable. On a daily basis defence, counsel can challenge the behaviour of police officers. Where there are patterns of inclusion despite police breaches, there will be less incentive for police to take the *Charter* seriously. In considering exclusion remedies, courts must be concerned with the long-term integrity of the justice system if *Charter* standards for accused are ignored or operate unequally against vulnerable groups, such as persons of colour and those who are young.[158]

In *Hudson v. U.S.*,[159] Scalia J., writing for a 5:4 majority, refused to apply the exclusionary rule to a violation of the Fourth Amendment "knock-and-announce" rule. In the course of doing so he suggested that exclusion may no longer be necessary because of the increasing professionalism of police forces, with wide-ranging reforms in education, training, and supervision, better internal discipline, and various forms of citizen review.

Policing and review standards have also improved in Canada. However, those preferring alternative remedies, such as civil suits and police complaints procedures, now bear a heavy burden of demonstrating their comparative efficacy. In Canada they have thus far generally proved to be a poor and low visibility response to systemic problems of police abuse or ignorance of their powers under an entrenched *Charter*. Police are rarely, if ever, disciplined for *Charter* breaches that uncover evidence of criminality. Civil litigation is expensive, uncertain in outcome, and, if successful, likely to be subject to confidentiality agreements. Civil litigation is also highly unlikely where the plaintiff is in prison.

Thankfully, our Supreme Court in *Grant* and *Harrison* still sees the need for a vigorous remedy of exclusion for serious *Charter* breaches, however serious the crime. In this area, as in others, an activist Supreme Court, mindful of its role as guardian of our Constitution, has given our criminal justice system a welcome balance against law and order expediency.

6) Bail to Maintain Public Confidence: *Hall*

In *R. v. Hall* (2002),[160] the Supreme Court was unanimous in ruling that the opening phrases "on any other just cause being shown and, without limiting

158 In developing standards for strip searches, the majority of the Court in *R. v. Golden*, [2001] 3 S.C.R. 679 at para. 83, took into account Commission findings of over-representation of African Canadians and Aboriginals in the Canadian criminal justice system and likely disproportionality in arrests and searches.

159 547 U.S. 586 (2006).

160 (2002), 4 C.R. (6th) 197 (S.C.C.) [*Hall*]. My full review and analysis of *Hall* was first published in the Criminal Reports and in "Zigzags on Rights of Accused: Brittle Majorities

the generality of the foregoing" in subsection 515(10)(c) of the *Criminal Code* were too general to survive *Charter* challenge and had to be struck down. The division in the Court came with the further 5:4 ruling that subsection 515(10)(c) is constitutional to the extent that it allows bail to be denied not because the accused is a flight or public safety risk, but to "maintain confidence in the administration of justice."

For reasons powerfully expressed by Iacobucci J. in dissent,[161] this is a deeply disappointing ruling. *Hall* effectively overrules the earlier *Morales* rulings that detaining in the public interest is too vague and that section 11(e) requires grounds of detention to be limited to assessment of flight risk and public safety. The surprise is that the majority judgment was written by McLachlin C.J.,[162] who had joined the majority in *Morales*, and who had also authored a strong dissent in *R. v. Pearson*[163] on the basis that the reverse onus for narcotic traffickers in question was too broad.

According to the majority, the portion of subsection 515(10)(c) which permits denial of bail where necessary to maintain confidence in the administration of justice was neither unduly vague nor overbroad with regard to the four specified factors. The chief justice saw the provision as representing a separate and distinct basis for bail denial not covered by the other two categories of flight risk and public safety in subsections (a) and (b):

> It [was] neither superfluous nor unjustified. It [served] a very real need to permit a bail judge to detain an accused [person] pending trial for the purpose of maintaining the public's confidence if the circumstances of the case so [warranted]. Without public confidence, the bail system and the justice system generally [stood compromised].

Denial of bail "to maintain confidence in the administration of justice" with regard to the factors set out in subsection 515(10)(c) complied with section 11(e)'s requirement of no denial of bail without just cause. According to McLachlin C.J., this was an "excellent example"[164] of the courts' constitutional dialogue with Parliament.

The dissent is conspicuously blunt. For Iacobucci J., liberty is at the heart of a free and democratic society, and our justice system must mini-

---

Manipulate Weasel Words of Dialogue, Deference and *Charter* Values" (2003) 20 Sup. Ct. L. Rev. 267 at 281–88.

161 Major, Arbour, and LeBel JJ. concurred.

162 L'Heureux-Dubé, Gonthier, Bastarache, and Binnie JJ. concurred.

163 [1992] 3 S.C.R. 665.

164 *Hall*, above note 160 at para. 43.

mize unwarranted denials of that liberty. In the criminal law context, this freedom is seen to be embodied generally in the right to be presumed innocent until proven guilty, and specifically in the right under section 11(e) of the *Charter* (not to be denied "reasonable bail without just cause"). It was impossible to justify the sweeping discretion to abrogate liberty that subsection 515(10)(c) afforded and it should be struck down in its entirety. In the view of the dissenting justices,

> fear that a bail judge will be unable to protect the public without subsection 515(10)(c) [was] without reasonable foundation. There [was] no evidence that the bail system was lacking in any way before the introduction of the provision in 1997, five years after the "public interest" ground for denying bail had been struck down as unconstitutionally vague. The Crown could not even raise a convincing hypothetical scenario that would require pre-trial detention

where there were no flight risk or public safety concerns addressed by subsection 515(10)(a) or (b). Indeed,

> [w]hether the phrase "maintain confidence in the administration of justice" had been given a workable standard by courts or Parliament in other contexts, in the context of subsection 515(10)(c), it was impermissibly vague because of the failure to establish plausible and valid grounds for denying bail which would serve the proper administration of the bail system, and which were not already covered under the more specific grounds in subsections 515(10)(a) and (b).[165]

Subsection 515(10)(c) was ripe for misuse and allowed irrational public fears to be elevated above an accused's *Charter* rights. According to Iacobucci J., the majority had transformed "dialogue with Parliament" into "abdication."[166]

In my view, the minority had it exactly right. The decision shows how the "dialogue" metaphor is strained and likely to be used to erode rights of accused. The amendment inserted into a criminal omnibus amendment bill resulted in no Parliamentary debate on the floor or in committee. Some debate.

---

165 The minority relied heavily on the analysis of the leading text by Justice Gary Trotter, *The Law of Bail in Canada* (Toronto: Carswell, 1999). The majority ignored it. See *Hall, ibid.* at para. 110.

166 *Ibid.* at para. 137.

A proper reading of the majority *Hall* ruling is that the tertiary ground should rarely be used, given that:

1) McLachlin C.J. remarks that there are "relatively rare cases where it can be properly invoked" (citing Hall J.A. of the B.C.C.A.) (para. 27) and that "the circumstances in which recourse to this ground for bail denial may not arise frequently."[167]
2) McLachlin C.J. accepts that the reasonable person making the assessment of the need to maintain public confidence must be properly informed about the philosophy of the legislative provisions, *Charter* values, and the actual circumstances of the case.[168]
3) *Hall* was an especially brutal offence and there was evidence that the community was fearful about this particular case.

Based on the above considerations, there is now substantial jurisprudence in lower courts and courts of appeal[169] for using the tertiary ground sparingly.

Ascertaining the true reality of the use of the tertiary ground since *Hall* would require expensive empirical research, given that so many bail decisions are made by provincial judges and justices of the peace and not recorded in available databases. An early survey[170] examined sixty-four higher-level decisions turning on the tertiary ground. It found that it was used to deny bail in thirty-five cases. This suggested that the ground was not being used sparingly. The trend was, however, already different in murder cases where judges often rejected it as a ground for detention.

A surprising and disappointing feature of the majority judgment in *Hall* is the failure of the majority to consider the issue of context. Often the Supreme Court has an expansive view of context and is guided by a variety of secondary sources. Here the majority puts on blinkers.

Bail decisions in high profile cases such as guns and drug cases in Toronto are now sometimes made on the unruly basis that a bail judge thinks that the offence is serious, and that a law and order community would get

---

167 *Ibid.* at para. 31.

168 *Ibid.* at para. 41. "*Charter* values" are certainly weasel words here in that the majority of the Supreme Court is showing such little respect for its previous standards.

169 See especially *R. v. Brotherston*, 2009 BCCA 43. After some earlier vacillation, the Ontario Court of Appeal has now reached the same position in *R. v. Heyden* (2009), 67 C.R. (6th) 174 (Ont. C.A.). But see earlier *R. v. M (E. W.)* (2007), 41 C.R. (6th) 259 (Ont. C.A.), and *R. v. S. B.* (2007), 49 C.R. (6th) 197 (Ont. C.A.).

170 Don Stuart & Joanna Harris, "Is the Public Confidence Ground to Deny Bail Used Sparingly?" (2004) 21 C.R. (6th) 232.

upset by a release. The issue ought to be reconsidered in the Supreme Court, given this reality and findings of systemic racism in the bail process.[171] For similar reasons, the Supreme Court ought also to consider the constitutionality of reverse onus clauses which are proliferating and threatening to completely undermine the 1972 *Bail Reform Act*.[172] This major initiative sought to restrict pretrial custody by placing the onus on the Crown to show cause for detention. Parliament has chosen to ignore evidence of appalling conditions in detention gaols. In 2006, Reinhardt J. of the Ontario Court of Justice found that conditions in the Don Jail in Toronto fell short of the United Nations' minimum rules for treatment of prisoners.[173]

7) Disclosure and Production: *McNeil*

In *R. v. McNeil*,[174] Charron J., speaking for a unanimous Court, provided a clear and comprehensive review of both the current *Stinchcombe* disclosure regime and of the procedures and principles for production of third party records. In either case, this important judgment should now be the first point of call.

In a balanced way, Charron J. clarifies the issue of access to police disciplinary records, which has led to protracted and conflicting litigation in lower courts. Records relating to findings of serious misconduct by police must be disclosed if "related to the investigation or if they could reasonably impact on the case against the accused." If not, the *O'Connor* procedure is to be applied. At a time when politicians are talking about somehow putting limits on disclosure, especially in mega trials, it is pleasing to see the Supreme Court standing firm, and indeed, expanding the constitutional obligation to disclose.

As for the procedures for the production of third party records, the Supreme Court in *McNeil* also makes it crystal clear that there are two quite distinct procedures—Parliament's scheme respecting records of sexual

---

171 *The Report of the Commission on Systemic Racism in the Ontario Criminal Justice System* (Toronto: Commission on Systemic Racism in the Ontario Criminal Justice System, 1995) found that the black detention rate for drug trafficking/importing was twenty-seven times higher than that for others accused..

172 S.C. 1970-71-72, c. 37.

173 *R. v. Prince* (2006), 41 C.R. (6th) 389 (Ont. S.C.J.). See too Justice Rosenberg, "The Attorney General and the Administration of Criminal Justice" (2009) 39 Queen's L.J. 813 at 856–59 (inconsistent with *Charter* rights and Canada's obligations under the *International Covenant on Civil and Political Rights*).

174 (2009), 62 C.R. (6th) 1 (S.C.C.). See David Paciocco, "*Stinchcombe* on Steroids: The Surprising Legacy of *McNeil*" (2009) 62 C.R. (6th) 26.

assault complainants upheld in *Mills*, and the *O'Connnor* common law regime for all other records. Details of both procedures are carefully clarified.

8) Trial by Jury: *Cinous, Fontaine, Krieger*

This issue of whether weak defences should be withdrawn from juries has divided the Supreme Court. In *R. v. Cinous* (2002),[175] McLachlin C.J. and Bastarache J., writing for a 6:3 majority,[176] rejected the argument of Arbour J. in dissent.[177] Her view was that the "air of reality" test developed in the context of the mistaken belief defence in sexual assault cases had departed from the common law "no evidence" test for withdrawal of the case from the jury. She believed that replacing it with a test of sufficiency of evidence had usurped the fact-finding function of juries. According to the minority, the "no evidence" test should be adopted for defences such as self-defence, especially where there were no special technical or policy considerations, no alternative defences, and where it was the accused's only defence.

The majority in *Cinous* firmly decided that the same test of air of reality should be applied to all defences. The test for whether there is an evidential foundation warranting that a defence be put to a jury was whether there is evidence upon which a properly instructed jury, acting reasonably, could acquit if it believed the evidence to be true. A trial judge must consider the totality of the evidence, and assumes the evidence relied upon by the accused to be true. The majority spoke of the "positive duty" to keep from the jury lacking an evidentiary foundation. However the trial judge

> [did] not make determinations about the credibility of witnesses, weigh the evidence, make findings of fact, or draw determinate factual inferences . . . Nor is the air of reality test intended to assess whether the defence is likely, unlikely, somewhat likely, or very likely to succeed at the end of the day. The question for the trial judge is whether the evidence discloses a real issue to be decided by the jury, and not how the judge should ultimately decide the issue.[178]

The message from the majority in *Cinous* in deciding that a defence of self-defence should not be put in a murder case where the accused testi-

---

175 (2002), 49 C.R. (5th) 209 (S.C.C.) [*Cinous*].

176 L'Heureux-Dubé, Gonthier, and LeBel JJ. concurred, as did Binnie J. in a short concurring opinion.

177 Iacobucci and Major JJ. concurred.

178 *Cinous*, above note 175 at para. 54.

fied he shot because he was in fear of being assassinated by a fellow gang member, was that weak defences should not be left to a jury. The short concurring opinion of Binnie J. (Gonthier J. concurring) is particularly blunt and dismissive:

> A *Criminal Code* that permitted preemptive killings within a criminal organization on the bare assertion by the killer that no course of action was reasonably available to him while standing outside a motor vehicle other than to put a shot in the back of the head of another member sitting inside the parked vehicle at a well-lit and populated gas station is a criminal code that would fail in its most basic purpose of promoting public order . . . [The] only way the defence could succeed was if the jury climbed into the skin of the [accused] and accepted as reasonable a sociopathic view of appropriate dispute resolution.[179]

This seems to deny the contextual aspect of the individualized objective approach which requires the court to let the jury consider whether, given the situation and experience of the accused, his fear was reasonable. The majority ruling of no air of reality was contrary to that of the trial judge, three justices of the Quebec Court of Appeal, and the three dissenters in the Supreme Court. It seemed to treat the accused's testimony as "second class" evidence, as Arbour J. put it, and to show a lack of trust in the jury system.

Subsequently, the Supreme Court appears to have lowered the *Cinous* bar in several decisions[180] that defences should have been left where the evidence appeared weak. In the automatism case of *R. v. Fontaine*,[181] Fish J. relies on *dicta* from Arbour J.'s dissenting opinion in *Cinous* to order a new trial to consider the defence. Justice Fish's respect for the autonomy of the jury system is also evident in his judgment for the Court in *R. v. Krieger*,[182] where he stated that a trial judge cannot direct a jury to convict.

In *Gunning*,[183] Charron J. held that the air of reality test had no application to the issue of proof of essential ingredients of an offence.[184] Absent a plea of guilt or admission of fact, such essentials were, under the presump-

179 *Ibid.* at paras. 128 and 130.

180 See, for example, *R. v. Fontaine* (2004), 18 C.R. (6th) 203 (S.C.C.) (automatism), and *R. v. Gunning*, [2005] 1 S.C.R. 627 (defence of property) [*Gunning*].

181 *Fontaine, ibid.*

182 [2006] 2 S.C.R. 501.

183 *Gunning*, above note 180.

184 *Ibid.* at paras. 30–31.

tion of innocence, necessarily at play and had to be left to the jury. This would appear to make anomalous the extensive jurisprudence respecting tough air of reality tests for mistaken belief in consent defences to charges of assault and sexual assault.

D. EVIDENCE

1) Assessing Reasonable Doubt: *W.D.* and *J.H.S.*

In *R. v. J.H.S.*,[185] the Supreme Court makes it clear that the much-quoted *W.D.* formula[186] for explaining reasonable doubt does not have to be followed. In *R v. W.D.*, Cory J. suggested the following three-step approach could be followed for instructions as to credibility:

> First, if you believe the evidence of the accused, obviously you must acquit.
>
> Second, if you do not believe the testimony of the accused but you are left in reasonable doubt by it, you must acquit.
>
> Third, even if you are not left in doubt by the evidence of the accused, you must ask yourself whether, on the basis of the evidence which you do accept, you are convinced beyond a reasonable doubt by that evidence of the guilt of the accused.[187]

In *J.H.S.*, Binnie J., without identifying the many critics (or supporters) of the *W.D.* questions, pithily and powerfully acknowledges their weaknesses as follows:

> As to the first question, the jury may believe inculpatory elements of the statements of an accused but reject the exculpatory explanation . . . . The principle that a jury may believe some, none, or all of the testimony of any witness, including that of an accused, suggests to some critics that the first *W.(D.)* question is something of an oversimplification.
>
> As to the second question, some jurors may wonder how, if they believe none of the evidence of the accused, such rejected evidence may nevertheless of itself raise a reasonable doubt. Of course, some elements of the evidence of an accused may raise a reasonable doubt, even though the bulk of it is rejected. Equally, the jury may simply conclude that they do not know whether to believe the accused's testimony or not. In either circumstance the accused is entitled to an acquittal.

185 2008 SCC 30 [*J.H.S.*].

186 [1991] 1 S.C.R. 742.

187 *Ibid.* at para. 28.

The third question, again, is taken by some critics as failing to contemplate a jury's acceptance of inculpatory bits of the evidence of an accused but not the exculpatory elements. In light of these possible sources of difficulty, Wood J.A. in *H.(C.W.)* suggested an additional instruction:

> I would add one more instruction in such cases, which logically ought to be second in the order, namely: "If, after a careful consideration of all the evidence, you are unable to decide whom to believe, you must acquit." [p. 155][188]

Given these weaknesses, it is unfortunate that the Supreme Court did not expressly and clearly abandon the *W.D.* approach, as it has just done in civil cases in the context of sexual assault.[189] *W.D.* has been responsible for many, many prolix appeals and orders of new trials. The main problem is that the second question is potentially confusing or too generous to the accused.[190] Justice Binnie might have mentioned the following remark of McLachlin J., dissenting in *R. v. S.(W.D.)*

> Certainly if the jury rejected (as opposed to being merely undecided about) *all* of the evidence of the accused, it is difficult to see how that very evidence, having been rejected, could raise a reasonable doubt. [191]

Trial judges are at least now free to reject the complexity of *W.D.* as long as they make sure that the jury is warned of the Crown's burden of proof, that it is not just a choice between competing versions, and that they may believe some, none, or all of any witnesses, including the accused. These principles, of course, apply equally to judge-only trials. In *R. v. Dinardo*,[192] the Court also warns that sufficient reasons must be provided to justify findings of credibility.

2) Similar Fact Evidence Exceptionally Admissible as Specific Propensity: *Handy*

Justice Binnie led the Court in *R. v. Handy*[193] to re-examine the similar fact evidence rule. In a comprehensive judgment he decided that such evidence

---

188 *J.H.S.*, above note 185 at paras. 10–12.

189 *F.H. v. McDougall* (2008), 61 C.R. (6th) 1 (S.C.C.), Rothstein J.

190 See especially the late Jack Gibson, "*R. v. W(.D.)* Revisited: Is Step Two a Misdirection?" (2003) 11 C.R. (6th) 323.

191 [1994] 3 S.C.R. 521.

192 (2008), 57 C.R. (6th) 48 (S.C.C.).

193 [2002] 2 S.C.R. 908.

is presumptively inadmissible but that exceptionally, it can be admitted to show specific, but not general, propensity. No longer is it necessary to artificially manufacture a purpose distinct from propensity. Notwithstanding the careful attention to criteria Binnie J. was at such pains to set out, it is uncertain whether *Handy* has really made the law clearer or easier to apply and whether similar fact evidence is more or less likely to be admitted.

The unanimous ruling in *R. v. Trochym*,[194] holding that the similar fact evidence had been wrongly admitted, confirms that the Supreme Court intends that it be admitted only in exceptional cases. In *Trochym*, the purpose was to show identity. It is intriguing that the majority reached its ruling on the "improbability of coincidence" test of *R. v. Arp*[195] without mentioning the *Arp* catchphrase of "strikingly similar." The Court in *R. v. C.R.B.*[196] and *Handy* had previously warned against the use of catchwords to solve this difficult weighing exercise. The Court did, however, return to the language of "striking similarity" in *R. v. Perrier*[197] in fashioning a special and complex test for the admissibility of similar fact evidence to show identity in gang cases.

3) Hearsay Principles of Necessity and Reliability: *Khelawon, Mapara*

The judgment of Charron J. in *R. v. Khelawon*[198] on the hearsay rule is a *tour de force*. She provides a detailed and instructive review of the current law of hearsay and in particular of the Court's principled approach which requires proof of necessity and reliability before hearsay evidence can be admitted. She takes us all back to first principles in rehearsing how hearsay should be identified and why judges should be mindful about admitting presumptively inadmissible hearsay. In identifying a "functional" approach she emphasizes the need for flexibility in the approach to the factor of reliability. She finds this largely reflected in the Supreme Court's jurisprudence, which she fully reviews.

The most important change in the law is that the Court in *Khelawon* expressly reversed *R. v. Starr*[199] to the extent that it divided factors into categories relevant to threshold and those relevant to ultimate reliability and

194 (2007), 43 C.R. (6th) 217 (S.C.C.).
195 [1998] 3 S.C.R. 339.
196 [1990] 1 S.C.R. 717.
197 2004 SCC 56.
198 (2006), 42 C.R. (6th) 1 (S.C.C.).
199 [2000] 2 S.C.R. 144.

forbade consideration of evidence extrinsic to the making of the statement. As the Court recognizes without providing citations, most judges and commentators have found no wisdom in those quick and restrictive *obita*. Laurie Lacelle[200] long ago pointed out that not allowing consideration of extrinsic evidence, such as medical evidence of bruises, would have a detrimental and undesirable effect on the prosecution of domestic assault cases where, for example, the complainant's out of court statement speaks of assault causing bruises, but she has now recanted. Of course the existence of corroborating physical evidence will not necessarily be determinative on the issue of sufficient reliability. So too the Court stresses in its ruling on the facts that just because there are striking similarities in other statements, there is to be no "rigid pigeonhole" admission. The catchphrase is case-by-case flexibility looking to all the facts. For those concerned by the length of pretrial *voir dires*, it is noteworthy that in *Khelawon* itself it was agreed that the *voir dire* on the statements would determine the result at trial.

In passing, the Court in *Khelawon* confirms the ruling in *R. v. Mapara*[201] on the relationship between traditional exceptions and the principled approach. The majority ruling in *Starr* promised that there would be a thorough review of each existing exception to see whether the principled requirements of necessity and reliability were met. Here the Court again accepts the *Mapara* ruling that traditional exceptions are presumptively valid. The bottom line of *Mapara* is that the co-conspirators' exception set out in the *Carter*[202] rules remain unaffected by *Starr*.

In *Mapara* the minority's difference of opinion with the majority turns out to be limited to the majority's view that the trial judge should only intervene to assess necessity and reliability in highly exceptional cases. According to the minority, this set the bar too high. Rather, an inquiry should occur when the circumstances in which the evidence was obtained or given raise real and serious concerns as to reliability or necessity. In such cases the trial judge should be required to scrutinize the evidence to ensure that it meets the criteria of the principled approach. However, even the minority judges emphasize that a *voir dire* to assess the hearsay evidence will remain the exception.[203]

200 "The Role of Corroborating Evidence in Assessing the Reliability of Hearsay Statements for Substantive Purposes" (1999) 19 C.R. (5th) 376.

201 [2005] 1 S.C.R. 358.

202 [1982] 1 S.C.R. 938.

203 In *R. v. Simpson* (2007), 53 C.R. (6th) 1 (Ont. C.A.), a new trial was ordered because the trial judge erred in admitting co-conspirator hearsay where necessity was not met because

When the majority in *Starr* called for existing hearsay exceptions to be reviewed according to the requirements of necessity and reliability, many writers, as the minority acknowledge, suggested that the complex and inherently circular co-conspirator's exception was a prime candidate for review and reform. The major problem is that it seems more consistent with *Starr* to have the issues of threshold liability and necessity determined by a trial judge at a *voir dire* before the jury hears the evidence.[204]

The trumping consideration for the majority is the need to ensure that conspiracy trials are "effective" and not unduly complicated by hearsay *voir dires*. That seems at odds with the concern of the majority in *Starr* to ensure that necessity and reliability criteria are taken seriously before the admission of any hearsay. Chief Justice McLachlin was a dissenter in *Starr* and appears to have found a new majority much more accepting of the status quo of existing categories of exceptions to the hearsay rule, including the one sometimes known as "the prosecutor's darling."

With the Court's acceptance of the wide co-conspirator's exception in *Mapara* there seems little likelihood that existing exceptions will be reconfigured. The only change so far is the reliability requirement of not being under "circumstances of suspicion," which the majority in *Starr* itself imposed on the exception of present intent.[205]

On the other hand, where an exception is narrow or technical, the principled approach is available as an avenue to admission in an appropriate case. For example, in *R. v. West*[206] Casey Hill J. avoided the rigours of statutory business records requirements by going straight to the principled approach to admit a forensic report from an expert who was deceased.

Lower courts[207] have differed as to whether admissions of parties should also be subject to the necessity and reliability determination. In passing,

---

the declarant was available to testify, and reliability was not met because of the manner of recording the statements. Lisa Dufraimont, "Annotation" (2008) 53 C.R. (6th) 2 suggests this ruling is more in keeping with the minority view in *Mapara*.

204 See especially the detailed analysis of David Layton, "*R. v. Pilarinos*: Evaluating the Co-conspirators or Joint Venture Exception to the Hearsay Rule" (2002) 2 C.R. (6th) 293. Layton points out that the co-conspirator exception has been applied in many contexts other than conspiracy and is best named the joint venture exception. He addresses concerns about rationale, reliability, and necessity, the issue of corroboration inherent in the rule, the lack of a *voir dire*, and the reality of the doctrine's dangerous reliance on conditional relevancy. See too Marvin Bloos & Michael Plaxton, "A Co-conspirators' Exception to the Standing Rule Keeping Out Hearsay in Gang Trials" (2003) 47 Crim. L.Q. 286.

205 See similarly Romilly J. in *R. v. Larsen* (2001), 42 C.R. (5th) 49 (B.C.S.C.) (hospital records).

206 (2001), 45 C.R. (5th) 307 (S.C.J.).

207 See, for example, *R. v. Terrico* (2005), 199 C.C.C. (3d) 126 (B.C.C.A.).

Charron J. in *Khelawon* makes an enigmatic comment that seems to suggest that such an inquiry should not occur:

> Some of the traditional exceptions stand on a different footing, such as admissions from parties (confessions in the criminal context) and co-conspirators' statements: see *Mapara*, at para. 21. In those cases, concerns about reliability are based on considerations other than the party's inability to test the accuracy of his or her own statement or that of his or her co-conspirators. Hence, the criteria for admissibility are not established in the same way.[208]

4) Judicial Notice: *Spence*

R. v. Spence[209] is now the controlling authority on judicial notice. Justice Binnie is clearly at pains to establish principles upon which all issues of judicial notice are to be based. On the one hand the Court is cautious; the closer any issue is to the dispositive issue, the less scope there is for judicial notice. If the matter relates to adjudicative issues, the strict Morgan criteria of notorious or indisputable govern. When it comes to social or legislative facts, the Court opens the door a little wider. However, a judge must still ask whether the alleged fact would be accepted by a properly informed reasonable person as not subject to reasonable dispute. This latter test is new.

In the course of reiterating that the Morgan approach is the "gold standard," Binnie J. criticizes the Thayer view that courts should take judicial notice of what "everyone knows." He sees at least three difficulties:

> Firstly what "everybody knows" may be wrong . . . . Secondly, there is the problem of trial fairness. Where do these facts come from and how are the parties going to address them? How can parties who are prejudiced by the taking of judicial notice rebut what "everybody" knows unless a plausible source is put to them for their comment and potential disagreement? A third problem is that judges occasionally contradict each other about some "fact" that "everybody" knows, even on the same court in the same case.[210]

Justice Binnie also notes that for the majority of the Court in *R. v. Malmo-Levine*[211] he expressed a preference for social science evidence to be pre-

208 *R. v. Khelawon*, [2006] 2 S.C.R. 787 at para. 65.

209 [2005] 3 S.C.R. 458.

210 *Ibid.* at para. 51.

211 [2003] 3 S.C.R. 571.

sented through an expert witness who could be cross-examined as to what value and weight should be given to such studies and reports.

These views appear to diverge considerably from those of L'Heureux-Dubé J. who championed the need for a wide approach to judicial notice to bring social context into the courtroom.[212] Justice L'Heureux-Dubé saw no distinction between the role of trial or appeal judges, did not stress the distinction between adjudicative and other facts, and indicated that it was not necessary to alert counsel as to when judicial notice may be taken. She also wrote that family law matters require an especially generous approach to judicial notice.

Justice Binnie's view is much more respectful of the adversarial process and the role and value of lawyers. It will be interesting to see whether the Supreme Court extends its new approach to judicial notice to contexts other than criminal matters and whether it will be able to satisfactorily distinguish between adjudicative facts, where there is to be a strict standard for judicial notice, and social and legal facts, where there is now a slightly relaxed standard. In the meantime, trial judges in particular would be well advised to alert counsel as to matters seen to be subject to judicial notice. Alerting counsel requires a delicate balance and the judge must avoid taking on the role of a research director.[213]

5) Expert Evidence: *Mohan, J.-L.J., Trochym*

In a series of decisions, the majority of the Supreme Court has adopted an increasingly cautious approach to the admission of expert testimony. Trial judges are expected to exercise the role of a gatekeeper and insist on criteria of necessity and reliability before admitting the evidence of experts.[214] Here, the Court is commendably protective of fair trial rights and the danger that the mystic infallibility of experts will overwhelm the fact-finding process. It is also concerned about time-wasting and that it is unfair that the Crown

---

212 *Moge v. Moge*, [1992] 3 S.C.R. 813 (taking judicial notice of the disproportionate economic impact of divorce on women), *Willick v. Willick*, [1994] 3 S.C.R. 670 (social science research on child support), and *R. v. S.(R.D.)*, [1997] 3 S.C.R. 484 (a black judge taking into account racial context in assessing credibility respecting the arrest of a black youth in Halifax). See too the following articles by L'Heureux-Dubé J.: "Re-examining the Doctrine of Judicial Notice in the Family Law Context" (1994) 26 Ottawa L. Rev. 551 and "Making Equality Work in Family Law" (1997) 14 Can. J. Fam. L. 103.

213 See Doherty J.A. in *R. v. Hamilton* (2004), 186 C.C.C. (3d) 129 (Ont. C.A.).

214 See especially *R. v. Mohan*, [1994] 2 S.C.R. 9; *R. v. J.-L.J.*, [2002] 2 S.C.R. 600; *R. v. D.D.*, [2000] 2 S.C.R. 275; and *R. v. Trochym* (2007), 43 C.R. (6th) 217 (S.C.C.) [*Trochym*].

typically has more resources to hire experts.[215] The scepticism is mostly directed to soft science, but recent wrongful convictions squarely blamed on faulty forensic pathology[216] will no doubt now attract the same caution.

In *R. v. Trochym*,[217] Deschamps J. made it clear that the criteria of necessity and reliability are to be applied whether the expertise reflects new science or old. She decided that evidence recovered by hypnosis was too unreliable to be admitted. The minority is concerned about the lack of evidentiary foundation. This characterization is debatable given that hypnosis experts did testify at trial and were subject to cross-examination, and the Court was considering a wealth of secondary sources. The dissenters say the majority should not have done its own research, and judges should not have taken judicial notice of experts. In the Court's controlling decision on judicial notice in *Spence* the unanimous Court did recognize that the strict *Morgan* test of notorious or indisputable can be relaxed where the court is dealing with social or legislative facts. However, Binnie J. added that even in such cases there should be a requirement that reasonably informed people would not reasonably dispute the evidence. It does seem that in *Trochym* the overwhelming opinion of researchers was that memory revived by hypnosis is much less reliable than previously thought. It would be odd if the Court had, as Deschamps J. put it, been "frozen" with old knowledge. It certainly seems within the Court's role to decide whether the evidence should be received with caution or, as the majority decided, be excluded altogether.

There is some doublespeak in the Court's approach where it indicates that unreliable devices such as polygraph tests and hypnosis can be used for other purposes, such as police investigations. If those tests are too unreliable for a court of law why is the Court condoning such devices in police investigation and interrogation where there are no lawyers present?

---

215 David Paciocco, "Unplugging Juke Box Testimony in an Adversarial System: Strategies for Changing the Tune on Partial Expects" (2009) 34 Queen's L.J. 565, suggests that the *Mohan* tests do not address the issue of bias directly enough. He calls for codes of conduct to recognize experts owe a special duty to courts of impartial advice and for exclusion after a *voir dire* if an opposing party can provide a realistic foundation that the testimony may be biased.

216 *Report of Inquiry into Pediatric Forensic Pathology in Ontario* (Goudge Report) (2008). The Commission's recommendations heavily influenced the revised approach to the admission of expert evidence set out by Doherty J.A. in *R. v. Abbey* (2009), 68 C.R. (6th) 201 (Ont. C.A.).

217 Above note 214.

6) Privilege against Self-Incrimination (section 13): *Henry*

In *R. v. Henry*,[218] Binnie J., speaking for the Court, introduced a fundamental, sensible, and well-justified new distinction that section 13 of the *Charter* only protects against the use of prior compelled testimony, and not against the use of testimony previously volunteered. This resulted in the reversal of *R. v. Mannion*[219] and, in the non-compelled situations, no *Charter* protection for accused. Like the majority judges in the BC Court of Appeal, the Supreme Court could not see why section 13 should protect an accused from cross-examination where he chose to testify one way at his first trial and then differently on the retrial.

Some had thought that the Court might have been prepared to reverse the *R. v. Dubois*[220] ruling that where a new trial is ordered, the new trial does not constitute "other proceedings" such as to trigger section 13 protection. The Court did not accept this view. The accused has a right not to be compelled to testify at the second trial and, in such cases, section 13 protected against indirect compulsion through the Crown introducing the accused's testimony from the first trial.

When it comes to situations where the accused was earlier compelled to testify when she was not the accused, the Supreme Court now gives the accused greater section 13 protection. Such earlier testimony cannot be used to incriminate or to attack credibility. The courts will now be spared the task of trying to draw a distinction that the Supreme Court now says has been, in this context, too difficult to draw.

The further pronouncement in *Henry* that not all *obiter dicta* of the Supreme Court are binding is expressly intended to foster creativity by the lower courts. However the Court does still insist[221] that some *obiter dicta* "obviously intended to give guidance should be accepted as authoritative." In contrast, *obiter* that are "commentary, examples or exposition that are intended to be helpful and may be found to be persuasive" are not binding. This may well be a difficult distinction to make! It seems clear that the lower courts have been given the green light to try.

218 [2005] 3 S.C.R. 609 [*Henry*].

219 [1986] 2 S.C.R. 272.

220 (1990), 64 C.R. (3d) 216 (S.C.C.).

221 *Henry*, above note 218 at para. 57.

7) Rape Shield Law: *Darrach*

The key issue in examining the rape shield law is whether prior sexual history is ever properly admitted on the issue of consent under sections 276 (1) and (2) of the *Criminal Code*. Our rape shield protection is, of course, built around the twin myth hypotheses established by McLachlin J. in *R. v. Seaboyer*[222] and now found in section 276(1) of the *Criminal Code* that prior sexual history cannot be used to show the complainant was more likely to have consented or less worthy of belief. Unlike any country in the Western world, this protection applies equally to prior sexual history with the accused ever since a further assertion by McLachlin J. in *Seaboyer* which has now been included in the *Criminal Code*.

The Supreme Court in *R. v. Darrach*[223] upheld the statutory regime as constitutional, but it left ambiguities, rendering the law unclear. The Court found that the rules in section 276(1) are not blanket exclusions and may lead to admission under the criteria of section 276(2). Can that lead to admission on the issue of consent? Consent is often the central issue in sexual assault trials, especially since the Supreme Court's decision in *R. v. Ewanchuk*[224] so drastically narrowed the defence of mistaken belief in consent. The problem is that *Darrach* is not at all clear; indicating at one point that such evidence would never be admissible on the issue of consent as it is not relevant, and at another that such evidence is rarely admissible to show consent.

If we assume or know that a sexual assault was committed, there can of course be no question of the relevance of prior sexual conduct, either to the issue of consent or mistaken belief. But trial judges cannot make such an assumption. Relevance is a low threshold test of whether the evidence would assist in proving a matter at issue. Nor can a trial judge simply assert the *Ewanchuk* proposition that there is no implied consent in sexual assault, given that Major J. in *Ewanchuk* also said that consent can be inferred from words and conduct.

There is a consistent line of authority, especially in the Ontario Superior Court (reviewed in *R. v. Strickland*[225] and earlier *R. v. Temertzoglou*[226]) to admit prior evidence of sexual conduct with the accused to show "context." In *Strickland*, Heeney J. was forthright in seeing prior sexual history

222 [1991] 2 S.C.R. 577.

223 [2000] 2 S.C.R. 443.

224 [1999] 1 S.C.R. 330.

225 (2007), 45 C.R. (6th) 183 (S.C.J.).

226 (2002), 11 C.R. (6th) 179 (S.C.J.).

as relevant to proof of consent on the basis that it is more probable that someone would consent to sexual activity with one whom there has been prior consensual sexual behaviour. But he hastens to say that such evidence, while probative, is certainly not conclusive and may not meet the "significant probative value" test set out in section 276(2). The solution he holds is to admit it as "part of the context."

Admitting evidence as "part of the context" seems very like the "part of the narrative" ruse sometimes resorted to bypass unwelcome evidentiary rules.[227] The real problem is that the twin myth hypotheses are too rigid. Professor David Paciocco[228] suggests judges read them down to forbid only general stereotypical inferences and to allow inferences specific to the case. This was the approach taken by Fuerst J. in *Temertzoglou.* This solution is rather like that adopted in the Supreme Court in *R. v. Handy*[229] for similar fact evidence: pattern evidence of the accused can exceptionally be admitted as evidence of specific, rather than general, propensity. The Paciocco analysis found favour in the lower courts but was not squarely addressed by the Supreme Court in *Darrach.* The Supreme Court further speaks of Parliament having clarified that the sexual nature of the previous activity can never be referred to. This seems bizarre. It is only the sexual nature of the prior relationship evidence that could give it any probative force.

In *R. v. A. (no.2)*[230] the House of Lords somehow read *Darrach* as not applying rape shield principles equally to prior sexual history with the accused. The Law Lords unanimously declared that new UK rape shield laws offended fair trial rights in the European Convention for the Protection of Human Rights and Fundamental Freedoms in applying with equal force to prior sexual history with the accused. Lord Steyn, for example, reasoned as follows:

> As a matter of common sense, a prior sexual relationship between the complainant and the accused may, depending on the circumstances, be relevant to the issue of consent. It is a species of prospectant evidence which may throw light on the complainant's state of mind. It cannot, of course, prove that she consented on the occasion in question. Relevancy and sufficiency are different things . . . . It is true that each decision to engage in

227 See Christopher Nowlin, "A Wolf in Sheep's Clothing" (2006) 51 Crim. L.Q. 238 at 271.

228 "The New Rape Shield Provisions in Section 276 Should Survive *Charter* Challenge" (1993) 21 C.R. (4th) 223.

229 [2002] 2 S..C.R. 908.

230 [2001] 2 W.L.R. 1546 (H.L.).

> sexual activity is always made afresh. On the other hand, the mind does not usually blot out all memories. What one has engaged on in the past may influence what choice one makes on a future occasion. Accordingly, a prior relationship between a complainant and an accused is sometimes relevant to what decision was made on the particular occasion.

Presently, rape shield law protection in the United States does not extend to prior sexual history with the accused. Following the Kobe Bryant rape trial acquittal, Dean Michelle Anderson has called for restrictions on such evidence.[231] But she accepts it as a given that

> prior negotiations between the complainant and the defendant regarding the specific acts at issue or customs and practices about those acts should be admissible. Those negotiations, customs, and practices between the parties reveal their legitimate expectations on the incident in question.[232]

Until the Supreme Court speaks more clearly on this issue my sympathy is with trial judges attempting to ensure that sexual assault trials are fair to both the accused and the accuser.

---

231 "Time to Reform Rape Shields Laws. Kobe Bryant Case Highlights Holes in the Armour" (2004) Criminal Justice 14.

232 *Ibid.* at 19.

International Law in the Jurisprudence of the McLachlin Court

JOHN H. CURRIE

A. INTRODUCTION

In its first decade under the leadership of Beverley McLachlin C.J., the Supreme Court of Canada has continued to make frequent and perhaps increased use of international law and other international sources in its judgments.[1] Indeed, in some instances, international law has proved pivotal to the outcome of the case under consideration. This has sent a clear signal to lower courts that international law will often be a relevant and perhaps even critical consideration in resolving domestic legal issues, a development widely considered desirable by international lawyers, one emblematic of Canada's commitment to the global rule of law.[2]

Members of the Court still, on occasion, invoke international legal sources without explicitly adverting to rules or principles of "reception"[3] justifying and guiding application of the international source to the specific case or issue under consideration. This practice makes the distillation, from the Court's judgments, of the rules or principles governing the domestic reception of international law in various contexts a necessarily inferential process, subject to the vagaries of individual interpretation and, hence, potential confusion. Happily,

---

1 This writer has identified at least fifty-six cases decided by the Court between 1 July 1999 and 31 July 2009 (the period covered by this article) in which one or more members of the Court refer to or rely upon international law in one form or another.

2 See, for example, Gib van Ert, *Using International Law in Canadian Courts*, 2d ed. (Toronto: Irwin Law, 2008) at 2 and 6–7 [van Ert, *International Law*].

3 See Gib van Ert, "What Is Reception Law?" [van Ert, "Reception Law"] in Oonagh E. Fitzgerald, ed., *The Globalized Rule of Law: Relationships between International and Domestic Law* (Toronto: Irwin Law, 2006) 85 [Fitzgerald].

however, this is increasingly a rarity. Recognizing the important implications of its reliance upon a source of law that until recently was often considered foreign, in recent years the McLachlin Court has made conscious efforts to address explicitly the nature of the relationship between international and Canadian law—efforts seldom found in the Court's earlier jurisprudence. The McLachlin Court's efforts in this regard are the subject of this article.

In particular, significant developments in the McLachlin Court's understanding of the relationship between international and Canadian law in four distinct areas, two in each of the non-constitutional and constitutional contexts, will be reviewed. First, the Court's substantial extension of the scope of the interpretive presumption of statutory conformity with Canada's international legal obligations will be discussed. Potential rigidification of that presumption in some of the Court's recent jurisprudence will also be considered. Second, the Court's first attempt to clarify the relationship between customary international law and Canadian common law since the issue was last explicitly considered by the Court in 1943[4] will be reviewed and critiqued. Third, the perplexing variability in the Court's approach to using international law in interpreting the *Canadian Charter of Rights and Freedoms*[5] will be assessed. Fourth, the possible emergence in the Court's jurisprudence of a doctrine of adoption of international legal principles as unwritten principles of the Canadian Constitution will be examined. Finally, some concluding thoughts on future challenges facing the Court in further defining the relationship between international and Canadian law will be offered.

It should be noted that this article does not focus on those of the McLachlin Court's cases that merely mention or make use of international law in various ways. Rather, the focus is on those cases that explicitly discuss rules governing the reception or application of international law in Canadian law. Nor does this paper analyze the Court's understanding of the substantive content of the various rules and doctrines of international law upon which it relies in many of its judgments. In other words, the purpose of this article is to examine the normative framework developed by the Court for the use of international law in domestic cases, rather than to conduct a behavioural study of the Court's reliance on or understanding of international law. As we shall see, even so confined, consideration of the Court's approach to international law is a rich and multi-faceted topic.

4 See *Reference Re Powers of Ottawa (City) and Rockcliffe Park*, [1943] S.C.R. 208 [*Foreign Legations*].

5 *Canadian Charter of Rights and Freedoms*, Part I of the *Constitution Act, 1982*, being Schedule B of the *Canada Act 1982* (U.K.) 1982, c. 11.

RÉSUMÉ

Ce chapitre discute du développement par la Cour McLachlin des règles régissant l'utilisation du droit international par les tribunaux canadiens. Quatre grands volets de l'évolution de ces « règles de la réception » font l'objet d'analyse, soit : (1) l'agrandissement de la portée de la présomption de la conformité législative avec les obligations internationales du Canada; (2) une ambivalence soutenue quant au rapport entre le droit international coutumier et la « common law » canadienne; (3) l'incertitude croissante au regard de l'utilisation appropriée du droit international par les tribunaux en interprétant la *Charte canadienne des droits et libertés*; et (4) l'émergence possible d'une doctrine selon laquelle des règles de droit international pourraient dorénavant constituer des éléments non-écrits de la constitution canadienne. Tout en applaudissant l'attention accrue qu'a portée la Cour McLachlin à ces aspects du droit de la réception, l'auteur préconise davantage d'éclaircissement, de rationalisation et d'intégration des règles applicables dans sa jurisprudence future.

B. THE ROLE OF INTERNATIONAL LAW IN NON-CONSTITUTIONAL CASES

1) The Presumption of Statutory Conformity with International Law

Turning first to the non-constitutional context, perhaps the most significant development in the Court's stance *vis-à-vis* international law over the past ten years has been its entrenchment and extension of the interpretive "presumption of conformity" of Canadian legislation with Canada's binding international legal obligations.[6] In one of its earliest clear articulations by a majority of the Court, in the 1990 decision in *National Corn Growers*,[7] this presumption was originally conceived as a means of reconciling Canada's treaty commitments and domestic legislation implementing them. In its origins, therefore, the presumption was premised on respect for legislative intent:

6 See generally van Ert, *International Law*, above note 2 at 130–81; John H. Currie, *Public International Law*, 2d ed. (Toronto: Irwin Law, 2008) at 248–59 [Currie].

7 *National Corn Growers Assn. v. Canada (Import Tribunal)*, [1990] 2 S.C.R. 1324, Gonthier J. for the majority [*National Corn Growers*].

> In interpreting legislation *which has been enacted with a view towards implementing international obligations*, as is the case here, it is reasonable for a tribunal to examine the domestic law in the context of the relevant agreement to clarify any uncertainty. Indeed where the text of the domestic law lends itself to it, one should also strive to expound an interpretation which is consonant with the relevant international obligations.[8]

This original, narrow scope of the presumption, applicable essentially to the interpretation of implementing legislation only, was repeated and applied in such cases as *Ward* (1993),[9] *Thomson v. Thomson* (1994),[10] *Pushpanathan* (1998),[11] and *Ordon Estate v. Grail* (1998).[12]

Even so narrowly construed, the principle that a domestic court should have recourse to treaties in interpreting domestic implementing legislation signalled a partial departure from the formerly strict rule of transformation applied by the Court in *Capital Cities Communications*[13] and introduced a monist vein into the Canadian legal system's posture towards treaties. It did so by allowing a treaty to have at least indirect domestic effect through the interpretive device of reconciliation of domestic implementing legislation with the corresponding treaty. The result was in some sense to place the onus on a legislature purporting to implement a treaty to indicate explicitly and clearly any departures from the treaty's provisions it intends to enact in domestic law. While this technically preserved legislative supremacy, a failure to express such statutory intent clearly would often mean that the treaty itself would govern the domestic legal effect of the implementing legislation.[14]

---

8 *Ibid.* at 1371 [emphasis added].

9 *Canada (A.G.) v. Ward*, [1993] 2 S.C.R. 689.

10 *Thomson v. Thomson*, [1994] 3 S.C.R. 551.

11 *Pushpanathan v. Canada*, [1998] 1 S.C.R. 982 at 1029–35 [*Pushpanathan*].

12 *Ordon Estate v. Grail*, [1998] 3 S.C.R. 437 at para. 137, Iacobucci and Major JJ. [*Ordon Estate*].

13 *Capital Cities Communications v. Canadian Radio-Television Commission*, [1978] 2 S.C.R. 141 at 173 [*Capital Cities Communications*]. See also *Francis v. The Queen*, [1956] S.C.R. 618 at 621; *A.-G. Canada v. A.-G. Ontario*, [1937] A.C. 326 [*Labour Conventions Case*]; *R. v. Canada Labour Relations Board* (1964), 44 D.L.R. (2d) 440 at 453–56 (Man. Q.B.), Smith J. It should be recalled, however, that not every treaty requires domestic transformation. If no changes to domestic law are required in order to permit performance of a treaty (for example, if it may be performed by previously authorized executive action, or if existing domestic law is already sufficient to give effect to the treaty's requirements), no transformation is required: see H.M. Kindred, "The Use and Abuse of International Legal Sources by Canadians Courts" in Fitzgerald, above note 3 at 10–17 [Kindred].

14 An effect enhanced by the Court's finding in *National Corn Growers*, above note 7 at 1371, that resort to the treaty text is not limited to situations where the domestic legislation

However, the presumption of conformity has not remained confined to the implementing legislation context in the jurisprudence of the McLachlin Court. In particular, in the 1999 majority decision in *Baker*,[15] the seeds were sown for an eventual, radical extension of the scope of the presumption. As is well known, the majority in *Baker* looked to Canada's unimplemented treaty obligations in the *Convention on the Rights of the Child*[16] to interpret the scope of a ministerial discretion provided for in the *Immigration Act*[17]—manifestly not legislation implementing the *Convention*. The majority relied on the *Convention* in highly cautious terms, reasserting the traditional rule, from *Capital Cities Communications*,[18] that unimplemented treaties are not part of Canadian law.[19] It also avoided any assertion of a presumption of conformity in this context. Rather, the majority found that the "values reflected in international human rights law may help inform the contextual approach to statutory interpretation and judicial review," and described the *Convention* as an "aid in interpreting domestic law."[20] Notwithstanding this cautious approach, the result was nevertheless effectively to read Canada's *Convention* obligation to consider the best interests of children, when decisions are

---

is ambiguous on its face but is, rather, permissible at the outset of the inquiry in order to *reveal* an ambiguity in the domestic legislation; as well as the Court's subsequent determination that international rules of treaty interpretation, pursuant to the *Vienna Convention on the Law of Treaties*, 23 May 1969, 1155 U.N.T.S. 331, should be applied in interpreting domestic implementing legislation: see *Pushpanathan*, above note 11 at 1019–20.

15 *Baker v. Canada (Minister of Citizenship and Immigration)*, [1999] 2 S.C.R. 817 [*Baker*].

16 *Convention on the Rights of the Child*, 20 November 1989, 1577 U.N.T.S. 3 (entered into force 2 September 1990), art. 3(1), requiring states' parties to consider the best interests of children when decisions are made that affect their future. It should be noted that throughout this paper I apply the term "implemented" to treaties that have unequivocally been the subject of express and purposeful legislative implementation, whereas I apply the term "unimplemented" to treaties that have not. This shorthand usage is without prejudice to the broader issue of whether certain treaties may nevertheless be considered "implemented" even if not the subject of such express and purposeful legislative implementation. For discussion of the many possible understandings of treaty "implementation," see Elisabeth Eid & Hoori Hamboyan, "Implementation by Canada of its International Human Rights Treaty Obligations: Making Sense Out of the Nonsensical" in Fitzgerald, above note 3 at 449; and Armand L.C. de Mestral & Evan Fox-Decent, "Implementation and Reception: The Congeniality of Canada's Legal Order to International Law" in Fitzgerald, above note 3 at 31 [de Mestral & Fox-Decent].

17 *Immigration Act*, R.S.C. 1985, c. I-2, s. 114(2) (now the *Immigration and Refugee Protection Act*, S.C. 2001, c. 27).

18 *Capital Cities Communications*, above note 13 at 173.

19 *Baker*, above note 15 at para. 69.

20 *Ibid.* at para. 70.

made that affect their future, into the factors that must be considered when exercising the relevant ministerial discretion under the *Immigration Act*.[21]

The majority in *Baker* did not elaborate on what was meant by "values reflected in international human rights law,"[22] as distinct from "international human rights law" *per se*. Was the distinction meant to suggest that the content of the *Convention* could also be found in customary international law and thus in common law principles directly applicable in construing the ministerial discretion?[23] If not, was it meant to signal that the presumption of conformity only operated with respect to the "values," rather than the rules, reflected in Canada's binding international legal obligations?[24] Were these distinctions meant to preserve, at least formally, the requirement of legislative transformation before a treaty may have domestic legal effect?[25] If so, this did not dissuade Iacobucci J. (writing for himself and Cory J. in a concurring judgment) from voicing strong concern for the effects of such an approach on the rule of transformation:

> I do not share my colleague's confidence that the Court's precedent in *Capital Cities* . . . survives intact following the adoption of a principle of law which permits reference to an unincorporated convention during the process of statutory interpretation. Instead, the result will be that the appellant is able to achieve indirectly what cannot be achieved directly, namely, to give force and effect within the domestic legal system to international obligations undertaken by the executive alone that have yet to be subject to the democratic will of Parliament.[26]

While the result, if not the reasoning, of the majority in *Baker* might thus be considered a departure from the traditional rule that treaties must be

21 *Ibid.* at para. 73.

22 *Ibid.* at para. 70.

23 See William A. Schabas, "Twenty-Five Years of Public International Law at the Supreme Court of Canada" (2000) 79 Can. Bar Rev. 174 at 182; Jutta Brunnée & Stephen J. Toope, "A Hesitant Embrace: The Application of International Law by Canadian Courts" (2002) 40 Can. Y.B. Int'l Law 3 at 45 [Brunnée & Toope]. On the status of customary international law in Canadian common law, see further below and see generally van Ert, *International Law*, above note 2 at 182–227; Currie, above note 6 at 226–35.

24 See Brunnée & Toope, *ibid.* at 37–38.

25 See authorities collected above, note 13.

26 *Baker*, above note 15 at 866, Iacobucci J. concurring. It should be noted, however, that Iacobucci J. had himself, the year before, endorsed the rule that "a court must presume that legislation is intended to comply with Canada's obligations under international instruments": see *Ordon Estate*, above note 12 at para. 137, Iacobucci and Major JJ. Admittedly, however, *Ordon Estate* involved interpretation of implementing legislation.

legislatively implemented to have domestic legal effect, a majority revisited and arguably extended the *Baker* approach in 2001 in *Spraytech*.[27] *Spraytech* required interpretation of provincial and municipal legislation to ensure that the latter came within the grant of delegated legislative authority provided in the former. Recalling the majority ruling in *Baker*, the *Spraytech* majority suggested that international environmental law's "precautionary principle" may be customary international law.[28] It also noted that its interpretation of the bylaw in issue "respected"—and its interpretation of the enabling provincial legislation was "consistent" with—that principle.[29] Again, therefore, the majority used very cautious language: the precautionary principle was described merely as "context"; no presumption of conformity of domestic legislation with that arguable principle of international law was asserted. Rather, conformity was merely noted to exist, almost as a fortuitous coincidence. But the *Spraytech* majority's invocation of *Baker* seemed at least to suggest that the permissible use of international law to interpret domestic legislation was not limited to treaty law, and could also extend to customary international law—perhaps even if not clearly established.

The Court's cautious, some might even say timid, approach in *Baker* and *Spraytech* to using international law in interpreting domestic non-implementing legislation led some commentators to suggest that the Court was in fact not asserting any particularly revolutionary or new role for international law at all. Rather, it was suggested, the Court was simply referring to international law as part of a much broader array of contextual factors that could, optionally, on occasion and as the Court saw fit, assist it in the process of statutory interpretation.[30] However, the Court's subsequent decisions decisively went much further, clearly overtaking *Baker* and *Spraytech*, and dramatically extending the role of the presumption of conformity well beyond its *National Corn Growers* roots.

---

27 *114957 Canada Ltée (Spraytech, Société d'arrosage) v. Hudson (Ville)*, [2001] 2 S.C.R. 241 [*Spraytech*].

28 *Ibid.* at para. 32.

29 *Ibid.* at paras. 30–31.

30 See, for example, Stéphane Beaulac, "National Application of International Law: The Statutory Interpretation Perspective" (2003) 41 Can. Y.B. Int'l Law 225 at 259 [Beaulac]; Stéphane Beaulac, "International Law and Statutory Interpretation: Up with Context, Down with Presumption" in O. Fitzgerald, ed., *The Globalized Rule of Law: Relationships between International and Domestic Law* (Toronto: Irwin Law, 2007) 331. See also Brunnée & Toope, above note 23 at 38–39, 41–42, and 45–46, fearing that such a conclusion might be drawn from the cases, even if not intended.

Schreiber (2002)[31] offered a first, terse but clear inkling of such an extension.[32] In *Schreiber*, the Court had been invited by one of the interveners to apply international law in construing the *State Immunity Act*.[33] The Court demurred on the ground that the domestic legislation was clearer and more detailed than international law and that nothing was therefore to be gained from considering the latter.[34] However, in doing so the Court also endorsed a much earlier dictum of Pigeon J., writing for himself in the 1968 case of *Daniels v. White*:[35]

> Parliament is not presumed to legislate in breach of a treaty or in any manner inconsistent with the comity of nations and the established rules of international law . . . [although] if a statute is unambiguous, its provisions must be followed even if they are contrary to international law.[36]

The majority in *Schreiber* characterized this dictum as the rule governing "when international law is appropriately used to interpret domestic legislation."[37] Remarkably, it did so without tying such a presumption to the interpretation of domestic *implementing* legislation. However, it also did not address how such an extension of the presumption of conformity could be reconciled with the requirement of legislative implementation of treaty obligations before they can have domestic legal effect.[38] In construing implementing legislation, the courts are guided by evidence that the legislature has at least made the decision to implement a treaty. In this context, the presumption of conformity does not do away at all with the need for implementation but merely facilitates it. But this is plainly not so in the absence of legislation purporting to implement the relevant treaty obligation. *Schreiber* did not address this conundrum.

---

31 *Schreiber v. Canada (Attorney General)*, [2002] 3 S.C.R. 269 [*Schreiber*].

32 It is arguable that the judgment of Dickson J., writing for the Court in *Zingre v. The Queen*, [1981] 2 S.C.R. 392 at 406–7 and 409–10 [*Zingre*], had already implicitly applied a presumption of conformity to the interpretation of non-implementing legislation. However, the language used in the judgment could also support the view that its use of the relevant treaty as an interpretive aid was confined to the particular facts of the case and that no general principle was being adumbrated by the Court; and it has not been cited by the Court as support for the presumption of conformity in the non-implementation context until very recently: see, for example, *R. v. Hape*, [2007] 2 S.C.R. 292 at para. 54 [*Hape*].

33 *State Immunity Act*, R.S.C. 1985, c. S-18.

34 *Schreiber*, above note 31 at para. 51.

35 *Daniels v. White and The Queen*, [1968] S.C.R. 517 [*Daniels*].

36 *Ibid.* at 541, Pigeon J. concurring.

37 *Schreiber*, above note 31 at para. 50.

38 See authorities collected above, note 13.

Nevertheless, following *Schreiber*, the McLachlin Court relied upon this much broader presumption of conformity in numerous cases and contexts. For example, in *Canadian Foundation for Children* (2004),[39] albeit a *Charter* case, the majority referred without qualification to the presumption that "[s]tatutes should be interpreted to comply with Canada's international obligations."[40] It accordingly applied a number of Canada's international treaty obligations, most unimplemented, in order to construe section 43 of the *Criminal Code*[41] in a way that avoided unconstitutionality on the basis of vagueness.

In *Mugesera* (2005),[42] the Court was called upon to interpret the elements of the *Criminal Code* offence of genocide.[43] Admittedly, this was likely a case of construing treaty implementing legislation, given the Court's observation that the relevant *Criminal Code* provision "incorporates, almost word for word, the definition of genocide found in art. II of the *Genocide Convention*."[44] Nevertheless, the Court underlined "[t]he importance of interpreting domestic law in a manner that accords with the principles of customary international law and with Canada's treaty obligations."[45] Notably, this formulation of the rule is not limited to the interpretation of domestic implementing legislation. Also notably, the Court credited the majority judgment in *Baker* for this rule, although it seems plain that the *Mugesera* formulation goes considerably further than *Baker*'s precise and circumspect language.

As a final example, in *Hape* (2007),[46] a majority of the Court affirmed, albeit in *obiter*, the presumption of conformity in unequivocal and broad terms:

> It is a well-established principle of statutory interpretation that legislation will be presumed to conform to international law .... The presumption applies equally to customary international law and treaty obligations.[47]

Again, here the presumption is stated without limiting its application to implementing legislation or to treaty obligations that have been implemented domestically.

---

39 *Canadian Foundation for Children, Youth and the Law v. Canada (Attorney General)*, [2004] 1 S.C.R. 76 [*Canadian Foundation for Children*].

40 *Ibid.* at para. 31, McLachlin C.J. for the majority.

41 *Criminal Code*, R.S.C. 1985, c. C-46.

42 *Mugesera v. Canada (Minister of Citizenship and Immigration)*, [2005] 2 S.C.R. 100 [*Mugesera*].

43 *Criminal Code*, above note 41, s. 318(1).

44 *Mugesera*, above note 42 at para. 82.

45 *Ibid.*

46 *Hape*, above note 32.

47 *Ibid.* at paras. 53–54.

Thus, the McLachlin Court has expanded the scope of the presumption of statutory conformity well beyond its origins as a device for reconciling Canada's treaty obligations and legislation implementing those obligations domestically. Rather, the presumption now clearly requires Canadian courts to interpret all domestic legislation, whether or not it purports to implement treaty obligations, in a manner consistent with all of Canada's international legal obligations, whether or not they take the form of treaty obligations. Of course, the presumption is rebuttable where the terms of the domestic rule cannot, through interpretive ingenuity, be reconciled with the international legal obligation.[48]

The academic literature has varied in its understanding of the theoretical underpinnings of this very broad presumption of conformity. On one hand, some commentators have regarded the presumption as resting on a judicial policy or even duty to ensure that judicial interpretation of statutes does not place Canada in violation of its international legal obligations.[49] The more orthodox view, however, is rooted essentially in a theory of legislative intent. As Sullivan explains it, the twin bases for the presumption are, first, that Canada's binding international legal obligations form part of the legal context in which legislatures act and, second, that legislatures should be taken not to intend to violate binding international law unless they make such intention clear.[50] Accordingly, where more than one interpretation of domestic law is possible, the interpretation that accords with Canada's international legal obligations will be preferred.[51] The Court has not clearly rejected either of these theoretical approaches in favour of the other, but has tended to rely principally on the latter.[52]

---

48 *Ibid.* at para. 53. See also van Ert, *International Law*, above note 2 at 131–32; Ruth Sullivan, *Sullivan on the Construction of Statutes*, 5th ed. (Markham, ON: Butterworths, 2008) at 548–49 [Sullivan]; Pierre Andre Côté, *The Interpretation of Legislation in Canada*, 3d ed. (Scarborough, ON: Carswell, 2000) at 367–68 [Côté].

49 See, for example, van Ert, *ibid.* at 132–33; and van Ert, "Reception Law," above note 3 at 89. In the English context, see Murray Hunt, *Using Human Rights Law in English Courts* (Oxford: Hart Publishing, 1998) at c. 8.

50 Sullivan, above note 48 at 538–39.

51 *Ibid.* See also John Mark Keyes & Ruth Sullivan, "A Legislative Perspective on the Interaction of International and Domestic Law" in Fitzgerald, above note 3 at 277.

52 See, for example, *Hape*, above note 32 at para. 53; *GreCon Dimter inc. v. J.R. Normand inc.*, [2005] 2 S.C.R. 401 at para. 39 [*GreCon Dimter*]. Note, however, that some support for the "judicial policy" approach may also be gleaned from the majority judgment in *Hape*, above note 32 at para. 53, LeBel J.: "The presumption of conformity is based on the rule of judicial policy that, as a matter of law, courts will strive to avoid constructions of domestic

At first blush, the extension of the presumption of conformity beyond the legislative implementation context poses challenges for an explanation of the presumption based on legislative intent. In construing implementing legislation, the courts have the benefit of knowing that the legislature intended to implement a treaty. In this sense and as suggested above, the presumption does not do away at all with the need for implementation of the treaty but merely gives effect to the legislative intent to implement by interpretatively easing the treaty's entry into Canadian law.[53] This is plainly not so, however, in the absence of legislation that purports to implement the relevant treaty obligation at all. Must legislative intent therefore be abandoned as an explanation for the presumption of statutory conformity? The McLachlin Court has not squarely faced this apparent difficulty.

One way of reconciling the theory of legislative intent with the broader understanding of the presumption of conformity adopted by the McLachlin Court, however, might be to take a broader view of manifestations of legislative intent. When the legislative branch[54] does not adopt legislation implementing one of Canada's treaty obligations, but the courts apply the presumption of conformity to existing legislation in order to avoid a conflict with those obligations, the legislative branch remains free to override such judicial reconciliation.[55] Its failure to do so may then fairly be taken as evidence for one of two conclusions. The first possibility is that the legislative failure to adopt legislation implementing any particular treaty flows from a legislative determination that no such implementing legislation is necessary in order to bring Canadian domestic law into line with the relevant treaty obligations. That is, the legislature may be presumed to have determined that the existing state of the law already permitted treaty compliance.[56] The interpretation of existing statute law by the courts in a manner compliant

---

law pursuant to which the state would be in violation of its international obligations, unless the wording of the statute clearly compels that result."

53 See Currie, above note 6 at 253–54.

54 It will be recalled that the constitutional authority to adopt legislation implementing Canada's treaty obligations is distributed between Parliament and the provincial legislatures according to whether the subject matter of the treaty corresponds to the classes of subjects assigned to one or the other orders of the legislative branch under ss. 91 and 92 of the *Constitution Act, 1867*: see *Labour Conventions Case*, above note 13 at paras. 12 and 15, Lord Atkin. See also Currie, above note 6 at 241–46.

55 See Kindred, above note 13 at 8–9. Admittedly, however, the exercise of such legislative power would often be factually dependent on executive concurrence, given that few non-government bills are ever enacted.

56 Thus obviating the need for legislative implementation: see Kindred, *ibid.* at 10–17.

with Canada's international legal obligations therefore merely amounts to confirmation of that legislative determination. The second possibility is that no such legislative determination may fairly be imputed and judicial application of the presumption of conformity has in fact led to a modification of the meaning of domestic statute law in order to reconcile it with Canada's international legal obligations. If this is so and the legislature fails to "correct" this effective judicial amendment of domestic statute law, it may be presumed that the legislature has acquiesced therein. On either explanation, a form of legislative "intent" is, more or less directly, respected.

Nevertheless, if domestic law is wherever possible to be interpretively reconciled with Canada's international legal obligations—including treaty obligations that have not been implemented—it is difficult to see what practical scope remains for the requirement of legislative implementation of treaty obligations. If all legislation—not merely that which purports to implement treaty obligations—should wherever possible be interpreted in conformity with Canada's international obligations, including treaty obligations that have not been implemented, does this not in effect require Canadian courts to read those treaty obligations into legislative ambiguities and voids left by Canadian legislators? If so, is the need for explicit legislative implementation of treaties not obviated? Have the courts not, in effect, assumed the role of domestic implementers of Canada's treaty obligations, at least in those cases where the legislatures have not? If so, it would seem that the requirement of treaty implementation has in fact been reduced to nothing more than the well-known, residual discretion of the legislative branch to violate international law as long as it does so in express statutory terms.[57]

While the Court continues to periodically rehearse the requirement of treaty implementation,[58] it has not to date addressed the foregoing questions or clearly explained how or why legislative implementation remains practically relevant in light of the Court's broad understanding of the presumption of statutory conformity.

This is not to say that the foregoing questions are unanswerable. In this writer's view, it is likely that the *Capital Cities Communication* requirement

---

57 See *Hape*, above note 32 at paras. 39, 53, and 68. See also Ronald St. J. Macdonald, "The Relationship between International Law and Domestic Law in Canada" in Ronald St. J. Macdonald, Gerald L. Morris, and Douglas M. Johnston, eds., *Canadian Perspectives on International Law and Organization* (Toronto: University of Toronto Press, 1974) 88 at 119 [Macdonald, "Relationship"]; van Ert, *International Law*, above note 2 at 131–32; Sullivan, above note 48 at 548–49; Côté, above note 48 at 367–68.

58 See, for example, *Baker*, above note 15 at para. 69.

of legislative treaty implementation indeed has effectively, if not formally, been rendered a dead letter by the McLachlin Court's expansion of the presumption of conformity. However, this is neither necessarily problematic nor objectionable in principle. While it is beyond the scope of this paper to develop this position fully here, in essence this issue requires consideration of the underlying rationale for the requirement of treaty implementation in the first place. Essentially, that rationale is rooted in the democratic principle: the executive branch, while competent to conclude treaties without legislative consent, is not constitutionally competent to make domestic law without legislative consent.[59] However, it does not follow from these premises that treaties require *legislative* implementation in order to have domestic legal effect. Such a conclusion would ignore the fact that legislatures are not the only constitutionally competent domestic lawmakers in our system. The courts too, through their common law jurisdiction, have the power to make domestic law (albeit subject to legislative override).[60] And there would seem to be no insuperable barrier, in principle, to the exercise of that common law power in order to give Canada's legislatively unimplemented but binding international legal obligations domestic legal effect—subject always, of course, to the power of the legislative branch to override such common law "implementation." It may be that legislative implementation is a more practical or otherwise preferred alternative in specific instances, for example, in the case of complex treaty schemes calling for substantial changes to domestic legal infrastructure, or for the expenditure of public funds.[61] However, this poses no barrier to the general proposition that, in appropriate circumstances and in keeping with the generally incremental approach of the courts in developing the common law,[62] Canadian courts may be considered legitimate "implementers" of Canada's international legal obligations. Indeed, this is arguably precisely the role that the McLachlin Court has been playing, in effect if not in form, since its understanding of

---

59 See Ian Brownlie, *Principles of Public International Law*, 7th ed. (Oxford: Oxford University Press, 2008) at 45 [Brownlie]; van Ert, *International Law*, above note 2 at 229–32.

60 See Peter W. Hogg, *Constitutional Law of Canada*, 5th ed., supp. looseleaf (Scarborough, ON: Thomson Carswell, 2007) at para. 12.2 [Hogg]. See also *R. v. Salituro*, [1991] 3 S.C.R. 654 at 670 and 678; *Watkins v. Olafson*, [1989] 2 S.C.R. 750, 61 D.L.R. 4th 577 at 584; and *Friedmann Equity Developments Inc. v. Final Note Ltd.*, [2000] 1 S.C.R. 842 at para. 42.

61 I am grateful to Gib van Ert for suggesting this limitation to me in private conversation following presentation of this paper at the Canadian Bar Association conference, "The McLachlin Court's First Decade: Reflections on the Past and Projections for the Future," Ottawa, 19 June 2009.

62 See authorities collected above, note 60.

the presumption of conformity began to expand in *Baker*. It may therefore be time for the Court to recognize this effect for what it is and explicitly formalize it as such.

Turning now to another feature of the McLachlin Court's jurisprudence on the presumption of statutory conformity, that presumption appears not only to have been extended in its scope by the Court, but arguably the rigidity of the presumption may also be increasing in the Court's jurisprudence.

This observation arises particularly from the Court's 2005 decision in *GreCon Dimter*,[63] where the Court had to determine which of two apparently inconsistent provisions of the *Civil Code of Québec*[64] should prevail in determining whether the Québec courts had jurisdiction over an action brought by a Québec importer against a German manufacturer. Noting that Canada (and thus Québec) is a party to the *New York Convention on the Recognition and Enforcement of Foreign Arbitral Awards*[65] and that the "legislature has incorporated the principles of the *New York Convention* . . . into Quebec law by enacting the substance of the Convention,"[66] the Court found that the "*New York Convention* is therefore a formal source for interpreting the domestic law provisions."[67]

As an aside, this is an interesting finding in itself, given the somewhat indirect evidence that the relevant provisions of the *Québec Civil Code* were intended to implement the *New York Convention*. In particular, the Court noted that the *Civil Code*'s rules governing international arbitration agreements were based on those of the *UNCITRAL Model Law on International Commercial Arbitration*.[68] As these "closely follow the provisions of the *New York Convention*," the Court concluded that the *Civil Code* implemented "the substance" of the *New York Convention*.[69] This seems to signal that the Court, in determining whether or not a given treaty has been legislatively implemented, will look to the substance of domestic legislation rather than more

63 *GreCon Dimter*, above note 52.

64 *Civil Code of Québec*, S.Q. 1991, c. 64, arts. 3139 & 3148(2).

65 *Convention on the Recognition and Enforcement of Foreign Arbitral Awards*, 10 June 1958, 330 U.N.T.S. 3, [1986] Can. T.S. No. 43 [*New York Convention*]; see *GreCon Dimter*, above note 52 at para. 40.

66 *GreCon Dimter*, *ibid.* at para. 41.

67 *Ibid.* See also *Dell Computer Corp. v. Union des consommateurs*, [2007] 2 S.C.R. 801 at paras. 38–41, 44–47, and 73–75, Deschamps J. [*Dell Computer*]; and at para. 175, Bastarache and LeBel JJ. dissenting.

68 *UNCITRAL Model Law on International Commercial Arbitration*, 21 June, 1985, U.N. Doc. A/40/17 (1985), Ann. I.

69 *GreCon Dimter*, above note 52 at para. 41.

formal indicators of legislative intent to implement.[70] It is also not clear why this step was necessary in the reasoning, in light of the now-broad scope of the presumption of conformity; conformity is required whether or not treaty obligations have been implemented and thus, even if unimplemented, the *New York Convention* would have been a "formal source for interpreting the domestic law provisions."[71]

In any case, the finding that the *New York Convention* was a formal source for the interpretation of the *Civil Code*, on the assumption that the latter implemented the former, is essentially consistent with the presumption of conformity originally set out in *National Corn Growers* and other cases in the legislative implementation context. However, in *GreCon Dimter* the Court went further in characterizing the role of the relevant treaty provisions in interpreting the domestic legislation. The Court wrote:

> The interpretation of the provisions in issue, and the resolution of the conflict between them, *must necessarily be harmonized* with the international commitments of Canada and Quebec.[72]

National Corn Growers articulated a rebuttable presumption of conformity of implementing legislation with international treaty obligations, one that courts "should . . . strive" to apply "where the text of the domestic law lends itself to it."[73] Subsequent articulations of the presumption of conformity, which asserted that courts "should" strive to interpret domestic legislation in conformity with Canada's international legal obligations, also implied its rebuttable nature.[74] The language quoted from *GreCon Dimter* above, by contrast, appears on its face to make such conformity mandatory and arguably to give the treaty controlling effect. The Court tied this rule to the "presumption that the legislature is deemed not to intend to legislate in a manner that cannot be reconciled with the state's international obligations,"[75] but did not explain why such a "presumption" entails a restatement of the *National*

---

70 On the increasingly flexible approach taken by Canadian courts in determining whether or not a treaty has been implemented, see Brunnée & Toope, above note 23 at 22–31; Kindred, above note 13 at 10–17; de Mestral & Fox-Decent, above note 16 at 42–56. But see Beaulac (2003), above note 30 at 245–48.

71 *GreCon Dimter*, above note 52 at para. 41.

72 *Ibid.* at para. 39 [emphasis added]

73 *National Corn Growers*, above note 7 at 1371.

74 See, for example, *Canadian Foundation for Children*, above note 39 at para. 31, per McLachlin C.J.: "Statutes *should* be construed to comply with Canada's international obligations" [emphasis added].

75 *GreCon Dimter*, above note 52 at para. 39, citing Côté, above note 48 at 367.

Corn Growers rule in such unqualified, compulsory terms. Did the Court in *GreCon Dimter* intend, by holding without qualification that domestic implementing legislation "must necessarily be harmonized" with treaty obligations, to remove the legislature's power to enact implementing legislation that cannot be so reconciled? Or may it simply be that, as there was no evidence in that case of a legislative intent to depart from the treaty's provisions, there was no need to add a qualification in that regard?

While both the majority and dissenting judgments in the subsequent *Dell Computer* (2007) case[76] relied on *GreCon Dimter*'s conclusion that the *New York Convention* was a formal source for the interpretation of domestic law, neither addressed the seemingly mandatory conformity rule enunciated by the Court in *GreCon Dimter*. Clarification of whether the Court intended in *GreCon Dimter* to "harden" the presumption of conformity, potentially privileging treaty compliance over legislative intent (at least in the treaty implementation context), will therefore have to await future cases.[77]

2) The Relationship between Customary International Law and Canadian Common Law

We turn now to consider the Court's only recent explicit consideration of the relationship between customary international law and domestic common law.[78] While the British courts have clearly taken an adoptionist stance[79] on this issue for some time,[80] the Canadian approach has perennially remained

76 See *Dell Computer*, above note 67 at paras. 38–41, 44–47, and 73–75, Deschamps J.; and at para. 175, Bastarache and LeBel JJ. dissenting.

77 It is perhaps notable that the majority in *Hape*, above note 32 at para. 53, affirmed in *obiter* the rebuttable nature of the presumption of conformity in general terms.

78 *Hape*, above note 32. It should be noted that while the Court relied extensively on customary international law in *Mugesera*, above note 42, it did so in the context of statutory interpretation, and (at least in considering the definition of "crimes against humanity") in light of the express incorporation of customary international law in s. 7(3.76) of the *Criminal Code*, above note 41. Accordingly, the question of the relationship between customary international law and Canadian common law did not arise in that case.

79 The term "incorporationist" is more common in British practice whereas "adoptionist" tends to be used in Canadian practice. On the vagaries of the terminology used in this area of the law, see van Ert, *International Law*, above note 2 at 3–5.

80 See, for example, *Trendtex Trading Corp. v. Central Bank of Nigeria*, [1977] Q.B. 529 (Eng. C.A.). In this judgment, Lord Denning traces the origins of this rule to the early eighteenth century and provides a succinct overview of the relevant precedents. *Ibid.* at 553. See also *Buvot v. Barbuit* (1737), 25 E.R. 777 (Ch.); *Heathfield v. Chilton* (1767), 4 Burrow 2015, Lord Mansfield; Shaheed Fatima, *Using International Law in Domestic Courts* (Oxford: Hart Publishing, 2005) at 403–36 [Fatima]; and Brownlie, above note 59 at 41–44. A similar

much less certain.[81] The principal reason for this is that, notwithstanding (or perhaps because of) the absence of any provisions in Canada's constitutional documents expressly governing the matter, Canadian courts have tended to refrain from addressing the issue squarely and clearly. Rather, Canadian courts have for many years implicitly taken an adoptionist stance, giving rise to the cautious conclusion that "there is room for the view that the law on the relationship of customary international law to domestic law in Canada is the same as it is in England."[82] More recently, a number of lower Canadian courts have been more explicit in their support for the adoptionist approach to customary international law,[83] leading some commentators to take a more robust view of Canadian law's embrace of the doctrine of adoption.[84]

As for the Supreme Court, it too has remained tentative on this issue ever since Lyman Poore Duff C.J.'s judgment in the Court's landmark 1943 decision in *Reference Re Powers of Ottawa (City) and Rockcliffe Park*.[85] While the chief justice's judgment in that case is widely interpreted as espousing

---

position is taken in the United States. See, for example, *The Paquette Habana*, (1900) 175 U.S. 688 at 700 (S. Ct.).

81 See generally Currie, above note 6 at 226–31.

82 See Macdonald, "Relationship," above note 57 at 111. See also Brunnée & Toope, above note 23 at 42–51, reviewing the ambiguous and sometimes conflicting Canadian caselaw and tentatively concluding that "the best view appears to be that customary law can operate directly within the Canadian legal system" (at 44).

83 For example, in litigation arising from the 1995 boarding and arrest by Canadian officials of the Spanish fishing trawler *Estai* in international waters (during the so-called turbot war), the Federal Court (Trial Division) considered "well settled" the proposition that "accepted principles of customary international law are recognized and are applied in Canadian courts, as part of the domestic law unless, of course, they are in conflict with domestic law": see *Jose Pereira E Hijos S.A. v. Canada (Attorney General)*, [1997] 2 F.C. 84 at para. 20 (T.D.). Similarly, in addressing a lawsuit brought by an Iranian expatriate against Iran for torture, the Ontario Court of Appeal accepted that "customary rules of international law are directly incorporated into Canadian domestic law unless explicitly ousted by contrary legislation": *Bouzari v. Islamic Republic of Iran* (2004), 71 O.R. (3d) 675 at para. 65 (C.A.), leave to appeal ref'd, [2005] 1 S.C.R. vi. See also *Mack v. Canada (Attorney General)* (2002), 60 O.R. (3d) 737 at para. 32 (C.A.), leave to appeal ref'd, [2003] 1 S.C.R. xiii.

84 See in particular the excellent analyses of the law in this area by van Ert, *International Law*, above note 2 at 182–227; and Francois Larocque & Martin Kreuser, "L'incorporation de la coutume internationale en common law canadienne" [2007] 45 Can. Y.B. Int'l Law 173.

85 *Foreign Legations*, above note 4. In this case, the Supreme Court of Canada was asked to give an advisory opinion on whether the Ontario *Assessment Act*, R.S.O. 1937, c. 272 (now R.S.O. 1990, c. A-31), applied to diplomatic property owned by foreign states in the national capital region, notwithstanding immunities from local taxation granted to foreign states by customary international law.

the adoptionist model, the Court's subsequent judgments only ever implicitly did so.[86] Perhaps sensing that clarification on the issue was long overdue, a majority of the McLachlin Court ventured an opinion on the topic in its 2007 decision in *Hape*[87]—interestingly, a case turning solely on interpretation of the *Charter*, such that its discussion of the doctrine of adoption must likely be considered *obiter dicta*.[88] Nevertheless, after reviewing the British position as well as the somewhat ambiguous adoptionist stance taken by the Canadian courts to date, the majority wrote:

> Despite the Court's silence in some recent cases, the doctrine of adoption has never been rejected in Canada. Indeed, there is a long line of cases in which the Court has either formally accepted it or at least applied it. In my view, following the common law tradition, it appears that the doctrine of adoption operates in Canada such that prohibitive rules of customary international law should be incorporated into domestic law in the absence of conflicting legislation. The automatic incorporation of such rules is justified on the basis that international custom, as the law of nations, is also the law of Canada unless, in a valid exercise of its sovereignty, Canada declares that its law is to the contrary. Parliamentary sovereignty dictates that a legislature may violate international law, but that it must do so expressly. Absent an express derogation, the courts may look to prohibitive rules of customary international law to aid in the interpretation of Canadian law and the development of the common law.[89]

---

86 See, for example, *Saint John v. Fraser-Brace Overseas Corp.*, [1958] S.C.R. 263 at 268–69, Rand J. (again dealing with the effect of the customary international law of state immunities from municipal taxation); and *Pushpanathan*, above note 11 at 1029–35 (referring to the customary international legal meaning attributed to the words "contrary to the principles of the United Nations" in interpreting legislation implementing treaty obligations relating to refugee status). See also *The Ship "North" v. The King* (1906), 37 S.C.R. 385 at 394, Davies J.; *Reference as to Whether Members of the Military or Naval Forces of the United States of America Are Exempt from Criminal Proceedings in Canadian Criminal Courts*, [1943] S.C.R. 483 at 502, Kerwin J.; *Re Newfoundland Continental Shelf*, [1984] 1 S.C.R. 86; *Reference re Secession of Québec*, [1998] 2 S.C.R. 217 at 276 [*Québec Secession Reference*]; *Spraytech*, above note 27 at paras. 30–32; *Suresh v. Canada (Minister of Citizenship and Immigration)*, [2002] 1 S.C.R. 3 at paras. 61–65 [*Suresh*]; and *Schreiber*, above note 31 at paras. 48–50, LeBel J. But see *Gouvernement de la République démocratique du Congo v. Venne*, [1971] S.C.R. 997.

87 *Hape*, above note 32.

88 See discussion of this point in John H. Currie, "Weaving a Tangled Web: *Hape* and the Obfuscation of Canadian Reception Law" [2007] 45 Can. Y.B. Int'l Law 55 at 85–86 and at n. 136 [Currie, "Weaving"].

89 *Hape*, above note 32 at para. 39.

While this attempt to clarify the direct domestic effect of customary international law is laudable, this paragraph, and the majority's subsequent application of the "doctrine of adoption" in *Hape*, gives rise to considerable uncertainties as to the true interpretation of that doctrine.[90] In particular it is submitted that this and other passages from *Hape* could be read to endorse as many as five different understandings of the relationship between customary international law and Canadian common law, as follows:

1) customary international law *is automatically part of* the common law of Canada in the absence of conflicting legislation;[91]
2) customary international law *should be incorporated into* the common law of Canada in the absence of conflicting legislation;
3) customary international law *may be incorporated into* the common law of Canada in the absence of conflicting legislation;[92]
4) customary international law *may aid in the development of* the common law of Canada; and
5) customary international law *may aid in the interpretation of* the common law of Canada.[93]

In other words, *Hape* arguably formulates several mutually inconsistent versions of the doctrine of adoption, both monist and dualist in nature,[94] without clearly articulating which one prevails. Some clarification as to whether the majority's intention was indeed to endorse the first of these alternative formulations—the only one clearly consistent with the doctrine of adoption applied in English law[95]—would therefore seem to be necessary.

---

90 See discussion in Currie, "Weaving," above note 88 at 63–66.

91 See also *Hape*, above note 32 at para. 56, where the majority refers to the principle of "the direct application of international custom."

92 See also *ibid.* at para. 46, holding that principles of customary international law "may be adopted into the common law of Canada in the absence of conflicting legislation"; and at para. 36, where the English position is paraphrased thus: "Prohibitive rules of international law may be incorporated directly into domestic law through the common law . . . . According to the doctrine of adoption, the courts may adopt rules of customary international law as common law rules."

93 See also *ibid.* at para. 70, where the majority refers to the "context and interpretive assistance set out in the foregoing discussion."

94 On the distinction between monist and dualist models for the reception of international law in domestic law, see van Ert, *International Law*, above note 2 at 3–5; Currie, above note 6 at 220–24. See also Gerald Fitzmaurice, "The General Principles of International Law: Considered from the Standpoint of the Rule of Law" (1957) 92:II Rec. des Cours 5 at 68–85; and Joseph G. Starke, "Monism and Dualism in the Theory of International Law" (1936) 17 Brit. Y.B. Int'l L. 66.

95 See authorities collected above, note 80.

If, on the other hand, the Court intended to endorse one or more of the latter, more discretionary, formulations of the doctrine of adoption, this may give rise to inconsistencies in principle with other rules of reception now recognized in Canadian law.

For example, the last understanding of the doctrine of adoption listed above would seem to accord customary international law a role inferior, in Canadian law, to that of Canada's unimplemented treaty obligations. As seen above, such obligations theoretically have no direct domestic effect in Canadian law.[96] However, as also seen above,[97] it is a well-established presumption of statutory construction that Canadian legislation is to be interpreted so as to comply with Canada's international legal obligations, whether or not domestically implemented, unless the relevant statutory language cannot bear such an interpretation.[98] That presumption effectively requires courts to reconcile, in the absence of clearly inconsistent statutory language, their interpretation of Canadian legislation with Canada's treaty obligations, including those that are not domestically implemented.[99] By contrast, the majority's assertion in *Hape* that customary international law merely "*may* . . . aid in the interpretation of Canadian law" states no such presumption or requirement.[100] Rather, judicial resort to customary international law in this version of the doctrine of adoption would appear to be purely voluntary. This apparent inconsistency of approach is not explained by the majority in *Hape*.

Similarly, it is arguable that the doctrine of adoption endorsed by the majority in *Hape*—whatever its correct interpretation—is an unnecessary

---

96 See authorities collected above, note 13. For the similar position taken in the United Kingdom, see *Maclaine Watson v. Department of Trade and Industry*, [1989] 3 All E.R. 523 at 531 (H.L.), Lord Oliver; *R. v. Secretary of State for the Home Department, ex parte Ahmed and Patel*, [1999] Imm. A.R. 22 at 36 (C.A.); and Fatima, above note 80 at 269–382.

97 *Hape*, above note 32 at paras. 53–54.

98 See, for example, *Daniels*, above note 35 at 541, Pigeon J.; *Zingre*, above note 32 at 409–10, Dickson J.; *Ordon Estate*, above note 12 at para. 137, Iacobucci and Major JJ.; *Schreiber*, above note 31 at para. 50; *Canadian Foundation for Children*, above note 39 at para. 31, McLachlin C.J. See also Sullivan, above note 48 at 538–49; Côté, above note 48 at 367–68; Brunnée & Toope, above note 23 at 25–26 and 32; van Ert, *International Law*, above note 2 at 130–81; and van Ert, "Reception Law," above note 3 at 89 (characterizing this presumption as a "basic doctrine of reception law").

99 See *Ordon Estate*, above note 12 at para. 137, Iacobucci and Major JJ.: "[A] court *must* presume that legislation is intended to comply with Canada's obligations under international instruments" [emphasis added]; and *Canadian Foundation for Children*, above note 39 at para. 31, McLachlin C.J.: "Statutes *should be* construed to comply with Canada's international obligations" [emphasis added].

100 *Hape*, above note 32 at para. 39 [emphasis added].

departure from the basic structure of the presumption of statutory conformity reviewed above. If the correct approach to the interpretation of domestic statute law is to presume its conformity, so far as textually possible, with Canada's international legal obligations—whether in the form of treaty or customary international law—why is there any need for a different "rule of adoption" guiding the relationship of domestic common law and customary international law specifically? Is there anything special about customary international law, as compared to Canada's treaty obligations, that justifies its differential treatment in terms of more direct domestic reception via the common law? Should the same underlying theoretical considerations not simply lead to extension of the presumption of conformity from the statutory to the common law contexts? Are Canada's international legal obligations not part of the legal context in which courts also act? Should courts not also be presumed to intend to respect those obligations when they formulate common law rules (unless they explicitly say otherwise)?[101] Assuming they are and should, why would interpretation of the common law not be subject to a presumption of conformity with customary international law *and* treaty law that is no more and no less robust than that applicable to the construction of statutes?

Answers to these questions, and clarification of what the *Hape* majority meant when it endorsed the "doctrine of adoption," must await further guidance from the Court in future cases.

C. THE ROLE OF INTERNATIONAL LAW IN CONSTITUTIONAL CASES

1) International Law and *Charter* Interpretation

We turn now to the McLachlin Court's use of international law in constitutional, and in particular, *Charter* cases. While it is widely accepted that the *Charter* does not, at least formally, implement any of Canada's international treaty obligations,[102] the Court has liberally taken account of such obligations, particularly in the human rights area, when construing the fundamental

101 See text accompanying above notes 49–52.

102 See, for example, *Ahani v. Canada (Attorney General)* (2002), 58 OR (3d) 107 at para. 31 (C.A.); William A. Schabas & Stéphane Beaulac, *International Human Rights and Canadian Law: Legal Commitment, Implementation and the Charter*, 3d ed. (Toronto: Thomson Carswell, 2007) at 59–67; Hogg, above note 60 at para. 36.9(c). For criticism of the *Ahani* decision, see Joanna Harrington, "Punting Terrorists, Assassins and Other Undesirables" (2003) 48 McGill L.J. 55.

guarantees set out in the *Charter*.[103] That in itself is, of course, not an innovation of the McLachlin Court, but is a longstanding practice stretching back to the 1989 majority judgment of the Court in *Slaight Communications Inc. v. Davidson*,[104] where it was held that:

> [T]he *Charter* should generally be presumed to provide protection at least as great as that afforded by similar provisions in international human rights documents which Canada has ratified.
>
> Canada's international human rights obligations should inform not only the interpretation of the content of the rights guaranteed by the *Charter* but also the interpretation of what can constitute pressing and substantial s. 1 objectives which may justify restrictions upon those rights.[105]

This approach, of course, is not really a rule of reception, in the sense that it does not contemplate judicial incorporation or transformation of Canada's international legal obligations into Canadian law *per se*. Rather, the Court in *Slaight Communications* was articulating a rule of construction, sometimes described as the "minimum content presumption," to the effect that the *Charter* should generally be interpreted to provide protections no less generous than those found in Canada's international human rights treaty obligations.[106]

Thus, resorting to international law in interpreting the *Charter* is not new. What has distinguished the McLachlin Court in this area, however, is the surprising—some might even say, disconcerting—variability in the role international law has played in its interpretation of the *Charter*, as well as in the range of international "legal" sources that have been called upon for this purpose. An exhaustive review of the relevant jurisprudence is not possible in the space available, but the main highlights may be noted.

---

103 See generally Schabas & Beaulac, *ibid.*

104 *Slaight Communications Inc. v. Davidson*, [1989] 1 S.C.R. 1038 [*Slaight Communications*].

105 *Ibid.* at 1056–57, Dickson C.J., quoting his earlier comment in *Reference re Public Service Employee Relations Act (Alta.)*, [1987] 1 S.C.R. 313 at 349 (dissenting on another point).

106 See Walter S. Tarnopolsky, "A Comparison between the *Canadian Charter of Rights and Freedoms* and the *International Covenant on Civil and Political Rights*" (1982–83) 8 Queen's L.J. 211; Hogg, above note 60 at paras. 33.8(c) and 36.9(c); Schabas & Beaulac, above note 102 at 61. See also John Claydon, "International Human Rights Law and the Interpretation of the *Canadian Charter of Rights and Freedoms*" (1982) 4 Sup. Ct. L. Rev. 287. But see the cautionary note sounded with respect to such a "minimum content" presumption by Irit Weiser, "Effect in Domestic Law of International Human Rights Treaties Ratified without Implementing Legislation" (1998) 27 Can. Council Int'l L. Proc. 132 at 138–39.

In *Burns* (2001),[107] for example, the Court had to consider whether extradition without guarantees against imposition of the death penalty was consistent with the principles of fundamental justice under section 7, and if not, whether it could be justified under section 1. In concluding that it was not and could not in the circumstances of that case, the Court endorsed the views that "international law and opinion is of use" in interpreting the *Charter*;[108] that "Canada's international human rights obligations should inform" *Charter* interpretation;[109] and that

> various sources of international human rights law—declarations, covenants, conventions, judicial and quasi-judicial decisions of international tribunals, customary norms—must . . . be relevant and persuasive sources for interpretation of the *Charter*'s provisions.[110]

Burns' endorsement of these various propositions was remarkable in a number of ways: first, in quoting selectively from *Slaight Communications*, it appeared to avoid that case's minimum content presumption.[111] Second, it broadened the range of international law that may be used in interpreting the *Charter* beyond Canada's international human rights obligations—although it did seem to imply that different weight may be attributed to different categories of international law: whereas Canada's international human rights obligations "must" be "relevant and persuasive," international law generally was merely "of use."[112] Third, the range of international materials that may be relevant was not limited to Canada's legal *obligations* at all: international "opinion" was considered equally useful as international law; and merely material sources of international human rights "law," such as non-binding declarations or judgments of international tribunals, were treated as just as relevant and persuasive as Canada's binding international legal obligations.[113] This was underscored by the Court's subsequent reliance on international initiatives to abolish the death penalty, notwithstanding its conclusion that such initiatives had not led to binding rules of international law.[114]

---

107 *United States v. Burns*, [2001] 1 S.C.R. 283 [*Burns*].

108 *Ibid.* at para. 79, citing *Re B.C. Motor Vehicle Act*, [1985] 2 S.C.R. 486 at 512, Lamer J.

109 *Burns*, above note 107 at para. 80, citing *Slaight Communications*, above note 104 at 1056–57, Dickson C.J.

110 *Burns*, above note 107 at para. 80, citing *Reference re Public Service Employee Relations Act (Alta.)*, above note 105 at 348, Dickson C.J. dissenting.

111 *Burns*, above note 107 at para. 80.

112 *Ibid.* at paras. 79–80.

113 *Ibid.*

114 *Ibid.* at paras. 81–92 and 127–28.

The following year, in *Suresh* (2002),[115] the Court again appeared to alter its approach to using international law in interpreting the *Charter. Suresh* raised the issue of whether deportation to a risk of torture, on national security grounds, was consistent with the *Charter.* In describing the role that international law should play in answering this question, the Court held that *Charter* interpretation "is *informed* . . . by international law, including *jus cogens*";[116] that "in seeking the meaning of the Canadian Constitution, the courts *may be informed* by international law";[117] and that international law was "evidence" of the meaning of the *Charter,* but "not . . . controlling in itself."[118]

A number of innovations are immediately apparent here. First, while *Burns'* embrace of international law of a non-human rights character is confirmed, the differential weight seemingly attributed to such international law by *Burns* is not mentioned. According to *Suresh,* interpretation of the *Charter* is "informed" no less by international law in general than it is by international human rights law in particular; and no distinction is drawn between general rules of international law and *jus cogens,* or peremptory norms of international law.[119] Second, one misses any language suggesting that international law—of whatever character—"should" or "must" be considered. Rather, interpretation of the *Charter,* according to *Suresh,* merely "*may be* informed" by international law.[120] Third, *Slaight Communications'* minimum content presumption is again not mentioned, an omission underscored by the Court's conclusion on the main issue before it. While accepting that deportation to torture is categorically prohibited by the *International Covenant on Civil and Political Rights,*[121] and the *Convention against Torture and Other Cruel, Inhuman or Degrading Treatment or Punishment,*[122] to both of which Canada was and is a party,[123] the Court nevertheless concluded that "in

---

115 *Suresh,* above note 86.

116 *Ibid.* at para. 46 [emphasis added].

117 *Ibid.* at para. 60.

118 *Ibid.*

119 *Ibid.* at para. 46, where the Court accords the same interpretive weight to international law generally, "sources" of international human rights law in particular, and even *jus cogens* norms. See also para. 60. For comment, see Brunnée & Toope, above note 23 at 49–50.

120 *Ibid.* at para. 60. See discussion in Brunnée & Toope, *ibid.* at 33–35; and Beaulac, above note 30.

121 *International Covenant on Civil and Political Rights,* 16 December 1966, 999 U.N.T.S. 171 (entered into force 23 March 1976; art. 41 entered into force 28 March 1979) [*Civil Rights Covenant*].

122 *Convention against Torture and Other Cruel, Inhuman or Degrading Treatment or Punishment,* 10 December 1984, 1465 U.N.T.S. 85 (entered into force 26 June 1987).

123 *Suresh,* above note 86 at paras. 66–75.

exceptional circumstances, deportation to face torture might be justified, either as a consequence of the balancing process mandated by s. 7 of the *Charter* or under s. 1."[124] In other words, *Charter* protections may fall below those called for in Canada's international human rights treaty obligations, at least in "exceptional circumstances." This is either an implicit repudiation of *Slaight Communications*' minimum content presumption, or a vivid illustration of its qualified and rebuttable nature.[125]

Five years later, the Court's majority judgment in *Hape* (2007)[126] appeared to announce a complete break with these earlier cases and to adopt still another, quite different, approach. In particular, after briefly recalling and summarizing the Court's previous rulings on the topic, the majority in *Hape* wrote:

> In interpreting the scope of application of the *Charter*, the courts should seek to ensure compliance with Canada's binding obligations under international law where the express words are capable of supporting such a conclusion.[127]

The first thing to note about this rule is that it apparently confirms the *Suresh* approach of giving Canada's international human rights and non-human rights obligations equal weight in interpreting the *Charter*.[128] Aside from this, however, the *Hape* rule appears to be wholly novel. Neither *Slaight Communications* nor any of its successors asserted a presumption of conformity, when interpreting the *Charter*, with Canada's international legal obligations. At the most, the Court's prior judgments suggested that international law only established a "floor" of human rights protection below which *Charter* interpretation should not, "generally" and absent "exceptional circumstances," drop—a floor, moreover, only established with reference to Canada's international *human rights* obligations.[129] Moreover, as we have just seen, *Suresh* appeared to eschew any such minimum content presumption or indeed any particular persuasive role for international law at all in interpreting the *Charter*, relegating it to the status of mere "evidence" that "*may* inform" such interpretation.[130] By contrast, the rule asserted by the majority

---

124 *Ibid.* at para. 78.

125 See also *Canadian Foundation for Children*, above note 39 at paras. 9–10.

126 *Hape*, above note 32.

127 *Ibid.* at para. 56.

128 *Suresh*, above note 86 at paras. 46 and 60.

129 See *Slaight Communications*, above note 104 at 1056–57.

130 See *Suresh*, above note 86 at paras. 46 and 60 [emphasis added].

in *Hape* would seem to require that Canadian courts, in interpreting the *Charter*, "ensure compliance" with Canada's international legal obligations.[131] Accordingly, *Charter* protections do not simply benefit from an interpretive floor based on a minimum content presumption; they are also subject to any "ceiling" or "walls" implied by *any* of Canada's international legal obligations. This indeed was vividly illustrated in the outcome of *Hape*, where the majority concluded that Canada's international legal obligations of a non-human rights character precluded application of the *Charter* to the actions of Canadian officials abroad.[132]

The *Hape* rule is also novel in that it considerably narrows any judicial discretion to adopt a *Charter* interpretation that does not conform to Canada's international legal obligations.[133] Whereas the pre-*Hape* jurisprudence accorded discretion to courts to depart from international law in interpreting the *Charter* that was either vaguely limited (in the case of *Slaight Communications*[134]) or unfettered (in the case of *Suresh*[135]), the rule in *Hape* seems to narrow the grounds for departure from international law to situations where the express wording of the relevant *Charter* provision makes "compliance" impossible. Accordingly, given the *Charter*'s silence on the issue, Canada's international legal obligations to respect the territorial sovereignty of other states were found to control the *Charter*'s extraterritorial reach. This seems a considerable departure from the Court's prior, cautious approach to the role of international law in interpreting the *Charter*, which looked to international law as evidence of the meaning of the *Charter* but—to quote *Suresh*—"not as con-

131 It is conceivable that the majority was not in fact purporting to state a general rule of *Charter* interpretation but, rather, one applicable only to s. 32(1) (see *Hape*, above note 32 at para. 56: "*In interpreting the scope of application of the* Charter, the courts should seek to ensure compliance with . . .") [emphasis added]. This seems highly unlikely, however, given the majority's indication that the courts must interpret the *Charter*'s jurisdictional reach "as with the substantive provisions of the *Charter*" (*ibid.* at para. 33); its references to prior decisions governing *Charter* interpretation generally (*ibid.* at paras. 54–55); and its subsequent unqualified reference to the "presumption of conformity" (*ibid.* at para. 56). Further, a subsequent description of *Hape*'s presumption of conformity in the *Charter* context by the Court recasts it thus: "The Court [in *Hape*] held that in interpreting the scope *and* application of the *Charter*, the courts should seek to ensure compliance with Canada's binding obligations under international law" [emphasis added]: see *Canada (Justice) v. Khadr*, 2008 SCC 28 at para. 18 [*Khadr*]. This reformulation may confirm the intended applicability of the presumption to interpretation of the *Charter* generally, and not merely s. 32(1).

132 See discussion in Currie, "Weaving," above note 88 at 75–77.

133 On the dangers of allowing international law to act as a limit on the protections afforded by the *Charter*, see *R. v. Cook*, [1998] 2 S.C.R. 597 at para. 148, Bastarache J.

134 *Slaight Communications*, above note 104 at 1056.

135 *Suresh*, above note 86 at para. 60.

trolling in itself."[136] Unfortunately, no explanation was given by the majority in *Hape* for these significant departures from the Court's earlier approaches.

The day after *Hape* was released, the Court also released its judgment in *Health Services* (2007).[137] Here the majority applied international human rights law to support its conclusion that the *Charter*'s guarantee of freedom of association includes a right to collective bargaining. However, in doing so, the majority again seemed to change its mind on the rules governing the use of international law in *Charter* interpretation. First, the majority in *Health Services* recalled and endorsed the equivocal *Suresh* approach, according to which "international law . . . *may inform* the interpretation of *Charter* guarantees";[138] and "Canada's international obligations *can assist* courts charged with interpreting the *Charter*'s guarantees."[139] However, it also explicitly reasserted *Slaight Communications'* minimum content presumption—albeit, significantly, without any of its qualifications:[140]

> [T]he *Charter* should be presumed to provide at least as great a level of protection as is found in the international human rights documents that Canada has ratified.[141]

This presumption was in fact applied by the majority to support its conclusion that section 2(d) of the *Charter* included collective bargaining rights. The majority also added, using language reminiscent of *Burns*, that "Canada's current international law commitments and the current state of international thought on human rights provide a *persuasive* source for interpreting the scope of the *Charter*."[142] Puzzlingly, however, nowhere in *Health Services* is *Hape*'s presumption of conformity mentioned at all.

Finally, brief mention should be made of the Court's 2008 judgment in *Khadr*.[143] *Khadr* introduced an exception to *Hape*'s holding that the *Charter*

---

136 *Ibid.*

137 *Health Services and Support—Facilities Subsector Bargaining Assn. v. British Columbia*, [2007] 2 S.C.R. 391, 2007 SCC 27 [*Health Services*].

138 *Ibid.* at para. 20 [emphasis added].

139 *Ibid.* at para. 69 [emphasis added].

140 See also *ibid.* at para. 79: "[Section] 2(d) of the *Charter* should be interpreted as recognizing at least the same level of protection [as international conventions to which Canada is a party]." Note the absence of the qualification "generally," which accompanied the articulation of the minimum content presumption in *Slaight Communications*, above note 104 at 1056–57.

141 *Ibid.* at para. 70.

142 *Ibid.* at para. 78.

143 *Khadr*, above note 131.

does not apply to the actions of Canadian officials abroad. According to *Khadr*, this territorial limitation does not apply if the extraterritorial actions of Canadian officials amount to violations of Canada's international legal obligations.[144] While in the course of its reasons in *Khadr* the Court does quote the presumption of conformity from *Hape*,[145] it does not clearly endorse it or relate it to the formulation of the *Khadr* exception.[146] Moreover, the Court also cites the much more discretionary "may inform" approach propounded in *Suresh*.[147] However, it does not purport to reconcile these different approaches or otherwise amplify on the rules governing the use of international law in interpreting the *Charter*. *Khadr*'s effect on those rules accordingly remains unclear.

What all of this would seem to demonstrate is that the McLachlin Court's approach to how and when international law is to be used in interpreting the *Charter* has fluctuated quite considerably over the past decade. The reasons for this variability are not clear; nor is there a clearly discernible trend in the Court's approach to the issue. On one hand, the *Hape* approach, subsequently quoted but not clearly endorsed by the Court in *Khadr*, would apply a rigid presumption of conformity of the *Charter* with Canada's international legal obligations, whether of a human rights character or not. On the other hand, *Health Services* (which postdates *Hape* by a day) appears to favour a robust, *Slaight*-type minimum content presumption with specific reference to Canada's international human rights obligations. And on still another hand, the Court in *Hape*, *Health Services*, and *Khadr* appears simultaneously to endorse *Suresh*'s highly discretionary contextual approach, in which international law and other sources merely "may inform" *Charter* interpretation.[148] Clarification of which of these approaches should prevail (or indeed whether an entirely different set of rules should be adopted) is therefore presumably something to be anticipated in future cases.

In expectation of the Court's further consideration of this issue, a number of observations and suggestions may be made.

First, in this writer's view, caution should be exercised before extending the presumption of conformity from the statutory to the *Charter* interpreta-

144 *Ibid.* at para. 19.

145 *Ibid.* at para. 18.

146 See discussion in John H. Currie, "*Khadr*'s Twist on *Hape*: Tortured Determinations of the Extraterritorial Reach of the *Canadian Charter*" (2008) 46 Can. Y.B. Int'l Law 307.

147 *Khadr*, above note 131 at para. 29.

148 See *Hape*, above note 32 at para. 55; *Health Services*, above note 137 at paras. 20 and 69; *Khadr*, *ibid.* at para. 29.

tion contexts. The *Hape* majority dealt with these two distinct issues as one, treating the presumption of conformity as a monolithic concept equally applicable to statutory and *Charter* interpretation.[149] But while consistency may be a virtue, that is so only where different circumstances do not call for different rules. The presumption of conformity poses no threat to, for example, democratic values in the statutory interpretation context, in part because courts form an integral part of Canada's democratic system, but also because legislatures retain the power, should they disapprove of interpretive "implementation" of Canada's international legal obligations by the courts, to override such implementation through the passage of countervailing legislation.[150] In contrast, applying the presumption of conformity in the *Charter* context is obviously not so readily subject to democratic override by the legislative branch,[151] a fact of no small moment given the enormous democratic deficit inherent in the processes of formation of international law itself.[152]

Second, a presumption of conformity in the *Charter* context is of particular concern if conformity is to be required with all of Canada's international legal obligations. The simple reason for this is that a large number of Canada's international legal obligations—treaty obligations in particular—are entirely within the control of the executive branch.[153] Accordingly,

149 Under a single heading entitled "Conformity with International Law as an Interpretive Principle of Domestic Law," the majority first reviews the well-established interpretive presumption of conformity of legislation with Canada's international legal obligations and then asserts that an identical presumption operates in the *Charter* interpretation context. The majority subsequently refers to both, compendiously, as "*the* presumption of conformity": *Hape*, above note 32 at paras. 53–56 [emphasis added].

150 See Kindred, above note 13 at 8–9.

151 See Irit Weiser, "Undressing the Window: A Proposal for Making International Human Rights Law Meaningful in the Canadian Commonwealth System" (2004) 37 U.B.C.L. Rev. 113 at 147–48.

152 Customary international law is the result of the practice and opinions of states, predominantly that of their executive branches: see Currie, above note 6 at c. 5. Treaty law is similarly the product of the negotiated positions of the executive branches of states: see Currie, above note 6 at c. 4. Moreover, the extent to which international treaty obligations are created for Canada rests entirely in the hands of the federal executive branch: see authorities collected below at note 153; and Currie, above note 6 at 239–40.

153 It will be recalled that the federal executive branch has constitutional authority to commit Canada to international treaties without the need for any legislative concurrence. See Allan E. Gotlieb, *Canadian Treaty-Making* (Toronto: Butterworths, 1968) at 4–6 and 14; Hogg, above note 60 at paras. 11.2 and 11.3(c); Hon. P. Martin, Secretary of State for External Affairs, *Federalism and International Relations* (Ottawa: Queen's Printer, 1968) at 11–33; and Gerald L. Morris, "The Treaty-Making Power: A Canadian Dilemma" (1967) 45 Can. Bar Rev. 478 at 484. One is reminded of the admonition of LaForest J. in *Douglas/Kwantlen*

requiring rigid *Charter* conformity with international legal obligations that may be brought into existence or modified solely at the instance of the federal executive branch would seem tantamount to placing the fox in charge of the henhouse.[154]

Third, even a presumption of conformity with Canada's international human rights obligations is fraught with potential dangers. In many areas, international human rights law may be considered rudimentary or even retrograde when compared with parallel human rights protections traditionally enjoyed under Canadian law.[155] In this context, a minimum content presumption of the sort endorsed by the Court in *Health Services* may be innocuous and even useful, but it is not clear that a presumption of *Charter* conformity with international human rights law would always lead to the enjoyment by Canadians of the "full benefit of the *Charter*'s protection."[156]

Assuming that *Hape*'s presumption of conformity in the *Charter* context may be set aside, on these and other bases, can *Health Services*' simultaneous embrace of *Suresh*'s "may inform" approach and of *Slaight Communications*' minimum content presumption be reconciled? Arguably it can. In particular, the majority in *Health Services* appeared to apply the *Suresh* "may inform" approach to international law generally, whereas the *Slaight Communications*' minimum content presumption was applied to international human rights law in particular.[157] This differential treatment of each category of international law is arguably analogous to a similar approach taken in *Burns*.[158] Was this the intent of the majority in *Health Services*? If so, the outlines of a consolidation of the McLachlin Court's jurisprudence in this area

---

Faculty Assn. v. Douglas College, [1990] 3 S.C.R. 570 at 585: "To permit government to pursue policies violating *Charter* rights by means of contracts or agreements with other persons or bodies cannot be tolerated."

154 See further discussion of this concern in Currie, "Weaving," above note 88 at 77–79.

155 See *Hape*, above note 32 at para. 186, Binnie J. concurring.

156 *R. v. Big M. Drug Mart*, [1985] 1 S.C.R. 295 at 344. See further discussion on this point in Currie, "Weaving," above note 88 at 78–79.

157 *Health Services*, above note 137: contrast para. 70 ("the *Charter should be presumed* to provide at least as great a level of protection as is found in the *international human rights documents* that Canada has ratified") with para. 20 ("*international law . . . may inform* the interpretation of *Charter* guarantees") [emphasis added].

158 See *Burns*, above note 107 at paras. 79–81 (international law is "of use" in interpreting the *Charter*, but international human rights law "*should* inform" and "*must be* relevant and *persuasive*" to such interpretation [emphasis added]). On the other hand, *Suresh*, above note 86, appeared to contradict this differential approach by according (at para. 46) the same interpretive weight to international law generally, "sources" of international human rights law in particular, and even *jus cogens* norms; see also *Suresh*, above note 86 at para. 60; and *Hape*, above note 32 at para. 56.

begin to suggest themselves. Yet *Khadr*'s subsequent, ambivalent reference to *Hape*'s presumption of conformity,[159] and its application of *Suresh*'s "may inform" approach to Canada's international human rights obligations,[160] fails to confirm, and indeed would appear to undermine, this suggestion. It therefore remains to be seen whether the Court chooses to pursue the reconciliation strategy suggested here.

Finally, an area that also calls out for clarification by the Court is whether and why *non*-binding international sources should be given the same weight in *Charter* interpretation as Canada's *binding* international obligations. This has been a consistent feature of the Court's jurisprudence in this area since, as seen above, it was pioneered in *Burns.*[161] It was endorsed in *Suresh*[162] and even in *Health Services,* where the majority accorded the same weight to Canada's international human rights commitments and "the current state of international thought on human rights."[163] Quite why these "various sources of international human rights law"—some internationally binding on Canada, others not[164]—should all be treated equally in interpreting the *Charter* has never been clarified by the Court. Intuitively, it would seem that binding obligations should carry more weight than non-binding ones, which is not to say that non-binding obligations may not have some appropriate role to play in *Charter* interpretation.[165] However, if the Court were to address this perennial sore point for many international lawyers,[166] this would be very

159 *Khadr,* above note 131 at para. 18.

160 *Ibid.* at para. 29.

161 *Burns,* above note 107 at para. 80, adopting the enumeration of sources by Dickson C.J. (dissenting) in *Public Service Employee Relations Act Reference,* above note 105 at 348: "The various sources of international human rights law—declarations, covenants, conventions, judicial and quasi-judicial decisions of international tribunals, customary norms—must, in my opinion, be relevant and persuasive sources for interpretation of the *Charter*'s provisions."

162 *Suresh,* above note 86 at para. 46.

163 *Health Services,* above note 137 at para. 78.

164 On the distinction between binding and non-binding "sources" of international "law" (sometimes differentiated by use of such terms as "formal" and "material" sources, "hard" and "soft" law, or *lex lata* and *lex ferenda*), see Currie, above note 6 at c. 3.

165 In particular, while concern that Canada not be placed in breach of its international legal obligations would support *Charter* interpretations that take account of Canada's binding international legal obligations, it would not with respect to other "sources" of international "law" that are not binding. Why, therefore, should treaty rules to which Canada has not adhered, customary rules to which it has persistently objected, or "soft law" sources that are not binding at all in international law, necessarily influence interpretation of the *Charter*?

166 See discussion in Kindred, above note 13 at 25–28; Brunnée & Toope, above note 23 at 49–55; and Beaulac, above note 30 at 264–67.

beneficial to a fuller understanding of the role of international law in *Charter* interpretation.

2) International Law as a Source of Unwritten, Non-*Charter* Constitutional Principles?

Finally, we touch upon a further potential innovation in *Hape*: the apparent use of international law as a source of unwritten principles of the Canadian Constitution.[167]

It may be remembered that in *Hape*, the majority held that "extraterritorial application of the *Charter* is impossible."[168] The majority's primary basis for that holding were Canada's international legal obligations flowing from the principles of the sovereign equality of states and non-intervention.[169] Holding that these principles of international law generally forbid states from exercising extraterritorial enforcement jurisdiction,[170] the majority concluded (applying the presumption of *Charter* conformity with Canada's international legal obligations reviewed above) that the *Charter* could have no application to the actions of Canadian officials abroad. However, the majority also relied upon a secondary, alternative argument to reach this same conclusion. In particular, the majority reasoned that, in light of international law's constraints on the exercise of extraterritorial enforcement jurisdiction, Parliament "has no jurisdiction to authorize enforcement abroad."[171]

---

167 See generally, for a more detailed discussion of this potential innovation, Currie, "Weaving," above note 88 at 87–94.

168 *Hape*, above note 32 at para. 85.

169 *Ibid.* at paras. 40–46 and 57–65. While the majority in *Hape* did also refer in the course of its reasons to the principle of comity, it made clear that it did not consider comity to be legally binding. Rather, "comity is more a principle of interpretation than a rule of law, because it does not arise from formal obligations": *ibid.* at para. 47. See also *ibid.* at para. 50: "International law is a positive legal order, whereas comity, which is of the nature of a principle of interpretation, is based on a desire for states to act courteously towards one another."

170 *Ibid.* at paras. 40–46, 57–65, and 96–101.

171 *Ibid.* at para. 94. See also para. 69: "In the absence of consent Canada cannot exercise its enforcement jurisdiction over a matter situated outside Canadian territory." In fact, the core of the international legal prohibition on extraterritorial exercises of enforcement jurisdiction is limited in its application to enforcement *in another's state's territory*, not outside one's own: see, for example, *The Case of the SS "Lotus" (France v. Turkey)* (1927), P.C.I.J. (Ser. A) No. 10 at 18–19 [*Lotus*]: "Now the first and foremost restriction imposed by international law upon a State is that—failing the existence of a permissive rule to the contrary—it may not exercise its power in any form *in the territory of another State*" [emphasis added]. Furthermore, international law is rife with rules, not based on consent, that permit states to exercise enforcement jurisdiction outside their own territory. To

As a result, enforcement abroad fell outside the "authority of Parliament," as that expression is used in section 32(1) of the *Charter*, and, hence, the reach of the *Charter*'s application provision.[172] It is this secondary, alternative argument that is of interest here.

In particular, the critical premise of this argument—that Parliament has no jurisdiction to authorize enforcement abroad[173]—appears to be premised entirely on the majority's understanding of Canada's international legal obligations rather than on any previously recognized rule of domestic constitutional law. The majority cites no constitutional authority for the proposition, which is perhaps not surprising given that it is axiomatic in Canadian constitutional law that the authority of Parliament is plenary within the classes of subjects enumerated in section 91 of the *Constitution Act, 1867*,[174] that it extends to the authorization of extraterritorial enforcement action,[175] and that it even includes the power to violate international law itself.[176] Rather,

---

cite but two examples by way of illustration: the right of states to arrest ships flying their flag, or engaged in piracy, on the high seas (see *United Nations Convention on the Law of the Sea*, 10 December 1982, 1833 U.N.T.S. 3 [entered into force 16 November 1994], arts. 94, 97, 99, 101–9, and 113–14); and the right of states to use armed force against other states in self-defence (see *Charter of the United Nations*, 26 June 1945, Can. T.S. 1945 No. 7 [in force 24 October 1945], art. 51).

172 *Hape*, above note 32 at paras. 69, 94, and 103–6. Section 32(1) of the *Charter*, above note 5, provides that it applies to "the Parliament and government of Canada in respect of *all matters within the authority of Parliament*" [emphasis added].

173 *Hape*, *ibid.* at para. 69.

174 *Constitution Act, 1867* (U.K.), 30 & 31 Vict., c. 3, reprinted in R.S.C. 1985, App. II, No. 5. See, on the plenary authority of Parliament, *Statute of Westminster 1931 (U.K.)*, 22 Geo. 5, c. 4, s. 3, which confers on Parliament "*full power* to make laws having extra-territorial *operation*" [emphasis added]; *Interpretation Act*, R.S.C. 1985, c. I-21, s. 8(3); *Croft v. Dunphy*, [1933] A.C. 156 (J.C.P.C.) [*Croft*]; *Society of Composers, Authors and Music Publishers of Canada v. Canadian Assn. of Internet Providers*, [2004] 2 S.C.R. 427 at para. 141, LeBel J.; Hogg, above note 60 at paras. 12.2 and 13.2; and Ruth Sullivan, *Statutory Interpretation* (Concord, ON: Irwin Law, 1997) at 34 [Sullivan, *Statutory*].

175 *Croft*, *ibid.* at 167 (affirming the *vires* of anti-smuggling legislation that authorized the seizure of vessels outside Canadian territory, and holding that the *British North America Act, 1867* "imposed no territorial restriction in terms and their Lordships see no justification for inferring it"). There are in fact many examples of federal legislation authorizing enforcement outside Canada's territory. See, for example, *National Defence Act*, R.S.C. 1985, c. N-5, ss. 31, 68, 196.17(2), and 273.65(2)(a); *Royal Canadian Mounted Police Act*, R.S.C. 1985, c. R-10, ss. 4 and 39; *Arctic Waters Pollution Prevention Act*, R.S.C. 1985, c. A-12, s. 15(4); *Oceans Act*, S.C. 1996, c. 31, ss. 12(1), 14, and 20; *Coastal Fisheries Protection Act*, R.S.C. 1985, c. C-33, ss. 7–9.

176 See Macdonald, "Relationship," above note 57 at 119; *Hape*, above note 32 at paras. 39, 53, and 68.

the sole source relied upon by the majority for the purported limitation on the authority of Parliament was customary international law.

The question that therefore arises is how and why a rule of customary international law comes to be applied, by a Canadian court, as a binding rule of domestic constitutional law that purportedly curtails the authority of Parliament itself. Did the majority implicitly adapt or extend the "doctrine of adoption" from a rule providing for the incorporation of customary international law as part of the common law into one also providing for its incorporation as part of the Canadian Constitution?[177] The majority does not explicitly say so, and so the question must remain rhetorical until the Court clarifies whether this was its intent.[178]

If and when the Court does clarify this issue, it may wish to address a number of important questions and concerns that are raised by the possibility described above.[179] Among these is the fact that the degree of democratic control over the adoption of customary international law as common law, through the legislative branch's ability to override common law rules,[180] would plainly be absent in the case of incorporation of customary international law as a rule of constitutional law. The ramifications of this for the principle of democracy, which the Court has elsewhere described as a fundamental, organizing principle of the Canadian Constitution,[181] would require consideration.

Moreover, it is submitted that there is a qualitative difference between the courts' function in developing the common law generally[182] and their function in elucidating the unwritten Constitution in particular.[183] Unlike the common law, the unwritten Constitution is not invented by the courts—it is

177 *Quaere* whether support for such an approach might implicitly be gleaned from the Court's prior reliance on customary international law in answering reference questions having constitutional significance: see, for example, *Re Newfoundland Continental Shelf*, above note 86; *Québec Secession Reference*, above note 86. However, in neither of these cases did the Court purport to premise limitations on the constitutional authority of a branch of government on customary international law alone. Nor does the majority in *Hape* premise its reasoning here on these cases.

178 This possibility might also explain the majority's otherwise *obiter* foray into the more traditional doctrine of adoption of customary international law as common law, reviewed above.

179 See generally Currie, "Weaving," above note 88 at 90–93.

180 See Kindred, above note 13 at 8–9; Sullivan, *Statutory*, above note 174 at 34; Sullivan, above note 48 at 449–51; and Hogg, above note 60 at para. 12.2.

181 *Québec Secession Reference*, above note 86 at paras. 33, 48, and 61–69.

182 See authorities collected above note 60.

183 See generally Hogg, above note 60 at paras. 1.8 and 15.9(g).

necessarily implied by the written Constitution.[184] The role of the courts is thus to unravel and explain the Constitution's necessarily implied elements in order to "fill . . . [the] gaps in the express terms of the constitutional text."[185] It is not, it is submitted, to introduce wholly new rules of constitutional law,[186] particularly if these would contradict some of the Constitution's most fundamental principles, such as the supremacy of Parliament.[187]

D. CONCLUSION

In conclusion, it can be seen from the foregoing that the McLachlin Court has indeed been very active in seeking to define, in various contexts, the rules governing the interaction of Canada's domestic law and its obligations under international law. In light of the dearth of such consideration that traditionally characterized much of the Court's prior jurisprudence, this interest and activity on the part of the McLachlin Court is very much welcomed and encouraged. The status and influence of international law in Canadian law is an area of the law of constitutional significance that is, nevertheless, not expressly addressed in Canada's written Constitution.[188] As such, it is governed entirely by unwritten principles of the Constitution, as interpreted from time to time by the courts.[189] Guidance from the Court on the "rules of reception" is therefore of critical importance to the operation in Canada of the rule of law itself.

The foregoing analysis also shows, however, that the Court's work in this area is not complete. Important theoretical and practical uncertainties and questions remain in spite of (and perhaps occasionally, due to) the Court's

184 In particular, by the preambular reference, in the *Constitution Act, 1867*, to Canada having "a constitution similar in principle to that of the United Kingdom." See *Fraser v. Public Service Staff Relations Board*, [1985] 2 S.C.R. 455 at 462–63; *Reference re Remuneration of Judges of the Provincial Court of Prince Edward Island*, [1997] 3 S.C.R. 3 at paras. 93 and 104 [*Judges Reference*]; *Québec Secession Reference*, above note 86 at para. 49.

185 *Judges Reference*, *ibid.* at para. 104.

186 See also *British Columbia v. Imperial Tobacco*, [2005] 2 S.C.R. 473 at para. 65; *Babcock v. Canada*, [2002] 3 S.C.R. 3 at para. 55; *Ocean Port Hotel v. British Columbia*, [2001] 2 S.C.R. 781; and *Reference re Manitoba Language Rights*, [1985] 1 S.C.R. 721 at 752.

187 See authorities collected above, notes 174–76.

188 With the notable exception of the largely spent s. 132 of the *Constitution Act, 1867*, above note 174, setting out Parliament's authority to implement "Empire Treaties" negotiated on Canada's behalf by the Imperial government prior to Canada's accession to independent statehood.

189 See van Ert, *International Law*, above note 2 at 73–129, treating Canadian reception law as an element of its unwritten constitution.

attempts to define the appropriate role of international law in resolving domestic legal issues. This is to be expected. The interaction of legal systems, particularly those involving largely different subjects, sources, institutions, and subject-matter, must inevitably be complex. So too must be the questions that will necessarily arise in elaborating a framework governing such interaction. In other words, the uncertainties and questions that have been identified in this paper as still requiring elucidation by the Court do not attest to shortcomings in the Court's analysis so much as they do to the fundamental importance that that analysis continue.

It is therefore critical that the Court build upon its prior work in order to bring increased clarity to the normative structure governing the application, in Canadian law, of Canada's international legal obligations. It is submitted that the Court's future efforts in this regard should be directed to addressing a number of key needs.

First, there continues to be a need for *clarification* of the precise meaning of some of the fundamental rules of reception already identified by the Court. For example, as discussed above, the Court's embrace in *Hape* of the doctrine of adoption to govern the relationship of customary international law and Canadian common law leaves the precise content of that doctrine uncertain. Similarly, the Court's variable approach to the interpretive weight to be given to Canada's international legal obligations in construing the *Charter* renders concise articulation of the applicable rule elusive. And in the non-*Charter* constitutional context, it remains unclear from the majority's reasoning in *Hape* whether a doctrine of adoption of international legal principles as unwritten principles of the Canadian Constitution is operative in Canadian constitutional law.

Second, there is a need for *rationalization* of the domestic impact of various orders of international rules, norms, and sources. As seen above, for example, the Court at present invokes binding and non-binding international "legal" sources in interpreting the *Charter*, seemingly attributing equal weight to both. In a similar manner, the presumption of statutory conformity appears to attribute the same weight to Canada's treaty obligations, whether legislatively implemented or not. The Court also appears not to draw any distinction between the domestic legal effects of norms considered "peremptory" or "non-derogable" in international law and those that are not.[190] Whether the failure to distinguish between these various

190 See Brunnée & Toope, above note 23 at 35 and 55–59; van Ert, *International Law*, above note 2 at 227. On the concept of peremptory (or "non-derogable" or *jus cogens*) norms, see Currie, above note 6 at 174–76.

international legal sources when applying them domestically is appropriate, and on what basis, requires further consideration by the Court.

Third and perhaps most ambitiously, as the rules of reception operating in various contexts gain clarity, there is an emerging need for *integration* of those rules. That is, the Court may be called upon to consider whether and how different rules of reception may be integrated in order to constitute an overall scheme for the reception of international law in Canadian law that is both internally coherent and "externally" consistent with other fundamental constitutional principles. For example and as suggested above, considerations of internal coherence may require explanation of the need for different rules governing the impact of international law on statutes and the common law respectively; yet not compel, due to contextual differences identified above, extension of the presumption of conformity from the statutory to the *Charter* interpretation contexts. Similarly, considerations of "external" consistency with prevailing fundamental constitutional principles may provide a justification for not extending the doctrine of adoption from the common law to the constitutional contexts; or require consideration of the effects of ready judicial reception of international law on the separation or even distribution of powers under the Canadian Constitution. In other words, "integration" need not necessarily lead to the identification of a single, monolithic rule of reception applicable in all contexts. Rather, the objective should be to promote uniformity of approach where contextual factors justify such; but also particularized approaches where they do not. The result may be to settle on a body of rules of reception that spring from common underlying policy objectives (such as enhancing Canada's international stature through increased adherence to its international legal obligations),[191] yet respect the fundamental constitutional principles (such as democracy, federalism, constitutionalism and the rule of law, respect for individual and collective rights and freedoms)[192] that help shape Canada's role in the world.

International lawyers, and Canadians generally, accordingly have much to look forward to during the McLachlin Court's second decade of consideration of the relationship between international and Canadian law.

191 See van Ert, *International Law*, above note 2 at 6–7.

192 See, for example, *Québec Secession Reference*, above note 86 at para. 32.

List of Contributors

Marie-Claire Belleau is a professor at the Faculty of Law, Université Laval.

John H. Currie is a professor at the Faculty of Law, University of Ottawa (Common Law Section).

Adam Dodek is an associate professor at the Faculty of Law, University of Ottawa (Common Law Section).

Susan L. Gratton is a former partner at McCarthy Tetrault LLP and an SJD candidate at the University of Toronto.

Thomson Irvine is senior Crown counsel in the constitutional law branch of the Saskatchewan Ministry of Justice and Attorney General.

Rebecca Johnson is a professor at the Faculty of Law, University of Victoria.

Freya Kristjanson is a partner with Cavalluzzo Hayes Shilton McIntyre & Cornish LLP in Toronto.

Thomas Kuttner, Q.C. is Ron Ianni Visiting Scholar, Faculty of Law, University of Windsor, and formerly was a professor of law at the University of New Brunswick.

Anik Lamontagne is an LLL student at the Faculty of Law, Université Laval.

Peter Landmann is counsel with the Ontario Ministry of the Attorney General.

Constance MacIntosh is an associate professor, Schulich School of Law, Dalhousie University.

The Rt. Hon. Beverley McLachlin, P.C. has been chief justice of Canada since 7 January 2000 and has been a justice of the Supreme Court of Canada since 1989.

David J. Mullan is Professor Emeritus, Faculty of Law, Queen's University.

Peter C. Oliver is a full professor at the Faculty of Law, University of Ottawa (Common Law Section).

Daniel Proulx is a professor and the Dean of the Faculty of Law at the University of Sherbrooke.

Nathalie Des Rosiers is general counsel of the Canadian Civil Liberties Association and executive director of the Canadian Civil Liberties Education Trust.

Lorne Sossin is a professor and Dean, Osgoode Hall Law School.

Lori Sterling is Deputy Minister at the Ontario Ministry of Aboriginal Affairs.

Don Stuart is a professor, Faculty of Law, Queen's University.

David A. Wright is the Associate Chair, Human Rights Tribunal of Ontario.

Printed and bound by CPI Group (UK) Ltd, Croydon, CR0 4YY

15/09/2026

14962400-0005